Financial Accounting
for Decision Makers

Visit the *Financial Accounting for Decision Makers*, sixth edition
Companion Website at **www.pearsoned.co.uk/atrillmclaney**
to find valuable **student** learning material including:

- Self assessment questions to test your learning
- A study guide to aid self-learning
- Revision questions and exercises to help you check your understanding
- Extensive links to valuable resources on the web
- Comments on case studies to aid interpretative and analytical skills

6th Edition

Financial Accounting
for Decision Makers

Peter Atrill
and
Eddie McLaney

Financial Times
Prentice Hall
is an imprint of

Harlow, England • London • New York • Boston • San Francisco • Toronto
Sydney • Tokyo • Singapore • Hong Kong • Seoul • Taipei • New Delhi
Cape Town • Madrid • Mexico City • Amsterdam • Munich • Paris • Milan

Pearson Education Limited
Edinburgh Gate
Harlow
Essex CM20 2JE
England

and Associated Companies throughout the world

Visit us on the World Wide Web at:
www.pearsoned.co.uk

Second edition published 1999 by Prentice Hall Europe
Third edition published 2002 by Pearson Education Limited
Fourth edition 2005
Fifth edition 2008
Sixth edition 2011

ISBN: 978-0-273-74039-1

British Library Cataloguing-in-Publication Data
A catalogue record for this book is available from the British Library

Library of Congress Cataloging-in-Publication Data
Atrill, Peter.
  Financial accounting for decision makers / Peter Atrill and Eddie
McLaney. — 6th ed.
    p. cm.
  ISBN 978-0-273-74039-1 (pbk.)
  1. Accounting. 2. Decision making. I. McLaney, E. J. II. Title.
  HF5636.A884 2010
  658.15—dc22

                                              2010018255

10 9 8 7 6 5 4 3 2 1
14 13 12 11 10

Typeset in 9.5/12.5pt Stone Serif by 35
Printed and bound by Rotolito Lombarda, Italy

Brief contents

Contents

3 Measuring and reporting financial performance   69

4 Accounting for limited companies (1)   114

5 Accounting for limited companies (2)   149

6 Measuring and reporting cash flows   186

7 Analysing and interpreting financial statements (1)   217

8 Analysing and interpreting financial statements (2)   261

Supporting resources

Visit **www.pearsoned.co.uk/atrillmclaney** to find valuable online resources

Companion Website for students
- Self assessment questions to test your learning
- A study guide to aid self-learning
- Revision questions and exercises to help you check your understanding
- Extensive links to valuable resources on the web
- Comments on case studies to aid interpretative and analytical skills

For instructors
- Complete, downloadable Instructor's Manual
- PowerPoint slides that can be downloaded and used for presentations
- Progress tests, consisting of various questions and exercise material with solutions
- Tutorial/seminar questions and solutions

Also: The Companion Website provides the following features:
- Search tool to help locate specific items of content
- Online help and support to assist with website usage and troubleshooting

For more information please contact your local Pearson Education sales representativeor visit **www.pearsoned.co.uk/atrillmclaney**

Guided tour of the book

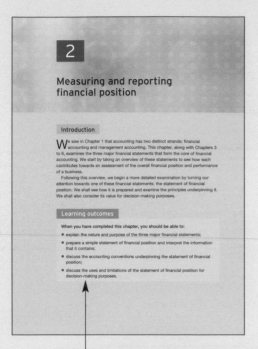

Learning outcomes Bullet points at the start of each chapter show what you can expect to learn from that chapter, and highlight the core coverage.

Activities These short questions, integrated throughout each chapter, allow you to check your understanding as you progress through the text. They comprise either a narrative question requiring you to review or critically consider topics, or a numerical problem requiring you to deduce a solution. A suggested answer is given immediately after each activity.

Key terms The key concepts and techniques in each chapter are highlighted in colour where they are first introduced, with an adjacent icon in the margin to help you refer back to them.

Examples At frequent intervals throughout most chapters, there are numerical examples that give you step-by-step workings to follow through to the solution.

'Real World' illustrations Integrated throughout the text, these illustrative examples highlight the practical application of accounting concepts and techniques by real businesses, including extracts from company reports and financial statements, survey data and other insights from business.

Self-assessment questions   Towards the end of most chapters you will encounter one of these questions, allowing you to attempt a comprehensive question before tackling the end-of-chapter assessment material. To check your understanding and progress, solutions are provided at the end of the book.

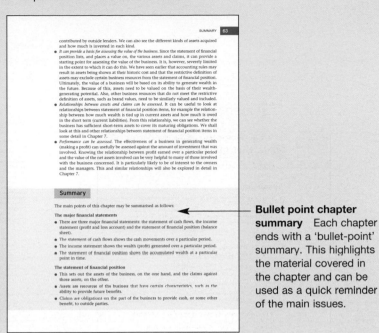

Bullet point chapter summary   Each chapter ends with a 'bullet-point' summary. This highlights the material covered in the chapter and can be used as a quick reminder of the main issues.

Key terms summary   At the end of each chapter, there is a listing (with page references) of all the key terms introduced in that chapter, allowing you to refer back easily to the most important points.

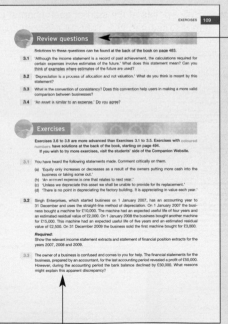

Review questions These short questions encourage you to review and/or critically discuss your understanding of the main topics covered in each chapter, either individually or in a group. Solutions to these questions can be found at the back of the book.

Further reading   This section comprises a listing of relevant chapters in other textbooks that you might refer to in order to pursue a topic in more depth or gain an alternative perspective.

References   Provides full details of sources of information referred to in the chapter.

Exercises   These comprehensive questions at the end of most chapters. The more advanced questions are separately identified. Solutions to five of the questions (those with coloured numbers) are provided at the end of the book, enabling you to assess your progress. Solutions to the remaining questions are available online for lecturers only. Additional exercises can be found on the Companion Website at **www.pearsoned.co.uk/atrillmclaney**.

Guided tour of the Companion Website

Extra material has been prepared to help you study using *Financial Accounting for Decision Makers*. This material can be found on the book's Companion Website at **www.pearsoned.co.uk/atrillmclaney**.

Self assessment questions

For each chapter there is a set of interactive self assessment questions, including multiple choice and fill-in-the-blanks questions. Test your learning and get automatic grading on your answers.

Revision questions

Sets of questions covering the whole book are designed to help you check your overall learning while you are revising.

Weblinks

A full set of relevant weblinks allows further study of each particular topic.

Preface

This text provides a comprehensive introduction to financial accounting. It is aimed both at students who are not majoring in accounting and at those who are. Those studying introductory-level financial accounting as part of their course in business, economics, hospitality management, tourism, engineering, or some other area, should find that the book provides complete coverage of the material at the level required. Students who are majoring in accounting should find the book a useful introduction to the main principles, which can serve as a foundation for further study. The text does not focus on the technical aspects, but rather examines the basic principles and underlying concepts. The ways in which financial statements and information can be used to improve the quality of decision making are the main focus of the book. To reinforce this practical emphasis, there are, throughout the text, numerous illustrative extracts with commentary from company reports, survey data and other sources.

In this sixth edition, we have taken the opportunity to make improvements that have been suggested by both students and lecturers who used the previous edition. We have brought up to date and expanded the number of examples from real life. We have incorporated the many changes that have occurred with International Financial Reporting Standards since the last edition. We have also picked up on developments that have arisen in the area of corporate governance.

We have also greatly expanded the coverage of financial reports beyond the income statement, statement of financial position (balance sheet) and statement of cash flows. This expanded coverage forms a new chapter, Chapter 10. The financial reports covered in Chapter 10 include both those that are mandatory for certain businesses as well as those that individual businesses may choose to prepare.

The text is written in an 'open-learning' style. This means that there are numerous integrated activities, worked examples and questions throughout the text to help you to understand the subject fully. You are encouraged to interact with the material and to check your progress continually. Irrespective of whether you are using the book as part of a taught course or for personal study, we have found that this approach is more 'user-friendly' and makes it easier for you to learn.

We recognise that most of you will not have studied financial accounting before, and, therefore, we have tried to write in a concise and accessible style, minimising the use of technical jargon. We have also tried to introduce topics gradually, explaining everything as we go. Where technical terminology is unavoidable we try to provide clear explanations. In addition, you will find all of the key terms highlighted in the text, and then listed at the end of each chapter with a page reference. All of these key terms are also listed alphabetically, with a concise definition, in the glossary given in Appendix B towards the end of the book. This should provide a convenient point of reference from which to revise.

A further important consideration in helping you to understand and absorb the topics covered is the design of the text itself. The page layout and colour scheme have been carefully considered to allow for the easy navigation and digestion of material.

The layout features a large page format, an open design, and clear signposting of the various features and assessment material. More detail about the nature and use of these features is given in the 'How to use this book' section below; and the main points are also summarised, using example pages from the text, in the 'Guided tour' on pp. xiv–xv.

We hope that you will find the book both readable and helpful.

Peter Atrill
Eddie McLaney

How to use this book

We have organised the chapters to reflect what we consider to be a logical sequence and, for this reason, we suggest that you work through the text in the order in which it is presented. We have tried to ensure that earlier chapters do not refer to concepts or terms that are not explained until a later chapter. If you work through the chapters in the 'wrong' order, you will probably encounter concepts and terms that were explained previously.

Irrespective of whether you are using the book as part of a lecture/tutorial-based course or as the basis for a more independent mode of study, we advocate following broadly the same approach.

Integrated assessment material

Interspersed throughout each chapter are numerous **activities**. You are strongly advised to attempt all of these questions. They are designed to simulate the sort of quick-fire questions that your lecturer might throw at you during a lecture or tutorial. Activities serve two purposes:

● to give you the opportunity to check that you understand what has been covered so far;
● to encourage you to think about the topic just covered, either to see a link between that topic and others with which you are already familiar, or to link the topic just covered to the next.

The answer to each activity is provided immediately after the question. This answer should be covered up until you have deduced your solution, which can then be compared with the one given.

Towards the middle/end of Chapters 2–11 there is a **self-assessment question**. This is more comprehensive and demanding than most of the activities, and is designed to give you an opportunity to check and apply your understanding of the core coverage of the chapter. The solution to each of these questions is provided in Appendix C at the end of the book. As with the activities, it is important that you attempt each question thoroughly before referring to the solution. If you have difficulty with a self-assessment question, you should go over the relevant chapter again.

End-of-chapter assessment material

At the end of each chapter there are four **review questions**. These are short questions requiring a narrative answer or discussion within a tutorial group. They are intended to help you assess how well you can recall and critically evaluate the core terms and concepts covered in each chapter. Answers to these questions are provided in Appendix D at the end of the book.

At the end of each chapter, except for Chapter 1, there is a set of **exercises**. These are mostly computational and are designed to reinforce your knowledge and understanding. Exercises are graded as either 'basic' or 'more advanced' according to their level of difficulty. The basic-level questions are fairly straightforward; the more advanced ones can be quite demanding but can be successfully completed if you have worked conscientiously through the chapter and have attempted the basic exercises. Solutions to some of the exercises in each chapter are provided in Appendix E at the end of the book. A coloured exercise number identifies these questions. Here, too, a thorough attempt should be made to answer each exercise before referring to the solution.

Solutions to the other exercises are provided in a separate *Instructors' Manual*.

To familiarise yourself with the main features and how they will benefit your study from this text, an illustrated 'Guided tour' is provided on pp. xiv–xv.

Content and structure

The text comprises eleven main chapters. The market research for this text revealed a divergence of opinions, given the target market, on whether or not to include material on double-entry bookkeeping techniques. So as to not interrupt the flow and approach of the main chapters, Appendix A on recording financial transactions (including activities and three exercise questions) has been placed after Chapter 11.

Acknowledgements

We are grateful to the following for permission to reproduce copyright material:

Figures

Figure 10.4 from The 2009 Value Added Scoreboard, www.innovation.go.uk, Department for Business Innovation and Skills, Crown Copyright material is reproduced with permission under the terms of the Click-Use Licence; Figure 8.4 from Financial Ratios as Predictors of Failure, Empirical Research in Accounting: Selected Studies, *Journal of Accounting Research*, Supplement to Volume 5, pp. 71–111 (Beaver, W.H. 1966).

Text

Real World 1.2 from *The Times, Business Section*, 26/09/2002, 25, The Times, Business Section, 26 September 2002. nisyndication.com; Real World 1.3 from Business big shot, *The Times*, 27/01/2009, 39, The Times, 27 January 2009. nisyndication.com; Real World 2.1 adapted from Balance sheets: the basics, accessed 19 October 2009, www.businesslink.gov.uk; Real World 3.2 from TUI Travel plc, Annual Report and Accounts 2008, p. 68; Real World 3.8 from Findel shares plunge as Yorkshire home shopping firm's bad debts rise, *Yorkshire Evening Post*, 17/04/2008 (Scott, N.), reproduced by kind permission of the Yorkshire Evening Post; Real World 4.7 from Rolls-Royce plc, Annual Report and Accounts 2008, note 14; Real World 4.8 from Eurotunnel pays first dividend since 1987 float, Ian King, 4 March 2009, www.timesonline.co.uk, 4 March 2009. nisyndication.com; Real World 5.2 from Tottenham Hotspur plc Annual Report 2009, p. 57; Real World 5.4 from Dirty laundry: how companies fudge the numbers, *The Times, Business Section*, 22/09/2002, The Times, Business Section, 22 September 2002. nisyndication.com; Real World 6.2 from www.tescocorporate.com, Tesco Annual Review 2009, p. 24; Real World 6.3 adapted from LiDCO Group plc, Annual Report 2009; Real World 8.4 from Marks and Spencer plc, Annual Report 2009; Real World 9.4 from Forbes, T. Technical update – Inadequate IFRS 3, Finance Week 30 January 2007, www.financeweek.co.uk, www.financeweek.co.uk/item/4760; Real World 10.2, 11.10 from Tesco plc, www.tesco.com, Annual Report and Financial Statements 2009; Real World 10.3, 10.4, 10.5, 10.6, 10.7 from Tesco plc, www.tesco.com, Annual Report and Financial Statements 2009, Business Review; Real World 11.7 from Marks and Spencer plc, Annual Report 2009, p. 55; Real World 11.8 from Tesco plc, www.tesco.com, Annual Report and Financial Statements 2009, Business Review, p. 51; Real World 11.12 adapted from SSL International plc, Annual Report and Accounts 2009, pp. 44–5; Real World 11.16 from Corporate Governance and Voting Policy January 2008, p. 14, www.jupiteronline.co.uk.

The Financial Times

Real World 1.1 from Morrison in uphill battle to integrate Safeway, *Financial Times*, 26/05/2005 (Elizabeth Rigby); Real World 1.5 from Fair shares?, *Financial Times*, 11/06/2005 (Michael Skapinker); Real World 1.6 from How we've poisoned the well of wealth, *Financial Times*, 15/02/2009 (Goyder, M.); Real World 2.5 from Akzo Nobel defends ICI takeover, *Financial Times*, 24/02/2009 (Michael Steen); Real World 4.1 from Monotub Industries in a spin as founder gets Titan for £1, *Financial Times*, 23/01/2003 (Urquhart, L.); Real World 5.3 from Battlelines are drawn up for fight on standards, *Financial Times*, 7/01/2008 (Bruce, R.); Real World 5.5 from Dell to lower writedowns on restated earnings, *Financial Times*, 30/10/2007 (Allison, K.); Real World 5.10 from It pays to read between the lines, *Financial Times*, 17/09/2005; Real World 6.1 from Rations cut for army of buyers, *Financial Times*, 20/10/2008; Real World 7.4 from Investing in Bollywood, Lex column, *Financial Times*, 25/06/2007; Real World 7.5 from Payment squeeze on suppliers, *Financial Times*, 22/12/2008 (Grant, J.); Real World 7.6 from Gearing levels set to plummet, *Financial Times*, 10/02/2009 (Grant, J.); Real World 8.1 adapted from *Financial Times*, 14/11/2009; Real World 8.6 from New study re-writes the A to Z of value investing, *Financial Times*, 14/08/2009 (Mathurin, P.); Real World 11.3 from M&S shareholders give Rose a dressing down, *Financial Times*, 9/07/2009 (Braithwaite, T., Rigby, E. and Burgess, K.); Real World 11.4 from An expert hand behind the scenes, *Financial Times*, 30/09/2008 (Willman, J.); Real World 11.5 from Hefty pay rises for non-executives, *Financial Times*, 15/02/2009 (Kelleher, E.); Real World 11.9 from Shake-up at Shell after pay backlash, *Financial Times*, 11/09/2009 (Burgess, K.); Real World 11.13 from Ebay seeks to alter terms of stock options, *Financial Times*, 11/03/2009 (Gelles, D.); Real World 11.15 from Shareholders revolt over C&W pay, *Financial Times*, 18/07/2009 (Parker, A.).

In some instances we have been unable to trace the owners of copyright material, and we would appreciate any information that would enable us to do so.

1

Introduction to accounting

Introduction

In this opening chapter we begin by considering the role of accounting. We shall see that it can be a valuable tool for decision-making. We shall identify the main users of accounting and financial information and discuss the ways in which this information can improve the quality of decisions that those users make. We shall then go on to consider the particular role of financial accounting and the differences between financial and management accounting. Since this book is concerned with accounting and financial decision making for private-sector businesses, we shall also examine the main forms of business enterprise and consider what are likely to be the key objectives of a business.

Learning outcomes

When you have completed this chapter, you should be able to:

- explain the nature and roles of accounting;

- identify the main users of financial information and discuss their needs;

- distinguish between financial and management accounting;

- explain the purpose of a business and describe how businesses are organised and structured.

What is accounting?

→ **Accounting** is concerned with collecting, analysing and communicating financial information. The purpose is to help people who use this information to make more informed decisions. If the financial information that is communicated is not capable of improving the quality of decisions made, there would be no point in producing it. Sometimes the impression is given that the purpose of accounting is simply to prepare financial reports on a regular basis. While it is true that accountants undertake this kind of work, it does not represent an end in itself. The ultimate purpose of the accountant's work is to give people better financial information on which to base their decisions. This decision-making perspective of accounting fits in with the theme of this book and shapes the way in which we deal with each topic.

Who are the users of accounting information?

For accounting information to be useful, the accountant must be clear *for whom* the information is being prepared and *for what purpose* the information will be used. There are likely to be various groups of people (known as 'user groups') with an interest in a particular organisation, in the sense of needing to make decisions about it. For the typical private-sector business, the more important of these groups are shown in Figure 1.1. Take a look at this figure and then try Activity 1.1.

Figure 1.1	Main users of financial information relating to a business

Several user groups have an interest in accounting information relating to a business. The majority of these are outside the business but, nevertheless, have a stake in it. This is not meant to be an exhaustive list of potential users; however, the groups identified are normally the most important.

Activity 1.1

Ptarmigan Insurance plc (PI) is a large motor insurance business. Taking the user groups identified in Figure 1.1, suggest, for each group, the sorts of decisions likely to be made about PI and the factors to be taken into account when making these decisions.

Your answer may be along the following lines:

User group	Decision
Customers	Whether to take further motor policies with PI. This might involve an assessment of PI's ability to continue in business and to meet their needs, particularly in respect of any insurance claims made.
Competitors	How best to compete against PI or, perhaps, whether to leave the market on the grounds that it is not possible to compete profitably with PI. This might involve competitors using PI's performance in various aspects as a 'benchmark' when evaluating their own performance. They might also try to assess PI's financial strength and to identify significant changes that may signal PI's future actions (for example, raising funds as a prelude to market expansion).
Employees	Whether to continue working for PI and, if so, whether to demand higher rewards for doing so. The future plans, profits and financial strength of the business are likely to be of particular interest when making these decisions.
Government	Whether PI should pay tax and, if so, how much, whether it complies with agreed pricing policies, whether financial support is needed and so on. In making these decisions an assessment of its profits, sales revenues and financial strength would be made.
Community representatives	Whether to allow PI to expand its premises and/or whether to provide economic support for the business. PI's ability to continue to provide employment for the community, the extent to which it is likely to use community resources and its likely willingness to help fund environmental improvements are likely to be considered when arriving at such decisions.
Investment analysts	Whether to advise clients to invest in PI. This would involve an assessment of the likely risks and future returns associated with PI.
Suppliers	Whether to continue to supply PI and, if so, whether to supply on credit. This would involve an assessment of PI's ability to pay for any goods and services supplied.
Lenders	Whether to lend money to PI and/or whether to require repayment of any existing loans. PI's ability to pay the interest and to repay the principal sum would be important factors in such decisions.
Managers	Whether the performance of the business needs to be improved. Performance to date would be compared with earlier plans or some other 'benchmark' to decide whether action needs to be taken. Managers may also wish to decide whether there should be a change in PI's future direction. This would involve looking at PI's ability to perform and at the opportunities available to it.
Owners	Whether to invest more in PI or to sell all, or part, of the investment currently held. This would involve an assessment of the likely risks and returns associated with PI. Owners may also be involved with decisions on rewarding senior managers. The financial performance of the business would normally be considered when making such a decision.

Although this answer covers many of the key points, you may have identified other decisions and/or other factors to be taken into account by each group.

The conflicting interests of users

We have seen above that each user group looks at a business from a different perspective and has its own particular interests. This means that there is always the risk that the interests of one group will collide with those of another group. Conflict between user groups is most likely to occur over the way in which the wealth of the business is generated and/or distributed. A good example is the conflict that may arise between the managers and the owners of the business. Although managers are appointed to act in the best interests of the owners, there is always a danger that they will not do so. Instead, managers may use the wealth of the business to award themselves large pay rises, to furnish large offices or to buy expensive cars for their own use. Accounting information has an important role to play in reporting the extent to which various groups have benefited from the business. Thus, owners may rely on accounting information to check whether the pay and benefits of managers are in line with agreed policy.

A further example is the potential conflict of interest between lenders and owners. There is a risk that the funds loaned to a business will not be used for purposes that have been agreed. Lenders may, therefore, rely on accounting information to check that the funds have been applied in an appropriate manner and that the terms of the loan agreement are not being broken.

Activity 1.2

Can you think of other examples where accounting information may be used to monitor potential conflicts of interest between the various user groups identified?

Two possible examples that spring to mind are:

● employees (or their representatives) wishing to check that they are receiving a 'fair share' of the wealth created by the business and that agreed profit-sharing schemes are being adhered to;
● government wishing to check that the profits made from a contract that it has given to a business are not excessive.

You may have thought of other examples.

How useful is accounting information?

No one would seriously claim that accounting information fully meets all of the needs of each of the various user groups. Accounting is still a developing subject and we still have much to learn about user needs and the ways in which these needs should be met. Nevertheless, the information contained in accounting reports should help users make decisions relating to the business. The information should reduce uncertainty about the financial position and performance of the business. It should help to answer questions concerning the availability of funds to pay owners a return, to repay loans, to reward employees and so on.

Typically, there is no close substitute for the information provided by the financial statements. Thus, if users cannot glean the required information from the financial statements, it is often unavailable to them. Other sources of information concerning the financial health of a business are normally much less useful.

Activity 1.3

What other sources of information might, say, an investment analayst use in an attempt to gain an impression of the financial position and performance of a business? What kind of information might be gleaned from these sources?

Other sources of information available include:

- meetings with managers of the business;
- public announcements made by the business;
- newspaper and magazine articles;
- websites, including the website of the business;
- radio and TV reports;
- information-gathering agencies (for example, agencies that assess businesses' credit-worthiness or credit ratings);
- industry reports;
- economy-wide reports.

These sources can provide information on various aspects of the business, such as new products or services being offered, management changes, new contracts offered or awarded, the competitive environment within which the business operates, the impact of new technology, changes in legislation, changes in interest rates and future levels of inflation. However, the various sources of information identified are not really substitutes for accounting reports. Rather, they are best used in conjunction with the reports in order to obtain a clearer picture of the financial health of a business.

Evidence on the usefulness of accounting

There are arguments and convincing evidence that accounting information is at least *perceived* as being useful to users. Numerous research surveys have asked users to rank the importance of accounting information, in relation to other sources of information, for decision-making purposes. Generally, these studies have found that users rank accounting information very highly. There is also considerable evidence that businesses choose to produce accounting information that exceeds the minimum requirements imposed by accounting regulations. (For example, businesses often produce a considerable amount of accounting information for managers, which is not required by any regulations.) Presumably, the cost of producing this additional accounting information is justified on the grounds that users find it useful. Such arguments and evidence, however, leave unanswered the question of whether the information produced is actually used for decision-making purposes, that is: does it affect people's behaviour?

It is normally very difficult to assess the impact of accounting on decision making. One situation arises, however, where the impact of accounting information can be observed and measured. This is where the **shares** (portions of ownership of a business) are traded on a stock exchange. The evidence reveals that, when a business makes an announcement concerning its accounting profits, the prices at which shares are traded and the volume of shares traded often change significantly. This suggests that investors are changing their views about the future prospects of the business as a result of this new information becoming available to them and that this, in turn, leads them to make a decision either to buy or to sell shares in the business.

Although there is evidence that accounting reports are perceived as being useful and are used for decision-making purposes, it is impossible to measure just how useful accounting reports are to users. As a result we cannot say with certainty whether the cost of producing those reports represents value for money. Accounting information will usually represent only one input to a particular decision and so the precise weight attached to the accounting information by the decision maker and the benefits which flow as a result cannot be accurately assessed. We shall now go on to see, however, that it is at least possible to identify the kinds of qualities which accounting information must possess in order to be useful. Where these qualities are lacking, the usefulness of the information will be diminished.

Providing a service

One way of viewing accounting is as a form of service. Accountants provide economic information to their 'clients', who are the various users identified in Figure 1.1. The quality of the service provided is determined by the extent to which the needs of the various user groups have been met. To meet these users' needs, it can be argued that accounting information should possess certain key qualities, or characteristics: relevance, reliability, comparability and understandability.

→ ● **Relevance**. Accounting information must have the ability to influence decisions. Unless this characteristic is present, there is really no point in producing the information. The information may be relevant to the prediction of future events (for example, in predicting how much profit is likely to be earned next year) or relevant in helping to confirm past events (for example, in establishing how much profit was earned last year). The role of accounting in confirming past events is important because users often wish to check the accuracy of earlier predictions that they have made. The accuracy (or inaccuracy) of earlier predictions may help users to judge the accuracy of current predictions. To influence a decision, the information must, of course, be available when the decision is being made. Thus, relevant information must be timely.

→ ● **Reliability**. Accounting should be free from significant error or bias. It should be capable of being relied upon by managers to represent what it is supposed to represent.

Though both relevance and reliability are very important, the problem that we often face in accounting is that information that is highly relevant may not be very reliable. Similarly, that which is reliable may not be very relevant.

Activity 1.4

To illustrate this last point, let us assume that a manager has to sell a custom-built machine owned by their business and has recently received a bid for it. This machine is very unusual and there is no ready market for it.

What information would be relevant to the manager when deciding whether to accept the bid? How reliable would that information be?

The manager would probably like to know the current market value of the machine before deciding whether or not to accept the bid. The current market value would be highly relevant to the final decision, but it might not be very reliable because the machine is unique and there is likely to be little information concerning market values.

When seeking to strike the right balance between relevance and reliability, the needs of users should be the overriding consideration.

→ ● **Comparability.** This quality will enable users to identify changes in the business over time (for example, the trend in sales revenue over the past five years). It will also help them to evaluate the performance of the business in relation to similar businesses. Comparability is achieved by treating items that are basically the same in the same manner for accounting purposes. Comparability may also be enhanced by making clear the policies that have been adopted in measuring and presenting the information.

→ ● **Understandability.** Accounting reports should be expressed as clearly as possible and should be understood by those at whom the information is aimed.

Activity 1.5

Do you think that accounting reports should be understandable to those who have not studied accounting?

It would be very useful if accounting reports could be understood by everyone. This, however, is unrealistic as complex financial events and transactions cannot normally be expressed in simple terms. It is probably best that we regard accounting reports in the same way that we regard a report written in a foreign language. To understand either of these, we need to have had some preparation. Generally speaking, accounting reports assume that the user not only has a reasonable knowledge of business and accounting but is also prepared to invest some time in studying the reports.

Despite the answer to Activity 1.5, the onus is clearly on accountants to provide information in a way that makes it as understandable as possible to non-accountants.

But . . . is it material?

The qualities, or characteristics, that have just been described will help us to decide whether accounting information is potentially useful. If a particular piece of information has these qualities then it may be useful. However, this does not automatically mean that it should be reported to users. We also have to consider whether the information is material, or significant. This means that we should ask whether its omission or misrepresentation in the accounting reports would really alter the decisions that users make. Thus, in addition to possessing the characteristics mentioned above,
→ accounting information must also cross the threshold of **materiality**. If the information is not regarded as material, it should not be included within the reports as it will merely clutter them up and, perhaps, interfere with the users' ability to interpret the financial results. The type of information and amounts involved will normally determine whether it is material.

Weighing up the costs and benefits

Having read the previous sections you may feel that, when considering a piece of accounting information, provided the four main qualities identified are present and it is material it should be gathered and made available to users. Unfortunately, there is one more hurdle to jump. Something may still exclude a piece of accounting information from the reports even when it is considered to be useful. Consider Activity 1.6.

Activity 1.6

Suppose an item of information is capable of being provided. It is relevant to a particular decision; it is also reliable, comparable, can be understood by the decision maker concerned and is material.
   Can you think of a reason why, in practice, you might choose not to produce the information?

The reason that you may decide not to produce, or discover, the information is that you judge the cost of doing so to be greater than the potential benefit of having the information. This cost–benefit issue will limit the extent to which accounting information is provided.

In theory, a particular item of accounting information should only be produced if the costs of providing it are less than the benefits, or value, to be derived from its use. Figure 1.2 shows the relationship between the costs and value of providing additional accounting information.

Figure 1.2   Relationship between costs and the value of providing additional accounting information

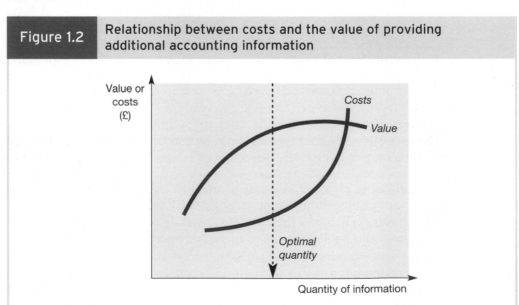

The benefits of accounting information eventually decline. The cost of providing information, however, will rise with each additional piece of information. The optimal level of information provision is where the gap between the value of the information and the cost of providing it is at its greatest.

The figure shows how the value of information received by the decision maker eventually begins to decline. This is, perhaps, because additional information becomes less relevant, or because of the problems that a decision maker may have in processing the sheer quantity of information provided. The costs of providing the information, however, will increase with each additional piece of information. The broken line indicates the point at which the gap between the value of information and the cost of providing that information is at its greatest. This represents the optimal amount of information that can be provided. This theoretical model, however, poses a number of problems in practice. We shall now go on to discuss these.

To illustrate the practical problems of establishing the value of information, let us assume that someone has collided with our car in a car park and dented and scraped the paint from one of the doors. We wish to have the dent taken out and the door resprayed at a local garage. We know that the nearest garage would charge £250 but believe that other local garages may offer to do the job for a lower price. The only way of finding out the prices at other garages is to visit them, so that they can see the extent of the damage. Visiting the garages will involve using some petrol and will take up some of our time. Is it worth the cost of finding out the price for the job at the various local garages? The answer, as we have seen, is that if the cost of discovering the price is less than the potential benefit, it is worth having that information.

To identify the various prices for the job, there are several points to be considered, including:

● How many garages shall we visit?
● What is the cost of petrol to visit each garage?
● How long will it take to make all the garage visits?
● At what price do we value our time?

The economic benefit of having the information on the price of the job is probably even harder to assess. The following points need to be considered:

● What is the cheapest price that we might be quoted for the job?
● How likely is it that we shall be quoted a price cheaper than £250?

As we can imagine, the answers to these questions may be far from clear – remember that we have only contacted the local garage so far. When assessing the value of accounting information we are confronted with similar problems.

The provision of accounting information can be very costly; however, the costs are often difficult to quantify. The direct, out-of-pocket, costs such as salaries of accounting staff are not really a problem to identify, but these are only part of the total costs involved. There are also less direct costs such as the cost of the user's time spent on analysing and interpreting the information contained in reports.

The economic benefit of having accounting information is even harder to assess. It is possible to apply some 'science' to the problem of weighing the costs and benefits, but a lot of subjective judgement is likely to be involved. No one would seriously advocate that the typical business should produce no accounting information. At the same time, no one would advocate that every item of information that could be seen as possessing one or more of the key characteristics should be produced, irrespective of the cost of producing it.

The characteristics that influence the usefulness of accounting information and which have been discussed in this section and the preceding section are set out in Figure 1.3.

Figure 1.3 The characteristics that influence the usefulness of accounting information

There are four main qualitative characteristics that influence the usefulness of accounting information. In addition, however, accounting information should be material and the benefits of providing the information should outweigh the costs.

Accounting as an information system

We have already seen that accounting can be seen as the provision of a service to 'clients'. Another way of viewing accounting is as a part of the business's total information system. Users, both inside and outside the business, have to make decisions concerning the allocation of scarce economic resources. To ensure that these resources are efficiently allocated, users need economic information on which to base decisions. It is the role of the accounting system to provide that information and this will involve information gathering and communication.

 The **accounting information system** should have certain features that are common to all valid information systems within a business. These are:

- identifying and capturing relevant information (in this case financial information);
- recording the information collected in a systematic manner;
- analysing and interpreting the information collected;
- reporting the information in a manner that suits the needs of users.

The relationship between these features is set out in Figure 1.4.

Figure 1.4   The accounting information system

Information identification → Information recording → Information analysis → Information reporting

There are four sequential stages of an accounting information system. The first two stages are concerned with preparation, whereas the last two stages are concerned with using the information collected.

Given the decision-making emphasis of this book, we shall be concerned primarily with the final two elements of the process: the analysis and reporting of accounting information. We shall consider the way in which information is used by, and is useful to, users rather than the way in which it is identified and recorded.

Efficient accounting systems are an essential ingredient of an efficient business. When the accounting systems fail, the results can be disastrous. **Real World 1.1** provides an example of a systems failure when two businesses combined and then attempted to integrate their respective systems.

Real World 1.1

Blaming the system

FT

When Sir Ken Morrison bought Safeway for £3.35bn in March 2004, he almost doubled the size of his supermarket chain overnight and went from being a regional operator to a national force. His plan was simple enough. He had to sell off some Safeway stores – Morrison has to date sold off 184 stores for an estimated £1.3bn – and convert the remaining 230 Safeway stores into Morrison's. Sir Ken has about another 50 to sell. But, nearly fifteen months on, and the integration process is proving harder in practice than it looked on paper. Morrison, once known for its robust performance, has issued four profit warnings in the past ten months. Each time the retailer has blamed Safeway. Last July, it was because of a faster-than-expected sales decline in Safeway stores. In March – there were two warnings that month – it was the fault of Safeway's accounting systems, which left Morrison with lower supplier incomes. This month's warning was put down to higher-than-expected costs from running parallel store systems. At the time of the first warning last July, Simon Procter, of the stockbrokers Charles Stanley, noted that the news 'has blown all profit forecasts out of the water and visibility is very poor from here on out'. But if it was difficult then to predict where Morrison's profits were heading, it is impossible now. Morrison itself cannot give guidance. 'No one envisaged this,' says Mr Procter. 'When I made that comment about visibility last July, I was thinking on a twelve-month time frame, not a two-year one.' Morrison says the complexity of the Safeway deal has put a 'significant strain' on its ability to cope with managing internal accounts. 'This is impacting the ability of the board to forecast likely trends in profitability and the directors are therefore not currently in a position to provide reliable guidance on the level of profitability as a whole,' admits the retailer.

Source: 'Morrison in uphill battle to integrate Safeway', Elizabeth Rigby, *Financial Times*, 26 May 2005.

As a footnote to Real World 1.1, though Morrison had its problems, these were quickly overcome and the Safeway takeover has proved to be a success.

Management accounting and financial accounting

Accounting is usually seen as having two distinct strands. These are:

 • **management accounting**, which seeks to meet the accounting needs of managers; and

 • **financial accounting**, which seeks to meet the accounting needs of all of the other users identified earlier in the chapter (see Figure 1.1).

The difference in their targeted user groups has led to each strand of accounting developing along different lines. The main areas of difference are as follows.

- *Nature of the reports produced.* Financial accounting reports tend to be general-purpose, that is, they contain financial information that will be useful for a broad range of users and decisions rather than being specifically designed for the needs of a particular group or set of decisions. Management accounting reports, on the other hand, are often specific-purpose reports. They are designed with a particular decision in mind and/or for a particular manager.

- *Level of detail.* Financial accounting reports provide users with a broad overview of the performance and position of the business for a period. As a result, information is aggregated and detail is often lost. Management accounting reports, however, often provide managers with considerable detail to help them with a particular operational decision.

- *Regulations.* Financial accounting reports, for many businesses, are subject to accounting regulations that try to ensure they are produced with standard content and in a standard format. The law and accounting rule makers impose these regulations. As management accounting reports are for internal use only, there are no regulations from external sources concerning the form and content of the reports. They can be designed to meet the needs of particular managers.

- *Reporting interval.* For most businesses, financial accounting reports are produced on an annual basis, though some large businesses produce half-yearly reports and a few produce quarterly ones. Management accounting reports may be produced as frequently as required by managers. In many businesses, managers are provided with certain reports on a daily, weekly or monthly basis, which allows them to check progress frequently. In addition, special-purpose reports will be prepared when required (for example, to evaluate a proposal to purchase a piece of equipment).

- *Time orientation.* Financial accounting reports reflect the performance and position of the business for the past period. In essence, they are backward looking. Management accounting reports, on the other hand, often provide information concerning future performance as well as past performance. It is an oversimplification, however, to suggest that financial accounting reports never incorporate expectations concerning the future. Occasionally, businesses will release projected information to other users in an attempt to raise capital or to fight off unwanted takeover bids. Even preparation of the routine financial accounting reports typically requires making some judgements about the future, as we shall see in Chapter 3.

- *Range and quality of information.* Financial accounting reports concentrate on information that can be quantified in monetary terms. Management accounting also produces such reports, but is also more likely to produce reports that contain information of a non-financial nature, such as physical volume of inventories, number of sales orders received, number of new products launched, physical output per employee and so on. Financial accounting places greater emphasis on the use of objective, verifiable evidence when preparing reports. Management accounting reports may use information that is less objective and verifiable, but nevertheless provide managers with the information they need.

We can see from this that management accounting is less constrained than financial accounting. It may draw from a variety of sources and use information that has varying degrees of reliability. The only real test to be applied when assessing the value of the information produced for managers is whether or not it improves the quality of the decisions made.

The distinctions between management and financial accounting suggest that there are differences between the information needs of managers and those of other users. While differences undoubtedly exist, there is also a good deal of overlap between these needs.

Activity 1.7

Can you think of any areas of overlap between the information needs of managers and those of other users?

We thought of two points:

- Managers will, at times, be interested in receiving a historical overview of business operations of the sort provided to other users.
- Other users would be interested in receiving information relating to the future, such as the planned level of profits and non-financial information such as the state of the sales order book and the extent of product innovations.

The distinction between the two areas of accounting reflects, to some extent, the differences in access to financial information. Managers have much more control over the form and content of information they receive. Other users have to rely on what managers are prepared to provide or what the financial reporting regulations require to be provided. Though the scope of financial accounting reports has increased over time, fears concerning loss of competitive advantage and user ignorance concerning the reliability of forecast data have led businesses to resist providing other users with the same detailed and wide-ranging information available to managers.

In the past, it has been argued that accounting systems are far too geared to meeting the regulatory requirements of financial accounting to be able to provide the information most helpful to managers. This is to say that financial accounting requirements have been the main priority and management accounting has suffered as a result. Recent survey evidence suggests, however, that this argument has lost its force. Modern management accounting systems tend to provide managers with information that is relevant to their needs rather than what is determined by external reporting requirements. Financial reporting cycles, however, retain some influence over management accounting and managers are aware of expectations of external users (see the reference at the end of the chapter).

Scope of this book

This book is concerned with financial accounting rather than management accounting. In Chapter 2 we begin by introducing the three principal financial statements:

- the statement of financial position (sometimes known as the balance sheet);
- the income statement (also called the profit and loss account); and
- the statement of cash flows.

These statements are briefly reviewed before we go on to consider the statement of financial position in more detail. We shall see that the statement of financial position provides information concerning the wealth held by a business at a particular point in time and the claims against this wealth. Included in our consideration of the statement of financial position will be an introduction to the **conventions of accounting**. Conventions are the generally accepted rules that accountants tend to follow when preparing financial statements.

Chapter 3 introduces the second of the major financial statements, the income statement. This provides information concerning the wealth created by a business during a period. In this chapter we shall be looking at such issues as how profit is measured, the point in time at which we recognise that a profit has been made and the accounting conventions that apply to this particular statement.

In the UK and throughout much of the industrialised world, the limited company is the major form of business unit. In Chapter 4 we consider the accounting aspects of limited companies. Although there is nothing of essence that makes the accounting aspects of companies different from other types of private-sector business, there are some points of detail that we need to consider. In Chapter 5 we continue our examination of limited companies and, in particular, consider the framework of rules that must be adhered to when presenting accounting reports to owners and external users.

Chapter 6 deals with the last of the three principal financial statements, the statement of cash flows. This financial statement is important in identifying the financing and investing activities of the business over a period. It sets out how cash was generated and how cash was used during a period.

Reading the three statements will provide information about the performance and position of a business. It is possible, however, to gain even more helpful insights about the business by analysing the statements using financial ratios and other techniques. Combining two figures in the financial statements in a ratio and comparing this with a similar ratio for, say, another business, can often tell us much more than just reading the figures themselves. Chapters 7 and 8 are concerned with techniques for analysing financial statements.

The typical large business in the UK is a group of companies rather than just a single company. A group of companies will exist where one company controls one or more other companies. In Chapter 9 we shall see why groups exist and consider the accounting issues raised by the combination of companies into groups.

The scope of financial reporting has tended to alter over the years. In Chapter 10 we shall consider where financial reporting has come from and how it seems to be developing. Finally, in Chapter 11, we shall consider the way in which larger businesses are managed and how directors and other senior managers are accountable to the owners and to other groups with an interest in the business.

Has accounting become too interesting?

In recent years, accounting has become front-page news and has been a major talking point among those connected with the world of business. Unfortunately, the attention that accounting has attracted has been for all the wrong reasons. We have seen that investors rely on financial reports to help to keep an eye both on their investment and on the performance of the managers. What, though, if the managers provide misleading financial reports to investors? Recent revelations suggest that the managers of some large businesses have been doing just this.

Two of the most notorious cases have been those of:

● Enron, an energy-trading business based in Texas, which was accused of entering into complicated financial arrangements in an attempt to obscure losses and to inflate profits; and
● WorldCom, a major long-distance telephone operator in the US, which was accused of reclassifying $3.9 billion of expenses so as to falsely inflate the profit figures that the business reported to its owners (shareholders) and to others.

In the wake of these scandals, there was much closer scrutiny by investment analysts and investors of the financial reports that businesses produce. This led to further businesses, in both the US and Europe, being accused of using dubious accounting practices to bolster reported profits.

Accounting scandals can have a profound effect on all those connected with the business. The Enron scandal, for example, ultimately led to the collapse of the company, which, in turn, resulted in lost jobs and large financial losses for lenders, suppliers and investors. Confidence in the world of business can be badly shaken by such events and this can pose problems for society as a whole. Not surprisingly, therefore, the relevant authorities tend to be severe on those who perpetrate such scandals. In the US, Bernie Ebbers, the former chief executive of WorldCom, received 25 years in prison for his part in the fraud.

Various reasons have been put forward to explain this spate of scandals. Some may have been caused by the pressures on managers to meet unrealistic expectations of investors for continually rising profits, others by the greed of unscrupulous executives whose pay is linked to financial performance. However, they may all reflect a particular economic environment.

Real World 1.2 gives some comments suggesting that when all appears to be going well with a business, people can be quite gullible and over-trusting.

Real World 1.2

The thoughts of Warren Buffett

Warren Buffett is one of the world's shrewdest and most successful investors. He believes that the accounting scandals mentioned above were perpetrated during the 'new economy boom' of the late 1990s when confidence was high and exaggerated predictions were being made concerning the future. He states that during that period

> You had an erosion of accounting standards. You had an erosion, to some extent, of executive behaviour. But during a period when everybody 'believes', people who are inclined to take advantage of other people can get away with a lot.

He believes that the worst is now over and that the 'dirty laundry' created during this heady period is being washed away and that the washing machine is now in the 'rinse cycle'.

Source: The Times, Business Section, 26 September 2002, p. 25. nisyndication.com.

Whatever the causes, the result of these accounting scandals has been to undermine the credibility of financial statements and to introduce much stricter regulations concerning the quality of financial information. We shall return to this issue in later chapters when we consider the financial statements.

The changing face of accounting

Over the past 25 years, the environment within which businesses operate has become increasingly turbulent and competitive. Various reasons have been identified to explain these changes, including:

- the increasing sophistication of customers;
- the development of a global economy where national frontiers become less important;
- rapid changes in technology;
- the deregulation of domestic markets (for example, electricity, water and gas);
- increasing pressure from owners (shareholders) for competitive economic returns;
- the increasing volatility of financial markets.

This new, more complex, environment has brought new challenges for managers and other users of accounting information. Their needs have changed and both financial accounting and management accounting have had to respond. To meet the changing needs of users there has been a radical review of the kind of information to be reported.

The changing business environment has given added impetus to the search for a clear framework and principles upon which to base financial accounting reports. Various attempts have been made to clarify the purpose of financial accounting reports and to provide a more solid foundation for the development of accounting rules. The frameworks and principles that have been developed try to address fundamental questions such as:

- Who are the users of financial accounting information?
- What kinds of financial accounting reports should be prepared and what should they contain?
- How should items (such as profit and asset values) be measured?

In response to criticisms that the financial reports of some businesses are not clear enough to users, accounting rule makers have tried to improve reporting rules to ensure that the accounting policies of businesses are more comparable and more transparent, and that they portray economic reality more faithfully. While this has had a generally beneficial effect, the recent accounting scandals have highlighted the limitations of accounting rules in protecting investors and others.

The internationalisation of businesses has created a need for accounting rules to have an international reach. It can no longer be assumed that users of accounting information relating to a particular business are based in the country in which the business operates or are familiar with the accounting rules of that country. Thus, there has been increasing harmonisation of accounting rules across national frontiers. A more detailed review of these developments is included in Chapter 5.

Management accounting has also changed by becoming more outward looking in its focus. In the past, information provided to managers has been largely restricted to that collected within the business. However, the attitude and behaviour of customers and rival businesses have now become the object of much information gathering. Increasingly, successful businesses are those that are able to secure and maintain competitive advantage over their rivals.

To obtain this advantage, businesses have become more 'customer driven' (that is, concerned with satisfying customer needs). This has led to management accounting information that provides details of customers and the market, such as customer evaluation of services provided and market share. In addition, information about the costs and profits of rival businesses, which can be used as 'benchmarks' by which to gauge competitiveness, is gathered and reported.

To compete successfully, businesses must also find ways of managing costs. The cost base of modern businesses is under continual review and this, in turn, has led to the development of more sophisticated methods of measuring and controlling costs.

What kinds of business ownership exist?

The particular form of business ownership has important implications for accounting purposes and so it is useful to be clear about the main forms of ownership that can arise. There are basically three arrangements:

- sole proprietorship;
- partnership; and
- limited company.

Each of these is considered below.

Sole proprietorship

→ **Sole proprietorship**, as the name suggests, is where an individual is the sole owner of a business. This type of business is often quite small in terms of size (as measured, for example, by sales revenue generated or number of staff employed); however, the number of such businesses is very large indeed. Examples of sole-proprietor businesses can be found in most industrial sectors but particularly within the service sector. Hence, services such as electrical repairs, picture framing, photography, driving instruction, retail shops and hotels have a large proportion of sole-proprietor businesses. The sole-proprietor business is easy to set up. No formal procedures are required and operations can often commence immediately (unless special permission is required because of the nature of the trade or service, such as running licensed premises). The owner can decide the way in which the business is to be conducted and has the flexibility to restructure or dissolve the business whenever it suits. The law does not recognise the sole-proprietor business as being separate from the owner, so the business will cease on the death of the owner.

Although the owner must produce accounting information to satisfy the taxation authorities, there is no legal requirement to produce accounting information relating to the business for other user groups. However, some user groups may demand accounting information about the business and may be in a position to have their demands met (for example, a bank requiring accounting information on a regular basis as a condition of a loan). The sole proprietor will have unlimited liability which means that no distinction will be made between the proprietor's personal wealth and that of the business if there are business debts that must be paid.

Partnership

→ A **partnership** exists where at least two individuals carry on a business together with the intention of making a profit. Partnerships have much in common with sole-proprietor businesses. They are usually quite small in size (although some, such as partnerships of accountants and solicitors, can be large). Partnerships are also easy to set up as no formal procedures are required (and it is not even necessary to have a written agreement between the partners). The partners can agree whatever arrangements suit them concerning the financial and management aspects of the business. Similarly, the partnership can be restructured or dissolved by agreement between the partners.

Partnerships are not recognised in law as separate entities and so contracts with third parties must be entered into in the name of individual partners. The partners of a business usually have unlimited liability.

Activity 1.8

What are the main advantages and disadvantages that should be considered when deciding between a sole proprietorship and a partnership?

The main advantages of a partnership over a sole-proprietor business are:

● sharing the burden of ownership;
● the opportunity to specialise rather than cover the whole range of services (for example, in a solicitors' practice each partner may specialise in a different aspect of the law);
● the ability to raise capital where this is beyond the capacity of a single individual.

The main disadvantages of a partnership compared with a sole proprietorship are:

● the risks of sharing ownership of a business with unsuitable individuals;
● the limits placed on individual decision making that a partnership will impose.

Limited company

→ **Limited companies** can range in size from quite small to very large. The number of individuals who subscribe capital and become the owners may be unlimited, which provides the opportunity to create a very large-scale business. The liability of owners, however, is limited (hence 'limited' company), which means that those individuals subscribing capital to the company are liable only for debts incurred by the company up to the amount that they have agreed to invest. This cap on the liability of the owners is designed to limit risk and to produce greater confidence to invest. Without such limits on owner liability, it is difficult to see how a modern capitalist economy could operate. In many cases, the owners of a limited company are not involved in the day-to-day running of the business and will, therefore, invest in a business only if there is a clear limit set on the level of investment risk.

The benefit of limited liability, however, imposes certain obligations on such companies. To start up a limited company, documents of incorporation must be prepared that set out, among other things, the objectives of the business. Furthermore, a framework of regulations exists that places obligations on limited companies concerning the way in which they conduct their affairs. Part of this regulatory framework requires annual financial reports to be made available to owners and lenders and usually an annual general meeting of the owners has to be held to approve the reports. In addition, a copy of the annual financial reports must be lodged with the Registrar of Companies for public inspection. In this way, the financial affairs of a limited company enter the public domain. With the exception of small companies, there is also a requirement for the annual financial reports to be subject to an audit. This involves an independent firm of accountants examining the annual reports and underlying records to see whether the reports provide a true and fair view of the financial health of the company and whether they comply with the relevant accounting rules established by law and by accounting rule makers.

All of the large household-name UK businesses (Marks and Spencer, Tesco, Shell, BSkyB, BA, BT, easyJet and so on) are limited companies.

Limited companies are considered in more detail in Chapters 4 and 5.

Activity 1.9

What are the main advantages and disadvantages that should be considered when deciding between a partnership business and a limited liability company?

The main advantages of a partnership over a limited company are:

- the ease of setting up the business;
- the degree of flexibility concerning the way in which the business is conducted;
- the degree of flexibility concerning restructuring and dissolution of the business;
- freedom from administrative burdens imposed by law (for example, the annual general meeting and the need for an independent audit).

The main disadvantage of a partnership compared with a limited company is the fact that it is not possible to limit the liability of all of the partners.

This book concentrates on the accounting aspects of limited liability companies because this type of business is by far the most important in economic terms. The early chapters will introduce accounting concepts through examples that do not draw a distinction between the different types of business. Once we have dealt with the basic accounting principles, which are the same for all three types of business, we can then go on to see how they are applied to limited companies. It must be emphasised that there are no differences in the way that these three forms of business keep their day-to-day accounting records. In preparing their periodic financial statements, there are certain differences that need to be considered. These differences are not ones of principle, however, but of detail.

How are businesses organised?

As we have just seen, nearly all businesses that involve more than a few owners and/or employees are set up as limited companies. This means that the finance will come from the owners (shareholders) both in the form of a direct cash investment to buy shares (in the ownership of the business) and through the owners allowing past profits, which belong to them, to be reinvested in the business. Finance will also come from lenders (banks, for example), who earn interest on their loans and from suppliers of goods and services being prepared to supply on credit, with payment occurring a month or so after the date of supply, usually on an interest-free basis.

In larger limited companies, the owners (shareholders) are not involved in the daily running of the business; instead they appoint a board of directors to manage the business on their behalf. The board is charged with three major tasks:

- setting the overall direction and strategy for the business;
- monitoring and controlling its activities; and
- communicating with owners and others connected with the business.

Each board has a chairman, elected by the directors, who is responsible for running the board in an efficient manner. In addition, each board has a chief executive officer (CEO), or managing director, who is responsible for running the business on a day-to-day basis. Occasionally, the roles of chairman and CEO are combined, although it is usually considered to be a good idea to separate them in order to prevent a single individual having excessive power. We shall come back to consider the relationship between directors and shareholders in more detail in Chapter 4.

The board of directors represents the most senior level of management. Below this level, managers are employed, with each manager given responsibility for a particular part of the business's operations.

What is the financial objective of a business?

A business is created to enhance the wealth of its owners. Throughout this book we shall assume that this is its main objective. This may come as a surprise, as there are other objectives that a business may pursue that are related to the needs of others associated with the business. For example, a business may seek to provide good working conditions for its employees, or it may seek to conserve the environment for the local community. While a business may pursue these objectives, it is normally set up with a view to increasing the wealth of its owners. In practice, the behaviour of businesses over time appears to be consistent with this objective.

Real World 1.3 reveals how one well-known business has changed its focus in order to improve profitability.

Real World 1.3

Profiting from change

It speaks volumes for the work done by Kate Swann in turning around W H Smith that when she became chief executive five years ago, the company was being spoken of in similar tems to Woolworths. Comments such as 'You wouldn't invent it if you were starting out today' and 'What is it actually for these days?' were typical among analysts, as they were with Woolies. Indeed, many thought that W H Smith was beyond help and argued that the supermarkets were eating away at sales.

Ms Swann has defied the sceptics, achieving an impressive turnaround. The company's magazine and newspaper distribution division was hived off as a separate entity and new outlets were opened at airports and railway stations – so much so that sales by W H Smith's travel unit now threaten to overtake those of its traditional high street stores. Lower-[profit-]margin lines, such as CDs and DVDs, have been cleared from the shelves to make way for higher-margin items, such as stationery.

The last plank of the strategy was in evidence again in yesterday's update, in which Ms Swann reported that sales in the nine weeks to January 17 were down by 7 per cent in the high street stores and by 2 per cent in the travel stores, partly because W H Smith is continuing to reduce its exposure to the entertainment category.

That was the bad news. The good news was that, although sales overall were down, the reduced focus on entertainment was good for profits. W H Smith made an extra 2p of profit in every £1 of sales, compared with the same period a year earlier, a stunning achievement given the deflation hitting the high street.

Source: 'Business big shot', Ian King, *The Times*, 27 January 2009, p. 39. nisyndication.com.

Within a market economy there are strong competitive forces at work that ensure that failure to enhance owners' wealth will not be tolerated for long. Competition for the funds provided by the owners and competition for managers' jobs will normally mean that the owners' interests will prevail. If the managers do not provide the expected increase in ownership wealth, the owners have the power to replace the existing management team with a new team that is more responsive to owners' needs.

Does this mean that the needs of other groups associated with the business (employees, customers, suppliers, the community and so on) are not really important? The answer to this question is certainly no, if the business wishes to survive and prosper over the longer term. Satisfying the needs of other groups will normally be consistent with increasing the wealth of the owners over the longer term.

The importance of customers to a business cannot be overstated. Dissatisfied customers will take their business to another supplier and this will, in turn, lead to a loss of wealth for the owners of the business losing the customers. **Real World 1.4** provides an illustration of the way in which one business acknowledges the link between customer satisfaction and creating wealth for its owners.

Real World 1.4

Checking out Sainsbury's objectives

J Sainsbury plc is a leading food retailer that recognises the importance of customers to increasing the wealth of the owners (shareholders) as follows:

> Our objective is to serve customers well and thereby provide shareholders with good, sustainable financial returns.

Source: Investor FAQs, www.j-sainsbury.co.uk, 8 January 2009, p. 1.

A dissatisfied workforce may result in low productivity, strikes and so forth, which will in turn have an adverse effect on owners' wealth. Similarly, a business that upsets the local community by unacceptable behaviour, such as polluting the environment, may attract bad publicity, resulting in a loss of customers and heavy fines.

Real World 1.5 provides an example of how two businesses responded to potentially damaging allegations.

Real World 1.5

The price of clothes   **FT**

US clothing and sportswear manufacturers Gap and Nike have many of their clothes produced in Asia where labour tends to be cheap. However, some of the contractors that produce clothes on behalf of the two companies have been accused of unacceptable practices.

> Campaigners visited the factories and came up with damaging allegations. The factories were employing minors, they said, and managers were harassing female employees.
>
> Nike and Gap reacted by allowing independent inspectors into the factories. They promised to ensure their contractors obeyed minimum standards of employment. Earlier this year, Nike took the extraordinary step of publishing the names and addresses of all its contractors' factories on the internet. The company said it could not be sure all the abuse had stopped. It said that if campaigners visited its contractors' factories and found examples of continued malpractice, it would take action.
>
> Nike and Gap said the approach made business sense. They needed society's approval if they were to prosper. Nike said it was concerned about the reaction of potential US recruits to the campaigners' allegations. They would not want to work for a company that was constantly in the news because of the allegedly cruel treatment of those who made its products.

Source: 'Fair shares?', Michael Skapinker, *Financial Times*, 11 June 2005.

It is important to recognise that generating wealth for the owners is not the same as seeking to maximise the current year's profit. Wealth creation is a longer-term concept, which relates not only to this year's profit but to that of future years as well. In the short term, corners can be cut and risks taken that improve current profit at the expense of future profit. **Real World 1.6** gives some examples of how emphasis on short-term profit can be damaging.

Real World 1.6

Short-term gains, long-term problems   FT

Human beings are bad at learning and changing. It takes a good crisis to drive home what may have been staring us in the face.

So what in particular are the lessons for all those concerned with saving, investment, borrowing and lending?

For many years, under the guise of defending capitalism, we have been allowing ourselves to degrade it. We have been poisoning the well from which we have drawn wealth.

We have misunderstood the importance of values to capitalism. We have surrendered to the idea that success is pursued by making as much money as the law allowed without regard to how it was made.

Thirty years ago, retailers would be quite content to source the shoes they wanted to sell as cheaply as possible. The working conditions of those who produced them was not their concern.

Then headlines and protests developed. Society started to hold them responsible for previously invisible working conditions.

Companies like Nike went through a transformation. They realised they were polluting their brand. Global sourcing became visible. It was no longer viable to define success simply in terms of buying at the lowest price and selling at the highest.

Financial services and investment are today where footwear was 30 years ago. Public anger at the crisis will make visible what was previously hidden.

Take the building up of huge portfolios of loans to poor people on US trailer parks. These loans were authorised without proper scrutiny of the circumstances of the borrowers. Somebody else then deemed them fit to be securitised . . . and so on through credit default swaps and the rest without anyone seeing the transaction in terms of its ultimate human origin.

Each of the decision makers thought it okay to act like the thoughtless footwear buyer of the 1970s. The price was attractive. There was money to make on the deal. Was it responsible? Irrelevant. It was legal, and others were making money that way.

And the consequences for the banking system if everybody did it? Not our problem.

Now we are paying the price in trillions of dollars for that imprudent attitude.

One senior investment banker whose business has survived the crisis in good shape recently confirmed this analysis to me. Again and again new product ideas had been put in front of him, without any prior thought about their ethical content.

The consumer has had a profound shock. Surely we could have expected the clever and wise people who invested our money to be better at risk management than they have shown themselves to be in the present crisis?

How could they have been so gullible in not challenging the bankers whose lending proved so flaky? How could they have believed that the levels of bonuses that were, at least in part, coming out of their savings could have been justified in 'incentivising' a better performance? How could they have believed that a 'better' performance would be one that is achieved for one bank without regard to its effect on the whole banking system? Where was the stewardship from those exercising investment on their behalf?

The answer has been that very few of them do exercise that stewardship. Most have stood back and said it doesn't really pay them to do so.

The failure of stewardship comes from the same mindset that created the irresponsible lending in the first place. We are back to the mindset that has allowed us to poison the well: never mind the health of the system as a whole, I'm making money out of it at the moment.

Responsibility means awareness for the system consequences of our actions. It is not a luxury. It is the cornerstone of prudence.

Source: 'How we've poisoned the well of wealth', Mark Goyder, *Financial Times*, 15 February 2009.

Balancing risk and return

All decision making involves the future and business decision making is no exception. The only thing certain about the future, however, is that we cannot be sure what will happen. Things may not turn out as planned and this risk should be carefully considered when making financial decisions.

As in other aspects of life, risk and return tend to be related. Evidence shows that returns relate to risk in something like the way shown in Figure 1.5.

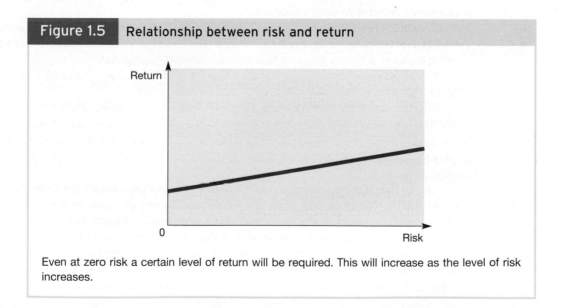

| Figure 1.5 | Relationship between risk and return |

Even at zero risk a certain level of return will be required. This will increase as the level of risk increases.

This relationship between risk and return has important implications for setting financial objectives for a business. The owners will require a minimum return to induce them to invest at all, but will require an additional return to compensate for taking risks; the higher the risk, the higher the required return. Managers must be aware of this and must strike the appropriate balance between risk and return when setting objectives and pursuing particular courses of action.

Real World 1.7 below describes how some businesses have been making higher risk investments in pursuit of higher returns.

Real World 1.7

Appetite for risk drives businesses   FT

Over the last few years, companies from the US and western Europe, joined increasingly by competitors from China and India, have looked to new markets abroad both to source and sell their products.

Driven by intensifying competition at home, companies have been drawn into direct investment in markets that not long ago were considered beyond the pale. But in the drive to increase returns, they have also been forced to accept higher risks.

Over time, the balance between risk and reward changes. For example, companies flooded into Russia early in the decade. But recently returns have fallen, largely due to booming raw materials prices. Meanwhile the apparent risk of investing in Russia has grown significantly.

As the risk-reward calculation has changed in Russia, companies have looked to other countries such as Libya and Vietnam where the rewards may be substantial, and the threats, though high, may be more manageable.

Source: Adapted from 'Appetite for risk drives industry', Stephen Fidler, FT.com site 27 June, 2007.

Not-for-profit organisations

Though the focus of this book is accounting as it relates to private-sector businesses, there are many organisations that do not exist mainly for the pursuit of profit. Examples include:

- charities
- clubs and associations
- universities
- local government authorities
- national government departments
- churches
- trade unions.

Such organisations also need to produce accounting information for decision-making purposes. Various user groups need accounting information about these types of organisation to help them to make decisions. These groups are often the same as, or similar to, those identified for private-sector businesses. They may have a stake in the future viability of the organisation and may use accounting information to check that the wealth of the organisation is being properly controlled and used in a way that is consistent with its objectives.

Real World 1.8 provides an example of the importance of accounting to relief agencies.

Accounting for disasters

FT

In the aftermath of the Asian tsunami more than £400 million was raised from charitable donations. It was important that this huge amount of money for aid and reconstruction was used as efficiently and effectively as possible. That did not just mean medical staff and engineers. It also meant accountants.

The charity that exerts financial control over aid donations is Mango: Management Accounting for Non-Governmental Organisations (NGOs). It provides accountants in the field and it provides the back-up, such as financial training, and all the other services that should result in really robust financial management in a disaster area.

The world of aid has changed completely as a result of the tsunami. According to Mango's director, Alex Jacobs, 'Accounting is just as important as blankets. Agencies have been aware of this for years. But when you move on to a bigger scale there is more pressure to show the donations are being used appropriately.'

Source: Adapted from 'Tsunami: finding the right figures for disaster relief', Robert Bruce, FT.com, 7 March 2005 and 'The work of Mango: Coping with generous donations', Robert Bruce, FT.com, 27 February 2006.

Summary

The main points of this chapter may be summarised as follows:

What is accounting?

● Accounting provides financial information for a range of users to help them make better judgements and decisions concerning a business.

Accounting and user needs

● For accounting to be useful, there must be a clear understanding of *for whom* and *for what purpose* the information will be used.

● There may be conflicts of interest between users over the ways in which the wealth of a business is generated or distributed.

● There is evidence to suggest that accounting is both used and useful for decision-making purposes.

Providing a service

● Accounting can be viewed as a form of service as it involves providing financial information required by the various users.

● To provide a useful service, accounting must possess certain qualities, or characteristics. These are relevance, reliability, comparability and understandability. In addition, accounting information must be material.

● Providing a service to users can be costly and financial information should be produced only if the cost of providing the information is less than the benefits gained.

Accounting information

● Accounting is part of the total information system within a business. It shares the features that are common to all information systems within a business, which are the identification, recording, analysis and reporting of information.

Management accounting and financial accounting

● Accounting has two main strands – management accounting and financial accounting.

● Management accounting seeks to meet the needs of the business's managers and financial accounting seeks to meet the needs of the other user groups.

● These two strands differ in terms of the types of reports produced, the level of reporting detail, the time horizon, the degree of standardisation and the range and quality of information provided.

Is accounting too interesting?

● In recent years, there has been a wave of accounting scandals in the US and Europe.

● This appears to reflect a particular economic environment, although other factors may also play a part.

The changing face of accounting

● Changes in the economic environment have led to changes in the nature and scope of accounting.

● Financial accounting has improved its framework of rules and there has been greater international harmonisation of accounting rules.

● Management accounting has become more outward looking and new methods for managing costs have emerged.

What kinds of business ownership exist?

There are three main forms of business unit:

- Sole proprietorship – easy to set up and flexible to operate but the owner has unlimited liability.
- Partnership – easy to set up and spreads the burdens of ownership, but partners usually have unlimited liability and there are ownership risks if the partners are unsuitable.
- Limited company – limited liability for owners but obligations imposed on the way a company conducts its affairs.

How are businesses organised and managed?

- Most businesses of any size are set up as limited companies.
- A board of directors is appointed by owners (shareholders) to oversee the running of the business.

What is the financial objective of a business?

- A business may pursue a variety of objectives but the main objective for virtually all businesses is to enhance the wealth of their owners. This does not mean, however, that the needs of other groups connected with the business, such as employees, should be ignored.
- When setting financial objectives the right balance must be struck between risk and return.

 Key terms

accounting p. 2	accounting information system p. 10
shares p. 5	management accounting p. 12
relevance p. 6	financial accounting p. 12
reliability p. 6	conventions of accounting p. 14
comparability p. 7	sole proprietorship p. 17
understandability p. 7	partnership p. 17
materiality p. 7	limited company p. 18

Reference

Dugdale, D., Jones, C. and Green, S., *Contemporary Management Accounting Practices in UK Manufacturing*, CIMA Research Publication, vol. 1, no. 13, 2005.

Further reading

If you would like to explore the topics covered in this chapter in more depth, we recommend the following books:

Alexander, D. and Nobes, C., *Financial Accounting: An International Introduction*, 3rd edn, Financial Times Prentice Hall, 2007, Chapter 1.

Elliot, B. and Elliot, J., *Financial Accounting and Reporting*, 13th edn, Financial Times Prentice Hall, 2009, Chapter 7.

Riahi-Belkaoui, A., *Accounting Theory*, 5th edn, Thomson Learning, 2004, Chapters 1, 2 and 6.

Review questions

Solutions to these questions can be found at the back of the book on pages 481–482.

1.1 What is the purpose of producing accounting information?

1.2 Identify the main users of accounting information for a university. For what purposes would different user groups need information? Is there a major difference in the ways in which accounting information for a university would be used compared with that of a private-sector business?

1.3 What, in economic principle, should be the determinant of what accounting information is produced? Should economics be the only issue here? (Consider who are the users of accounting information.)

1.4 Financial accounting statements tend to reflect past events. In view of this, how can they be of any assistance to a user in making a decision when decisions, by their very nature, can only be made about future actions?

2

Measuring and reporting financial position

Introduction

We saw in Chapter 1 that accounting has two distinct strands: financial accounting and management accounting. This chapter, along with Chapters 3 to 6, examines the three major financial statements that form the core of financial accounting. We start by taking an overview of these statements to see how each contributes towards an assessment of the overall financial position and performance of a business.

Following this overview, we begin a more detailed examination by turning our attention towards one of these financial statements: the statement of financial position. We shall see how it is prepared and examine the principles underpinning it. We shall also consider its value for decision-making purposes.

Learning outcomes

When you have completed this chapter, you should be able to:

● explain the nature and purpose of the three major financial statements;

● prepare a simple statement of financial position and interpret the information that it contains;

● discuss the accounting conventions underpinning the statement of financial position;

● discuss the uses and limitations of the statement of financial position for decision-making purposes.

Making financial decisions

We have just seen that a key purpose of this chapter is to show how the statement of financial position is constructed and how it may help users. So, let us begin by considering a practical situation where this statement may be of benefit. **Real World 2.1** describes how the statement of financial position of a small business was used by a bank when deciding whether to grant a loan.

Real World 2.1

A sound education

Sandeep Sud is a qualified solicitor who also runs a school uniform business based in Hounslow, in partnership with his parents. The company, which has four full-time employees, uses its statement of financial position (balance sheet) to gauge how the business is progressing. It has also been a key factor in securing a bank loan for the improvement and expansion of the company premises.

According to Sandeep,

> Having a strong statement of financial position helped when it came to borrowing. When we first applied for a refurbishment loan we couldn't provide up-to-date accounts to the bank manager. This could have been a problem, but we quickly got our accounts in order and the loan was approved straight away. Because our statement of financial position was strong, the bank thought we were a good risk. Although we decided not to draw down on the loan – because we used cash flow instead – it did open our eyes to the importance of a strong statement of financial position.

Source: Adapted from 'Balance sheets: the basics', www.businesslink.gov.uk, accessed 19 October 2009.

Before we consider the statement of financial position in detail, however, we shall first gain an overview of all three major financial accounting statements. This should help us to understand the role of each one as well as their inter-relationships.

The major financial statements – an overview

The major financial accounting statements aim to provide a picture of the financial position and performance of a business. To achieve this, a business's accounting system will normally produce three particular statements on a regular, recurring basis. These three statements are concerned with answering the following questions:

- What cash movements (that is, cash in and cash out) took place over a particular period?
- How much wealth (that is, profit) was generated, or lost, by the business over that period? (Profit (or loss) is defined as the increase (or decrease) in wealth arising from trading activities.)
- What is the accumulated wealth of the business at the end of that period and what form does the wealth take?

To address each of the above questions, there is a separate financial statement. The financial statements are:

→   ● the **statement of cash flows**;
→   ● the **income statement** (also known as the profit and loss account); and
→   ● the **statement of financial position** (also known as the balance sheet).

Together they provide an overall picture of the financial health of the business.

Perhaps the best way to introduce these financial statements is to look at an example of a very simple business. From this we shall be able to see the sort of information that each of the statements can usefully provide. It is, however, worth pointing out that, while a simple business is our starting point, the principles for preparing the financial statements apply equally to the largest and most complex businesses. This means that we shall frequently encounter these principles again in later chapters.

Example 2.1

Paul was unemployed and unable to find a job. He therefore decided to embark on a business venture. Christmas was approaching, and so he decided to buy gift wrapping paper from a local supplier and to sell it on the corner of his local high street. He felt that the price of wrapping paper in the high street shops was too high. This provided him with a useful business opportunity.

He began the venture with £40 of his own money, in cash. On Monday, Paul's first day of trading, he bought wrapping paper for £40 and sold three-quarters of it for £45 cash.

● **What cash movements took place during Monday?**

For Monday, a *statement of cash flows* showing the cash movements for the day can be prepared as follows:

Statement of cash flows for Monday

	£
Opening balance (cash introduced)	40
Cash from sales of wrapping paper	45
Cash paid to buy wrapping paper	(40)
Closing balance of cash	45

The statement shows that Paul placed £40 cash into the business. The business received £45 cash from customers, but paid £40 cash to buy the wrapping paper. This left £45 of cash by Monday evening. Note that we are taking the standard approach found in the financial statements of showing figures to be deducted (in this case the £40 paid out) in brackets. We shall take this approach consistently throughout the chapters dealing with financial statements.

● **How much wealth (that is, profit) was generated by the business during Monday?**

An *income statement (profit and loss account)* can be prepared to show the wealth (profit) generated on Monday. The wealth generated will represent the difference between the value of the sales made and the cost of the goods (that is, wrapping paper) sold.

Income statement (profit and loss account) for Monday

	£
Sales revenue	45
Cost of goods sold ($\frac{3}{4}$ of £40)	(30)
Profit	15

Note that it is only the cost of the wrapping paper *sold* that is matched against (and deducted from) the sales revenue in order to find the profit, not the whole of the cost of wrapping paper acquired. Any unsold inventories (in this case $\frac{1}{4}$ of £40 = £10) will be charged against the future sales revenue that they generate.

● **What is the accumulated wealth at Monday evening?**
To establish the accumulated wealth at the end of Monday's trading, we can draw up a *statement of financial position (balance sheet)*. This will list the resources held at the end of that day.

Statement of financial position (balance sheet) as at Monday evening

	£
Cash (closing balance)	45
Inventories of goods for resale ($\frac{1}{4}$ of £40)	10
Total assets	55
Equity	55

Note the terms 'assets' and 'equity' that appear in the above statement. 'Assets' are business resources (things of value to the business) and include cash and inventories. 'Equity' is the word used in accounting to describe the investment, or stake, of the owner(s) – in this case Paul – in the business. Both of these terms will be discussed in some detail a little later in this chapter.

We can see from the financial statements in Example 2.1 that each statement provides part of a picture portraying the financial performance and position of the business. We begin by showing the cash movements. Cash is a vital resource that is necessary for any business to function effectively. Cash is required to meet debts that may become due and to acquire other resources (such as inventories). Cash has been described as the 'lifeblood' of a business. Movements in cash are usually closely scrutinised by users of financial statements.

However, it is clear that reporting cash movements alone would not be enough to portray the financial health of the business. The changes in cash over time do not tell us how much profit was generated. The income statement provides us with information concerning this aspect of performance. For example, we saw that during Monday the cash balance increased by £5, but the profit generated, as shown in the income statement, was £15. The cash balance did not increase by the amount of the profit made because part of the wealth generated (£10) was held in the form of inventories.

The statement of financial position that was drawn up as at the end of Monday's trading provides an insight into the total wealth of the business. Cash is only one form in which wealth may be held. In the case of this business, wealth is also held in the form of inventories (also known as stock). Hence, when drawing up the statement of financial position, both forms of wealth held will be listed. In the case of a large business, there may be many other forms in which wealth will be held, such as land and buildings, equipment, motor vehicles and so on.

Let us now continue with our example.

Example 2.2

On Tuesday, Paul bought more wrapping paper for £20 cash. He managed to sell all of the new inventories and all of the earlier inventories, for a total of £48.

The statement of cash flows for Tuesday will be as follows:

Statement of cash flows for Tuesday

	£
Opening balance (from Monday evening)	45
Cash from sales of wrapping paper	48
Cash paid to buy wrapping paper	(20)
Closing balance	73

The income statement for Tuesday will be as follows:

Income statement for Tuesday

	£
Sales revenue	48
Cost of goods sold (£20 + £10)	(30)
Profit	18

The statement of financial position as at Tuesday evening will be:

Statement of financial position as at Tuesday evening

	£
Cash (closing balance)	73
Inventories	–
Total assets	73
Equity	73

We can see that the total business wealth increased to £73 by Tuesday evening. This represents an increase of £18 (that is, £73 – £55) over Monday's figure – which, of course, is the amount of profit made during Tuesday as shown on the income statement.

Activity 2.1

On Wednesday, Paul bought more wrapping paper for £46 cash. However, it was raining hard for much of the day and sales were slow. After Paul had sold half of his total inventories for £32, he decided to stop trading until Thursday morning.

Have a go at drawing up the three financial statements for Paul's business for Wednesday.

Statement of cash flows for Wednesday

	£
Opening balance (from Tuesday evening)	73
Cash from sales of wrapping paper	32
Cash paid to buy wrapping paper	(46)
Closing balance	59

Income statement for Wednesday

	£
Sales revenue	32
Cost of goods sold ($\frac{1}{2}$ of £46)	(23)
Profit	9

Statement of financial position as at Wednesday evening

	£
Cash (closing balance)	59
Inventories ($\frac{1}{2}$ of £46)	23
Total assets	82
Equity	82

Note that the total business wealth had increased by £9 (that is, the amount of Wednesday's profit) even though the cash balance had declined. This is because the business is holding more of its wealth in the form of inventories rather than cash, compared with the position on Tuesday evening.

The equity by Wednesday evening stood at £82. This arose from Paul's initial investment of £40, plus his profits for Monday (£15), Tuesday (£18) and Wednesday (£9). This represents Paul's total investment in his business at that time. Typical of most businesses, the equity partly consists of specific injections of funds by the owner, plus profits that the owner has allowed to accumulate.

We can see that the income statement and statement of cash flows are both concerned with measuring flows (of wealth and cash respectively) during a particular period (for example, a particular day, a particular month or a particular year). The statement of financial position, however, is concerned with the financial position at a particular moment in time.

Figure 2.1 illustrates this point. The financial statements (income statement, statement of cash flows and statement of financial position) are often referred to as the **final accounts** of the business.

Figure 2.1   The relationship between the statement of financial position, the income statement and the statement of cash flows

The income statement and statement of cash flows are concerned with measuring flows of wealth and cash (respectively) over time. The statement of financial position, however, is concerned with measuring the amount of wealth at a particular moment in time.

For external users (that is, virtually all users except the managers of the business concerned), these statements are normally backward looking because they are based on information concerning past events and transactions. This can be useful in providing feedback on past performance and in identifying trends that provide clues to future performance. However, the statements can also be prepared using projected data to help assess likely future profits, cash flows and so on. The financial statements are normally prepared on a projected basis for internal decision-making purposes only. Managers are usually reluctant to publish these projected statements for external users, as they may reveal valuable information to competitors.

Now that we have an overview of the financial statements, we shall consider each statement in more detail. We shall go straight on to look at the statement of financial position. Chapter 3 looks at the income statement; Chapter 6 goes into more detail on the statement of cash flows. (Chapters 4 and 5 consider the statements of financial position and income statements of limited companies.)

The statement of financial position

This sets out the financial position of a business at a particular moment in time. We saw a little earlier in the chapter that the statement shows the forms in which the wealth of the business is held and how much wealth is held in each form. We can, however, be more specific about the nature of this statement by saying that it sets out the **assets** of the business, on the one hand, and the **claims** against the business, on the other. Before looking at the statement of financial position in more detail, we need to be clear about what these terms mean.

Assets

An asset is essentially a resource held by the business. For a particular item to be treated as an asset for accounting purposes it should have the following characteristics:

- *A probable future benefit must exist.* This simply means that the item must be expected to have some future monetary value. This value can arise through its use within the business or through its hire or sale. Thus, an obsolete piece of equipment that could be sold for scrap would still be considered an asset, whereas an obsolete piece of equipment that could not be sold for scrap would not be regarded as one.
- *The business must have the right to control the resource.* Unless the business controls the resource, it cannot be regarded as an asset for accounting purposes. Thus, for a business offering holidays on barges, the canal system may be a very valuable resource, but as the business will not be able to control the access of others to the canal system, it cannot be regarded as an asset of the business. (However, the barges owned by the business would be regarded as assets.)
- *The benefit must arise from some past transaction or event.* This means that the transaction (or other event) giving rise to the business's right to the benefit must have already occurred, not be one which will arise at some future date. Thus an agreement by a business to buy a piece of equipment at some future date would not mean that the item is currently an asset of the business.
- *The asset must be capable of measurement in monetary terms.* Unless the item can be measured in monetary terms, with a reasonable degree of reliability, it will not be regarded as an asset for inclusion on the statement of financial position. Thus, the title of a magazine (for example *Hello!* or *Vogue*) that was created by its publisher may be extremely valuable to that publishing business, but this value is usually difficult to quantify. It will not, therefore, be treated as an asset.

Note that all four of these conditions must apply. If one of them is missing, the item will not be treated as an asset for accounting purposes and will, therefore, not appear on the statement of financial position.

We can see that these conditions will strictly limit the kind of items that may be referred to as 'assets' in the statement of financial position. Certainly not all resources exploited by a business will be assets of the business for accounting purposes. Some, like the canal system or the magazine title *Hello!*, may well be assets in a broader sense, but not for accounting purposes. Once an asset has been acquired by a business, it will continue to be considered an asset until the benefits are exhausted or the business disposes of it in some way.

Activity 2.2

Indicate which of the following items could appear as an asset on the statement of financial position of a business. Explain your reasoning in each case.

1 £1,000 owed to the business by a customer who is unable to pay.
2 A patent, bought from an inventor, that gives the business the right to produce a new product. Production of the new product is expected to increase profits over the period during which the patent is held.
3 A new marketing director, whom the business had recently hired, who is confidently expected to increase profits by over 30 per cent during the next three years.

Activity 2.2 continued

4 A recently purchased machine that will save the business £10,000 each year. It is already being used by the business but it has been acquired on credit and is not yet paid for.

Your answer should be along the following lines:

1 Under normal circumstances, a business would expect a customer to pay the amount owed. Such an amount is therefore typically shown as an asset under the heading 'trade receivables' (or 'debtors'). However, in this particular case the customer is unable to pay. As a result, the item is incapable of providing future benefits and the £1,000 owing would not be regarded as an asset. Debts that are not paid are referred to as 'bad debts'.

2 The patent would meet all of the conditions set out above and would therefore be regarded as an asset.

3 The new marketing director would not be considered as an asset. One argument for this is that the business does not have exclusive rights of control over the director. (Nevertheless, it may have an exclusive right to the services that the director provides.) Perhaps a stronger argument is that the value of the director cannot be measured in monetary terms with any degree of reliability.

4 The machine would be considered an asset even though it is not yet paid for. Once the business has agreed to buy the machine and has accepted it, the machine represents an asset even though payment is still outstanding. (The amount outstanding would be shown as a claim, as we shall see below.)

The sorts of items that often appear as assets in the statement of financial position of a business include:

● property
● plant and equipment
● fixtures and fittings
● patents and trademarks
● trade receivables (debtors)
● investments outside the business.

Activity 2.3

Can you think of two additional items that might appear as assets in the statement of financial position of a typical business?

You may be able to think of a number of other items. Two that we have met so far, because they were the only types of asset that were held by Paul's wrapping-paper business (in Examples 2.1 and 2.2), are inventories and cash.

Note that an asset does not have to be a physical item – it may be a non-physical item that gives a right to certain benefits. Assets (such as inventories) that have a physical substance and can be touched are referred to as **tangible assets**. Assets (such as patents) that have no physical substance but which, nevertheless, provide expected future benefits are referred to as **intangible assets**.

Claims

A claim is an obligation of the business to provide cash, or some other form of benefit, to an outside party. It will normally arise as a result of the outside party providing assets for use by the business. There are essentially two types of claim against a business:

→ • **Equity**. This represents the claim of the owner(s) against the business. This claim is sometimes referred to as the *owner's capital*. Some find it hard to understand how the owner can have a claim against the business, particularly when we consider the example of a sole-proprietor-type business where the owner *is*, in effect, the business. However, for accounting purposes, a clear distinction is made between the business (whatever its size and form) and the owner(s). The business is viewed as being quite separate from the owner and this is equally true for a sole proprietor like Paul, the wrapping-paper seller in the examples above or a large company like Marks and Spencer plc. It is seen as a separate entity with its own separate existence, and when financial statements are prepared they relate to the business rather than to the owner(s). This means that the statement of financial position will reflect the position of the business as a separate entity. Viewed from this perspective, any funds contributed by the owner will be seen as coming from outside the business and will appear as a claim against the business in its statement of financial position.

As we have just seen, the business and the owner are separate for accounting purposes, irrespective of the type of business concerned. It is also true that the equity section of the statement of financial position is broadly the same irrespective of the type of business concerned. We shall see in Chapter 4 that, with limited companies, the total equity figure must be analysed according to how each part of it first arose. For example, companies must make a distinction between that part of it that arose from retained profits and that part that arose from the owners putting in cash to start up the business, usually by buying shares in the company.

→ • **Liabilities**. Liabilities represent the claims of all individuals and organisations, apart from the owner(s). They arise from past transactions or events such as supplying goods or lending money to the business. When a liability is settled it can only be through an outflow of assets (usually cash).

Once a claim from the owners or outsiders has been incurred by a business, it will remain as an obligation until it is settled.

Now that the meaning of the terms *assets*, *equity* and *liabilities* has been established, we can go on and discuss the relationship between them. This relationship is quite straightforward. If a business wishes to acquire assets, it will have to raise the necessary funds from somewhere. It may raise the funds from the owner(s) or from other outside parties or from both. Example 2.3 illustrates this relationship.

Example 2.3

Jerry and Company start a business by depositing £20,000 in a bank account on 1 March. This amount was raised partly from the owner (£6,000) and partly from borrowing (£14,000). Raising funds in this way will give rise to a claim on the business by both the owner (equity) and the lender (liability). If a statement of financial position of Jerry and Company is prepared following the above transactions, it will appear as follows:

→

Example 2.3 continued

Jerry and Company
Statement of financial position as at 1 March

	£
ASSETS	
Cash at bank	20,000
Total assets	20,000
EQUITY AND LIABILITIES	
Equity	6,000
Liabilities – borrowing	14,000
Total equity and liabilities	20,000

We can see from the statement of financial position that the total claims are the same as the total assets. Thus:

Assets = Equity + Liabilities

This equation – which we shall refer to as the *accounting equation* – will always hold true. Whatever changes may occur to the assets of the business or the claims against it, there will be compensating changes elsewhere that will ensure that the statement of financial position always 'balances'. By way of illustration, consider the following transactions for Jerry and Company:

2 March   Bought a motor van for £5,000, paying by cheque.
3 March   Bought inventories (that is, goods to be sold) on one month's credit for £3,000. (This means that the inventories were bought on 3 March, but payment will not be made to the supplier until 3 April.)
4 March   Repaid £2,000 of the amount borrowed to the lender, by cheque.
6 March   Owner introduced another £4,000 into the business bank account.

A statement of financial position may be drawn up after each day in which transactions have taken place. In this way, the effect can be seen of each transaction on the assets and claims of the business. The statement of financial position as at 2 March will be:

Jerry and Company
Statement of financial position as at 2 March

	£
ASSETS	
Cash at bank (20,000 – 5,000)	15,000
Motor van	5,000
Total assets	20,000
EQUITY AND LIABILITIES	
Equity	6,000
Liabilities – borrowing	14,000
Total equity and liabilities	20,000

As can be seen, the effect of buying the motor van is to decrease the balance at the bank by £5,000 and to introduce a new asset – a motor van – to the statement of financial position. The total assets remain unchanged. It is only the 'mix' of assets that has changed. The claims against the business remain the same because there has been no change in the way in which the business has been funded.

The statement of financial position as at 3 March, following the purchase of inventories, will be:

Jerry and Company
Statement of financial position as at 3 March

	£
ASSETS	
Cash at bank	15,000
Motor van	5,000
Inventories	3,000
Total assets	23,000
EQUITY AND LIABILITIES	
Equity	6,000
Liabilities – borrowing	14,000
Liabilities – trade payable	3,000
Total equity and liabilities	23,000

The effect of buying inventories has been to introduce another new asset (inventories) to the statement of financial position. In addition, the fact that the goods have not yet been paid for means that the claims against the business will be increased by the £3,000 owed to the supplier, who is referred to as a *trade payable* (or trade creditor) on the statement of financial position.

Activity 2.4

Try drawing up a statement of financial position for Jerry and Company as at 4 March.

The statement of financial postion as at 4 March, following the repayment of part of the borrowing, will be:

Jerry and Company
Statement of financial position as at 4 March

	£
ASSETS	
Cash at bank (15,000 – 2,000)	13,000
Motor van	5,000
Inventories	3,000
Total assets	21,000
EQUITY AND LIABILITIES	
Equity	6,000
Liabilities – borrowing (14,000 – 2,000)	12,000
Liabilities – trade payable	3,000
Total equity and liabilities	21,000

The repayment of £2,000 of the borrowing will result in a decrease in the balance at the bank of £2,000 and a decrease in the lender's claim against the business by the same amount.

Activity 2.5

Try drawing up a statement of financial position as at 6 March for Jerry and Company.

The statement of financial position as at 6 March, following the introduction of more funds, will be:

Jerry and Company
Statement of financial position as at 6 March

	£
ASSETS	
Cash at bank (13,000 + 4,000)	17,000
Motor van	5,000
Inventories	3,000
Total assets	25,000
EQUITY AND LIABILITIES	
Equity (6,000 + 4,000)	10,000
Liabilities – borrowing	12,000
Liabilities – trade payable	3,000
Total equity and liabilities	25,000

The introduction of more funds by the owner will result in an increase in the equity of £4,000 and an increase in the cash at bank by the same amount.

Example 2.3 illustrates the point that the accounting equation (assets equals equity plus liabilities) will always hold true, because it reflects the fact that, if a business wishes to acquire more assets, it must raise funds equal to the cost of those assets. The funds raised must be provided by the owners (equity), or by others (liabilities), or by a combination of the two. Hence the total cost of assets acquired should always equal the total equity plus liabilities.

It is worth pointing out that in real life businesses do not normally draw up a statement of financial position after each day, as shown in the example above. Such an approach is not likely to be useful, given the relatively small number of transactions each day. We have done this in our examples to see the effect on the statement of financial position, transaction by transaction. In real life, a statement of financial position for the business is usually prepared at the end of a defined reporting period.

Determining the length of the reporting interval will involve weighing up the costs of producing the information against the perceived benefits of the information for decision-making purposes. In practice, the reporting interval will vary between businesses; it could be monthly, quarterly, half-yearly or annually. For external reporting purposes, an annual reporting cycle is the norm (although certain businesses, typically larger ones, report more frequently than this). However, for purposes of internal reporting to managers, many businesses produce monthly financial statements.

The effect of trading transactions

In Example 2.3, we dealt with the effect on the statement of financial position of a number of different types of transactions that a business might undertake. These transactions covered the purchase of assets for cash and on credit, the repayment of borrowing and the injection of equity. However, one form of transaction, trading, has not yet been considered. To deal with the effect of trading transactions on the statement of financial position, let us return to that example.

Example 2.4

The statement of financial position that we drew up for Jerry and Company as at 6 March was as follows:

Jerry and Company
Statement of financial position as at 6 March

	£
ASSETS	
Cash at bank	17,000
Motor van	5,000
Inventories	3,000
Total assets	25,000
EQUITY AND LIABILITIES	
Equity	10,000
Liabilities – borrowing	12,000
Liabilities – trade payable	3,000
Total equity and liabilities	25,000

On 7 March, the business managed to sell all of the inventories for £5,000 and received a cheque immediately from the customer for this amount. The statement of financial position on 7 March, after this transaction has taken place, will be:

Jerry and Company
Statement of financial position as at 7 March

	£
ASSETS	
Cash at bank (17,000 + 5,000)	22,000
Motor van	5,000
Inventories (3,000 – 3,000)	–
Total assets	27,000
EQUITY AND LIABILITIES	
Equity (10,000 + (5,000 – 3,000))	12,000
Liabilities – borrowing	12,000
Liabilities – trade payable	3,000
Total equity and liabilities	27,000

We can see that the inventories (£3,000) have now disappeared from the statement of financial position, but the cash at bank has increased by the selling price of the inventories (£5,000). The net effect has therefore been to increase assets by £2,000 (that is, £5,000 less £3,000). This increase represents the net increase in wealth (the profit) that has arisen from trading. Also note that the equity of the business has increased by £2,000, in line with the increase in assets. This increase in equity reflects the fact that increases in wealth, as a result of trading or other operations, will be to the benefit of the owners and will increase their stake in the business.

Activity 2.6

What would have been the effect on the statement of financial position if the inventories had been sold on 7 March for £1,000 rather than £5,000?

The statement of financial position on 7 March would then have been:

Jerry and Company
Statement of financial position as at 7 March

	£
ASSETS	
Cash at bank (17,000 + 1,000)	18,000
Motor van	5,000
Inventories (3,000 − 3,000)	–
Total assets	23,000
EQUITY AND LIABILITIES	
Equity (10,000 + (1,000 − 3,000))	8,000
Liabilities – borrowing	12,000
Liabilities – trade payable	3,000
Total equity and liabilities	23,000

As we can see, the inventories (£3,000) will disappear from the statement of financial position but the cash at bank will rise by only £1,000. This will mean a net reduction in assets of £2,000. This reduction represents a loss arising from trading and will be reflected in a reduction in the equity of the owners.

We can see that any decrease in wealth (that is, a loss) arising from trading or other transactions will lead to a reduction in the owner's stake in the business. If the business wished to maintain the level of assets as at 6 March, it would be necessary to obtain further funds from the owners or from borrowing, or both.

What we have just seen means that the accounting equation can be extended as follows:

Assets (at the end of the period) = Equity (amount at the start of the period)
+ Profit (or − Loss) (for the period)
+ Liabilities (at the end of the period)

(This is assuming that the owner makes no injections or withdrawals of equity during the period.)

As we have seen, the profit (or loss) for the period is shown on the statement of financial position as an addition to (or a reduction of) equity. Any funds introduced or withdrawn by the owner for living expenses or other reasons also affect equity. If the owners withdrew £1,500 for their own use, the equity of the owners would be reduced by £1,500. If the drawings were in cash, the balance of cash would decrease by £1,500 in the statement of financial position.

Note that, like all statement of financial position items, the amount of equity is cumulative. This means that any profit made that is not taken out as drawings by the owner(s) remains in the business. These retained (or 'ploughed-back') profits have the effect of expanding the business.

Classifying assets

If the items on the statement of financial position are listed haphazardly, with assets at the top of the statement and equity and liabilities underneath, it can be confusing, even though it may contain all of the information and be mathematically correct. To help users to understand the information, it is normally presented in a more systematic manner; assets and claims are usually grouped into categories.

Assets may be categorised as being either current or non-current.

Current assets

→ **Current assets** are basically assets that are held for the short term. To be more precise, they are assets that meet any of the following conditions:

● they are held for sale or consumption during the business's normal operating cycle;
● they are expected to be sold within the next year;
● they are held principally for trading;
● they are cash, or near cash such as easily marketable, short-term investments.

The operating cycle of a business is the time between buying and/or creating a product or service and receiving the cash on its sale. For most businesses, this will be less than a year.

The most common current assets are inventories (stock), trade receivables (amounts owed for goods or services supplied on credit) and cash.

Perhaps it is worth making the point here that most sales made by most businesses are made on credit. This is to say that the goods pass to, or the service is rendered to, the customer at one point but the customer pays later. Retail sales are the only significant exception to this general point.

For businesses that sell goods, rather than render a service, the current assets of inventories, trade receivables and cash are interrelated. They circulate within a business as shown in Figure 2.2. We can see that cash can be used to buy inventories, which are then sold on credit. When the credit customers (trade receivables) pay, the business receives an injection of cash and so on.

Figure 2.2	The circulating nature of current assets

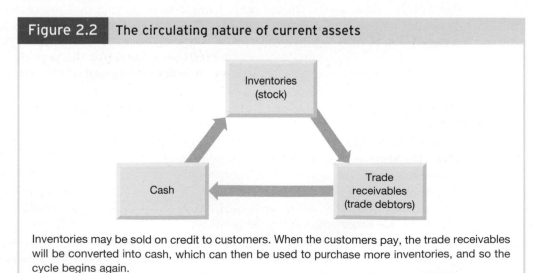

Inventories may be sold on credit to customers. When the customers pay, the trade receivables will be converted into cash, which can then be used to purchase more inventories, and so the cycle begins again.

For purely service businesses, the situation is similar, except that inventories are not involved.

Non-current assets

 Non-current assets (also called fixed assets) are simply assets that do not meet the definition of current assets. They tend to be held for long-term operations.

This distinction between assets that are continuously circulating within the business (current) and assets used for long-term operations (non-current) may be helpful when trying to assess the appropriateness of the mix of assets held. Most businesses will need a certain amount of both types of asset to operate effectively.

Activity 2.7

Can you think of two examples of assets that may be classified as non-current assets for an insurance business?

Examples of assets that may be defined as being non-current are:

- property
- furniture
- motor vehicles
- computers
- computer software
- reference books.

This is not an exhaustive list. You may have thought of others.

It is important to appreciate that how a particular asset is classified (that is, between current and non-current) may vary according to the nature of the business. This is because the *purpose* for which a particular type of asset is held may differ from business to business. For example, a motor vehicle manufacturer will normally hold inventories of the finished motor vehicles produced for resale; it would, therefore, classify them as part of the current assets. On the other hand, a business that uses motor vehicles for delivering its goods to customers (that is, as part of its long-term operations) would classify them as non-current assets.

Activity 2.8

The assets of Kunalun and Co., a large advertising agency, are as follows:

- cash at bank
- fixtures and fittings
- office equipment
- motor vehicles
- property
- computer equipment
- work in progress (that is, partly completed work for clients).

Which of these do you think should be defined as non-current assets and which should be defined as current assets?

Your answer should be as follows:

Non-current assets	*Current assets*
Fixtures and fittings	Cash at bank
Office equipment	Work in progress
Motor vehicles	
Property	
Computer equipment	

Classifying claims

As we have already seen, claims are normally classified into equity (owner's claim) and liabilities (claims of outsiders). Liabilities are further classified as either current or non-current.

Current liabilities

→ **Current liabilities** are basically amounts due for settlement in the short term. To be more precise, they are liabilities that meet any of the following conditions:

● they are expected to be settled within the business's normal operating cycle;
● they are held principally for trading purposes;
● they are due to be settled within a year after the date of the relevant statement of financial position;
● there is no right to defer settlement beyond a year after the date of the relevant statement of financial position.

Non-current liabilities

→ **Non-current liabilities** represent amounts due that do not meet the definition of current liabilities and so represent longer-term liabilities.

Note that it is quite common for non-current liabilities to become current liabilities. For example, borrowings that are due to be repaid within eighteen months following the date of a particular statement of financial position will appear as a non-current liability, but if the borrowings have not been paid off in the meantime, they will appear as a current liability in the statement of financial position as at one year later.

This classification of liabilities can help gain a clearer impression of the ability of the business to meet its maturing obligations (that is, claims that must shortly be met). The value of the current liabilities (that is, the amounts that must be paid within the normal operating cycle), can be compared with the value of the current assets (that is, the assets that either are cash or will turn into cash within the normal operating cycle).

The classification of liabilities should also help to highlight how the long-term finance of the business is raised. If a business relies on long-term borrowings to finance the business, the financial risks associated with the business will increase. This is because these borrowings will bring a commitment to make periodic interest payments and capital repayments. The business may be forced to stop trading if this commitment is not fulfilled. Thus, when raising long-term finance, a business must try to strike the right balance between non-current liabilities and owner's equity. We shall consider this issue in more detail in Chapter 7.

Activity 2.9

Can you think of one example of a current liability and one of a non-current liability?

An example of a current liability would be amounts owing to suppliers for goods supplied on credit (trade payables) or a bank overdraft (a form of short-term bank borrowing that is repayable on demand). An example of a non-current liability would be long-term borrowings.

Statement layouts

Now that we have looked at the classification of assets and liabilities, we shall consider the layout of the statement of financial position. Although there is an almost infinite number of ways in which the same information on assets and claims could be presented, we shall consider two basic layouts. The first of these follows the style that we adopted with Jerry and Company earlier (see pages 39–41). A more comprehensive example of this style is shown in Example 2.5.

Example 2.5

Brie Manufacturing
Statement of financial position as at 31 December 2009

	£000
ASSETS	
Non-current assets	
Property	45
Plant and equipment	30
Motor vans	19
	94
Current assets	
Inventories	23
Trade receivables	18
Cash at bank	12
	53
Total assets	147
EQUITY AND LIABILITIES	
Equity	60
Non-current liabilities	
Long-term borrowings	50
Current liabilities	
Trade payables	37
Total equity and liabilities	147

The non-current assets have a total of £94,000, which together with the current assets total of £53,000 gives a total of £147,000 for assets. Similarly, the equity totals £60,000, which together with the £50,000 for non-current liabilities and £37,000 for current liabilities gives a total for equity and liabilities of £147,000.

Within each category of asset (non-current and current) shown in Example 2.5, the items are listed in reverse order of liquidity (nearness to cash). Thus, the assets that are furthest from cash come first and the assets that are closest to cash come last. In the case of non-current assets, property is listed first as this asset is usually the most difficult to turn into cash and motor vans are listed last as there is usually a ready market for them. In the case of current assets, we have already seen that inventories are converted to trade receivables and then trade receivables are converted to cash. Hence, under the heading of current assets, inventories are listed first, followed by trade receivables and finally cash itself. This ordering of assets is a normal practice, which is followed irrespective of the layout used.

Note that, in addition to a grand total for assets held, subtotals for non-current assets and current assets are shown. Subtotals are also used for non-current liabilities and current liabilities when more than one item appears within these categories.

This layout is the most popular in practice in the UK.

A slight variation from the standard layout illustrated in Example 2.5 is as shown in Example 2.6.

Example 2.6

Brie Manufacturing
Statement of financial position as at 31 December 2009

	£000
ASSETS	
Non-current assets	
Property	45
Plant and equipment	30
Motor vans	19
	94
Current assets	
Inventories	23
Trade receivables	18
Cash at bank	12
	53
Total assets	147
LIABILITIES	
Non-current liabilities	
Long-term borrowings	(50)
Current liabilities	
Trade payables	(37)
Total liabilities	(87)
Net assets	60
EQUITY	60

We can see that the total liabilities are deducted from the total assets. This derives a figure for net assets – which is equal to equity. Using this format, the basic accounting equation is rearranged so that

$$\text{Assets} - \text{Liabilities} = \text{Equity}$$

This rearranged equation highlights the fact that equity represents the residual interest of the owner(s) after deducting all liabilities of the business.

Self-assessment question 2.1

The following information relates to Simonson Engineering as at 30 September 2010:

	£
Plant and equipment	25,000
Trade payables	18,000
Short-term borrowings	26,000
Inventories	45,000
Property	72,000
Long-term borrowings	51,000
Trade receivables	48,000
Equity at 1 October 2009	117,500
Cash in hand	1,500
Motor vehicles	15,000
Fixtures and fittings	9,000
Profit for the year to 30 September 2010	18,000
Drawings for the year to 30 September 2010	15,000

Required:
Prepare a statement of financial position for the business using the standard layout illustrated in Example 2.5.

The solution to this question can be found at the back of the book on pages 482–483.

Capturing a moment in time

As we have already seen, the statement of financial position reflects the assets, equity and liabilities of a business at *a specified point in time*. It has been compared to a photograph. A photograph 'freezes' a particular moment in time and will represent the situation only at that moment. Hence, events may be quite different immediately before and immediately after the photograph was taken. When examining this statement, therefore, it is important to establish the date for which it has been drawn up. This information should be prominently displayed in the statement of financial position heading, as shown above in Examples 2.5 and 2.6. When we are trying to assess current financial position, the more recent the statement of financial position date, the better.

A business will normally prepare a statement of financial position as at the close of business on the last day of its accounting year. In the UK, businesses are free to choose their accounting year. When making a decision on which year-end date to choose, commercial convenience can often be a deciding factor. For example, a business operating in the retail trade may choose to have a year-end date early in the calendar year (for example, 31 January) because trade tends to be slack during that period and more staff time is available to help with the tasks involved in the preparation of the annual financial statements (such as checking the amount of inventories held). Since trade is slack, it is also a time when the amount of inventories held by the retail business is likely to be unusually low as compared with other times of the year. Thus the statement of financial position, though showing a fair view of what it purports to show, may not show a picture of what is more typically the position of the business over the rest of the year.

The role of accounting conventions

As we saw in Chapter 1, accounting has a number of rules or conventions that have evolved over time. They have evolved as attempts to deal with practical problems experienced by preparers and users of financial statements, rather than to reflect some theoretical ideal. In preparing the statements of financial position earlier, we have followed various accounting conventions, though they have not been explicitly mentioned. We shall now identify and discuss the major conventions that we have applied.

Business entity convention

For accounting purposes, the business and its owner(s) are treated as being quite separate and distinct. This is why owners are treated as being claimants against their own business in respect of their investment in the business. The **business entity convention** must be distinguished from the legal position that may exist between businesses and their owners. For sole proprietorships and partnerships, the law does not make any distinction between the business and its owner(s). For limited companies, on the other hand, there is a clear legal distinction between the business and its owners. (As we shall see in Chapter 4, the limited company is regarded as having a separate legal existence.) For accounting purposes these legal distinctions are irrelevant and the business entity convention applies to all businesses.

Historic cost convention

The **historic cost convention** holds that the value of assets shown on the statement of financial position should be based on their acquisition cost (that is, historic cost). This method of measuring asset value takes preference over other methods based on some form of current value. Many people, however, find the historic cost convention difficult to support, as outdated historic costs are unlikely to help in the assessment of current financial position. It is often argued that recording assets at their current value would provide a more realistic view of financial position and would be relevant for a wide range of decisions. However, a system of measurement based on current values can present a number of problems.

Activity 2.10

Plumber and Company has some motor vans that are used by staff when visiting customers' premises to carry out work. It is now the last day of the business's accounting year.

If it were decided to show the vans on the statement of financial position at a current value (rather than a value based on their historic cost), how might the business arrive at a suitable value and how reliable would this figure be?

Two ways of deriving a current value are to find out

- how much would have to be paid to buy vans of a similar type and condition; or
- how much a motor van dealer would pay for the vans, were the business to sell them.

Both options will normally rely on opinion and so a range of possible values could be produced for each. For example, both the cost to replace the vans and the proceeds of selling them is likely to vary from one dealer to another. Moreover, the range of values for each option could be significantly different from one option to the other. (The selling prices of the vans are likely to be lower than the amount required to replace them.) Thus, any value finally decided upon could arouse some debate.

Activity 2.10 illustrates that the term 'current value' can be defined in different ways. It can be defined broadly as either the current replacement cost or the current realisable value (selling price) of an asset. These two types of valuation may result in quite different figures being produced to represent the current value of an item. Furthermore, the broad terms 'replacement cost' and 'realisable value' can be defined in different ways. We must therefore be clear about what kind of current value accounting we wish to use.

Activity 2.10 also illustrates the practical problems associated with current value accounting. Current values, however defined, are often difficult to establish with any real degree of objectivity. The figures produced may be heavily dependent on the opinion of managers. Unless current value figures are capable of some form of independent verification, there is a danger that the financial statements will lose their credibility among users. In fact, motor vans probably pose a less severe problem than do many other types of asset. This is because there tends to be a ready market for motor vans, which means that a value can be identified by contacting a dealer. For a highly specialised piece of equipment, perhaps one that was created to meet the precise needs of the particular business, identifying a replacement cost, or worse still a selling price, could be very difficult.

By reporting assets at their historic cost, it is argued that more reliable information is produced. Reporting in this way reduces the need for judgements, as the amount paid for a particular asset is usually a matter of demonstrable fact. Information based on past costs, however, may not always be relevant to the needs of users.

Later in the chapter, we shall consider the valuation of assets in the statement of financial position in more detail. We shall see that the historic cost convention is not always rigidly adhered to. Departures from this convention are becoming more frequent.

Prudence convention

→ The **prudence convention** holds that caution should be exercised when making accounting judgements. This means that liabilities and losses should not be understated while assets and profits should not be overstated. The application of this convention usually involves recording all losses at once and in full; this refers to both actual losses and expected losses. Profits, on the other hand, are recognised only when they actually arise. Greater emphasis is, therefore, placed on expected losses than on expected profits. To illustrate the application of this convention, let us assume that certain inventories held by a business prove unpopular with customers and so a decision is made to sell them below their original cost. The prudence convention requires that the expected loss from future sales be recognised immediately rather than when the goods are eventually sold. If, however, these inventories could have been sold above their original cost, profit would only be recognised at the time of sale.

The prudence convention evolved to counteract the excessive optimism of some managers and owners and is designed to prevent an overstatement of financial position. There is, however, a risk that it will introduce a bias towards understatement of both financial position and profit.

Activity 2.11

What problems might arise if an excessively prudent view is taken of the financial position and performance of a business?

Excessive prudence will lead to an overstatement of losses and an understatement of profits and financial position. This will obscure the underlying financial reality and may lead users to make bad decisions. The owners, for example, may sell their stake in the business at a lower price than they would have received if a fairer picture of the financial health of the business had been presented.

In recent years, the prudence convention has weakened its grip on accounting and has become a less dominant force. Nevertheless, it remains an important convention.

Going concern convention

→ The **going concern convention** holds that the financial statements should be prepared on the assumption that the business will continue operations for the foreseeable future, unless this is known not to be true. In other words, it is assumed that there is no intention, or need, to sell off the non-current assets of the business. Such a sale may arise where the business is in financial difficulties and needs to pay amounts borrowed that are due for repayment. This convention is important because the market (sale) value of many non-current assets is often low in relation to the values at which they appear in the statement of financial position. This means that were a forced sale to occur, there is the likelihood that assets will be sold for less than their statement of financial position value. Such anticipated losses should be fully recorded as soon as the business's going concern status is called into question. However, where there is no expectation of a need to sell off non-current assets, they can continue to be shown at their recorded values.

Dual aspect convention

→ The **dual aspect convention** asserts that each transaction has two aspects, both of which will affect the statement of financial position. Thus the purchase of a motor car for cash results in an increase in one asset (motor car) and a decrease in another (cash). The repayment of borrowings results in the decrease in a liability (borrowings) and the decrease in an asset (cash).

Activity 2.12

What are the two aspects of each of the following transactions?

1   Purchase £1,000 inventories on credit.
2   Owner withdraws £2,000 in cash.
3   Repayment of borrowings of £3,000.

Your answer should be as follows:

1   Inventories increase by £1,000, trade payables increase by £1,000.
2   Equity reduces by £2,000, cash reduces by £2,000.
3   Borrowings reduce by £3,000, cash reduces by £3,000.

Recording the dual aspect of each transaction ensures that the statement of financial position will continue to balance.

Figure 2.3 summarises the main accounting conventions that exert an influence on the construction of the statement of financial position.

| Figure 2.3 | Accounting conventions influencing the statement of financial position |

These are the key accounting conventions relating to the statement of financial position.

Money measurement

We saw earlier that a resource will only be regarded as an asset and included on the statement of financial position if it can be measured in monetary terms, with a reasonable degree of reliability. Some resources of a business, however, do not meet this criterion and so are excluded from the statement of financial position. As a result, the scope of this statement is limited.

Activity 2.13

Can you think of resources of a business that cannot usually be measured reliably in monetary terms?

You may have thought of the following:

- the quality of the human resources of the business
- the reputation of the business's products
- the location of the business
- the relationship a business enjoys with its customers.

There have been occasional attempts to measure and report resources of a business that are normally excluded from the statement of financial position so as to provide a more complete picture of its financial position. These attempts, however, invariably fail the reliability test. We saw in Chapter 1 that a lack of reliability affects the quality of financial statements. Unreliable measurement can lead to inconsistency in reporting and can create uncertainty among users, which in turn undermines the credibility of the financial statements.

Some key resources of a business that normally defy reliable measurement are now discussed.

Goodwill and brands

Some intangible non-current assets are similar to tangible non-current assets: they have a clear and separate identity and the cost of acquiring them can be reliably measured. Examples normally include patents, trademarks, copyrights and licences. Other intangible non-current assets, however, are quite different. They lack a clear and separate identity and reflect a hotchpotch of attributes, which are part of the essence of the business. Goodwill and product brands are often examples of assets that lack a clear and separate identity.

The term 'goodwill' is often used to cover various attributes such as the quality of the products, the skill of employees and the relationship with customers. The term 'product brands' is also used to cover various attributes, such as the brand image, the quality of the product, the trademark and so on. Where goodwill and product brands have been generated internally by the business, it is often difficult to determine their cost or to measure their current market value or even to be clear that they really exist. They are, therefore, excluded from the statement of financial position.

When they are acquired through an arm's-length transaction, however, the problems of uncertainty about their existence and measurement are resolved. (An 'arm's-length' transaction is one that is undertaken between two unconnected parties.) If goodwill is acquired when taking over another business, or if a business acquires a particular product brand from another business, these items will be separately identified and a price agreed for them. Under these circumstances, they can be regarded as assets (for accounting purposes) by the business that acquired them and included on the statement of financial position.

To agree a price for acquiring goodwill or product brands means that some form of valuation must take place and this raises the question as to how it is done. Usually, the valuation will be based on estimates of future earnings from holding the asset, a process that is fraught with difficulties. Nevertheless, a number of specialist businesses now exist that are prepared to take on this challenge. **Real World 2.2** reveals how one specialist business ranked and valued the top ten brands in the world for 2009.

Real World 2.2

Brand leaders

Millward Brown Optimor, part of WPP marketing services group, recently produced a report that ranked and valued the top ten world brands for 2009 as follows:

Ranking	Brand	Value ($m)
1	Google	100,039
2	Microsoft	76,249
3	Coca-Cola	67,625
4	IBM	66,622
5	McDonald's	66,575
6	Apple	63,113
7	China Mobile	61,283
8	GE (General Electric)	59,793
9	Vodafone	53,727
10	Marlboro	49,460

We can see that the valuations placed on the brands owned are quite staggering.

Source: 'Brandz Top 100 Most Valuable Global Brands 2009', Millward Brown Optimor, www.millwardbrown.com, 2009.

Human resources

Attempts have been made to place a monetary measurement on the human resources of a business, but without any real success. There are, however, certain limited circumstances in which human resources are measured and reported in the statement of financial position. These circumstances normally arise with professional football clubs. While football clubs cannot own players, they can own the rights to the players' services. Where these rights are acquired by compensating other clubs for releasing the players from their contracts, an arm's-length transaction arises and the amounts paid provide a reliable basis for measurement. This means that the rights to services can be regarded as an asset of the club for accounting purposes (assuming, of course, the player will also bring benefits to the club).

Real World 2.3 describes how one leading club reports its investment in players on the statement of financial position.

Real World 2.3

Spurs players appear on the pitch and on the statement of financial position

Tottenham Hotspur Football Club (Spurs) has acquired several key players as a result of paying transfer fees to other clubs. In common with most UK football clubs, Spurs reports the cost of acquiring the rights to the players' services on its statement of financial position. The club's statement as at 30 June 2009 shows the cost of registering its squad of players at about £197 million. The club treats a proportion of each player's transfer fee as an expense each year. The exact proportion depends on the length of the particular player's contract.

The £197 million does not include 'home-grown' players such as Ledley King, because Spurs did not pay a transfer fee for them and so no clear-cut value can be placed on their services. During the year to 30 June 2009, the club was very active in the transfer market and fifteen players were signed, including Robbie Keane for the sum of £12 million. Keane had previously been with the club and was only away at Liverpool for a few months. Fifteen players left the club (including Keane), earning it transfer fees totalling £73 million.

The item of players' registrations is shown as an intangible asset in the statement of financial position as it is the rights to services, not the players, that are the assets. It is shown net of depreciation (or *amortisation*, as it is usually termed for intangible non-current assets). The carrying amount at 30 June 2009 was £128 million and represented 44 per cent of Spurs' assets, as shown in the statement of financial position.

Source: Tottenham Hotspur plc Annual Report 2009.

Monetary stability

When using money as the unit of measurement, we normally fail to recognise the fact that it will change in value over time. In the UK and throughout much of the world, however, inflation has been a persistent problem. This has meant that the value of money has declined in relation to other assets. In past years, high rates of inflation have resulted in statements of financial position which were prepared on a historic cost basis reflecting figures for assets that were much lower than if current values were employed. Rates of inflation have been relatively low in recent years and so the disparity between historic cost values and current values has been less pronounced. Nevertheless, it can still be significant and has added fuel to the debate concerning how to measure asset values on the statement of financial position. It is to this issue that we now turn.

Valuing assets

It was mentioned earlier that, when preparing the statement of financial position, the historic cost convention is normally applied for the reporting of assets. However, this point requires further elaboration as, in practice, it is not simply a matter of recording each asset on the statement of financial position at its original cost. We shall see that things are a little more complex than this. Before discussing the valuation rules in some detail, however, we should point out that these rules are based on international accounting standards, which are rules that are generally accepted throughout much of the world. The nature and role of accounting standards will be discussed in detail in Chapter 5.

Tangible non-current assets (property, plant and equipment)

→ Tangible non-current assets normally consist of **property, plant and equipment**. We shall refer to them in this way from now on. This is a rather broad term that includes items such as land and buildings, motor vehicles and fixtures and fittings. All of these items are, in essence, the 'tools' used by the business to generate wealth, that is, they are used to produce or supply goods and services or for administration purposes. They tend to be held for the longer term, which means for more than one accounting period.

Initially these items are recorded at their historic cost, which will include any amounts spent on getting them ready for use. However, they will normally be used up over time as a result of wear and tear, obsolescence and so on. The amount used up, which is referred to as *depreciation*, must be measured for each accounting period for which the assets are held. Although we shall leave a detailed examination of depreciation until Chapter 3, we need to know that when an asset has been depreciated, this must be reflected in the statement of financial position.

The total depreciation that has accumulated over the period since the asset was acquired must be deducted from its cost. This net figure (that is, the cost of the asset less the total depreciation to date) is referred to as the *carrying amount*, *net book value*, or *written down value*. The procedure just described is not really a contravention of the historic cost convention. It is simply recognition of the fact that a proportion of the historic cost of the non-current asset has been consumed in the process of generating benefits for the business.

Although using historic cost (less any depreciation) is the 'benchmark treatment' for recording these assets, an alternative is allowed. Property, plant and equipment can be
→ recorded using **fair values** provided that these values can be measured reliably. The fair values, in this case, are the current market values (that is, the exchange values in an arm's-length transaction). The use of fair values, rather than depreciated cost figures, can provide users with more up-to-date information, which may well be more relevant to their needs. It may also place the business in a better light, as assets such as property may have increased significantly in value over time. Of course, increasing the statement of financial position value of an asset does not make that asset more valuable. However, perceptions of the business may be altered by such a move.

One consequence of revaluing non-current assets is that the depreciation charge will be increased. This is because the depreciation charge is based on the increased value of the asset.

Real World 2.4 shows that one well-known business revalued its land and buildings and, by doing so, greatly improved the look of its statement of financial position.

Real World 2.4

Marks marks up land and buildings

The statement of financial position of Marks and Spencer plc, a major high street retailer, as at 28 March 2009 reveals land and buildings at a carrying amount, or net book value, of £2,458 million. These land and buildings were revalued by a firm of independent surveyors five years earlier and this has been reflected in subsequent statements of financial position. The effect of the revaluation was to give an uplift of £530.9 million against the previous carrying amount.

Source: Marks and Spencer plc Annual Report 2009, Notes to the financial statements, Note 14, www.marksandspencer.com.

Activity 2.14

Refer to the statement of financial position of Brie Manufacturing shown earlier in Example 2.5 (pages 48–49). What would be the effect of revaluing the property to a figure of £110,000 on the statement of financial position?

The effect on the statement of financial position would be to increase the property to £110,000 and the gain on revaluation (that is, £110,000 − £45,000 = £65,000) would be added to the equity of the owner, as it is the owner who will benefit from the gain. The revised statement of financial position would therefore be as follows:

Brie Manufacturing
Statement of financial position as at 31 December 2009

	£000
ASSETS	
Non-current assets (property, plant and equipment)	
Property	110
Plant and equipment	30
Motor vans	19
	159
Current assets	
Inventories	23
Trade receivables	18
Cash at bank	12
	53
Total assets	212
EQUITY AND LIABILITIES	
Equity (60 + 65)	125
Non-current liabilities	
Long-term borrowings	50
Current liabilities	
Trade payables	37
Total equity and liabilities	212

Once assets are revalued, the frequency of revaluation then becomes an import-ant issue as assets recorded at out-of-date values can mislead users. Using out-of-date revaluations on the statement of financial position is the worst of both worlds. It lacks the objectivity and verifiability of historic cost; it also lacks the realism of current values. Where fair values are used, revaluations should therefore be frequent enough to ensure that the carrying amount of the revalued asset does not differ materially from its fair value at the statement of financial position date.

When an item of property, plant, or equipment is revalued on the basis of fair values, all assets within that particular group must be revalued. Thus, it is not acceptable to revalue some property but not others. Although this provides some degree of consistency within a particular group of assets, it does not, of course, prevent the statement of financial position from containing a mixture of valuations.

Intangible non-current assets

For these assets, the 'benchmark treatment' is, once again, that they are measured initially at historic cost. What follows, however, will depend on whether the asset has a finite or an infinite useful life. (Purchased goodwill is an example of an asset that could have an infinitely useful life, though the life of purchased goodwill can be limited.) Where the asset has a finite life, any amortisation that has arisen since it was acquired will be deducted from its cost. Where, however, the asset has an infinite life, it will not be amortised. Instead, it will be tested annually to see whether there has been any fall in value. This point is discussed in more detail in the following section.

Once again, the alternative of revaluing intangible assets using fair values is available. However, this can only be used where an active market exists, which allows fair values to be properly determined. In practice, this is a rare occurrence.

The impairment of non-current assets

There is always a risk that both types of non-current asset (tangible and intangible) may suffer a significant fall in value. This may be due to factors such as changes in market conditions, technological obsolescence and so on. In some cases, this fall in value may lead to the carrying amount, or net book value, of the asset being higher than the amount that could be recovered from the asset through its continued use or through its sale. When this occurs, the asset value is said to be impaired and the general rule is to reduce the value on the statement of financial position to the recoverable amount. Unless this is done, the asset value will be overstated. This type of impairment in value should not be confused with routine depreciation, arising from, say, wear and tear due to normal usage.

Activity 2.15

With which one of the accounting conventions that we discussed earlier is this accounting treatment consistent?

The answer is the prudence convention, which states that actual or anticipated losses should be recognised in full.

In many situations, a business may use either historic cost, less any depreciation, or a value-based measure when reporting its non-current assets. However, where the value-based measure is the impaired value and is smaller than the historic-cost-based value, the business has no choice; the use of depreciated historic cost is not an option.

Real World 2.5 provides an example of where the application of the 'impairment rule', as it is called, resulted in huge write-downs (that is, reductions in the statement of financial position value of the assets) for one large business.

Real World 2.5

Painting a rosy picture

FT

Akzo Nobel, the Dutch paints and chemicals company, on Tuesday defended its £8bn ($11.6bn) acquisition of ICI in 2007 after it took a €1.2bn ($1.5bn) impairment charge on the former UK industrial giant because of sharply lower paint sales.

The company saw the volume of paint sold fall by 10 per cent in the fourth quarter, with even steeper declines in Asia, one of the areas where ICI had been strong. This prompted the move to slash growth estimates and fair value for ICI.

'It's not a world of high growth any more, it's a world with completely different challenges,' said Hans Wijers, chief executive. 'We expect 2009 to be an uncertain year with a lot of volatility [and] with challenging volume circumstances.'

The €1.2bn impairment charge cuts into the €4.4bn of goodwill the company recorded when it acquired ICI and its Dulux brand name, but Akzo defended its previous assumptions as conservative.

'Could we have anticipated that the world economy would go down so much?' Mr Wijers said. 'I'm not sorry about [the ICI] transaction. It was the right thing to do at the right time and the company has become much stronger because of it.'

Source: 'Akzo Nobel defends ICI takeover', Michael Steen, *Financial Times*, 24 February 2009.

We saw earlier that intangible, non-current assets with infinite lives must be tested annually to see whether there has been any impairment. Other non-current assets, however, must also be tested where events suggest that impairment has taken place.

We should bear in mind that impairment reviews involve making judgements concerning the appropriate value to place on assets. Employing independent valuers to make these judgements may give users greater confidence in the information reported. There is always a risk that managers will manipulate impairment values to portray a picture that they would like users to see.

Inventories

It is not only non-current assets that run the risk of a significant fall in value. The inventories of a business could also suffer this fate, which could be caused by factors such as reduced selling prices, obsolescence, deterioration, damage and so on. Where a fall in value means that the amount likely to be recovered from the sale of the inventories will be lower than their cost, this loss must be reflected in the statement of financial position. Thus, if the net realisable value (that is, selling price less any selling costs) falls below the historic cost of inventories held, the former should be used as the basis of valuation. This reflects, once again, the influence of the prudence convention on the statement of financial position.

Real World 2.6 reveals how one well-known business wrote down the inventories of one of its products following a sharp reduction in selling prices.

Real World 2.6

You're fired!

'You're fired!' is what some investors might like to tell Amstrad, run by *Apprentice* star Sir Alan Sugar. . . . Shares in the company fell nearly 10 per cent as it revealed that sales of its much-vaunted videophone have failed to take off.

Amstrad launched the E3, a phone allowing users to hold video calls with each other, in a blaze of publicity last year. But, after cutting the price from £99 to £49, Amstrad sold just 61,000 E3s in the year to June and has taken a £5.7 million stock [inventories] write down.

Source: 'Amstrad (AMT)', *Investors Chronicle*, 7 October 2005.

The published financial statements of large businesses will normally show the basis on which inventories are valued. **Real World 2.7** shows how one business reports this information.

Real World 2.7

Reporting inventories

The 2009 annual report of Ted Baker plc, a leading designer clothes brand, includes the following explanation concerning inventories:

> Inventories and work in progress are stated at the lower of cost and net realisable value. Cost includes materials, direct labour and inward transportation costs. Net realisable value is based on estimated selling price, less further costs expected to be incurred to completion and disposal. Provision is made for obsolete, slow moving or defective items where appropriate.

Source: Ted Baker plc Report and Accounts 2009, p. 44.

Meeting user needs

The statement of financial position is the oldest of the three main financial statements and many businesses have prepared one on a regular basis, even when there was no regulation requiring it to be produced. This suggests that it is regarded as providing useful information. There are various ways in which the statement of financial position may help users, including the following:

- *It provides an insight into how the business is financed and how its funds are deployed.* We can see how much finance is contributed by the owners and how much is contributed by outside lenders. We can also see the different kinds of assets acquired and how much is invested in each kind.

- *It can provide a basis for assessing the value of the business.* Since the statement of financial position lists, and places a value on, the various assets and claims, it can provide a starting point for assessing the value of the business. It is, however, severely limited in the extent to which it can do this. We have seen earlier that accounting rules may result in assets being shown at their historic cost and that the restrictive definition of assets may exclude certain business resources from the statement of financial position. Ultimately, the value of a business will be based on its ability to generate wealth in the future. Because of this, assets need to be valued on the basis of their wealth-generating potential. Also, other business resources that do not meet the restrictive definition of assets, such as brand values, need to be similarly valued and included.

- *Relationships between assets and claims can be assessed.* It can be useful to look at relationships between statement of financial position items, for example the relationship between how much wealth is tied up in current assets and how much is owed in the short term (current liabilities). From this relationship, we can see whether the business has sufficient short-term assets to cover its maturing obligations. We shall look at this and other relationships between statement of financial position items in some detail in Chapter 7.

- *Performance can be assessed.* The effectiveness of a business in generating wealth (making a profit) can usefully be assessed against the amount of investment that was involved. Knowing the relationship between profit earned over a particular period and the value of the net assets involved can be very helpful to many of those involved with the business concerned. It is particularly likely to be of interest to the owners and the managers. This and similar relationships will also be explored in detail in Chapter 7.

Summary

The main points of this chapter may be summarised as follows:

The major financial statements

- There are three major financial statements: the statement of cash flows, the income statement (profit and loss account) and the statement of financial position (balance sheet).

- The statement of cash flows shows the cash movements over a particular period.

- The income statement shows the wealth (profit) generated over a particular period.

- The statement of financial position shows the accumulated wealth at a particular point in time.

The statement of financial position

- This sets out the assets of the business, on the one hand, and the claims against those assets, on the other.

- Assets are resources of the business that have certain characteristics, such as the ability to provide future benefits.

- Claims are obligations on the part of the business to provide cash, or some other benefit, to outside parties.

- Claims are of two types: equity and liabilities.
- Equity represents the claim(s) of the owner(s) and liabilities represent the claims of others, apart from the owner.

Classification of assets and liabilities

- Assets are normally categorised as being current or non-current.
- Current assets are cash or near cash or are held for sale or consumption in the normal course of business, or for trading, or for the short term.
- Non-current assets are assets that are not current assets. They are normally held for the long-term operations of the business.
- Liabilities are normally categorised as being current or non-current liabilities.
- Current liabilities represent amounts due in the normal course of the business's operating cycle, or are held for trading, or are to be settled within a year of, or cannot be deferred for at least a year after, the end of the reporting period.
- Non-current liabilities represent amounts due that are not current liabilities.

Statement of financial position layouts

- The standard layout begins with assets at the top of the statement of financial position and places equity and liabilities underneath.
- A variation of the standard layout begins with the assets at the top of the statement of financial position. From the total assets figure are deducted the non-current and current liabilities to arrive at a net assets figure. Equity is placed underneath.

Accounting conventions

- Accounting conventions are the rules of accounting that have evolved to deal with practical problems experienced by those preparing financial statements.
- The main conventions relating to the statement of financial position include the business entity, historic cost, prudence, going concern and dual aspect conventions.

Money measurement

- Using money as the unit of measurement limits the scope of the statement of financial position.
- Certain resources such as goodwill, product brands and human resources are difficult to measure. An 'arm's-length transaction' is normally required before such assets can be reliably measured and reported on the statement of financial position.
- Money is not a stable unit of measurement – it changes in value over time.

Asset valuation

- The 'benchmark treatment' is to show property, plant and equipment at historic cost less any amounts written off for depreciation. However, fair values may be used rather than depreciated cost.
- The 'benchmark treatment' for intangible non-current assets is to show the items at historic cost. Only assets with a finite life will be amortised (depreciated) and fair values will rarely be used.
- Where the recoverable amount from tangible non-current assets is below their carrying amount, this lower amount is reflected in the statement of financial position.
- Inventories are shown at the lower of cost or net realisable value.

The usefulness of the statement of financial position

- It shows how finance has been raised and how it has been been deployed.
- It provides a basis for valuing the business, though the conventional statement of financial position can only be a starting point.
- Relationships between various statement of financial position items can usefully be explored.
- Relationships between wealth generated and wealth invested can be helpful indicators of business effectiveness.

 Key terms

statement of cash flows p. 32	**non-current assets** p. 46
income statement p. 32	**current liabilities** p. 47
statement of financial position p. 32	**non-current liabilities** p. 47
final accounts p. 35	**business entity convention** p. 51
assets p. 36	**historic cost convention** p. 51
claims p. 36	**prudence convention** p. 52
tangible assets p. 38	**going concern convention** p. 53
intangible assets p. 38	**dual aspect convention** p. 53
equity p. 39	**property, plant and equipment**
liabilities p. 39	p. 58
current assets p. 45	**fair values** p. 58

Further reading

If you would like to explore the topics covered in this chapter in more depth, we recommend the following books:

Elliott, B. and Elliott, J., *Financial Accounting and Reporting*, 13th edn, Financial Times Prentice Hall, 2009, Chapters 16 and 18.

IASC Foundation Education, *A Guide through International Financial Reporting Standards (IFRSs) 2008*, July 2008, IAS 16, IAS 36 and IAS 38.

KPMG, *Insights into IFRS*, 6th edn, 2009/10, Sweet and Maxwell, 2009, Sections 1.2, 3.2, 3.3, 3.8 and 3.10.

Review questions

Solutions to these questions can be found at the back of the book on pages 482–483.

2.1   An accountant prepared a statement of financial position for a business. In this statement, the equity of the owner was shown next to the liabilities. This confused the owner, who argued: 'My equity is my major asset and so should be shown as an asset on the statement of financial position.' How would you explain this misunderstanding to the owner?

2.2   'The statement of financial position shows how much a business is worth.' Do you agree with this statement? Explain the reasons for your response.

2.3   What is meant by the accounting equation? How does the form of this equation differ between the two statement of financial position layouts mentioned in the chapter?

2.4   In recent years there have been attempts to place a value on the 'human assets' of a business in order to derive a figure that can be included on the statement of financial position. Do you think humans should be treated as assets? Would 'human assets' meet the conventional definition of an asset for inclusion on the statement of financial position?

Exercises

Exercises 2.5 to 2.8 are more advanced than 2.1 to 2.4. Exercises with coloured numbers have solutions at the back of the book, starting on page 491.
    If you wish to try more exercises, visit the students' side of the Companion Website.

2.1   On Thursday, the fourth day of his business venture, Paul, the street trader in wrapping paper (see earlier in the chapter, pages 32–33), bought more inventories for £53 cash. During the day he sold inventories that had cost £33 for a total of £47.

Required:
Draw up the three financial statements for Paul's business venture for Thursday.

2.2   The equity of Paul's business belongs to him because he is the sole owner of the business. Can you explain how the figure for equity by Thursday evening has arisen? You will need to look back at the events of Monday, Tuesday and Wednesday (pages 32–35) to do this.

2.3   While on holiday in Bridlington, Helen had her credit cards and purse stolen from the beach while she was swimming. She was left with only £40, which she had kept in her hotel room, but she had three days of her holiday remaining. She was determined to continue her holiday and decided to make some money to enable her to do so. She decided to sell orange juice to holidaymakers using the local beach. On the first day she bought 80 cartons of orange juice at £0.50 each for cash and sold 70 of these at £0.80 each. On the following day she bought 60 cartons at £0.50 each for cash and sold 65 at £0.80 each. On the third and final day she bought another 60 cartons at £0.50 each for cash. However, it rained and, as a result, business was poor. She managed to sell 20 at £0.80 each but sold off the rest of her inventories at £0.40 each.

Required:
Prepare an income statement and statement of cash flows for each day's trading and prepare a statement of financial position at the end of each day's trading.

2.4 On 1 March, Joe Conday started a new business. During March he carried out the following transactions:

1 March Deposited £20,000 in a bank account.
2 March Bought fixtures and fittings for £6,000 cash and inventories £8,000 on credit.
3 March Borrowed £5,000 from a relative and deposited it in the bank.
4 March Bought a motor car for £7,000 cash and withdrew £200 in cash for his own use.
5 March A further motor car costing £9,000 was bought. The motor car bought on 4 March was given in part exchange at a value of £6,500. The balance of the purchase price for the new car was paid in cash.
6 March Conday won £2,000 in a lottery and paid the amount into the business bank account. He also repaid £1,000 of the borrowings.

Required:
Draw up a statement of financial position for the business at the end of each day.

2.5 The following is a list of the assets and claims of Crafty Engineering Ltd at 30 June last year:

	£000
Trade payables	86
Motor vehicles	38
Long-term loan from Industrial Finance Co.	260
Equipment and tools	207
Short-term borrowings	116
Inventories	153
Property	320
Trade receivables	185

Required:
(a) Prepare the statement of financial position of the business as at 30 June last year from the above information using the standard layout. (*Hint*: There is a missing item that needs to be deduced and inserted.)
(b) Discuss the significant features revealed by this financial statement.

2.6 The statement of financial position of a business at the start of the week is as follows:

	£
ASSETS	
Property	145,000
Furniture and fittings	63,000
Inventories	28,000
Trade receivables	33,000
Total assets	**269,000**
EQUITY AND LIABILITIES	
Equity	203,000
Short-term borrowing (bank overdraft)	43,000
Trade payables	23,000
Total equity and liabilities	**269,000**

During the week the following transactions take place:

(a) Inventories sold for £11,000 cash; these inventories had cost £8,000.
(b) Sold inventories for £23,000 on credit; these inventories had cost £17,000.
(c) Received cash from trade receivables totalling £18,000.
(d) The owners of the business introduced £100,000 of their own money, which was placed in the business bank account.

(e) The owners brought a motor van, valued at £10,000, into the business.
(f) Bought inventories on credit for £14,000.
(g) Paid trade payables £13,000.

Required:
Show the statement of financial position after all of these transactions have been reflected.

2.7   The following is a list of assets and claims of a manufacturing business at a particular point in time:

	£
Short-term borrowing	22,000
Property	245,000
Inventories of raw materials	18,000
Trade payables	23,000
Plant and equipment	127,000
Loan from Manufacturing Finance Co. (long-term borrowing)	100,000
Inventories of finished goods	28,000
Delivery vans	54,000
Trade receivables	34,000

Required:
Write out a statement of financial position in the standard format incorporating these figures. (*Hint*: There is a missing item that needs to be deduced and inserted.)

2.8   You have been talking to someone who had read a few chapters of an accounting text some years ago. During your conversation the person made the following statements:
(a) The income statement shows how much cash has come into and left the business during the accounting period and the resulting balance at the end of the period.
(b) In order to be included in the statement of financial position as an asset, an item needs to be worth something in the market – that is all.
(c) The accounting equation is:

$$\text{Assets} + \text{Equity} = \text{Liabilities}$$

(d) Non-current assets are things that cannot be moved.
(e) Goodwill has an infinite life and so should not be amortised.

Required:
Comment critically on each of the above statements, going into as much detail as you can.

3

Measuring and reporting financial performance

Introduction

In this chapter, we continue our examination of the major financial statements by looking at the income statement. This statement was briefly considered in Chapter 2 and we shall now look at it in some detail. We shall see how it is prepared and how it links with the statement of financial position. We shall also consider some of the key measurement problems to be faced when preparing the income statement.

Learning outcomes

When you have completed this chapter, you should be able to:

- discuss the nature and purpose of the income statement;

- prepare an income statement from relevant financial information and interpret the information that it contains;

- discuss the main recognition and measurement issues that must be considered when preparing the income statement;

- explain the main accounting conventions underpinning the income statement.

What does it mean?

Tate and Lyle plc, whose business is sweeteners, starches and sugar refining, reported sales revenue of £3,553 million and a profit of £70 million for the year ending on 31 March 2009. To understand fully the significance of these figures, we must be clear about the nature of revenue and profit. This means that we must be able to answer questions such as:

- Does the sales revenue of £3,553 million represent the cash generated from sales for the period?
- What is the relationship between the sales revenue and the profit for the period?
- Can the profit for the period of £70 million be measured with complete accuracy and certainty?
- Does the profit figure of £70 million mean that the business had £70 million *more* in the bank at the end of the year than it had at the beginning?
- How can the sales revenue and profit figures help in assessing performance?

The answers to these and other questions are covered in the chapter.

The income statement

In Chapter 2 we considered the statement of financial position (balance sheet). We saw that it sets out the wealth of a business, and who contributed that wealth, at a particular moment in time. However, it is not usually enough for users of financial statements to have information relating only to this aspect of financial health. Businesses exist for the primary purpose of generating wealth, or profit, and it is the profit generated *during a period* that is the concern of many users. The main purpose of the income statement – or profit and loss account, as it is sometimes called – is to measure and report how much **profit** (wealth) the business has generated over a period. It also helps users to gain some impression of how that profit was made. As with the statement of financial position, which we examined in Chapter 2, the principles of preparation are the same irrespective of whether the income statement is for a sole proprietorship business or for a limited company.

The measurement of profit requires that the total revenue of the business, generated during a particular period, be identified. **Revenue** is simply a measure of the inflow of economic benefits arising from the ordinary activities of a business. These benefits will result in either an increase in assets (such as cash or amounts owed to the business by its customers) or a decrease in liabilities. Different forms of business enterprise will generate different forms of revenue. Some examples of the different forms that revenue can take are as follows:

- sales of goods (for example, by a manufacturer)
- fees for services (for example, of a solicitor)
- subscriptions (for example, of a club)
- interest received (for example, on an investment fund).

Real World 3.1 shows the various forms of revenue generated by a leading football club.

Real World 3.1

Gunning for revenue

Arsenal Football Club generated total revenue of £313 million for the year ended 31 May 2009. Like other leading clubs, it relies on various forms of revenue to sustain its success. Figure 3.1 below shows the contribution of each form of revenue for the year. The high level of revenue from property development is unusual for a football club, even for Arsenal. It arises from the fact that the club is developing its former home Highbury Stadium for residential accommodation following its move to the Emirates Stadium.

Figure 3.1	Arsenal's revenue for the year ended 31 May 2009

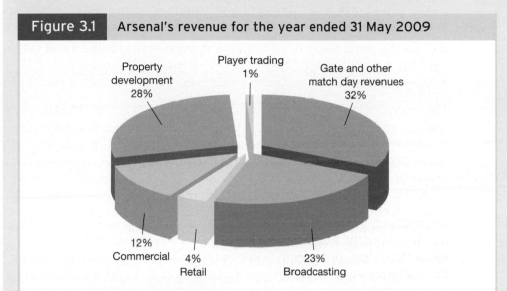

Gate receipts and broadcasting tend to be Arsenal's main forms of revenue, although commercial activities (including sponsorship and events) are also significant. During this particular year, there was a lot of income from property development. Between them, gate receipts, broadcasting and commercial activities accounted for 93 per cent of total revenue, excluding property development.

Source: Based on information in Arsenal Holdings plc Annual Report 2009, Note 3 to the financial statements.

→ The total expenses relating to each period must also be identified. **Expense** is really the opposite of revenue. It represents the outflow of economic benefits arising from the ordinary activities of a business. This loss of benefits will result in either a decrease in assets (such as cash) or an increase in liabilities (such as amounts owed to suppliers). Expenses are incurred in the process of generating, or attempting to generate, revenue. The nature of the business will again determine the type of expenses that will be incurred. Examples of some of the more common types of expense are:

● the cost of buying or making the goods that are sold during the period concerned – known as *cost of sales* or *cost of goods sold*
● salaries and wages
● rent and rates
● motor vehicle running expenses
● insurance

- printing and stationery
- heat and light
- telephone and postage.

The income statement simply shows the total revenue generated during a particular period and deducts from this the total expenses incurred in generating that revenue. The difference between the total revenue and total expenses will represent either profit (if revenue exceeds expenses) or loss (if expenses exceed revenue). Thus, we have:

> **Profit (or loss) for the period = Total revenue for the period − Total expenses incurred in generating that revenue**

The period over which profit or loss is normally measured is usually known as the **accounting period**, but it is sometimes called the 'reporting period' or 'financial period'.

Different roles

The income statement and the statement of financial position should not be viewed in any way as substitutes for one another. Rather they should be seen as performing different roles. The statement of financial position, as we have seen, sets out the position at a single moment in time: it is a 'snapshot' of the make-up of the wealth held by the business. The income statement, on the other hand, is concerned with the *flow* of wealth over a period of time. The two statements are, however, closely related.

The income statement links the statements of financial position at the beginning and the end of an accounting period. Thus, at the start of a new accounting period, the statement of financial position shows the opening wealth position of the business. After an appropriate period, an income statement is prepared to show the wealth generated over that period. A statement of financial position is then also prepared to reveal the new wealth position at the end of the period. This statement of financial position will reflect the changes in wealth that have occurred since the previous statement of financial position was drawn up.

We saw in Chapter 2 (pages 36–42) that the effect on the statement of financial position of making a profit (or loss) means that the accounting equation can be extended as follows:

> **Assets (at the end of the period) = Equity (amount at the start of the period + profit (or − loss) for the period) + Liabilities (at the end of the period)**

(This is assuming that the owner makes no injections or withdrawals of equity during the period.)

The amount of profit or loss for the period affects the statement of financial position as an adjustment to equity.

The above equation can be extended to:

> **Assets (at the end of the period) = Equity (amount at the start of the period) + (sales revenue − expenses) (for the period) + Liabilities (at the end of the period)**

In theory, it would be possible to calculate the profit (or loss) for the period by making all adjustments for revenue and expenses through the equity section of the statement of financial position. However, this would be rather cumbersome. A better solution is to have an 'appendix' to the equity section, in the form of an income statement. By deducting expenses from revenue for the period, the income statement derives the profit (or loss) by which the equity figure in the statement of financial position needs to be adjusted. This profit (or loss) figure represents the net effect of trading for the period. By providing this 'appendix', users are presented with a detailed and more informative view of performance.

Income statement layout

The layout of the income statement will vary according to the type of business to which it relates. To illustrate an income statement, let us consider the case of a retail business (that is, a business that buys goods in their completed state and resells them). This type of business usually has straightforward operations and, as a result, the income statement is relatively easy to understand.

Example 3.1 sets out a typical layout for the income statement of a retail business.

Example 3.1

Better-Price Stores
Income statement for the year ended 31 October 2009

	£
Sales revenue	232,000
Cost of sales	(154,000)
Gross profit	78,000
Salaries and wages	(24,500)
Rent and rates	(14,200)
Heat and light	(7,500)
Telephone and postage	(1,200)
Insurance	(1,000)
Motor vehicle running expenses	(3,400)
Depreciation – fixtures and fittings	(1,000)
Depreciation – motor van	(600)
Operating profit	24,600
Interest received from investments	2,000
Interest on borrowings	(1,100)
Profit for the year	25,500

We saw in Chapter 2 that brackets are used to denote when an item is to be deducted. This convention is used by accountants in preference to + or − signs and will be used throughout the text.

Gross profit

→ The first part of the income statement is concerned with calculating the **gross profit** for the period. We can see that revenue, which arises from selling the goods, is the first item to appear. Deducted from this item is the cost of sales (also called cost of goods sold) during the period. This gives the gross profit, which represents the profit from buying and selling goods, without taking into account any other revenues or expenses associated with the business.

Operating profit

From the gross profit, other expenses (overheads) that have been incurred in operating the business (salaries and wages, rent and rates and so on) are deducted.

→   The resulting figure is known as the **operating profit** for the accounting period. This represents the wealth generated during the period from the normal activities of the business. It does not take account of any income that the business may have from activities that are not included in its normal operations. Better-Price Stores in Example 3.1 is a retailer, so the interest on some spare cash that the business has invested is not part of its operating profit. Costs of financing the business are also ignored in the calculation of the operating profit.

Profit for the year

Having established the operating profit, we add any non-operating income (such as interest receivable) and deduct any interest payable on borrowings made by the business,

→   to arrive at the **profit for the year** (or net profit). This is the income that is attributable to the owner(s) of the business and which will be added to the equity figure in the statement of financial position. As can be seen, profit for the year is a residual: that is, the amount remaining after deducting all expenses incurred in generating the sales revenue for the period and taking account of non-operating income.

Further issues

Having set out the main principles involved in preparing an income statement, we need to consider some further points.

Cost of sales

→   The **cost of sales** (or cost of goods sold) figure for a period can be identified in different ways. In some businesses, the cost of sales amount for each individual sale is identified at the time of the transaction. Each item of sales revenue is closely matched with the relevant cost of that sale and so identifying the cost of sales figure for inclusion in the income statement is not a problem. Many large retailers (for example, supermarkets) have point-of-sale (checkout) devices that not only record each sale but also simultaneously pick up the cost of the goods that are the subject of the particular sale. Other businesses that sell a relatively small number of high-value items (for example, an engineering business that produces custom-made equipment) also tend to match sales revenue with the cost of the goods sold, at the time of the sale. However, some businesses (for example, small retailers) do not usually find it practical to match each sale to a particular cost of sales figure as the accounting period progresses. Instead, therefore, they identify the cost of sales figure at the end of the accounting period.

Deriving the cost of sales after the end of the accounting period

To understand how this is done, we need to remember that the cost of sales figure represents the cost of goods that were *sold* by the business during the period rather than the cost of goods that were *bought* by that business during the period. Part of the goods bought during a particular period may remain in the business, as inventories, at the accounting period end. These will normally be sold in the next period. To derive the cost of sales for a period, we need to know the amount of opening and closing inventories for the period and the cost of goods bought during the period. Example 3.2 illustrates how the cost of sales is derived.

Example 3.2

Better-Price Stores, which we considered in Example 3.1 above, began the accounting year with unsold inventories of £40,000 and during that year bought inventories at a cost of £189,000. At the end of the year, unsold inventories of £75,000 were still held by the business.

The opening inventories at the beginning of the year *plus* the goods bought during the year will represent the total goods available for resale. Thus:

	£
Opening inventories	40,000
Purchases (goods bought)	189,000
Goods available for resale	229,000

The closing inventories will represent that portion of the total goods available for resale that remains unsold at the end of the period. Thus, the cost of goods actually sold during the period must be the total goods available for resale *less* the inventories remaining at the end of the period. That is:

	£
Goods available for resale	229,000
Closing inventories	(75,000)
Cost of sales (or cost of goods sold)	154,000

These calculations are sometimes shown on the face of the income statement as in Example 3.3.

Example 3.3

	£	£
Sales revenue		232,000
Cost of sales:		
Opening inventories	40,000	
Purchases (goods bought)	189,000	
Closing inventories	(75,000)	(154,000)
Gross profit		78,000

This is just an expanded version of the first section of the income statement for Better-Price Stores, as set out in Example 3.1. We have simply included the additional information concerning inventories balances and purchases for the year provided in Example 3.2.

Classifying expenses

The classifications for the revenue and expense items, as with the classifications of various assets and claims in the statement of financial position, are often a matter of judgement by those who design the accounting system. Thus, the income statement set out in Example 3.1 could have included the insurance expense with the telephone and postage expense under a single heading – say, 'general expenses'. Such decisions are normally based on how useful a particular classification will be to users. This will usually mean that expense items of material size will be shown separately. For businesses that trade as limited companies, however, there are rules that dictate the classification of various items appearing in the financial statements for external reporting purposes. These rules will be discussed in Chapters 4 and 5.

Activity 3.1

The following information relates to the activities of H & S Retailers for the year ended 30 April 2010:

	£
Motor vehicle running expenses	1,200
Closing inventories	3,000
Rent and rates payable	5,000
Motor vans – cost less depreciation	6,300
Annual depreciation – motor vans	1,500
Heat and light	900
Telephone and postage	450
Sales revenue	97,400
Goods purchased	68,350
Insurance	750
Loan interest payable	620
Balance at bank	4,780
Salaries and wages	10,400
Opening inventories	4,000

Prepare an income statement for the year ended 30 April 2010. (*Hint*: Not all items listed should appear on this statement.)

Your answer to this activity should be as follows:

H & S Retailers
Income statement for the year ended 30 April 2010

	£	£
Sales revenue		97,400
Cost of sales:		
Opening inventories	4,000	
Purchases	68,350	
Closing inventories	(3,000)	(69,350)
Gross profit		28,050
Salaries and wages		(10,400)
Rent and rates		(5,000)
Heat and light		(900)
Telephone and postage		(450)
Insurance		(750)
Motor vehicle running expenses		(1,200)
Depreciation – motor vans		(1,500)
Operating profit		7,850
Loan interest		(620)
Profit for the year		7,230

Note that neither the motor vans nor the bank balance are included in this statement, because they are both assets and so neither revenues nor expenses.

The accounting period

We have seen already that for reporting to those outside the business, a financial reporting cycle of one year is the norm, though some large businesses produce a half-yearly, or interim, financial statement to provide more frequent feedback on progress. For those who manage a business, however, it is probably essential to have much more frequent feedback on performance. Thus it is quite common for income statements to be prepared on a quarterly, monthly, weekly or even daily basis in order to show how things are progressing.

Recognising revenue

A key issue in the measurement of profit concerns the point at which revenue is recognised. Revenue arising from the sale of goods or provision of a service could be recognised at various points. Where, for example, a motor car dealer receives an order for a new car from one of its customers, the associated revenue could be recognised by the dealer

● at the time that the order is placed by the customer;
● at the time that the car is collected by the customer; or
● at the time that the customer pays the dealer.

These three points could well be quite far apart, particularly where the order relates to a specialist car that is sold to the customer on credit.

The point chosen is not simply a matter of academic interest: it can have a profound impact on the total revenues reported for a particular accounting period. This, in turn, could have a profound effect on profit. If the sale transaction straddled the end of an accounting period, the choice made between the three possible times for recognising the revenue could determine whether it is included as revenue of an earlier accounting period or a later one.

When dealing with the sale of goods or the provision of services, the main criteria for recognising revenue are that

- the amount of revenue can be measured reliably; and
- it is probable that the economic benefits will be received.

An additional criterion, however, must be applied where the revenue comes from the sale of goods, which is that

- ownership and control of the items should pass to the buyer.

Activity 3.2 provides an opportunity to apply these criteria to a practical problem.

Activity 3.2

A manufacturing business sells goods on credit (that is, the customer pays for the goods some time after they are received). Below are four points in the production/selling cycle at which revenue might be recognised by the business:

1 when the goods are produced;
2 when an order is received from the customer;
3 when the goods are delivered to, and accepted by, the customer;
4 when the cash is received from the customer.

A significant amount of time may elapse between these different points. At what point do you think the business should recognise revenue?

All of the three criteria mentioned above will usually be fulfilled at point 3: when the goods are passed to, and accepted by, the customer. This is because

- the selling price and the settlement terms will have been agreed and therefore the amount of revenue can be reliably measured;
- delivery and acceptance of the goods leads to ownership and control passing to the buyer;
- transferring ownership gives the seller legally enforceable rights that makes it probable that the buyer will pay.

We can see that the effect of applying these criteria is that a sale on credit is usually recognised *before* the cash is received. Thus, the total sales revenue figure shown in the income statement may include sales transactions for which the cash has yet to be received. The total sales revenue figure in the income statement for a period will often, therefore, be different from the total cash received from sales during that period.

For cash sales (that is, sales where cash is paid at the same time as the goods are transferred), there will be no difference in timing between reporting sales revenue and cash received. **Real World 3.2** sets out the revenue recognition criteria for the travel business TUI Travel plc (which owns First Choice, Thomson, Exodus and many other well-known names). We can see that, although clients may pay for flights or holidays some time before they go, any money received in advance of the departure date, or use of the service, is not treated as revenue until later.

Real World 3.2

Selling point

(i) *Revenue recognition*

Revenue is recognised in the income statement when the significant risks and rewards of ownership have been transferred to the buyer.

Revenue in respect of in-house product is recognised on the date of departure. Travel agency commissions and other revenues received from the sale of third-party product are recognised when they are earned, typically on receipt of final payment. Revenue from individual travel modules directly booked by the customer with airline, hotels and incoming agencies is recognised when the customer departs or uses the respective service.

No revenue is recognised if there are significant uncertainties regarding recovery of the consideration due, associated costs or possible return of goods.

(ii) *Client monies received in advance (deferred income)*

Client monies received at the balance sheet [statement of financial position] date relating to holidays commencing and flights departing after the year end is deferred and included within trade and other payables.

Source: TUI Travel plc Annual Report and Accounts 2008, p. 68.

Long-term contracts

Some contracts, both for goods and for services, can last for more than one accounting period. If the business providing the goods or service were to wait until the contract is completely fulfilled before recognising revenue, the income statement could give a misleading impression of the wealth generated in the various accounting periods covered by the contract. This is a particular problem for businesses that undertake major long-term contracts, where a single contract could represent a large proportion of their total activities.

Construction contracts

Construction contracts often extend over a long period of time. Suppose that a customer enters into a contract with a builder to have a new factory built that will take three years to complete. In such a situation, it is possible to recognise revenue *before* the factory is completed provided that the building work can be broken down into a number of stages and each stage can be measured reliably. Let us assume that building the factory could be broken down into the following stages:

Stage 1 – clearing and levelling the land and putting in the foundations.
Stage 2 – building the walls.
Stage 3 – putting on the roof.
Stage 4 – putting in the windows and completing all the interior work.

Each stage can be awarded a separate price with the total for all the stages being equal to the total contract price for the factory. This means that, as each stage is completed, the builder can recognise the price for that stage as revenue and bill the customer accordingly. This is provided that the outcome of the contract as a whole can be estimated reliably.

If the builder were to wait until the factory was completed before recognising revenue, the income statement covering the final year of the contract would recognise all of the revenue on the contract and the income statements for each preceding year would recognise no revenue. This would give a misleading impression, as it would not reflect the work done during each period.

Real World 3.3 sets out the revenue recognition criteria for one large construction business.

Real World 3.3

Tracking revenue

Jarvis plc is a business operating in the areas of road and rail infrastructure renewal, facilities management and plant hire. The point at which revenue on long-term contracts is recognised by the business is as follows:

> When the outcome of a long-term contract can be estimated reliably, contract revenue is recognised by reference to the degree of completion of each contract, based on the amounts certified and to be certified by the customer.

Source: Jarvis plc Annual Report and Accounts 2009, p. 41.

Services

Revenue from contracts for services may also be recognised in stages. Suppose a consultancy business has a contract to install a new computer system for the government, which will take several years to complete. Revenue can be recognised *before* the contract is completed as long as the contract can be broken down into stages and the particular stages of completion can be measured reliably. This is really the same approach as that used in the construction contract mentioned above.

Sometimes a continuous service is provided to a customer; for example, a telecommunications business may provide open access to the internet to those who subscribe to the service. In this case, revenue is usually recognised as the service is rendered. Benefits from providing the service are usually assumed to flow evenly over time and so revenue is recognised evenly over the subscription period.

Where it is not possible to break down a service into particular stages of completion, or to assume that benefits from providing the service accrue evenly over time, revenue will not usually be recognised until the service is fully completed. The work done by a solicitor on a house purchase for a client would normally be one such example.

Real World 3.4 provides an example of how one major business recognises revenue from providing services.

Real World 3.4

Sky-high broadcasting revenue

British Sky Broadcasting Group plc is a major satellite broadcaster that generates various forms of revenue. Here are the ways in which some of its revenues are recognised:

- pay-per-view revenues – when the event (movie or football match) is viewed
- subscription services, including Sky TV and Sky Broadband – as the services are provided
- advertising revenues – when the advertising is broadcast
- installation, hardware and service revenue – when the goods and services are delivered.

Source: Based on information in British Sky Broadcasting Group plc Annual Report and Accounts 2009, p. 78.

When a service is provided, there will normally be a timing difference between the recognition of revenue and the receipt of cash. Revenue for providing services is often recognised *before* the cash is received, as with the sale of goods on credit. However, there are occasions when it is the other way around, usually because the business demands payment before providing the service.

Activity 3.3

Can you think of any examples where cash may be demanded in advance of a service being provided? (*Hint*: Try to think of services that you may use.)

Examples of cash being received in advance of the service being provided may include:

- rent received from letting premises
- telephone line rental charges
- TV licence (BBC) or subscription (for example, Sky) fees
- subscriptions received for the use of health clubs or golf clubs.

You may have thought of others.

Recognising expenses

Having decided on the point at which revenue is recognised, we can now turn to the issue of the recognition of expenses. The **matching convention** in accounting is designed to provide guidance concerning the recognition of expenses. This convention states that expenses should be matched to the revenue that they helped to generate. In other words, the expenses associated with a particular item of revenue must be taken into account in the same accounting period as that in which the item of revenue is included. Applying this convention may mean that a particular expense reported in the income statement for a period may not be the same figure as the cash paid for that item during the period. The expense reported might be either more or less than the cash paid during the period. Let us consider two examples that illustrate this point.

When the expense for the period is more than the cash paid during the period

Example 3.4

Domestic Ltd, a retailer, sells household electrical appliances. It pays its sales staff a commission of 2 per cent of sales revenue generated. Total sales revenue for last year amounted to £300,000. This will mean that the commission to be paid in respect of the sales for the year will be £6,000. However, by the end of the year, the amount of sales commission that had actually been paid to staff was £5,000. If the business reported only the amount paid, it would mean that the income statement would not reflect the full expense for the year. This would contravene the *matching convention* because not all of the expenses associated with the revenue of the year would have been matched in the income statement. This will be remedied as follows:

- Sales commission expense in the income statement will include the amount paid plus the amount outstanding (that is, £6,000 = £5,000 + £1,000).
- The amount outstanding (£1,000) represents an outstanding liability at the end of the year and will be included under the heading **accrued expenses**, or 'accruals', in the statement of financial position. As this item will have to be paid within twelve months of the year end, it will be treated as a current liability.
- The cash will already have been reduced to reflect the commission paid (£5,000) during the period.

These points are illustrated in Figure 3.2.

Figure 3.2   Accounting for sales commission

This illustrates the main points of Example 3.4. We can see that the sales commission expense of £6,000 (which appears in the income statement) is made up of a cash element of £5,000 and an accrued element of £1,000. The cash element appears in the statement of cash flows and the accrued element will appear as a year-end liability in the statement of financial position.

In principle, all expenses should be matched to the period in which the sales revenue to which they relate is reported. However, it is sometimes difficult to match certain expenses to sales revenue in the same precise way that we have matched sales commission to sales revenue. It is unlikely, for example, that electricity charges incurred can be linked directly to particular sales in this way. As a result, the electricity charges incurred by, say, a retailer would be matched to the *period* to which they relate. Example 3.5 illustrates this.

Example 3.5

Domestic Ltd has reached the end of its accounting year and has only paid for electricity for the first three quarters of the year (amounting to £1,900). This is simply because the electricity company has yet to send out bills for the quarter that ends on the same date as Domestic Ltd's year end. The amount of Domestic Ltd's bill for the last quarter is £500. In this situation, the amount of the electricity expense outstanding is dealt with as follows:

● Electricity expense in the income statement will include the amount paid, plus the amount of the bill for the last quarter (that is, £1,900 + £500 = £2,400) in order to cover the whole year.
● The amount of the outstanding bill (£500) represents a liability at the end of the year and will be included under the heading 'accruals' or 'accrued expenses' in the statement of financial position. This item would normally have to be paid within twelve months of the year end and will, therefore, be treated as a current liability.
● The cash will already have been reduced to reflect the amount (£1,900) paid for electricity during the period.

This treatment will mean that the correct figure for the electricity expense for the year will be included in the income statement. It will also have the effect of showing that, at the end of the accounting year, Domestic Ltd owed the amount of the last quarter's electricity bill. Dealing with the outstanding amount in this way reflects the dual aspect of the item and will ensure that the accounting equation is maintained.

Domestic Ltd may wish to draw up its income statement before it is able to discover how much it owes for the last quarter's electricity. In this case it is quite normal to make a reasonable estimate of the amount of the bill and to use this estimated amount as described above.

Activity 3.4

How will the payment of the electricity bill for the last quarter be dealt with in the accounting records of Domestic Ltd?

When the electricity bill is eventually paid, it will be dealt with as follows:

● Reduce cash by the amount of the bill.
● Reduce the amount of the accrued expense as shown on the statement of financial position by the same amount.

If an estimated figure is used and there is a slight error in the estimate, a small adjustment (either negative or positive depending on the direction of the error) can be made to the following year's expense. Dealing with the estimation error in this way is not strictly correct, but the amount is likely to be insignificant.

Activity 3.5

Can you think of other expenses for a retailer, apart from electricity charges, that cannot be linked directly to sales revenue and for which matching will therefore be done on a time basis?

You may have thought of the following examples:

- rent and rates
- insurance
- interest payments
- licence fees payable.

This is not an exhaustive list. You may have thought of others.

When the amount paid during the period is more than the full expense for the period

It is not unusual for a business to be in a situation where it has paid more during the year than the full expense for that year. Example 3.6 illustrates how we deal with this.

Example 3.6

Images Ltd, an advertising agency, normally pays rent for its premises quarterly in advance (on 1 January, 1 April, 1 July and 1 October). On the last day of the last accounting year (31 December), it paid the next quarter's rent (£4,000) to the following 31 March, which was a day earlier than required. This would mean that a total of five quarters' rent was paid during the year. If Images Ltd reports all of the cash paid as an expense in the income statement, this would be more than the full expense for the year. This would contravene the matching convention because a higher figure than the expenses associated with the revenue of the year would appear in the income statement.

The problem is overcome by dealing with the rental payment as follows:

- Show the rent for four quarters as the appropriate expense in the income statement (that is, $4 \times £4,000 = £16,000$).
- The cash (that is, $5 \times £4,000 = £20,000$) would already have been paid during the year.
- Show the quarter's rent paid in advance (£4,000) as a prepaid expense under assets in the statement of financial position. (The rent paid in advance will appear as a current asset in the statement of financial position, under the heading **prepaid expenses** or 'prepayments'.)

In the next accounting period, this prepayment will cease to be an asset and will become an expense in the income statement of that period. This is because the rent prepaid relates to the next period and will be 'used up' during it.

These points are illustrated in Figure 3.3.

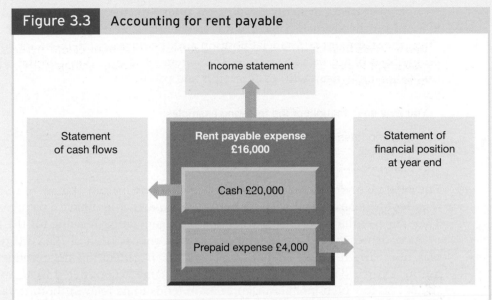

Figure 3.3   Accounting for rent payable

This illustrates the main points of Example 3.6. We can see that the rent expense of £16,000 (which appears in the income statement) is made up of four quarters' rent at £4,000 per quarter. This is the amount that relates to the period and is 'used up' during the period. The cash paid of £20,000 (which appears in the statement of cash flows) is made up of the cash paid during the period, which is five quarters at £4,000 per quarter. Finally, the prepayment of £4,000 (which appears on the statement of financial position) represents the payment made on 31 December and relates to the next financial year.

In practice, the treatment of accruals and prepayments will be subject to the **materiality convention** of accounting. This convention states that, where the amounts involved are immaterial, we should consider only what is reasonable. This may mean that an item will be treated as an expense in the period in which it is paid, rather than being strictly matched to the revenue to which it relates. For example, a business may find that, at the end of an accounting period, a bill of £5 has been paid for stationery that has yet to be delivered. For a business of any size, the time and effort involved in recording this as a prepayment would not be justified by the little effect that this would have on the measurement of profit or financial position. The amount would, therefore, be treated as an expense when preparing the income statement for the current period and ignored in the following period.

Profit, cash and accruals accounting

As we have just seen, revenue does not usually represent cash received and expenses are not the same as cash paid. As a result, the profit figure (that is, total revenue minus total expenses) will not normally represent the net cash generated during a period. It is therefore important to distinguish between profit and liquidity. Profit is a measure of achievement, or productive effort, rather than a measure of cash generated. Although making a profit will increase wealth, as we have already seen in Chapter 2, cash is only one form in which that wealth may be held.

→ The above points are reflected in the **accruals convention** of accounting, which asserts that profit is the excess of revenue over expenses for a period, not the excess of cash receipts over cash payments. Leading on from this, the approach to accounting that

→ is based on the accruals convention is frequently referred to as **accruals accounting**. Thus, the statement of financial position and the income statement are both prepared on the basis of accruals accounting. The statement of cash flows, on the other hand, is not, as it simply deals with cash receipts and payments.

Depreciation

→ The expense of **depreciation**, which appeared in the income statement in Activity 3.1, requires further explanation. Most non-current assets do not have a perpetual existence. They are eventually used up in the process of generating revenue for the business. In essence, depreciation is an attempt to measure that portion of the cost (or fair value) of a non-current asset that has been used up in generating the revenue recognised during a particular period. The depreciation charge is considered to be an expense of the period to which it relates. Depreciation tends to be relevant both to tangible non-current assets (property, plant and equipment) and to intangible non-current assets. We should be clear that the principle is the same for both types of non-current asset. We shall deal with each of the two in turn.

Depreciating tangible non-current assets (property, plant and equipment)

To calculate a depreciation charge for a period, four factors have to be considered:

- the cost (or fair value) of the asset
- the useful life of the asset
- the residual value of the asset
- the depreciation method.

The cost (or fair value) of the asset

The cost of an asset will include all costs incurred by the business to bring the asset to its required location and to make it ready for use. Thus, in addition to the costs of acquiring the asset, any delivery costs, installation costs (for example, setting up a new machine) and legal costs incurred in the transfer of legal title (for example, in purchasing property) will be included as part of the total cost of the asset. Similarly, any costs incurred in improving or altering an asset in order to make it suitable for its intended use within the business will also be included as part of the total cost.

Activity 3.6

Andrew Wu (Engineering) Ltd bought a new motor car for its marketing director. The invoice received from the motor car supplier showed the following:

	£
New BMW 325i	26,350
Delivery charge	80
Alloy wheels	660
Sun roof	200
Petrol	30
Number plates	130
Road fund licence	120
	27,570
Part exchange – Reliant Robin	(1,000)
Amount outstanding	26,570

What is the total cost of the new car that will be treated as part of the business's property, plant and equipment?

The cost of the new car will be as follows:

	£
New BMW 325i	26,350
Delivery charge	80
Alloy wheels	660
Sun roof	200
Number plates	130
	27,420

This cost includes delivery charges, which are necessary to bring the asset into use, and it includes number plates, as they are a necessary and integral part of the asset. Improvements (alloy wheels and sun roof) are also regarded as part of the total cost of the motor car. The petrol and road fund licence, however, represent costs of operating the asset rather than a part of the total cost of acquiring it and making it ready for use: hence these amounts will be charged as an expense in the period incurred (although part of the cost of the licence may be regarded as a prepaid expense in the period incurred).

The part-exchange figure shown is part payment of the total amount outstanding and so is not relevant to a consideration of the total cost.

The fair value of an asset was defined in Chapter 2 as the exchange value that could be obtained in an arm's-length transaction. As we saw, assets may be revalued to fair value only if this can be measured reliably. When a revaluation is carried out, all items within the same class must be revalued and revaluations must be kept up to date.

The useful life of the asset

A tangible non-current asset has both a *physical life* and an *economic life*. The physical life will be exhausted through the effects of wear and tear and/or the passage of time. It is possible, however, for the physical life to be extended considerably through careful maintenance, improvements and so on. The economic life is decided by the effects of technological progress and by changes in demand. After a while, the benefits of using the asset may be less than the costs involved. This may be because the asset is unable to compete with newer assets, or because it is no longer relevant to the needs of the business. The economic life of a non-current tangible asset may be much shorter than its physical life. For example, a computer may have a physical life of eight years and an economic life of three years.

It is the economic life that will determine the expected useful life for the purpose of calculating depreciation. Forecasting the economic life, however, may be extremely difficult in practice: both the rate at which technology progresses and shifts in consumer tastes can be swift and unpredictable.

Residual value (disposal value)

When a business disposes of a tangible non-current asset that may still be of value to others, some payment may be received. This payment will represent the **residual value**, or *disposal value*, of the asset. To calculate the total amount to be depreciated, the residual value must be deducted from the cost (or fair value) of the asset. The likely amount to be received on disposal can, once again, be difficult to predict. The best guide is often past experience of similar assets sold.

Depreciation method

Once the amount to be depreciated (that is, the cost, or fair value, of the asset less any residual value) has been estimated, the business must select a method of allocating this depreciable amount between the accounting periods covering the asset's useful life. Although there are various ways in which the total depreciation may be allocated and, from this, a depreciation charge for each period derived, there are really only two methods that are commonly used in practice.

The first of these is known as the **straight-line method**. This method simply allocates the amount to be depreciated evenly over the useful life of the asset. In other words, an equal amount of depreciation is charged for each year that the asset is held.

Example 3.7

To illustrate this method, consider the following information:

Cost of machine	£78,124
Estimated residual value at the end of its useful life	£2,000
Estimated useful life	4 years

To calculate the depreciation charge for each year, the total amount to be depreciated must be calculated. This will be the total cost less the estimated residual value: that is, £78,124 − £2,000 = £76,124. Having done this, the annual depreciation charge can be derived by dividing the amount to be depreciated by the estimated useful life of the asset of four years. The calculation is therefore:

$$\frac{£76,124}{4} = £19,031$$

Thus, the annual depreciation charge that appears in the income statement in relation to this asset will be £19,031 for each of the four years of the asset's life.

The amount of depreciation relating to the asset will be accumulated for as long as the asset continues to be owned by the business. This accumulated depreciation figure will increase each year as a result of the annual depreciation amount charged to the income statement. This accumulated amount will be deducted from the cost of the asset on the statement of financial position. At the end of the second year, for example, the accumulated depreciation will be £19,031 × 2 = £38,062. The asset details will appear on the statement of financial position as follows:

	£
Machine at cost	78,124
Accumulated depreciation	(38,062)
	40,062

The balance of £40,062 shown above is referred to as the **carrying amount** (sometimes also known as the **written-down value** or **net book value**) of the asset. It represents that portion of the cost (or fair value) of the asset that has still to be charged as an expense (written off) in future years. It must be emphasised that this figure does not, unless by coincidence, represent the current market value, which may be quite different. The only point at which the carrying amount is intended to equal the market value of the asset is immediately before it is to be disposed of. Thus in Example 3.7, at the end of the four-year life of the machine, the carrying amount would be £2,000 – its estimated disposal value.

The straight-line method derives its name from the fact that the carrying amount of the asset at the end of each year, when plotted against time, will result in a straight line, as shown in Figure 3.4.

Figure 3.4 **Graph of carrying amount against time using the straight-line method**

Carrying amount (£000)

(Graph: y-axis Carrying amount (£000) from 0 to 80; x-axis Asset life (years) from 0 to 4. Line declining from 80 at year 0 to about 2 at year 4.)

Asset life (years)

The carrying amount of the asset declines by a constant amount each year. This is because the straight-line method provides a constant depreciation charge each year. The result, when plotted on a graph, is a straight line.

The second approach found in practice to calculating depreciation for a period is referred to as the **reducing-balance method**. This method applies a fixed percentage rate of depreciation to the carrying amount of the asset each year. The effect of this will be high annual depreciation charges in the early years and lower charges in the later years. To illustrate this method, let us take the same information that was used in Example 3.7. By using a fixed percentage of 60 per cent of the carrying amount to determine the annual depreciation charge, the effect will be to reduce the carrying amount to £2,000 after four years.

The calculations will be as follows:

	£
Cost of machine	78,124
Year 1 depreciation charge (60%* of cost)	(46,874)
Carrying amount	31,250
Year 2 depreciation charge (60% of carrying amount)	(18,750)
Carrying amount	12,500
Year 3 depreciation charge (60% of carrying amount)	(7,500)
Carrying amount	5,000
Year 4 depreciation charge (60% of carrying amount)	(3,000)
Residual value	2,000

* See the box below for an explanation of how to derive the fixed percentage.

Deriving the fixed percentage

Deriving the fixed percentage to be applied requires the use of the following formula:

$$P = (1 - \sqrt[n]{R/C}) \times 100\%$$

where: P = the depreciation percentage
n = the useful life of the asset (in years)
R = the residual value of the asset
C = the cost, or fair value, of the asset.

The fixed percentage rate will, however, be given in all examples used in this text.

We can see that the pattern of depreciation is quite different between the two methods. If we plot the carrying amount of the asset, which has been derived using the reducing-balance method, against time, the result will be as shown in Figure 3.5.

Figure 3.5	Graph of carrying amount against time using the reducing-balance method

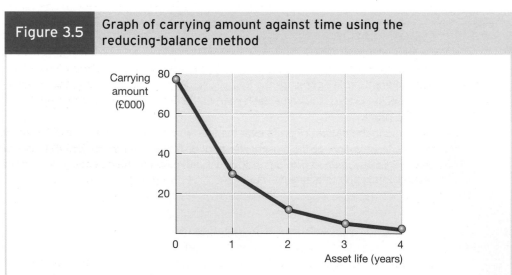

Under the reducing-balance method, the carrying amount of an asset falls by a larger amount in the earlier years than in the later years. This is because the depreciation charge is based on a fixed-rate percentage of the carrying amount.

Activity 3.7

Assume that the machine used in the example above was owned by a business that made a profit before depreciation of £40,000 for each of the four years in which the asset was held.

Calculate the profit for the business for each year under each depreciation method, and comment on your findings.

Your answer should be as follows:

Straight-line method

	(a) Profit before depreciation £	(b) Depreciation £	(a – b) Profit £
Year 1	40,000	19,031	20,969
Year 2	40,000	19,031	20,969
Year 3	40,000	19,031	20,969
Year 4	40,000	19,031	20,969

Reducing-balance method

	(a) Profit before depreciation £	(b) Depreciation £	(a – b) Profit/(loss) £
Year 1	40,000	46,874	(6,874)
Year 2	40,000	18,750	21,250
Year 3	40,000	7,500	32,500
Year 4	40,000	3,000	37,000

The straight-line method of depreciation results in the same profit figure for each year of the four-year period. This is because both the profit before depreciation and the depreciation charge are constant over the period. The reducing-balance method, however, results in very different profit figures for the four years, despite the fact that in this example the pre-depreciation profit is the same each year. In the first year a loss is reported and, thereafter, a rising profit.

Although the *pattern* of profit over the four-year period will be quite different, depending on the depreciation method used, the *total* profit for the period (£83,876) will remain the same. This is because both methods of depreciating will allocate the same amount of total depreciation (£76,124) over the four-year period. It is only the amount allocated *between years* that will differ.

In practice, the use of different depreciation methods may not have such a dramatic effect on profits as suggested in Activity 3.7. This is because businesses typically have more than one depreciating non-current asset. Where a business replaces some of its assets each year, the total depreciation charge calculated under the reducing-balance method will reflect a range of charges (from high through to low), as assets will be at different points in the replacement cycle. This could mean that each year's total depreciation charge may not be significantly different from the total depreciation charge that would be derived under the straight-line method.

Selecting a depreciation method

How does a business choose which depreciation method to use for a particular asset? The answer is the one that best matches the depreciation expense to the pattern of economic benefits that the asset provides. Where these benefits are provided evenly over time (buildings, for example), the straight-line method is usually appropriate. Where assets lose their efficiency (as with certain types of machinery), the benefits provided will decline over time and so the reducing-balance method may be more appropriate. Where the pattern of economic benefits provided by the asset is uncertain, the straight-line method is normally chosen.

There is an international financial reporting standard (or international accounting standard) to deal with the depreciation of property, plant and equipment. As we shall see in Chapter 5, the purpose of accounting standards is to narrow areas of accounting difference and to try to ensure that information provided to users is transparent and comparable. The relevant standard endorses the view that the depreciation method chosen should reflect the pattern of economic benefits provided but does not specify particular methods to be used. It states that the useful life, depreciation method and residual values of non-current assets should be reviewed at least annually and adjustments made where appropriate.

Real World 3.5 sets out the depreciation policies of Thorntons plc.

Real World 3.5

Sweet talk on depreciation policies

Thorntons plc, the manufacturer and retailer of confectionery, uses the straight-line method to depreciate all its property, plant and equipment, other than land and assets in the course of construction. The financial statements for the year ended 30 June 2009 show the period over which different classes of assets are depreciated as follows:

Long leasehold and freehold premises	50 years
Short leasehold land and buildings	Period of the lease
Other plant, vehicles and equipment	3 to 15 years
Retail fixtures and fittings	Up to 10 years

We can see that there are wide variations in the expected useful lives of the various assets held.

Source: Thorntons plc Annual Report and Accounts 2009, p. 49.

It seems that Thorntons plc is typical of UK businesses in that most use the straight-line approach. The reducing-balance method is not very much used.

The approach taken to calculating depreciation is summarised in Figure 3.6.

Figure 3.6   Calculating the annual depreciation charge

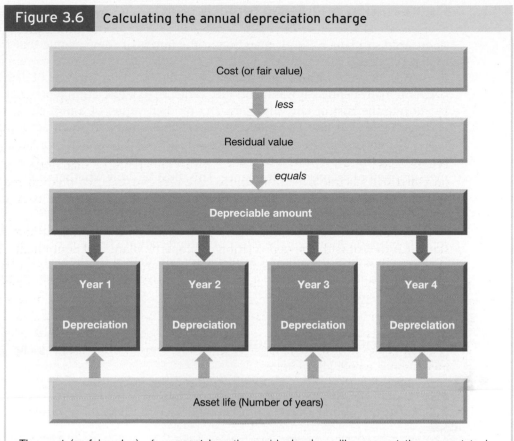

The cost (or fair value) of an asset less the residual value will represent the amount to be depreciated. This amount is depreciated over the useful life (four years in this particular case) of the asset using an appropriate depreciation method.

Depreciating intangible assets

Where an intangible asset has a finite life, the approach taken for the depreciation (or **amortisation** as it is usually called with intangibles) is broadly the same as that for property, plant and equipment (tangible non-current assets). The asset is amortised (depreciated) over its useful life and the amortisation method used should reflect the pattern of benefits provided. Some differences arise, however, because of the valuation problems surrounding these assets. Intangible assets are reported initially at cost but can, in principle, be revalued to fair value. However, this rarely occurs as there is usually no active market from which to establish fair values. For similar reasons, the residual value of an intangible asset is normally assumed to be zero.

We saw in Chapter 2 that some intangible assets, which may include acquired goodwill, could have infinite useful lives. These assets are not amortised but instead are tested for impairment at least annually. While intangible assets with finite lives and property, plant and equipment are also subject to impairment testing, this will only occur when there is some indication that impairment may actually have taken place; it does not take place on a routine basis.

Depreciation and asset replacement

There seems to be a misunderstanding in the minds of some people that the purpose of depreciation is to provide the funds for the replacement of a non-current asset when it reaches the end of its useful life. However, this is not the purpose of depreciation as conventionally defined. It was mentioned earlier that depreciation represents an attempt to allocate the cost or fair value (less any residual value) of a non-current asset over its expected useful life. The resulting depreciation charge in each accounting period represents an expense, which is then used in the calculation of profit for the period. Calculating the depreciation charge for a period is therefore necessary for the proper measurement of financial performance. This must be done whether or not the business intends to replace the asset in the future.

If there is an intention to replace the asset, the depreciation charge in the income statement will not ensure that liquid funds are set aside by the business specifically for this purpose. Although the effect of a depreciation charge is to reduce profit, and therefore to reduce the amount available for withdrawal by the owners, the amounts retained within the business as a result may be invested in ways that are unrelated to the replacement of the particular asset.

Depreciation and judgement

From what we have just seen about depreciation, it seems that accounting is not as precise and objective as it sometimes appears to be. There are areas where subjective judgement is required; depreciation provides a good illustration of this.

Activity 3.8

What kinds of judgements must be made to calculate a depreciation charge for a period?

You may have thought of the following:

- the expected residual or disposal value of the asset
- the expected useful life of the asset
- the choice of depreciation method.

Making different judgements on these matters would result in a different pattern of depreciation charges over the life of the asset and, therefore, in a different pattern of reported profits. However, underestimations or overestimations that are made in relation to the above will be adjusted for in the final year of an asset's life. As a result, the total depreciation charge (and total profit) over the asset's life will not be affected by estimation errors.

Real World 3.6 describes the effect of extending the useful life of property, plant and equipment on the short-term profits of one large business.

Real World 3.6

Sports massage

JJB Sports plc, a leading retailer, reported interim financial results for the six months ended 30 June 2005 that caused some disquiet among investors and analysts. The business changed the estimates for the useful life of its property, plant and equipment when calculating depreciation. It explained that this was due to new requirements to adopt International Financial Reporting Standards (IFRSs) when preparing financial statements. The article below, however, suggests that not everyone believed this.

JJB massages results to boost profits

High street retailer JJB Sports massaged last week's disappointing interim results by changing its depreciation calculations, in order to boost flagging profits by £4.3 million.

Analysts admitted that they were caught on the hop, as the company reported a 35.8% drop in operating profits from £27.4 million to £17.6 million for six months ended June 2005 on revenues down 6% to £340.4 million. Operating profits would have plummeted even further [to £13.3 million] had the company not changed its accounting for depreciation. 'The company explained the change as coming out of its IFRS conversion review, but it was clearly there for other reasons,' said Teather & Greenwood retail analyst Sanjay Vidyarthi.

JJB said that an impairment review ahead of its IFRS transition had forced a rethink on the carrying value of property, plant and equipment.

It concluded that these items had useful economic lives that more closely matched the length of the short-term lease of the property, rather than the 10-year economic life, which had formed the basis of the depreciation charge in previous accounting periods.

Richard Ratner, head of equity research at Seymour Pierce, said: 'They said the way they had depreciated assets previously was not correct but I haven't seen any other companies make this kind of change.'

JJB's share price fell from 168.2p before the results to 164.7p at the end of last week.

Source: 'JJB massages results to boost profits', *Accountancy Age*, 20 October 2005, p. 3.

Activity 3.9

Sally Dalton (Packaging) Ltd bought a machine for £40,000. At the end of its useful life of four years, the amount received on sale was £4,000. When the asset was bought the business received two estimates of the likely residual value of the asset, which were: (a) £8,000 and (b) zero.

Show the pattern of annual depreciation charges over the four years and the total depreciation charges for the asset under each of the two estimates. The straight-line method should be used to calculate the annual depreciation charges.

The depreciation charge, assuming estimate (a), will be £8,000 a year (that is, (£40,000 – £8,000)/4). The depreciation charge, assuming estimate (b), will be £10,000 a year (that is, £40,000/4). As the actual residual value is £4,000, estimate (a) will lead to underdepreciation of £4,000 (that is, £8,000 – £4,000) over the life of the asset and estimate (b) will lead to overdepreciation of £4,000 (that is, £0 – £4,000). These under- and overestimations will be dealt with in year 4.

Activity 3.9 continued

The pattern of depreciation and total depreciation charges will therefore be:

		Estimate	
		(a) £	(b) £
Year			
1	Annual depreciation	8,000	10,000
2	Annual depreciation	8,000	10,000
3	Annual depreciation	8,000	10,000
4	Annual depreciation	8,000	10,000
		32,000	40,000
4	Under/(over)depreciation	4,000	(4,000)
	Total depreciation	36,000	36,000

The final adjustment for underdepreciation of an asset is often referred to as 'loss (or deficit) on sale of non-current asset', as the amount actually received is less than the residual value. Similarly, the adjustment for overdepreciation is often referred to as 'profit (or surplus) on sale of non-current asset'. These final adjustments are normally made as an extra expense (or a reduction in the expense) for depreciation in the year of disposal of the asset.

Costing inventories

The way in which we measure the cost of inventories (or stock) is important because the cost of inventories sold during a period will affect the calculation of profit and the remaining inventories held at the end of the period will affect the portrayal of wealth in the statement of financial position. In the previous chapter, we saw that historic cost is often the basis for reporting assets. It is, therefore, tempting to think that determining the cost of inventories held or used is very straightforward. However, in a period of changing prices, the costing of inventories can be a problem.

A business must determine the cost of the inventories sold during the period and the cost of the inventories remaining at the end of the period. To do this, some assumption must be made about the way in which the inventories are physically handled. The assumption made need not have anything to do with how the inventories are *actually* handled. The assumption is concerned only with providing useful accounting information.

Three assumptions used are:

→ 1 **first in, first out (FIFO)** – the earliest inventories held are the first to be used;
→ 2 **last in, first out (LIFO)** – the latest inventories held are the first to be used;
→ 3 **weighted average cost (AVCO)** – inventories entering the business lose their separate identity and go into a 'pool'. Any issues of inventories then reflect the average cost of the inventories that are held.

Example 3.8 provides a simple illustration of the way in which each method is applied.

Example 3.8

A business which supplies grass seed to farmers and horticulturalists has the following transactions during a period:

		Tonnes	Cost/tonne £
1 May	Opening inventories	100	100
2 May	Bought	500	110
3 May	Bought	800	120
		1,400	
6 May	Sold	(900)	
	Closing inventories	500	

First in, first out (FIFO)

Using the first in, first out approach, the first 900 tonnes of seed bought are treated as if these are the ones that are sold. This will consist of the opening inventories (100 tonnes), the purchases made on 2 May (500 tonnes) and some of the purchases made on 3 May (300 tonnes). The remainder of the 3 May purchases (500 tonnes) will comprise the closing inventories. Thus we have:

	Cost of sales			Closing inventories		
	Tonnes	Cost/tonne £	Total £000	Tonnes	Cost/tonne £	Total £000
1 May	100	100	10.0			
2 May	500	110	55.0			
3 May	300	120	36.0	500	120	60.0
Cost of sales			101.0	Closing inventories		60.0

Last in, first out (LIFO)

Using the last in, first out approach, the later purchases will be treated as if these were the first to be sold. This is the 3 May purchases (800 tonnes) and some of the 2 May purchases (100 tonnes). The earlier purchases (the rest of the 2 May purchase and the opening inventories) will comprise the closing inventories. Thus we have:

	Cost of sales			Closing inventories		
	Tonnes	Cost/tonne £	Total £000	Tonnes	Cost/tonne £	Total £000
3 May	800	120	96.0			
2 May	100	110	11.0	400	110	44.0
1 May				100	100	10.0
Cost of sales			107.0	Closing inventories		54.0

Figure 3.7 contrasts LIFO and FIFO.

Example 3.8 continued

Figure 3.7	FIFO and LIFO treatment of the inventories in Example 3.8

Using FIFO, the oldest purchases of inventories are treated as the first to be used leaving the later purchases in closing inventories. With LIFO it is the opposite.

Weighted average cost (AVCO)

Using this approach, a weighted average cost will be determined that will be used to derive both the cost of goods sold and the cost of the remaining inventories held. This simply means that the total cost of the opening inventories, the 2 May and 3 May purchases, are added together and divided by the total number of tonnes to obtain the weighted average cost per tonne. Both the cost of sales and closing inventories values are based on that average cost per tonne. Thus we have:

		Purchases	
	Tonnes	Cost/tonne	Total
		£	£000
1 May	100	100	10.0
2 May	500	110	55.0
3 May	800	120	96.0
	1,400		161.0

Average cost = £161,000/1,400 = £115 per tonne.

Cost of sales			Closing inventories		
Tonnes	Cost/tonne	Total	Tonnes	Cost/tonne	Total
	£	£000		£	£000
900	115	103.5	500	115	57.5

Activity 3.10

Suppose the 900 tonnes of inventories in Example 3.8 were sold for £150 per tonne.

(a) Calculate the gross profit for this sale under each of the three methods.
(b) What observations concerning the portrayal of financial position and performance can you make about each method when prices are rising?

Your answer should be along the following lines:

(a) Gross profit calculation:

	FIFO £000	LIFO £000	AVCO £000
Sales revenue (900 @ £150)	135.0	135.0	135.0
Cost of sales	(101.0)	(107.0)	(103.5)
Gross profit	34.0	28.0	31.5
Closing inventories figure	60.0	54.0	57.5

(b) These figures reveal that FIFO will give the highest gross profit during a period of rising prices. This is because sales revenue is matched with the earlier (and cheaper) purchases. LIFO will give the lowest gross profit because sales revenue is matched against the more recent (and dearer) purchases. The AVCO method will normally give a figure that is between these two extremes.

   The closing inventories figure in the statement of financial position will be highest with the FIFO method. This is because the cost of goods still held will be based on the more recent (and dearer) purchases. LIFO will give the lowest closing inventories figure as the goods held will be based on the earlier (and cheaper) purchases. Once again, the AVCO method will normally give a figure that is between these two extremes.

Activity 3.11

Assume that prices in Activity 3.10 are falling rather than rising. How would your observations concerning the portrayal of financial performance and position be different for the various costing methods?

When prices are falling, the positions of FIFO and LIFO are reversed. FIFO will give the lowest gross profit as sales revenue is matched against the earlier (and dearer) goods bought. LIFO will give the highest gross profit as sales revenue is matched against the more recent (and cheaper) goods bought. AVCO will give a cost of sales figure between these two extremes. The closing inventories figure in the statement of financial position will be lowest under FIFO as the cost of inventories will be based on the more recent (and cheaper) purchases. LIFO will provide the highest closing inventories figure and AVCO will provide a figure between the two extremes.

The different costing methods will only have an effect on the reported profit from one year to the next. The figure derived for closing inventories will be carried forward and matched with sales revenue in a later period. Thus, if the cheaper purchases of inventories are matched to sales revenue in the current period, it will mean that the dearer purchases will be matched to sales revenue in a later period. Over the life of the business, therefore, the total profit will be the same whichever costing method has been used.

Inventories – some further issues

We saw in Chapter 2 that the convention of prudence requires that inventories be valued at the lower of cost and net realisable value. (The net realisable value of inventories is the estimated selling price less any further costs that may be necessary to complete the goods and any costs involved in selling and distributing the goods.) This rule may mean that the valuation method applied to inventories (cost or net realisable value) could switch each year, depending on which of cost and net realisable value is the lower. In practice, however, the cost of the inventories held is usually below the current net realisable value – particularly during a period of rising prices. It is, therefore, the cost figure that will normally appear in the statement of financial position.

Activity 3.12

Can you think of any circumstances where the net realisable value will be lower than the cost of inventories held, even during a period of generally rising prices?

The net realisable value may be lower where:

- goods have deteriorated or become obsolete;
- there has been a fall in the market price of the goods;
- the goods are being used as a 'loss leader';
- bad buying decisions have been made.

There is an international financial reporting standard that deals with inventories. It states that, when preparing financial statements for external reporting, the cost of inventories should normally be determined using either FIFO or AVCO. The LIFO approach is not an acceptable method to use for external reporting, but a business could use it for reports to management. The standard also requires the 'lower of cost and net realisable value' rule to be used and so endorses the application of the prudence convention.

Real World 3.7 sets out the inventories costing methods of one well-known super-market business.

Real World 3.7

Buy one, get one free

J Sainsbury plc, the supermarket chain, employs two methods of costing inventories and the particular method applied depends on where the inventories are located. The business reports:

> Inventories are valued at the lower of cost and net realisable value. Inventories at warehouses are valued on a first-in, first-out basis. Those at retail outlets are valued at calculated average cost prices.

Source: J Sainsbury plc Annual Report and Financial Statements 2009, p. 49.

→ Costing inventories and depreciation provide two examples where the **consistency convention** must be applied. This convention holds that once a particular method of accounting is selected, it should be applied consistently over time. Thus, it would not be acceptable to switch from, say, FIFO to AVCO between periods (unless exceptional circumstances make it appropriate). The purpose of this convention is to help users make valid comparisons of performance and position from one period to the next.

Activity 3.13

Reporting inventories in the financial statements provides a further example of the need to apply subjective judgement. For the inventories of a retail business, what are the main areas where judgement is required?

The main areas are:

● the choice of cost method (FIFO, LIFO, AVCO);
● deducing the net realisable value figure for inventories held.

Trade receivables problems

We have seen that, when businesses sell goods or services on credit, revenue will usually be recognised before the customer pays the amounts owing. Recording the dual aspect of a credit sale will involve increasing sales revenue and increasing trade receivables by the amount of the revenue from the credit sale.

With this type of sale there is always the risk that the customer will not pay the amount due, however reliable they might have appeared to be at the time of the sale. When it becomes reasonably certain that the customer will never pay, the debt owed
→ is considered to be a **bad debt** and this must be taken into account when preparing the financial statements.

Activity 3.14

When preparing the financial statements, what would be the effect on the income statement and on the statement of financial position of not taking into account the fact that a debt is bad?

The effect would be to overstate the assets (trade receivables) on the statement of financial position and to overstate profit in the income statement, as the revenue (which has been recognised) will not result in any future benefit.

To provide a more realistic picture of financial performance and position, the bad debt must be 'written off'. This will involve reducing the trade receivables and increasing expenses (by creating an expense known as 'bad debts written off') by the amount of the bad debt.

The matching convention requires that the bad debt is written off in the same period as the sale that gave rise to the debt is recognised.

Note that, when a debt is bad, the accounting response is not simply to cancel the original sale. If this were done, the income statement would not be so informative. Reporting the bad debts as an expense can be extremely useful in assessing management performance.

At the end of the accounting period, it may not be possible to identify with reasonable certainty all the bad debts that have been incurred during the period. It may be that some trade receivables appear doubtful, but only at some later point in time will the true position become clear. The uncertainty that exists does not mean that, when preparing the financial statements, we should ignore the possibility that some of the trade receivables outstanding will eventually prove to be bad. It would not be prudent to do so, nor would it comply with the need to match expenses to the period in which the associated sale is recognised. As a result, the business will normally try to identify all those trade receivables that, at the end of the period, can be classified as doubtful (that is, there is a possibility that they may eventually prove to be bad). This can be done by examining individual trade receivables accounts or by taking a proportion of the total trade receivables outstanding based on past experience.

  Once a figure has been derived, an expense known as an **allowance for trade receivables** can be created. This will be shown as an expense in the income statement and deducted from the total trade receivables figure in the statement of financial position.

By doing this, full account is taken, in the appropriate accounting period, of those trade receivables where there is a risk of non-payment. This accounting treatment of these trade receivables will be in addition to the treatment of bad debts described above.

Example 3.9 illustrates the reporting of bad debts and allowances for trade receivables.

Example 3.9

Desai Enterprises had trade receivables of £350,000 outstanding at the end of the accounting year to 30 June 2010. Investigation of these trade receivables revealed that £10,000 would probably be irrecoverable and that a further £30,000 were doubtful of being recoverable. Relevant extracts from the income statement for that year would be as follows:

Income statement (extracts) for the year ended 30 June 2010

	£
Bad debts written off	10,000
Allowances for trade receivables	30,000

Statement of financial position (extracts) as at 30 June 2010

	£
Trade receivables	340,000*
Allowances for trade receivables	(30,000)
	310,000

* That is, £350,000 – £10,000 irrecoverable trade receivables.

The allowances for trade receivables figure is, of course, an estimate; it is quite likely that the actual amount of trade receivables that prove to be bad will be different from the estimate. Let us say that, during the next accounting period, it was discovered that, in fact, £26,000 of the trade receivables considered doubtful proved to be irrecoverable. These trade receivables must now be written off as follows:

- reduce trade receivables by £26,000; and
- reduce allowances for trade receivables by £26,000.

However, allowances for trade receivables of £4,000 will remain. This amount represents an overestimate made when creating the allowance as at 30 June 2010. As the allowance is no longer needed, it should be eliminated. Remember that the allowance was made by creating an expense in the income statement for the year to 30 June 2010. As the expense was too high, the amount of the overestimate should be 'written back' in the next accounting period. In other words, it will be treated as revenue for the year to 30 June 2011. This will mean

- reducing the allowances for trade receivables by £4,000; and
- increasing revenue by £4,000.

Ideally, of course, the amount should be written back to the 2010 income statement; however, it is too late to do this. At the end of the year to 30 June 2011, not only will 2010's overestimate be written back but a new allowance should be created to take account of the trade receivables arising from 2011's credit sales that are considered doubtful.

Activity 3.15

Clayton Conglomerates had trade receivables of £870,000 outstanding at the end of the accounting year to 31 March 2009. The chief accountant believed that £40,000 of those trade receivables were irrecoverable and that a further £60,000 were doubtful of being recoverable. In the subsequent year, it was found that an over-pessimistic estimate of those trade receivables considered doubtful had been made and that only a further £45,000 of trade receivables had actually proved to be bad.

Show the relevant income statement extracts for both 2009 and 2010 to report the bad debts written off and the allowances for trade receivables. Also show the relevant statement of financial position extract as at 31 March 2009.

Your answer should be as follows:

Income statement (extract) for the year ended 31 March 2009

	£
Bad debts written off	40,000
Allowances for trade receivables	60,000

Income statement (extract) for the year ended 31 March 2010

	£
Allowances for trade receivables written back (revenue)	15,000

(*Note*: This figure will usually be netted off against any allowances for trade receivables created in respect of 2010.)

Statement of financial position (extract) as at 31 March 2009

	£
Trade receivables	830,000
Allowances for trade receivables	(60,000)
	770,000

Activity 3.16

Bad debts and allowances for trade receivables are two further examples where judgement is needed to derive an appropriate expense figure.

What will be the effect of different judgements concerning the appropriate amount of bad debts expense and allowances for trade receivables expense on the profit for a particular period and on the total profit reported over the life of the business?

Judgement is often required in deriving a figure for bad debts incurred during a period. There may be situations where views will differ concerning whether or not a debt is irrecoverable. The decision concerning whether or not to write off a bad debt will have an effect on the expenses for the period and, hence, the reported profit. However, over the life of the business the total reported profit would not be affected, as incorrect judgements in one period will be adjusted for in a later period.

Suppose that a debt of £100 was written off in a period and that, in a later period, the amount owing was actually received. The increase in expenses of £100 in the period in which the bad debt was written off would be compensated for by an increase in revenue of £100 when the amount outstanding was finally received (bad debt recovered). If, on the other hand, the amount owing of £100 was never written off in the first place, the profit for the two periods would not be affected by the bad debt adjustment and would, therefore, be different – but the total profit for the two periods would be the same.

A similar situation would apply where there are differences in judgements concerning allowances for trade receivables.

Real World 3.8 describes the rise in bad debts of one business.

Real World 3.8

Shopping for bad debts

Shares in Yorkshire home shopping firm Findel dived by nearly 40 per cent after profits were hit by an increase in customers slipping behind on payments. The company, which sells a range of household goods under names such as The Cotswold Company, Kitbag and Ace, said it was adding £5 million to its bad debt provision (allowances for trade receivables) for the year ended 31 March 2008, with profits hit as a result.

This came after the group experienced a 'softening' in repayments from credit customers during the past two months. Around 1.5 million customers use credit to buy goods through Findel's home shopping arm, with another one million paying by cash. The group's bad debt provision (allowances for trade receivables) before the £5 million change is understood to have been £83 million.

Findel, which is based at Burley-in-Wharfedale, West Yorkshire, said: 'In light of the deteriorating economic climate the company has conducted a further review of the Home Shopping debt book and now estimates that the bad debt provision will be £5 million higher than had previously been anticipated.'

The company warned that profits would be down as a result, but would come in higher than last year's £56 million.

Source: 'Findel shares plunge as Yorkshire home shopping firm's bad debts rise', Nigel Scott, *Yorkshire Evening Post*, 17 April 2008. Reproduced by kind permission of the Yorkshire Evening Post.

Let us now try to bring together some of the points that we have raised in this chapter through a self-assessment question.

Self-assessment question 3.1

TT and Co. is a new business that started trading on 1 January 2009. The following is a summary of transactions that occurred during the first year of trading:

1   The owners introduced £50,000 of equity, which was paid into a bank account opened in the name of the business.
2   Premises were rented from 1 January 2009 at an annual rental of £20,000. During the year, rent of £25,000 was paid to the owner of the premises.
3   Rates (a tax on business premises) were paid during the year as follows:

    For the period 1 January 2009 to 31 March 2009   £500
    For the period 1 April 2009 to 31 March 2010   £1,200

4   A delivery van was bought on 1 January 2009 for £12,000. This is expected to be used in the business for four years and then to be sold for £2,000.
5   Wages totalling £33,500 were paid during the year. At the end of the year, the business owed £630 of wages for the last week of the year.
6   Electricity bills for the first three quarters of the year were paid totalling £1,650. After 31 December 2009, but before the financial statements had been finalised for the year, the bill for the last quarter arrived showing a charge of £620.
7   Inventories totalling £143,000 were bought on credit.
8   Inventories totalling £12,000 were bought for cash.
9   Sales revenue on credit totalled £152,000 (cost of sales £74,000).
10   Cash sales revenue totalled £35,000 (cost of sales £16,000).
11   Receipts from trade receivables totalled £132,000.
12   Payments to trade payables totalled £121,000.
13   Van running expenses paid totalled £9,400.

At the end of the year it was clear that a credit customer (trade receivable) who owed £400 would not be able to pay any part of the debt. All of the other trade payables were expected to settle in full.

The business uses the straight-line method for depreciating non-current assets.

Required:
Prepare a statement of financial position as at 31 December 2009 and an income statement for the year to that date.

The solution to this question can be found at the back of the book on pages 473–474.

Uses and usefulness of the income statement

The income statement, like the statement of financial position, has been around for a long time. Most major businesses seem to prepare an income statement on a frequent basis (monthly or even more frequently). This is despite there being no rule requiring an income statement to be produced more frequently than once, or in some cases twice, a year. The income statement is, therefore, regarded as providing useful information. In particular, this statement may help in providing information on:

● *How effective the business has been in generating wealth.* Since wealth generation is the primary reason for most businesses to exist, assessing how much wealth has been created is an important issue. Although we have seen that different judgements concerning depreciation, inventories and bad debts may affect the calculation of profit for a period, this problem should not be overstated. For most businesses in most years, the effect of making different judgements would probably not significantly affect the final profit figure.

● *How the profit was derived.* For some users, the only item of concern may be the final profit figure, or *bottom line* as it is sometimes called. While this is a primary measure of performance, and its importance is difficult to overstate, the income statement contains other information that should also be of interest. To evaluate business performance effectively, it is important to discover how the profit figure was derived. Thus the level of sales revenue, the nature and amount of expenses incurred, and the profit in relation to sales revenue are important factors in understanding the performance of the business over a period. The analysis and interpretation of financial statements are considered in detail in Chapters 7 and 8.

Summary

The main points of this chapter may be summarised as follows:

The income statement (profit and loss account)

● The income statement measures and reports how much profit (or loss) has been generated over a period.

● Profit (or loss) for the period is the difference between the total revenue and total expenses for the period.

● The income statement links the statements of financial position at the beginning and end of an accounting period.

● The income statement will normally first calculate gross profit and then deduct any overheads for the period. The final figure derived is the profit (or loss) for the period.

● Gross profit represents the difference between the sales revenue for the period and the cost of sales.

Expenses and revenue

● Cost of sales may be identified either by matching the cost of each sale to the particular sale or, in the case of retail and wholesaling businesses, by adjusting the goods bought during the period to take account of opening and closing inventories.

● Classifying expenses is often a matter of judgement, although there are rules for businesses that trade as limited companies.

● Revenue is recognised when the amount of revenue can be measured reliably and it is probable that the economic benefits will be received.

● Where there is a sale of goods, there is an additional criterion that ownership and control must pass to the buyer before revenue can be recognised.

● Revenue can be recognised after partial completion provided that a particular stage of completion can be measured reliably.

● The matching convention states that expenses should be matched to the revenue that they help generate.

- A particular expense reported in the income statement may not be the same as the cash paid. This will result in accruals or prepayments appearing in the statement of financial position.
- The materiality convention states that where the amounts are immaterial, we should consider only what is expedient.
- 'Accruals accounting' is preparing the income statement and statement of financial position following the accruals convention, which says that profit = revenue – expenses (not cash receipts – cash payments).

Depreciation of non-current assets

- Depreciation requires a consideration of the cost (or fair value), useful life and residual value of an asset. It also requires a consideration of the method of depreciation.
- The straight-line method of depreciation allocates the amount to be depreciated evenly over the useful life of the asset.
- The reducing-balance method applies a fixed percentage rate of depreciation to the carrying amount of an asset each year.
- The depreciation method chosen should reflect the pattern of benefits associated with the asset.
- Depreciation is an attempt to allocate the cost (or fair value), less the residual value, of an asset over its useful life. It does not provide funds for replacement of the asset.

Costing inventories

- The way in which we derive the cost of inventories is important in the calculation of profit and the presentation of financial position.
- The first in, first out (FIFO) method approaches matters as if the earliest inventories held are the first to be used.
- The last in, first out (LIFO) method approaches matters as if the latest inventories are the first to be used.
- The weighted average cost (AVCO) method applies an average cost to all inventories used.
- When prices are rising, FIFO gives the lowest cost of sales figure and highest closing inventories figure and LIFO gives the highest cost of sales figure and the lowest closing inventories figure. AVCO gives figures for cost of sales and closing inventories that lie between FIFO and LIFO.
- When prices are falling, the positions of FIFO and LIFO are reversed.
- Inventories are shown at the lower of cost and net realisable value.
- When a particular method of accounting, such as an inventories costing method, is selected, it should be applied consistently over time.

Bad debts

- Where it is reasonably certain that a credit customer will not pay, the debt is regarded as 'bad' and written off.
- Where it is doubtful that a credit customer will pay, an allowance for trade receivables expense should be created.

Uses of the income statement

- It provides a profit figure.
- It provides information on how the profit was derived.

→ **Key terms**

profit p. 70
revenue p. 70
expense p. 71
accounting period p. 72
gross profit p. 73
operating profit p. 74
profit for the year p. 74
cost of sales p. 74
matching convention p. 81
accrued expenses p. 82
prepaid expenses p. 84
materiality convention p. 85
accruals convention p. 86
accruals accounting p. 86
depreciation p. 86

residual value p. 88
straight-line method p. 88
carrying amount p. 89
written-down value p. 89
net book value p. 89
reducing-balance method p. 89
amortisation p. 93
first in, first out (FIFO) p. 96
last in, first out (LIFO) p. 96
weighted average cost (AVCO)
  p. 96
consistency convention p. 101
bad debt p. 101
allowance for trade receivables
  p. 102

Further reading

If you would like to explore the topics covered in this chapter in more depth, we recommend the following books:

Elliott, B. and Elliott, J., *Financial Accounting and Reporting*, 13th edn, Financial Times Prentice Hall, 2009, Chapters 2, 16, 19 and 20.

IASC Foundation Education, *A Guide through International Financial Reporting Standards (IFRSs) 2008*, July 2008, IAS 2, IAS 16, IAS 18, IAS 36 and IAS 38.

KPMG, *Insights into IFRS*, 6th edn, 2009/10, Sweet and Maxwell, 2009, Sections 3.2, 3.3, 3.8, 3.10 and 4.2.

Review questions

Solutions to these questions can be found at the back of the book on page 483.

3.1 'Although the income statement is a record of past achievement, the calculations required for certain expenses involve estimates of the future.' What does this statement mean? Can you think of examples where estimates of the future are used?

3.2 'Depreciation is a process of allocation and not valuation.' What do you think is meant by this statement?

3.3 What is the convention of consistency? Does this convention help users in making a more valid comparison between businesses?

3.4 'An asset is similar to an expense.' Do you agree?

Exercises

Exercises 3.6 to 3.8 are more advanced than Exercises 3.1 to 3.5. Exercises with coloured numbers have solutions at the back of the book, starting on page 494.

If you wish to try more exercises, visit the students' side of the Companion Website.

3.1 You have heard the following statements made. Comment critically on them.

(a) 'Equity only increases or decreases as a result of the owners putting more cash into the business or taking some out.'
(b) 'An accrued expense is one that relates to next year.'
(c) 'Unless we depreciate this asset we shall be unable to provide for its replacement.'
(d) 'There is no point in depreciating the factory building. It is appreciating in value each year.'

3.2 Singh Enterprises, which started business on 1 January 2007, has an accounting year to 31 December and uses the straight-line method of depreciation. On 1 January 2007 the business bought a machine for £10,000. The machine had an expected useful life of four years and an estimated residual value of £2,000. On 1 January 2008 the business bought another machine for £15,000. This machine had an expected useful life of five years and an estimated residual value of £2,500. On 31 December 2009 the business sold the first machine bought for £3,000.

Required:
Show the relevant income statement extracts and statement of financial position extracts for the years 2007, 2008 and 2009.

3.3 The owner of a business is confused and comes to you for help. The financial statements for the business, prepared by an accountant, for the last accounting period revealed a profit of £50,000. However, during the accounting period the bank balance declined by £30,000. What reasons might explain this apparent discrepancy?

3.4   Spratley Ltd is a builders' merchant. On 1 September the business had, as part of its inventories, 20 tonnes of sand at a cost of £18 per tonne and, therefore, at a total cost of £360. During the first week in September, the business bought the following amounts of sand:

September	Tonnes	Cost per tonne £
2	48	20
4	15	24
6	10	25

On 7 September the business sold 60 tonnes of sand to a local builder.

Required:

Calculate the cost of goods sold and of the remaining inventories using the following costing methods:

(a) first in, first out
(b) last in, first out
(c) weighted average cost.

3.5   Fill in the values (a) to (f) in the following table on the assumption that there were no opening balances involved.

| | Relating to period | | At end of period | |
	Paid/Received	Expense/revenue for period	Prepaid	Accruals/deferred revenues
	£	£	£	£
Rent payable	10,000	(a)	1,000	
Rates and insurance	5,000	(b)		1,000
General expenses	(c)	6,000	1,000	
Interest payable on borrowings	3,000	2,500	(d)	
Salaries	(e)	9,000		3,000
Rent receivable	(f)	1,500		1,500

3.6 The following is the statement of financial position of TT and Co. (see Self-assessment question 3.1 on page 105) at the end of its first year of trading:

Statement of financial position as at 31 December 2009

	£
ASSETS	
Non-current assets	
Property, plant and equipment	
Delivery van at cost	12,000
Depreciation	(2,500)
	9,500
Current assets	
Inventories	65,000
Trade receivables	19,600
Prepaid expenses*	5,300
Cash	750
	90,650
Total assets	100,150
EQUITY AND LIABILITIES	
Equity	
Original	50,000
Retained earnings	26,900
	76,900
Current liabilities	
Trade payables	22,000
Accrued expenses†	1,250
	23,250
Total equity and liabilities	100,150

* The prepaid expenses consisted of rates (£300) and rent (£5,000).
† The accrued expenses consisted of wages (£630) and electricity (£620).

During 2010, the following transactions took place:

1 The owners withdrew equity in the form of cash of £20,000.
2 Premises continued to be rented at an annual rental of £20,000. During the year, rent of £15,000 was paid to the owner of the premises.
3 Rates on the premises were paid during the year as follows: for the period 1 April 2010 to 31 March 2011 £1,300.
4 A second delivery van was bought on 1 January 2010 for £13,000. This is expected to be used in the business for four years and then to be sold for £3,000.
5 Wages totalling £36,700 were paid during the year. At the end of the year, the business owed £860 of wages for the last week of the year.
6 Electricity bills for the first three quarters of the year and £620 for the last quarter of the previous year were paid totalling £1,820. After 31 December 2010, but before the financial statements had been finalised for the year, the bill for the last quarter arrived showing a charge of £690.
7 Inventories totalling £67,000 were bought on credit.
8 Inventories totalling £8,000 were bought for cash.
9 Sales revenue on credit totalled £179,000 (cost £89,000).
10 Cash sales revenue totalled £54,000 (cost £25,000).
11 Receipts from trade receivables totalled £178,000.
12 Payments to trade payables totalled £71,000.
13 Van running expenses paid totalled £16,200.

The business uses the straight-line method for depreciating non-current assets.

Required:

Prepare a statement of financial position as at 31 December 2010 and an income statement for the year to that date.

3.7   The following is the statement of financial position of WW Associates as at 31 December 2008:

Statement of financial position as at 31 December 2008

	£
ASSETS	
Non-current assets	
Machinery	25,300
Current assets	
Inventories	12,200
Trade receivables	21,300
Prepaid expenses (rates)	400
Cash	8,300
	42,200
Total assets	67,500
EQUITY AND LIABILITIES	
Equity	
Original	25,000
Retained earnings	23,900
	48,900
Current liabilities	
Trade payables	16,900
Accrued expenses (wages)	1,700
	18,600
Total equity and liabilities	67,500

During 2009, the following transactions took place:

1 The owners withdrew equity in the form of cash of £23,000.
2 Premises were rented at an annual rental of £20,000. During the year, rent of £25,000 was paid to the owner of the premises.
3 Rates on the premises were paid during the year for the period 1 April 2009 to 31 March 2010 and amounted to £2,000.
4 Some machinery (a non-current asset), which was bought on 1 January 2008 for £13,000, has proved to be unsatisfactory. It was part-exchanged for some new machinery on 1 January 2009 and WW Associates paid a cash amount of £6,000. The new machinery would have cost £15,000 had the business bought it without the trade-in.
5 Wages totalling £23,800 were paid during the year. At the end of the year, the business owed £860 of wages.
6 Electricity bills for the four quarters of the year were paid totalling £2,700.
7 Inventories totalling £143,000 were bought on credit.
8 Inventories totalling £12,000 were bought for cash.
9 Sales revenue on credit totalled £211,000 (cost £127,000).
10 Cash sales revenue totalled £42,000 (cost £25,000).
11 Receipts from trade receivables totalled £198,000.
12 Payments to trade payables totalled £156,000.
13 Van running expenses paid totalled £17,500.

The business uses the reducing-balance method of depreciation for non-current assets at the rate of 30 per cent each year.

Required:

Prepare a statement of financial position as at 31 December 2009 and an income statement for the year to that date.

3.8 The following is the income statement for Nikov and Co. for the year ended 31 December 2009, along with information relating to the preceding year.

Income statement for the year ended 31 December

	2009 £000	2008 £000
Sales revenue	420.2	382.5
Cost of sales	(126.1)	(114.8)
Gross profit	294.1	267.7
Salaries and wages	(92.6)	(86.4)
Selling and distribution costs	(98.9)	(75.4)
Rent and rates	(22.0)	(22.0)
Bad debts written off	(19.7)	(4.0)
Telephone and postage	(4.8)	(4.4)
Insurance	(2.9)	(2.8)
Motor vehicle expenses	(10.3)	(8.6)
Depreciation – Delivery van	(3.1)	(3.3)
– Fixtures and fittings	(4.3)	(4.5)
Operating profit	35.5	56.3
Loan interest	(4.6)	(5.4)
Profit for the year	30.9	50.9

Required:

Analyse the performance of the business for the year to 31 December 2009 in so far as the information allows.

4

Accounting for limited companies (1)

Introduction

Most businesses in the UK, except the very smallest, operate in the form of limited companies. More than 2 million limited companies now exist and they account for the majority of UK business activity and employment. The economic significance of this type of business is not confined to the UK; it can be seen in many of the world's developed countries.

In this chapter we consider the nature of limited companies and how they differ from sole proprietorship businesses and partnerships. This expands the brief discussion of various business forms in Chapter 1. We examine the ways in which the owners provide finance as well as the rules governing the way in which limited companies must account to their owners and to other interested parties. We shall also see how the financial statements, which were discussed in the previous two chapters, are prepared for this type of business.

Learning outcomes

When you have completed this chapter, you should be able to:

- discuss the nature of the limited company;

- describe the main features of the equity (owners' claim) in a limited company;

- discuss the framework of rules designed to safeguard the interests of shareholders;

- explain how the income statement and statement of financial position of a limited company differ in detail from those of sole proprietorships and partnerships.

Why limited companies?

Although there are very many businesses in the UK that trade as sole proprietorships, as partnerships and in other forms, overwhelmingly the most important business form is the limited company. In terms of sales revenue generated, wealth created, number of people employed, exports achieved and virtually any other measure, limited companies dominate the business scene. We shall be seeing in this chapter that limited companies are subject to a great deal of regulation, particularly in the areas of finance and accounting. This is particularly true of those limited companies whose shares are traded on the London Stock Exchange. All of this regulation can be very tiresome for the companies and, importantly, very expensive.

In this chapter we shall be looking at a number of issues, including:

● What is a limited company?
● Why are limited companies so popular?
● What regulation must limited companies accept?
● Why do some limited companies have their shares traded on the London Stock Exchange, when this leads to even more regulation, at great expense?

We shall be answering these and other questions during this chapter.

The main features of limited companies

Legal nature

Let us begin our examination of limited companies by discussing their legal nature. A *limited company* has been described as an artificial person that has been created by law. This means that a company has many of the rights and obligations that 'real' people have. It can, for example, sue or be sued by others and can enter into contracts in its own name. This contrasts sharply with other types of businesses, such as sole proprietorships and partnerships (that is, unincorporated businesses), where it is the owner(s) rather than the business that must sue, enter into contracts and so on, because the business has no separate legal identity.

With the rare exceptions of those that are created by Act of Parliament or by Royal Charter, all UK companies are created (or *incorporated*) by registration. To create a company the person or persons wishing to create it (usually known as *promoters*) fill in a few simple forms and pay a modest registration fee. After having ensured that the necessary formalities have been met, the Registrar of Companies, a UK government official, enters the name of the new company on the Registry of Companies. Thus, in the UK, companies can be formed very easily and cheaply (for about £100).

A limited company may be owned by just one person, but most have more than one owner and some have many owners. The owners are usually known as *members* or *shareholders*. The ownership of a company is normally divided into a number, frequently a large number, of shares, each of equal size. Each owner, or shareholder, owns one or more shares in the company. Large companies typically have a very large number of shareholders. For example, at 31 March 2009, BT Group plc, the telecommunications business, had nearly 1.2 million different shareholders.

Since a limited company has its own legal identity, it is regarded as being quite separate from those that own and manage it. It is worth emphasising that this legal separateness of owners and the company has no connection whatsoever with the business entity convention of accounting, which we discussed in Chapter 2. This accounting convention applies equally well to all business types, including sole proprietorships and partnerships where there is certainly no legal distinction between the owner(s) and the business.

The legal separateness of the limited company and its shareholders leads to two important features of the limited company: perpetual life and limited liability. These are now explained.

Perpetual life

A company is normally granted a perpetual existence and so will continue even where an owner of some, or even all, of the shares in the company dies. The shares of the deceased person will simply pass to the beneficiary of his or her estate. The granting of perpetual existence means that the life of a company is quite separate from the lives of those individuals who own or manage it. It is not, therefore, affected by changes in ownership that arise when individuals buy and sell shares in the company.

Though a company may be granted a perpetual existence when it is first formed, it is possible for either the shareholders or the courts to bring this existence to an end. When this is done, the assets of the company are usually sold to generate cash to meet the outstanding liabilities. Any surplus arising after all liabilities have been met will then be used to pay the shareholders. Shareholders may agree to end the life of a company where it has achieved the purpose for which it was formed or where they feel that the company has no real future. The courts may bring the life of a company to an end where creditors have applied to the courts for this to be done because they have not been paid amounts owing.

Where shareholders agree to end the life of a company, it is referred to as a 'voluntary liquidation'. **Real World 4.1** describes the demise of one company by this method.

 Real World 4.1

Monotub Industries in a spin as founder gets Titan for £1

Monotub Industries, maker of the Titan washing machine, yesterday passed into corporate history with very little ceremony and with only a whimper of protest from minority shareholders.

At an extraordinary meeting held in a basement room of the group's West End headquarters, shareholders voted to put the company into voluntary liquidation and sell its assets and intellectual property to founder Martin Myerscough for £1. [The shares in the company were at one time worth 650p each.]

The only significant opposition came from Giuliano Gnagnatti who, along with other shareholders, has seen his investment shrink faster than a wool twin-set on a boil wash.

The not-so-proud owner of 100,000 Monotub shares, Mr Gnagnatti, the managing director of an online retailer, described the sale of Monotub as a 'free gift' to Mr Myerscough. This assessment was denied by Ian Green, the chairman of Monotub, who said the closest the beleaguered company had come to a sale was an offer for £60,000 that gave no guarantees against liabilities, which are thought to amount to £750,000.

The quiet passing of the washing machine, eventually dubbed the Titanic, was in strong contrast to its performance in many kitchens.

Originally touted as the 'great white goods hope' of the washing machine industry with its larger capacity and removable drum, the Titan ran into problems when it kept stopping during the spin cycle, causing it to emit a loud bang and leap into the air.

Summing up the demise of the Titan, Mr Green said: 'Clearly the machine had some revolutionary aspects, but you can't get away from the fact that the machine was faulty and should not have been launched with those defects.'

The usually-vocal Mr Myerscough, who has promised to pump £250,000 into the company and give Monotub shareholders £4 for every machine sold, refused to comment on his plans for the Titan or reveal who his backers were. But . . . he did say that he intended to 'take the Titan forward'.

Source: 'Monotub Industries in a spin as founder gets Titan for £1', Lisa Urquhart, *Financial Times*, 23 January 2003.

Limited liability

Since the company is a legal person in its own right, it must take responsibility for its own debts and losses. This means that, once the shareholders have paid what they have agreed to pay for the shares, their obligation to the company, and to the company's creditors, is satisfied. Thus shareholders can limit their losses to the amount that they have paid, or agreed to pay, for their shares. This is of great practical importance to potential shareholders since they know that what they can lose, as part owners of the business, is limited.

Contrast this with the position of sole proprietors or partners. They cannot 'ring-fence' assets that they do not want to put into the business. If a sole proprietorship or partnership business finds itself in a position where liabilities exceed the business assets, the law gives unsatisfied creditors the right to demand payment out of what the sole proprietor or partner may have regarded as 'non-business' assets. Thus the sole proprietor or partner could lose everything – house, car, the lot. This is because the law sees Jill, the sole proprietor, as being the same as Jill the private individual. The shareholder, by contrast, can lose only the amount committed to that company. Legally, the business operating as a limited company, in which Jack owns shares, is not the same as Jack himself. This is true even if Jack were to own all of the shares in the company.

Real World 4.2 gives an example of a well-known case where the shareholders of a particular company were able to avoid any liability to those that had lost money as a result of dealing with the company.

Real World 4.2

Carlton and Granada 1 – Nationwide Football League 0

Two television broadcasting companies, Carlton and Granada, each owned 50 per cent of a separate company, ITV Digital (formerly ON Digital). ITV Digital signed a contract to pay the Nationwide Football League (in effect the three divisions of English football below the Premiership) more than £89 million on both 1 August 2002 and 1 August 2003 for the rights to broadcast football matches over three seasons. ITV Digital was unable to sell enough subscriptions for the broadcasts and collapsed because it was unable to meet its liabilities. The Nationwide Football League tried to force Carlton and Granada (ITV Digital's only shareholders) to meet ITV Digital's contractual obligations. It was unable to do so because the shareholders could not be held legally liable for the amounts owing.

Carlton and Granada merged into one business in 2003, but at the time of ITV Digital were two independent companies.

Activity 4.1

The fact that shareholders can limit their losses to that which they have paid, or have agreed to pay, for their shares is of great practical importance to potential shareholders.

Can you think of any practical benefit to a private-sector economy, in general, of this ability of shareholders to limit losses?

Business is a risky venture – in some cases very risky. People will usually be happier to invest money when they know the limit of their liability. If investors are given limited liability, new businesses are more likely to be formed and existing ones are likely to find it easier to raise more finance. This is good for the private-sector economy and may ultimately lead to the generation of greater wealth for society as a whole.

→ Although **limited liability** has this advantage to the providers of equity finance (the shareholders), it is not necessarily to the advantage of all others who have a stake in the business, as we saw in the case of the Nationwide Football League clubs in Real World 4.2. Limited liability is attractive to shareholders because they can, in effect, walk away from the unpaid debts of the company if their contribution has not been sufficient to meet those debts. This is likely to make any individual, or another business, that is considering entering into a contract, wary of dealing with the limited company. This can be a real problem for smaller, less established companies. Suppliers may insist on cash payment before delivery of goods or the rendering of a service. Alternatively, they may require a personal guarantee from a major shareholder that the debt will be paid before allowing trade credit. In the latter case, the supplier circumvents the company's limited liability status by demanding the personal liability of an individual. Larger, more established companies, on the other hand, tend to have built up the confidence of suppliers.

Legal safeguards

Various safeguards exist to protect individuals and businesses contemplating dealing with a limited company. These include the requirement to indicate limited liability status in the name of the company. By doing this, an alert is issued to prospective suppliers and lenders.

A further safeguard is the restrictions placed on the ability of shareholders to withdraw their equity from the company. These restrictions are designed to prevent shareholders from protecting their own investment and, as a result, leaving lenders and suppliers in an exposed position. We shall consider this point in more detail later in the chapter.

Finally, limited companies are required to produce annual financial statements (income statements, statements of financial position and statements of cash flows) and make these publicly available. This means that anyone interested can gain an impression of the financial performance and position of the company. The form and content of the first two of these statements are considered in some detail later in the chapter. Chapter 6 is devoted to the statement of cash flows.

Public and private companies

When a company is registered with the Registrar of Companies, it must be registered either as a public or as a private company. The main practical difference between these is that a **public limited company** can offer its shares for sale to the general public, but a **private limited company** is restricted from doing so. A public limited company must signal its status to all interested parties by having the words 'public limited company', or its abbreviation 'plc', in its name. For a private limited company, the word 'limited' or 'Ltd' must appear as part of its name.

Private limited companies tend to be smaller businesses where the ownership is divided among relatively few shareholders who are usually fairly close to one another – for example, a family company. Numerically, there are vastly more private limited companies in the UK than there are public ones. Of the 2.25 million UK limited companies now in existence, only 9,600 (representing 0.4 per cent of the total) are public limited companies. Figure 4.1 shows the trend in the numbers of public and private limited companies in recent years.

Figure 4.1	Numbers of public and private limited companies registered 2004 to 2009

Public limited companies

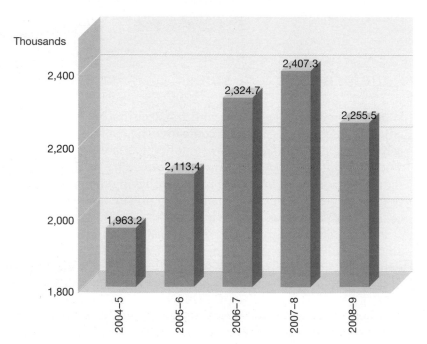

Private limited companies

There was a steady rise in the number of private limited companies over the period, until 2008/9 when there was a decline. Over the same period there has been a gradual decline in the number of public limited companies.

Source: Based on information in Companies Register Activities 2008, statistical tables on companies registration activities 2008/9, www.companieshouse.gov.uk.

Since individual public companies tend to be larger, they are often economically more important. In some industry sectors, such as banking, insurance, oil refining and grocery retailing, they are completely dominant. Although some large private limited companies exist, many private limited companies are little more than the vehicle through which one-person businesses operate.

Real World 4.3 shows the extent of market dominance of public limited companies in one particular business sector.

Real World 4.3

A big slice of the market

The grocery sector is dominated by four large players: Tesco, Sainsbury, Morrison and Asda. The first three are public limited companies and the fourth, Asda, is owned by a large US public company, Wal-Mart. Figure 4.2 shows the share of the grocery market enjoyed by each during the twelve-week period to 4 October 2009.

Figure 4.2	Market share of the four largest grocery companies: 12 weeks to 4 October 2009

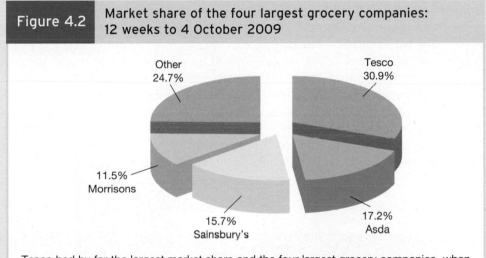

Tesco had by far the largest market share and the four largest grocery companies, when taken together, had more than 75 per cent of the total market during the period.

Source: Compiled from information in 'Falling inflation brings growth challenge', www.kamcity.com, 14 October 2009.

Taxation

Another consequence of the legal separation of the limited company from its owners is that companies must be accountable to the tax authorities for tax on their profits and gains. This leads to the reporting of tax in the financial statements of limited companies. The charge for tax is shown in the income statement (profit and loss account). The tax charge for a particular year is based on that year's profit. Since only 50 per cent of a company's tax liability is due for payment during the year concerned, the other 50 per cent will appear on the end-of-year statement of financial position (balance sheet) as a short-term liability. This will be illustrated a little later in the chapter. The tax position of companies contrasts with that of sole proprietorships and partnerships, where tax is levied not on the business but on the owner(s). Thus tax does not impact on the financial statements of unincorporated businesses, but is an individual matter between the owner(s) and the tax authorities.

Companies are charged **corporation tax** on their profits and gains. The percentage rates of tax tend to vary from year to year, but have recently been 28 per cent for larger companies and 21 per cent for smaller companies. These rates of tax are levied on the company's taxable profit, which is not necessarily the same as the profit shown on the income statement. This is because tax law does not, in every respect, follow the normal accounting rules. Generally, however, the taxable profit and the company's accounting profit are pretty close to one another.

Transferring share ownership: the role of the Stock Exchange

We have already seen that shares in a company may be transferred from one owner to another. The desire of some shareholders to sell their shares, coupled with the desire of others to buy those shares, has led to the existence of a formal market in which shares can be bought and sold. The London Stock Exchange and similar organisations around the world provide a marketplace in which shares in public companies may be bought and sold. Share prices are determined by the laws of supply and demand, which are, in turn, determined by investors' perceptions of the future economic prospects of the companies concerned. Only the shares of certain companies (*listed* companies) may be traded on the London Stock Exchange. Less than 1,100 UK companies are listed. This represents only about 1 in 2,000 of all UK companies (public and private) and roughly one in nine public limited companies. However, many of these listed companies are massive. Nearly all of the 'household-name' UK businesses (for example, Tesco, Next, BT, Vodafone, BP and so on) are listed companies.

Activity 4.2

If, as has been pointed out earlier, the change in ownership of shares does not directly affect the particular company, why do many public companies actively seek to have their shares traded in a recognised market?

The main reason is that investors are generally very reluctant to pledge their money unless they can see some way in which they can turn their investment back into cash. In theory, the shares of a particular company may be very valuable because the company has bright prospects. However, unless this value is capable of being turned into cash, the benefit to the shareholders is dubious. After all, we cannot spend shares; we normally need cash.

This means that potential shareholders are much more likely to be prepared to buy new shares from the company (thereby providing the company with new investment finance) where they can see a way of liquidating their investment (turning it into cash) as and when they wish. Stock Exchanges provide the means of liquidation.

Although the buying and selling of 'second-hand' shares does not provide the company with cash, the fact that the buying and selling facility exists will make it easier for the company to raise new share capital when it needs to do so.

Managing a company

A limited company may have legal personality, but it is not a human being capable of making decisions and plans about the business and exercising control over it. People must undertake these management tasks. The most senior level of management of a company is the board of directors.

→   The shareholders elect **directors** (by law there must be at least one director for a private limited company and two for a public limited company) to manage the company on a day-to-day basis on behalf of those shareholders. In a small company, the board may be the only level of management and consist of all of the shareholders. In larger companies, the board may consist of ten or so directors out of many thousands of shareholders. Indeed, directors are not even required to be shareholders. Below the board of directors of the typical large company could be several layers of management comprising thousands of people.

→   In recent years, the issue of **corporate governance** has generated much debate. The term is used to describe the ways in which companies are directed and controlled. The issue of corporate governance is important because, with larger companies, those who own the company (that is, the shareholders) are usually divorced from the day-to-day control of the business. The shareholders employ the directors to manage the company for them. Given this position, it may seem reasonable to assume that the best interests of shareholders will guide the directors' decisions. However, in practice this does not always seem to be the case. The directors may be more concerned with pursuing their own interests, such as increasing their pay and 'perks' (such as expensive motor cars, overseas visits and so on) and improving their job security and status. As a result, a conflict can occur between the interests of shareholders and the interests of directors.

The problems and issues associated with corporate governance will be explored in detail in Chapter 11.

Financing limited companies

Equity (the owners' claim)

The equity of a sole proprietorship is normally encompassed in one figure on the statement of financial position. With companies, this is usually a little more complicated, although in essence the same broad principles apply. With a company, equity is divided
→   between shares (for example, the original investment), on the one hand, and **reserves** (that is, profits and gains subsequently made), on the other. There is also the possibility that there will be more than one type of shares and of reserves. Thus, within the basic divisions of share capital and reserves, there might well be further subdivisions. This might seem quite complicated, but we shall shortly consider the reasons for these subdivisions and all should become clearer.

The basic division

When a company is first formed, those who take steps to form it (the promoters) will decide how much needs to be raised by the potential shareholders to set the company up with the necessary assets to operate. Example 4.1 acts as a basis for illustration.

Example 4.1

Some friends decide to form a company to operate an office cleaning business. They estimate that the company will need £50,000 to obtain the necessary assets. Between them, they raise the cash, which they use to buy shares in the company, on 31 March 2010, with a **nominal value** (or **par value**) of £1 each.

At this point the statement of financial position of the company would be:

Statement of financial position as at 31 March 2010

	£
Net assets (all in cash)	50,000
Equity	
Share capital	
50,000 shares of £1 each	50,000

The company now buys the necessary non-current assets (vacuum cleaners and so on) and inventories (cleaning materials) and starts to trade. During the first year, the company makes a profit of £10,000. This, by definition, means that the equity expands by £10,000. During the year, the shareholders (owners) make no drawings of their equity, so at the end of the year the summarised statement of financial position looks like this:

Statement of financial position as at 31 March 2011

	£
Net assets (various assets less liabilities*)	60,000
Equity	
Share capital	
50,000 shares of £1 each	50,000
Reserves (revenue reserve)	10,000
Total equity	60,000

* We saw in Chapter 2 that Assets = Equity + Liabilities. We also saw that this can be rearranged so that Assets – Liabilities = Equity.

The profit is shown in a reserve, known as a **revenue reserve**, because it arises from generating revenue (making sales). Note that we do not simply merge the profit with the share capital: we must keep the two amounts separate (to satisfy company law). The reason for this is that there is a legal restriction on the maximum drawings of their equity (or payment of a **dividend**) that the shareholders can make. This is defined by the amount of revenue reserves and so it is helpful to show these separately. We shall look at why there is this restriction, and how it works, a little later in the chapter.

Share capital

Ordinary shares

Shares represent the basic units of ownership of a business. All companies issue **ordinary shares**. Ordinary shares are often known as *equities*. The nominal value of such shares is at the discretion of the people who start up the company. For example, if the initial share capital is to be £50,000, this could be two shares of £25,000 each, 5 million shares of one penny each or any other combination that gives a total of £50,000. All shares must have equal value.

Activity 4.3

The initial financial requirement for a new company is £50,000. There are to be two equal shareholders. Would you advise them to issue two shares of £25,000 each? Why?

Such large-denomination shares tend to be unwieldy. Suppose that one of the shareholders wanted to sell her shareholding. She would have to find one buyer. If there were shares of smaller denomination, it would be possible to sell part of the shareholding to various potential buyers. Furthermore, it would be possible to sell just part of the holding and retain a part.

In practice, £1 is the normal maximum nominal value for shares. Shares of 25 pence each and 50 pence each are probably the most common.

Altering the nominal value of shares

As we have already seen, the promoters of a new company may make their own choice of the nominal or par value of the shares. This value need not be permanent. At a later date the shareholders can decide to change it.

Suppose that a company has 1 million ordinary shares of £1 each and a decision is made to change the nominal value of the shares from £1 to £0.50, in other words to halve the value. This would lead the company to issue each shareholder with a new share certificate (the shareholders' evidence of ownership of their shares) for exactly twice as many shares, each with half the nominal value. The result would be that each shareholder retains a holding of the same total nominal value. This process is known, not surprisingly, as **splitting** the shares. The opposite, reducing the number of shares and increasing their nominal value per share to compensate, is known as **consolidating**. Since each shareholder would be left, after a split or consolidation, with exactly the same proportion of ownership of the company's assets as before, the process should not increase the value of the total shares held.

Splitting is fairly common. The objective is probably to avoid individual shares becoming too valuable and therefore unwieldy, as was discussed in Activity 4.3. If a company trades successfully, the value of each share is likely to rise and, in time, could increase to a level that makes the shares less marketable. Splitting would solve this problem. Consolidating is relatively rare.

Real World 4.4 provides an example of a share split by one business.

Real World 4.4

Doing the splits

A G Barr, the Scottish based maker of soft drinks, including Tizer and Irn Bru, had a share split in September 2009, as announced by the business in its half-yearly report:

As previously announced, the 2 for 1 share split, which is aimed at improving liquidity and marketability of the company's shares became effective on 21 September.

Source: A G Barr plc Interim Report August 2009, p. 3.

Preference shares

→ Some companies not only issue ordinary shares, but also have other classes of shares, **preference shares** being the most common. Preference shares guarantee that *if a dividend is paid*, the preference shareholders will be entitled to the first part of it up to a maximum value. This maximum is normally defined as a fixed percentage of the nominal value of the preference shares. If, for example, a company issues 10,000 preference shares of £1 each with a dividend rate of 6 per cent, this means that the preference shareholders are entitled to receive the first £600 (that is, 6 per cent of £10,000) of any dividend that is paid by the company for a year. The excess over £600 goes to the ordinary shareholders. Normally, any undistributed profits and gains also accrue to the ordinary shareholders.

The ordinary shareholders are the primary risk-takers as they are entitled to share in the profits of the company only after other claims have been satisfied. There are no upper limits, however, on the amount by which they may benefit. The potential rewards available to ordinary shareholders reflect the risks that they are prepared to take. Since ordinary shareholders take most of the risks, power normally resides in their hands. Usually, only the ordinary shareholders are able to vote on issues that affect the company, such as who the directors should be.

It is open to the company to issue shares of various classes – perhaps with some having unusual and exotic conditions – but in practice it is rare to find other than straightforward ordinary and preference shares. Although a company may have different classes of shares whose holders have different rights, within each class all shares must be treated equally. The rights of the various classes of shareholders, as well as other matters relating to a particular company, are contained in that company's set of rules, known as the 'articles and memorandum of association'. A copy of these rules must be lodged with the Registrar of Companies, who makes it available for inspection by the general public.

Reserves

As we have already seen, reserves are profits and gains that a company has made and which still form part of the shareholders' equity. One reason that past profits and gains may not continue to be part of equity is that they have been paid out to shareholders (as dividends and so on). Another reason is that reserves will be reduced by the amount of any losses that the company might suffer. In the same way that profits increase equity, losses reduce it.

Activity 4.4

Are reserves amounts of cash? Can you think of a reason why this is an odd question?

To deal with the second point first, it is an odd question because reserves are a claim, or part of one, on the assets of the company, whereas cash is an asset. So reserves cannot be cash.

→ Reserves are classified as either revenue reserves or **capital reserves**. In Example 4.1 we came across one type of reserve, the revenue reserve. We should recall that this reserve represents the company's retained trading profits and gains on the disposal of non-current assets. It is worth mentioning that retained earnings, as they are most often called, represent overwhelmingly the largest source of new finance for UK companies. For most companies they amount to more than share issues and borrowings combined.

Capital reserves arise for two main reasons:

● issuing shares at above their nominal value (for example, issuing £1 shares at £1.50);
● revaluing (upwards) non-current assets.

Where a company issues shares at above their nominal value, UK law requires that the excess of the issue price over the nominal value be shown separately.

Activity 4.5

Can you think why shares might be issued at above their nominal value? (*Hint*: This would not usually happen when a company is first formed and the initial shares are being issued.)

Once a company has traded and has been successful, the shares would normally be worth more than the nominal value at which they were issued. If additional shares are to be issued to new shareholders to raise finance for further expansion, unless they are issued at a value higher than the nominal value, the new shareholders will be gaining at the expense of the original ones.

Example 4.2 shows how this works.

Example 4.2

Based on future prospects, the net assets of a company are worth £1.5 million. There are currently 1 million ordinary shares in the company, each with a face (nominal) value of £1. The company wishes to raise an additional £0.6 million of cash for expansion and has decided to raise it by issuing new shares. If the shares are issued for £1 each (that is 600,000 shares), the total number of shares will be

$$1.0m + 0.6m = 1.6m$$

and their total value will be the value of the existing net assets plus the new injection of cash:

$$£1.5m + £0.6m = £2.1m.$$

This means that the value of each share after the new issue will be

$$£2.1m/1.6m = £1.3125.$$

The current value of each share is

$$£1.5m/1.0m = £1.50$$

so the original shareholders will lose

$$£1.50 - £1.3125 = £0.1875 \text{ a share}$$

and the new shareholders will gain

$$£1.3125 - £1.0 = £0.3125 \text{ a share}.$$

The new shareholders will, no doubt, be delighted with this outcome; the original ones will not.

Things could be made fair between the two sets of shareholders described in Example 4.2 by issuing the new shares at £1.50 each. In this case it would be necessary to issue 400,000 shares to raise the necessary £0.6 million. £1 a share of the £1.50 is the nominal value and will be included with share capital in the statement of financial position (£400,000 in total). The remaining £0.50 is a share premium, which will be shown as a capital reserve known as the **share premium account** (£200,000 in total).

It is not clear why UK company law insists on the distinction between nominal share values and the premium. In some other countries (for example, the United States) with similar laws governing the corporate sector, there is not the necessity of distinguishing between share capital and share premium. Instead, the total value at which shares are issued is shown as one comprehensive figure on the company's statement of financial position. **Real World 4.5** shows the equity of one well-known business.

Real World 4.5

Funding Thorntons

Thorntons plc, the chocolate maker and retailer, had the following share capital and reserves as at 27 June 2009:

	£m
Share capital (10p ordinary shares)	6,835
Share premium	13,752
Retained earnings	8,151
Total equity	**28,738**

Note how the nominal share capital figure is only about one-half of the share premium account figure. This implies that Thorntons has issued shares at higher prices than the 10p a share nominal value. This reflects its trading success since the company was first formed. In 2008, retained earnings (profits) had made up over 40 per cent of the total for share capital and reserves. By 2009, this had reduced to around 28 per cent. This reduction was mainly caused by a loss suffered by the company pension fund during the year.

Source: Thorntons plc Annual Report 2009, p. 45.

Bonus shares

It is always open to a company to take reserves of any kind (irrespective of whether they are capital or revenue) and turn them into share capital. This will involve transferring the desired amount from the reserve concerned to share capital and then distributing the appropriate number of new shares to the existing shareholders. New shares arising from such a conversion are known as **bonus shares**. Issues of bonus shares used to be quite frequently encountered in practice, but more recently they are much less common. Example 4.3 illustrates this aspect of share issues.

Example 4.3

The summary statement of financial position of a company at a particular point in time is as follows:

Statement of financial position

	£
Net assets (various assets less liabilities)	128,000
Equity	
Share capital	
50,000 shares of £1 each	50,000
Reserves	78,000
Total equity	128,000

The company decides that it will issue existing shareholders with one new share for every share currently owned by each shareholder. The statement of financial position immediately following this will appear as follows:

Statement of financial position

	£
Net assets (various assets less liabilities)	128,000
Equity	
Share capital	
100,000 shares of £1 each (50,000 + 50,000)	100,000
Reserves (78,000 − 50,000)	28,000
Total equity	128,000

We can see that the reserves have decreased by £50,000 and share capital has increased by the same amount. Share certificates for the 50,000 ordinary shares of £1 each, which have been created from reserves, will be issued to the existing shareholders to complete the transaction.

Activity 4.6

A shareholder of the company in Example 4.3 owned 100 shares before the bonus issue. How will things change for this shareholder as regards the number of shares owned and the value of the shareholding?

The answer should be that the number of shares would double, from 100 to 200. Now the shareholder owns one five-hundredth of the company (that is, 200/100,000). Before the bonus issue, the shareholder also owned one five-hundredth of the company (that is, 100/50,000). The company's assets and liabilities have not changed as a result of the bonus issue and so, logically, one five-hundredth of the value of the company should be identical to what it was before. Thus, each share is worth half as much.

A *bonus issue* simply takes one part of the equity (a reserve) and puts it into another part (share capital). The transaction has no effect on the company's assets or liabilities, so there is no effect on shareholders' wealth.

Note that a bonus issue is not the same as a share split. A split does not affect the reserves.

Activity 4.7

Can you think of any reasons why a company might want to make a bonus issue if it has no economic consequence?

We think that there are three possible reasons:

- *Share price*. To lower the value of each share without reducing the shareholders' collective or individual wealth. This has a similar effect to share splitting.
- *Shareholder confidence*. To provide the shareholders with a 'feel-good factor'. It is believed that shareholders like bonus issues because they seem to make them better off, although in practice they should not affect their wealth.
- *Lender confidence*. Where reserves arising from operating profits and/or realised gains on the sale of non-current assets are used to make the bonus issue, it has the effect of taking part of that portion of the shareholders' equity that could be drawn by the shareholders, as drawings (or dividends), and locking it up. The amount transferred becomes part of the permanent equity base of the company. (We shall see a little later in this chapter that there are severe restrictions on the extent to which shareholders may make drawings from their equity.) An individual or business contemplating lending money to the company may insist that the dividend payment possibilities are restricted as a condition of making the loan. This point will be explained shortly.

Real World 4.6 provides an example of a bonus share issue.

Real World 4.6

It's a bonus

Henry Boot plc is a leading property and construction business. In March 2007 the business announced a four-for-one bonus issue of shares. The bonus issue increased the number of shares in issue from 26 million to 130 million and left each shareholder with five times as many shares as before the issue. The directors believed that the bonus issue would benefit shareholders by enhancing the liquidity and marketability of the ordinary shares.

Source: Based on information contained in an announcement published by Henry Boot plc on 12 April 2007, www.henryboot.co.uk.

Share capital jargon

Before leaving our detailed discussion of share capital, it might be helpful to clarify some of the jargon relating to shares that is used in company financial statements.

→   Share capital that has been issued to shareholders is known as the **issued share capital** (or **allotted share capital**). Sometimes, but not very often, a company may not require shareholders to pay the whole amount that is due to be paid for the shares at the time of issue. This may happen where the company does not need the money all at once. Some money would normally be paid at the time of issue and the company would 'call' for further instalments until the shares were **fully paid shares**. That part of the total issue price that has been called is known as the **called-up share capital**. That part that has been called and paid is known as the **paid-up share capital**.

Raising share capital

Once the company has made its initial share issue to start business (usually soon after the company is first formed) it may decide to make further issues of new shares. These may be:

- *Rights issues* – issues made to existing shareholders, in proportion to their existing shareholding
- *Public issues* – issues made to the general investing public
- *Private placings* – issues made to selected individuals who are usually approached and asked if they would be interested in taking up new shares.

During its lifetime a company may use all three of these approaches to raising funds through issuing new shares (although only public companies can make appeals to the general public).

Borrowings

Most companies borrow money to supplement that raised from share issues and ploughed-back profits. Company borrowing is often on a long-term basis, perhaps on a ten-year contract. Lenders may be banks and other professional providers of loan finance. Many companies borrow in such a way that small investors, including private individuals, are able to lend small amounts. This is particularly the case with the larger, Stock Exchange listed, companies and involves them making an issue of **loan notes**, which, though large in total, can be taken up in small slices by individual investors, both private individuals and investing institutions such as pension funds and insurance companies. In some cases, these slices of loans can be bought and sold through the Stock Exchange. This means that investors do not have to wait the full term of their loan to obtain repayment, but can sell their slice of it to another would-be lender at intermediate points in the term of the loan. Loan notes are often known as *loan stock* or *debentures*.

Some of the features of financing by loan notes, particularly the possibility that the loan notes may be traded on the Stock Exchange, can lead to confusing loan notes with shares. We should be clear that shares and loan notes are not the same thing. It is the shareholders who own the company and, therefore, who share in its losses and profits. Holders of loan notes lend money to the company under a legally binding contract that normally specifies the rate of interest, the interest payment dates and the date of repayment of the loan itself.

Usually, long-term loans are secured on assets of the company. This would give the lender the right to seize the assets concerned, sell them and satisfy the repayment obligation, should the company fail to pay either its interest payments or the repayment of the loan itself, on the dates specified in the contract between the company and the lender. A mortgage granted to a private individual buying a house or a flat is a very common example of a secured loan.

Long-term financing of companies can be depicted as in Figure 4.3.

Figure 4.3	Sources of long-term finance for a typical limited company

Companies derive their long-term finance from three sources: new share issues, retained earnings and long-term borrowings. For a typical company, the sum of the first two (jointly known as 'equity finance') exceeds the third. Retained earnings usually exceed either of the other two in terms of the amount of finance raised in most years.

It is important to the prosperity and stability of a company that it strikes a suitable balance between finance provided by the shareholders (equity) and from borrowing. This topic will be explored in Chapter 7.

Real World 4.7 shows the long-term borrowings of Rolls-Royce plc, the engine-building business, at 31 December 2008.

 Real World 4.7

Borrowing at Rolls-Royce

The following extract from the annual financial statements of Rolls-Royce plc sets out the sources of the company's long-term borrowing as at 31 December 2008.

	£m
Unsecured	
Bank loans	5
$7\frac{3}{8}$% Notes 2016	200
5.84% Notes 2010	136
6.38% Notes 2013	178
6.55% Notes 2015	67
$4\frac{1}{2}$% Notes 2011	738
Secured	
Obligations under finance leases payable after five years	1
	1,325
Repayable	
Between one and two years – by instalments	2
– otherwise	136
Between two and five years – by instalments	1
– otherwise	916
After five years – by instalments	3
– otherwise	267
	1,325

Source: Rolls-Royce plc Annual Report and Accounts 2008, note 14.

Note the large number of sources of the company borrowings. This is typical of most large companies and probably reflects a desire to exploit all available means of raising finance, each of which may have some advantages and disadvantages. 'Secured' in this context means that the lender would have the right, should Rolls-Royce fail to meet its interest and/or capital repayment obligations, to seize a specified asset of the business (probably some land) and use it to raise the sums involved. Normally, a lender would accept a lower rate of interest where the loan is secured as there is less risk involved. It should be said that whether a loan to a company like Rolls-Royce is secured or unsecured is usually pretty academic. It is unlikely that such a large and profitable company would fail to meet its obligations.

'Finance leases' are, in effect, arrangements where Rolls-Royce needs the use of a non-current asset (such as an item of machinery) and, instead of buying the asset itself, it arranges for a financier to buy the asset. The financier then leases it to the business, probably for the entire economic life of the asset. Though legally it is the financier who owns the asset, from an accounting point of view the essence of the arrangement is that, in effect, Rolls-Royce has borrowed cash from the financier to buy the asset. Thus, the asset appears among the business's non-current assets and the financial obligation to the financier is shown here as long-term borrowing. This is a good example of how accounting tries to report the economic *substance* of a transaction, rather than its strict legal *form*. Finance leasing is a fairly popular means of raising long-term funds.

Withdrawing equity

Companies, as we have seen, are legally obliged to distinguish, on the statement of financial position, between that part of the shareholders' equity that may be withdrawn and that part which may not. The withdrawable part consists of profits arising from trading and from the disposal of non-current assets. It is represented in the statement of financial position by *revenue reserves*.

It is important to appreciate that the total of revenue reserves appearing in the statement of financial position is rarely the total of all trading profits and profits on disposals of non-current assets generated by the company. This total will normally have been reduced by at least one of the following three factors:

● corporation tax paid on those profits
● any dividends paid
● any losses from trading and the disposal of non-current assets.

The non-withdrawable part consists of share capital plus profits arising from shareholders buying shares in the company and from upward revaluations of assets still held. It is represented in the statement of financial position by *share capital* and *capital reserves*.

Figure 4.4 shows the important division between the part of the shareholders' equity that can be withdrawn as a dividend and the part that cannot.

Figure 4.4	Availability for dividends of various parts of the shareholders' equity

Total equity finance of limited companies consists of share capital, capital reserves and revenue reserves. Only the revenue reserves (which arise from realised profits and gains) can be used to fund a dividend. In other words, the maximum legal dividend is the amount of the revenue reserves.

The law does not specify how large the non-withdrawable part of a particular company's shareholders' equity should be. However, when seeking to impress prospective lenders and credit suppliers, the larger this part, the better. Those considering doing business with the company must be able to see from the company's statement of financial position how large it is.

Activity 4.8

Why are limited companies required to distinguish different parts of their shareholders' equity, whereas sole proprietorship and partnership businesses are not?

The reason stems from the limited liability that company shareholders enjoy but which owners of unincorporated businesses do not. If a sole proprietor or partner withdraws all of the equity, or even an amount in excess of this, the position of the lenders and credit suppliers of the business is not weakened since they can legally enforce their claims against the sole proprietor or partner as an individual. With a limited company, the business and the owners are legally separated and such a right to enforce claims against individuals does not exist. To protect the company's lenders and credit suppliers, however, the law insists that the shareholders cannot normally withdraw a specific part of their equity.

Let us now look at an example that illustrates how this protection of creditors works.

Example 4.4

The summary statement of financial position of a company at a particular date is as follows:

Statement of financial position

	£
Total assets	43,000
Equity	
Share capital	
20,000 shares of £1 each	20,000
Reserves (revenue)	23,000
Total equity	43,000

A bank has been asked to make a £25,000 long-term loan to the company. If the loan were to be made, the statement of financial position immediately following would appear as follows:

Statement of financial position (after the loan)

	£
Total assets (£43,000 + £25,000)	68,000
Equity	
Share capital	
20,000 shares of £1 each	20,000
Reserves (revenue)	23,000
	43,000
Non-current liability	
Borrowings – loan	25,000
Total equity and liabilities	68,000

As things stand, there are assets with a total carrying amount of £68,000 to meet the bank's claim of £25,000. It would be possible and perfectly legal, however, for the company to pay a dividend (withdraw part of the shareholders' equity) equal to the total revenue reserves (£23,000). The statement of financial position would then appear as follows:

Statement of financial position

	£
Total assets (£68,000 – £23,000)	45,000
Equity	
Share capital	
20,000 shares of £1 each	20,000
Reserves [revenue (£23,000 – £23,000)]	–
	20,000
Non-current liabilities	
Borrowings – bank loan	25,000
Total equity and liabilities	45,000

This leaves the bank in a very much weaker position, in that there are now total assets with a carrying amount of £45,000 to meet a claim of £25,000. Note that the difference between the amount of the borrowings (bank loan) and the total assets equals the equity (share capital and reserves) total. Thus, the equity represents a margin of safety for lenders and suppliers. The larger the amount of the equity withdrawable by the shareholders, the smaller is the potential margin of safety for lenders and suppliers.

As we have already seen, the law says nothing about how large the margin of safety must be. It is up to each company to decide what is appropriate.

As a practical footnote to Example 4.4, it is worth pointing out that long-term lenders would normally seek to secure a loan against an asset of the company, such as land.

Activity 4.9

Would you expect a company to pay all of its revenue reserves as a dividend? What factors might be involved with a dividend decision?

It would be rare for a company to pay all of its revenue reserves as a dividend: the fact that it is legally possible does not necessarily make it a good idea. Most companies see ploughed-back profits as a major – usually *the* major – source of new finance. The factors that tend most to influence the dividend decision are likely to include:

- the availability of cash to pay a dividend: it would not be illegal to borrow to pay a dividend, but it would be unusual, and possibly imprudent;
- the needs of the business for finance for new investment;
- the expectations of shareholders concerning the amount of dividends to be paid.

You may have thought of others.

If we look back at Real World 4.5 (page 128), we can see that at 27 June 2009, Thorntons plc could legally have paid a dividend totalling £8,151 million. Of course, the company did not do this, presumably because the funds concerned were tied up in property, plant and equipment and other assets, not lying around in the form of unused cash.

Activity 4.10

Can you remember the circumstances in which the non-withdrawable part of a company's capital could be reduced, without contravening the law? This was mentioned earlier in the chapter.

It can be reduced as a result of the company sustaining trading losses, or losses on disposal of non-current assets, which exceed the withdrawable amount of shareholders' equity. It cannot be reduced by shareholders making withdrawals.

Though payment of a cash dividend is the standard way for shareholders to withdraw equity from a company, it is not the only way. Provided that certain conditions are met, it is perfectly legal for a company to redeem some of its shares or to buy some of its shares, from particular shareholders who are willing to sell, and cancel them. These conditions are generally not difficult to meet for profitable companies.

The main financial statements

As we might expect, the financial statements of a limited company are, in essence, the same as those of a sole proprietor or partnership. There are, however, some differences of detail. We shall now consider these. Example 4.5 sets out the income statement and statement of financial position of a limited company.

Example 4.5

Da Silva plc
Income statement for the year ended 31 December 2010

	£m
Revenue	840
Cost of sales	(520)
Gross profit	320
Wages and salaries	(98)
Heat and light	(18)
Rent and rates	(24)
Motor vehicle expenses	(20)
Insurance	(4)
Printing and stationery	(12)
Depreciation	(45)
Audit fee	(4)
Operating profit	95
Interest payable	(10)
Profit before taxation	85
Taxation	(24)
Profit for the year	61

Statement of financial position as at 31 December 2010

	£m
ASSETS	
Non-current assets	
Property, plant and equipment	203
Intangible assets	100
	303
Current assets	
Inventories	65
Trade receivables	112
Cash	36
	213
Total assets	516
EQUITY AND LIABILITIES	
Equity	
Ordinary shares of £0.50 each	200
Share premium account	30
Other reserves	50
Retained earnings	25
	305
Non-current liabilities	
Borrowings	100
Current liabilities	
Trade payables	99
Taxation	12
	111
Total equity and liabilities	516

Let us now go through these statements and pick up those aspects that are unique to limited companies.

The income statement

The main points for consideration in the income statement are as follows:

Profit

We can see that, following the calculation of operating profit, two further measures of profit are shown.

- The first of these is the **profit before taxation**. Interest charges are deducted from the operating profit to derive this figure. In the case of a sole proprietor or partnership business, the income statement would end here.
- The second measure of profit is the *profit for the year*. As the company is a separate legal entity, it is liable to pay tax (known as corporation tax) on the profits generated. (This contrasts with the sole-proprietor business where it is the owner rather than the business that is liable for the tax on profits, as we saw earlier in the chapter.) This measure of profit represents the amount that is available for the shareholders.

Audit fee

Companies beyond a certain size are required to have their financial statements audited by an independent firm of accountants, for which a fee is charged. As we shall see in Chapter 5, the purpose of the audit is to lend credibility to the financial statements. Although it is also open to sole proprietorships and partnerships to have their financial statements audited, relatively few do, so this is an expense that is most often seen in the income statement of a company.

The statement of financial position

The main points for consideration in the statement of financial position are as follows:

Taxation

The amount that appears as part of the current liabilities represents 50 per cent of the tax on the profit for the year 2010. It is, therefore, 50 per cent (£12 million) of the charge that appears in the income statement (£24 million); the other 50 per cent (£12 million) will already have been paid. The unpaid 50 per cent will be paid shortly after the statement of financial position date. These payment dates are set down by law.

Other reserves

This will include any reserves that are not separately identified on the face of the statement of financial position. It may include a *general reserve*, which normally consists of trading profits that have been transferred to this separate reserve for reinvestment ('ploughing back') into the operations of the company. It is not at all necessary to set up a separate reserve for this purpose. The trading profits could remain unallocated and still swell the retained earnings of the company. It is not entirely clear why directors decide to make transfers to general reserves, since the profits concerned remain part of the revenue reserves, and as such they still remain available for dividend. The most plausible explanation seems to be that directors feel that placing profits in a separate reserve indicates an intention to invest the funds, represented by the reserve, permanently in the company and, therefore, not to use them to pay a dividend. Of course, the retained earnings appearing on the statement of financial position are also a reserve, but that fact is not indicated in its title.

Dividends

We have already seen that dividends represent drawings by the shareholders of the company. Dividends are paid out of the revenue reserves and should be deducted from these reserves (usually retained earnings) when preparing the statement of financial position. Shareholders are often paid an annual dividend, perhaps in two parts. An 'interim' dividend may be paid part way through the year and a 'final' dividend shortly after the year end.

Dividends declared by the directors during the year but still unpaid at the year end *may* appear as a liability in the statement of financial position. To be recognised as a liability, however, they must be properly authorised before the year-end date. This normally means that the shareholders must approve the dividend.

Large companies tend to have a clear and consistent policy towards the payment of dividends. Any change in the policy provokes considerable interest and is usually interpreted by shareholders as a signal of the directors' views concerning the future. For example, an increase in dividends may be taken as a signal from the directors that future prospects are bright: a higher dividend is seen as tangible evidence of their confidence.

Real World 4.8 provides an example of one well-known business that paid a dividend after more than twenty years of trading.

Real World 4.8

At last!

Eurotunnel is to pay its first-ever dividend to its long-suffering shareholders, it revealed today. The Channel tunnel operator announced the €0.04-a-share payout (3.56p) as it reported net profits for the year of €40 million (£35.6 million), compared with a loss for 2007 of €12 million.

Eurotunnel floated on the London stock market in November 1987 when it it raised £770 million from investors. This included some 574,000 small shareholders, who, if they invested more than £500 worth of shares at 350p each, were offered perks including free travel and discounts on hotels and car hire provided they held their shares beyond 1993, when the tunnel was expected to open.

However, as the project over-ran more cash was required on top of the company's credit facilities, leading to a £532 million rights issue in December 1990.

Commenting on today's results, Jacques Gounon, the chairman and chief executive of Eurotunnel, said:

Despite the incident in September [following a fire in one of the tunnels], the year 2008 clearly marks the end of financial uncertainty for Eurotunnel. Through its efficiency and the control of its costs, the group has recorded a solid profit which, for the first time in our history, allows us to pay a dividend to our loyal shareholders.

Source: 'Eurotunnel pays first dividend since 1987 float', Ian King, 4 March 2009, www.timesonline.co.uk. nisyndication.com.

Self-assessment question 4.1

The summarised statement of financial position of Dev Ltd at a particular point in time is as follows:

Statement of financial position

	£
Net assets (various assets less liabilities)	235,000
Equity	
Share capital: 100,000 shares of £1 each	100,000
Share premium account	30,000
Revaluation reserve	37,000
Retained earnings	68,000
Total equity	235,000

Required:

(a) Without any other transactions occurring at the same time, the company made a one-for-five rights share issue at £2 per share payable in cash. This means that each shareholder was offered one share for every five already held. All shareholders took up their rights. Immediately afterwards, the company made a one-for-two bonus issue. Show the statement of financial position immediately following the bonus issue, assuming that the directors wanted to retain the maximum dividend payment potential for the future.

(b) Explain what external influence might cause the directors to choose not to retain the maximum dividend payment possibilities.

(c) Show the statement of financial position immediately following the bonus issue, assuming that the directors wanted to retain the *minimum* dividend payment potential for the future.

(d) What is the maximum dividend that could be paid before and after the events described in (a) if the minimum dividend payment potential is achieved?

(e) Lee owns 100 shares in Dev Ltd before the events described in (a). Assuming that the net assets of the company have a value equal to their carrying amount on the statement of financial position, show how these events will affect Lee's wealth.

(f) Looking at the original statement of financial position of Dev Ltd, shown above, what four things do we know about the company's status and history that are not specifically stated on the statement of financial position?

The solution to this question can be found at the back of the book on pages 474–475.

Summary

The main points of this chapter may be summarised as follows:

Main features of a limited company

● It is an artificial person that has been created by law.

● It has a separate life to its owners and is granted a perpetual existence.

- It must take responsibility for its own debts and losses but its owners are granted limited liability.
- A public company can offer its shares for sale to the public; a private company cannot.
- It is governed by a board of directors, which is elected by the shareholders.
- Corporate governance is a major issue.

Financing the limited company

- The share capital of a company can be of two main types: ordinary shares and preference shares.
- Holders of ordinary shares (equities) are the main risk-takers and are given voting rights; they form the backbone of the company.
- Holders of preference shares are given a right to a fixed dividend before ordinary shareholders receive a dividend.
- Reserves are profits and gains made by the company and form part of the ordinary shareholders' equity.
- Borrowings provide another major source of finance.

Share issues

- Bonus shares are issued to existing shareholders when part of the reserves of the company is converted into share capital. No funds are raised.
- Rights issues give existing shareholders the right to buy new shares in proportion to their existing holding.
- Public issues are made direct to the general investing public.
- Private placings are share issues to particular investors.
- The shares of public companies may be bought and sold on a recognised Stock Exchange.

Reserves

- Reserves are of two types: revenue reserves and capital reserves.
- Revenue reserves arise from trading profits and from realised profits on the sale of non-current assets.
- Capital reserves arise from the issue of shares above their nominal value or from the upward revaluation of non-current assets.
- Revenue reserves can be withdrawn as dividends by the shareholders whereas capital reserves normally cannot.

Financial statements of limited companies

- The financial statements of limited companies are based on the same principles as those of sole proprietorship and partnership businesses. However, there are some differences in detail.
- The income statement has three measures of profit displayed after the gross profit figure: operating profit, profit before taxation and profit for the year.
- The income statement also shows audit fees and tax on profits for the year.
- Any unpaid tax and unpaid, but authorised, dividends will appear in the statement of financial position as current liabilities.
- The share capital plus the reserves make up 'equity'.

→ **Key terms**

limited liability   p. 118
public limited company   p. 119
private limited company   p. 119
corporation tax   p. 122
directors   p. 123
corporate governance   p. 123
reserves   p. 123
nominal value   p. 124
par value   p. 124
revenue reserve   p. 124
dividend   p. 124
ordinary shares   p. 124
splitting   p. 125

consolidating   p. 125
preference shares   p. 126
capital reserves   p. 126
share premium account   p. 128
bonus shares   p. 128
issued share capital   p. 130
allotted share capital   p. 130
fully paid shares   p. 131
called-up share capital   p. 131
paid-up share capital   p. 131
loan notes   p. 131
profit before taxation   p. 138

Further reading

If you would like to explore the topics covered in this chapter in more depth, we recommend the following books:

Elliott, B. and Elliott, J., *Financial Accounting and Reporting*, 13th edn, Financial Times Prentice Hall, 2009, Chapter 10.

Thomas, A. and Ward, A. M., *Introduction to Financial Accounting*, 6th edn, McGraw Hill, 2009, Chapter 29.

Review questions

Solutions to these questions can be found at the back of the book on page 484.

4.1 How does the liability of a limited company differ from the liability of a real person, in respect of amounts owed to others?

4.2 Some people are about to form a company, as a vehicle through which to run a new business. What are the advantages to them of forming a private limited company rather than a public one?

4.3 What is a reserve? Distinguish between a revenue reserve and a capital reserve.

4.4 What is a preference share? Compare the main features of a preference share with those of

(a) an ordinary share; and
(b) loan notes.

Exercises

Exercises 4.6 to 4.8 are more advanced than Exercises 4.1 to 4.5. Those with coloured numbers have answers at the back of the book, starting on page 498.
   If you wish to try more exercises, visit the students' side of the Companion Website.

4.1 Comment on the following quote:

> Limited companies can set a limit on the amount of debts that they will meet. They tend to have reserves of cash, as well as share capital and they can use these reserves to pay dividends to the shareholders. Many companies have preference as well as ordinary shares. The preference shares give a guaranteed dividend. The shares of many companies can be bought and sold on the Stock Exchange. Shareholders selling their shares can represent a useful source of new finance to the company.

4.2 Comment on the following quotes:

(a) 'Bonus shares increase the shareholders' wealth because, after the issue, they have more shares, but each one of the same nominal value as they had before.'
(b) 'By law, once shares have been issued at a particular nominal value, they must always be issued at that value in any future share issues.'
(c) 'By law, companies can pay as much as they like by way of dividends on their shares, provided that they have sufficient cash to do so.'
(d) 'Companies do not have to pay tax on their profits because the shareholders have to pay tax on their dividends.'

4.3 Briefly explain each of the following expressions that you have seen in the financial statements of a limited company:

(a) dividend
(b) audit fee
(c) share premium account.

4.4 Iqbal Ltd started trading on 1 January 2006. During the first five years of trading, the following occurred:

Year ended 31 December	Trading profit/(loss) £	Profit/(loss) on sale of non-current assets £	Upward revaluation of non-current assets £
2006	(15,000)	–	–
2007	8,000	–	10,000
2008	15,000	5,000	–
2009	20,000	(6,000)	–
2010	22,000	–	–

Required:
Assume that the company paid the maximum legal dividend each year. Under normal circumstances, how much would each year's dividend be?

4.5 Hudson plc's outline statement of financial position as at a particular date was as follows:

	£m
Net assets (assets less liabilities)	72
Equity	
£1 ordinary shares	40
General reserve	32
Total equity	72

The directors made a one-for-four bonus issue, immediately followed by a one-for-four rights issue at a price of £1.80 per share.

Required:
Show the statement of financial position of Hudson plc immediately following the two share issues.

4.6 Presented below is a draft set of simplified financial statements for Pear Limited for the year ended 30 September 2010.

Income statement for the year ended 30 September 2010

	£000
Revenue	1,456
Cost of sales	(768)
Gross profit	688
Salaries	(220)
Depreciation	(249)
Other operating costs	(131)
Operating profit	88
Interest payable	(15)
Profit before taxation	73
Taxation at 30%	(22)
Profit for the year	51

Statement of financial position as at 30 September 2010

	£000
ASSETS	
Non-current assets	
Property, plant and equipment	
Cost	1,570
Depreciation	(690)
	880
Current assets	
Inventories	207
Trade receivables	182
Cash at bank	21
	410
Total assets	1,290
EQUITY AND LIABILITIES	
Equity	
Share capital	300
Share premium account	300
Retained earnings at beginning of year	104
Profit for year	51
	755
Non-current liabilities	
Borrowings (10% loan notes repayable 2014)	300
Current liabilities	
Trade payables	88
Other payables	20
Taxation	22
Borrowings (bank overdraft)	105
	235
Total equity and liabilities	1,290

The following information is available:

1 Depreciation has not been charged on office equipment with a carrying amount of £100,000. This class of assets is depreciated at 12 per cent a year using the reducing-balance method.

2 A new machine was purchased, on credit, for £30,000 and delivered on 29 September 2010 but has not been included in the financial statements. (Ignore depreciation.)

3 A sales invoice to the value of £18,000 for September 2010 has been omitted from the financial statements. (The cost of sales figure is stated correctly.)

4 A dividend of £25,000 had been approved by the shareholders before 30 September 2010, but was unpaid at that date. This is not reflected in the financial statements.

5 The interest payable on the loan notes for the second half-year was not paid until 1 October 2010 and has not been included in the financial statements.

6 An allowance for trade receivables is to be made at the level of 2 per cent of trade receivables.

7 An invoice for electricity to the value of £2,000 for the quarter ended 30 September 2010 arrived on 4 October and has not been included in the financial statements.

8 The charge for taxation will have to be amended to take account of the above information. Make the simplifying assumption that tax is payable shortly after the end of the year, at the rate of 30 per cent of the profit before tax.

***Required*:**

Prepare a revised set of financial statements for the year ended 30 September 2010 incorporating the additional information in 1 to 8 above. (Work to the nearest £1,000.)

4.7 Presented below is a draft set of financial statements for Chips Limited.

Chips Limited
Income statement for the year ended 30 June 2010

	£000
Revenue	1,850
Cost of sales	(1,040)
Gross profit	810
Depreciation	(220)
Other operating costs	(375)
Operating profit	215
Interest payable	(35)
Profit before taxation	180
Taxation	(60)
Profit for the year	120

Statement of financial position as at 30 June 2010

	Cost £000	Depreciation £000	£000
ASSETS			
Non-current assets			
Property, plant and equipment			
Buildings	800	(112)	688
Plant and equipment	650	(367)	283
Motor vehicles	102	(53)	49
	1,552	(532)	1,020
Current assets			
Inventories			950
Trade receivables			420
Cash at bank			16
			1,386
Total assets			2,406
EQUITY AND LIABILITIES			
Equity			
Ordinary shares of £1, fully paid			800
Reserves at beginning of the year			248
Profit for the year			120
			1,168
Non-current liabilities			
Borrowings (secured 10% loan notes)			700
Current liabilities			
Trade payables			361
Other payables			117
Taxation			60
			538
Total equity and liabilities			2,406

The following additional information is available:

1 Purchase invoices for goods received on 29 June 2010 amounting to £23,000 have not been included. This means that the cost of sales figure in the income statement has been understated.

2 A motor vehicle costing £8,000 with depreciation amounting to £5,000 was sold on 30 June 2010 for £2,000, paid by cheque. This transaction has not been included in the company's records.

3 No depreciation on motor vehicles has been charged. The annual rate is 20 per cent of cost at the year end.

4 A sale on credit for £16,000 made on 1 July 2010 has been included in the financial statements in error. The cost of sales figure is correct in respect of this item.

5 A half-yearly payment of interest on the secured loan due on 30 June 2010 has not been paid.

6 The tax charge should be 30 per cent of the reported profit before taxation. Assume that it is payable, in full, shortly after the year end.

Required:

Prepare a revised set of financial statements incorporating the additional information in 1 to 6 above. (Work to the nearest £1,000.)

4.8 Rose Limited operates a small chain of retail shops that sell high-quality teas and coffees. Approximately half of sales are on credit. Abbreviated and unaudited financial statements are given below.

Rose Limited
Income statement for the year ended 31 March 2010

	£000
Revenue	12,080
Cost of sales	(6,282)
Gross profit	5,798
Labour costs	(2,658)
Depreciation	(625)
Other operating costs	(1,003)
Operating profit	1,512
Interest payable	(66)
Profit before taxation	1,446
Taxation	(434)
Profit for the year	1,012

Statement of financial position as at 31 March 2010

	£000
ASSETS	
Non-current assets	2,728
Current assets	
Inventories	1,583
Trade receivables	996
Cash	26
	2,605
Total assets	5,333
EQUITY AND LIABILITIES	
Equity	
Share capital (50p shares, fully paid)	750
Share premium	250
Retained earnings	1,468
	2,468
Non-current liabilities	
Borrowings – secured loan notes (2014)	300
Current liabilities	
Trade payables	1,118
Other payables	417
Tax	434
Borrowings – overdraft	596
	2,565
Total equity and liabilities	5,333

Since the unaudited financial statements for Rose Limited were prepared, the following information has become available:

1 An additional £74,000 of depreciation should have been charged on fixtures and fittings.
2 Invoices for credit sales on 31 March 2010 amounting to £34,000 have not been included; cost of sales is not affected.
3 Trade receivables totalling £21,000 are recognised as having gone bad, but they have not yet been written off.
4 Inventories which had been purchased for £2,000 have been damaged and are unsaleable. This is not reflected in the financial statements.
5 Fixtures and fittings to the value of £16,000 were delivered just before 31 March 2010, but these assets were not included in the financial statements and the purchase invoice had not been processed.
6 Wages for Saturday-only staff, amounting to £1,000, have not been paid for the final Saturday of the year. This is not reflected in the financial statements.
7 Tax is payable at 30 per cent of profit after taxation. Assume that it is payable shortly after the year end.

Required:
Prepare revised financial statements for Rose Limited for the year ended 31 March 2010, incorporating the information in 1 to 7 above. (Work to the nearest £1,000.)

5

Accounting for limited companies (2)

Introduction

This chapter continues our examination of the financial statements of limited companies. We begin by identifying the legal responsibilities of directors and then go on to discuss the main sources of accounting rules governing published financial statements. Although a detailed consideration of these accounting rules is beyond the scope of this book, the key rules that shape the form and content of the published financial statements are discussed. We also consider the efforts made to ensure that these rules are underpinned by a coherent framework of principles.

Accounting rules enjoy widespread support and are generally considered to have had a beneficial effect on the quality of financial information provided to users. There are, however, potential problems with a rule-based approach. In this chapter, we consider these problems and their impact on the presentation of financial statements and on the future development of accounting.

Despite the proliferation of accounting rules, concerns have been expressed over the quality of some published financial reports. This chapter ends by considering some well-publicised accounting scandals and the problem of creative accounting.

Learning outcomes

When you have completed this chapter, you should be able to:

- describe the responsibilities of directors and auditors concerning the annual financial statements provided to shareholders and others;

- discuss both the framework of regulation and the framework of principles that help to shape the form and content of annual financial statements;

- prepare a statement of financial position, statement of comprehensive income and statement of changes in equity in accordance with International Financial Reporting Standards;

- discuss the arguments for and against the use of accounting rules when preparing financial statements;

- discuss the threat posed by creative accounting and identify the areas that are vulnerable to creative accounting techniques.

The directors' duty to account

With most large companies, it is not possible for all shareholders to be involved in the management of the company, nor do most of them wish to be involved. Instead, they appoint directors to act on their behalf. This separation of ownership from day-to-day control creates a need for directors to be accountable for their stewardship (management) of the company's assets. To fulfil this need, the directors must prepare (or have prepared on their behalf) financial statements that provide a fair representation of the financial position and performance of the business. This means that they must select appropriate accounting policies, make reasonable accounting estimates and adhere to all relevant accounting rules when preparing the statements. To avoid misstatements on the financial statements, whether from fraud or error, the directors must also maintain appropriate internal control systems.

Each of the company's shareholders has the right to be sent a copy of the financial statements produced by the directors. The financial statements must also be made available to the general public. This is achieved by the company submitting a copy to the Registrar of Companies (Department of Trade and Industry), which allows anyone who wishes to do so to inspect them. In addition, listed companies are required to publish their financial statements on their website.

Activity 5.1

It can be argued that the publication of financial statements is vital to a well-functioning private sector. Why might this be the case?

There are at least two reasons:

- Unless shareholders receive regular information about the performance and position of a business they will have problems in appraising their investment. Under these circumstances, they would probably be reluctant to invest, which would adversely affect the functioning of a private enterprise economy.
- Suppliers of labour, goods, services and finance, particularly those supplying credit (loans) or goods and services on credit, need information about the financial health of a business. They would be reluctant to engage in commercial relationships where a company does not provide information. The fact that a company has limited liability increases the risks involved in dealing with it. An unwillingness to engage in commercial relationships with limited companies will, again, adversely affect the functioning of the private sector of the economy.

The need for accounting rules

If we accept the need for directors to prepare and publish financial statements, we should also accept the need for a framework of rules concerning how these statements are prepared and presented. Without rules, there is a much greater risk that unscrupulous directors will adopt accounting policies and practices that portray an unrealistic view of financial health. There is also a much greater risk that the financial statements will not be comparable over time or with those of other businesses. Accounting rules can narrow areas of differences and reduce the variety of accounting methods. This should help ensure that businesses treat similar transactions in a similar way.

Example 5.1 below illustrates the problem of comparability where businesses can exercise choice over the accounting methods used.

Example 5.1

Rila plc and Pirin plc are both wholesalers of electrical goods. Both commenced trading on 1 March 2009 with an identical share capital. Both acquired identical property, plant and equipment on 1 March and both achieved identical trading results during the first year of trading. The following financial information relating to both businesses is available:

	£m
Ordinary £1 shares contributed on 1 March 2009	60
Non-current assets at cost acquired on 1 March 2009	40
Revenue for the year to 28 February 2010	100
Purchases of inventories during the year to 28 February 2010	70
Expenses for the year to 28 February 2010 (excluding depreciation)	20
Trade receivables as at 28 February 2010	37
Trade payables as at 28 February 2010	12
Cash as at 28 February 2010	5

The non-current assets are leasehold buildings that have five years left on the lease to run. Inventories at the year end have been valued at £16 million on a FIFO basis and £12 million on a LIFO basis.

When preparing their financial statements at the year end,

- Rila plc decided to write off the cost of the leasehold premises at the end of the lease period. Pirin plc adopted the straight-line basis of depreciation for the leasehold buildings.
- Rila plc adopted the FIFO method of inventories valuation and Pirin plc adopted the LIFO method.

The income statements and the statements of financial position for the two businesses, ignoring taxation, will be as follows:

Income statements for the year to 28 February 2010

	Rila plc £m	Pirin plc £m
Revenue	100	100
Cost of sales		
Rila plc (£70m – £16m)	(54)	
Pirin plc (£70m – £12m)		(58)
Gross profit	46	42
Expenses (excluding depreciation)	(20)	(20)
Depreciation		
Rila plc	(–)	
Pirin plc (£40m/5)		(8)
Profit for the year	26	14

Example 5.1 continued

Statements of financial position as at 28 February 2010

	Rila plc £m	Pirin plc £m
ASSETS		
Non-current assets		
Property, plant and equipment at cost	40	40
Accumulated depreciation	(–)	(8)
	40	32
Current assets		
Inventories	16	12
Trade receivables	37	37
Cash	5	5
	58	54
Total assets	98	86
EQUITY AND LIABILITIES		
Equity		
Share capital	60	60
Retained earnings	26	14
	86	74
Current liabilities		
Trade payables	12	12
Total equity and liabilities	98	86

Although the two businesses are identical in terms of funding and under-lying trading performance, the financial statements create an impression that the financial health of each business is quite different. The accounting methods selected by Rila plc help to portray a much rosier picture. We can see that Rila plc reports a significantly higher profit for the year and higher assets at the year end.

Depreciation and inventories valuation are not the only areas where choices might be exercised. They nevertheless illustrate the potential impact of different accounting choices over the short term.

Accounting rules should help to provide greater confidence in the integrity of financial statements. This, in turn, may help a business to raise funds and to build stronger relationships with customers and suppliers. Users must be realistic, however, about what can be achieved through regulation. Problems of manipulation and of concealment can still occur even within a highly regulated environment and examples of both will be considered later in the chapter. The scale of these problems, however, should be reduced where there is a practical set of rules.

Problems of comparability can also still occur as accounting is not a precise science. Judgements and estimates must be made when preparing financial statements and these may hinder comparisons. Furthermore, no two companies are identical (unlike the companies in Example 5.1) and the accounting policies adopted may vary between companies for valid reasons.

Sources of accounting rules

In recent years there have been increasing trends towards the internationalisation of business and the integration of financial markets. These trends have helped to strengthen the case for the international harmonisation of accounting rules. When a common set of rules is followed, users of financial statements should be better placed to compare the financial health of companies based in different countries. The existence of such rules should also relieve international companies of some of the burden of preparing financial statements as different financial statements will no longer have to be prepared to comply with the rules of different countries in which a particular company operates.

The International Accounting Standards Board (IASB) is an independent body that is at the forefront of the move towards harmonisation. The Board, which is based in the UK, is dedicated to developing a single set of high-quality, global accounting rules that provide transparent and comparable information in financial statements. These rules, which are known as **International Accounting Standards** (IASs) or **International Financial Reporting Standards** (IFRSs), deal with key issues such as:

- what information should be disclosed;
- how information should be presented;
- how assets should be valued; and
- how profit should be measured.

Activity 5.2

We have already come across some IASs and IFRSs in earlier chapters. Try to recall at least two topics where financial reporting standards were mentioned.

We came across financial reporting standards when considering:

- the valuation and impairment of assets (Chapter 2);
- depreciation and impairment of non-current assets (Chapter 3); and
- the valuation of inventories (Chapter 3).

In recent years, several important developments have greatly increased the authority of the IASB. The first major boost came when the European Commission required nearly all companies listed on the stock exchanges of EU member states to adopt IFRSs for accounting periods commencing on or after 1 January 2005. As a result, nearly 7,000 companies in 25 different countries switched to IFRSs. This was followed in 2006 by the IASB and the US Financial Accounting Standards Board agreeing a roadmap for convergence between IFRSs and US accounting rules. In that same year, China closely aligned its financial reporting standards with IFRSs. Finally, in 2007, Brazil, Canada, Chile, India, Japan and Korea all announced their intention to adopt, or converge with, IFRSs.

There are now over 100 countries that either require or permit the use of IFRSs. It seems increasingly likely that those countries that have not joined in using IFRSs will do so sooner or later. Although non-listed UK companies are not currently required to adopt IFRSs, they have the option to do so. Some informed observers believe, however, that IFRSs will soon become a requirement for all UK companies.

The EU requirement to adopt IFRSs, mentioned earlier, overrides any laws in force in member states that could either hinder or restrict compliance with them. The ultimate aim is to achieve a single framework of accounting rules for companies from all member states. The EU recognises that this will be achieved only if individual governments do not add to the requirements imposed by the various IFRSs. Thus, it seems that accounting rules developed within individual EU member countries will eventually disappear. For the time being, however, the EU accepts that the governments of member states may need to impose additional disclosures for some corporate governance matters and regulatory requirements.

In the UK, company law requires disclosure relating to various corporate governance issues. There is, for example, a requirement to disclose details of directors' remuneration in the published financial statements, which goes beyond anything required by IFRSs. Furthermore, the Financial Services Authority (FSA), in its role as the UK (Stock Exchange) listing authority, imposes rules on Stock Exchange listed companies. These include the requirement to publish a condensed set of interim (half-year) financial statements in addition to the annual financial statements. (These statements are not required by the IASB, although there is a standard providing guidance on their form and content. The statements and the standard will be considered in Chapter 10.)

Figure 5.1 sets out the main sources of accounting rules for Stock Exchange listed companies discussed above. While company law and the FSA still play an important role, in the longer term IFRSs seem set to become the sole source of company accounting rules.

Figure 5.1 Sources of external accounting rules for a UK public limited company listed on the London Stock Exchange

International Financial Reporting Standards provide the basic framework of accounting rules for nearly all Stock Exchange listed companies. These rules are augmented by company law and by the Financial Services Authority (FSA) in its role as the UK listing authority.

Real World 5.1 is a list of IASB standards that were in force as at 1 January 2009. This gives some idea of the range of topics that are covered.

Real World 5.1

International standards

The following is a list of the International Accounting Standards (IASs) and International Financial Reporting Standards (IFRSs) in issue as at 3 May 2010. (The latter term is used for standards issued from 2003 onwards.) Several standards have been issued and subsequently withdrawn, which explains the gaps in the numerical sequence. In addition, several have been revised and reissued.

IAS 1   *Presentation of Financial Statements*
IAS 2   *Inventories*
IAS 7   *Statement of Cash Flows*
IAS 8   *Accounting Policies, Changes in Accounting Estimates and Errors*
IAS 10   *Events after the Reporting Period*
IAS 11   *Construction Contracts*
IAS 12   *Income Taxes*
IAS 16   *Property, Plant and Equipment*
IAS 17   *Leases*
IAS 18   *Revenue*
IAS 19   *Employee Benefits*
IAS 20   *Accounting for Government Grants and Disclosure of Government Assistance*
IAS 21   *The Effects of Changes in Foreign Exchange Rates*
IAS 23   *Borrowing Costs*
IAS 24   *Related Party Disclosures*
IAS 26   *Accounting and Reporting by Retirement Benefit Plans*
IAS 27   *Consolidated and Separate Financial Statements*
IAS 28   *Investments in Associates*
IAS 29   *Financial Reporting in Hyperinflationary Economies*
IAS 31   *Interests in Joint Ventures*
IAS 32   *Financial Instruments: Presentation*
IAS 33   *Earnings per Share*
IAS 34   *Interim Financial Reporting*
IAS 36   *Impairment of Assets*
IAS 37   *Provisions, Contingent Liabilities and Contingent Assets*
IAS 38   *Intangible Assets*
IAS 40   *Investment Property*
IAS 41   *Agriculture*
IFRS 1   *First-time Adoption of International Financial Reporting Standards*
IFRS 2   *Share-based Payment*
IFRS 3   *Business Combinations*
IFRS 4   *Insurance Contracts*
IFRS 5   *Non-current Assets Held for Sale and Discontinued Operations*
IFRS 6   *Exploration for and Evaluation of Mineral Resources*
IFRS 7   *Financial Instruments: Disclosures*
IFRS 8   *Operating Segments*
IFRS 9   *Financial Instruments*

Source: International Accounting Standards Board, www.iasb.org.uk.

The IASB has an ambitious agenda and so significant changes to the above list are likely to occur in the future.

Presenting the financial statements

Now that we have gained an impression of the sources of rules affecting limited companies, let us turn our attention to the main rules to be followed in the presentation of financial statements. We shall focus on the IASB rules and, in particular, those contained in IAS 1 *Presentation of Financial Statements*. This standard is very important as it sets out the structure and content of financial statements and the principles to be followed in preparing these statements.

It might be helpful to have a set of the most recent financial statements of a Stock Exchange listed company available as you work through this section. They should all be available on the internet. Select a listed company that interests you and go to its website.

According to IAS 1, the financial statements consist of:

● a statement of financial position
● a statement of comprehensive income
● a statement of changes in equity
● a statement of cash flows
● notes on accounting policies and other explanatory notes.

The standard states that these financial statements should normally cover a one-year period and should be accompanied by comparative information for the previous year. Thus, at the end of each accounting year companies should normally produce two of each of the statements, plus the related notes. In practice, virtually all companies satisfy this requirement by showing the equivalent figures for the previous year in a separate column in the current year's statements.

Comparative narrative information should also be provided if needed for a better grasp of current period results – for example, as background to an ongoing legal dispute.

Fair representation

Before we consider the financial statements in detail, it is important to emphasise that the standard requires that they provide a fair representation of a company's financial position, financial performance and cash flows. There is a presumption that this will be achieved where they are drawn up in accordance with the various IASB standards that are currently in force. It is only in very rare circumstances that compliance with a standard would not result in a fair representation of the financial health of a company. Where the financial statements have been prepared in accordance with IASB standards, it should be clearly stated in the notes.

Activity 5.3

IAS 1 does not say that the requirement is for the financial statements to show a 'correct' or an 'accurate' representation of financial health. Why, in your opinion, does it not use those words? (*Hint*: Think of depreciation of non-current assets.)

Accounting can never really be said to be 'correct' or 'accurate' as these words imply that there is a precise value that an asset, claim, revenue or expense could have. This is simply not true in many, if not most, cases.

Depreciation provides a good example. The annual depreciation expense is based on judgements about the future concerning the expected useful life and residual value of an asset. If all relevant factors are taken into account and reasonable judgements are applied, it may be possible to achieve a fair representation of the amount of the cost or fair value of the asset that is consumed for a particular period. However, a precise figure for depreciation for a period cannot be achieved.

Let us now consider each of the financial statements in turn.

Statement of financial position

IAS 1 does not prescribe the format (or layout) for this financial statement but does set out the *minimum* information that should be presented on the face of the statement of financial position. This includes the following:

- property, plant and equipment
- investment property
- intangible assets
- financial assets (such as shares and loan notes of other companies held)
- inventories
- trade and other receivables
- cash and cash equivalents
- trade and other payables
- provisions (a provision is a liability that is of uncertain timing or amount – such as a possible obligation arising from a legal case against the company that has yet to be determined)
- financial liabilities (excluding payables and provisions shown above)
- tax liabilities
- issued share capital and reserves (equity).

Additional information should be also shown where it is relevant to an understanding of the financial position of the business.

The standard requires that a distinction is normally made on the statement of financial position between current assets and non-current assets and between current liabilities and non-current liabilities. However, for certain types of business, such as financial institutions, the standard accepts that it may be more appropriate to order items according to their liquidity (that is, their nearness to cash).

Some of the items shown above may have to be sub-classified to comply with particular standards or because of their size or nature. Thus, sub-classifications are required for assets such as property, plant and equipment, receivables and inventories as well as for claims such as provisions and reserves. Certain details relating to share capital, such as the number of issued shares and their nominal value, must also be shown. To avoid cluttering up the statement of financial position, however, this additional information can be shown in the notes. In practice, most companies use notes for this purpose.

Statement of comprehensive income

This statement extends the conventional income statement to include certain other gains and losses that affect shareholders' equity. It may be presented either in the form

of a single statement or as two separate statements, comprising an income statement and
→   a **statement of comprehensive income**. This choice of presentation, however, seems to
be a transitional arrangement as the IASB's clear preference is for a single statement.

Again the format of the statement of comprehensive income is not prescribed, but
IAS 1 sets out the *minimum* information to be presented on the face of the statement.
This includes:

- revenue
- finance costs
- profits or losses arising from discontinued operations
- tax expense
- profit or loss
- each component of other comprehensive income classified by its nature
- any share of the comprehensive income of associates or joint ventures
- total comprehensive income.

The standard makes it clear that further items should be shown on the face of the
income statement where they are relevant to an understanding of performance. If,
for example, a business is badly affected by flooding and inventories are destroyed as
a result, the cost of the flood damage should be shown.

As a further aid to understanding, all material expenses should be separately disclosed.
However, they need not be shown on the face of the income statement: they can
appear in the notes to the financial statements. The kind of material items that may
require separate disclosure include:

- write-down of inventories to net realisable value
- write-down of property, plant and equipment
- disposals of investments
- restructuring costs
- discontinued operations
- litigation settlements.

This is not an exhaustive list and, in practice, other material expenses may require
separate disclosure.

The standard suggests two possible ways in which expenses can be presented on
the face of the income statement. Expenses can be presented either according to their
nature, for example as depreciation, employee expenses and so on, or according to
business functions, such as administrative activities and distribution. The choice between
the two possible ways of presenting expenses will depend on which one the directors
believe will provide the more relevant and reliable information.

To understand what other information must be presented in this statement, apart
from that already contained in a conventional income statement, we should remember
that, broadly, the conventional income statement shows all *realised* gains and losses
for the period. It also includes some unrealised losses (that is, losses relating to assets
still held). However, unrealised gains, and some unrealised losses do not pass through
the income statement, but go directly to a reserve. We saw, in an earlier chapter, an
example of an unrealised gain (which, therefore, would not have passed through the
conventional income statement).

Activity 5.4

Can you think of this example?

The example that we met earlier is where a business revalues its land and buildings. The gain arising is not shown in the conventional income statement, but is transferred to a revaluation reserve, which forms part of the equity. (We met this example in Activity 2.14 on page 59.) Land and buildings are not the only assets to which this rule relates, but these types of asset are, in practice, the most common examples of unrealised gains.

An example of an unrealised gain, or loss, that has not been mentioned so far, arises from exchange differences when the results of foreign operations are translated into UK currency. Any gain, or loss, bypasses the income statement and is taken directly to a currency translation reserve. A weakness of conventional accounting is that there is no robust principle that we can apply to determine precisely what should, and what should not, be included in the income statement. For example, losses arising from the impairment of non-current assets normally appear in the income statement. On the other hand, losses arising from translating the carrying amount of assets expressed in an overseas currency (because they are owned by an overseas branch) do not. There is no real difference in principle between the two types of loss, but the difference in treatment is ingrained in conventional accounting practice.

The statement of comprehensive income includes *all* gains and losses for a period and so will also take into account unrealised gains and any remaining unrealised losses. It extends the conventional income statement by including these items immediately below the measure of profit for the year. An illustration of this statement is shown in Example 5.2. In this example, expenses are presented according to business function and comparative figures for the previous year are shown alongside the figures for the current year.

Example 5.2

Malik plc
Statement of comprehensive income for the year ended 31 December 2009

	2009 £m	2008 £m
Revenue	100.6	97.2
Cost of sales	(60.4)	(59.1)
Gross profit	40.2	38.1
Other income	4.0	3.5
Distribution expenses	(18.2)	(16.5)
Administration expenses	(10.3)	(11.2)
Other expenses	(2.1)	(2.4)
Operating profit	13.6	11.5
Finance charges	(2.0)	(1.8)
Profit before tax	11.6	9.7
Tax	(2.9)	(2.4)
Profit for the year	8.7	7.3
Other comprehensive income		
Revaluation of property, plant and equipment	20.3	6.6
Foreign currency translation differences for foreign operations	12.5	4.0
Tax on other comprehensive income	(6.0)	(2.6)
Other comprehensive income for the year, net of tax	26.8	8.0
Total comprehensive income for the year	35.5	15.3

This example adopts a single-statement approach to presenting comprehensive income. The alternative two-statement approach simply divides the information shown above into two separate parts. The income statement, which is the first statement, begins with the revenue for the year and ends with the profit for the year. The statement of comprehensive income, which is the second statement, begins with the profit for the year and ends with the total comprehensive income for the year.

Statement of changes in equity

→ The **statement of changes in equity** aims to help users to understand the changes in share capital and reserves that took place during the period. It reconciles the figures for these items at the beginning of the period with those at the end of the period. This is achieved by showing the effect on the share capital and reserves of total comprehensive income as well as the effect of share issues and purchases during the period. The effect of dividends during the period may also be shown in this statement, although dividends can be shown in the notes instead.

To see how a statement of changes in equity may be prepared, let us consider Example 5.3.

Example 5.3

At 1 January 2010 Miro plc had the following equity:

Miro plc

	£m
Share capital (£1 ordinary shares)	100
Revaluation reserve	20
Translation reserve	40
Retained earnings	150
Total equity	310

During 2010, the company made a profit for the year from normal business operations of £42 million and reported an upward revaluation of property, plant and equipment of £120 million (net of any tax that would be payable were the unrealised gains to be realised). A loss on exchange differences on translating the results of foreign operations of £10 million was also reported. To strengthen its financial position, the company issued 50 million ordinary shares during the year at a premium of £0.40. Dividends for the year were £27 million.

This information for 2010 can be set out in a statement of changes in equity as follows:

Statement of changes in equity for the year ended 31 December 2010

	Share capital £m	Share premium £m	Revaluation reserve £m	Translation reserve £m	Retained earnings £m	Total £m
Balance as at 1 January 2010	100	–	20	40	150	310
Changes in equity for 2010						
Issue of ordinary shares (Note 1)	50	20	–	–	–	70
Dividends (Note 2)	–	–	–	–	(27)	(27)
Total comprehensive income for the year (Note 3)	–	–	120	(10)	42	152
Balance at 31 December 2010	150	20	140	30	165	505

Notes:

1 The premium on the share price is transferred to a specific reserve.
2 We have chosen to show dividends in the statement of changes in equity rather than in the notes. They represent an appropriation of equity and are deducted from retained earnings.
3 The effect of each component of comprehensive income on the various components of shareholders' equity must be separately disclosed. The revaluation gain and the loss on translating foreign operations are each allocated to a specific reserve. The profit for the year is added to retained earnings.

Statement of cash flows

The statement of cash flows should help users to assess the ability of a company to generate cash and to assess the company's need for cash. The presentation requirements for this statement are set out in IAS 7 *Statement of Cash Flows*, which we shall consider in some detail in the next chapter.

Notes

The notes play an important role in helping users to understand the financial statements. They will normally contain the following information:

- a statement that the financial statements comply with relevant IFRSs;
- a summary of the measurement bases used and other significant accounting policies applied (for example, the basis of inventories valuation);
- supporting information relating to items appearing on the statement of financial position, statement of comprehensive income, statement of changes in equity and statement of cash flows; and
- other significant disclosures such as future contractual commitments that have not been recognised and financial risk management objectives and policies.

General points

The standard provides support for three key accounting conventions when preparing the financial statements. These are:

- the going concern convention;
- the accruals convention (except for the statement of cash flows); and
- the consistency convention.

These conventions were discussed in Chapters 2 and 3.

Finally, to improve the transparency of financial statements, the standard states that:

● offsetting liabilities against assets, or expenses against income, is not allowed. Thus it is not acceptable, for example, to offset a bank overdraft against a positive bank balance (where a company has both); and
● material items must be shown separately.

Selected financial reporting standards

If we look back at Real World 5.1 on page 155, we can see that we have looked at the matters covered by a number of standards (for example IAS 1 and IAS 2). There are others that we shall consider in later chapters (for example IAS 7 and IAS 27). There are also other standards that deal with quite technical areas that we need not concern ourselves with (for example, IAS 12 and IAS 19).

In this section we are going to consider two standards that we have not considered, but which have a more general application and which also have a significant influence over the way in which financial statements are prepared.

IAS 8 *Accounting Policies, Changes in Accounting Estimates and Errors*

IAS 8 sets out the criteria for selecting and changing accounting policies and the appropriate treatment for disclosing these policies. It also sets out the treatment for disclosing changes in accounting estimates and for the correction of errors. A key aim of the standard is to improve the comparability of financial statements both over time and between different businesses.

Accounting policies

Accounting policies are the principles, rules and conventions used to prepare the financial statements. Wherever possible, they should be determined by reference to an appropriate accounting standard. (The standard on inventories, for example, will provide policies to be adopted in this area.) In the absence of an appropriate standard, managers must make suitable judgements to ensure that users receive relevant and reliable information.

The general rule is that, once a particular policy has been selected and applied, it should not be changed. However, an accounting policy may be changed where

1 it is required by a new financial reporting standard; or
2 it will result in more relevant and reliable information being provided to users.

If a new accounting standard requires changes to be made, the name of the standard, and any transitional arrangements, should be disclosed. If a change is voluntary, the reasons why it will result in more relevant and reliable information should be disclosed. In both cases, the nature of the change in policy and the amount of the adjustment on relevant items and on earnings per share for both the current and the prior period should be disclosed.

Changes in accounting estimates

Managers are normally required to make various estimates when preparing financial statements.

These estimates may need revision in the light of new information. If a revised estimate affects assets, liabilities or equity, it should be adjusted in the period of the change. If it affects profit, it should be revised in the period affected. This may be in the period of change and/or in future periods.

Both the nature and amount of a change in estimate affecting the current period or future periods should be disclosed. If it is impracticable to estimate the amount, this fact must be disclosed.

Errors

Errors are omissions or misstatements in the financial statements. They may arise for a variety of reasons, which include mathematical mistakes, oversights, misinterpretation of facts and fraud. Sometimes these errors are significant in nature and/or size and are not discovered until a later period. In such a situation, the general rule is that the relevant figures for the earlier period(s) in which the errors occurred should be restated for comparison purposes. If the errors occurred before the prior periods presented for comparison, then the opening balances of assets, liabilities and equity for the earliest prior period presented should be restated. The nature of the errors and their effect on relevant items and on earnings per share for the current and the prior period(s) should also be disclosed.

IAS 10 *Events after the Reporting Period*

The main aim of IAS 10 is to clarify when financial statements should be adjusted for events that took place after the reporting period (or accounting period). The standard deals with events that occur between the end of the reporting period and the date when the financial statements are authorised to be issued both to the shareholders and to the general public. Two types of events are identified:

1 those providing evidence of conditions that existed before the end of the reporting period (adjusting events); and
2 those indicating conditions arising after the end of the reporting period (non-adjusting events).

The standard requires that financial statements should incorporate only the adjusting events.

Activity 5.7

Vorta plc received the following information between the end of the reporting period and the date at which the financial statements were authorised for issue:

1 Inventories which were reported in the statement of financial position at an estimated net realisable value of £250,000 were sold shortly after the year end for £200,000.
2 There was a decline of £150,000 in the market value of investments after the end of the reporting period.
3 An error was discovered which indicated that the trade receivables figure on the statement of financial position was understated by £220,000.

Which of the above are adjusting events?

Items 1 and 3 meet the definition of an adjusting event whereas item 2 meets the definition of a non-adjusting event. This is because, with items 1 and 3, we have received additional information on the position at the year end. With item 2, a change has occurred *after* the year end.

The standard clarifies two important points concerning events after the reporting period. First, if a dividend is declared for equity shareholders after the reporting period, it should not be treated as a liability in the financial statements. In the past it was normal practice to treat such dividends as liabilities. Second, if it becomes clear after the reporting period that the business will cease trading, the going concern assumption will not apply. As a result the financial statements must be prepared using a fundamentally different basis for valuation. It will mean, for example, that assets will be shown at their estimated realisable values.

The date at which the financial statements were authorised for issue must be disclosed as it is important to understanding what should and should not be included. There should also be disclosure of who authorised the issue.

Activity 5.8

Who do you think will normally authorise the issue of the financial statements?

It is normally the board of directors.

Where non-adjusting events are significant, they may influence users' decisions. The standard therefore requires significant non-adjusting events to be disclosed by way of a note. A major restructuring, a plan to discontinue an operation and the proposed purchase of a major asset are examples of non-adjusting events that might be disclosed. The standard requires that the nature of the event and its likely financial effect be disclosed. If the financial effect cannot be reliably estimated, this fact should be disclosed.

Real World 5.2 is the note to the financial statements of Tottenham Hotspur plc that deals with non-adjusting events that occurred between the statement of financial position date (30 June 2009) and the date of issue of the financial statements (9 November 2009). It relates mainly to transfers of players during the Summer 2009 transfer window.

Real World 5.2

A window of opportunity for Spurs

Since the balance sheet [statement of financial position] date the following events have occurred:

P Crouch was bought from Portsmouth
K Naughton was bought from Sheffield United
K Walker was bought from Sheffield United
S Bassong was bought from Newcastle United
N Kranjcar was bought from Portsmouth
J Walker joined
D Zokora was sold to Sevilla
C Gunter was sold to Nottingham Forest
D Bent was sold to Sunderland
P Chimbonda was sold to Blackburn Rovers
KP Boateng was sold to Portsmouth
Y Berchiche was transferred to Real Valladolid
Gilberto was released

Including Football League levies, the uncontingent net costs of these transactions amounted to approximately £8,640,000.

The contingent liability from these transactions amounts to approximately £4,770,000 and the contingent asset amounts to approximately £10,541,000.

Post year end there was a placing of £15m issuing an additional 30 million ordinary shares. ENIC Group subscribed for 27.8m of these new ordinary shares.

These contingent liabilities and assets relate to additional transfer fees that will be payable or receivable, respectively, dependent on the performance of particular players in the above list. These additional fees will be specified in the transfer contracts of these players.

Source: Tottenham Hotspur plc Annual Report 2009, p. 59.

Figure 5.2 summarises the main points to be considered when applying IAS 10.

Figure 5.2   Applying IAS 10

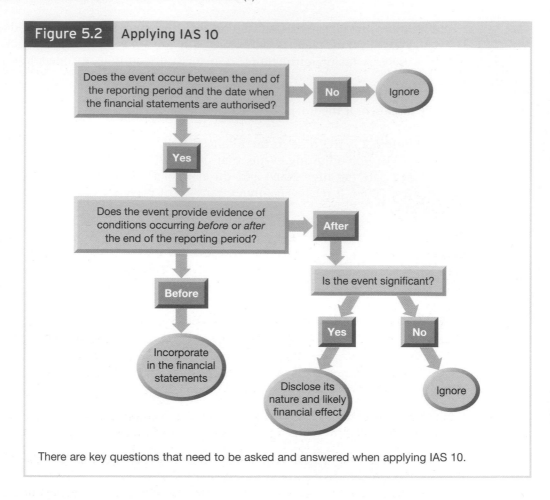

There are key questions that need to be asked and answered when applying IAS 10.

The framework of principles

In Chapters 2 and 3 we came across various accounting conventions such as the prudence, historic cost and going concern conventions. These conventions were developed as a practical response to particular problems that were confronted when preparing financial statements. They have stood the test of time and are still of value to preparers today. However, they do not provide, and were never designed to provide, a framework of principles to guide the development of financial statements. As we grapple with increasingly complex financial reporting problems, the need to have a sound understanding of *why* we account for things in a particular way becomes more pressing. Knowing *why* we account, rather than simply *how* we account, is vital if we are to improve the quality of financial statements.

In recent years, much effort has been expended in various countries, including the UK, to develop a clear **framework of principles** that will guide us in the development of accounting. Such a framework should provide clear answers to such fundamental questions as:

● Who are the main users of financial statements?
● What is the purpose of financial statements?
● What qualities should financial information possess?

- What are the main elements of financial statements?
- How should these elements be defined, recognised and measured?

If these questions can be answered, accounting rule makers, such as the IASB, will be in a stronger position to identify best practice and to develop more coherent rules. This should, in turn, increase the credibility of financial reports in the eyes of users. It may even help reduce the possible number of rules, because some issues may be resolved by reference to the application of general principles rather than by the generation of further rules.

The IASB framework

The quest for a framework of accounting principles began in earnest in the 1970s when the Financial Accounting Standards Board (FASB) in the US devoted a very large amount of time and resources to this endeavour. This resulted in a broad framework of principles, which other rule-making bodies, including the IASB, have drawn upon when developing their own frameworks.

The IASB has produced the *Framework for the Preparation and Presentation of Financial Statements*, which begins by discussing the main user groups and their needs. This is well-trodden territory and the various groups and needs identified are in line with those set out in the sections on this topic in Chapter 1. The framework goes on to identify the objective of financial statements, which is

> to provide information about the financial position, performance and changes in financial position of an enterprise that is useful to a wide range of users in making economic decisions.

This reflects the mainstream view and is similar to the objective of financial statements that others have developed in recent years.

The IASB framework sets out the qualitative characteristics that make financial statements useful. The main characteristics identified are relevance, reliability, comparability and understandability; these were also discussed in Chapter 1. The framework also identifies the main elements of financial statements as assets, liabilities, equity, income and expense; and a definition of each element is provided. The definitions adopted hold no surprises and are similar to those adopted by other rule-making bodies and to those that we discussed earlier, in Chapters 2 and 3.

The IASB framework identifies different valuation bases in use such as historic cost, current cost and realisable value, but does not indicate a preference for a particular valuation method. It simply notes that historic cost is the most widely used method of valuation (although fair values are now increasingly used in International Financial Reporting Standards). Finally, the framework discusses the type of capital base that a business should try to maintain. It includes a discussion of the two main types of capital base – financial capital and physical capital – but, again, expresses no preference as to which should be maintained. The IASB framework does not have the same legal status as the IASB standards. Nevertheless, it offers guidance for dealing with accounting issues, particularly where no relevant accounting standard exists.

Overall, the IASB framework has provoked little debate and the principles and definitions adopted appear to enjoy widespread acceptance. There has been some criticism, mainly from academics, that the framework is really a descriptive document and does not provide theoretical underpinning to the financial statements. There has also been some criticism of the definitions of the elements of the financial statements. However, these criticisms have not sparked any major controversies.

In 2004, the IASB and the US FASB agreed to undertake a joint project for the development of a common conceptual framework. This project revisits many of the areas covered by the existing IASB framework and has already led to the publication of various drafts and discussion papers. However, the project is still continuing.

Problems with standards

There is broad agreement that financial reporting standards have improved the quality of financial statements. Nevertheless, we should be alert to the potential problems associated with their use. Some of these problems are discussed below.

Standards may inhibit change

By setting out rigid procedures to be followed, standards may stifle the development of new and better procedures. Progress in financial reporting may require that businesses have the freedom to experiment and innovate. Unless they have this freedom, accounting practice may become ossified.

Although this problem cannot be easily dismissed, history has shown that financial reporting standards are changed when they prove to be ineffective or inadequate. Over the years, numerous standards have been either modified or withdrawn. Furthermore, developing a new standard involves wide consultation with interested parties and much debate about what constitutes best practice. Financial reporting standards can, therefore, provide the stimulus for new thinking.

Standards may impose false conformity

No two businesses are identical: each will have its own characteristics and operating methods. By insisting on common standards, there is a danger that the unique aspects of each business will be obscured.

Although this argument has some merit, it can be taken too far. Differences between businesses can be overstated and their common features understated. Furthermore, there is nothing to stop standards allowing a limited choice between accounting methods, which may help in reflecting individual characteristics.

Activity 5.9

Think back to Chapter 3. Can you recall an area of accounting where the relevant standard allowed some choice of accounting method?

The inventories standard permits some choice over inventories costing methods and the depreciation standard permits some choice over depreciation methods.

Finally, a business can, in exceptional circumstances, depart from an accounting standard where it conflicts with the requirement to provide a fair presentation of financial health. Businesses do not, therefore, have to comply with unreasonable rules.

Standards involve consensus-seeking

Financial reporting standards affect certain groups who must be willing to accept them. Unless this happens, standards cannot be implemented effectively. The development of standards may, therefore, be influenced more by the need to achieve consensus than by technical considerations of what is the best approach to adopt. When this occurs, the quality of financial statements will suffer.

To date, there is no evidence to suggest this has been a major problem. In order to command authority, standard-setters must be responsive to the groups affected. In a democracy this is how authority is legitimised. The trick that they must achieve, however, is to make rules that are both technically sound and broadly acceptable.

Standards can be costly

There is now an intricate web of financial reporting standards surrounding large businesses. The costs of complying with these rules are high and are borne by shareholders. Each additional standard that incurs costs for businesses means that less money is available for distribution to shareholders. There is an assumption that the benefits to shareholders of these standards outweigh their costs, but what if this is not the case? It is reasonable to expect standard-setters to carry out an assessment of costs and benefits before adding to the burden of rules.

Standards can be complex

There is a growing concern that international financial reporting standards are making financial statements too complex to be useful to shareholders. This has led to calls for better regulation. International standards are meant to be based on principles rather than on legalistic rules, and this should help to prevent excessive complexity. Many, however, question whether this principles-based approach is working effectively. **Real World 5.3** gives a flavour of the problem.

Real World 5.3

Complexity is standard practice

FT

Every year when the Finance Bill is published the accountancy profession takes a look at the number of pages it has grown to and complains about being overwhelmed with detail. The same is becoming true of manuals to deal with the growing minutiae of international financial reporting standards (IFRS). In February accounting firm Ernst & Young will publish its annual volume. 'Our book will be 3,200 pages long,' explains Will Rainey, the firm's global director of IFRS services. 'That hardly suggests principles have triumphed over rules.'

And this is the problem.

Sir David Tweedie, chairman of the International Accounting Standards Board (IASB), which promulgates IFRS, is fond of stating the principles that should lie behind a leasing standard, for example. He puts the fundamental principle in one sentence – and then says

Real World 5.3 continued

the only other guidance that ought to exist in the standard is: 'If in doubt, read the first sentence again'. Sadly, the accountancy profession has not attained that nirvana.

However, the pendulum is swinging towards a more principles-based approach. At a round table organised by the Institute of Chartered Accountants of Scotland (ICAS) in Brussels last autumn, it became clear that complexity and detail were still at the root of worries about IFRS. Most of the Europeans present blamed the detail on the influence of US financial reporting that has tended to be entangled in the detail created by a more legalistic culture.

Stig Enevoldsen is chairman of the technical expert group of the European Financial Reporting Advisory Group (EFRAG), which advises the EU on whether each new IFRS that comes along is technically valid and advances European interests. He praises moves towards principles but says the greater complexity often came from the IASB itself. Regulators need to recognise that it is possible to have more than one solution to an accounting problem, but much of the confusion is down to the Big Four accounting firms for providing more guidance to audit staff. He wanted companies and auditors to take ownership of judgements they made.

The efforts of ICAS, which has been a highly-effective cheerleader for the argument that principles-based standards should outweigh rules, are bearing fruit. Its president, Isobel Sharp of Deloitte, is in no doubt the battle has virtually been won as an argument. What is needed now is tangible efforts to bring about the change. 'There is a great consensus wherever you go,' she says, 'but now a principled approach needs to be achieved.'

That is the next step. But there are inherent dangers in that process. In the US, moves are afoot that will, eventually, allow US companies to follow the rest of the world and adopt IFRS as their financial reporting system. But the problem is that the US system is founded on a mass of complex rules and it will be hard to change that culture. Likewise, many Europeans fear that bringing the US into the fold will entail too many concessions to a rule-based system.

Source: 'Battlelines are drawn up for fight on standards', Robert Bruce, *Financial Times*, 7 January 2008.

Accounting rules or accounting choice?

The alternative to a rule-based approach is to allow businesses freedom of choice in the accounting methods adopted. Instead of creating standards for all to follow, shareholders of each business should decide how much and what kind of information they require. It is argued that competitive forces should help to ensure that managers are responsive to shareholders' requirements.

Activity 5.10

What sort of competitive forces may encourage managers to be responsive?

They may include competition for funds and competition for managers' jobs.

It would be nice to think that the supply of financial information could be left to competitive forces. There are times, however, when these forces are weak. There are also times when managers have an incentive to conceal relevant information from shareholders.

Activity 5.11

What sort of information might managers have an incentive to conceal?

Managers may wish to conceal information that would cast doubt on their ability or integrity or might prevent the business from obtaining funds. This may include information relating to excessive management rewards, poor business performance or weak financial health.

Managers also have an incentive to select accounting methods and policies that enhance reported profits, particularly if they are linked to managerial rewards. This point will be discussed further when we discuss creative accounting later in the chapter.

Given the management incentives described, there is always a risk that shareholders will not receive relevant and reliable information. Financial reporting standards combat this risk by imposing discipline on managers in financial reporting. This disciplinary role provided a major impetus for the creation of standards.

With freedom of choice comes the problem of comparability. Differences between businesses in terms of shareholder needs and in the strength of competitive forces will result in differences in the quantity and quality of information disclosed – which leads us back to one of the key aims of financial reporting standards.

The auditors' role

Shareholders are required to elect a qualified and independent person or, more usually, a firm to act as **auditors**. The auditors' main duty is to report whether, in their opinion, the financial statements do what they are supposed to do, namely to show a true and fair view of the financial performance, position and cash flows of the company. To be able to form such an opinion, auditors must carefully scrutinise the annual financial statements and the underlying evidence upon which they are based. In particular, they will examine the accounting principles followed, the accounting estimates made and the robustness of the company's internal control systems. The auditors' opinion must be included with the financial statements sent to the shareholders and to the Registrar of Companies.

The relationship between the shareholders, the directors and the auditors is illustrated in Figure 5.3. This shows that the shareholders elect the directors to act on their behalf, in the day-to-day running of the company. The directors are then required to 'account' to the shareholders on the performance, position and cash flows of the company, on an annual basis. The shareholders also elect auditors, whose role it is to give the shareholders an independent view of the truth and fairness of the financial statements prepared by the directors.

Figure 5.3	The relationship between the shareholders, the directors and the auditors

The directors are appointed by the shareholders to manage the company on the shareholders' behalf. The directors are required to report each year to the shareholders, principally by means of financial statements, on the company's performance, position and cash flows. To give greater confidence in the statements, the shareholders also appoint auditors to investigate the reports and to express an opinion on their reliability.

Directors' report

In addition to preparing the financial statements, UK law requires the directors to prepare an annual report to shareholders and other interested parties. The **directors' report** will contain both financial and non-financial information, which goes beyond that contained in the financial statements. The information to be disclosed is diverse and will include the names of those who were directors during the year, the principal activities of the company and any recommended dividend. The most important element of the report, however, is probably the **business review**. This is aimed at helping shareholders to assess how well the directors have performed. It should provide an analysis of financial performance and position and should also set out the principal risks and uncertainties facing the business. We shall consider this review in some detail in Chapter 10.

In addition to disclosing the above information, the directors' report must contain a declaration that the directors are not aware of any other information that the auditors might need in preparing their audit report. Furthermore, the report must declare that the directors have taken steps to ensure that the auditors are aware of all relevant information. The auditors do not carry out an audit of the directors' report. However, they will check to see that the information in the report is consistent with that contained in the audited financial statements.

For companies listed on the Stock Exchange, the law also requires the publication of an annual directors' remuneration report. This should help shareholders to assess whether the rewards received by directors are appropriate.

Summary financial statements

We saw earlier that the directors must provide each shareholder with a copy of the annual financial statements. For large businesses, these financial statements can be extremely detailed and complicated. Along with the accompanying notes, they may extend over many pages. It is possible, however, for the directors to provide a summarised version of the full financial statements as an alternative.

→ The main advantages of providing **summary financial statements** are that:

- many shareholders do not wish to receive the full version because they may not have the time, interest or skill necessary to be able to gain much from it;
- directors could improve their communication with their shareholders by providing something closer to the needs of many shareholders;
- reproducing and posting copies of the full version is expensive and a waste of resources where particular shareholders do not wish to receive it.

It has now become common practice for large businesses to send all of their shareholders who are private individuals a copy of the summary financial statements, with a clear message that a copy of the full version is available on request. Institutional investors (insurance companies, pension funds and so on) tend to receive a full version as a matter of routine.

Critics of summary financial statements, however, argue that it is dangerous for shareholders to receive financial reports that attempt to simplify complexity. Any attempt to do so runs the risk of discarding important information and distorting the message. If a shareholder is unwilling or unable to develop the necessary accounting skills, or to spend the necessary time to examine the full version of the financial statements, the proper solution is either to seek expert advice or to invest in mutual funds managed by experts. Viewed from this perspective, the best thing that a business can do to help less sophisticated shareholders is to provide more detailed information to experts, such as investment analysts.

Creative accounting

Despite the proliferation of accounting rules and the independent checks that are imposed, concerns over the quality of published financial statements surface from time to time. There are occasions when directors apply particular accounting policies, or structure particular transactions, in such a way as to portray a picture of financial health that is in line with what they want users to see, rather than what is a true and fair view of financial position and performance. Misrepresenting the performance and
→ position of a business in this way is referred to as **creative accounting** and it poses a major problem for accounting rule makers and for society generally.

Activity 5.12

Why might the directors of a company engage in creative accounting?

There are many reasons including:

- to get around restrictions (for example, to report sufficient profit to pay a dividend);
- to avoid government action (for example, the taxation of excessive profits);
- to hide poor management decisions;
- to achieve sales revenue or profit targets, thereby ensuring that performance bonuses are paid to the directors;
- to attract new share capital or long-term borrowing by showing an apparently healthy financial position; and
- to satisfy the demands of major investors concerning levels of return.

Creative accounting methods

The ways in which unscrupulous directors can manipulate the financial statements are many and varied. However, they usually involve adopting novel or unorthodox practices for reporting key elements of the financial statements such as revenue, expenses, assets and liabilities. They may also involve the use of complicated or obscure transactions in an attempt to hide the underlying economic reality. The manipulation carried out may be designed either to bend the rules or to break them. Below we consider some of the more important ways in which rules may be bent or broken.

Misstating revenue

Some creative accounting methods are designed to overstate the revenue for a period. These methods often involve the early recognition of sales revenue or the reporting of sales transactions that have no real substance. **Real World 5.4** provides examples of both types of revenue manipulation.

 Real World 5.4

Overstating revenue

Hollow swaps: telecoms companies sell useless fibre optic capacity to each other in order to generate revenues on their income statements. Example: Global Crossing.

Channel stuffing: a company floods the market with more products than its distributors can sell, artificially boosting its sales. SSL, the condom maker, shifted £60 million in excess inventories on to trade customers. Also known as 'trade loading'.

Round tripping: also known as 'in-and-out trading'. Used to notorious effect by Enron. Two or more traders buy and sell energy among themselves for the same price and at the same time. Inflates trading volumes and makes participants appear to be doing more business than they really are.

Pre-dispatching: goods such as carpets are marked as 'sold' as soon as an order is placed. . . . This inflates sales and profits.

Note that some of the techniques used, such as round tripping, may inflate the sales revenue for a period but will not inflate reported profits. Nevertheless, this may still benefit the business. Sales revenue growth has become an important yardstick of performance for some investors and can affect the value they place on the business.

Source: 'Dirty laundry: how companies fudge the numbers', *The Times*, Business Section, 22 September 2002. nisyndication.com.

The manipulation of revenue has been at the heart of many of the accounting scandals recently exposed. Given its critical role in the measurement of performance, this is, perhaps, not surprising. **Real World 5.5** provides an example of how the financial results of one well-known business were distorted by the overstatement of sales revenues.

Real World 5.5

Recomputing the numbers

FT

In August 2007, Dell (the computer manufacturer) admitted that some unnamed 'senior executives' had been involved in a scheme to overstate sales revenue figures during the period 2003 to 2007. This was done in an attempt to make it appear that quarterly sales targets had been met, when in fact this was not the case. The overstatement of sales revenue was estimated to amount to $92m; about 1 per cent of total profit over the period concerned.

Source: 'Dell to lower writedowns on restated earnings', Kevin Allison, *Financial Times*, 30 October 2007.

Massaging expenses

Some creative accounting methods focus on the manipulation of expenses. Those expenses that rely on directors' estimates of the future or their choice of accounting policy are particularly vulnerable to manipulation.

Activity 5.13

Can you identify the kind of expenses where the directors make estimates or choices in the ways described?

These include certain expenses that we discussed in Chapter 3, such as:

- depreciation of property, plant and equipment
- amortisation of intangible assets, such as goodwill
- inventories (cost of sales)
- allowances for trade receivables.

By changing estimates about the future (for example, the useful life or residual value of an asset), or by changing accounting policies (for example, switching from FIFO to AVCO), it may be possible to derive an expense figure, and consequently a profit figure, that suits the directors.

The incorrect 'capitalisation' of expenses may also be used as a means of manipulation. This involves treating expenses as if they were amounts incurred to acquire or develop non-current assets, rather than amounts consumed during the period. The net effect of this is that the expenses will be unfairly understated and profit will, therefore, be unfairly boosted. Businesses that build their own assets are often best placed to undertake this form of malpractice.

Activity 5.14

What would be the effect on the profits and total assets of a business of incorrectly capitalising expenses?

Both would be artificially inflated. Reported profits would increase because expenses would be reduced. Total assets would be increased because the expenses would be incorrectly treated as non-current assets.

Real World 5.6 provides an example of one business that capitalised expenses on a huge scale.

Real World 5.6

Sorry - wrong numbers   **FT**

One particularly notorious case of capitalising expenses is alleged to have occurred in the financial statements of WorldCom (now renamed MCI). This company, which is a large US telecommunications business, is alleged to have overstated profits by treating certain operating expenses, such as basic network maintenance, as capital expenditure. This happened over a fifteen-month period during 2001 and 2002. To correct for this overstatement, profits had to be reduced by a massive $3.8 billion.

Source: Based on two personal views on WorldCom posted on the FT.com site, 27 June 2002.

Concealing 'bad news'

Some creative accounting methods focus on the concealment of losses or liabilities. The financial statements can look much healthier if these can somehow be eliminated. One way of doing this is to create a 'separate' entity that will take over the losses or liabilities.

Real World 5.7 describes how one large business concealed losses and liabilities.

Real World 5.7

For a very special purpose

Perhaps the most well-known case of concealment of losses and liabilities concerned the Enron Corporation. This was a large US energy business that used 'special purpose entities' (SPEs) as a means of concealment. SPEs were used by Enron to rid itself of problem assets that were falling in value, such as its broadband operations. In addition, liabilities were transferred to these entities to help Enron's statement of financial position look healthier. The company had to keep its gearing ratios (the relationship between borrowing and equity) within particular limits to satisfy credit-rating agencies and SPEs were used to achieve this. The SPEs used for concealment purposes were not independent of the company and should have been consolidated in the statement of financial position of Enron, along with their losses and liabilities.

When these, and other accounting irregularities, were discovered in 2001, there was a restatement of Enron's financial performance and position to reflect the consolidation of the SPEs, which had previously been omitted. As a result of this restatement, the company recognised $591 million in losses over the preceding four years and an additional $628 million worth of liabilities at the end of 2000.

The company collapsed at the end of 2001.

Source: 'The rise and fall of Enron', C. William Thomas, *Journal of Accountancy*, vol. 194, no. 3, 2002. This article represents the opinions of the author, which are not necessarily those of the Texas Society of Certified Public Accountants.

Misstating assets

There are various ways in which assets may be misstated. These include:

- using asset values that are higher than their fair market values;
- capitalising costs that should have been written off as expenses, as described earlier;
- recording assets that are not owned or which do not exist.

Real World 5.8 describes how one large business reported an asset that did not exist.

Real World 5.8

When things go sour

Parmalat, a large Italian dairy-and-food business, announced in December 2003 that a bank account held in the Cayman Islands with the Bank of America did not have, as had been previously reported, a balance of €3.95 billion. The fake balance turned out to be part of a web of deception: it had simply been 'invented' in order to help offset more than €16 billion of outstanding borrowings. According to Italian prosecutors, the business had borrowed heavily on the strength of fictitious sales revenues.

A Cayman Islands subsidiary, which was supposed to hold the fake bank balance, engaged in fictitious trading in an attempt to conceal the true nature of the deception. This included the supply of 300,000 tons of milk powder from a fake Singapore-based business to a Cuban business through the subsidiary.

Source: Based on 'How it all went so sour', Peter Gumbel, *Time Europe Magazine*, 21 November 2004.

Inadequate disclosure

Directors may misrepresent or try to conceal certain information. This may relate to commitments made, key changes in accounting policies or estimates, significant events and so on. The information may also relate to financial transactions between the directors and the business. **Real World 5.9** provides such an example.

Real World 5.9

Banking on a loan

Anglo Irish Bank chairman Sean Fitzpatrick dramatically resigned last night, admitting he had hidden a massive €87 million in loans from the bank. Mr Fitzpatrick's personal borrowings from the bank were more than twice the amount shown for loans to all thirteen directors in last year's annual accounts. Another high-profile director, Lar Bradshaw, until recently chairman of Dublin Docklands Development Authority, also resigned from the board. Anglo Irish Bank said that a loan Mr Bradshaw held jointly with Mr Fitzpatrick was temporarily transferred to another bank prior to a year-end audit. 'While Mr Bradshaw was unaware that this transfer took place, he believed that it was in the bank's best interest that he should resign', Anglo said. . . .

   As required under accounting rules, company figures showed that directors had loans of €41 million from Anglo Irish. Analysts were shocked to learn last night that the true figure of directors' borrowings at present is actually €150 million. Mr Fitzpatrick's €87 million makes up more than half of this. A statement from the bank said Mr Fitzpatrick would move his loans to another bank, understood to be Irish Nationwide, before the end of each financial year, so that they would not be recorded by the auditors. The loans were then moved back to Anglo Irish in a practice which continued for eight years.

Source: 'Anglo Irish bank chief quits over hiding €87m loan', www.belfasttelegraph.co.uk, 19 December 2008.

Figure 5.4 summarises the main methods of creative accounting.

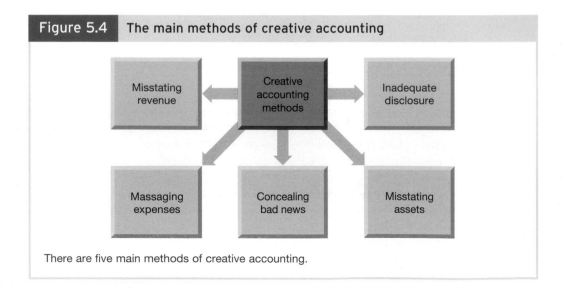

Figure 5.4 **The main methods of creative accounting**

There are five main methods of creative accounting.

Checking for creative accounting

When examining the financial statements of a business, a number of checks may be carried out on the financial statements to help gain a feel for their reliability. These can include checks to see whether

- the reported profits are significantly higher than the operating cash flows for the period, which may suggest that profits have been overstated;
- the tax charge is low in relation to reported profits, which may suggest, again, that profits are overstated, although there may be other, more innocent explanations;
- the valuation methods used for assets held are based on historic cost or fair values and, if the latter approach has been used, why and how the fair values were determined;
- there have been changes in accounting policies over the period, particularly in key areas such as revenue recognition, inventories valuation and depreciation;
- the accounting policies adopted are in line with those adopted by the rest of the industry;
- the auditors' report gives a 'clean bill of health' to the financial statements; and
- the 'small print', that is the notes to the financial statements, is not being used to hide significant events or changes.

Real World 5.10 describes the emphasis that one analyst places on this last check.

Real World 5.10

Taking note   FT

Alistair Hodgson, investment manager at private client stockbroker Pilling and Co, says:

> I almost look at the notes more than I look at the main figures at first. The notes tend to hold the key to anything that looks strange. I look to pick out things that the auditor has told the company to declare – the kind of thing they might not want to declare, but they have got to do so in order to make the accounts honest.

Source: 'It pays to read between the lines', *Financial Times*, 17 September 2005.

Checks may also be carried out to provide confirmation of positive financial health. These may include checks to see whether

- the business is paying increased dividends;
- the directors are buying shares in the business.

Although the various checks described are useful, they cannot be used to guarantee the reliability of the financial statements. Some creative accounting practices may be very deeply seated and may go undetected for years.

Creative accounting and economic growth

Some years ago there was a wave of creative accounting scandals, particularly in the US but also in Europe; however, it seems that this wave has now subsided. The quality of financial statements is improving and, it is to be hoped, trust among investors and others is being restored. As a result of the actions taken by various regulatory bodies and by accounting rule makers, creative accounting has become a more risky and difficult process for those who attempt it. However, it will never disappear completely and a further wave of creative accounting scandals may occur in the future.

The recent wave coincided with a period of strong economic growth and, during good economic times, investors and auditors become less vigilant. Thus, the opportunity to manipulate the figures becomes easier. We must not, therefore, become too complacent. Things may change again when we next experience a period of strong growth.

Self-assessment question 5.1

You have overheard the following statements:

(a) 'Dividends announced between the end of the reporting period and the date at which the financial reports are authorised for publication, which relate to the reporting period just ended, should be treated as a liability in the statement of financial position at the end of that period.'

(b) 'IAS 1 provides support for three key accounting conventions – accruals, historic cost and consistency.'

(c) 'IAS 1 permits bank overdrafts to be offset against positive bank balances when preparing the statement of financial position.'

(d) 'Accounting policies can only be changed if it is required by a new financial reporting standard.'

(e) 'All non-adjusting events occurring between the end of the reporting period and the date at which the financial statements are authorised for issue should be ignored.'

(f) 'All companies must publish an annual directors' remuneration report.'

Required:
Critically comment on each of these statements.

The solution to this question can be found at the back of the book on pages 475–476.

Summary

The main points of this chapter may be summarised as follows:

Directors' duty

- Separation of ownership from day-to-day control creates a need for directors to be accountable.
- To fulfil this need, the directors have a duty to prepare and publish financial statements.
- These financial statements must provide a fair representation of the financial health of the business.

The need for accounting rules

- Accounting rules are necessary in order to avoid unacceptable accounting practices and to improve the comparability of financial statements.
- This should give greater confidence in the integrity of financial statements.

Accounting rules

- The International Accounting Standards Board (IASB) has become an important source of rules.
- Company law and the London Stock Exchange are also sources of rules for UK companies.

Presenting financial statements

- IAS 1 sets out the structure and content of financial statements.
- It identifies four financial statements: the statement of financial position, statement of comprehensive income, statement of changes in equity and statement of cash flows. In addition notes are required.
- The financial statements must provide a fair representation of the financial health of a company and this will only normally be achieved by adherence to relevant IASB standards.
- IAS 1 identifies information to be shown in the various financial statements and some of the principles to be followed in preparing the statements.

Selected financial reporting standards

- IAS 8 sets out the criteria for selecting and changing accounting policies.
- It also sets out the treatment for disclosing changes in accounting estimates and for the correction of errors.
- IAS 10 aims to clarify when financial statements should be adjusted for events that took place after the reporting period.
- Only events that provide evidence of conditions before the end of the reporting period lead to adjustments to the financial statements.

Framework of principles

- This helps to underpin accounting rules.
- The IASB framework identifies and discusses: the users of financial statements, the objective of financial statements, the qualitative characteristics of financial statements, the elements of financial statements, different valuation bases and different capital maintenance bases.
- The IASB framework draws on earlier work by other rule-making bodies.

Problems with standards

- Standards may inhibit change.
- They may impose false conformity.
- They involve consensus-seeking.
- They can be costly.
- They can introduce complexity.
- The alternative is to allow accounting choice. This, however, leads to the risk of manipulation, inadequate disclosure and lack of comparability.

Other statutory reports

- The auditors' report provides an opinion by an independent auditor concerning whether the financial statements provide a true and fair view of the financial health of a business.

- The directors' report contains information of a financial and a non-financial nature, which goes beyond that contained in the financial statements.
- For companies quoted on the Stock Exchange, an annual directors' remuneration report must also be prepared.

Summary financial statements

- Summary financial statements offer a condensed version of the full financial statements.
- They are designed to improve communication between the directors and shareholders with less sophisticated needs.
- Critics argue, however, that it is dangerous to try to simplify complexity.

Creative accounting

- Despite the accounting rules in place there have been examples of creative accounting by directors.
- This involves using accounting practices to show what the directors would like users to see rather than what is a fair representation of reality.
- The main forms of creative accounting involve misstating revenues, massaging expenses, concealing bad news, misstating assets, and inadequate disclosure.
- There are various checks that can be carried out to the financial statements to see whether creative accounting practices may have been used.

 Key terms

International Accounting Standards p. 153	**framework of principles** p. 166
	auditors p. 171
International Financial Reporting Standards p. 153	**directors' report** p. 172
	business review p. 172
statement of comprehensive income p. 158	**summary financial statements** p. 173
statement of changes in equity p. 160	**creative accounting** p. 173

Further reading

If you would like to explore the topics covered in this chapter in more depth, we recommend the following books:

Elliott, B. and Elliott, J., *Financial Accounting and Reporting*, 13th edn, Financial Times Prentice Hall, 2009, Chapters 5 to 8.

IASC Foundation Education, *A Guide through International Financial Reporting Standards (IFRSs) 2009*, September 2009.

KPMG, *Insights into IFRS*, 6th edn, 2009/10, Sweet and Maxwell, 2009.

Melville, A., *International Financial Reporting*, 2nd edn, Financial Times Prentice Hall, 2009, Chapters 1 to 4.

Review questions

Solutions to these questions can be found at the back of the book on pages 484–485.

5.1 When preparing financial statements for the current period, Woden plc found that it had under-stated its revenue in error by £2 million in the previous period. How should the business report this error?

5.2 What are accounting policies and how should they be determined?

5.3 Why do we need accounting rules?

5.4 What are the main methods of creative accounting?

Exercises

Exercises 5.6 to 5.8 are more advanced than 5.1 to 5.5. Those with coloured numbers have answers at the back of the book, starting on page 500.
    If you wish to try more exercises, visit the students' side of the Companion Website.

5.1 'Searching for an agreed framework of principles for accounting rules is likely to be a journey without an ending.' Discuss.

5.2 'Financial reporting standards eliminate the need for accountants to make judgements and so lower their professional status.' Do you agree?

5.3 Thor plc has the following events occur between the end of the reporting period and the date the financial statements were authorised for issue:

1 The discovery that, during the reporting period, an employee had defrauded the business of £120,000.
2 The bankruptcy of a customer who owes the business £280,000. This sum was outstanding at the end of the reporting period.
3 A fire occurring after the reporting period that destroyed a large factory owned by Thor plc.
4 An increase in the value of land held by Thor plc by £10 million resulted from a change in the planning laws, which occurred after the end of the reporting period.

According to IAS 10 (*Events after the Reporting Period*), how should each of these events be treated?

5.4 What problems are likely to be encountered when preparing summary financial statements for shareholders?

5.5   The following information was extracted from the financial statements of I. Ching (Booksellers) plc for the year to 31 December 2009:

	£m
Finance charges	40
Cost of sales	460
Distribution expenses	110
Revenue	943
Administrative expenses	212
Other expenses	25
Gain on revaluation of property, plant and equipment	20
Loss on foreign currency translations on foreign operations	15
Tax on profit for the year	24
Tax on other components of comprehensive income	1

Prepare a statement of comprehensive income for the year ended 31 December 2009 that is set out in accordance with the requirements of IAS 1 *Presentation of Financial Statements*.

5.6   Manet plc had the following share capital and reserves as at 1 January 2009:

	£m
Share capital (£0.25 ordinary shares)	250
Share premium account	50
Revaluation reserve	120
Currency translation reserve	15
Retained earnings	380
Total equity	815

During the year to 31 December 2009, the company revalued property, plant and equipment upwards by £30 million and made a loss on foreign exchange translation of foreign operations of £5 million. The company made a profit for the year from normal operations of £160 million and the dividend was £80 million.

Prepare a statement of changes in equity in accordance with the requirements of IAS 1 *Presentation of Financial Statements*.

5.7   Professor Myddleton argues that financial reporting standards should be limited to disclosure requirements and should not impose rules on companies as to how to measure particular items in the financial statements. He states:

> The volume of accounting instructions is already high. If things go on like this, where will we be in 20 or 30 years' time? On balance I conclude we would be better off without any standards on accounting measurement. There could still be some disclosure requirements for listed companies, though probably less than now.

Do you agree with this idea? Discuss.

5.8 You have overheard the following statements:

(a) 'The role of independent auditors is to prepare the financial statements of the company.'

(b) 'International Accounting Standards (IASs) apply to all companies, but Stock Exchange listed companies must also adhere to International Financial Reporting Standards (IFRSs).'

(c) 'All listed companies in European Union states must follow IASs and IFRSs.'

(d) 'According to IAS 1, companies' financial statements must show an "accurate representation" of what they purport to show.'

(e) 'IAS 1 leaves it to individual companies to decide the format that they use in the statement of financial position.'

(f) 'The statement of changes in equity deals with unrealised profits and gains, for example an upward revaluation of a non-current asset.'

(g) 'If a majority of the shareholders of a listed company agree, the company need not produce a full set of financial statements, but can just produce summary financial statements.'

Critically comment on each of these statements.

6

Measuring and reporting cash flows

Introduction

This chapter is devoted to the third major financial statement identified in Chapter 2: the statement of cash flows. This statement reports the movements of cash over a period and the effect of these movements on the cash position of the business. It is an important financial statement because cash is vital to the survival of a business. Without cash, a business cannot operate.

In this chapter, we shall see how the statement of cash flows is prepared and how the information that it contains may be interpreted. We shall also see why the deficiencies of the income statement in identifying and explaining cash flows make a separate statement necessary.

The statement of cash flows is being considered after the chapters on limited companies because the format of the statement requires an understanding of this type of business. Nearly all limited companies are required to provide a statement of cash flows for shareholders and other users as part of their annual financial reports.

Learning outcomes

When you have completed this chapter, you should be able to:

- discuss the crucial importance of cash to a business;
- explain the nature of the statement of cash flows and discuss how it can be helpful in identifying cash flow problems;
- prepare a statement of cash flows;
- interpret a statement of cash flows.

The statement of cash flows

The statement of cash flows is a fairly recent addition to the annual published financial statements. Companies were only required to publish an income statement and a statement of financial position (balance sheet). The prevailing view seems to have been that all the financial information needed by users would be contained within these two statements. This view may have been based partly on the assumption that if a business were profitable, it would also have plenty of cash. Although in the long run this is likely to be true, it is not necessarily true in the short to medium term.

We saw in Chapter 3 that the income statement sets out the revenue and expenses, rather than the cash receipts and cash payments, for the period. This means that the profit (or loss), which represents the difference between the revenue and expenses for the period, may have little or no relation to the cash generated for the period. To illustrate this point, let us take the example of a business making a sale (generating a revenue). This may well lead to an increase in wealth that will be reflected in the income statement. However, if the sale is made on credit, no cash changes hands – at least not at the time of sale. Instead, the increase in wealth is reflected in another asset: an increase in trade receivables. Furthermore, if an item of inventories is the subject of the sale, wealth is lost to the business through the reduction in inventories. This means an expense is incurred in making the sale, which will be shown in the income statement. Once again, however, no cash has changed hands at the time of sale. For such reasons, the profit and the cash generated for a period will rarely go hand in hand.

The following activity should help to underline how profit and cash for a period may be affected differently by particular transactions or events.

Activity 6.1

The following is a list of business/accounting events. In each case, state the effect (increase, decrease or none) on both profit and cash:

		Effect	
		on profit	*on cash*
1	Repayment of borrowings	_____	_____
2	Making a profitable sale on credit	_____	_____
3	Buying a current asset on credit	_____	_____
4	Receiving cash from a credit customer (trade receivable)	_____	_____
5	Depreciating a non-current asset	_____	_____
6	Buying some inventories for cash	_____	_____
7	Making a share issue for cash	_____	_____

You should have come up with the following:

		Effect	
		on profit	*on cash*
1	Repayment of borrowings	none	decrease
2	Making a profitable sale on credit	increase	none
3	Buying a current asset on credit	none	none
4	Receiving cash from a credit customer (trade receivable)	none	increase
5	Depreciating a non-current asset	decrease	none
6	Buying some inventories for cash	none	decrease
7	Making a share issue for cash	none	increase

Activity 6.1 continued

The reasons for these answers are as follows:

1 Repaying borrowings requires that cash be paid to the lender. This means that two figures in the statement of financial position will be affected, but none in the income statement.
2 Making a profitable sale on credit will increase the sales revenue and profit figures. No cash will change hands at this point, however.
3 Buying a current asset on credit affects neither the cash balance nor the profit figure.
4 Receiving cash from a credit customer increases the cash balance and reduces the credit customer's balance. Both of these figures are on the statement of financial position. The income statement is unaffected.
5 Depreciating a non-current asset means that an expense is recognised. This causes the carrying amount of the asset, as it is recorded on the statement of financial position, to fall by an amount equal to the amount of the expense. No cash is paid or received.
6 Buying some inventories for cash means that the value of the inventories will increase and the cash balance will decrease by a similar amount. Profit is not affected.
7 Making a share issue for cash increases the shareholders' equity and increases the cash balance; profit is unaffected.

It is clear from the above that if we are to gain insights about cash movements over time, the income statement is not the place to look. Instead we need a separate financial statement. This fact has become widely recognised in recent years and in 1991 a UK financial reporting standard, FRS 1, emerged that required all but the smallest companies to produce and publish a statement of cash flows. This standard has been superseded for listed companies from 2005 by the international standard IAS 7. The two standards have broadly similar requirements. This chapter follows the provisions of IAS 7.

Why is cash so important?

It is worth asking why cash is so important. After all, cash is just an asset that the business needs to help it to function. In that sense, it is no different from inventories or non-current assets.

The reason for the importance of cash is that people and organisations will not normally accept anything other than cash in settlement of their claims. If a business wants to employ people, it must pay them in cash. If it wants to buy a new non-current asset to exploit a business opportunity, the seller of the asset will normally insist on being paid in cash, probably after a short period of credit. When businesses fail, it is their inability to find the cash to pay the amounts owed that really pushes them under. These factors lead to cash being the pre-eminent business asset. Cash is what analysts tend to watch most carefully when assessing the ability of businesses to survive and/or to take advantage of commercial opportunities.

During an economic downturn, the ability to generate cash takes on even greater importance. Banks become more cautious in their lending and those businesses with weak cash flows often find it difficult to obtain finance. **Real World 6.1** describes how the recent financial crisis has led banks in China to place greater emphasis on cash flows when considering loan applications.

Real World 6.1

Cash flow is in top three places

FT

'The banks are tightening the screws,' says K. B. Chan, chairman of Surface Mount Technology, which supplies consumer electronics companies. 'A lot of companies are strapped for cash.'

Stanley Wong, business development director at Man Yue Electronics, the world's fifth largest maker of aluminium capacitors, says: 'Banks don't even trust each other. They are being a lot more careful.' Mr Wong says that companies such as his, with strong cash flows, will still get working capital and other loans but bankers who used to lend to Man Yue and other manufacturers sight unseen are now tramping out to their factories for a closer look.

'The banks only look at cash flow – number one is cash flow, number two is cash flow and number three is cash flow,' says Mr Chan. 'Profit is only an accounting statement.'

Source: 'Rations cut for army of buyers', *Financial Times*, 20 October 2008.

The main features of the statement of cash flows

The statement of cash flows is a summary of the cash receipts and payments over the period concerned. All payments of a particular type, for example cash payments to acquire additional non-current assets or other investments, are added together to give just one figure that appears in the statement. The net total of the statement is the net increase or decrease of the cash (and cash equivalents) of the business over the period. The statement is basically an analysis of the business's cash (and cash equivalents) movements for the period.

A definition of cash and cash equivalents

IAS 7 defines cash as notes and coins in hand and deposits in banks and similar institutions that are accessible to the business on demand. Cash equivalents are short-term, highly liquid investments that are readily convertible to known amounts of cash and which are subject to an insignificant risk of changes of value. Cash equivalents are held for the purpose of meeting short-term cash commitments rather than for investment or other purposes.

Activity 6.2 should clarify the types of items that fall within the definition of 'cash equivalents'.

Activity 6.2

At the end of its accounting period, Zeneb plc's statement of financial position included the following items:

1 *A bank deposit account where one month's notice of withdrawal is required*. This deposit was made because the business has a temporary cash surplus that it will need to use in the short term for operating purposes.
2 *Ordinary shares in Jones plc (a Stock Exchange listed business)*. These were acquired because Zeneb plc has a temporary cash surplus and its directors believed that the shares represent a good short-term investment. The funds invested will need to be used in the short term for operating purposes.
3 *A bank deposit account that is withdrawable instantly*. This represents an investment of surplus funds that are not seen as being needed in the short term.
4 *An overdraft on the business's bank current account*.

Which (if any) of these four items would be included in the figure for cash and cash equivalents?

Your response should have been as follows:

1 A cash equivalent because the deposit is part of the business's normal cash management activities and there is little doubt about how much cash will be obtained when the deposit is withdrawn.
2 Not a cash equivalent. Although the investment was made as part of normal cash management, there is a significant risk that the amount expected (hoped for!) when the shares are sold may not actually be forthcoming.
3 Not a cash equivalent because this represents an investment rather than a short-term surplus amount of cash.
4 This is cash itself, though a negative amount of it. The only exception to this classification would be where the business is financed in the longer term by an overdraft, when it would be part of the financing of the business, rather than negative cash.

As can be seen from the responses to Activity 6.2, whether a particular item falls within the definition of cash and cash equivalent depends on two factors:

● the nature of the item; and
● why it has arisen.

In practice, it is not usually difficult to decide whether an item is a cash equivalent.

The relationship between the main financial statements

The statement of cash flows is now accepted, along with the income statement and the statement of financial position, as a major financial statement. The relationship between the three statements is shown in Figure 6.1. The statement of financial position reflects the combination of assets (including cash) and claims (including the shareholders' equity) of the business *at a particular point in time*. The statement of cash flows and the income statement explain the *changes over a period* to two of the items in the statement of financial position. The statement of cash flows explains the changes to cash. The income statement explains changes to equity, arising from trading operations.

Figure 6.1   The relationship between the statement of financial position, the income statement and the statement of cash flows

The statement of financial position shows the relationship, at a particular point in time, between the business's assets and claims. The income statement explains how, over a period between two statements of financial position, the equity figure in the first statement of financial position has altered as a result of trading operations. The statement of cash flows also looks at changes over the accounting period, but this statement explains the alteration in the cash (and cash equivalent) balances from the first to the second of the two consecutive statements of financial position.

The form of the statement of cash flows

The standard layout of the statement of cash flows is summarised in Figure 6.2. Explanations of the terms used in the statement of cash flows are given below.

Figure 6.2   Standard layout of the statement of cash flows

This is the standard layout for the statement of cash flows as required by IAS 7 *Statement of Cash Flows*.

Cash flows from operating activities

This is the net inflow or outflow from trading operations, after tax payments (or receipts) and cash paid to meet financing costs. It is equal to the sum of cash receipts from trade receivables and cash receipts from cash sales, where relevant, less the sums paid to buy inventories, to pay rent, to pay wages and so on. From this are also deducted payments for interest on the business's borrowings, corporation tax and dividends paid.

Note that it is the amounts of cash received and paid during the period that feature in the statement of cash flows, not the revenue and expenses for that period. It is, of course, the income statement that deals with the revenue and expenses. Similarly the tax and dividend payments that appear in the statement of cash flows are those made in the period of the statement. Companies normally pay tax on their profits in four equal instalments. Two of these are during the year concerned and the other two are during the following year. As a result, by the end of each accounting year, half of the tax will have been paid and the remainder will be a current liability at the end of the year, to be paid off during the following year. During any particular year, therefore, the tax payment would normally equal 50 per cent of the previous year's tax charge and 50 per cent of that of the current year.

The net figure for this section is intended to indicate the net cash flows for the period that arose from normal day-to-day trading activities after taking account of the tax that has to be paid on them and the cost of servicing the finance (equity and borrowings) needed to support them.

Cash flows from investing activities

This section of the statement is concerned with cash payments made to acquire additional non-current assets and with cash receipts from the disposal of non-current assets. These non-current assets will tend to be the usual items such as buildings and machinery. They might also be loans made by the business or shares in another company bought by the business.

This section also includes cash receipts *arising from* financial investments (loans and equities) made outside the business. These receipts are interest on loans made by the business and dividends from shares in other companies that are owned by the business.

Cash flows from financing activities

This part of the statement is concerned with the long-term financing of the business. So here we are considering borrowings (other than very short-term borrowings) and finance from share issues. This category is concerned with repayment/redemption of finance as well as with the raising of it. It is permissible under IAS 7 to include dividend payments made by the business here, as an alternative to including them in 'Cash flows from operating activities' (above).

This section shows the net cash flows from raising and/or paying back long-term finance.

Net increase or decrease in cash and cash equivalents

The total of the statement must, of course, be the net increase or decrease in cash and cash equivalents over the period concerned.

The effect on a business's cash and cash equivalents of its various activities is shown in Figure 6.3. As explained, the arrows show the *normal* direction of cash flow for the typical healthy, profitable business in a typical year.

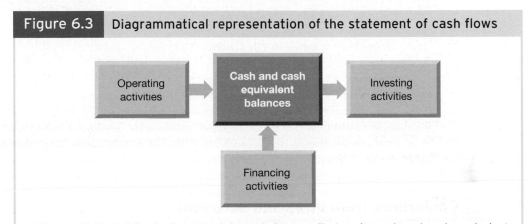

Figure 6.3   Diagrammatical representation of the statement of cash flows

Various activities of the business each have their own effect on its cash and cash equivalent balances, either positive (increasing them) or negative (reducing them). The net increase or decrease in the cash and cash equivalent balances over a period will be the sum of these individual effects, taking account of the direction (cash in or cash out) of each activity.

Note that the direction of the arrow shows the *normal* direction of the cash flow in respect of each activity. In certain circumstances, each of these arrows could be reversed in direction.

The normal direction of cash flows

Normally 'operating activities' provide positive cash flows, that is, they help to increase the business's cash resources. In fact, for most UK businesses, in most time periods, cash generated from day-to-day trading, even after deducting tax, interest and dividends, is overwhelmingly the most important source of new finance.

Activity 6.3

Last year's statement of cash flows for Angus plc showed a negative cash flow from operating activities. What could be the reason for this and should the business's management be alarmed by it? (*Hint*: We think that there are two broad possible reasons for a negative cash flow.)

The two reasons are:

1 The business is unprofitable. This leads to more cash being paid out to employees, to suppliers of goods and services, for interest and so on than is received from trade receivables in respect of sales. This would be particularly alarming, because a major expense for most businesses is depreciation of non-current assets. Since depreciation does not lead to a cash flow, it is not considered in 'net cash inflows from operating activities'. This means that a negative operating cash flow might well indicate a very much larger trading loss – in other words, a significant loss of the business's wealth; something to concern management.

2 The other reason might be less alarming. A business that is expanding its activities (level of sales revenue) would tend to spend quite a lot of cash relative to the amount of cash coming in from sales. This is because it will probably be expanding its assets (non-current and current) to accommodate the increased demand. For example, a business may well need to have inventories in place before additional sales can be made. Similarly staff have to be employed and paid. Even when the additional sales are made, those sales would normally be made on credit, with the cash inflow lagging behind the sales. All of this means that, in the first instance, in cash flow terms, the business would not necessarily benefit from the additional sales revenue. This is particularly likely to be true of a new business, which would be expanding inventories and other assets from zero. It would also need to employ and pay staff. Expansion typically causes cash flow strains for the reasons just explained. This can be a particular problem because the business's increased profitability might encourage a feeling of optimism, which could lead to lack of attention being paid to the cash flow problem.

Investing activities typically cause net negative cash flows. This is because many types of non-current asset wear out and many that do not wear out become obsolete. Also, businesses tend to seek to expand their asset base. When a business sells some non-current assets, the sale will give rise to positive cash flows, but in net terms the cash flows are normally negative with cash spent on new assets outweighing that received from disposal of old ones.

Financing can go in either direction, depending on the financing strategy at the time. Since businesses seek to expand, there is a general tendency for this area to lead to cash coming into the business rather than leaving it.

Real World 6.2 shows the summarised statement of cash flows of Tesco plc, the UK-based supermarket company.

Real World 6.2

Cashing in

Like many larger companies, Tesco produces summary versions of its financial statements for users who do not want all of the detail. The summary statement of cash flows for the business for the year ended 28 February 2009 shows the cash flows of the business under each of the headings described above.

Summarised statement of cash flows for the year ended 28 February 2009

	£m
Cash generated from operations	4,978
Interest paid	(562)
Corporation tax paid	(456)
Net cash from operating activities	3,960
Net cash used in investing activities	(5,974)
Cash flows from financing activities	
Dividends paid	(883)
Other net cash flows from financing activities	4,498
Net cash from financing activities	3,615
Net increase in cash and cash equivalents	1,601

Source: Tesco Annual Review 2009, p. 24, www.tescocorporate.com.

As we shall see shortly, more detailed information under each of the main headings is provided in the statement of cash flows presented to shareholders and other users.

Preparing the statement of cash flows

Deducing net cash flows from operating activities

The first section of the statement of cash flows is the 'cash flows from operating activities'. There are two approaches that can be taken to deriving this figure: the direct method and the indirect method.

The direct method

→ The **direct method** involves an analysis of the cash records of the business for the period, picking out all payments and receipts relating to operating activities. These are summarised to give the total figures for inclusion in the statement of cash flows. Done on a computer, this is a simple matter, but not many businesses adopt the direct method.

The indirect method

→ The **indirect method** is the more popular method. It relies on the fact that, broadly, sales revenue gives rise to cash inflows and expenses give rise to outflows. This means that the figure for profit for the year will be closely linked to the net cash flows from operating activities. Since businesses have to produce an income statement in any case, information from it can be used as a starting point to deduce the cash flows from operating activities.

Of course, within a particular accounting period, profit for the year will not normally equal the net cash inflows from operating activities. We saw in Chapter 3 that, when sales are made on credit, the cash receipt occurs some time after the sale. This means that sales revenue made towards the end of an accounting year will be included in that year's income statement. However, most of the cash from those sales will flow into the business, and should be included in the statement of cash flows, in the following year. Fortunately it is easy to deduce the cash received from sales if we have the relevant income statement and statements of financial position, as we shall see in Activity 6.4.

Activity 6.4

How can we deduce the cash inflows from sales using the income statement and statement of financial position for the business?

The statement of financial position will tell us how much was owed in respect of credit sales at the beginning and end of the year (trade receivables). The income statement tells us the sales revenue figure. If we adjust the sales revenue figure by the increase or decrease in trade receivables over the year, we deduce the cash from sales for the year.

Example 6.1

The sales revenue figure for a business for the year was £34 million. The trade receivables totalled £4 million at the beginning of the year, but had increased to £5 million by the end of the year.

Basically, the trade receivables figure is dictated by sales revenue and cash receipts. It is increased when a sale is made and decreased when cash is received from a credit customer. If, over the year, the sales revenue and the cash receipts had been equal, the beginning-of-year and end-of-year trade receivables figures would have been equal. Since the trade receivables figure increased, it must mean that less cash was received than sales revenues were made. This means that the cash receipts from sales must be £33 million (that is, 34 − (5 − 4)).

Put slightly differently, we can say that as a result of sales, assets of £34 million flowed into the business during the year. If £1 million of this went to increasing the asset of trade receivables, this leaves only £33 million that went to increase cash.

The same general point is true in respect of nearly all of the other items that are taken into account in deducing the operating profit figure. The exception is depreciation. This is not necessarily associated with any movement in cash during the accounting period.

All of this means that we can take the profit before taxation (that is, the profit after interest but before taxation) for the year, add back the depreciation and interest expense charged in arriving at that profit, and adjust this total by movements in inventories, trade (and other) receivables and payables. If we then go on to deduct payments made during the accounting period for taxation, interest on borrowings and dividends, we have the net cash from operating activities.

Example 6.2

The relevant information from the financial statements of Dido plc for last year is as follows:

	£m
Profit before taxation (after interest)	122
Depreciation charged in arriving at profit before taxation	34
Interest expense	6
At the beginning of the year:	
Inventories	15
Trade receivables	24
Trade payables	18
At the end of the year:	
Inventories	17
Trade receivables	21
Trade payables	19

The following further information is available about payments during last year:

	£m
Taxation paid	32
Interest paid	5
Dividends paid	9

The cash flow from operating activities is derived as follows:

	£m
Profit before taxation (after interest)	122
Depreciation	34
Interest expense	6
Increase in inventories (17 – 15)	(2)
Decrease in trade receivables (21 – 24)	3
Increase in trade payables (19 – 18)	1
Cash generated from operating activities	164
Interest paid	(5)
Taxation paid	(32)
Dividends paid	(9)
Net cash from operating activities	118

As we can see, the net increase in **working capital*** (that is, current assets less current liabilities) as a result of trading was £162 million (that is, 122 + 34 + 6). Of this, £2 million went into increased inventories. More cash was received from trade receivables than sales revenue was made. Similarly, less cash was paid to trade payables than purchases of goods and services on credit. Both of these had a favourable effect on cash. Over the year, therefore, cash increased by £164 million. When account was taken of the payments for interest, tax and dividends, the net cash from operating activities was £118 million (inflow).

Note that we needed to adjust the profit before taxation (after interest) by the depreciation and interest expenses to derive the profit before depreciation, interest and taxation.

* Working capital is a term widely used in accounting and finance, not just in the context of the statement of cash flows. We shall encounter it several times in later chapters.

We should be clear why it is necessary to add back an amount for interest at the start of the derivation of cash flow from operating activities only to deduct an amount for interest further down. The reason is that the first is the interest expense for the year, whereas the second is the amount of cash paid out for interest during the year. These may well be different amounts, as was the case in Example 6.2.

The indirect method of deducing the net cash flow from operating activities is summarised in Figure 6.4.

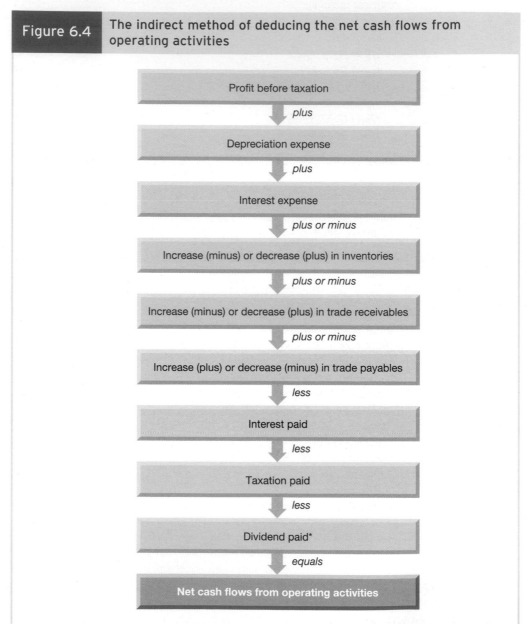

Figure 6.4   The indirect method of deducing the net cash flows from operating activities

Determining the net cash from operating activities firstly involves adding back the depreciation and the interest expense to the profit before taxation. Next, adjustment is made for increases or decreases in inventories, trade receivables and trade payables. Lastly, cash paid for interest, taxation and dividends is deducted.

* Note that dividends could alternatively be included under the heading 'Cash flows from financing activities'.

Activity 6.5

The relevant information from the financial statements of Pluto plc for last year is as follows:

	£m
Profit before taxation (after interest)	165
Depreciation charged in arriving at operating profit	41
Interest expense	21
At the beginning of the year:	
Inventories	22
Trade receivables	18
Trade payables	15
At the end of the year:	
Inventories	23
Trade receivables	21
Trade payables	17

The following further information is available about payments during last year:

	£m
Taxation paid	49
Interest paid	25
Dividends paid	28

What figure should appear in the statement of cash flows for 'Cash flows from operating activities'?

Net cash inflows from operating activities:

	£m
Profit before taxation (after interest)	165
Depreciation	41
Interest expense	21
Increase in inventories (23 − 22)	(1)
Increase in trade receivables (21 − 18)	(3)
Increase in trade payables (17 − 15)	2
Cash generated from operating activities	225
Interest paid	(25)
Taxation paid	(49)
Dividends paid	(28)
Net cash from operating activities	123

Deducing the other areas of the statement of cash flows

We can now go on to take a look at the preparation of a complete statement of cash flows through Example 6.3.

Example 6.3

Torbryan plc's income statement for the year ended 31 December 2010 and the statements of financial position as at 31 December 2009 and 2010 are as follows:

Income statement for the year ended 31 December 2010

	£m
Revenue	576
Cost of sales	(307)
Gross profit	269
Distribution expenses	(65)
Administrative expenses	(26)
	178
Other operating income	21
Operating profit	199
Interest receivable	17
	216
Interest payable	(23)
Profit before taxation	193
Taxation	(46)
Profit for the year	147

Statements of financial position as at 31 December 2009 and 2010

	2009 £m	2010 £m
ASSETS		
Non-current assets		
Property, plant and equipment		
Land and buildings	241	241
Plant and machinery	309	325
	550	566
Current assets		
Inventories	44	41
Trade receivables	121	139
	165	180
Total assets	715	746
EQUITY AND LIABILITIES		
Equity		
Called-up ordinary share capital	150	200
Share premium account	–	40
Retained earnings	26	123
	176	363
Non-current liabilities		
Borrowings – loan notes	400	250
Current liabilities		
Borrowings (all bank overdraft)	68	56
Trade payables	55	54
Taxation	16	23
	139	133
Total equity and liabilities	715	746

During 2010, the business spent £95 million on additional plant and machinery. There were no other non-current-asset acquisitions or disposals. A dividend of £50 million was paid on ordinary shares during the year. The interest receivable revenue and the interest payable expense for the year were equal to the cash inflow and outflow respectively.

The statement of cash flows would be as follows:

Torbryan plc
Statement of cash flows for the year ended 31 December 2010

	£m
Cash flows from operating activities	
Profit before taxation (after interest) (see Note 1 below)	193
Adjustments for:	
Depreciation (Note 2)	79
Interest receivable (Note 3)	(17)
Interest payable (Note 4)	23
Increase in trade receivables (139 – 121)	(18)
Decrease in trade payables (55 – 54)	(1)
Decrease in inventories (44 – 41)	3
Cash generated from operations	262
Interest paid	(23)
Taxation paid (Note 5)	(39)
Dividend paid	(50)
Net cash from operating activities	150
Cash flows from investing activities	
Payments to acquire tangible non-current assets	(95)
Interest received (Note 3)	17
Net cash used in investing activities	(78)
Cash flows from financing activities	
Repayments of loan notes (Note 6)	(150)
Issue of ordinary shares (Note 7)	90
Net cash used in financing activities	(60)
Net increase in cash and cash equivalents	12
Cash and cash equivalents at 1 January 2010 (Note 8)	(68)
Cash and cash equivalents at 31 December 2010	(56)

To see how this relates to the cash of the business at the beginning and end of the year it can be useful to provide a reconciliation as follows:

Analysis of cash and cash equivalents during the year ended
31 December 2010

	£m
Overdraft balance at 1 January 2010	(68)
Net cash inflow	12
Overdraft balance at 31 December 2010	(56)

Notes:

1 This is simply taken from the income statement for the year.

2 Since there were no disposals, the depreciation charges must be the difference between the start and end of the year's plant and machinery (non-current assets) values, adjusted by the cost of any additions.

Example 6.3 continued

	£m
Carrying amount at 1 January 2010	309
Additions	95
	404
Depreciation (balancing figure)	(79)
Carrying amount at 31 December 2010	325

3 Interest receivable must be taken away to work towards the profit before crediting it, because it is not part of operations but of investing activities. The cash inflow from this source appears under the 'Cash flows from investing activities' heading.

4 Interest payable expense must be taken out, by adding it back to the profit figure. We subsequently deduct the cash paid for interest payable during the year. In this case the two figures are identical.

5 Taxation is paid by companies 50 per cent during their accounting year and 50 per cent in the following year. As a result the 2010 payment would have been half the tax on the 2009 profit (that is, the figure that would have appeared in the current liabilities at the end of 2008), plus half of the 2010 taxation charge (that is, $16 + (\frac{1}{2} \times 46) = 39$). Probably the easiest way to deduce the amount paid during the year to 31 December 2010 is by following this approach:

	£m
Taxation owed at start of the year (from the statement of financial position as at 31 December 2009)	16
Taxation charge for the year (from the income statement)	46
	62
Taxation owed at the end of the year (from the statement of financial position as at 31 December 2010)	(23)
Taxation paid during the year	39

This follows the logic that if we start with what the business owed at the beginning of the year, add the increase in what was owed as a result of the current year's taxation charge and then deduct what was owed at the end, the resulting figure must be what was paid during the year.

6 It has been assumed that the loan notes were redeemed for the value shown on the statement of financial position. This is not, however, always the case.

7 The share issue raised £90 million, of which £50 million went into the share capital total on the statement of financial position and £40 million into share premium.

8 There were no 'cash equivalents', just cash (though negative).

What does the statement of cash flows tell us?

The statement of cash flows tells us how the business has generated cash during the period and where that cash has gone. Since cash is properly regarded as the lifeblood of just about any business, this is potentially very useful information.

Tracking the sources and uses of cash over several years could show financing trends that a reader of the statements could use to help to make judgements about the likely future behaviour of the business.

Looking specifically at the statement of cash flows for Torbryan plc, in Example 6.3, we can see the following:

● Net cash flow from operations was strong, much larger than the profit for the year figure, after taking account of the dividend paid. This would be expected because depreciation is deducted in arriving at profit. Working capital has absorbed some cash, which would be unsurprising if there had been an expansion of activity (sales revenue) over the year. From the information supplied, however, we do not know whether there was an expansion or not. (We have only one year's income statement.)

- There were net outflows of cash for investing activities, but this would not be unusual. Many items of property, plant and equipment have limited lives and need to be replaced with new ones. The expenditure during the year was not out of line with the depreciation expense for the year, which is to be expected for a business with a regular replacement programme for non-current assets.
- There was a fairly major outflow of cash to redeem some borrowings, partly offset by the proceeds of a share issue. This presumably represents a change of financing strategy. Together with the ploughed-back profit from trading, there has been a significant shift in the equity/borrowings balance.

Real World 6.3 looks at the statement of cash flows of an emerging business, LiDCO Group plc, that is experiencing negative cash flows as it seeks to establish a profitable market for its products.

Real World 6.3

Not losing heart

LiDCO Group plc has its shares listed on the Alternative Investment Market (AIM). AIM is a junior market of the London Stock Exchange that specialises in the shares of smaller, up-and-coming businesses.

LiDCO makes highly sophisticated equipment for monitoring the hearts of cardiac patients, typically in hospitals and clinics. The business was started by doctors and scientists. It has spent £6.8 million over ten years developing its products, obtaining registration for their use from both the UK and US authorities and creating manufacturing facilities.

LiDCO's statement of cash flows for the year to 31 January 2009 was as follows:

	£000
Net cash outflow from operating activities	(1,204)
Cash flows from investing activities	
Purchase of property, plant and equipment	(208)
Purchase of intangible fixed assets	(447)
Interest received	57
Net cash used in investing activities	(598)
Cash flows from financing activities	
Convertible loan repayment	(553)
Invoice discounting financing facility	364
Net cash outflow from financing activities	(189)
Net decrease in cash and cash equivalents	(1,991)

[Note that this was adapted from the statement that appeared in the business's annual report. Some more detail was supplied in the way of notes to the accounts.]

To put these figures into context, the sales revenue for the year was £4.53 million. This means that the net cash outflow from operating activities was equal to 27 per cent of the revenue figure. (This was an improvement, since it was 30 per cent in 2008, nearly 40 per cent in 2007 and over 50 per cent in 2006.) Such cash flow profiles are fairly typical of 'high-tech' businesses that have enormous start-up costs to bring their products to the market in sufficient quantities to yield a profit. Of course, not all such businesses achieve this, but LiDCO seems confident of success.

Sources: LiDCO Group plc Annual Report 2009 and AIM company profile, www.londonstockexchange.com.

Problems with IAS 7

IAS 7 *Statement of Cash Flows* does not enjoy universal acclaim. Its critics argue that the standard is too permissive in the description and classification of important items.

Some believe that the standard would inspire greater confidence among users if it insisted that only the direct method be used to calculate cash flows from operating activities. Supporters of the direct method argue that, being cash-based, it provides greater clarity by setting out operating cash receipts and payments. No accrual-based adjustments are made, which means that it is less susceptible to manipulation than the indirect approach, which has been described as 'a gift to dodgy companies'. (See the reference at the end of the chapter.) In its defence, however, it should be said that the indirect approach may help to shed light on the quality of reported profits by reconciling profit with the net cash from operating activities for a period. A business must demonstrate an ability to convert profits into cash and so revealing the link between profits and cash is important.

IAS 7 is also criticised for failing to require cash flows to be reconciled with movements in net debt, which may be defined as borrowings less any cash and cash equivalents. This reconciliation, so it is argued, would help users to gain a better understanding of movements in net debt and the management of cash flows. Net debt is often seen as a useful indicator of business solvency and so linking movements in this figure to the statement of cash flows may be important. Although not required to do so, many listed UK businesses provide this reconciliation as additional information. This is, at least partly, for historical reasons: the standard that preceded IAS 7 required this information.

Example 6.4 below illustrates how this reconciliation may be carried out.

Example 6.4

Based on the information set out in the financial statements of Torbryan plc for the financial years ended 31 December 2009 and 2010 (see Example 6.3), the following reconciliation of net cash flow to movement in net debt for the year to 31 December 2010 can be carried out.

Reconciliation of net cash flow to movement in net debt for the year to 31 December 2010

	£m
Net increase in cash and cash equivalents during the year	12
Repayment of loan notes	150
Decrease in net debt during the year	162
Net debt at 1 January 2010 (400 + 68*)	468
Net debt at 31 December 2010 (250 + 56)	(306)
Decrease in net debt during the year	162

* We saw earlier that a bank overdraft is normally viewed as negative cash. An overdraft is added to other borrowings to derive the net debt, whereas a positive cash balance would be deducted.

We can see that the net debt has been reduced largely through the repayment of loan notes but partly through a reduction in the overdraft.

Self-assessment question 6.1

Touchstone plc's income statements for the years ended 31 December 2009 and 2010 and statements of financial position as at 31 December 2009 and 2010 are as follows:

Income statements for the years ended 2009 and 2010

	2009 £m	2010 £m
Revenue	173	207
Cost of sales	(96)	(101)
Gross profit	77	106
Distribution expenses	(18)	(20)
Administrative expenses	(24)	(26)
Other operating income	3	4
Operating profit	38	64
Interest payable	(2)	(4)
Profit before taxation	36	60
Taxation	(8)	(16)
Profit for the year	28	44

Statements of financial position as at 31 December 2009 and 2010

	2009 £m	2010 £m
ASSETS		
Non-current assets		
Property, plant and equipment		
Land and buildings	94	110
Plant and machinery	53	62
	147	172
Current assets		
Inventories	25	24
Treasury bills (short-term investments)	–	15
Trade receivables	16	26
Cash at bank and in hand	4	4
	45	69
Total assets	192	241
EQUITY AND LIABILITIES		
Equity		
Called-up ordinary share capital	100	100
Retained earnings	30	56
	130	156
Non-current liabilities		
Borrowings – loan notes (10%)	20	40
Current liabilities		
Trade payables	38	37
Taxation	4	8
	42	45
Total equity and liabilities	192	241

→

Self-assessment question 6.1 continued

Included in 'cost of sales', 'distribution expenses' and 'administrative expenses', depreciation was as follows:

	2009 £m	2010 £m
Land and buildings	5	6
Plant and machinery	6	10

There were no non-current asset disposals in either year.

The interest payable expense equalled the cash payment made during the year, in both cases.

The business paid dividends on ordinary shares of £14 million during 2009 and £18 million during 2010.

The Treasury bills represent a short-term investment of funds that will be used shortly in operations. There is insignificant risk that this investment will lose value.

Required:

Prepare a statement of cash flows for the business for 2010.

The solution to this question can be found at the back of the book on pages 476–477.

Summary

The main points of this chapter may be summarised as follows:

The need for a statement of cash flows

- Cash is important because no business can operate without it.
- The statement of cash flows is specifically designed to reveal movements in cash over a period.
- Cash movements cannot be readily detected from the income statement, which focuses on revenue and expenses rather than on cash receipts and cash payments.
- Profit (or loss) and cash generated for the period are rarely equal.
- The statement of cash flows is a primary financial statement, along with the income statement and the statement of financial position.

Preparing the statement of cash flows

- The layout of the statement contains three categories of cash movement: cash flows from operating activities, cash flows from investing activities, and cash flows from financing activities.
- The total of the cash movements under these three categories will provide the net increase or decrease in cash and cash equivalents for the period.
- A reconciliation can be undertaken to check that the opening balance of cash and cash equivalents plus the net increase (or decrease) for the period equals the closing balance.

Calculating the cash generated from operations

- The net cash flows from operating activities can be derived by either the direct method or the indirect method.
- The direct method is based on an analysis of the cash records for the period, whereas the indirect method uses information contained within the income statement and statements of financial position of the business.
- The indirect method takes the net operating profit for the period, adds back any depreciation charge and then adjusts for changes in inventories, receivables and payables during the period.

Interpreting the statement of cash flows

- The statement of cash flows shows the main sources and uses of cash.
- Tracking the cash movements over several periods may reveal financing and investing patterns and may help predict future management action.

Problems with IAS 7

- IAS 7 has been criticised for being too permissive in the description and classification of important items and for allowing businesses to adopt the indirect method for determining net cash from operating activities.
- There have also been calls for movements in net debt to be reconciled with cash flows.

 Key terms

direct method   p. 195   **working capital**   p. 197
indirect method   p. 195

Reference

'Cash flow statements', *Financial Times*, 25 August 2005, FT.com.

Further reading

If you would like to explore the topics covered in this chapter in more depth, we recommend the following books:

Elliott, B. and Elliott, J., *Financial Accounting and Reporting*, 13th edn, Financial Times Prentice Hall, 2009, Chapter 27.

IASC Foundation Education, *A Guide through International Financial Reporting Standards (IFRSs) 2008*, July 2008, IAS 7.

KPMG, *Insights into IFRS*, 6th edn, 2009/10, Sweet and Maxwell, 2009, Section 2.3.

Review questions

Solutions to these questions can be found at the back of the book on pages 485–486.

6.1 The typical business outside the service sector has about 50 per cent more of its resources tied up in inventories than in cash, yet there is no call for a 'statement of inventories flows' to be prepared. Why is cash regarded as more important than inventories?

6.2 What is the difference between the direct and indirect methods of deducing cash generated from operations?

6.3 Taking each of the categories of the statement of cash flows in turn, in which direction would you normally expect the cash flow to be? Explain your answer.

(a) Cash flows from operating activities
(b) Cash flows from investing activities
(c) Cash flows from financing activities.

6.4 What causes the profit for the year not to equal the net cash inflow?

Exercises

Exercises 6.3 to 6.8 are more advanced than 6.1 and 6.2. Those with coloured numbers have solutions at the back of the book, starting on page 502.
    If you wish to try more exercises, visit the students' side of the Companion Website.

6.1 How will each of the following events ultimately affect the amount of cash?

(a) An increase in the level of inventories
(b) A rights issue of ordinary shares
(c) A bonus issue of ordinary shares
(d) Writing off part of the value of some inventories
(e) The disposal of a large number of the business's shares by a major shareholder
(f) Depreciating a non-current asset.

6.2 The following information has been taken from the financial statements of Juno plc for last year and the year before last:

	Year before last £m	Last year £m
Operating profit	156	187
Depreciation charged in arriving at operating profit	47	55
Inventories held at end of year	27	31
Trade receivables at end of year	24	23
Trade payables at end of year	15	17

Required:
What is the figure for cash generated from the operations for Juno plc for last year?

6.3 Torrent plc's income statement for the year ended 31 December 2010 and the statements of financial position as at 31 December 2009 and 2010 are as follows:

Income statement for the year ended 31 December 2010

	£m
Revenue	623
Cost of sales	(353)
Gross profit	270
Distribution expenses	(71)
Administrative expenses	(30)
Rental income	27
Operating profit	196
Interest payable	(26)
Profit before taxation	170
Taxation	(36)
Profit for the year	134

Statements of financial position as at 31 December 2009 and 2010

	2009 £m	2010 £m
ASSETS		
Non-current assets		
Property, plant and equipment		
Land and buildings	310	310
Plant and machinery	325	314
	635	624
Current assets		
Inventories	41	35
Trade receivables	139	145
	180	180
Total assets	815	804
EQUITY AND LIABILITIES		
Equity		
Called-up ordinary share capital	200	300
Share premium account	40	–
Revaluation reserve	69	9
Retained earnings	123	197
	432	506
Non-current liabilities		
Borrowings – loan notes	250	150
Current liabilities		
Borrowings (all bank overdraft)	56	89
Trade payables	54	41
Taxation	23	18
	133	148
Total equity and liabilities	815	804

During 2010, the business spent £67 million on additional plant and machinery. There were no other non-current asset acquisitions or disposals.

There was no share issue for cash during the year. The interest payable expense was equal in amount to the cash outflow. A dividend of £60 million was paid.

Required:
Prepare the statement of cash flows for Torrent plc for the year ended 31 December 2010.

6.4 Chen plc's income statements for the years ended 31 December 2009 and 2010 and the statements of financial position as at 31 December 2009 and 2010 are as follows:

Income statements for the years ended 31 December 2009 and 2010

	2009 £m	2010 £m
Revenue	207	153
Cost of sales	(101)	(76)
Gross profit	106	77
Distribution expenses	(22)	(20)
Administrative expenses	(20)	(28)
Operating profit	64	29
Interest payable	(4)	(4)
Profit before taxation	60	25
Taxation	(16)	(6)
Profit for the year	44	19

Statements of financial position as at 31 December 2009 and 2010

	2009 £m	2010 £m
ASSETS		
Non-current assets		
Property, plant and equipment		
Land and buildings	110	130
Plant and machinery	62	56
	172	186
Current assets		
Inventories	24	25
Trade receivables	26	25
Cash at bank and in hand	19	–
	69	50
Total assets	241	236
EQUITY AND LIABILITIES		
Equity		
Called-up ordinary share capital	100	100
Retained earnings	56	57
	156	157
Non-current liabilities		
Borrowings – loan notes (10%)	40	40
Current liabilities		
Borrowings (all bank overdraft)	–	2
Trade payables	37	34
Taxation	8	3
	45	39
Total equity and liabilities	241	236

Included in 'cost of sales', 'distribution expenses' and 'administrative expenses', depreciation was as follows:

	2009 £m	2010 £m
Land and buildings	6	10
Plant and machinery	10	12

There were no non-current asset disposals in either year. The amount of cash paid for interest equalled the expense in both years. Dividends were paid totalling £18 million in each year.

Required:

Prepare a statement of cash flows for the business for 2010.

6.5   The following are the financial statements for Nailsea plc for the years ended 30 June 2009 and 2010:

Income statement for years ended 30 June

	2009 £m	2010 £m
Revenue	1,230	2,280
Operating expenses	(722)	(1,618)
Depreciation	(270)	(320)
Operating profit	238	342
Interest payable	–	(27)
Profit before taxation	238	315
Taxation	(110)	(140)
Profit for the year	128	175

Statements of financial position as at 30 June

	2009 £m	2010 £m
ASSETS		
Non-current assets		
Property, plant and equipment (at carrying amount)		
Land and buildings	1,500	1,900
Plant and machinery	810	740
	2,310	2,640
Current assets		
Inventories	275	450
Trade receivables	100	250
Bank	–	118
	375	818
Total assets	2,685	3,458
EQUITY AND LIABILITIES		
Equity		
Share capital (fully paid £1 shares)	1,400	1,600
Share premium account	200	300
Retained profits	828	958
	2,428	2,858
Non-current liabilities		
Borrowings – 9% loan notes (repayable 2011)	–	300
Current liabilities		
Borrowings (all bank overdraft)	32	–
Trade payables	170	230
Taxation	55	70
	257	300
Total equity and liabilities	2,685	3,458

There were no disposals of non-current assets in either year. Dividends were paid in 2009 and 2010 of £40 million and £45 million, respectively.

Required:

Prepare a statement of cash flows for Nailsea plc for the year ended 30 June 2010.

6.6   The following financial statements for Blackstone plc are a slightly simplified set of published accounts. Blackstone plc is an engineering business that developed a new range of products in 2007. These products now account for 60 per cent of its turnover.

Income statement for the years ended 31 March

	Notes	2009 £m	2010 £m
Revenue		7,003	11,205
Cost of sales		(3,748)	(5,809)
Gross profit		3,255	5,396
Operating expenses		(2,205)	(3,087)
Operating profit		1,050	2,309
Interest payable	1	(216)	(456)
Profit before taxation		834	1,853
Taxation		(210)	(390)
Profit for the year		624	1,463

Statements of financial position as at 31 March

	Notes	2009 £m	2010 £m
ASSETS			
Non-current assets			
Property, plant and equipment	2	4,300	7,535
Intangible assets	3	–	700
		4,300	8,235
Current assets			
Inventories		1,209	2,410
Trade receivables		641	1,173
Cash at bank		123	–
		1,973	3,583
Total assets		6,273	11,818
EQUITY AND LIABILITIES			
Equity			
Share capital		1,800	1,800
Share premium		600	600
Capital reserves		352	352
Retained earnings		685	1,748
		3,437	4,500
Non-current liabilities			
Borrowings – Bank loan (repayable 2013)		1,800	3,800
Current liabilities			
Trade payables		931	1,507
Taxation		105	195
Borrowings (all bank overdraft)		–	1,816
		1,036	3,518
Total equity and liabilities		6,273	11,818

Notes:

1 The expense and the cash outflow for interest payable are equal.

2 The movements in property, plant and equipment during the year are set out below.

	Land and buildings £m	Plant and machinery £m	Fixtures and fittings £m	Total £m
Cost				
At 1 April 2009	4,500	3,850	2,120	10,470
Additions	–	2,970	1,608	4,578
Disposals	–	(365)	(216)	(581)
At 31 March 2010	4,500	6,455	3,512	14,467
Depreciation				
At 1 April 2009	1,275	3,080	1,815	6,170
Charge for year	225	745	281	1,251
Disposals	–	(305)	(184)	(489)
At 31 March 2010	1,500	3,520	1,912	6,932
Carrying amount				
At 31 March 2010	3,000	2,935	1,600	7,535

3 Intangible assets represent the amounts paid for the goodwill of another engineering business acquired during the year.

4 Proceeds from the sale of non-current assets in the year ended 31 March 2010 amounted to £54 million.

5 Dividends were paid on ordinary shares of £300 million in 2009 and £400 million in 2010.

Required:

Prepare a statement of cash flows for Blackstone plc for the year ended 31 March 2010. (*Hint:* A loss (deficit) on disposal of non-current assets is simply an additional amount of depreciation and should be dealt with as such in preparing the statement of cash flows.)

6.7 Simplified financial statements for York plc are as follows:

Income statement for the year ended 30 September 2010

	£m
Revenue	290.0
Cost of sales	(215.0)
Gross profit	75.0
Operating expenses (Note 1)	(62.0)
Operating profit	13.0
Interest payable (Note 2)	(3.0)
Profit before taxation	10.0
Taxation	(2.6)
Profit for the year	7.4

Statement of financial position as at 30 September

	2009 £m	2010 £m
ASSETS		
Non-current assets (Note 4)	80.0	85.0
Current assets		
Inventories and trade receivables	119.8	122.1
Cash at bank	9.2	16.6
	129.0	138.7
Total assets	209.0	223.7
EQUITY AND LIABILITIES		
Equity		
Share capital	35.0	40.0
Share premium account	30.0	30.0
Reserves	31.0	34.9
	96.0	104.9
Non-current liabilities		
Borrowings	32.0	35.0
Current liabilities		
Trade payables	80.0	82.5
Taxation	1.0	1.3
	81.0	83.8
Total equity and liabilities	209.0	223.7

Notes:

1 Operating expenses include depreciation of £13 million and a surplus of £3.2 million on the sale of non-current assets.
2 The expense and the cash outflow for interest payable are equal.
3 A dividend of £3.5 million was paid during 2010.
4 Non-current asset costs and depreciation:

	Cost £m	Accumulated depreciation £m	Carrying amount £m
At 1 October 2009	120.0	40.0	80.0
Disposals	(10.0)	(8.0)	(2.0)
Additions	20.0		20.0
Depreciation		13.0	(13.0)
At 30 September 2010	130.0	45.0	85.0

Required:

Prepare a statement of cash flows for York plc for the year ended 30 September 2010.

6.8 The statements of financial position of Axis plc as at 31 December 2009 and 2010 and the income statement for the year ended 31 December 2010 were as follows:

Statements of financial position as at 31 December

	2009		2010	
	£m	£m	£m	£m
ASSETS				
Non-current assets				
Property, plant and equipment				
Land and building at cost	130		130	
Accumulated depreciation	(30)	100	(32)	98
Plant and machinery at cost	70		80	
Accumulated depreciation	(17)	53	(23)	57
		153		155
Current assets				
Inventories		25		24
Trade receivables		16		26
Short-term investments		–		12
Cash at bank and in hand		–		7
		41		69
Total assets		194		224
EQUITY AND LIABILITIES				
Equity				
Share capital		100		100
Retained earnings		36		40
		136		140
Non-current liabilities				
Borrowings – 10% loan notes		20		40
Current liabilities				
Trade payables		31		36
Taxation		7		8
		38		44
Total equity and liabilities		194		224

Income statement for the year ended 31 December 2010

	£m
Revenue	173
Cost of sales	(96)
Gross profit	77
Sundry operating expenses	(24)
Deficit on sale of non-current asset	(1)
Depreciation – buildings	(2)
– plant	(16)
Operating profit	34
Interest receivable	2
Interest payable	(2)
Profit before taxation	34
Taxation	(16)
Profit for the year	18

During the year, plant (a non-current asset) costing £15 million and with accumulated depreciation of £10 million was sold.

The short-term investments were government securities, where there was little or no risk of loss of value.

The expense and the cash outflow for interest payable were equal.

During 2010 a dividend of £14 million was paid.

Required:

Prepare a statement of cash flows for Axis plc for the year ended 31 December 2010.

7

Analysing and interpreting financial statements (1)

Introduction

In this chapter we shall consider the analysis and interpretation of the financial statements that we discussed in Chapters 2, 3 and 6. We shall see how financial (or accounting) ratios can help in assessing the financial health of a business.

Financial ratios can be employed to examine various aspects of financial position and performance. They are widely used by external users and can also be helpful to managers in a wide variety of decision areas, such as profit planning, pricing, working-capital management and financial structure.

We shall continue our examination of the analysis and interpretation of financial statements in Chapter 8.

Learning outcomes

When you have completed this chapter, you should be able to:

● explain how ratios can be used to assess the position and performance of a business;

● identify the major categories of ratios that can be used for analysis purposes;

● calculate key ratios for assessing the profitability, efficiency, liquidity and gearing of a business;

● explain the significance of the ratios calculated.

Financial ratios

Financial ratios provide a quick and relatively simple means of assessing the financial health of a business. A ratio simply relates one figure appearing in the financial statements to some other figure appearing there (for example, operating profit in relation to the amount invested in the business (capital employed)) or, perhaps, to some resource of the business (for example, operating profit per employee, sales revenue per square metre of selling space and so on).

Ratios can be very helpful when comparing the financial health of different businesses. Differences may exist between businesses in the scale of operations. This means that a direct comparison of, say, the operating profit generated by each business may be misleading. By expressing operating profit in relation to some other measure (for example, capital employed), the problem of scale is eliminated. A business with an operating profit of, say, £10,000 and capital employed of £100,000 can be compared with a much larger business with an operating profit of, say, £80,000 and capital employed of £1,000,000 by the use of a simple ratio. The operating profit to capital employed ratio for the smaller business is 10 per cent (that is, $(10,000/100,000) \times 100\%$) and the same ratio for the larger business is 8 per cent (that is, $(80,000/1,000,000) \times 100\%$). These ratios can be directly compared whereas comparison of the absolute operating profit figures would be much less meaningful. The need to eliminate differences in scale through the use of ratios can also apply when comparing the performance of the same business over time.

By calculating a small number of ratios it is often possible to build up a good picture of the position and performance of a business. It is not surprising, therefore, that ratios are widely used by those who have an interest in businesses and business performance. Although ratios are not difficult to calculate, they can be difficult to interpret. It is important to appreciate that they are really only the starting point for further analysis.

Ratios help to highlight the financial strengths and weaknesses of a business, but they cannot, by themselves, explain why those strengths or weaknesses exist or why certain changes have occurred. Only a detailed investigation will reveal these underlying reasons. Ratios tend to enable us to know which questions to ask, rather than provide the answers.

Ratios can be expressed in various forms, for example as a percentage or as a proportion. The way that a particular ratio is presented will depend on the needs of those who will use the information. Although it is possible to calculate a large number of ratios, only a few, based on key relationships, tend to be helpful to a particular user. Many ratios that could be calculated from the financial statements (for example, rent payable in relation to current assets) may not be considered because there is no clear or meaningful relationship between the two items.

There is no generally accepted list of ratios that can be applied to the financial statements, nor is there a standard method of calculating many ratios. Variations in both the choice of ratios and their calculation will be found in practice. However, it is important to be consistent in the way in which ratios are calculated for comparison purposes. The ratios that we shall discuss here are those that are widely used. They are popular because many consider them to be among the more important for decision-making purposes.

Financial ratio classifications

Ratios can be grouped into categories, with each category relating to a particular aspect of financial performance or position. The following broad categories provide a useful basis for explaining the nature of the financial ratios to be dealt with. There are five of them:

- *Profitability*. Businesses generally exist with the primary purpose of creating wealth for their owners. Profitability ratios provide insights relating to the degree of success in achieving this purpose. They express the profit made (or figures bearing on profit, such as sales revenue or overheads) in relation to other key figures in the financial statements or to some business resource.
- *Efficiency*. Ratios may be used to measure the efficiency with which particular resources have been used within the business. These ratios are also referred to as *activity* ratios.
- *Liquidity*. It is vital to the survival of a business that there are sufficient liquid resources available to meet maturing obligations (that is, amounts owing that must be paid in the near future). Some liquidity ratios examine the relationship between liquid resources held and amounts due for payment in the near future.
- *Financial gearing*. This is the relationship between the contribution to financing the business made by the owners of the business and the amount contributed by others, in the form of loans. The level of gearing has an important effect on the degree of risk associated with a business, as we shall see. Gearing is, therefore, something that managers must consider when making financing decisions. Gearing ratios tend to highlight the extent to which the business uses borrowings.
- *Investment*. Certain ratios are concerned with assessing the returns and performance of shares in a particular business from the perspective of shareholders who are not involved with the management of the business.

The analyst must be clear *who* the target users are and *why* they need the information. Different users of financial information are likely to have different information needs, which will in turn determine the ratios that they find useful. For example, shareholders are likely to be particularly interested in their returns in relation to the level of risk associated with their investment. Profitability, investment and gearing ratios will, therefore, be of particular interest. Long-term lenders are concerned with the long-term viability of the business and, to help them to assess this, the profitability and gearing ratios of the business are also likely to be of particular interest. Short-term lenders, such as suppliers of goods and services on credit, may be interested in the ability of the business to repay the amounts owing in the short term. As a result, the liquidity ratios should be of interest.

We shall consider ratios falling into the first four of these five categories (profitability, efficiency, liquidity and gearing) a little later in the chapter. The remaining category (investment) takes a rather different perspective and will be considered in Chapter 8, along with other interpretation issues.

The need for comparison

Merely calculating a ratio will not tell us very much about the position or performance of a business. For example, if a ratio revealed that a retail business was generating £100 in sales revenue per square metre of floor space, it would not be possible to deduce from this information alone whether this particular level of performance was good, bad or indifferent. It is only when we compare this ratio with some 'benchmark' that the information can be interpreted and evaluated.

Activity 7.1

Can you think of any bases that could be used to compare a ratio you have calculated from the financial statements of your business for a particular period?
   We feel that there are three sensible possibilities.

You may have thought of the following bases:

- past periods for the same business
- similar businesses for the same or past periods
- planned performance for the business.

We shall now take a closer look at these three bases of comparison.

Past periods

By comparing the ratio we have calculated with the same ratio, but for a previous period, it is possible to detect whether there has been an improvement or deterioration in performance. Indeed, it is often useful to track particular ratios over time (say, five or ten years) to see whether it is possible to detect trends. The comparison of ratios from different periods brings certain problems, however. In particular, there is always the possibility that trading conditions were quite different in the periods being compared. There is the further problem that, when comparing the performance of a single business over time, operating inefficiencies may not be clearly exposed. For example, the fact that sales revenue per employee has risen by 10 per cent over the previous period may at first sight appear to be satisfactory. This may not be the case, however, if similar businesses have shown an improvement of 50 per cent for the same period or had much better sales revenue per employee ratios to start with. Finally, there is the problem that inflation may have distorted the figures on which the ratios are based. Inflation can lead to an overstatement of profit and an understatement of asset values, as will be discussed in Chapter 8 and Chapter 10.

Similar businesses

In a competitive environment, a business must consider its performance in relation to that of other businesses operating in the same industry. Survival may depend on its ability to achieve comparable levels of performance. A useful basis for comparing a particular ratio, therefore, is the ratio achieved by similar businesses during the same period. This basis is not, however, without its problems. Competitors may have different year ends and so trading conditions may not be identical. They may also have different accounting policies, which can have a significant effect on reported profits and asset values (for example, different methods of calculating depreciation or valuing inventories). Finally, it may be difficult to obtain the financial statements of competitor businesses. Sole proprietorships and partnerships, for example, are not obliged to make their financial statements available to the public. In the case of limited companies, there is a legal obligation to do so. However, a diversified business may not provide a breakdown of activities that is sufficiently detailed to enable analysts to compare the activities with those of other businesses.

Planned performance

Ratios may be compared with the targets that management developed before the start of the period under review. The comparison of planned performance with actual performance may therefore be a useful way of revealing the level of achievement attained. However, the planned levels of performance must be based on realistic assumptions if they are to be useful for comparison purposes.

Planned performance is likely to be the most valuable benchmark against which managers may assess their own business. Businesses tend to develop planned ratios for each aspect of their activities. When formulating its plans, a business may usefully take account of its own past performance and the performance of other businesses. There is no reason, however, why a particular business should seek to achieve either its own previous performance or that of other businesses. Neither of these may be seen as an appropriate target.

Analysts outside the business do not normally have access to the business's plans. For these people, past performance and the performances of other, similar, businesses may provide the only practical benchmarks.

Calculating the ratios

Probably the best way to explain financial ratios is through an example. Example 7.1 provides a set of financial statements from which we can calculate important ratios.

Example 7.1

The following financial statements relate to Alexis plc, which operates a whole-sale carpet business.

Statements of financial position (balance sheets) as at 31 March

	2009 £m	2010 £m
ASSETS		
Non-current assets		
Property, plant and equipment (at cost less depreciation)		
Land and buildings	381	427
Fixtures and fittings	129	160
	510	587
Current assets		
Inventories at cost	300	406
Trade receivables	240	273
Cash at bank	4	–
	544	679
Total assets	1,054	1,266
EQUITY AND LIABILITIES		
Equity		
£0.50 ordinary shares (Note 1)	300	300
Retained earnings	263	234
	563	534
Non-current liabilities		
Borrowings – 9% loan notes (secured)	200	300
Current liabilities		
Trade payables	261	354
Taxation	30	2
Short-term borrowings (all bank overdraft)	–	76
	291	432
Total equity and liabilities	1,054	1,266

Income statements for the year ended 31 March

	2009 £m	2010 £m
Revenue (Note 2)	2,240	2,681
Cost of sales (Note 3)	(1,745)	(2,272)
Gross profit	495	409
Operating expenses	(252)	(362)
Operating profit	243	47
Interest payable	(18)	(32)
Profit before taxation	225	15
Taxation	(60)	(4)
Profit for the year	165	11

Statement of cash flows for the year ended 31 March

	2009 £m	2010 £m
Cash flows from operating activities		
Profit, after interest, before taxation	225	15
Adjustments for:		
Depreciation	26	33
Interest expense	18	32
	269	80
Increase in inventories	(59)	(106)
Increase in trade receivables	(17)	(33)
Increase in trade payables	58	93
Cash generated from operations	251	34
Interest paid	(18)	(32)
Taxation paid	(63)	(32)
Dividend paid	(40)	(40)
Net cash from/(used in) operating activities	130	(70)
Cash flows from investing activities		
Payments to acquire property, plant and equipment	(77)	(110)
Net cash used in investing activities	(77)	(110)
Cash flows from financing activities		
Issue of loan notes	–	100
Net cash from financing activities	–	100
Net increase in cash and cash equivalents	53	(80)
Cash and cash equivalents at start of year		
Cash/(overdraft)	(49)	4
Cash and cash equivalents at end of year		
Cash/(overdraft)	4	(76)

Notes:

1 The market value of the shares of the business at the end of the year was £2.50 for 2009 and £1.50 for 2010.

2 All sales and purchases are made on credit.

3 The cost of sales figure can be analysed as follows:

	2009 £m	2010 £m
Opening inventories	241	300
Purchases (Note 2)	1,804	2,378
	2,045	2,678
Closing inventories	(300)	(406)
Cost of sales	1,745	2,272

4 At 31 March 2008, the trade receivables stood at £223 million and the trade payables at £183 million.

5 A dividend of £40 million has been paid to the shareholders in respect of each of the years.

6 The business employed 13,995 staff at 31 March 2009 and 18,623 at 31 March 2010.

7 The business expanded its capacity during 2010 by setting up a new warehouse and distribution centre in the north of England.

8 At 1 April 2008, the total of equity stood at £438 million and the total of equity and non-current liabilities stood at £638 million.

A brief overview

Before we start our detailed look at the ratios for Alexis plc (in Example 7.1), it is helpful to take a quick look at what information is obvious from the financial statements. This will usually pick up some issues that the ratios may not be able to identify. It may also highlight some points that could help us in our interpretation of the ratios. Starting at the top of the statement of financial position, the following points can be noted:

- *Expansion of non-current assets*. These have increased by about 15 per cent (from £510 million to £587 million). Note 7 mentions a new warehouse and distribution centre, which may account for much of the additional investment in non-current assets. We are not told when this new facility was established, but it is quite possible that it was well into the year. This could mean that not much benefit was reflected in terms of additional sales revenue or cost saving during 2010. Sales revenue, in fact, expanded by about 20 per cent (from £2,240 million to £2,681 million); this is greater than the expansion in non-current assets.

- *Major expansion in the elements of working capital*. Inventories increased by about 35 per cent, trade receivables by about 14 per cent and trade payables by about 36 per cent between 2009 and 2010. These are major increases, particularly in inventories and payables (which are linked because the inventories are all bought on credit – see Note 2).

- *Reduction in the cash balance*. The cash balance fell from £4 million (in funds) to a £76 million overdraft, between 2009 and 2010. The bank may be putting the business under pressure to reverse this, which could raise difficulties.

- *Apparent debt capacity*. Comparing the non-current assets with the long-term borrowings implies that the business may well be able to offer security on further borrowing. This is because potential lenders usually look at the value of assets that can be offered as security when assessing loan requests. Lenders seem particularly attracted to land and, to a lesser extent, buildings as security. For example, at 31 March 2010, non-current assets had a carrying amount (the value at which they appeared in the statement of financial position) of £587 million, but long-term borrowing was only £300 million (though there was also an overdraft of £76 million). Carrying amounts are not normally, of course, market values. On the other hand, land and buildings tend to have a market value higher than their value as shown on the statement of financial position due to inflation in property values.

- *Lower operating profit*. Though sales revenue expanded by 20 per cent between 2009 and 2010, both cost of sales and operating expenses rose by a greater percentage, leaving both gross profit and, particularly, operating profit massively reduced. The level of staffing, which increased by about 33 per cent (from 13,995 to 18,623 employees – see Note 6), may have greatly affected the operating expenses. (Without knowing when the additional employees were recruited during 2010, we cannot be sure of the effect on operating expenses.) Increasing staffing by 33 per cent must put an enormous strain on management, at least in the short term. It is not surprising, therefore that 2010 was not successful for the business.

Having had a quick look at what is fairly obvious, without calculating any financial ratios, we shall now go on to calculate and interpret those relating to profitability and efficiency, liquidity and gearing.

Profitability

The following ratios may be used to evaluate the profitability of the business:

● return on ordinary shareholders' funds
● return on capital employed
● operating profit margin
● gross profit margin.

We shall now look at each of these in turn.

Return on ordinary shareholders' funds (ROSF)

→ The **return on ordinary shareholders' funds ratio** compares the amount of profit for the period available to the owners with the owners' average stake in the business during that same period. The ratio (which is normally expressed in percentage terms) is as follows:

$$\text{ROSF} = \frac{\text{Profit for the year less any preference dividend}}{\text{Ordinary share capital + Reserves}} \times 100$$

The profit for the year (less preference dividend (if any)) is used in calculating the ratio, as this figure represents the amount of profit that is attributable to the owners.

In the case of Alexis plc, the ratio for the year ended 31 March 2009 is

$$\text{ROSF} = \frac{165}{(438 + 563)/2} \times 100 = 33.0\%$$

Note that, when calculating the ROSF, the average of the figures for ordinary shareholders' funds as at the beginning and at the end of the year has been used. It is preferable to use an average figure as this is likely to be more representative. This is because the shareholders' funds did not have the same total throughout the year, yet we want to compare it with the profit earned during the whole period. We know, from Note 8, that the total of the shareholders' funds at 1 April 2008 was £438 million. By a year later, however, it had risen to £563 million, according to the statement of financial position as at 31 March 2009.

The easiest approach to calculating the average amount of shareholders' funds is to take a simple average based on the opening and closing figures for the year. This is often the only information available, as is the case with Example 7.1. Averaging in this way is generally valid for all ratios that combine a figure for a period (such as profit for the year) with one taken at a point in time (such as shareholders' funds).

Where not even the beginning-of-year figure is available, it is usually acceptable to use just the year-end figure. This is not ideal but, provided that this approach is consistently adopted, it should provide ratios that are useful.

Activity 7.2

Calculate the ROSF for Alexis plc for the year to 31 March 2010.

The ratio for 2010 is

$$\text{ROSF} = \frac{11}{(563 + 534)/2} \times 100 = 2.0\%$$

Broadly, businesses seek to generate as high a value as possible for this ratio, provided that it is not achieved at the expense of potential future returns by, for example, taking on more risky activities. In view of this, the 2010 ratio is very poor by any standards; a bank deposit account will normally yield a better return than this. We need to try to find out why things went so badly wrong in 2010. As we look at other ratios, we should find some clues.

Return on capital employed (ROCE)

→ The **return on capital employed ratio** is a fundamental measure of business performance. This ratio expresses the relationship between the operating profit generated during a period and the average long-term capital invested in the business.

The ratio is expressed in percentage terms and is as follows:

$$\text{ROCE} = \frac{\text{Operating profit}}{\text{Share capital} + \text{Reserves} + \text{Non-current liabilities}} \times 100$$

Note, in this case, that the profit figure used is the operating profit (that is, the profit *before* interest and taxation), because the ratio attempts to measure the returns to all suppliers of long-term finance before any deductions for interest payable on borrowings, or payments of dividends to shareholders, are made.

For the year to 31 March 2009, the ratio for Alexis plc is

$$\text{ROCE} = \frac{243}{(638 + 763)/2} \times 100 = 34.7\%$$

(The capital employed figure at 1 April 2008 is given in Note 8).

ROCE is considered by many to be a primary measure of profitability. It compares inputs (capital invested) with outputs (operating profit). This comparison is vital in assessing the effectiveness with which funds have been deployed. Once again, an average figure for capital employed should be used where the information is available.

Activity 7.3

Calculate the ROCE for Alexis plc for the year to 31 March 2010.

For 2010, the ratio is

$$\text{ROCE} = \frac{47}{(763 + 834)/2} \times 100 = 5.9\%$$

This ratio tells much the same story as ROSF; namely a poor performance, with the return on the assets being less than the rate that the business has to pay for most of its borrowed funds (that is, 10 per cent for the loan notes).

Real World 7.1 shows how financial ratios are used by businesses as a basis for setting profitability targets.

Real World 7.1

Targeting profitability

The ROCE ratio is widely used by businesses when establishing targets for profitability. These targets are sometimes made public and here are some examples:

Tesco plc, the supermarket business, in 2004 set a target to achieve a growth in ROCE of 2 per cent from its 2004 figure of 10.4 per cent. It achieved this with 12.5 per cent in 2006 and increased it further in 2007. Tesco then set a further 2 per cent target growth for ROCE for 2008 and beyond. The business achieved a 13 per cent rate of ROCE in 2009. Tesco uses performance against a target ROCE as a basis of rewarding its senior managers, indicating the importance that the business attaches to this measure of performance.

BSkyB plc, the satellite broadcaster, has a target ROCE of 15 per cent by 2011 for its broadband operation.

Air France-KLM, the world's largest airline (on the basis of sales revenue), has set itself the target of achieving a ROCE of 7 per cent.

Sources: Information taken from Tesco plc Annual Report 2009, 'BSkyB/triple play', *Financial Times*, 12 July 2006 and Air France-KLM press release, 14 February 2008.

Real World 7.2 provides some indication of the levels of ROCE achieved by UK businesses.

Real World 7.2

Achieving profitability

UK businesses reported an average ROCE of 11.6 per cent for the second quarter of 2009. This was down on the record rate of 15.1 per cent for the first quarter of 2007, which was the highest level of ROCE since the Office of National Statistics first kept records.

Service sector businesses were much the more successful with an average ROCE of 15.6 per cent, compared with 6.7 per cent among manufacturers. These compare with 15.7 per cent for service businesses, and 10.2 per cent for manufacturers, averaged over 2006, 2007 and 2008. This suggests that despite the recession UK service businesses are maintaining their profitability quite well. Manufacturers, on the other hand, have suffered a large fall in profitability compared with recent years.

The difference in ROCE between the two sectors is accounted for by the higher capital intensity of manufacturing, according to the Office of National Statistics.

Source: Information taken from 'Corporate profitability', Office of National Statistics, www.statistics.gov.uk/cci, 17 October 2009.

Operating profit margin

→ The **operating profit margin ratio** relates the operating profit for the period to the sales revenue. The ratio is expressed as follows:

$$\text{Operating profit margin} = \frac{\text{Operating profit}}{\text{Sales revenue}} \times 100$$

The operating profit (that is, profit before interest and taxation) is used in this ratio as it represents the profit from trading operations before the interest payable expense is taken into account. This is often regarded as the most appropriate measure of operational performance, when used as a basis of comparison, because differences arising from the way in which the business is financed will not influence the measure.

For the year ended 31 March 2009, Alexis plc's operating profit margin ratio is

$$\text{Operating profit margin} = \frac{243}{2,240} \times 100 = 10.8\%$$

This ratio compares one output of the business (operating profit) with another output (sales revenue). The ratio can vary considerably between types of business. For example, supermarkets tend to operate on low prices and, therefore, low operating profit margins. This is done in an attempt to stimulate sales and thereby increase the total amount of operating profit generated. Jewellers, on the other hand, tend to have high operating profit margins but have much lower levels of sales volume. Factors such as the degree of competition, the type of customer, the economic climate and industry characteristics (such as the level of risk) will influence the operating profit margin of a business. This point is picked up again later in the chapter.

Activity 7.4

Calculate the operating profit margin for Alexis plc for the year to 31 March 2010.

The ratio for 2010 is

$$\text{Operating profit margin} = \frac{47}{2,681} \times 100 = 1.8\%$$

Once again, this shows a very weak performance compared with that of 2009. Whereas in 2009 for every £1 of sales revenue an average of 10.8p (that is, 10.8 per cent) was left as operating profit, after paying the cost of the carpets sold and other expenses of operating the business, for 2010 this had fallen to only 1.8p for every £1. It seems that the reason for the poor ROSF and ROCE ratios was partially, perhaps wholly, a high level of expenses relative to sales revenue. The next ratio should provide us with a clue as to how the sharp decline in this ratio occurred.

Real World 7.3 describes how one well-known business intends to increase its operating profit margin over time.

Operating profit margin taking off at BA

British Airways plc, the airline business, exceeded its 10 per cent operating profit margin target during the year to 31 March 2008. This target had been in existence since 2002.

The year to 31 March 2009 was rather less successful with the company sustaining an operating loss equal to 2.4 per cent of its sales revenue. The business put this down to 'incredibly difficult trading conditions' brought about by the recession.

Source: British Airways plc Annual Report 2009.

Gross profit margin

→ The **gross profit margin ratio** relates the gross profit of the business to the sales revenue generated for the same period. Gross profit represents the difference between sales revenue and the cost of sales. The ratio is therefore a measure of profitability in buying (or producing) and selling goods or services before any other expenses are taken into account. As cost of sales represents a major expense for many businesses, a change in this ratio can have a significant effect on the 'bottom line' (that is, the profit for the year). The gross profit margin ratio is calculated as follows:

$$\text{Gross profit margin} = \frac{\text{Gross profit}}{\text{Sales revenue}} \times 100$$

For the year to 31 March 2009, the ratio for Alexis plc is

$$\text{Gross profit margin} = \frac{495}{2,240} \times 100 = 22.1\%$$

Activity 7.5

Calculate the gross profit margin for Alexis plc for the year to 31 March 2010.

The ratio for 2010 is:

$$\text{Gross profit margin} = \frac{409}{2,681} \times 100 = 15.3\%$$

The decline in this ratio means that gross profit was lower *relative* to sales revenue in 2010 than it had been in 2009. Bearing in mind that

Gross profit = Sales revenue − Cost of sales (or cost of goods sold)

this means that cost of sales was higher *relative* to sales revenue in 2010, than in 2009. This could mean that sales prices were lower and/or that the purchase cost of carpets sold had increased. It is possible that both sales prices and carpets sold prices had reduced, but the former at a greater rate than the latter. Similarly they may both have increased, but with sales prices having increased at a lesser rate than the cost of the carpets.

Clearly, part of the decline in the operating profit margin ratio is linked to the dramatic decline in the gross profit margin ratio. Whereas, after paying for the carpets sold, for each £1 of sales revenue 22.1p was left to cover other operating expenses in 2009, this was only 15.3p in 2010.

The profitability ratios for the business over the two years can be set out as follows:

	2009 %	2010 %
ROSF	33.0	2.0
ROCE	34.7	5.9
Operating profit margin	10.8	1.8
Gross profit margin	22.1	15.3

Activity 7.6

What do you deduce from a comparison of the declines in the operating profit and gross profit margin ratios?

It occurs to us that the decline in the operating profit margin was 9 per cent (that is, 10.8 per cent to 1.8 per cent), whereas that of the gross profit margin was only 6.8 per cent (that is, from 22.1 per cent to 15.3 per cent). This can only mean that operating expenses were greater, compared with sales revenue in 2010, than they had been in 2009. The declines in both ROSF and ROCE were caused partly, therefore, by the business incurring higher inventories' purchasing costs relative to sales revenue and partly through higher operating expenses compared with sales revenue. We should need to compare these ratios with their planned levels before we could usefully assess the business's success.

The analyst must now carry out some investigation to discover what caused the increases in both cost of sales and operating expenses, relative to sales revenue, from 2009 to 2010. This will involve checking on what has happened with sales and inventories prices over the two years. Similarly, it will involve looking at each of the individual areas that make up operating expenses to discover which ones were responsible for the increase, relative to sales revenue. Here, further ratios, for example staff expenses (wages and salaries) to sales revenue, could be calculated in an attempt to isolate the cause of the change from 2009 to 2010. In fact, as we discussed when we took an overview of the financial statements, the increase in staffing may well account for most of the increase in operating expenses.

Real World 7.4 is a Financial Times article that discusses the reasons for improving profitability at 'Bollywood' .

Real World 7.4

Investing in Bollywood

FT

Alas for investors, the economics of Bollywood have long been about as predictable as, but rather less uplifting than, the plotline of the average Hindi movie. The world's biggest movie market in terms of number of tickets sold – a massive 3.7 billion – has traditionally offered miserable returns to its backers. Instead, revenues were swallowed up by a blend of piracy, taxes and inefficiencies.

Now the script appears to be changing. Big backers – in the shape of international entertainment giants such as Walt Disney and Viacom, and venture capitalists – are starting to enter Bollywood. With a brace of Indian film production companies listed on London's Alternative Investment Market and a third due to follow shortly, smaller investors are also getting in on the act. That is testament to improving industry dynamics. Digital technology and tougher regulation is helping reduce piracy while tax strains are being mitigated either by new rules at home – such as scrapping entertainment tax for multiplexes – or shifting production abroad.

Entertainment companies are also sharpening up their acts and evolving from one-stop shops to specialists in, say, production or distribution. Cleaner corporate structures enable them to access a broader range of financing. The economics of movie-making are improving too. Perhaps 40 per cent of Indian movies are now shot overseas, benefiting from tax breaks, 'captive' actors and producers and – in Europe – longer working days. As a result, a movie may be in the can in perhaps a quarter of the time it would normally take in India.

Evolution in other parts of the media world also plays into the hands of Bollywood moguls; for example, the growth in satellite TV means more channels to bid on movie licensing rights. Industry analysts reckon Bollywood now offers a return on capital employed of about 30 to 35 per cent, not too dissimilar from Hollywood. Years of tears followed by a happy ending? How Bollywood.

Source: 'Investing in Bollywood', Lex column, *Financial Times*, 25 June 2007.

Efficiency

Efficiency ratios are used to try to assess how successfully the various resources of the business are managed. The following ratios cover some of the more important aspects of resource management:

- average inventories turnover period
- average settlement period for trade receivables
- average settlement period for trade payables
- sales revenue to capital employed
- sales revenue per employee.

We shall now look at each of these in turn.

Average inventories turnover period

Inventories often represent a significant investment for a business. For some types of business (for example, manufacturers and certain retailers), inventories may account for a substantial proportion of the total assets held (see Real World 8.5, page 274). The **average inventories turnover period ratio** measures the average period for which inventories are being held. The ratio is calculated as follows:

$$\text{Average inventories turnover period} = \frac{\text{Average inventories held}}{\text{Cost of sales}} \times 365$$

The average inventories for the period can be calculated as a simple average of the opening and closing inventories levels for the year. However, in the case of a highly seasonal business, where inventories levels may vary considerably over the year, a monthly average may be more appropriate, should this information be available.

In the case of Alexis plc, the inventories turnover period for the year ended 31 March 2009 is

$$\text{Average inventories turnover period} = \frac{(241 + 300)/2}{1,745} \times 365 = 56.6 \text{ days}$$

(The opening inventories figure was taken from Note 3 to the financial statements.)

This means that, on average, the inventories held are being 'turned over' every 56.6 days. So, a carpet bought by the business on a particular day would, on average, have been sold about eight weeks later. A business will normally prefer a short inventories turnover period to a long one, because holding inventories has costs, for example the opportunity cost of the funds tied up. When judging the amount of inventories to carry, the business must consider such things as the likely demand for the inventories, the possibility of supply shortages, the likelihood of price rises, the amount of storage space available and the perishability and/or susceptibility to obsolescence of the inventories.

This ratio is sometimes expressed in terms of weeks or months rather than days. Multiplying by 52 or 12, rather than 365, will achieve this.

Activity 7.7

Calculate the average inventories turnover period for Alexis plc for the year ended 31 March 2010.

The ratio for 2010 is

$$\text{Average inventories turnover period} = \frac{(300 + 406)/2}{2,272} \times 365 = 56.7 \text{ days}$$

The inventories turnover period is virtually the same in both years.

Average settlement period for trade receivables

Selling on credit is the norm for most businesses, except for retailers. Trade receivables are a necessary evil. A business will naturally be concerned with the amount of funds tied up in trade receivables and try to keep this to a minimum. The speed of payment can have a significant effect on the business's cash flow. The **average settlement period for trade receivables ratio** calculates how long, on average, credit customers take to pay the amounts that they owe to the business. The ratio is as follows:

$$\text{Average settlement period for trade receivables} = \frac{\text{Average trade receivables}}{\text{Credit sales revenue}} \times 365$$

A business will normally prefer a shorter average settlement period to a longer one as, once again, funds are being tied up that may be used for more profitable purposes. Although this ratio can be useful, it is important to remember that it produces an *average* figure for the number of days for which debts are outstanding. This average may be badly distorted by, for example, a few large customers who are very slow or very fast payers.

Since all sales made by Alexis plc are on credit, the average settlement period for trade receivables for the year ended 31 March 2009 is

$$\text{Average settlement period for trade receivables} = \frac{(223 + 240)/2}{2,240} \times 365 = 37.7 \text{ days}$$

(The opening trade receivables figure was taken from Note 4 to the financial statements.)

Activity 7.8

Calculate the average settlement period for Alexis plc's trade receivables for the year ended 31 March 2010.

The ratio for 2010 is:

$$\text{Average settlement period for trade receivables} = \frac{(240 + 273)/2}{2,681} \times 365 = 34.9 \text{ days}$$

On the face of it, this reduction in the settlement period is welcome. It means that less cash was tied up in trade receivables for each £1 of sales revenue in 2010 than in 2009. Only if the reduction were achieved at the expense of customer goodwill or a high direct financial cost might the desirability of the reduction be questioned. For example, the reduction may have been due to chasing customers too vigorously or as a result of incurring higher expenses, such as discounts allowed to customers who pay quickly.

Real World 7.5 is an article that discusses how customers are unilaterally extending their payment terms as a result of the recession.

Real World 7.5

Taking credit where it's not due   **FT**

Two-thirds of suppliers are being forced to accept arbitrary extensions of payment terms by their customers as pressure on businesses to conserve cash becomes more acute, a survey by the Institute of Credit Management has found.

The findings provide more evidence of the speed with which the recession is prompting many businesses to focus on preserving cash and managing working capital more tightly.

The findings come after the Department for Business, Enterprise and Regulatory Reform last week unveiled a voluntary 'prompt payment code', designed with the ICM. It aims to help small businesses by discouraging bigger companies from using their purchasing power to ease pressures on their cash flow by squeezing their supply chain.

In a poll of 600 members last month, the ICM asked whether any of their customers had tried arbitrarily to extend their payment terms in the previous three months. Sixty-seven per cent said Yes with the rest saying No.

For those answering Yes, 61 per cent said the extension applied retroactively as well as to future business, with 39 per cent saying it applied to all future business.

Philip King, ICM director general, said: 'We were certainly staggered by the volume and the proportion of respondents who said they had experienced that. It's no surprise that it's happening but for the number to be that high is a real surprise.'

The ICM is the largest organisation in Europe representing credit managers in trade credit, credit insurance and insolvency.

In some cases, it said, there was 'anecdotal evidence' that some companies were trying to delay paying their suppliers by challenging their invoices, but it stressed there was 'no scientific evidence' of an increase.

Challenging the accuracy of invoices is common practice, but there are signs it is being used more regularly to delay payment.

The head of a global employment agency with operations in the UK said it had taken on more staff to process invoices. 'It used to be that if there was a mistake with one line, clients would pay the whole invoice and we'd resolve that one grey area. But now they're using one possible mistake as a way of withholding payment on the entire invoice,' said the executive.

Martin O'Donovan, an assistant director at the Association of Corporate Treasurers, said: 'People really are under strain and are pulling whatever levers they have got – even those that are not the most politic ones and perhaps not in the longer-term interest of the company.'

Source: 'Payment squeeze on suppliers', Jeremy Grant, *Financial Times*, 22 December 2008.

Average settlement period for trade payables

The **average settlement period for trade payables ratio** measures how long, on average, the business takes to pay those who have supplied goods and services on credit. The ratio is calculated as follows:

$$\text{Average settlement period for trade payables} = \frac{\text{Average trade payables}}{\text{Credit purchases}} \times 365$$

This ratio provides an average figure, which, like the average settlement period for trade receivables ratio, can be distorted by the payment period for one or two large suppliers.

As trade payables provide a free source of finance for the business, it is perhaps not surprising that some businesses attempt to increase their average settlement period for trade payables. However, such a policy can be taken too far and result in a loss of goodwill of suppliers.

For the year ended 31 March 2009, Alexis plc's average settlement period for trade payables is

$$\text{Average settlement period for trade payables} = \frac{(183 + 261)/2}{1,804} \times 365 = 44.9 \text{ days}$$

(The opening trade payables figure was taken from Note 4 to the financial statements and the purchases figure from Note 3.)

Activity 7.9

Calculate the average settlement period for trade payables for Alexis plc for the year ended 31 March 2010.

The ratio for 2010 is

$$\text{Average settlement period for trade payables} = \frac{(261 + 354)/2}{2,378} \times 365 = 47.2 \text{ days}$$

There was an increase, between 2009 and 2010, in the average length of time that elapsed between buying inventories and services and paying for them. On the face of it, this is beneficial because the business is using free finance provided by suppliers. If, however, this is leading to a loss of supplier goodwill it could have adverse consequences for Alexis plc.

Sales revenue to capital employed

→ The **sales revenue to capital employed ratio** (or net asset turnover ratio) examines how effectively the assets of the business are being used to generate sales revenue. It is calculated as follows:

$$\frac{\text{Sales revenue to capital}}{\text{employed ratio}} = \frac{\text{Sales revenue}}{\text{Share capital + Reserves + Non-current liabilities}}$$

Generally speaking, a higher net asset turnover ratio is preferred to a lower one. A higher ratio will normally suggest that assets are being used more productively in the generation of revenue. However, a very high ratio may suggest that the business is 'overtrading on its assets', that is, it has insufficient assets to sustain the level of sales revenue achieved. (Overtrading will be discussed in more detail in Chapter 8.) When comparing this ratio for different businesses, factors such as the age and condition of assets held, the valuation bases for assets and whether assets are leased or owned outright can complicate interpretation.

A variation of this formula is to use the total assets less current liabilities (which is equivalent to long-term capital employed) in the denominator (lower part of the fraction). The identical result is obtained.

For the year ended 31 March 2009 this ratio for Alexis plc is

$$\text{Sales revenue to capital employed} = \frac{2,240}{(638 + 763)/2} = 3.20 \text{ times}$$

Activity 7.10

Calculate the sales revenue to capital employed ratio for Alexis plc for the year ended 31 March 2010.

The sales revenue to capital employed ratio for 2010 is

$$\text{Sales revenue to capital employed} = \frac{2,681}{(763 + 834)/2} = 3.36 \text{ times}$$

This seems to be an improvement, since in 2010 more sales revenue was being generated for each £1 of capital employed (£3.36) than was the case in 2009 (£3.20). Provided that overtrading is not an issue and that the additional sales are generating an acceptable profit, this is to be welcomed.

Sales revenue per employee

The **sales revenue per employee ratio** relates sales revenue generated to a particular business resource, that is, labour. It provides a measure of the productivity of the workforce. The ratio is:

$$\text{Sales revenue per employee} = \frac{\text{Sales revenue}}{\text{Number of employees}}$$

Generally, businesses would prefer to have a high value for this ratio, implying that they are using their staff efficiently.

For the year ended 31 March 2009, the ratio for Alexis plc is

$$\text{Sales revenue per employee} = \frac{£2,240m}{13,995} = £160,057$$

Activity 7.11

Calculate the sales revenue per employee for Alexis plc for the year ended 31 March 2010.

The ratio for 2010 is

$$\text{Sales revenue per employee} = \frac{£2,681m}{18,623} = £143,962$$

This represents a fairly significant decline and probably one that merits further investigation. As we discussed previously, the number of employees had increased quite notably (by about 33 per cent) during 2010 and the analyst will probably try to discover why this had not generated sufficient additional sales revenue to maintain the ratio at its 2009 level. It could be that the additional employees were not appointed until late in the year ended 31 March 2010.

The efficiency, or activity, ratios may be summarised as follows:

	2009	2010
Average inventories turnover period	56.6 days	56.7 days
Average settlement period for trade receivables	37.7 days	34.9 days
Average settlement period for trade payables	44.9 days	47.2 days
Sales revenue to capital employed (net asset turnover)	3.20 times	3.36 times
Sales revenue per employee	£160,057	£143,962

Activity 7.12

What do you deduce from a comparison of the efficiency ratios over the two years?

We feel that maintaining the inventories turnover period at the 2009 level might be reasonable, though whether this represents a satisfactory period can probably only be assessed by looking at the business's planned inventories period. The inventories turnover period for other businesses operating in carpet retailing, particularly those regarded as the market leaders, may have been helpful in formulating the plans. On the face of things, a shorter receivables collection period and a longer payables payment period are both desirable. On the other hand, these may have been achieved at the cost of a loss of the goodwill of customers and suppliers, respectively. The increased net asset turnover ratio seems beneficial, provided that the business can manage this increase. The decline in the sales revenue per employee ratio is undesirable but, as we have already seen, is probably related to the dramatic increase in the level of staffing. As with the inventories turnover period, these other ratios need to be compared with the planned standard of efficiency.

Relationship between profitability and efficiency

In our earlier discussions concerning profitability ratios, we saw that return on capital employed (ROCE) is regarded as a key ratio by many businesses. The ratio is:

$$ROCE = \frac{Operating\ profit}{Long\text{-}term\ capital\ employed} \times 100$$

where long-term capital comprises share capital plus reserves plus long-term borrowings. This ratio can be broken down into two elements, as shown in Figure 7.1. The first ratio is the operating profit margin ratio and the second is the sales revenue to capital employed (net asset turnover) ratio, both of which we discussed earlier.

Figure 7.1	The main elements of the ROCE ratio

The ROCE ratio can be divided into two elements: operating profit to sales revenue and sales revenue to capital employed. By analysing ROCE in this way, we can see the influence of both profitability and efficiency on this important ratio.

By breaking down the ROCE ratio in this manner, we highlight the fact that the overall return on funds employed within the business will be determined both by the profitability of sales and by efficiency in the use of capital.

Example 7.2

Consider the following information, for last year, concerning two different businesses operating in the same industry:

	Antler plc	Baker plc
	£m	£m
Operating profit	20	15
Average long-term capital employed	100	75
Sales revenue	200	300

The ROCE for each business is identical (20 per cent). However, the manner in which that return was achieved by each business was quite different. In the case of Antler plc, the operating profit margin is 10 per cent and the sales revenue to capital employed ratio is 2 times (so ROCE = 10% × 2 = 20%). In the case of Baker plc, the operating profit margin is 5 per cent and the sales revenue to capital employed ratio is 4 times (and so ROCE = 5% × 4 = 20%).

Example 7.2 demonstrates that a relatively high sales revenue to capital employed ratio can compensate for a relatively low operating profit margin. Similarly, a relatively low sales revenue to capital employed ratio can be overcome by a relatively high operating profit margin. In many areas of retail and distribution (for example, supermarkets and delivery services), the operating profit margins are quite low but the ROCE can be high, provided that the assets are used productively (that is, low margin, high turnover).

Activity 7.13

Show how the ROCE ratio for Alexis plc can be analysed into the two elements for each of the years 2009 and 2010. What conclusions can you draw from your figures?

	ROCE =	Operating profit margin	× Sales revenue to capital employed
2009	34.7%	10.8%	3.20
2010	5.9%	1.8%	3.36

As we can see, the relationship between the three ratios holds for Alexis plc for both years. The small apparent differences arise because the three ratios are stated here only to one or two decimal places.

Although the business was more effective at generating sales revenue (sales revenue to capital employed ratio increased) in 2010 than in 2009, in 2010 it fell well below the level necessary to compensate for the sharp decline in the effectiveness of each sale (operating profit margin). As a result, the 2010 ROCE was well below the 2009 value.

Liquidity

Liquidity ratios are concerned with the ability of the business to meet its short-term financial obligations. The following ratios are widely used:

- current ratio
- acid test ratio
- operating cash flows to maturing obligations.

These three will now be considered.

Current ratio

→ The **current ratio** compares the 'liquid' assets (that is, cash and those assets held that will soon be turned into cash) of the business with the current liabilities. The ratio is calculated as follows:

$$\text{Current ratio} = \frac{\text{Current assets}}{\text{Current liabilities}}$$

Some people seem to believe that there is an 'ideal' current ratio (usually 2 times or 2:1) for all businesses. However, this fails to take into account the fact that different types of business require different current ratios. For example, a manufacturing business will often have a relatively high current ratio because it is necessary to hold inventories of finished goods, raw materials and work in progress. It will also normally sell goods on credit, thereby giving rise to trade receivables. A supermarket chain, on the other hand, will have a relatively low ratio, as it will hold only fast-moving inventories of finished goods and all of its sales will be made for cash (no credit sales). (See Real World 8.5 on page 274.)

The higher the ratio, the more liquid the business is considered to be. As liquidity is vital to the survival of a business, a higher current ratio might be thought to be preferable to a lower one. If a business has a very high ratio, however, it may be that funds are tied up in cash or other liquid assets and are not, therefore, being used as productively as they might otherwise be.

As at 31 March 2009, the current ratio of Alexis plc is

$$\text{Current ratio} = \frac{544}{291} = 1.9 \text{ times (or 1.9:1)}$$

Activity 7.14

Calculate the current ratio for Alexis plc as at 31 March 2010.

The ratio as at 31 March 2010 is

$$\text{Current ratio} = \frac{679}{432} = 1.6 \text{ times (or 1.6:1)}$$

Although this is a decline from 2009 to 2010, it is not necessarily a matter of concern. The next ratio may provide a clue as to whether there seems to be a problem.

Acid test ratio

→   The **acid test ratio** is very similar to the current ratio, but it represents a more stringent test of liquidity. It can be argued that, for many businesses, inventories cannot be converted into cash quickly. (Note that, in the case of Alexis plc, the inventories turnover period was about 57 days in both years (see page 237).) As a result, it may be better to exclude this particular asset from any measure of liquidity. The acid test ratio is a variation of the current ratio, but excluding inventories.

The minimum level for this ratio is often stated as 1.0 times (or 1:1; that is, current assets (excluding inventories) equals current liabilities). In many highly successful businesses that are regarded as having adequate liquidity, however, it is not unusual for the acid test ratio to be below 1.0 without causing particular liquidity problems. (See Real World 8.5 on page 274.)

The acid test ratio is calculated as follows:

$$\text{Acid test ratio} = \frac{\text{Current assets (excluding inventories)}}{\text{Current liabilities}}$$

The acid test ratio for Alexis plc as at 31 March 2009 is

$$\text{Acid test ratio} = \frac{544 - 300}{291} = 0.8 \text{ times (or 0.8:1)}$$

We can see that the 'liquid' current assets do not quite cover the current liabilities, so the business may be experiencing some liquidity problems.

Activity 7.15

Calculate the acid test ratio for Alexis plc as at 31 March 2010.

The ratio as at 31 March 2010 is

$$\text{Acid test ratio} = \frac{679 - 406}{432} = 0.6 \text{ times}$$

The 2010 ratio is significantly below that for 2009. The 2010 level may well be a cause for concern. The rapid decline in this ratio should lead to steps being taken, at least, to stop it falling further.

Cash generated from operations to maturing obligations

→ The **cash generated from operations to maturing obligations ratio** compares the cash generated from operations (taken from the statement of cash flows) with the current liabilities of the business. It provides a further indication of the ability of the business to meet its maturing obligations. The ratio is expressed as:

$$\frac{\textbf{Cash generated from operations}}{\textbf{to maturing obligations}} = \frac{\textbf{Cash generated from operations}}{\textbf{Current liabilities}}$$

The higher this ratio is, the better the liquidity of the business. This ratio has the advantage over the current ratio that the operating cash flows for a period usually provide a more reliable guide to the liquidity of a business than do the current assets held at the statement of financial position date. Alexis plc's ratio for the year ended 31 March 2009 is

$$\text{Cash generated from operations to maturing obligations ratio} = \frac{251}{291} = 0.9 \text{ times}$$

This indicates that the operating cash flows for the year are not quite sufficient to cover the current liabilities at the end of the year.

Activity 7.16

Calculate the cash generated from operations to maturing obligations ratio for Alexis plc for the year ended 31 March 2010.

$$\text{Cash generated from operations to maturing obligations ratio} = \frac{34}{432} = 0.1 \text{ times}$$

This shows an alarming decline in the ability of the business to meet its maturing obligations from its operating cash flows. This confirms that liquidity is a real cause for concern for the business.

The liquidity ratios for the two-year period may be summarised as follows:

	2009	2010
Current ratio	1.9	1.6
Acid test ratio	0.8	0.6
Cash generated from operations to maturing obligations	0.9	0.1

Activity 7.17

What do you deduce from the liquidity ratios set out above?

Although it is not possible to make a totally valid judgement without knowing the planned ratios, there appears to have been a worrying decline in liquidity. This is indicated by all three of these ratios. The most worrying is in the last ratio because it shows that the ability of the business to generate cash from trading operations has declined, relative to the short-term debts, from 2009 to 2010. The apparent liquidity problem may, however, be planned, short-term and linked to the expansion in non-current assets and staffing. It may be that when the benefits of the expansion come on stream, liquidity will improve. On the other hand, short-term claimants may become anxious when they see signs of weak liquidity. This anxiety may lead them to press for payment, which could cause problems for Alexis plc.

Operating cash cycle

→ When assessing the liquidity of a business, it is important to be aware of the **operating cash cycle (OCC)**. In the case of a business that purchases goods on credit for sub-sequent resale on credit (for example, a wholesaler), this may be defined as the time period between the outlay of cash necessary for the purchase of inventories and the ultimate receipt of cash from the credit customer. For such a business, the OCC is as shown in Figure 7.2.

Figure 7.2   The operating cash cycle

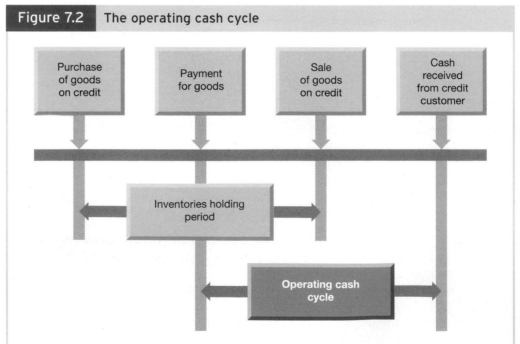

The OCC is the time period between paying for goods and receiving the cash from the sale of those goods. The length of the OCC has a significant impact on the amount of funds that the business needs to apply to working capital.

Figure 7.2 shows that payment for inventories acquired on credit occurs some time after those inventories have been purchased and, therefore, no immediate cash outflow arises from the purchase. Similarly, cash receipts from credit customers will occur some time after the sale is made. There will, therefore, be no immediate cash inflow as a result of the sale. The OCC is the time period between the payment made to the supplier for goods and the cash received from the credit customer. Though Figure 7.2 depicts the position for a wholesaling business, the definition of the OCC can easily be adapted for other types of businesses, such as retailers and manufacturers.

The OCC is important because it has a significant influence on the financing requirements of the business. Broadly speaking, the longer the cycle, the greater the financing requirements of the business and the greater the financial risks. For this reason, a business may wish to reduce the OCC to the minimum possible period.

For the type of business that buys inventories and then sells them on credit, the OCC can be calculated from the financial statements by using certain ratios. The calculation is as shown in Figure 7.3.

Figure 7.3	Calculating the operating cash cycle

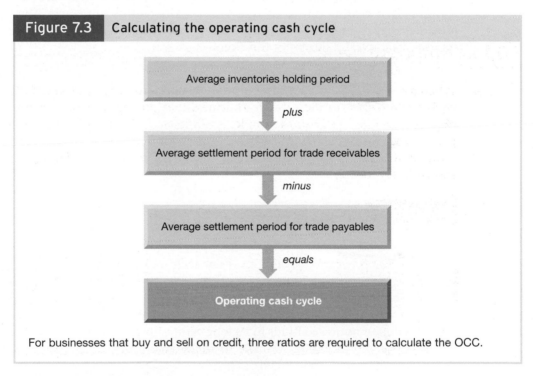

For businesses that buy and sell on credit, three ratios are required to calculate the OCC.

Activity 7.18

Calculate the length of the OCC for Alexis plc for the year ended 31 March 2010, using the values that you calculated in the relevant Activities earlier in this chapter.

The OCC for the year ended 31 March 2010 is as follows:

	Number of days
Average inventories turnover period (from Activity 7.7)	56.7
Average settlement period for trade receivables (from Activity 7.8)	34.9
	91.6
Average settlement period for trade payables (from Activity 7.9)	(47.2)
OCC	44.4

Financial gearing

→ **Financial gearing** occurs when a business is financed, at least in part, by borrowing instead of by finance provided by the owners (the shareholders) as equity. A business's level of gearing (that is, the extent to which it is financed from sources that require a fixed return) is an important factor in assessing risk. Where a business borrows, it takes on a commitment to pay interest charges and make capital repayments. Where the borrowing is heavy, this can be a significant financial burden; it can increase the risk of the business becoming insolvent. Nevertheless, most businesses are geared to some extent. (Costain Group plc, the builders and construction business, is a rare example of a UK business with no borrowings.)

Given the risks involved, we may wonder why a business would want to take on gearing (that is, to borrow). One reason may be that the owners have insufficient funds, so the only way to finance the business adequately is to borrow from others. Another reason is that gearing can be used to increase the returns to owners. This is possible provided that the returns generated from borrowed funds exceed the cost of paying interest. Example 7.3 illustrates this point.

Example 7.3

The long-term capital structures of two new businesses, Lee Ltd and Nova Ltd, are as follows:

	Lee Ltd	Nova Ltd
	£000	£000
£1 ordinary shares	100	200
10% loan notes	200	100
	300	300

In their first year of operations, they each make an operating profit (that is, profit before interest and taxation) of £50,000. The tax rate is 30 per cent of the profit before taxation but after interest.

Lee Ltd would probably be considered relatively highly geared, as it has a high proportion of borrowed funds in its long-term capital structure. Nova Ltd is much lower geared. The profit available to the shareholders of each business in the first year of operations will be:

	Lee Ltd	Nova Ltd
	£000	£000
Operating profit	50	50
Interest payable	(20)	(10)
Profit before taxation	30	40
Taxation (30%)	(9)	(12)
Profit for the year (available to ordinary shareholders)	21	28

The return on ordinary shareholders' funds (ROSF) for each business will be:

Lee Ltd	Nova Ltd
$\dfrac{21,000}{100,000} \times 100 = 21\%$	$\dfrac{28,000}{200,000} \times 100 = 14\%$

We can see that Lee Ltd, the more highly geared business, has generated a better ROSF than Nova Ltd. This is despite the fact that the ROCE (return on capital employed) is identical for both businesses (that is, (£50,000/£300,000) × 100 = 16.7%).

Note that at the £50,000 level of operating profit, the shareholders of both Lee Ltd and Nova Ltd benefit from gearing. Were the two businesses totally reliant on equity financing, the profit for the year (the profit after taxation) would be £35,000 (that is, £50,000 less 30 per cent taxation), giving a ROSF of 11.7 per cent (that is, £35,000/£300,000). Both businesses generate higher ROSFs than this as a result of financial gearing.

An effect of gearing is that returns to shareholders become more sensitive to changes in operating profits. For a highly geared business, a change in operating profits will lead to a proportionately greater change in the ROSF ratio.

Activity 7.19

Assume that the operating profit was 20 per cent higher for each business than stated above (that is, an operating profit of £60,000). What would be the effect of this on ROSF?

The revised profit available to the shareholders of each business in the first year of operations will be:

	Lee Ltd £000	Nova Ltd £000
Operating profit	60	60
Interest payable	(20)	(10)
Profit before taxation	40	50
Taxation (30%)	(12)	(15)
Profit for the year (available to ordinary shareholders)	28	35

The ROSF for each business will now be:

Lee Ltd $\frac{28,000}{100,000} \times 100 = 28\%$

Nova Ltd $\frac{35,000}{200,000} \times 100 = 17.5\%$

We can see that for Lee Ltd, the higher-geared business, the returns to shareholders have increased by one-third (from 21 per cent to 28 per cent), whereas for the lower-geared business, Nova Ltd, the benefits of gearing are less pronounced, increasing by only one-quarter (from 14 per cent to 17.5 per cent). The effect of gearing can, of course, work in both directions. So, for a highly geared business, a small decline in operating profit will bring about a much greater decline in the returns to shareholders.

The reason that gearing tends to be beneficial to shareholders is that interest rates for borrowings are low by comparison with the returns that the typical business can earn. On top of this, interest expenses are tax-deductible, as we saw in Example 7.3 and Activity 7.19, which makes the effective cost of borrowing quite cheap. It is debatable whether the apparent low interest rates really are beneficial to the shareholders. Some argue that since borrowing increases the risk to shareholders, there is a hidden cost of borrowing. What are not illusory, however, are the benefits to the shareholders of the tax-deductibility of interest on borrowings.

The effect of gearing is like that of two intermeshing cogwheels of unequal size (see Figure 7.4). The movement in the larger cog (operating profit) causes a more than proportionate movement in the smaller cog (returns to ordinary shareholders).

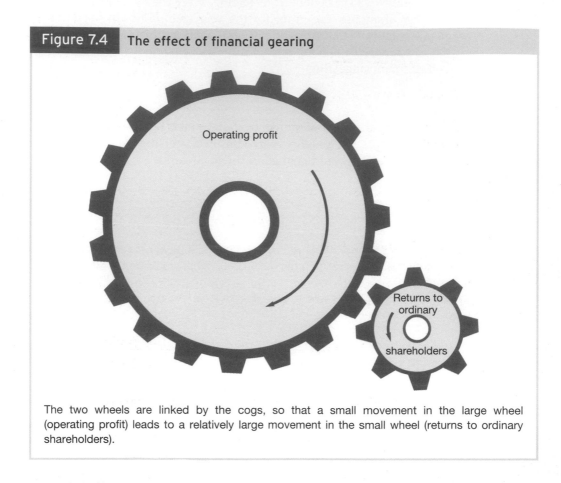

Figure 7.4   The effect of financial gearing

The two wheels are linked by the cogs, so that a small movement in the large wheel (operating profit) leads to a relatively large movement in the small wheel (returns to ordinary shareholders).

Two ratios are widely used to assess gearing:

● the gearing ratio, and
● the interest cover ratio.

Gearing ratio

→ The **gearing ratio** measures the contribution of long-term lenders to the long-term capital structure of a business:

$$\text{Gearing ratio} = \frac{\text{Long-term (non-current) liabilities}}{\text{Share capital} + \text{Reserves} + \text{Long-term (non-current) liabilities}} \times 100$$

The gearing ratio for Alexis plc, as at 31 March 2009, is

$$\text{Gearing ratio} = \frac{200}{(563 + 200)} \times 100 = 26.2\%$$

This is a level of gearing that would not normally be considered to be very high.

Activity 7.20

Calculate the gearing ratio of Alexis plc as at 31 March 2010.

The ratio as at 31 March 2010 is

$$\text{Gearing ratio} = \frac{300}{(534 + 300)} \times 100 = 36.0\%$$

This is a substantial increase in the level of gearing over the year.

Interest cover ratio

→   The **interest cover ratio** measures the amount of operating profit available to cover interest payable. The ratio may be calculated as follows:

$$\text{Interest cover ratio} = \frac{\text{Operating profit}}{\text{Interest payable}}$$

The ratio for Alexis plc for the year ended 31 March 2009 is

$$\text{Interest cover ratio} = \frac{243}{18} = 13.5 \text{ times}$$

This ratio shows that the level of operating profit is considerably higher than the level of interest payable. This means that a large fall in operating profit could occur before operating profit levels failed to cover interest payable. The lower the level of operating profit coverage, the greater the risk to lenders that interest payments will not be met. There will also be a greater risk for the shareholders that the lenders will take action against the business to recover the interest due.

Activity 7.21

Calculate the interest cover ratio of Alexis plc for the year ended 31 March 2010.

The ratio for the year ended 31 March 2010 is

$$\text{Interest cover ratio} = \frac{47}{32} = 1.5 \text{ times}$$

Alexis plc's gearing ratios are:

	2009	2010
Gearing ratio	26.2%	36.0%
Interest cover ratio	13.5 times	1.5 times

Activity 7.22

What do you deduce from a comparison of Alexis plc's gearing ratios over the two years?

The gearing ratio altered significantly. This is mainly due to the substantial increase in the contribution of long-term lenders to the financing of the business.

The interest cover ratio has declined dramatically from a position where operating profit covered interest 13.5 times in 2009, to one where operating profit covered interest only 1.5 times in 2010. This was partly caused by the increase in borrowings in 2010, but mainly caused by the dramatic decline in profitability in that year. The later situation looks hazardous; only a small decline in future profitability would leave the business with insufficient operating profit to cover the interest payments. The gearing ratio at 31 March 2010 would not necessarily be considered to be very high for a business that was trading successfully. It is the low profitability that is the problem.

Without knowing what the business planned these ratios to be, it is not possible to reach a valid conclusion on Alexis plc's gearing.

Real World 7.6 consists of extracts from an article that discusses the likely lowering of gearing levels in the face of the recession. It explains that many businesses seem likely to issue additional ordinary shares (equity), either through making a rights issue or some public issue, and using the resulting funds to reduce borrowing as a means of reducing gearing.

Real World 7.6

Changing gear   **FT**

When Stuart Siddall was corporate treasurer of Amec four years ago, analysts were critical when the engineering group swung from having substantial net debt on its balance sheet [statement of financial position] to sitting on a huge cash pile after completing disposals.

'The analysts were saying "this is inefficient balance sheet management",' says Mr Siddall.

Companies back then were expected to be highly geared, with net debt to shareholders' funds at historically high levels.

How times have changed. With a wave of rights issues and other equity issuance now expected from the UK's non-financial companies – and with funds from these being used to pay down debt – the pendulum is rapidly swinging back in favour of more conservative balance sheet management. Gearing levels are set to fall dramatically, analysts say. 'There is going to be an appreciable and material drop in gearing, by about a quarter or a third over the next three years', predicts Mr Siddall, now chief executive of the Association of Corporate Treasurers.

Historically, gearing levels – as measured by net debt as a proportion of shareholders' funds – have run at an average of about 30 per cent over the past twenty years.

Peak levels (around 45 per cent) were reached in the past few years as companies took advantage of cheap credit. Current predictions see it coming down to about 20 per cent – and staying there for a good while to come.

Graham Secker, managing director of equity research at Morgan Stanley, says: 'This is going to be a relatively long-term phenomenon.'

One of the most immediate concerns to heavily indebted companies is whether, in a recessionary environment, they will be able to generate the profit and cash flows to service their debts.

Gearing levels vary from sector to sector as well. Oil companies prefer low levels given their exposure to the volatility of oil prices. BP's net debt-shareholders' funds ratio of 21 per cent is at the low end of a 20 to 30 per cent range it considers prudent.

Miners' gearing is on a clear downward trend already. Xstrata, the mining group, stressed last month that its £4.1 billion rights issue would cut gearing from 40 per cent to less than 30 per cent. A week later, BHP said its $13 billion of first-half cash flows had cut gearing to less than 10 per cent. Rio Tinto, which had gearing of 130 per cent at the last count in August 2008, is desperately trying to cut it by raising fresh equity.

Utilities tend to be highly geared because they can afford to borrow more against their typically reliable cash flows. But even here the trend is downwards.

Severn Trent, the UK water group, says its appropriate long-term gearing level is 60 per cent. But 'given ongoing uncertainties . . . it is prudent in the near term to retain as much liquidity and flexibility as possible'. It does not expect to pursue that target until credit markets improve.

Reducing gearing is not easy, especially for the most indebted companies that need to the most: shareholders will be more reluctant to finance replacement equity in companies with highly leveraged balance sheets.

The supply of fresh equity will also be constrained, not only by a glut of demand from companies but by the squeeze on investor money from a wave of government bond issuance.

Richard Jeffrey, chief investment officer at Cazenove Capital Management, says there is a risk of the government making it more difficult to raise money to improve balance sheets. 'That is of extreme concern because that could become a limitation, longer term, in the capital that companies have to fund investment.'

Source: 'Gearing levels set to plummet', Jeremy Grant, *Financial Times*, 10 February 2009.

Self-assessment question 7.1

Both Ali plc and Bhaskar plc operate wholesale electrical stores throughout the UK. The financial statements of each business for the year ended 30 June 2010 are as follows:

Statements of financial position as at 30 June 2010

	Ali plc £m	Bhaskar plc £m
ASSETS		
Non-current assets		
Property, plant and equipment *(cost less depreciation)*		
Land and buildings	360.0	510.0
Fixtures and fittings	87.0	91.2
	447.0	601.2
Current assets		
Inventories	592.0	403.0
Trade receivables	176.4	321.9
Cash at bank	84.6	91.6
	853.0	816.5
Total assets	1,300.0	1,417.7
EQUITY AND LIABILITIES		
Equity		
£1 ordinary shares	320.0	250.0
Retained earnings	367.6	624.6
	687.6	874.6
Non-current liabilities		
Borrowings – loan notes	190.0	250.0
Current liabilities		
Trade payables	406.4	275.7
Taxation	16.0	17.4
	422.4	293.1
Total equity and liabilities	1,300.0	1,417.7

Income statements for the year ended 30 June 2010

	Ali plc £m	Bhaskar plc £m
Revenue	1,478.1	1,790.4
Cost of sales	(1,018.3)	(1,214.9)
Gross profit	459.8	575.5
Operating expenses	(308.5)	(408.6)
Operating profit	151.3	166.9
Interest payable	(19.4)	(27.5)
Profit before taxation	131.9	139.4
Taxation	(32.0)	(34.8)
Profit for the year	99.9	104.6

All purchases and sales were on credit. Ali plc had announced its intention to pay a dividend of £135 million and Bhaskar plc £95 million in respect of the year. The market values of a share in Ali plc and Bhaskar plc at the end of the year were £6.50 and £8.20 respectively.

Required:
For each business, calculate two ratios that are concerned with each of the following aspects:

- profitability
- efficiency
- liquidity
- gearing

(eight ratios in total).
What can you conclude from the ratios that you have calculated?

The solution to this question can be found at the back of the book on pages 477–478.

Summary

The main points of this chapter may be summarised as follows:

Ratio analysis

- Ratio analysis compares two related figures, usually both from the same set of financial statements.
- It is an aid to understanding what the financial statements really mean.
- It is an inexact science, so results must be interpreted cautiously.
- Past periods, the performance of similar businesses and planned performance are often used to provide benchmark ratios.
- A brief overview of the financial statements can often provide insights that may not be revealed by ratios and/or may help in the interpretation of them.

Profitability ratios

- Profitability ratios are concerned with effectiveness at generating profit.
- The profitability ratios covered are return on ordinary shareholders' funds (ROSF), return on capital employed (ROCE), operating profit margin, and gross profit margin.

Efficiency ratios

- Efficiency ratios are concerned with efficiency of using assets/resources.
- The efficiency ratios covered are the average inventories turnover period, the average settlement period for trade receivables, the average settlement period for trade payables, sales revenue to capital employed, and sales revenue per employee.

Liquidity ratios

- Liquidity ratios are concerned with the ability to meet short-term obligations.
- The liquidity ratios covered are the current ratio, the acid test ratio, and cash generated from operations to maturing obligations.

Operating cash cycle

● The operating cash cycle is the time period between paying for goods and receiving cash from the sale of those goods.

Gearing ratios

● Gearing ratios are concerned with the relationship between equity and debt financing.
● The ratios covered are the gearing ratio and the interest cover ratio.

 Key terms

Further reading

If you would like to explore the topics covered in this chapter in more depth, we recommend the following books:

Elliott, B. and Elliott, J., *Financial Accounting and Reporting*, 13th edn, Financial Times Prentice Hall, 2009, Chapter 28.

Schoenebeck, K. and Holtzman, M., *Interpreting and Analyzing Financial Statements*, 5th edn, Prentice Hall, 2009, Chapters 2 to 5.

Wild, J., Subramanyam, K. and Halsey, R., *Financial Statement Analysis*, 9th edn, McGraw-Hill, 2006, Chapters 8, 9 and 11.

Review questions

Solutions to these questions can be found at the back of the book on page 486.

7.1 Some businesses (for example, supermarket chains) operate on a low operating profit margin. Does this mean that the return on capital employed from the business will also be low?

7.2 What potential problems arise for the external analyst from the use of statement of financial position figures in the calculation of financial ratios?

7.3 Two businesses operate in the same industry. One has an inventories turnover period that is longer than the industry average. The other has an inventories turnover period that is shorter than the industry average. Give three possible explanations for each business's inventories turnover period ratio.

7.4 In the chapter it was mentioned that ratios help to eliminate some of the problems of comparing businesses of different sizes. Does this mean that size is irrelevant when interpreting and analysing the position and performance of different businesses?

Exercises

Exercises 7.5 to 7.8 are more advanced than 7.1 to 7.4. Those with coloured numbers have solutions at the back of the book, starting on page 507.

If you wish to try more exercises, visit the students' side of the Companion Website.

7.1 I. Jiang (Western) Ltd has recently produced its financial statements for the current year. The directors are concerned that the return on capital employed (ROCE) had decreased from 14 per cent last year to 12 per cent for the current year.

The following reasons were suggested as to why this reduction in ROCE had occurred:

1 an increase in the gross profit margin;
2 a reduction in sales revenue;
3 an increase in overhead expenses;
4 an increase in amount of inventories held;
5 the repayment of some borrowings at the year end; and
6 an increase in the time taken for credit customers (trade receivables) to pay.

Required:
Taking each of these six suggested reasons in turn, state, with reasons, whether each of them could lead to a reduction in ROCE.

7.2 Amsterdam Ltd and Berlin Ltd are both engaged in retailing, but they seem to take a different approach to it according to the following information:

Ratio	Amsterdam Ltd	Berlin Ltd
Return on capital employed (ROCE)	20%	17%
Return on ordinary shareholders' funds (ROSF)	30%	18%
Average settlement period for trade receivables	63 days	21 days
Average settlement period for trade payables	50 days	45 days
Gross profit margin	40%	15%
Operating profit margin	10%	10%
Average inventories turnover period	52 days	25 days

Required:

Describe what this information indicates about the differences in approach between the two businesses. If one of them prides itself on personal service and one of them on competitive prices, which do you think is which and why?

7.3 Conday and Co. Ltd has been in operation for three years and produces antique reproduction furniture for the export market. The most recent set of financial statements for the business is as follows:

Statement of financial position as at 30 November

	£000
ASSETS	
Non-current assets	
Property, plant and equipment (cost less depreciation)	
Land and buildings	228
Plant and machinery	762
	990
Current assets	
Inventories	600
Trade receivables	820
	1,420
Total assets	2,410
EQUITY AND LIABILITIES	
Equity	
Ordinary shares of £1 each	700
Retained earnings	365
	1,065
Non-current liabilities	
Borrowings – 9% loan notes (Note 1)	200
Current liabilities	
Trade payables	665
Taxation	48
Short-term borrowings (all bank overdraft)	432
	1,145
Total equity and liabilities	2,410

Income statement for the year ended 30 November

	£000
Revenue	2,600
Cost of sales	(1,620)
Gross profit	980
Selling and distribution expenses (Note 2)	(408)
Administration expenses	(194)
Operating profit	378
Finance expenses	(58)
Profit before taxation	320
Taxation	(95)
Profit for the year	225

Notes:

1 The loan notes are secured on the land and buildings.
2 Selling and distribution expenses include £170,000 in respect of bad debts.
3 A dividend of £160,000 was paid on the ordinary shares during the year.
4 The directors have invited an investor to take up a new issue of ordinary shares in the business at £6.40 each making a total investment of £200,000. The directors wish to use the funds to finance a programme of further expansion.

***Required*:**

(a) Analyse the financial position and performance of the business and comment on any features that you consider to be significant.
(b) State, with reasons, whether or not the investor should invest in the business on the terms outlined.

7.4 The directors of Helena Beauty Products Ltd have been presented with the following abridged financial statements:

Helena Beauty Products Ltd
Income statement for the year ended 30 September

	2009 £000	2009 £000	2010 £000	2010 £000
Sales revenue		3,600		3,840
Cost of sales				
Opening inventories	320		400	
Purchases	2,240		2,350	
	2,560		2,750	
Closing inventories	(400)	(2,160)	(500)	(2,250)
Gross profit		1,440		1,590
Expenses		(1,360)		(1,500)
Profit		80		90

Statement of financial position as at 30 September

	2009 £000	2010 £000
ASSETS		
Non-current assets		
Property, plant and equipment	1,900	1,860
Current assets		
Inventories	400	500
Trade receivables	750	960
Cash at bank	8	4
	1,158	1,464
Total assets	3,058	3,324
EQUITY AND LIABILITIES		
Equity		
£1 ordinary shares	1,650	1,766
Reserves	1,018	1,108
	2,668	2,874
Current liabilities	390	450
Total equity and liabilities	3,058	3,324

Required:

Using six ratios, comment on the profitability (three ratios) and efficiency (three ratios) of the business as revealed by the statements shown above.

7.5   Threads Limited manufactures nuts and bolts, which are sold to industrial users. The abbreviated financial statements for 2009 and 2010 are as follows:

Income statements for the year ended 30 June

	2009 £000	2010 £000
Revenue	1,180	1,200
Cost of sales	(680)	(750)
Gross profit	500	450
Operating expenses	(200)	(208)
Depreciation	(66)	(75)
Operating profit	234	167
Interest	(–)	(8)
Profit before taxation	234	159
Taxation	(80)	(48)
Profit for the year	154	111

Statements of financial position as at 30 June

	2009 £000	2010 £000
ASSETS		
Non-current assets		
Property, plant and equipment	702	687
Current assets		
Inventories	148	236
Trade receivables	102	156
Cash	3	4
	253	396
Total assets	955	1,083
EQUITY AND LIABILITIES		
Equity		
Ordinary share capital (£1 shares, fully paid)	500	500
Retained earnings	256	295
	756	795
Non-current liabilities		
Borrowings – bank loan	–	50
Current liabilities		
Trade payables	60	76
Other payables and accruals	18	16
Taxation	40	24
Short-term borrowings (all bank overdraft)	81	122
	199	238
Total equity and liabilities	955	1,083

Dividends were paid on ordinary shares of £70,000 and £72,000 in respect of 2009 and 2010, respectively.

Required:
(a) Calculate the following financial ratios for *both* 2009 and 2010 (using year-end figures for statement of financial position items):
   1 return on capital employed
   2 operating profit margin
   3 gross profit margin
   4 current ratio
   5 acid test ratio
   6 settlement period for trade receivables
   7 settlement period for trade payables
   8 inventories turnover period.
(b) Comment on the performance of Threads Limited from the viewpoint of a business considering supplying a substantial amount of goods to Threads Limited on usual trade credit terms.

7.6 Bradbury Ltd is a family-owned clothes manufacturer based in the south west of England. For a number of years the chairman and managing director was David Bradbury. During his period of office, sales revenue had grown steadily at a rate of 2 to 3 per cent each year. David Bradbury retired on 30 November 2009 and was succeeded by his son Simon. Soon after taking office, Simon decided to expand the business. Within weeks he had successfully negotiated a five-year contract with a large clothes retailer to make a range of sports and leisurewear items. The contract will result in an additional £2 million in sales revenue during each year of the contract. To fulfil the contract, Bradbury Ltd acquired new equipment and premises.

Financial information concerning the business is given below:

Income statements for the year ended 30 November

	2009	2010
	£000	£000
Revenue	9,482	11,365
Operating profit	914	1,042
Interest charges	(22)	(81)
Profit before taxation	892	961
Taxation	(358)	(386)
Profit for the year	534	575

Statements of financial position as at 30 November

	2009	2010
	£000	£000
ASSETS		
Non-current assets		
Property, plant and equipment at cost less depreciation		
Premises	5,240	7,360
Plant and equipment	2,375	4,057
	7,615	11,417
Current assets		
Inventories	2,386	3,420
Trade receivables	2,540	4,280
	4,926	7,700
Total assets	12,541	19,117
EQUITY AND LIABILITIES		
Equity		
Share capital	2,000	2,000
Reserves	7,813	8,268
	9,813	10,268
Non-current liabilities		
Borrowing – loans	1,220	3,675
Current liabilities		
Trade payables	1,157	2,245
Taxation	179	193
Short-term borrowings (all bank overdraft)	172	2,736
	1,508	5,174
Total equity and liabilities	12,541	19,117

Dividends of £120,000 were paid on ordinary shares in respect of each of the two years.

Required:
(a) Calculate, for each year (using year-end figures for statement of financial position items), the following ratios:
1 operating profit margin
2 return on capital employed
3 current ratio
4 gearing ratio
5 trade receivables settlement period
6 sales revenue to capital employed.
(b) Using the above ratios, and any other ratios or information you consider relevant, comment on the results of the expansion programme.

7.7 The financial statements for Harridges Ltd are given below for the two years ended 30 June 2009 and 2010. Harridges Limited operates a department store in the centre of a small town.

Harridges Ltd Income statement for the years ended 30 June

	2009 £000	2010 £000
Sales revenue	2,600	3,500
Cost of sales	(1,560)	(2,350)
Gross profit	1,040	1,150
Wages and salaries	(320)	(350)
Overheads	(260)	(200)
Depreciation	(150)	(250)
Operating profit	310	350
Interest payable	(50)	(50)
Profit before taxation	260	300
Taxation	(105)	(125)
Profit for the year	155	175

Statement of financial position as at 30 June

	2009 £000	2010 £000
ASSETS		
Non-current assets		
Property, plant and equipment	1,265	1,525
Current assets		
Inventories	250	400
Trade receivables	105	145
Cash at bank	380	115
	735	660
Total assets	2,000	2,185
EQUITY AND LIABILITIES		
Equity		
Share capital: £1 shares fully paid	490	490
Share premium	260	260
Retained earnings	350	450
	1,100	1,200
Non-current liabilities		
Borrowings – 10% loan notes	500	500
Current liabilities		
Trade payables	300	375
Other payables	100	110
	400	485
Total equity and liabilities	2,000	2,185

Dividends were paid on ordinary shares of £65,000 and £75,000 in respect of 2009 and 2010, respectively.

Required:
(a) Choose and calculate eight ratios that would be helpful in assessing the performance of Harridges Ltd. Use end-of-year values and calculate ratios for both 2009 and 2010.
(b) Using the ratios calculated in (a) and any others you consider helpful, comment on the business's performance from the viewpoint of a prospective purchaser of a majority of shares.

7.8 The financial statements of Freezeqwik Ltd, a distributor of frozen foods, are set out below for the year ended 31 December last year.

Income statement for the year ended 31 December last year

	£000	£000
Sales revenue		820
Cost of sales		
Opening inventories	142	
Purchases	568	
	710	
Closing inventories	(166)	(544)
Gross profit		276
Administration expenses		(120)
Distribution expenses		(95)
Operating profit		61
Financial expenses		(32)
Profit before taxation		29
Taxation		(7)
Profit for the year		22

Statement of financial position as at 31 December last year

	£000
Non-current assets	
Property, plant and equipment	
Premises at valuation less depreciation	180
Fixtures and fittings at cost less depreciation	82
Motor vans at cost less depreciation	102
	364
Current assets	
Inventories	166
Trade receivables	264
Cash	24
	454
Total assets	818
Equity	
Ordinary share capital	300
Share premium account	200
Retained earnings	152
	652
Current liabilities	
Trade payables	159
Taxation	7
	166
Total equity and liabilities	818

All purchases and sales are on credit. There has been no change in the level of trade receivables or payables over the period.

Required:
Calculate the length of the OCC for the business and go on to suggest how the business may seek to reduce this period.

8

Analysing and interpreting financial statements (2)

Introduction

In this chapter we shall continue our examination of the analysis and interpretation of financial statements. We shall start by taking a detailed look at investment ratios, that is, those that consider business performance from the perspective of a shareholder. We then go on to consider common-sized financial statements. This technique presents the financial statements themselves as ratios and can offer useful insights to performance and position.

We shall also consider the value of ratios in predicting the future. In particular, we shall examine the extent to which ratios can help predict financial collapse. Finally, we shall consider problems that are encountered when undertaking ratio analysis. Although ratios can be extremely useful in assessing financial health, it is important to be aware of their limitations when making decisions.

Learning outcomes

When you have completed this chapter, you should be able to:

- calculate and interpret key investment ratios;

- prepare and interpret common-sized financial statements;

- evaluate the use of ratios in helping to predict financial failure;

- discuss the limitations of ratios as a tool of financial analysis.

To demonstrate how particular ratios are calculated and interpreted, we shall continue to refer to Alexis plc, whose financial statements and other information are set out in Example 7.1 on pages 222–223.

Investment ratios

There are various ratios available that are designed to help shareholders assess the returns on their investment. The following are widely used:

- dividend payout ratio
- dividend yield ratio
- earnings per share
- cash generated from operations per share
- price/earnings ratio.

Dividend payout ratio

→ The **dividend payout ratio** measures the proportion of earnings that a business pays out to shareholders in the form of dividends. The ratio is calculated as follows:

$$\text{Dividend payout ratio} = \frac{\text{Dividends announced for the year}}{\text{Earnings for the year available for dividends}} \times 100$$

In the case of ordinary shares, the earnings available for dividend will normally be the profit for the year (that is, the profit after taxation) less any preference dividends relating to the year. This ratio is normally expressed as a percentage.

The dividend payout ratio for Alexis plc for the year ended 31 March 2009 is

$$\text{Dividend payout ratio} = \frac{40}{165} \times 100 = 24.2\%$$

→ The information provided by this ratio is often expressed slightly differently as the **dividend cover ratio**. Here the calculation is:

$$\text{Dividend cover ratio} = \frac{\text{Earnings for the year available for dividend}}{\text{Dividends announced for the year}}$$

In the case of Alexis plc (for 2009) it would be 165/40 = 4.1 times. That is to say, the earnings available for dividend cover the actual dividend paid by just over four times.

Activity 8.1

Calculate the dividend payout ratio of Alexis plc for the year ended 31 March 2010.

The ratio for 2010 is:

$$\text{Dividend payout ratio} = \frac{40}{11} \times 100 = 363.6\%$$

This would normally be considered to be a very alarming increase in the ratio over the two years. Paying a dividend of £40 million in 2010 would probably be widely regarded as very imprudent.

Dividend yield ratio

→ The **dividend yield ratio** relates the cash return from a share to its current market value. This can help investors to assess the cash return on their investment in the business. The ratio, expressed as a percentage, is

$$\text{Dividend yield} = \frac{\text{Dividend per share}/(1-t)}{\text{Market value per share}} \times 100$$

where t is the 'dividend tax credit' rate of income tax. This requires some explanation. In the UK, investors who receive a dividend from a business also receive a tax credit. As this tax credit can be offset against any tax liability arising from the dividends received, the dividends are effectively issued net of income tax, at the dividend tax credit rate.

Investors may wish to compare the returns from shares with the returns from other forms of investment. As these other forms of investment are usually quoted on a 'gross' (that is, pre-tax) basis it is useful to 'gross up' the dividend to make comparison easier. → We can achieve this by dividing the **dividend per share** by $(1-t)$, where t is the 'dividend tax credit' rate of income tax.

Using the 2009/10 dividend tax credit rate of 10 per cent, the dividend yield for Alexis plc for the year ended 31 March 2009 is

$$\text{Dividend yield} = \frac{0.067*/(1-0.10)}{2.50} \times 100 = 3.0\%$$

The shares' market value is given in Note 1 to Example 7.1 (page 223).

* Dividend proposed/number of shares = 40/(300 × 2) = £0.067 dividend per share (the 300 is multiplied by 2 because they are £0.50 shares).

Activity 8.2

Calculate the dividend yield for Alexis plc for the year ended 31 March 2010.

The ratio for 2010 is:

$$\text{Dividend yield} = \frac{0.067*/(1-0.10)}{1.50} \times 100 = 5.0\%$$

* 40/(300 × 2) = £0.067.

Earnings per share

→ The **earnings per share (EPS)** ratio relates the earnings generated by the business, and available to shareholders, during a period, to the number of shares in issue. For equity (ordinary) shareholders, the amount available will be represented by the profit for the year (profit after taxation) less any preference dividend, where applicable. The ratio for equity shareholders is calculated as follows:

$$\text{Earnings per share} = \frac{\text{Earnings available to ordinary shareholders}}{\text{Number of ordinary shares in issue}}$$

In the case of Alexis plc, the earnings per share for the year ended 31 March 2009 is as follows:

$$\text{EPS} = \frac{£165m}{600m} = 27.5p$$

Many investment analysts regard the EPS ratio as a fundamental measure of share performance. The trend in earnings per share over time is used to help assess the investment potential of a business's shares. Although it is possible to make total profit rise through ordinary shareholders investing more in the business, this will not necessarily mean that the profitability *per share* will rise as a result.

It is not usually very helpful to compare the EPS of one business with that of another. Differences in financing arrangements (for example, in the nominal value of shares issued) can render any such comparison meaningless. However, it can be very useful to monitor the changes that occur in this ratio for a particular business over time.

Activity 8.3

Calculate the earnings per share of Alexis plc for the year ended 31 March 2010.

The ratio for 2010 is

$$\text{EPS} = \frac{£11m}{600m} = 1.8p$$

Cash generated from operations per share

It can be argued that, in the short term at least, cash generated from operations (found in the statement of cash flows) provides a better guide to the ability of a business to pay dividends and to undertake planned expenditures than the earnings per share figure. The **cash generated from operations (CGO) per ordinary share ratio** is calculated as follows:

$$\text{Cash generated from operations per share} = \frac{\text{Cash generated from operations less preference dividend (if any)}}{\text{Number of ordinary shares in issue}}$$

The ratio for Alexis plc for the year ended 31 March 2009 is as follows:

$$\text{CGO per share} = \frac{£251m}{600m} = 41.8p$$

Activity 8.4

Calculate the CGO per ordinary share for Alexis plc for the year ended 31 March 2010.

The ratio for 2010 is:

$$\text{CGO per share} = \frac{£34m}{600m} = 5.7p$$

There has been a dramatic decrease in this ratio over the two-year period.

Note that, for both years, the CGO per share for Alexis plc is higher than the earnings per share. This is not unusual. The effect of adding back depreciation to derive the CGO figures will often ensure that a higher figure is derived.

Price/earnings (P/E) ratio

→ The **price/earnings ratio** relates the market value of a share to the earnings per share. This ratio can be calculated as follows:

$$\text{P/E ratio} = \frac{\textbf{Market value per share}}{\textbf{Earnings per share}}$$

The P/E ratio for Alexis plc as at 31 March 2009 is

$$\text{P/E ratio} = \frac{£2.50}{27.5p^*} = 9.1 \text{ times}$$

* The EPS figure (27.5p) was calculated on page 264.

This ratio indicates that the market value of the share is 9.1 times higher than its current level of earnings. The ratio is a measure of market confidence in the future of a business. The higher the P/E ratio, the greater the confidence in the future earning power of the business and, consequently, the more investors are prepared to pay in relation to the earnings stream of the business.

P/E ratios provide a useful guide to market confidence concerning the future and they can, therefore, be helpful when comparing different businesses. However, differences in accounting policies between businesses can lead to different profit and earnings per share figures. This can distort comparisons.

Activity 8.5

Calculate the P/E ratio of Alexis plc as at 31 March 2010.

The ratio for 2010 is

$$P/E \text{ ratio} = \frac{£1.50}{1.8p} = 83.3 \text{ times}$$

The investment ratios for Alexis plc over the two-year period are as follows:

	2009	2010
Dividend payout ratio	24.2%	363.6%
Dividend yield ratio	3.0%	5.0%
Earnings per share	27.5p	1.8p
Cash generated from operations per share	41.8p	5.7p
P/E ratio	9.1 times	83.3 times

Activity 8.6

What do you deduce from the investment ratios set out above?
Can you offer an explanation why the share price has not fallen as much as it might have done, bearing in mind the very poor (relative to 2009) trading performance in 2010?

Athough the EPS has fallen dramatically and the dividend payment for 2010 seems very imprudent, the share price seems to have held up remarkably well (fallen from £2.50 to £1.50). This means that dividend yield and P/E value for 2010 look better than those for 2009. This is an anomaly of these two ratios, which stems from using a forward-looking value (the share price) in conjunction with historic data (dividends and earnings). Share prices are based on investors' assessments of the business's future. It seems with Alexis plc that, at the end of 2010, the 'market' was not happy with the business, relative to 2009. This is evidenced by the fact that the share price had fallen by £1 a share. On the other hand, the share price has not fallen as much as profit for the year. It appears that investors believe that the business will perform better in the future than it did in 2010. This may well be because they believe that the large expansion in assets and employee numbers that occurred in 2010 will yield benefits in the future; benefits that the business was not able to generate during 2010.

Real World 8.1 gives some information about the shares of several large, well-known UK businesses. This type of information is provided on a daily basis by several newspapers, notably the *Financial Times*.

Real World 8.1

Market statistics for some well-known businesses   FT

The following data was extracted from the *Financial Times* of 14 November 2009, relating to the previous day's trading of the shares of some well-known businesses on the London Stock Exchange:

Share	Price (pence)	Change	2009 High	Low	Yield %	P/E	Volume 000s
BP	581.10	+2.70	599.30	400.00	6.4	17.1	40,071
J D Wetherspoon	489.70	+17.2	551.00	270.00	–	14.9	507
ITV	51.30	+0.6	58.65	16.50	–	2.3	18,277
Marks and Spencer	372.30	+3.40	388.40	209.50	4.0	11.6	18,241
Rolls-Royce	469.90	+2.70	495.04	242.81	2.8	41.6	5,376
Vodafone	137.10	+1.30	148.00	111.20	5.7	7.4	131,940

The column headings are as follows:

Price   Mid-market price in pence (that is, the price midway between buying and selling price) of the shares at the end of trading on 13 November 2009.

Change   Gain or loss in the mid-market price during 13 November 2009.

High/Low   Highest and lowest prices (in pence) reached by the share during the year ended on 13 November 2009.

Yield   Gross dividend yield, based on the most recent year's dividend and the current share price.

P/E   Price/earnings ratio, based on the most recent year's (after-tax) profit for the year and the current share price.

Volume   The number of shares (in thousands) that were bought/sold on 13 November 2009.

So, for example, for BP, the oil business:

● the shares had a mid-market price of £5.811 each at the close of Stock Exchange trading on 13 November 2009;
● the shares had increased in price by 2.70 pence during trading on 13 November 2009;
● the shares had highest and lowest prices during the previous year of £5.993 and £4.00, respectively;
● the shares had a dividend yield, based on the 13 November 2009 price (and the dividend for the most recent year) of 6.4 per cent;
● the shares had a P/E ratio, based on the 13 November 2009 price (and the after-taxation earnings per share for the most recent year) of 17.1;
● during trading in the shares on 13 November 2009, 40,071,000 of the business's shares had changed hands from one investor to another.

Note that two of the businesses shown above (Wetherspoon and ITV) do not have a dividend yield figure. This is because neither of them has paid a dividend recently.

Source: Financial Times, 14 November 2009.

Real World 8.2 shows how investment ratios can vary between different industry sectors.

Real World 8.2

Yielding dividends   **FT**

Investment ratios can vary significantly between businesses and between industries. To give some indication of the range of variations that occur, the average dividend yield ratios and average P/E ratios for listed businesses in twelve different industries are shown in Figures 8.1 and 8.2, respectively.

Real World 8.2 continued

| Figure 8.1 | Average dividend yield ratios for businesses in a range of industries |

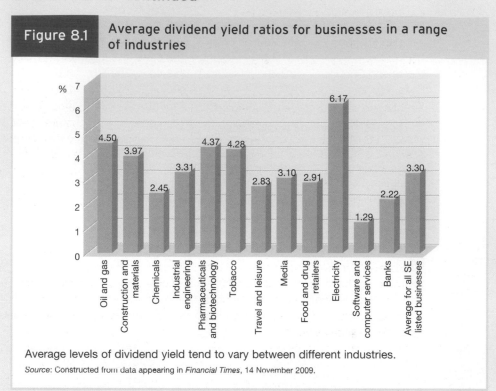

Average levels of dividend yield tend to vary between different industries.

Source: Constructed from data appearing in *Financial Times*, 14 November 2009.

| Figure 8.2 | Average price/earnings ratios for businesses in a range of industries |

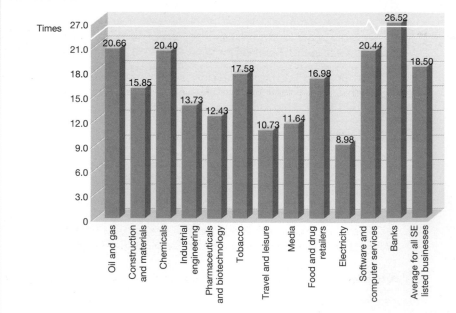

Average price/earnings ratios differ between different industries.

Source: Constructed from data appearing in *Financial Times*, 14 November 2009.

The dividend yield ratios are calculated from the current market value of the shares and the most recent year's dividend paid.

Some industries tend to pay out lower dividends than others, leading to lower dividend yield ratios. The average for all Stock Exchange listed businesses was 3.30 (as is shown in Figure 8.1), but there is a wide variation, with software and computer services at 1.29 and Electricity at 6.17.

Some types of businesses tend to invest heavily in developing new products, hence their tendency to pay low dividends compared with their share prices. Some of the inter-industry differences in the dividend yield ratio can be explained by the nature of the calculation of the ratio. The prices of shares at any given moment are based on expectations of their economic futures; dividends are actual past events. A business that had a good trading year recently may have paid a dividend that, in the light of investors' assessment of the business's economic future, may be high (a high dividend yield).

These P/E ratios are calculated from the current market value of the shares and the most recent year's earnings per share (EPS).

Businesses that have a high share price relative to their recent historic earnings have high P/E ratios. This may be because their future is regarded as economically bright, which may be the result of investing heavily in the future at the expense of recent profits (earnings). On the other hand, high P/Es also arise where businesses have recent low earnings but investors believe that their future is brighter. The average P/E for all Stock Exchange listed businesses was 18.5, but in the travel and leisure industry this was as low as 10.73 and for banks as high as 26.52.

At 13 November 2009, P/E ratios were at a fairly high level. Share prices were quite high, as a result of a strong recovery in share prices during 2009, from their low point in February 2009. At the same time, the recession had led to fairly low reported profits. (Remember that P/Es are based on current share prices and recent reported profits.)

Source: Financial Times, 14 November 2009.

Self-assessment question 8.1

Look back at the financial statements for Ali plc and Bhaskar plc for the year ended 30 June 2010 given in self-assessment question 7.1 on pages 250–251.

Required:
For each business, calculate the following ratios:

- Dividend payout ratio;
- Dividend yield ratio;
- Earnings per share;
- P/E ratio.

(The dividend income tax credit rate can be taken to be 10 per cent.)
What can you conclude from the ratios that you have calculated?

The solution to this question can be found at the back of the book on page 478.

Financial ratios and the problem of overtrading

→   **Overtrading** occurs where a business is operating at a level of activity that cannot be supported by the amount of finance that has been committed. For example, the business may have inadequate finance to fund the level of trade receivables and inventories necessary for the level of sales revenue that it is achieving. This situation usually reflects a poor level of financial control over the business. The reasons for overtrading are varied. It may occur:

● in young, expanding businesses that fail to prepare adequately for the rapid increase in demand for their goods or services;
● in businesses where the managers may have misjudged the level of expected sales demand or have failed to control escalating project costs;
● as a result of a fall in the value of money (inflation), causing more finance to have to be committed to inventories and trade receivables, even where there is no expansion in the real volume of trade;
● where the owners are unable to inject further funds into the business themselves and/or they cannot persuade others to invest in the business.

Whatever the reason, the problems that it brings must be dealt with if the business is to survive over the longer term.

Overtrading results in liquidity problems such as exceeding borrowing limits, or slow repayment of borrowings and trade payables. It can also result in suppliers withholding supplies, thereby making it difficult to meet customer needs. The managers of the business might be forced to direct all of their efforts to dealing with immediate and pressing problems, such as finding cash to meet interest charges due or paying wages. Longer-term planning becomes difficult as managers spend their time going from crisis to crisis. Ultimately, the business may fail because it cannot meet its maturing obligations.

Activity 8.7

If a business is overtrading, do you think the following ratios would be higher or lower than normally expected?

1 Current ratio
2 Average inventories turnover period
3 Average settlement period for trade receivables
4 Average settlement period for trade payables.

Your answer should be as follows:

1 The current ratio would be lower than normally expected. This is a measure of liquidity and lack of liquidity is a typical symptom of overtrading.
2 The average inventories turnover period would be lower than normally expected. Where a business is overtrading, the level of inventories held will be low because of the problems of financing them. In the short term, sales revenue may not be badly affected by the low inventories levels and therefore inventories will be turned over more quickly.
3 The average settlement period for trade receivables may be lower than normally expected. Where a business is suffering from liquidity problems it may chase credit customers more vigorously in an attempt to improve cash flows.
4 The average settlement period for trade payables may be higher than normally expected. The business may try to delay payments to its suppliers because of the liquidity problems arising.

To deal with the overtrading problem, a business must ensure that the finance available is consistent with the level of operations. Thus, if a business that is overtrading is unable to raise new finance, it should cut back its level of operations in line with the finance available. Although this may mean lost sales and lost profits in the short term, it may be necessary to ensure survival over the longer term.

Trend analysis

It is often helpful to see whether ratios are indicating trends. Key ratios can be plotted on a graph to provide a simple visual display of changes occurring over time. The trends occurring within a business may, for example, be plotted against trends for rival businesses or for the industry as a whole for comparison purposes. An example of trend analysis is shown in **Real World 8.3**.

Real World 8.3

Trend setting

In Figure 8.3 the current ratio of three of the UK's leading supermarkets is plotted over time. We can see that the current ratio of Tesco plc has risen over the period but it was, nevertheless, consistently lower than that of its main rivals until 2005, when it overtook Morrison; in 2009 it overtook Sainsbury. Sainsbury seems to be following the opposite trend, with its current ratio on a fairly consistent downward path. With well-managed businesses like Sainsbury and Tesco, it seems highly probable that these trends are the result of deliberate policy.

Figure 8.3	Graph plotting current ratio against time

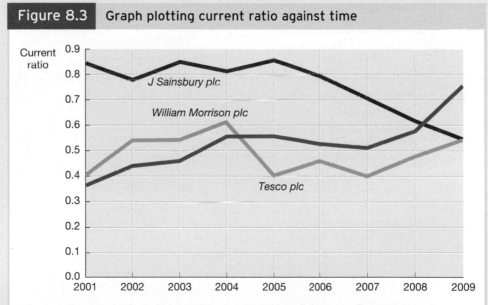

The current ratio for three leading UK supermarket businesses is plotted for the financial years ended during 2001 to 2009. This enables comparison to be made regarding the ratio, both for each of the three businesses over time and between the businesses.

Source: Ratios calculated from information in the annual reports of the three businesses for each of the years 2001 to 2009.

Many larger businesses publish certain key financial ratios as part of their annual reports to help users identify significant trends. These ratios typically cover several years' activities. **Real World 8.4** shows part of the table of 'key performance measures' of Marks and Spencer plc (M and S), the well-known UK retailer.

Real World 8.4

Key performance measures of Marks and Spencer plc

		2009 52 weeks	2008 52 weeks	2007 52 weeks	2006 53 weeks	2005 52 weeks
Gross margin	$\dfrac{\text{Gross profit}}{\text{Revenue}}$	37.2%	38.6%	38.9%	38.3%	34.7%
Net margin	$\dfrac{\text{Operating profit}}{\text{Revenue}}$	9.6%	13.4%	12.2%	10.9%	8.0%
Net margin excluding property disposals and exceptional items		8.5%	12.1%	12.2%	11.0%	8.7%
Profitability	$\dfrac{\text{Profit before tax}}{\text{Revenue}}$	7.8%	12.5%	10.9%	9.6%	6.7%
Profitability excluding property disposals and exceptional items		6.7%	11.2%	11.2%	9.6%	7.4%
Basic earnings per share $\dfrac{\text{Basic earnings}}{\text{Weighted average ordinary shares in issue}}$		32.3p	49.2p	39.1p	31.3p	17.6p
Earnings per share adjusted for property disposals and exceptional items		28.0p	43.6p	40.4p	31.4p	19.2p
Dividend per share declared in respect of the year		17.8p	22.5p	18.3p	14.0p	12.1p
Dividend cover $\dfrac{\text{Profit attributable to shareholders}}{\text{Dividends payable}}$		1.8×	2.3×	2.1×	2.2×	2.9×
Return on equity $\dfrac{\text{Profit attributable to shareholders}}{\text{Average equity shareholders' funds}}$		25.2%	45.6%	46.3%	50.0%	35.1%

Source: Marks and Spencer plc Annual Report 2009. Reproduced by kind permission of Marks and Spencer plc.

M and S's return on equity (return on ordinary shareholders' funds) in 2009 was significantly less good than it had been during the previous three years. The net margin fell significantly in 2009 from a recent peak in 2008, though the gross margin was fairly stable after 2005. M and S felt that its problems in 2009 were substantially related to difficult trading conditions in a major recession.

Common-sized financial statements

→ **Common-sized financial statements** are normal financial statements (such as the income statement, statement of financial position and statement of cash flows) which are expressed in terms of some base figure. The objective of presenting financial statements in this way is to help make better comparisons. The detection of differences and trends is often more obvious than may be the case when examining the original statements, which are expressed in financial values.

Vertical analysis

One approach to common-sized statements is to express all the figures in a particular statement in terms of one of the figures in that statement. This 'base' figure is typically one that is seen as a key figure in the statement, such as sales revenue in an income statement, total long-term funds in a statement of financial position and the cash flow from operating activities in the statement of cash flows.

Example 8.1 is a common-sized income statement that uses sales revenue as the base figure. Note that the base figure is set at 100 and all other figures are expressed as a percentage of this.

Example 8.1

The common-sized income statement of Alexis plc (see Example 7.1 on pages 222–223) for 2009 in abbreviated form, and using revenue as the base figure, will be as follows:

Common-sized income statement for the year ended 31 March 2009

		Calculation of figures
Revenue	100.0	Base figure
Cost of sales	(77.9)	$(1,745/2,240) \times 100\%$
Gross profit	22.1	$(495/2,240) \times 100\%$
Operating expenses	(11.3)	$(252/2,240) \times 100\%$
Operating profit	10.8	$(243/2,240) \times 100\%$
Interest payable	(0.8)	$(18/2,240) \times 100\%$
Profit before taxation	10.0	$(225/2,240) \times 100\%$
Taxation	(2.7)	$(60/2,240) \times 100\%$
Profit for the year	7.3	$(165/2,240) \times 100\%$

Each of the figures in the income statement is simply the original financial figure divided by the revenue figure and then expressed as a percentage. Since the revised values have been expressed to only one decimal place, it was necessary to adjust to make the income statement add up, despite rounding errors.

Of course, not much can be discerned from looking at just one common-sized statement. We need some benchmark for comparison. This could be other accounting periods for the same business.

Activity 8.8

The following is a set of common-sized income statements for a major high street department store for five consecutive accounting periods:

	Year 1	Year 2	Year 3	Year 4	Year 5
Revenue	100.0	100.0	100.0	100.0	100.0
Cost of sales	(68.9)	(68.5)	(67.2)	(66.5)	(66.3)
Gross profit	31.1	31.5	32.8	33.5	33.7
Operating expenses	(28.1)	(28.4)	(27.6)	(29.2)	(30.2)
Operating profit	3.0	3.1	5.2	4.3	3.5
Interest payable	(1.1)	(1.2)	(1.6)	(2.1)	(1.3)
Profit before taxation	1.9	1.9	3.6	2.2	2.2

What significant features are revealed by the common-sized income statements?

Operating profit, relative to revenue, rose in Year 3 but fell back again in Years 4 and 5 to end the five-year period at a higher level than it had been in Years 1 and 2. Although the gross profit margin rose steadily over the five-year period, so did the operating expenses, with the exception of Year 3. Clearly, the fall in operating expenses to revenue in Year 3 led to the improvement in operating profit to revenue.

The common-sized financial statements being compared do not have to be for the same business. They can be for different businesses. **Real World 8.5** gives common-sized statements of financial position for five UK businesses that are either very well known by name, or whose products are everyday commodities for most of us. These businesses were randomly selected, except that each one is high profile and from a different industry. For each business, the major statement of financial position items are expressed as a percentage of the total investment by the providers of long-term finance (equity and non-current liabilities).

Real World 8.5

A summary of the statements of financial position of five UK businesses

Business:	Next plc	British Airways plc	Rolls-Royce plc	Tesco plc	Severn Trent plc
Statement of financial position date:	24.1.09	31.3.09	31.12.08	28.2.09	31.3.09
Non-current assets	64	128	88	114	103
Current assets					
Inventories	30	2	39	10	–
Trade receivables	60	8	59	7	5
Other receivables	8	5	–	16	–
Cash and near cash	4	22	43	17	3
	102	37	141	50	8
Total assets	166	165	229	164	111
Equity and non-current liabilities	100	100	100	100	100
Current liabilities					
Trade payables	45	44	86	30	–
Taxation	8	–	3	1	–
Other short-term liabilities	2	10	3	–	7
Overdrafts and short-term borrowings	11	11	37	33	4
	66	65	129	64	11
Total equity and liabilities	166	165	229	164	111

The non-current assets, current assets and current liabilities are expressed as a percentage of the total net long-term investment (equity plus non-current liabilities) of the business concerned. Next plc is a major retail and home shopping business. British Airways plc (BA) is a major airline. Rolls-Royce plc is a major engineering business. Tesco plc is one of the major UK supermarket businesses. Severn Trent plc is a major supplier of water, sewerage services and waste management, mainly in the UK.

Source: Table constructed from information appearing in the financial statements for the year ended in late 2008 or early 2009 for each of the five businesses concerned.

It is quite striking, in Real World 8.5, how different is the make-up of the statement of financial position from one business to the next. Take the current assets and current liabilities for example. Though the totals for current assets are pretty large when compared with the total long-term investment, these percentages vary considerably from one type of business to the next. When we look at the nature of current assets held we can see that Next, Rolls-Royce and Tesco, which produce and/or sell goods, are the only ones that hold significant amounts of inventories. The other two businesses are service providers and so inventories are not a significant item. We can see from the table that Tesco does not sell a lot on credit and very few of BA's and Severn Trent's sales are on credit as these businesses have little or nothing invested in trade receivables. It is interesting to note that Tesco's trade payables are much higher than its inventories. Since most of these payables will be suppliers of inventories, it means that the business is able, on average, to have the cash from a particular sale in the bank before it needs to pay for the goods concerned.

→ So far we have been considering what is known as **vertical analysis**. That is, we have been treating all of the figures in each statement as a percentage of a figure in that statement. This 'baseline' figure has been the sales revenue figure, in the case of the income statement, and the total long-term investment, with the statement of financial position. Note that common-sized statements do not have to be expressed in terms of any particular factor; it is up to the individual carrying out the analysis.

Horizontal analysis

→ **Horizontal analysis** is an alternative to the vertical analysis that we have seen so far. Here the figures appearing in a particular financial statement are expressed as a base figure (that is 100) and the equivalent figures appearing in similar statements are expressed as a percentage of this base figure. So, for example, the inventories figure appearing in a particular statement of financial position may be set as the base figure (that is, set at 100) and then the inventories figures appearing in successive statements of financial position could each be expressed as a percentage of this base inventories figure. The 'base' statement would normally be the earliest (or latest) of a set of statements for the same business. Where the analysis was between businesses, as in Real World 8.5 (above), selecting which business should be the base one is not so obvious, unless one of the businesses is the one of most interest, perhaps because the objective is to compare a particular business with each of the others in turn.

Example 8.2 shows a horizontally analysed common-sized income statement for the business, a department store, which was the subject of Activity 8.8.

Example 8.2

The following is a set of common-sized income statements for a major high street department store for five consecutive accounting periods, using horizontal analysis and making Year 1 the base year:

	Year 1	Year 2	Year 3	Year 4	Year 5
Revenue	100.0	104.3	108.4	106.5	108.9
Cost of sales	(100.0)	(103.7)	(105.7)	(102.9)	(104.8)
Gross profit	100.0	105.5	114.4	114.5	118.0
Operating expenses	(100.0)	(105.4)	(106.7)	(110.4)	(117.2)
Operating profit	100.0	106.6	105.9	113.3	125.6
Interest payable	(100.0)	(111.9)	(157.1)	(202.4)	(127.4)
Profit before taxation	100.0	103.5	102.8	104.5	124.5

Year 1 is the base year so all of the figures in the Year 1 income statement are 100.0. All of the figures for the other years are that year's figure divided by the Year 1 figure for the same item and then expressed as a percentage. For example, the Year 4 profit before taxation, divided by the profit before taxation for Year 1 was 104.5 or the profit was 4.5 per cent greater in Year 4 than it had been for Year 1.

Activity 8.9

What are the significant features revealed by the common-sized income statement in Example 8.2?

Revenue did not show much of an increase over the five years, particularly if these figures are not adjusted for inflation. Years 2 and 3 saw increases, but Years 4 and 5 were less impressive. The rate of increase in the cost of sales was less than that for revenue and, therefore, the gross profit growth was greater, than the rate of increase of revenue. Operating expenses showed growth over the years. Interest payable increased strongly during the first four years of the period, but then fell back significantly in Year 5.

Activity 8.10

The vertical approach to common-sized financial statements has the advantage of enabling the analyst to see each figure expressed in terms of the same item (revenue, long-term finance and so on).

- What are the disadvantages of this approach?
- How do horizontally analysed common-sized statements overcome any problems?
- What problems do they bring?

The problem with the horizontal approach is that it is not possible to see, for example, that revenue values are different from one year or business to the next. Normally a vertically analysed common-sized income statement shows the revenue figure as 100 for all years or businesses. This is, of course, a problem of all approaches to ratio analysis.

Horizontally analysed common-sized statements overcome this problem because, say, revenue figures are expressed in terms of one year or one particular business. This makes differences in revenue levels crystal clear. Unfortunately, such an approach makes comparison within each year's, or within a particular business's, statement rather difficult.

Perhaps the answer is to produce two sets of common-sized statements, one analysed vertically and the other horizontally.

Using ratios to predict financial failure

Financial ratios, based on current or past performance, are often used to help predict the future. However, both the choice of ratios and the interpretation of results are normally dependent on the judgement and opinion of the analyst. In recent years, however, attempts have been made to develop a more rigorous and systematic approach to the use of ratios for prediction purposes. In particular, researchers have shown an interest in the ability of ratios to predict the financial failure of a business.

By financial failure, we mean a business either being forced out of business or being severely adversely affected by its inability to meet its financial obligations. It is often referred to as 'going bust' or 'going bankrupt'. This, of course, is an area with which all those connected with the business are likely to be concerned.

Using single ratios

Many approaches that attempt to use ratios to predict future financial failure have been developed. Early research focused on the examination of ratios on an individual basis to see whether they were good or bad predictors of financial failure. Here, a particular ratio (for example the current ratio) for a business that had failed was tracked over several years leading up to the date of the failure. This was to see whether it was possible to say that the ratio had shown a trend that could have been taken as a warning sign.

Beaver (see reference 1 at the end of the chapter) carried out the first research in this area. He identified 79 businesses that had failed. He then calculated the average (mean) of various ratios for these 79 businesses, going back over the financial statements of each business for each of the ten years leading up to each business's failure. Beaver then compared these average ratios with similarly derived ratios for a sample of 79 businesses that did not fail over this period. (The research used a matched-pair design, where each failed business was matched with a non-failed business of similar size and industry type.) Beaver found that some ratios exhibited a marked difference between the failed and non-failed businesses for up to five years prior to failure. This is shown in Figure 8.4.

Figure 8.4 Average (mean) ratios of failed and non-failed businesses plotted against the number of years before failure

Each of the ratios (a) to (f) above indicates a marked difference in the average ratio between the sample of failed businesses and a matched sample of non-failed businesses. The vertical scale of each graph is the average value of the particular ratio for each group of businesses (failed and non-failed). The horizontal axis is the number of years before failure. Thus Year 1 is the most recent year and Year 5 the earliest of the years. For each of the six ratios, the difference between the average for the failed and the non-failed businesses can be detected five years prior to the failure of the former group.

* The no-credit interval is the same as the cash generated from operations to maturing obligations ratio discussed in Chapter 7.

Source: Beaver (see reference 1 at the end of the chapter).

To explain Figure 8.4, let us take a closer look at graph (a). This plots the ratio, cash flow (presumably the operating cash flow figure, taken from the statement of cash flows) divided by total debt (borrowings). For the non-failed businesses this stayed fairly steady at just below +0.45 over the period. For the failed businesses, however, this was already well below the non-failed businesses, at about +0.15, even five years before those businesses eventually failed. It then declined steadily until, by one year before the failure, it was less than –0.15. Note that the scale of the horizontal axis shows the most recent year before the actual failure (Year 1) on the left and the earliest one (Year 5) on the right. The other graphs in Figure 8.4 show a similar picture for five other ratios. In each case there is a deteriorating average ratio for the failed businesses as the time of failure approaches.

What is shown in Figure 8.4 implies that failure could be predicted by careful assessment of the trend shown by particular key ratios.

Research by Zmijewski (see reference 2 at the end of the chapter), using a sample of 72 failed and 3,573 non-failed businesses over a six-year period, found that businesses that ultimately went on to fail were characterised by lower rates of return, higher levels of gearing, lower levels of coverage for their fixed interest payments and more variable returns on shares. While we may not find these results very surprising, it is interesting to note that Zmijewski, like a number of other researchers in this area, did not find liquidity ratios particularly useful in predicting financial failure. Intuition might have led us (wrongly it seems) to believe that the liquidity ratios would have been particularly helpful in this context.

→ The approach adopted by Beaver and Zmijewski is referred to as **univariate analysis** because it looks at one ratio at a time. Although this approach can produce interesting results, there are practical problems associated with its use. Let us say, for example, that past research has identified two ratios as being good predictors of financial failure. When applied to a particular business, however, it may be found that one ratio predicts financial failure whereas the other does not. Given these conflicting signals, how should the decision maker interpret the results?

Using combinations of ratios

The weaknesses of univariate analysis have led researchers to develop models that combine ratios in such a way as to produce a single index that can be interpreted more clearly. One approach to model development, much favoured by researchers, applies
→ **multiple discriminate analysis** (MDA). This is, in essence, a statistical technique that is similar to regression analysis and which can be used to draw a boundary between those businesses that fail and those businesses that do not. This boundary is referred to as the
→ **discriminate function**. In this context, MDA attempts to identify those factors likely to influence financial failure. However, unlike regression analysis, MDA assumes that the observations come from two different populations (for example, failed and non-failed businesses) rather than from a single population.

To illustrate this approach, let us assume that we wish to test whether two ratios (say, the current ratio and the return on capital employed) can help to predict failure. To do this, we can calculate these ratios, first for a sample of failed businesses and then for a matched sample of non-failed ones. From these two sets of data we can produce a scatter diagram that plots each business according to these two ratios to produce a single coordinate. Figure 8.5 illustrates this approach.

Figure 8.5	Scatter diagram showing the distribution of failed and non-failed businesses

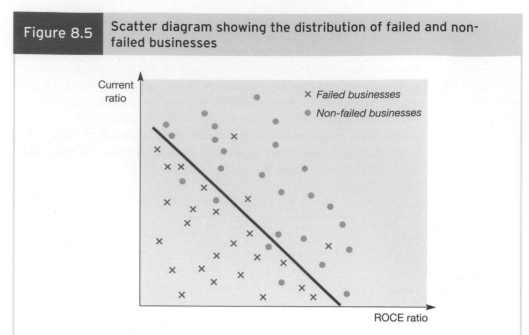

The distribution of failed and non-failed businesses is based on two ratios. The line represents a boundary between the samples of failed and non-failed businesses. Although there is some crossing of the boundary, the boundary represents the line that minimises the problem of misclassifying particular businesses.

Using the observations plotted on the diagram, we try to identify the boundary between the failed and the non-failed businesses. This is the diagonal line in Figure 8.5.

We can see that those businesses that fall below and to the left of the line are predominantly failed and those that fall to the right are predominantly non-failed ones. Note that there is some overlap between the two populations. The boundary produced is unlikely, in practice, to eliminate all errors. Some businesses that fail may fall on the side of the boundary with non-failed businesses. The opposite also happens. However, the analysis will *minimise* the misclassification errors.

The boundary shown in Figure 8.5 can be expressed in the form

$$Z = a + (b \times \text{Current ratio}) + (c \times \text{ROCE})$$

where a is a constant and b and c are weights to be attached to each ratio. A weighted average or total score (Z) is then derived. The weights given to the two ratios will depend on the slope of the line and its absolute position. Note that this example, using the current and ROCE ratios, is purely hypothetical and only intended to illustrate the approach.

Z-score models

Altman (see reference 3 at the end of the chapter) was the first to develop a model (in 1968), using financial ratios, that was able to predict financial failure. In 2000 he revised that model. In fact, the revisions necessary to make the model effective in present times were quite minor. Altman's revised model, the Z-score model, is based on five financial ratios and is as follows:

$$Z = 0.717a + 0.847b + 3.107c + 0.420d + 0.998e$$

where a = Working capital/Total assets

b = Accumulated retained profits/Total assets

c = Operating profit/Total assets

d = Book (statement of financial position) value of ordinary and preference shares/Total liabilities at book (statement of financial position) value

e = Sales revenue/Total assets

The coefficients (the numbers) in the above model reflect the importance to the Z-score of each of the ingredients (a to e).

In developing and revising this model, Altman carried out experiments using a paired sample of failed businesses and non-failed businesses and collected relevant data for each business for five years prior to failure. He found that the model represented by the formula above was able to predict failure for up to two years before it occurred. However, the predictive accuracy of the model became weaker the longer the time before the date of the actual failure.

The ratios used in this model were identified by Altman through a process of trial and error, as there is no underlying theory of financial failure to help guide researchers in their selection of appropriate ratios. According to Altman, those businesses with a Z-score of less than 1.23 tend to fail. The lower the score the greater is the probability of failure. Those with a Z-score greater than 4.14 tend not to fail. Those businesses with a Z-score between 1.23 and 4.14 occupied a 'zone of ignorance' and were difficult to classify. However, the model was able overall to classify 91 per cent of the businesses correctly; only 9 per cent fell into the 'zone of ignorance'. Altman based his model on US businesses.

In recent years, other models, using a similar approach, have been developed throughout the world. In the UK, Taffler has developed separate Z-score models for different types of business. (See reference 4 at the end of the chapter for a discussion of the work of Taffler and others.)

The prediction of financial failure is not the only area where research into the predictive ability of ratios has taken place. Researchers have also developed ratio-based models that claim to assess the vulnerability of a business to takeover by another. This is another area that is of vital importance to all those connected with the business.

Real World 8.6 discusses some research that showed that investing in shares in businesses with very low Z-scores is unsuccessful compared with investing in businesses with higher Z-scores. The research did not show, however, that the higher the Z-score, the more successful the investment.

Real World 8.6

From A to Z

Investors looking to profit during a recession should be targeting stocks with strong fundamentals, according to research by Morgan Stanley.

This 'value investing' approach – buying into companies where fundamental measures, such as book value and earnings, are not yet reflected in their share prices – is not new.

Real World 8.6 continued

But Morgan Stanley's analysis has found that the ability of this approach to deliver returns in downturns depends on the financial strength of the companies – in particular, the importance attached to the balance sheet [statement of financial position] by investors.

'If a stock's balance sheet is weak, the valuation multiple will be of little importance at this stage in the economic cycle,' says Graham Secker, Morgan Stanley strategy analyst.

He ranked a basket of European companies by their Altman Z-score – a measure of financial strength devised by US academic Edward Altman. A Z-score can be calculated for all non-financial companies and the lower the score, the greater the risk of the company falling into financial distress.

When Secker compared the companies' Z-scores with their share price movements, he discovered that the companies with weaker balance sheets underperformed the market more than two thirds of the time.

Morgan Stanley also found that a company with an Altman Z-score of less than 1 tends to underperform the wider market by more than 4 per cent over the year with an associated probability of 72 per cent.

'Given the poor performance over the last year by stocks with a low Altman Z-score, the results of our backtest are now even more compelling than they were 12 months ago,' argues Secker. 'We calculate that the median stock with an Altman Z-score of 1 or less has underperformed the wider market by 5–6 per cent per annum between 1990 and 2008.'

Secker sees this as logical. In a recession, companies with balance sheets that are perceived to be weak are deemed a higher risk by lenders and face a higher cost of capital. This turns market sentiment against them and will generally lead to their share prices falling below their peers.

In 2008, the share price performance for stocks with an Altman Z-score of less than 1 was the worst since Morgan Stanley's analysis began in 1991. Under the Morgan Stanley methodology, the 2008 score is calculated using 2007 company financials. Of all the companies with a 2008 Z-score of less than 1, the median share price performance was a loss of 49 per cent, compared with a wider market fall of 42 per cent.

When compound annual growth rates since 1991 are analysed, the results are more dramatic. On average, companies with Z-scores of less than 1 saw their shares fall 4.4 per cent, compared with an average rise of 1.3 per cent for their peers.

In only five of the last 18 years has a stock with an Altman score of 1 or less outperformed the market. These were generally years of strong economic growth.

However, companies with the highest Z-scores aren't necessarily the best performers. During the bear market of 2000 to 2002, companies that had a Z-score above 3 fell almost twice as much as the market.

Analysts say the 2009 Z-scores, based on 2008 balance sheets, are far lower than in previous years as companies absorb the strain of the downturn in their accounts. 'There's been a lot of change between 2007 and 2008 [accounting years], tightening of credit and a vast deterioration in corporate balance sheets,' says Secker. 'I'd expect 2009 [Z-scores] to be much worse.'

Analysis by the Financial Times and Capital IQ, the data provider, corroborates this – showing that the 2009 scores have been badly affected by the crisis.

Some 8 per cent of global companies with a market capitalisation of more than $500 million have Altman scores below 1 for 2009 – based on 2008 company financials. This is the highest percentage since 2002 and the largest annual increase since 2001 – showing the impact of the recession on the balance sheets of even the largest companies. If smaller companies were included, the results would be worse – as their earnings and market capitalisations have been affected far more.

European balance sheets were hit the hardest, with companies averaging a Z-score of 2.8, compared with 4.0 for Asia and the US, according to Capital IQ. This suggests the scores are not due to chance. A similar differential was recorded in 2001 during the last recession. On this evidence, US companies appear more resilient than their global peers in a downturn.

On a sector basis, healthcare and IT companies have the highest Z-scores. In 2008, their scores were more than three times higher than the average for the lowest scoring sector: utilities. A similar pattern was found in 2001 – suggesting that investors may want to think twice before buying into 'defensive' utilities in a downturn.

Source: 'New study re-writes the A to Z of value investing', Patrick Mathurin, *Financial Times*, 14 August 2009.

Limitations of ratio analysis

Although ratios offer a quick and useful method of analysing the position and performance of a business, they are not without their problems and limitations. We shall now review some of the shortcomings of financial ratio analysis.

Quality of financial statements

It must always be remembered that ratios are based on financial statements. The results of ratio analysis are, therefore, dependent on the quality of these underlying statements. Ratios will inherit the limitations of the financial statements on which they are based. In Chapter 2 we saw that one important limitation of financial statements is their failure to include all resources controlled by the business. Internally generated goodwill and brands, for example, are excluded from the statement of financial position because they fail to meet the strict definition of an asset. This means that, even though these resources may be of considerable value, key ratios such as ROSF, ROCE and the gearing ratio will fail to acknowledge their presence.

There is also the problem of deliberate attempts to make the financial statements misleading. We discussed this problem of *creative accounting* in Chapter 5.

Inflation

A persistent, though recently less severe, problem, in most countries is that the financial results of businesses can be distorted as a result of inflation. One effect of inflation is that the reported value of assets held for any length of time may bear little relation to current values. Generally speaking, the reported value of assets will be understated in current terms during a period of inflation as they are usually reported at their original cost (less any amounts written off for depreciation). This means that comparisons, either between businesses or between periods, will be hindered. A difference in, say, ROCE may simply be owing to the fact that assets shown in one of the statements of financial position being compared were acquired more recently (ignoring the effect of depreciation on the asset values). Another effect of inflation is to distort the measurement of profit. In the calculation of profit, sales revenue is often matched with costs incurred at an earlier time. This is because there is often a time lag between acquiring a particular resource and using it to help generate sales revenue. For example, inventories may well be acquired several months before they are sold. During a period of inflation, this will mean that the expense does not reflect prices that are current at the time of the sale. The cost of sales figure is usually based on the historic cost of the inventories concerned. As a result, expenses will be understated in the income statement and this, in turn, means that profit will be overstated. One effect of this will be to distort the profitability ratios discussed earlier. We shall take a look at attempts to correct for inflation, in financial statements, in Chapter 10.

The restricted view given by reliance on ratios

It is important not to rely exclusively on ratios, thereby losing sight of information contained in the underlying financial statements. As we saw in Chapter 7, and earlier in this chapter, some items reported in these statements can be vital in assessing position and performance. For example, the total sales revenue, capital employed and profit figures may be useful in assessing changes in absolute size that occur over time, or in assessing differences in scale between businesses. Ratios do not provide such information. When comparing one figure with another, ratios measure *relative* performance and position and, therefore, provide only part of the picture. When comparing two businesses, therefore, it will often be useful to assess the absolute size of profits, as well as the relative profitability of each business. For example, Business A may generate £1 million operating profit and have a ROCE of 15 per cent and Business B may generate £100,000 operating profit and have a ROCE of 20 per cent. Although Business B has a higher level of *profitability*, as measured by ROCE, it generates lower total operating profits.

The basis for comparison

We saw earlier that if ratios are to be useful they require a basis for comparison. Moreover, it is important that the analyst compares like with like. Where the comparison is with another business, there can be difficulties. No two businesses are identical. The greater the differences between the businesses being compared, the greater are the limitations of ratio analysis. Furthermore, any differences in accounting policies, financing methods (gearing levels) and financial year ends will add to the problems of making comparisons between businesses.

Ratios relating to the statement of financial position

Because the statement of financial position is only a 'snapshot' of the business at a particular moment in time, any ratios based on statement of financial position figures, such as the liquidity ratios, may not be representative of the financial position of the business for the year as a whole. For example, it is common for a seasonal business to have a financial year end that coincides with a low point in business activity. As a result, inventories and trade receivables may be low at the year end. This means that the liquidity ratios may also be low. A more representative picture of liquidity can only really be gained by taking additional measurements at other points in the year.

Real World 8.7 points out another way in which ratios are limited.

Real World 8.7

Remember, it's people that really count . . .

Lord Weinstock (1924–2002) was an influential industrialist whose management style and philosophy helped to shape management practice in many UK businesses. During his long and successful reign at GEC plc, a major engineering business, Lord Weinstock relied heavily on financial ratios to assess performance and to exercise control. In particular, he relied on ratios relating to sales revenue, expenses, trade receivables, profit margins and inventories turnover. However, he was keenly aware of the limitations of ratios and recognised that, ultimately, people produce profits.

In a memo written to GEC managers he pointed out that ratios are an aid to good management rather than a substitute for it. He wrote:

> The operating ratios are of great value as measures of efficiency but they are only the measures and not efficiency itself. Statistics will not design a product better, make it for a lower cost or increase sales. If ill-used, they may so guide action as to diminish resources for the sake of apparent but false signs of improvement.
>
> Management remains a matter of judgement, of knowledge of products and processes and of understanding and skill in dealing with people. The ratios will indicate how well all these things are being done and will show comparison with how they are done elsewhere. But they will tell us nothing about how to do them. That is what you are meant to do.

Source: Extract from *Arnold Weinstock and the Making of GEC*, Stephen Aris (Aurum Press, 1998), published in *The Sunday Times*, 22 February 1998, p. 3.

Summary

The main points of this chapter may be summarised as follows:

Investment ratios

- Investment ratios are concerned with returns to shareholders.
- The investment ratios covered are the dividend payout ratio, the dividend yield ratio, earnings per share (EPS), cash generated from operations per share, and the price/earnings ratio.

Uses of ratios

- Individual ratios can be tracked to detect trends, for example by plotting them on a graph.
- Ratios can be used to predict financial failure.
- Univariate analysis looks at just one ratio over time in an attempt to predict financial failure.
- Multiple discriminate analysis (that is, looking at several ratios, put together in a model, over time, in an attempt to predict financial failure) can produce Z-scores that can be used to assess financial strength.

Limitations of ratio analysis

● Ratios are only as reliable as the financial statements from which they derive.

● Inflation can distort the information.

● Ratios give a restricted view.

● It can be difficult to find a suitable benchmark (for example, another business) to compare with.

● Some ratios could mislead due to the 'snapshot' nature of the statement of financial position.

 Key terms

dividend payout ratio p. 262	**overtrading** p. 270
dividend cover ratio p. 262	**common-sized financial statements**
dividend yield ratio p. 263	p. 273
dividend per share p. 263	**vertical analysis** p. 275
earnings per share (EPS) p. 263	**horizontal analysis** p. 275
cash generated from operations per	**univariate analysis** p. 279
ordinary share ratio p. 264	**multiple discriminate analysis** p. 279
price/earnings ratio p. 265	**discriminate function** p. 279

References

1 Beaver, W. H., 'Financial Ratios as Predictors of Failure', in *Empirical Research in Accounting: Selected Studies*, 1966, pp. 71–111.

2 Zmijewski, M. E., 'Predicting Corporate Bankruptcy: An Empirical Comparison of the Extent of Financial Distress Models', Research Paper, State University of New York, 1983.

3 Altman, E. I., 'Predicting Financial Distress of Companies: Revisiting the Z-score and Zeta Models', New York University Working Paper, June 2000.

4 Neophytou, E., Charitou, A. and Charalamnous, C., 'Predicting Corporate Failure: Empirical Evidence for the UK', University of Southampton Department of Accounting and Management Science Working Paper 01-173, 2001.

Further reading

If you would like to explore the topics covered in this chapter in more depth, we recommend the following books:

Elliott, B. and Elliott, J., *Financial Accounting and Reporting*, 13th edn, Financial Times Prentice Hall, 2009, Chapter 29.

Revsine, L., Collins, D. and Bruce Johnson, W., *Financial Reporting and Analysis*, 3rd edn, Prentice Hall, 2007, Chapter 5.

Wild, J., Subramanyam, K. and Halsey, R., *Financial Statement Analysis*, 9th edn, McGraw-Hill, 2006, Chapters 8, 9 and 11.

Review questions

Solutions to these questions can be found at the back of the book on page 487.

8.1 What potential problems arise particularly for the external analyst from the use of statement of financial position figures in the calculation of financial ratios?

8.2 Identify and discuss three factors (apart from those mentioned in the chapter) that might influence the level of dividend per share a company decides to pay.

8.3 Identify and discuss three reasons why the P/E ratio of two businesses operating within the same industry may differ.

8.4 Identify and discuss three ratios (apart from those already mentioned in the chapter) that are likely to be affected by a business overtrading.

Exercises

Exercises 8.5 to 8.8 are more advanced than 8.1 to 8.4. Those with coloured numbers have answers at the back of the book, starting on page 510.

If you wish to try more exercises, visit the students' side of the Companion Website.

8.1 At the close of share trading on 13 November 2009, the market investor ratios for Next plc, the UK fashion and textiles retailer, and the averages for the 'general retailers' section, were as follows:

	Next plc	General retailers section
Dividend yield (%)	2.8	2.75
P/E ratio (times)	12.3	17.60
Dividend cover (times)	2.8	2.07

Source: *Financial Times*, 14 November 2009.

***Required*:**
Comment on what can be deduced about Next plc, relative to the general retailers sector, from an equity investor's point of view.

8.2   Telford Industrial Services plc is a medium-sized business.
      Extracts from the business's financial statements appear below.

Summary of statement of financial position at 31 December

	2007 £m	2008 £m	2009 £m	2010 £m
ASSETS				
Non-current assets	48	51	65	64
Current assets				
Inventories	21	22	23	26
Trade receivables	34	42	34	29
Cash	–	3	–	–
	55	67	57	55
Total assets	103	118	122	119
EQUITY AND LIABILITIES				
Equity	48	61	61	63
Non-current liabilities	30	30	30	30
Current liabilities				
Trade payables	20	27	25	18
Short-term borrowings	5	–	6	8
	25	27	31	26
Total equity and liabilities	103	118	122	119

Summary of income statements for years ended 31 December

	2007 £m	2008 £m	2009 £m	2010 £m
Sales revenue	152	170	110	145
Operating profit	28	40	7	15
Interest payable	(4)	(3)	(4)	(5)
Profit before taxation	24	37	3	10
Taxation	(12)	(16)	–	(4)
Profit for the year	12	21	3	6

Required:
Prepare a set of common-sized statements of financial position and common-sized income statements, on a vertical basis, using equity as the base figure for the statements of financial position and sales revenue as the base figure for the income statements.

8.3   *Required*:
      (a) Calculate the Z-scores for Ali plc and Bhaskar plc (see SAQ 7.1 on pages 250–251), using the Altman model set out on page 280.
      (b) Comment on the Z-scores for the two businesses and the validity of using this particular model to assess these particular businesses.

8.4 Diversified Industries plc (DI) is a business that has interests in engineering, caravan manufacturing and a chain of shops selling car accessories. DI has recently been approached by the directors of Automobile Care plc (AC), a smaller chain of accessory shops, who wish to negotiate the sale of their business to DI. The following information, which has been extracted from AC's financial statements, is available:

	Years ended 31 December		
	2008	2009	2010
	£m	£m	£m
Revenue	18.1	28.2	36.9
Profit before taxation	3.2	4.1	7.3
Taxation	(1.0)	(1.7)	(3.1)
Profit for the year	2.2	2.4	4.2
Dividend paid for the year	0.9	1.1	1.3
Issued share capital			
16 million shares of 25p each	4.0	4.0	4.0
Reserves	8.0	9.3	12.2

AC's market price per share at 31 December 2010 was £3.15.

Required:
(a) Calculate the following items for AC for 2010 and explain the use of each one:
   1 earnings per share
   2 price/earnings ratio
   3 dividend yield (assuming a 10 per cent dividend income tax credit rate)
   4 dividend payout ratio.
(b) Write some short notes on the factors the directors of DI should take into account when considering the possible purchase of AC. You should use the income statement details together with the figures that you calculated in your answer to part (a).

8.5 One of the main suppliers to your business is Green Ltd, a family-owned business. It is the only available supplier and your business buys 60 per cent of Green Ltd's output. Recently, Green Ltd has run into a severe cash shortage and it requires extra finance to re-equip its factory with modern machinery that is expected to cost £8 million. The machinery's life is expected to be ten years and savings, before depreciation, arising from its installation are expected to be £1 million a year. Green Ltd has approached your business to see if you are able to help with finance. The directors of Green Ltd have pointed out that, if it could acquire the new machinery, your business will be able to share in the benefits through reduced prices for supplies.

Extracts from Green Ltd's recent financial statements are as follows:

Income statement data for years ended 31 December

	2008	2009	2010
	£m	£m	£m
Revenue	11.5	8.0	9.5
Operating profit (loss)	(0.2)	(2.0)	1.9
Interest payable	(1.2)	(2.4)	(1.5)
Profit (loss) before taxation	(1.4)	(4.4)	0.4

There was no charge for taxation and no dividends were paid in respect of any of these three years.

Statements of financial position as at 31 December

	2008 £m	2009 £m	2010 £m
ASSETS			
Non-current assets			
Property, plant and equipment, at cost	22.1	23.9	24.0
Depreciation	(10.2)	(12.0)	(14.0)
	11.9	11.9	10.0
Current assets			
Inventories	4.3	3.5	3.8
Trade receivables	2.8	2.6	4.1
	7.1	6.1	7.9
Total assets	19.0	18.0	17.9
EQUITY AND LIABILITIES			
Equity			
Ordinary shares	1.0	1.0	1.0
Reserves	7.4	3.0	3.4
	8.4	4.0	4.4
Non-current liabilities			
Borrowings – loan notes	6.5	8.2	7.4
Current liabilities			
Trade payables	1.4	1.7	1.9
Short-term borrowings (all bank overdraft)	2.7	4.1	4.2
	4.1	5.8	6.1
Total equity and liabilities	19.0	18.0	17.9

Required:

(a) Calculate for each year and comment on each the following ratios for Green Ltd:
1 return on capital employed ratio
2 acid test ratio
3 trade receivables settlement period (months) ratio
4 interest cover ratio
5 gearing ratio.

(b) Write some short notes suggesting the level and nature of the financial assistance that your business might be prepared to provide for Green Ltd. Your notes should also suggest what terms and conditions you would seek to impose.

8.6 Russell Ltd installs and services heating and ventilation systems for commercial premises. The business's most recent statement of financial position and income statement are as follows:

Statement of financial position

ASSETS	£000	£000
Non-current assets		
Property, plant and equipment		
Machinery and equipment at cost	883.6	
Accumulated depreciation	(328.4)	555.2
Motor vehicles at cost	268.8	
Accumulated depreciation	(82.2)	186.6
		741.8
Current assets		
Inventories		293.2
Trade receivables		510.3
		803.5
Total assets		1,545.3
EQUITY AND LIABILITIES		
Equity		
£1 ordinary shares		400.0
General reserve		52.2
Retained earnings		380.2
		832.4
Non-current liabilities		
12% loan notes		250.0
Current liabilities		
Trade payables		199.7
Taxation		128.0
Short-term borrowings (bank overdraft)		135.2
		462.9
Total equity and liabilities		1,545.3

Income statement for the year

	£000
Revenue	5,207.8
Operating profit	542.0
Interest payable	(30.0)
Profit before taxation	512.0
Taxation (25%)	(128.0)
Profit for the year	384.0
Dividend paid during the year	153.6

The business wishes to invest in more machinery and equipment in order to cope with an upsurge in demand for its services. An additional operating profit of £120,000 a year is expected if an investment of £600,000 is made in machinery.

The directors are considering an offer from venture capitalists to finance the expansion programme. The finance will be made available immediately through either

1   an issue of £1 ordinary shares at a premium of £3 a share; or
2   an issue of £600,000 10 per cent loan notes at nominal value.

The directors wish to maintain the same dividend payout ratio in future years as in past years whichever method of finance is chosen.

Required:
(a) For each of the financing schemes:
    1   prepare a projected income statement for next year;
    2   calculate the projected earnings per share for next year;
    3   calculate the projected level of gearing as at the end of next year.
(b) Briefly assess both of the financing schemes under consideration from the viewpoint of the existing shareholders.

8.7   The following is the statement of financial position (in abbreviated form) of Projections Ltd as at the end of this year:

Statement of financial position as at 31 December

	£000
ASSETS	
Non-current assets	
Cost	290
Accumulated depreciation	(110)
	180
Current assets	
Inventories	26
Trade receivables	35
Cash	5
	66
Total assets	246
EQUITY AND LIABILITIES	
Equity	
Share capital	150
Retained earnings	48
	198
Current liabilities	
Trade payables	21
Taxation (payable during next year)	27
	48
Total equity and liabilities	246

The following plans have been made for next year:

1   Revenue is expected to total £350,000, all on credit. Sales will be made at a steady rate over the year and two months' credit will be allowed to customers.
2   £200,000 worth of inventories will be bought during the year, all on credit. Purchases will be made at a steady rate over the year and suppliers will allow one month's credit.
3   New non-current assets will be bought, and paid for, during the year at a cost of £30,000. No disposals of non-current assets are planned. The depreciation expense for the year will be 10 per cent of the cost of the non-current assets owned at the end of the year.

4 Inventories at the end of the year are expected to have a value double that which applied at the beginning of the year.

5 Operating expenses, other than depreciation, are expected to total £52,000, of which £5,000 will remain unpaid at the end of the year.

6 During the year, the tax noted in the start of the year statement of financial position will be paid.

7 The tax rate can be assumed to be 25 per cent of operating profit. The tax will not be paid during the year.

8 A dividend of £10,000 will be paid during the year.

Required:

Prepare a projected income statement for next year and a statement of financial position as at the end of next year, to the nearest £1,000.

8.8 Genesis Ltd was incorporated in 2007 and has grown rapidly over the past three years. The rapid rate of growth has created problems for the business, which the directors have found difficult to deal with. Recently, a firm of management consultants has been asked to help the directors to overcome these problems.

In a preliminary report to the board of directors, the management consultants state: 'Most of the difficulties faced by the business are symptoms of an underlying problem of overtrading.'

The most recent financial statements of the business are set out below.

Statement of financial position as at 31 October 2010

ASSETS	£000	£000
Non-current assets		
Property, plant and equipment		
Land and buildings at cost	530	
Accumulated depreciation	(88)	442
Fixtures and fittings at cost	168	
Accumulated depreciation	(52)	116
Motor vans at cost	118	
Accumulated depreciation	(54)	64
		622
Current assets		
Inventories		128
Trade receivables		104
		232
Total assets		854
EQUITY AND LIABILITIES		
Equity		
Ordinary £0.50 shares		60
General reserve		50
Retained earnings		74
		184
Non-current liabilities		
Borrowings – 10% loan notes (secured)		120
Current liabilities		
Trade payables		184
Taxation		8
Short-term borrowings (all bank overdraft)		358
		550
Total equity and liabilities		854

Income statement for the year ended 31 October 2010

	£000	£000
Revenue		1,640
Cost of sales		
Opening inventories	116	
Purchases	1,260	
	1,376	
Closing inventories	(128)	(1,248)
Gross profit		392
Selling and distribution expenses		(204)
Administration expenses		(92)
Operating profit		96
Interest payable		(44)
Profit before taxation		52
Taxation		(16)
Profit for the year		36

All purchases and sales were on credit.

A dividend was paid during the year on ordinary shares of £4,000.

Required:

(a) Calculate and discuss *five* financial ratios that might be used to establish whether the business is overtrading. Do these five ratios suggest that the business is overtrading?

(b) State the ways in which a business may overcome the problem of overtrading.

9

Reporting the financial results of groups of companies

Introduction

Many larger businesses, including virtually all of those that are household names in the UK, consist not just of one single company but of a group of companies. Here one company (the parent company) controls one or more other companies (the subsidiary companies). This usually arises because the parent owns more than 50% of the shares of the subsidiaries.

In this chapter we shall look at groups and, more particularly, at the accounting treatment that they usually receive. This will draw heavily on what we have already covered so far, particularly in Chapters 2 to 6. We shall also briefly consider associate companies.

Learning outcomes

When you have completed this chapter, you should be able to:

- discuss the nature of groups, and explain why they exist and how they are formed;

- prepare a group statement of financial position (balance sheet) and income statement;

- explain the nature of associate company status and its accounting implications;

- explain and interpret the contents of a set of group financial statements.

What is a group of companies?

→ It is quite common for one company to be able to exercise control over the activities of another. Control typically arises because the first company (the **parent company**) owns more than 50 per cent of the ordinary (voting) shares of the second company
→ (the **subsidiary company**). This leads to the directors of the parent company being able to appoint the directors of the subsidiary company and, therefore, being able
→ to dictate its policies. Where this relationship arises, a **'group' (of companies)** is said to exist. Where there is a group, the relevant International Financial Reporting Standards (IAS 27 *Consolidated and Separate Financial Statements* and IFRS 3 *Business Combinations*) normally require that a set of financial statements is drawn up annually not only for each individual company, but also for the group taken as a whole. Before we go on to
→ consider how the **group financial statements** (that is, the financial statements of a group of companies) are prepared, we shall look at the reasons why groups exist at all and at the types of group relationships that can exist.

Why do groups exist?

Companies have subsidiaries where:

1 The parent company creates a new company to operate some part of its business, perhaps a new activity.
2 The parent company buys a majority, perhaps all, of the shares of some other existing
→   company – that is, a **'takeover'**.

Many companies have subsidiaries as a result of both of these reasons.

Newly created companies

It is very common for large businesses to be made up of a number of individual companies. These companies are controlled by a parent company, sometimes known
→ as the **'holding' company**. In some cases, the only assets of the parent company are the shares that it owns in the subsidiary companies. Although the subsidiary companies own the land, buildings, machinery, inventories and so on, since the parent owns the subsidiaries, it effectively controls the productive assets of those companies. **Real World 9.1** looks at Associated British Foods plc, the major UK food manufacturer and retailer.

 Real World 9.1

Food for thought

Under the heading 'Non-current assets' in the statement of financial position of Associated British Foods plc, there is no property, plant and equipment, just 'goodwill' and 'investment in subsidiaries'. The productive assets of the group are owned by the more than eighty subsidiary companies. These include such well-known names as:

● British Sugar plc
● Twinings and Company Limited (tea producers)
● The Ryvita Company Limited
● Primart Stores Limited.

Source: Associated British Foods plc Annual Report and Accounts 2009.

An obvious question to ask is: why do businesses operate through subsidiaries? To put it another way, why do the parent companies not own all of the assets of the business directly, instead of them being owned by the subsidiaries? The answers to these questions are probably:

● *Limited liability*. Each individual company has limited liability. This means that if there is a financial failure of one subsidiary, neither the assets of other subsidiaries nor those of the parent could be legally demanded by any unsatisfied claimants (lenders, trade payables and so on) against the failed company. Thus the group can 'ring-fence' each part of the business by having separate companies, each with its own limited liability.

● *Individual identity*. A sense of independence and autonomy may be created that could, in turn, increase levels of commitment among staff. It may also help to develop, or perpetuate, a market image of a smaller, independent business. Customers, as well as staff, may prefer to deal with what they see as a smaller, specialist business than with a division of a large diversified business.

To create a subsidiary, the would-be parent may simply form a new company in the normal way. The new company would then issue shares to the parent, in exchange for some asset or assets of the parent. Where the new subsidiary has been formed to undertake a completely new activity, the asset may well be cash. If the subsidiary is to carry on some activity, which the parent had undertaken directly up to that point, the assets are likely to be such things as the non-current and current assets associated with the particular activity.

Example 9.1

The summarised statement of financial position of Baxter plc is as follows:

Statement of financial position

	£m
ASSETS	
Non-current assets	
Property, plant and equipment	
Land	43
Plant	15
Vehicles	8
	66
Current assets	
Inventories	15
Trade receivables	23
Cash	13
	51
Total assets	117
EQUITY AND LIABILITIES	
Equity	
Called-up share capital: ordinary shares of £1 each, fully paid	50
Retained earnings	16
	66
Non-current liabilities	
Borrowings – loan notes	40
Current liabilities	
Trade payables	11
Total equity and liabilities	117

Example 9.1 continued

Baxter plc has recently formed a new company, Nova Ltd, which is to undertake the work that has previously been done by the industrial fibres division of Baxter plc. The following assets are to be transferred to Nova Ltd at the values that currently are shown in the statement of financial position of Baxter plc:

	£m
Land	10
Plant	5
Vehicles	3
Inventories	6
Cash	3
	27

Nova Ltd is to issue £1 ordinary shares at their nominal value to Baxter plc in exchange for these assets.

Baxter plc's statement of financial position immediately after these transfers will be:

Statement of financial position

	£m
ASSETS	
Non-current assets	
Property, plant and equipment	
Land (43 – 10)	33
Plant (15 – 5)	10
Vehicles (8 – 3)	5
	48
Investments	
27 million ordinary £1 shares of Nova Ltd	27
	75
Current assets	
Inventories (15 – 6)	9
Trade receivables	23
Cash (13 – 3)	10
	42
Total assets	117
EQUITY AND LIABILITIES	
Equity	
Called-up share capital:	
ordinary shares of £1 each, fully paid	50
Retained earnings	16
	66
Non-current liabilities	
Borrowings – loan notes	40
Current liabilities	
Trade payables	11
Total equity and liabilities	117

As you have probably noted, the individual productive assets have simply been replaced by the asset of shares in Nova Ltd.

Activity 9.1

Try to prepare the statement of financial position of Nova Ltd, immediately following the transfers of the assets and the shares being issued.

It should look something like this:

Statement of financial position

	£m
ASSETS	
Non-current assets	
Property, plant and equipment (at transfer value)	
Land	10
Plant	5
Vehicles	3
	18
Current assets	
Inventories	6
Cash	3
	9
Total assets	27
EQUITY AND LIABILITIES	
Equity	
Called-up share capital:	
ordinary shares of £1 each, fully paid	27

Takeovers

A would-be parent company may also create a subsidiary by taking over an existing company. Here it buys more than 50 per cent of the shares of a hitherto, unconnected **target company** to enable it to exercise control, thereby making the target a subsidiary company. The shares are, of course, bought from the existing shareholders of the target company.

In many takeovers, the parent offers its own shares as all, or part of, the bid consideration. This means the target company shareholders who accept the offer will exchange their existing shares for shares in the parent. Thus, they cease to be shareholders of the target company and become shareholders in the parent.

Often the parent company offers cash or a combination of shares and cash.

Real World 9.2 outlines a recent, high-profile example of a 'share-for-share' takeover.

Real World 9.2

Banking on shares

FT

When Lloyds TSB Bank plc took over its banking rival HBOS plc in January 2009, in the midst of the UK's banking crisis, HBOS shareholders received 0.833 of a Lloyds share for every one share that they held in HBOS. So, a shareholder who owned 1,000 HBOS shares before the takeover would have held 833 Lloyds shares after it.

Source: 'Lloyds could rue HBOS haste', Jane Croft and Kate Burgess, *Financial Times*, 13 February 2009.

Example 9.2

The summarised statement of financial position of Adams plc is as follows:

Statement of financial position

	£m
ASSETS	
Non-current assets	
Property, plant and equipment	
Land	35
Plant	21
Vehicles	12
	68
Current assets	
Inventories	25
Trade receivables	28
Cash	22
	75
Total assets	143
EQUITY AND LIABILITIES	
Equity	
Called-up share capital: ordinary shares of £1 each, fully paid	60
Share premium account	5
Retained earnings	5
	70
Non-current liabilities	
Borrowings – loan notes	50
Current liabilities	
Trade payables	23
Total equity and liabilities	143

Adams plc has recently made an offer of £1 a share for all the share capital of Beta Ltd. Beta Ltd's issued share capital is 20 million shares of 50p each. Adams plc will 'pay' for this by issuing the appropriate number of new ordinary shares of Adams plc at an issue value of £2 a share.

All the Beta Ltd shareholders accepted the offer. This means that Adams plc will need to issue shares to the value of £20 million (that is, 20 million × £1).

Since the Adams plc shares are to be issued at £2 each, 10 million shares will need to be issued, at a share premium of £1 each.

Following the takeover, the statement of financial position of Adams plc will look as follows:

Statement of financial position

	£m
ASSETS	
Non-current assets	
Property, plant and equipment	
Land	35
Plant	21
Vehicles	12
	68
Investments	
Shares in Beta Ltd	20
	88
Current assets	
Inventories	25
Trade receivables	28
Cash	22
	75
Total assets	163
EQUITY AND LIABILITIES	
Equity	
Called-up share capital: ordinary shares of £1 each, fully paid (60 + 10)	70
Share premium account (5 + 10)	15
Retained earnings	5
	90
Non-current liabilities	
Borrowings – loan notes	50
Current liabilities	
Trade payables	23
Total equity and liabilities	163

Note that the assets have increased by £20 million and that this is balanced by the value of the shares issued (£10 million share capital and £10 million share premium).

Activity 9.2

If, instead of the consideration offered being all in shares, the offer had been 50 per cent in cash and 50 per cent in Adams plc shares, what would the statement of financial position of Adams plc have looked like after the takeover?

The total offer value would still be £20 million, but this would be met by paying cash totalling £10 million and by issuing shares worth £10 million (£5 million share capital and £5 million share premium). So the statement of financial position would be:

Activity 9.2 continued

Statement of financial position

		£m
ASSETS		
Non-current assets		
Property, plant and equipment		
Land		35
Plant		21
Vehicles		12
		68
Investments		
Shares in Beta Ltd		20
		88
Current assets		
Inventories		25
Trade receivables		28
Cash (22 − 10)		12
		65
Total assets		153
EQUITY AND LIABILITIES		
Equity		
Called-up share capital:		
ordinary shares of £1 each, fully paid (60 + 5)		65
Share premium account (5 + 5)		10
Retained earnings		5
		80
Non-current liabilities		
Borrowings – loan notes		50
Current liabilities		
Trade payables		23
Total equity and liabilities		153

Activity 9.3

How would the takeover affect the statement of financial position of Beta Ltd?

The statement of financial position of Beta Ltd would not be affected at all. A change of shareholders does not affect the financial statements of a company.

It is not necessary that the parent company should retain the target/subsidiary as a separate company, following the takeover. The subsidiary could be wound up and its assets owned directly by the parent. Normally this would not happen, however, for the reasons that we considered above; namely limited liability and individual identity. The latter may be particularly important in the case of a takeover. The new parent company may be very keen to retain the name and identity of its new subsidiary, where the subsidiary has a good marketing image.

TYPES OF GROUP RELATIONSHIP 303

Types of group relationship

So far we have considered a situation where there is the simple relationship between a parent and its subsidiary or subsidiaries that is shown in Figure 9.1.

Figure 9.1   A simple parent/subsidiaries relationship

The parent company exercises control directly by owning a majority of the voting shares in each of the four subsidiaries.

A slightly more complex relationship is shown in Figure 9.2.

Figure 9.2   A more complex parent/subsidiaries relationship

The parent company exercises control over Subsidiaries 1 and 3 directly by owning a majority of the voting shares in them. The parent also exercises control over Subsidiary 2 because Subsidiary 1 has control over Subsidiary 2.

Here Subsidiary 2 is a subsidiary by virtue of being controlled by another company (Subsidiary 1), that is, in turn, a subsidiary of the parent. In these circumstances, Subsidiary 2 is usually called a 'sub-subsidiary' of the parent. The parent company here is sometimes known as the 'ultimate' parent company of Subsidiary 2. Subsidiary 3 is a straightforward subsidiary.

Earlier in this chapter, it was pointed out that one company is a subsidiary of another because the latter *controls* the former. This is usually as a result of the parent owning a majority, or all, of the voting shares of the other, but this does not need to be the case. Consider Figure 9.2 and suppose that the parent owns 60 per cent of the voting shares of Subsidiary 1 and that Subsidiary 1 owns 60 per cent of the shares of Subsidiary 2. In effect, the parent only owns 36 per cent of the shares of Subsidiary 2 (that is, 60 per cent of 60 per cent), yet the latter is a subsidiary of the former. This is because the parent has complete control over (though not total ownership of) Subsidiary 1, which in turn has complete control over (though again not total ownership of) Subsidiary 2.

Activity 9.4

Company A owns 40 per cent of the voting shares of both Company B and Company C. The other 60 per cent of the voting shares of Company C are owned by Company B.
  Is Company C a subsidiary of Company A?

The answer is no. This is despite the fact that Company A can be seen to own 64 per cent of the shares of Company C; 40 per cent directly and 24 per cent (that is, 40 per cent × 60 per cent) through Company B. Since A does not control B, it cannot control B's shares in C.

Though ownership and control do not necessarily go hand-in-hand, in practice this tends to be the case.

The reason that we are concerned as to whether one company is a subsidiary of another is, of course, that group financial statements must be prepared where there is a parent/subsidiary relationship, but not otherwise.

Real World 9.3 shows the subsidiaries of the Go-Ahead Group plc. Most of us in the UK use the services of at least one of the subsidiaries, many of us on a daily basis. Most of the productive assets of the group are owned by the subsidiaries, rather than directly by the parent company. Note that Go-Ahead uses the word 'group' in its official name. This is not unusual, but is not a legal requirement. Many companies which operate mainly through subsidiaries do not indicate this in the company name.

Real World 9.3

Going ahead with subsidiaries

Go-Ahead Group plc
Principal subsidiaries

Name	Percentage of shares owned
Brighton & Hove Bus and Coach Company Limited	100
City of Oxford Motor Services Limited	100
Go North East Limited	100
London Central Bus Company Limited	100
London General Transport Services Limited	100
Docklands Minibuses Limited	100
Go Northern Limited	100
Go Wear Buses Limited	100
Metrobus Limited	100
New Southern Railway Limited	65
London and South Eastern Railway Limited	65
Govia Limited	65
Abingdon Bus Company Limited	100
Aviance UK Limited	100
Reed Aviation Limited	100
Meteor Parking Limited	100
PAS Direct Limited	100
Nicaria Limited	100
Chauffeured Parking Services Limited	100
Plane Handling Limited	100
Go South Coast Limited	100
Wilts and Dorset Bus Company Limited	100
Solent Blue Line Limited	100
The Southern Vectis Omnibus Company Limited	100
Marchwood Motorways (Services) Limited	100
Marchwood Motorways (Southampton) Limited	100
Hants and Dorset Motor Services Limited	100
Tourist Coaches Limited	100
Hants and Dorset Trim Limited	100
Go-Ahead Leasing Limited	100
London and Birmingham Railway Limited	65
Go-Ahead Holding Limited	100

Source: Go-Ahead Group plc Annual Report 2009.

Preparation of a group statement of financial position

→ We are now going to look at the preparation of a **group statement of financial position**. We shall do this by considering a series of examples, starting with the simplest possible case and gradually building on more and more of the complexities found in real life.

Each company within the group will prepare its own statement of financial position, which considers things from the perspective of that particular company. As well as this, the parent company will produce a statement of financial position that reflects the assets and claims of the group as a whole. In effect, the group statement of financial position looks at the group as if the parent company owned the assets and, therefore, was responsible for the outside liabilities of all the group members. This means, among other things, that whereas the *parent company* statement of financial position will include the assets of investments in the shares of the subsidiary companies, in the *group* statement of financial position, this will be replaced by the net assets (assets less claims of non-group liabilities). In other words, the group statement of financial position looks behind the subsidiary company shares to see what they represent, in terms of assets and liabilities. The assets and liabilities of subsidiaries are 'consolidated' into the statement of financial position of the parent company. This point should become clearer as we look at some examples.

Example 9.3

The statements of financial position of Parent plc and of Subsidiary Ltd, on the date that the former bought all the shares in the latter, were as follows:

Statements of financial position

	Parent plc £m	Subsidiary Ltd £m
ASSETS		
Non-current assets		
Property, plant and equipment		
Land	40	5
Plant	30	2
Vehicles	20	2
	90	9
Investment		
5 million shares of Subsidiary Ltd	10	–
	100	9
Current assets		
Inventories	20	3
Trade receivables	30	2
Cash	10	2
	60	7
Total assets	160	16
EQUITY AND LIABILITIES		
Equity		
Called-up share capital:		
ordinary shares of £1 each, fully paid	70	5
Share premium account	10	–
Retained earnings	30	5
	110	10
Non-current liabilities		
Borrowings – loan notes	30	–
Current liabilities		
Trade payables	20	6
Total equity and liabilities	160	16

To derive the group statement of financial position, we simply combine each of the like items by adding them together. For example, the group investment in land is £45 million, representing £40 million invested by Parent plc and £5 million invested by Subsidiary Ltd.

The only exceptions to the rule that we simply add like items together lies with the investment in the shares of Subsidiary Ltd in the statement of financial position of Parent plc, and with the equity (share capital plus reserves) in the statement of financial position of Subsidiary Ltd. In effect, these are two sides of the same coin, since Parent plc is the owner of Subsidiary Ltd. For this reason, it is logical simply to add these two items together and since one is an asset and the other is a claim and they are equal in amount, they will cancel each other out.

The group statement of financial position will be as follows:

Statement of financial position

	£m
ASSETS	
Non-current assets	
Property, plant and equipment	
Land (40 + 5)	45
Plant (30 + 2)	32
Vehicles (20 + 2)	22
	99
Current assets	
Inventories (20 + 3)	23
Trade receivables (30 + 2)	32
Cash (10 + 2)	12
	67
Total assets	166
EQUITY AND LIABILITIES	
Equity	
Called-up share capital:	
ordinary shares of £1 each, fully paid	70
Share premium account	10
Retained earnings	30
	110
Non-current liabilities	
Borrowings – loan notes (30 + 0)	30
Current liabilities	
Trade payables (20 + 6)	26
Total equity and liabilities	166

The 'Equity' section of the group statement of financial position is simply that of Parent plc. The £10 million Equity for Subsidiary Ltd cancels out with the £10 million that relates to '5 million shares of Subsidiary Ltd' in the non-current assets section of the parent company's statement of financial position. Since Parent owns all of Subsidiary's shares, all of Subsidiary's equity is attributable to Parent.

Activity 9.5

The statements of financial position of Large plc and of Small plc, on the date that Large plc bought all the shares in Small plc, were as follows:

Statements of financial position

	Large plc £m	Small plc £m
ASSETS		
Non-current assets		
Property, plant and equipment		
Land	55	–
Plant	43	21
Vehicles	25	17
Investment	123	38
20 million shares of Small plc	32	–
	155	38
Current assets		
Inventories	42	18
Trade receivables	18	13
Cash	24	13
	84	44
Total assets	239	82
EQUITY AND LIABILITIES		
Equity		
Called-up share capital:		
ordinary shares of £1 each, fully paid	100	20
Share premium account	–	5
Retained earnings	64	7
	164	32
Non-current liabilities		
Borrowings – loan notes	50	30
Current liabilities		
Trade payables	25	20
Total equity and liabilities	239	82

Have a try at deducing the group statement of financial position.

The group statement of financial position will be as follows:

Statement of financial position

	£m
ASSETS	
Non-current assets	
Property, plant and equipment	
Land (55 + 0)	55
Plant (43 + 21)	64
Vehicles (25 + 17)	42
	161
Current assets	
Inventories (42 + 18)	60
Trade receivables (18 + 13)	31
Cash (24 + 13)	37
	128
Total assets	289
EQUITY AND LIABILITIES	
Equity	
Called-up share capital: ordinary shares of £1 each, fully paid	100
Retained earnings	64
	164
Non-current liabilities	
Borrowings – loan notes (50 + 30)	80
Current liabilities	
Trade payables (25 + 20)	45
Total equity and liabilities	289

The 'equity' section of the group statement of financial position is simply that of Large plc. The £32 million for the equity (share capital and reserves) of Small plc cancels out with the £32 million relating to 'Investment in 20 million shares of Small plc' in the Non-current assets section of the statement of financial position of Large plc.

The example and the activity represent the simplest case because:

1 the parent owns all of the shares of the subsidiary;
2 the price paid for the shares (£10 million and £32 million, respectively) exactly equals the 'book value' or 'carrying amount' of the net assets of the subsidiary (that is the values at which they appear in the subsidiary's statement of financial position); and
3 no trading has taken place since the shares were acquired.

Frequently, in practice, not all of these three 'simplifications' exist; often none of them exists.

We shall now go on to look at the 'complications', first, one by one and then all together.

Complication 1: Less than 100 per cent ownership of the subsidiary by the parent

The problem here is that when we come to set the asset of 'shares of subsidiary', in the statement of financial position of the parent, against the 'equity' (owners' claim) in the statement of financial position of the subsidiary, they do not completely cancel one another.

Example 9.4

The statements of financial position of Parent plc and of Subsidiary Ltd, on the date that the former bought the shares in the latter, are the same as in the previous example (Example 9.3) except that Parent plc owns only 4 million (of the 5 million) shares of Subsidiary Ltd. Thus the investment is only £8 million, instead of £10 million. As a result, Parent plc's cash balance is £2 million greater than in the previous example.

The two statements of financial position were as follows:

Statements of financial position

	Parent plc £m	Subsidiary Ltd £m
ASSETS		
Non-current assets		
Property, plant and equipment		
Land	40	5
Plant	30	2
Vehicles	20	2
	90	9
Investment		
4 million shares of Subsidiary Ltd	8	–
	98	9
Current assets		
Inventories	20	3
Trade receivables	30	2
Cash	12	2
	62	7
Total assets	160	16
EQUITY AND LIABILITIES		
Equity		
Called-up share capital:		
ordinary shares of £1 each, fully paid	70	5
Share premium account	10	–
Retained earnings	30	5
	110	10
Non-current liabilities		
Borrowings – loan notes	30	–
Current liabilities		
Trade payables	20	6
Total equity and liabilities	160	16

As before, to prepare the group statement of financial position, we simply add like items together. The problem is that when we come to set the £8 million investment made by Parent plc against the £10 million equity of Subsidiary Ltd, they do not cancel. There is an owners' claim of £2 million in the statement of financial position of Subsidiary Ltd that has not been cancelled out.

Activity 9.6

Can you puzzle out what the £2 million represents?

It represents the extent to which Parent plc does not own all of the shares of Subsidiary Ltd. Parent plc only owns 80 per cent of the shares and, therefore, other investors must own the rest. Since we are including all of the assets and liabilities of Subsidiary Ltd as being those of the group, the group statement of financial position needs to acknowledge that there is another source of equity finance, as well as Parent plc.

→ This £2 million owners' claim is known as '**non-controlling interests**' or ('**minority interests**'). It is shown in the group statement of financial position as an addition to, but not part of, the equity.

The group statement of financial position will be as follows:

Statement of financial position

	£m
ASSETS	
Non-current assets	
Property, plant and equipment	
Land (40 + 5)	45
Plant (30 + 2)	32
Vehicles (20 + 2)	22
	99
Current assets	
Inventories (20 + 3)	23
Trade receivables (30 + 2)	32
Cash (12 + 2)	14
	69
Total assets	168
EQUITY AND LIABILITIES	
Equity	
Called-up share capital: ordinary shares of £1 each, fully paid	70
Share premium account	10
Retained earnings	30
	110
Non-controlling interests	2
	112
Non-current liabilities	
Borrowings – loan notes (30 + 0)	30
Current liabilities	
Trade payables (20 + 6)	26
	168

This statement of financial position reflects the fact that the group has control over net assets totalling £112 million (at statement of financial position values). Of this, £110 million is financed by the shareholders of the parent company and £2 million by others.

It may have occurred to you that an alternative approach to dealing with less than 100 per cent ownership is to scale down the assets and liabilities, to reflect this, before carrying out the 'consolidation' of the two sets of financial statements. Since Parent plc only owns 80 per cent of Subsidiary Ltd, we could multiply all of the figures in Subsidiary Ltd's statement of financial position by 0.8 before preparing the group financial statements. If we did this, the owners' claim would be reduced to £8 million, which would exactly cancel with the asset (shares of Subsidiary Ltd) in the statement of financial position of Parent plc.

Activity 9.7

Can you think of the (logical) reason why we do not 'scale down' for less than 100 per cent owned subsidiaries when preparing the group statement of financial position?

The reason that all of the assets and liabilities of the subsidiary are included in the group statement of financial position, in these circumstances, is that the parent company *controls* all of the subsidiaries' assets, even though it may not strictly own them all. Control is the key issue in group financial statements.

Activity 9.8

The statements of financial position of Large plc and of Small plc, on the date that Large plc bought the shares in Small plc, were as follows:

Statements of financial position

	Large plc £m	Small plc £m
ASSETS		
Non-current assets		
Property, plant and equipment		
Land	55	–
Plant	43	21
Vehicles	25	17
	123	38
Investment		
15 million shares of Small plc	24	–
	147	38
Current assets		
Inventories	42	18
Trade receivables	18	13
Cash	32	13
	92	44
Total assets	239	82

	Large plc £m	Small plc £m
EQUITY AND LIABILITIES		
Equity		
Called-up share capital:		
ordinary shares of £1 each, fully paid	100	20
Share premium account	–	5
Retained earnings	64	7
	164	32
Non-current liabilities		
Borrowings – loan notes	50	30
Current liabilities		
Trade payables	25	20
Total equity and liabilities	239	82

Have a go at preparing the group statement of financial position.

The group statement of financial position will be as follows:

Statement of financial position

	£m
ASSETS	
Non-current assets	
Property, plant and equipment	
Land (55 + 0)	55
Plant (43 + 21)	64
Vehicles (25 + 17)	42
	161
Current assets	
Inventories (42 + 18)	60
Trade receivables (18 + 13)	31
Cash (32 + 13)	45
	136
Total assets	297
EQUITY AND LIABILITIES	
Equity	
Called-up share capital:	
ordinary shares of £1 each, fully paid	100
Retained earnings	64
	164
Non-controlling interests	8
	172
Non-current liabilities	
Borrowings – loan notes (50 + 30)	80
Current liabilities	
Trade payables (25 + 20)	45
Total equity and liabilities	297

Large plc owns 75 per cent of the shares, costing £24 million. The £8 million for non-controlling interests represents the remaining 25 per cent of the Small plc shares owned by the 'outside' shareholders (that is, 25 per cent of £32 million).

Complication 2: Paying more or less than the underlying net asset value for the shares

Here the problem is that, even where the subsidiary is 100 per cent owned, the asset of 'shares of the subsidiary', in the statement of financial position of the parent, will not exactly cancel against the equity figure in the statement of financial position of the subsidiary. Anything paid in excess of the underlying net asset value of the subsidiary's shares must represent an undisclosed asset, which is normally referred to as '**goodwill arising on consolidation**'. Any amount paid below the underlying net asset value is normally referred to as '**negative goodwill arising on consolidation**'.

This situation tends only to arise where there is a takeover of an existing business. Where a would-be parent creates a new subsidiary, goodwill (positive or negative) will not usually arise.

For the sake of simplicity, we shall assume that the statement of financial position of a subsidiary reflects all of its assets and liabilities and that these are recorded at their fair values. We shall, however, consider the situation where this is not the case later in the chapter.

Example 9.5

We are returning to the original statements of financial position of Parent plc and Subsidiary Ltd (Example 9.3, page 306), on the date that the former bought the shares in the latter. So Parent plc owns all of the shares in Subsidiary Ltd, but we shall assume that they were bought for £15 million rather than £10 million. Parent plc's cash balance reflects the higher amount paid. The statements of financial position are as follows:

Statements of financial position

	Parent plc £m	Subsidiary Ltd £m
ASSETS		
Non-current assets		
Property, plant and equipment		
Land	40	5
Plant	30	2
Vehicles	20	2
	90	9
Investment		
5 million shares of Subsidiary Ltd	15	–
	105	9
Current assets		
Inventories	20	3
Trade receivables	30	2
Cash	5	2
	55	7
Total assets	160	16

	Parent plc £m	Subsidiary Ltd £m
EQUITY AND LIABILITIES		
Equity		
Called-up share capital:		
ordinary shares of £1 each, fully paid	70	5
Share premium account	10	–
Retained earnings	30	5
	110	10
Non-current liabilities		
Borrowings – loan notes	30	–
Current liabilities		
Trade payables	20	6
Total equity and liabilities	160	16

The normal routine of adding like items together and cancelling the investment in Subsidiary Ltd shares against the equity of that company is followed, except that the last two do not exactly cancel. The difference is, of course, goodwill arising on consolidation.

The group statement of financial position will be as follows:

Statement of financial position

	£m
Non-current assets	
Property, plant and equipment	
Land (40 + 5)	45
Plant (30 + 2)	32
Vehicles (20 + 2)	22
	99
Intangible asset	
Goodwill arising on consolidation (15 – 10)	5
	104
Current assets	
Inventories (20 + 3)	23
Trade receivables (30 + 2)	32
Cash (5 + 2)	7
	62
Total assets	166
Equity	
Called-up share capital:	
ordinary shares of £1 each, fully paid	70
Share premium account	10
Retained earnings	30
	110
Non-current liabilities	
Borrowings – loan notes (30 + 0)	30
Current liabilities	
Trade payables (20 + 6)	26
Total equity and liabilities	166

The goodwill represents the excess of what was paid by Parent plc for the shares over the fair value of their underlying net assets, at the time of the takeover.

Activity 9.9

The statements of financial position of Large plc and of Small plc, on the date that Large plc bought all the shares in Small plc, were as follows:

Statements of financial position

	Large plc £m	Small plc £m
ASSETS		
Non-current assets		
Property, plant and equipment		
Land	48	–
Plant	43	21
Vehicles	25	17
	116	38
Investment		
20 million shares of Small plc	35	–
	151	38
Current assets		
Inventories	42	18
Trade receivables	18	13
Cash	28	13
	88	44
Total assets	239	82
EQUITY AND LIABILITIES		
Equity		
Called-up share capital:		
ordinary shares of £1 each, fully paid	100	20
Share premium account	–	5
Retained earnings	64	7
	164	32
Non-current liabilities		
Borrowings – loan notes	50	30
Current liabilities		
Trade payables	25	20
Total equity and liabilities	239	82

Have a go at preparing the group statement of financial position.

The group statement of financial position will be as follows:

Statement of financial position

	£m
ASSETS	
Non-current assets	
Property, plant and equipment	
Land (48 + 0)	48
Plant (43 + 21)	64
Vehicles (25 + 17)	42
	154
Intangible asset	
Goodwill arising on consolidation (35 – 32)	3
	157
Current assets	
Inventories (42 + 18)	60
Trade receivables (18 + 13)	31
Cash (28 + 13)	41
	132
Total assets	289
EQUITY AND LIABILITIES	
Equity	
Called-up share capital:	
ordinary shares of £1 each, fully paid	100
Retained earnings	64
	164
Non-current liabilities	
Borrowings – loan notes (50 + 30)	80
Current liabilities	
Trade payables (25 + 20)	45
Total equity and liabilities	289

A little later in the chapter we shall see that there is a slightly different approach that can be taken in the valuation of goodwill arising on consolidation in the group statement of financial position. In practice, however, most businesses take the approach that we have just explored.

Complications 1 and 2 taken together

We shall now take a look at how we cope with a situation where the parent owns less than all of the shares of its subsidiary, *and* it has paid more or less than the underlying net asset value of the shares.

Example 9.6

Again we shall look at the statements of financial position of Parent plc and of Subsidiary Ltd, on the date that the former bought the shares in the latter. This time we shall combine both of the 'complications' that we have already met. Here, Parent plc now only owns 80 per cent of the shares of Subsidiary Ltd, for which it paid £3 a share, that is, £1 above their underlying net asset value.

Statements of financial position

	Parent plc £m	Subsidiary Ltd £m
ASSETS		
Non-current assets		
Property, plant and equipment		
Land	40	5
Plant	30	2
Vehicles	20	2
	90	9
Investment		
4 million shares of Subsidiary Ltd	12	–
	102	9
Current assets		
Inventories	20	3
Trade receivables	30	2
Cash	8	2
	58	7
Total assets	160	16
EQUITY AND LIABILITIES		
Equity		
Called-up share capital:		
ordinary shares of £1 each, fully paid	70	5
Share premium account	10	–
Retained earnings	30	5
	110	10
Non-current liabilities		
Borrowings – loan notes	30	–
Current liabilities		
Trade payables	20	6
Total equity and liabilities	160	16

The normal routine still applies. This means adding like items together and cancelling the investment in Subsidiary Ltd shares against the equity of that company. Again they will not cancel, but this time for a combination of two reasons; non-controlling interests *and* goodwill arising on consolidation.

We need to separate out these two issues before we go on to prepare the group financial statements.

To establish the non-controlling interests element, we need simply to calculate the part of the owners' claim of Subsidiary Ltd that is not owned by Parent plc. Parent plc owns 80 per cent of the shares, so others own the remaining 20 per cent. Twenty per cent of the equity of Subsidiary Ltd is £2 million (that is, 20 per cent × £10 million).

To discover the appropriate goodwill figure, we need to compare what Parent plc paid and what it got, in terms of the fair values reflected in the statement of financial position. It paid £12 million and got net assets with a fair value of £8 million (that is, 80 per cent × £10 million). Thus, goodwill is £4 million (that is, 12 – 8).

The group statement of financial position will be as follows:

Statement of financial position

	£m
ASSETS	
Non-current assets	
Property, plant and equipment	
Land (40 + 5)	45
Plant (30 + 2)	32
Vehicles (20 + 2)	22
	99
Intangible asset	
Goodwill arising on consolidation	
(12 – (80% × 10))	4
	103
Current assets	
Inventories (20 + 3)	23
Trade receivables (30 + 2)	32
Cash (8 + 2)	10
	65
Total assets	168
EQUITY AND LIABILITIES	
Equity	
Called-up share capital:	
ordinary shares of £1 each, fully paid	70
Share premium account	10
Retained earnings	30
	110
Non-controlling interests	2
	112
Non-current liabilities	
Borrowings – loan notes (30 + 0)	30
Current liabilities	
Trade payables (20 + 6)	26
Total equity and liabilities	168

Activity 9.10

The statements of financial position of Large plc and Small plc, on the date that Large plc bought the shares in Small plc, were as follows:

Statements of financial position

	Large plc £m	Small plc £m
ASSETS		
Non-current assets		
Property, plant and equipment		
Land	49	–
Plant	43	21
Vehicles	25	17
	117	38
Investment		
15 million shares of Small plc	27	–
	144	38
Current assets		
Inventories	42	18
Trade receivables	18	13
Cash	35	13
	95	44
Total assets	239	82
EQUITY AND LIABILITIES		
Equity		
Called-up share capital:		
ordinary shares of £1 each, fully paid	100	20
Share premium account	–	5
Retained earnings	64	7
	164	32
Non-current liabilities		
Borrowings – loan notes	50	30
Current liabilities		
Trade payables	25	20
Total equity and liabilities	239	82

Have a try at preparing the group statement of financial position.

The non-controlling interests will be £8 million (that is, 25 per cent of £32 million).

To discover goodwill, we need to compare what was paid (£27 million) with what was obtained (75 per cent of £32 million = £24 million). Thus, we have goodwill of £3 million.

The group statement of financial position will be as follows:

Statement of financial position

	£m
ASSETS	
Non-current assets	
Property, plant and equipment	
Land (49 + 0)	49
Plant (43 + 21)	64
Vehicles (25 + 17)	42
	155
Intangible asset	
Goodwill arising on consolidation	3
	158
Current assets	
Inventories (42 + 18)	60
Trade receivables (18 + 13)	31
Cash (35 + 13)	48
	139
Total assets	297
EQUITY AND LIABILITIES	
Equity	
Called-up share capital:	
ordinary shares of £1 each, fully paid	100
Retained earnings	64
	164
Non-controlling interests (25% × 32)	8
	172
Non-current liabilities	
Borrowings – loan notes (50 + 30)	80
Current liabilities	
Trade payables (25 + 20)	45
Total equity and liabilities	297

Complication 3: Trading has taken place since the shares were acquired

Except very rarely, most group statements of financial position will be prepared after some time has elapsed from the date that the parent company acquired the shares in the subsidiary. This does not in any way raise major difficulties, but we need to backtrack to the position at the time of the acquisition to establish the goodwill figure.

We shall look at another example. All three of our 'complications' exist here.

Example 9.7

The statements of financial position of Mega plc and Micro plc, as at 31 December, are set out below. Mega plc bought its shares in Micro plc some time ago, at a time at which the latter's share capital was exactly as shown below and the retained earnings balance stood at £30 million.

Statements of financial position as at 31 December

	Mega plc £m	Micro plc £m
ASSETS		
Non-current assets		
Property, plant and equipment		
Land	53	18
Plant	34	11
Vehicles	24	9
	111	38
Investment		
6 million shares of Micro plc	33	–
	144	38
Current assets		
Inventories	27	10
Trade receivables	29	11
Cash	11	1
	67	22
Total assets	211	60
EQUITY AND LIABILITIES		
Equity		
Called-up share capital:		
ordinary shares of £1 each, fully paid	100	10
Retained earnings	38	35
	138	45
Non-current liabilities		
Borrowings – loan notes	50	10
Current liabilities		
Trade payables	23	5
Total equity and liabilities	211	60

We can see that the investment in the statement of financial position of Mega plc (£33 million) comes nowhere near cancelling with the £45 million owners' claim of Micro plc. We need to separate out the elements.

Let us start with non-controlling interests. Here we are not concerned at all with the position at the date of the takeover. If the equity of Micro plc totals £45 million at the statement of financial position date and the minorities own 4 million of the 10 million shares, their contribution to the financing of the group's assets must be £18 million (that is, 40 per cent × £45 million).

Next let us ask ourselves what Mega plc got when it paid £33 million for the shares. At that time, the equity part of Micro plc's statement of financial position looked like this:

	£m
Called-up share capital:	
Ordinary shares of £1 each, fully paid	10
Retained earnings	<u>30</u>
	<u><u>40</u></u>

This means that the net assets of Micro plc must have also been worth (in terms of fair values reflected in the statement of financial position) £40 million; otherwise the statement of financial position would not have balanced. Since Mega plc bought 6 million of 10 million shares, it paid £33 million for net assets worth £24 million (that is, 60 per cent of £40 million). Thus, there is goodwill arising on consolidation of £9 million (that is, £33m – £24m).

We shall assume that no steps have been taken since the takeover to alter this goodwill figure. We shall consider why such steps may have been taken a little later in this chapter.

In dealing with non-controlling interests and goodwill we have, in effect, picked up the following parts of the owners' claim of Micro plc at 31 December:

● the minorities' share of both the equity (as non-controlling interests);
● Mega plc's share of the share capital and its share of the reserves as they stood at the date of the takeover (in the calculation of the goodwill figure).

The only remaining part of the owners' claim of Micro plc at 31 December is Mega plc's share of Micro plc's reserves that have built up since the takeover, that is, its share of (£35 million – £30 million) = £5 million. This share is £3 million (that is, 60 per cent of £5 million). This is Mega plc's share of the profits that have been earned by its subsidiary since the takeover, to the extent that profits have not already been paid out as dividends. As such, it is logical for this £3 million to be added to the retained earnings balance of the parent company in arriving at the group reserves.

This treatment of the equity of Micro plc can be represented in a tabular form as shown in Figure 9.3.

Figure 9.3 The treatment of the share equity of Micro plc in producing the group statement of financial position

	Total	Minorities 40%	Mega plc 60%	
	£m	£m	£m	
Share capital	10	4	6	Compare with the cost of the shares to deduce goodwill on consolidation
Retained profit:				
Pre-acquisition	30	12	18	
Post-acquisition	5	2	3	
	—	—	—	Add to the retained profit balance of Mega plc to deduce group revenue reserves
	45	18	27	
	—	—	—	

Non-controlling interests

The non-controlling interests total is simply the appropriate percentage of the subsidiary's total equity, without reference to when the reserves arose. The parent's share of the subsidiary's total of equity, at the date of the takeover, is compared with the price paid by the parent to deduce the goodwill arising on consolidation. The parent's share of the subsidiary's post-acquisition reserves is added to the parent's reserves to find the total reserves.

The group statement of financial position will be as follows:

Statement of financial position as at 31 December

	£m
ASSETS	
Non-current assets	
Property, plant and equipment	
Land (53 + 18)	71
Plant (34 + 11)	45
Vehicles (24 + 9)	33
	149
Intangible asset	
Goodwill arising on consolidation (33 − (6 + 18))	9
	158
Current assets	
Inventories (27 + 10)	37
Trade receivables (29 + 11)	40
Cash (11 + 1)	12
	89
Total assets	247
EQUITY AND LIABILITIES	
Equity	
Called-up share capital:	
ordinary shares of £1 each, fully paid	100
Retained earnings (38 + 3)	41
	141
Non-controlling interests (40% × 45)	18
	159
Non-current liabilities	
Borrowings – loan notes (50 + 10)	60
Current liabilities	
Trade payables (23 + 5)	28
Total equity and liabilities	247

Activity 9.11

The statements of financial position of Grand plc and Petit Ltd, as at 30 June, are set out below. Grand plc bought its shares in Petit Ltd some time ago at which time the latter's share capital was the same as it is currently and the retained earnings balance stood at £14 million.

Statements of financial position as at 30 June

	Grand plc £m	Petit Ltd £m
ASSETS		
Non-current assets		
Property, plant and equipment		
Land	12	10
Plant	14	8
Vehicles	3	6
	29	24
Investment		
7.5 million shares of Petit Ltd	21	–
	50	24
Current assets		
Inventories	10	5
Trade receivables	9	4
Cash	2	2
	21	11
Total assets	71	35
EQUITY AND LIABILITIES		
Equity		
Called-up share capital:		
ordinary shares of £1 each, fully paid	30	10
Retained earnings	14	22
	44	32
Non-current liabilities		
Borrowings – loan notes	20	–
Current liabilities		
Trade payables	7	3
Total equity and liabilities	71	35

Prepare the statement of financial position for the group as at 30 June.

Your answer should be something like this:

Non-controlling interests
25% × £32 million = £8 million

Goodwill arising on consolidation
£21 million − [75% × (£10 million + £14 million)] = £3 million

Grand plc's share of Petit Ltd's post-acquisition reserves
75% × (£22 million − £14 million) = £6 million

Activity 9.11 continued

Assuming that no steps have been taken since the takeover to alter the goodwill figure, the group statement of financial position will be as follows:

Statement of financial position as at 30 June

	£m
ASSETS	
Non-current assets	
Property, plant and equipment	
Land (12 + 10)	22
Plant (14 + 8)	22
Vehicles (3 + 6)	9
	53
Intangible asset	
Goodwill arising on consolidation	3
	56
Current assets	
Inventories (10 + 5)	15
Trade receivables (9 + 4)	13
Cash (2 + 2)	4
	32
Total assets	88
EQUITY AND LIABILITIES	
Equity	
Called-up share capital:	
ordinary shares of £1 each, fully paid	30
Retained earnings (14 + 6)	20
	50
Non-controlling interests	8
	58
Non-current liabilities	
Borrowings – loan notes (20 + 0)	20
Current liabilities	
Trade payables (7 + 3)	10
Total equity and liabilities	88

Goodwill arising on consolidation and asset carrying amounts

Goodwill arising on consolidation represents the difference between the cost of acquiring the shares in a subsidiary and the fair value of the net assets acquired. In the examples that we have considered so far, we have assumed that the values at which a subsidiary's assets appear in the subsidiary's statement of financial position are the same as the fair values of those assets. Thus, it has been possible to deduce goodwill by making a comparison of the cost of acquiring the subsidiary with the values appearing in the subsidiary's statement of financial position. Unfortunately, things are not usually that simple!

Carrying amounts often differ from the fair values of assets. Generally speaking, the values at which assets are shown in the statement of financial position are lower because accounting conventions such as prudence and historic cost conspire to produce a conservative bias. As a result, not only do assets tend to be shown on the statement of financial position at less than their fair value, but some assets are completely omitted from the normal statement of financial position. This is particularly true of intangible assets, such as brand values. This means that, to calculate goodwill arising on consolidation, we cannot rely on statement of financial position values. We must find out what the fair values of the assets acquired really are. This must include both assets that appear on the statement of financial position of the subsidiary and those that do not (such as brand values).

Example 9.8 seeks to illustrate this point.

Example 9.8

The statements of financial position of Parent plc and of Subsidiary Ltd (which we last met in Example 9.6), on the date that the former bought the shares in the latter, were as follows:

Statements of financial position

	Parent plc £m	Subsidiary Ltd £m
ASSETS		
Non-current assets		
Property, plant and equipment		
Land	40	5
Plant	30	2
Vehicles	20	2
	90	9
Investment		
5 million shares of Subsidiary Ltd	15	–
	105	9
Current assets		
Inventories	20	3
Trade receivables	30	2
Cash	5	2
	55	7
Total assets	160	16
EQUITY AND LIABILITIES		
Equity		
Called-up share capital:		
ordinary shares of £1 each, fully paid	70	5
Share premium account	10	–
Retained earnings	30	5
	110	10
Non-current liabilities		
Borrowings – loan notes	30	–
Current liabilities		
Trade payables	20	6
Total equity and liabilities	160	16

Example 9.8 continued

When Parent plc was valuing the shares of Subsidiary Ltd, it was judged that most of the statement of financial position values were in line with the fair values, but that the following fair values should be applied to the three categories of property, plant and equipment of the subsidiary:

	£m
Land	7
Plant	3
Vehicles	3

In addition it was recognised that the subsidiary has goodwill valued at £1 million. When these fair values are incorporated into the group statement of financial position, it will be as follows:

Statement of financial position

	£m
ASSETS	
Non-current assets	
Property, plant and equipment	
Land (40 + 7)	47
Plant (30 + 3)	33
Vehicles (20 + 3)	23
	103
Intangible asset	
Goodwill	1
	104
Current assets	
Inventories (20 + 3)	23
Trade receivables (30 + 2)	32
Cash (5 + 2)	7
	62
Total assets	166
EQUITY AND LIABILITIES	
Equity	
Called-up share capital:	
ordinary shares of £1 each, fully paid	70
Share premium account	10
Retained earnings	30
	110
Non-current liabilities	
Borrowings – loan notes (30 + 0)	30
Current liabilities	
Trade payables (20 + 6)	26
Total equity and liabilities	166

This example takes the simple case of no outside shareholdings in the subsidiary (that is, the subsidiary is 100 per cent owned by the parent) and no post-acquisition trading (the statements of financial position are at the date of acquisition), but these 'complications' would not alter the principles.

It should be noted that there is no need for the statement of financial position of the subsidiary to be adjusted for fair values, just the group statement of financial position. As far as the subsidiary is concerned, no change occurs with the takeover except a change in the names on the list of shareholders.

The financial reporting standard that deals with this area of group financial statements (IFRS 3) is clear that intangible assets of the subsidiary, at the date of the takeover, such as brand values and patent rights, must be separately identified at their fair value. These assets must then be incorporated at those values in the group statement of financial position.

The non-current assets of the subsidiary that have finite lives should have a depreciation (or amortisation) charge, based on their fair values, in the group income statement. This charge may well be different in amount to that which arises in the financial statements of the subsidiary.

Goodwill arising on consolidation is simply the excess of what the parent company paid for the subsidiary company's shares over their fair value, based on all of the identifiable assets (tangible and intangible) of the subsidiary. This means that what is identified as goodwill arising on consolidation tends to represent only the value of:

- having a workforce in place;
- cost synergies – arising from the fact that the combined business can make cost savings by, say, having just one head office instead of two; and
- sales synergies – arising, for example, from group members trading with one another.

These attributes that represent goodwill could well be enduring, but they can also be lost, either partially or completely. IFRS 3 recognises this and states that the value of goodwill should be reviewed annually, or even more frequently if circumstances dictate. Where its value has been impaired, it must be reduced accordingly in the group financial statements. It should be noted that goodwill arising on consolidation does not appear in the statements of financial position either of the parent or the subsidiary. It only appears on the group statement of financial position.

Despite the requirement of IFRS 3 that all subsidiary company assets, whether they appear on the subsidiary's statement of financial position or not, whether they are tangible or intangible, should be reflected at their fair value in the group statement of financial position, this seems not always to happen in reality. **Real World 9.4** relates an investigation into how some large, well-known businesses seem not to be following the spirit of IFRS 3.

 Real World 9.4

Where there's goodwill . . .

During the first year that IFRS 3 applied (2005), the largest 100 businesses listed on the London Stock Exchange between them spent £40 billion on taking over other businesses. This acquisition cost was treated as follows in the subsequent group statements of financial position:

	£ billion	per cent
Tangible assets	6.8	17
Intangible assets	12.0	30
Goodwill arising on consolidation	21.2	53

Real World 9.4 continued

The author of the report, Thayne Forbes, concluded that this treatment was counter to the spirit of IFRS 3. It seemed implausible that such a large proportion of the total should be treated as goodwill, when IFRS 3 limits what should be treated as goodwill quite severely.

Forbes identified some examples. Included is the takeover of RAC plc (the UK motoring organisation) by Aviva plc (the UK-based insurance business) in March 2005. Aviva paid £1.1 billion, of which the majority was treated as goodwill. RAC had 7 million customers and is one of the most trusted brands in the UK, yet these were valued at only £260 million and £132 million respectively.

Forbes identified four possible reasons for these apparent misapplications of IFRS 3. These are:

1 *To reduce depreciation charges and increase profits*. Since goodwill cannot be depreciated and intangible assets with finite lives should be, reported profit will tend to be enhanced by treating as much of the purchase price as possible as goodwill.
2 *To minimise impairment charges.* Though both intangible assets without finite lives and goodwill are subject to tests of impairment of value and a possible accounting charge as a result, the tests for goodwill are less stringent. So another intangible asset is more likely to lead to an impairment charge than is goodwill.
3 *Lack of skills.* Having to value intangibles following a takeover is a new requirement, so the skills to do so may not be so readily available.
4 *Failure to see the big picture*. Businesses may get so bogged down with the regulations that they fail to consider the key issues and effects of the takeover.

Forbes went on to say:

'The implications of this inadequate reporting are far reaching. It renders annual reports more useless than they currently are, it makes a standard ineffective when applied and the financial bodies that govern them, it sets a dangerous precedent for future years and it opens a new era of creative accounting that distances shareholders and investors further from reality.'

A year later, Forbes felt that the situation was improving, with more explanation and justification being given by businesses for the goodwill values included in group statements of financial position. He seemed not to believe, however, that practice was by that time totally satisfactory.

The position seemed not to have become satisfactory by 2009. The Financial Reporting Council looked at the financial reporting of twenty takeovers that had occurred in 2008 and were reported in the financial statements of the parent company concerned during 2009. The Council concluded that 'there is a need for improved compliance with the disclosure requirements of IFRS'.

Sources: 'Technical update – Inadequate IFRS 3', Thayne Forbes, *Finance Week*, 30 January 2007, www.financeweek.co.uk; 'Intangibles and IFRS 3: seen but not heard', Thayne Forbes, www.intangiblebusiness.com, 8 February 2008; and *Accounting for Acquisitions*, Financial Reporting Council, January 2010, p. 3.

In the cases that we have considered so far, goodwill arising on consolidation has always been a positive value (that is, more was paid for the parent's share of the net assets of the subsidiary than their fair values). It is possible for goodwill to be negative. This is where the parent pays less than the fair values. Where negative goodwill on consolidation arises, IFRS 3 says that fair values of all assets and liabilities of the subsidiary concerned should be reassessed. This reassessment is to try to ensure that no assets have been overstated or liabilities understated or omitted. If this reassessment still results in negative goodwill, the amount of this negative goodwill should be credited immediately to the group income statement of the year of the acquisition of the subsidiary. In practice negative goodwill would be pretty rare.

Goodwill arising on consolidation: an alternative approach

IFRS 3 *Business Combinations* was revised with effect from 1 July 2009. Most of the changes brought in by the revised standard were fairly technical. One, however, was more fundamental and intended to correct an anomaly with the way that goodwill arising on consolidation is valued.

Activity 9.12

Can you puzzle out what the anomaly is? Hint: It is concerned with the fact that goodwill arising on consolidation is treated differently from all other assets of the subsidiary that appear in the group statement of financial position.

The anomaly is that goodwill is the only subsidiary company asset that is not shown in full; it is scaled down according to the proportion of the subsidiary's shares that are owned by the parent. All other assets of the subsidiary are included in full, irrespective of the parent's proportion of the ownership.

As we saw earlier, it is a basic principle of preparing group financial statements that if the parent controls the assets of the subsidiary, even if it does not own them 100 per cent, all of their value should be included. The revised IFRS 3 allows, though does not require, that goodwill be shown in the statement of financial position at its full value.

Our Example 9.9 returns to Example 9.6, which included two of our 'complications' (the parent owning less than 100 per cent of the subsidiary's balance sheet and paying more than the fair value for them).

Example 9.9

The group statement of financial position for Parent plc and its subsidiary applying the 'old' IFRS 3 approach is as follows:

Statement of financial position

	£m
ASSETS	
Non-current assets	
Property, plant and equipment	
Land	45
Plant	32
Vehicles	22
	99
Intangible asset	
Goodwill arising on consolidation (12 − (80% × 10))	4
	103
Current assets	
Inventories	23
Trade receivables	32
Cash	10
	65
Total assets	168
EQUITY AND LIABILITIES	
Equity	
Called-up share capital:	
ordinary shares of £1 each, fully paid	70
Share premium account	10
Retained earnings	30
	110
Non-controlling interests	2
	112
Non-current liabilities	
Borrowings – loan notes	30
Current liabilities	
Trade payables	26
Total equity and liabilities	168

The goodwill (£4 million) represents the excess of what was paid by Parent plc for the shares (£12 million) over the fair value of its proportion of the underlying net assets, at the time of the takeover (£8 million).

Logically, if Parent's share of the goodwill is £4 million, the total value of it is £5 million. Including this total value in the group statement of financial position would be more in line with the general approach to preparing group financial statements. The revised IFRS 3 permits this.

Activity 9.13

If the goodwill figure in the statement of financial position in Example 9.9 is to be increased by £1 million, something else on the statement will also need to be adjusted to maintain equality between total assets and total claims (equity and liabilities). What would this adjustment logically be?

The answer is that the figure for non-controlling interests will need to be increased by that amount. This is because £1 million of the value of the goodwill belongs to outside shareholders and this needs to be reflected in their claim, as it appears in the group statement of financial position.

As mentioned above, groups may use this 'new' approach to the value of goodwill arising on consolidation if they wish. It is widely believed that relatively few groups will do so in practice. The new approach seems to be supported more by academics than by businesses.

In view of the likely limited take up of the new approach in practice, we shall use the 'old' approach (that is, the one explored earlier in this chapter) in all subsequent examples and exercises.

Inter-company assets and claims

Though members of a group are separate legal entities, the element of control exercised by the parent, and generally close relations between group members, tend to lead to inter-company trading and other inter-company transactions. This, in turn, means that a particular asset in one company's statement of financial position could relate to an equal-sized liability in the statement of financial position of another member of the same group.

The principle underlying the group statement of financial position is that it should represent the situation as if all the assets and claims of individual group members were directly the assets and claims of the parent company. Since the parent company cannot owe itself money, where there are inter-company balances these must be eliminated when preparing the group statement of financial position.

Example 9.10

Delta plc and its subsidiary Gamma plc are the only members of a group. Delta plc sells goods on credit to Gamma plc. At the statement of financial position date the following balances existed in the books of the companies:

	Trade receivables £m	Trade payables £m
Delta plc	34	26
Gamma plc	23	18

Included in the trade receivables of Delta plc, and the trade payables of Gamma plc, is £5 million in respect of some recent inter-company trading.

Example 9.10 continued

In deducing the figures to be included in the group statement of financial position, we have to eliminate the inter-company balance, as follows:

Trade receivables = 34 − 5 + 23 = £52 million
Trade payables = 26 + 18 − 5 = £39 million

Note that these consolidated trade receivables and trade payables figures represent what is, respectively, owed by and owed to individuals and organisations outside of the group. This is what they are intended to represent, according to the principles of group accounting.

Preparation of a group income statement

→ The **group income statement** follows very similar principles to those that apply to the statement of financial position. These are:

- Like items are added together. For example, the revenue of each subsidiary is added to that of the parent company to discover group revenue.
- All the amounts appearing under each heading in the income statements of subsidiaries are included in the total, even where they are not wholly owned subsidiaries. For example, the revenue of a subsidiary that is 60 per cent owned by the parent is included in full.
- The interests of outside shareholders (non-controlling interests) are separately identified towards the bottom of the income statement.

Example 9.11

Holder plc owns 75 per cent of the ordinary shares of Sub Ltd. The outline income statements of the two companies for the year ended on 31 December are as follows:

Income statements for the year ended 31 December

	Holder plc £m	Sub Ltd £m
Revenue	83	40
Cost of sales	(41)	(15)
Gross profit	42	25
Administration expenses	(16)	(9)
Distribution expenses	(6)	(3)
Operating profit	20	13
Interest payable	(2)	(1)
Profit before taxation	18	12
Taxation	(8)	(4)
Profit for the year	10	8

Preparing the group income statement is a very simple matter of adding like items together, except that not all of the profit for the year of the subsidiary 'belongs' to the group. Twenty-five per cent (£2 million) of it belongs to outside shareholders. We recognise this in the group income statement by deducting the 25 per cent of the profit for the year of the subsidiary from the combined profit for the year.

The group income statement will be as follows:

Income statement for the year ended 31 December

	£m
Revenue (83 + 40)	123
Cost of sales (41 + 15)	(56)
Gross profit	67
Administration expenses (16 + 9)	(25)
Distribution expenses (6 + 3)	(9)
Operating profit	33
Interest payable (2 + 1)	(3)
Profit before taxation	30
Taxation (8 + 4)	(12)
Profit for the year	18
Attributable to non-controlling interests	(2)
Profit for the year attributable to Holder plc shareholders	16

This statement says that the assets under the control of the group generated profit for the year of £18 million. Of this, £2 million is the share of the 'outside' shareholders of Sub Ltd. This follows the normal approach of group financial statements of treating all assets, claims, revenues and expenses of group companies as if they were those of the group. Where the subsidiaries are not 100 per cent owned by the parent, this fact is acknowledged by making an adjustment to reflect the non-controlling interests.

Activity 9.14

Ajax plc owns 60 per cent of the ordinary shares of Exeter plc. The outline income statements of the two companies for the year ended on 31 December are as follows:

Income statements for the year ended 31 December

	Ajax plc £m	Exeter plc £m
Revenue	120	80
Cost of sales	(60)	(40)
Gross profit	60	40
Administration expenses	(17)	(4)
Distribution expenses	(10)	(15)
Operating profit	33	21
Interest payable	(3)	(1)
Profit before taxation	30	20
Taxation	(12)	(10)
Profit for the year	18	10

Have a try at preparing a consolidated (group) income statement.

→

Activity 9.14 continued

Your answer should look something like this:

Group income statement for the year ended 31 December

	£m
Revenue (120 + 80)	200
Cost of sales (60 + 40)	(100)
Gross profit	100
Administration expenses (17 + 4)	(21)
Distribution expenses (10 + 15)	(25)
Operating profit	54
Interest payable (3 + 1)	(4)
Profit before taxation	50
Taxation (12 + 10)	(22)
Profit for the year	28
Attributable to non-controlling interests (40% × 10)	(4)
Profit for the year attributable to Ajax plc shareholders	24

The statement of comprehensive income

As we saw in Chapter 5, IAS 1 *Presentation of Financial Statements* requires listed companies to provide a statement of comprehensive income, which extends the conventional income statement to include certain other gains and losses that affect shareholders' equity. It may be presented either as a single statement or as two separate statements, an income statement and a statement of comprehensive income. IAS 1 demands that in the group's statement of comprehensive income, both the profit (or loss) for the year and the comprehensive income for the period distinguish between that which is attributable to non-controlling interests and that attributable to the shareholders of the parent company.

Inter-company trading

As we saw a little earlier in the chapter, it is very common for members of the group to trade with one another. As far as each member of the group is concerned such trading should be dealt with in the accounting records, including the income statement, in exactly the same way as trading with any other party. When we come to the group income statement, however, inter-company trading between group members must be eliminated. It is in the spirit of group accounting that the group income statement should only recognise trading with parties outside of the group, as if the group were one single business. Only sales to outsiders should be reflected in the group sales revenue figure; only purchases of goods and services from parties outside of the group should be reflected.

Group statement of cash flows

Groups must normally prepare a statement of cash flows that follows the same logic as the statement of financial position and income statement – that is, it has to show the movements in all of the cash that is in the control of the group, for the period under review.

The preparation of a **group statement of cash flows** follows the same rules as those that apply to the preparation of the statement for individual companies. In view of this we need not spend time looking separately at statements of cash flows in a group context.

Similarly to the statement of financial position and income statement, cash transfers between group members should not be reflected in the group statement of cash flows.

Self-assessment question 9.1

The statements of financial position, as at 31 December last year, and income statements, for the year ended last 31 December, of Great plc and Small plc are set out below. Great plc bought its shares in Small plc on 1 January last year at which time the latter's share capital was the same as it is currently and the retained earnings balance stood at £35 million.

At the time of the acquisition, the fair value of all the assets of Small plc was thought to be the same as that shown in their statement of financial position, except for land whose fair value was thought to be £5 million more than the statement of financial position value. It is believed that there has been no impairment in the value of the goodwill arising on consolidation since 1 January last year.

Statements of financial position as at 31 December last year

	Great plc £m	Small plc £m
ASSETS		
Non-current assets		
Property, plant and equipment		
Land	80	14
Plant	33	20
Vehicles	20	11
	133	45
Investment		
16 million shares of Small plc	53	–
	186	45
Current assets		
Inventories	20	9
Trade receivables	21	6
Cash	17	5
	58	20
Total assets	244	65
EQUITY AND LIABILITIES		
Equity		
Called-up share capital:		
ordinary shares of £1 each, fully paid	100	20
Retained earnings	77	40
	177	60
Non-current liabilities		
Borrowings – loan notes	50	–
Current liabilities		
Trade payables	17	5
Total equity and liabilities	244	65

Self-assessment question 9.1 continued

Income statements for the year ended 31 December last year

	Great plc £m	Small plc £m
Revenue	91	27
Cost of sales	(46)	(13)
Gross profit	45	14
Administration expenses	(8)	(3)
Distribution expenses	(6)	(2)
Operating profit	31	9
Interest payable	(3)	–
Profit before taxation	28	9
Taxation	(12)	(4)
Profit for the year	16	5

Required:

Prepare the statement of financial position and income statement for the group.

The solution to this question can be found at the back of the book on page 479.

Accounting for less than a controlling interest – associate companies

What happens when one company makes a substantial investment in another company but this does not provide the investing company with a controlling interest? In other words, the company whose shares have been acquired does not become a subsidiary of the investing company. One approach would simply include the investment of shares in the company at cost in the investing company's statement of financial position. Assuming that the shares are held on a long-term basis, they would be treated as a non-current asset. Any dividends received from the investment would be treated as income in the investing company's income statement.

The problem with this approach, however, is that companies normally pay dividends of much less than the profits earned for the period. The profits that are not distributed, but are ploughed back to help to generate more profits for the future, still belong to the shareholders. From the perspective of the investing company, the accounting treatment described would not, therefore, fully reflect the benefits from the investment made. Where the investment does not involve the purchase of a substantial shareholding in the company, this problem is overlooked and so the treatment of the investment described above (that is, showing the investment, at cost, as a non-current asset and taking account only of any dividends received) is applied. Where, however, the investment involves the purchase of a significant number of voting shares in the company, a different kind of accounting treatment seems more appropriate.

To deal with the problem identified above, a particular type of relationship between the two companies has been defined. An **associate company** is one in which an investing company or group has a substantial, but not controlling, interest. To be more precise, it is a company over which another company can exercise significant influence regarding its operating and financial policies. If a company holds 20 per cent or more of the voting shares of another company it is presumed to be able to exercise significant influence. This influence is usually demonstrated by the investing company being represented on the board of directors of the associate company or by participation in policy making. The relevant international accounting standard (IAS 28 *Investments in Associates*) provides the detailed guidelines concerning what constitutes an associate company.

The accounting treatment of an associate company falls somewhere between consolidation, as with group financial statements, and the treatment of small share investments, as described at the beginning of this section. Let us assume that a company invests in another company, so that the latter becomes an associate of the former. The accounting treatment will be as follows:

- The investing company will be required to produce consolidated financial statements that reflect not only its own performance and position, but also those of its associate company.
- In the consolidated income statement, the investing company's share of the operating profit of the associate company will be shown and will be added to the operating profit of the investing company. As operating profit represents the profit before interest and taxation, the investing company's share of any interest payable and tax relating to the associate company will also be shown. These will be deducted in deriving the profit for the year for the investing company and its associate company.
- In the consolidated statement of financial position, the investment made in the associate company will be shown and the investing company's share of any post-acquisition reserves will be added to the investment. In this way profits of the associate, that have not been paid to the investing company, will be recognised in the investing company's statement of financial position. This will have the effect of showing more fully the investment in the associate company.
- Dividends received by the investing company from the associate company will not be included in the consolidated income statement. This is because the investing company's share of the associate company's profit will already be fully reflected in the consolidated income statement.
- If the investing company also has subsidiaries, their financial statements will also have to be incorporated, in the manner that we saw for groups earlier in the chapter. Thus a company that has both subsidiary companies and associate companies will prepare just one set of consolidated financial statements reflecting all of these, irrespective of how many subsidiaries and associates it may have.

To illustrate these points, let us take a simple example.

Example 9.12

A plc owns 25 per cent of the ordinary shares of B plc. The price paid for the shares was £26 million. A plc bought its shares in B plc when the latter's reserves stood at £24 million. The reserves of B plc have increased to £40 million by 31 March last year.

Example 9.12 continued

The income statements for A plc and B plc for the year ended 31 March this year are as follows:

Income statements for the year ended 31 March this year

	A plc £m	B plc £m
Revenues	800	100
Cost of sales	(500)	(60)
Gross profit	300	40
Operating expenses	(120)	(12)
Operating profit	180	28
Interest payable	(30)	(8)
Profit before taxation	150	20
Taxation	(40)	(4)
Profit for the year	110	16

To comply with the relevant standard (IAS 28), A plc's share of the operating profit of B plc as well as its share of interest payable and taxation relating to B plc will be incorporated within A plc's consolidated income statement. A plc's consolidated income statement will, therefore, be as follows:

A plc
Consolidated income statement

	£m	
Revenues	800	
Cost of sales	(500)	
Gross profit	300	
Operating expenses	(120)	
	180	
Share of operating profit of associate – B plc	7	(25% × £28m)
Operating profit	187	
Interest payable:		
A plc	(30)	
Associate – B plc	(2)	(25% × £8m)
Profit before taxation	155	
Taxation:		
A plc	(40)	
Associate – B plc	(1)	(25% × £4m)
Profit for the year	114	

The consolidated statement of financial position of A plc, treating B plc as an associate company, would include an amount for the investment in B plc that is calculated as follows:

Extract from A plc's consolidated statement of financial position as at 31 March this year

	£m	
Cost of investment in associate company	26	
Share of post-acquisition reserves	4	(that is, 25% × (40 − 24))
	30	

Activity 9.15

What is the crucial difference between the approach taken when consolidating subsidiary company results and incorporating the results of associate companies, as far as the statement of financial position and income statement are concerned?

In preparing group financial statements, all of the items in the statements are added together, as if the parent owned them all, even when the subsidiary is less than 100 per cent owned. For example, the revenue figure in the consolidated income statement is the sum of all the revenues made by group companies; the inventories figure in the statement of financial position is the sum of all the inventories held by all members of the group.

When dealing with associate companies, we only deal with the shareholding company's share of the profit of the associate and its effect on the value of the shareholding.

Real World 9.5 is the list of the associate companies of Cadbury plc, the confectionery manufacturer, as at 31 December 2008. Three of the company's four associate companies are involved in some aspect of Cadbury's main activity. The fourth associate company, however, is Camelot Group plc, the business that operates the UK national lottery.

Real World 9.5

A bit of a lottery

Details of principal associate undertakings

	Country of incorporation and operation	Proportion of issued share capital held
Camelot Group plc	Great Britain	20%
Crystal Candy (Private) Ltd	Zimbabwe	49%
Meito Adams Company Ltd	Japan	50%
Xtrapack Ltd	Great Britain	30%

Cadbury was taken over by Kraft, the US food business, in January 2010. Cadbury, even before the takeover, had expressed a desire to sell its holding in Camelot. At the time of writing, however, Cadbury continued to own 20 per cent of the Camelot shares.

Source: Cadbury plc Annual Report 2008.

The argument against consolidation

There seems to be a compelling logic for consolidating the results of subsidiaries controlled by a parent company, to reflect the fact that the shareholders of the parent company effectively control all of the assets of all of the companies in the group. There is also, however, a fairly strong argument against doing so.

Anyone reading the consolidated financial statements of a group of companies could be misled into believing that trading with any member of the group would, in effect, be the same as trading with the group as a whole. It might be imagined that all of the group's assets could be called upon to meet any amounts owed by any member of the group. This would be untrue, however. Only the assets owned by the particular group member would be accessible to any creditor of that group member. The reason for this is, of course, the legal separateness of the limited company from its shareholder(s), which in turn leads to limited liability of individual group members. There would be absolutely no legal obligation on a parent company, or a fellow subsidiary, to meet the financial obligations of a struggling subsidiary. In fact this is a reason why some businesses operate through a series of subsidiaries, a point that was made early in this chapter.

Despite this criticism of consolidation, the requirement to prepare group financial statements is a very popular legal requirement throughout the world.

Summary

The main points of this chapter may be summarised as follows:

Groups

- A group exists where one company (parent) can exercise control over another (subsidiary), usually by owning more than 50% of the voting shares.
- Groups arise by a parent setting up a new company or taking over an existing one.
- Businesses operate as groups in order to have limited liability for each part of the business, and to give each part of the business an individual identity.
- Normally parent companies are required to produce financial statements for the group as a whole, as if all of the group members' assets, liabilities, revenues, expenses and cash flows were those of the parent company directly.

Group statements of financial position

- Group statements of financial position are derived by adding like items (assets and liabilities) together and setting the equity of each subsidiary (in the subsidiary's statement of financial position) against the investment in subsidiary figure (in the parent's statement of financial position).
- Where the equity of the subsidiary does not cancel the investment in subsidiary it will be for three possible reasons:
    1. more (or less) was paid for the subsidiary shares than their 'fair value', leading to 'goodwill arising on consolidation', an intangible non-current asset (or negative goodwill arising on consolidation) in the group statement of financial position;
    2. the parent does not own all of the shares of the subsidiary, leading to 'non-controlling (or minority) interests' (similar to equity in the group statement of financial position) reflecting the fact that the parent's shareholders do not supply all of the equity finance to fund the group's net assets;
    3. the subsidiary has made profits or losses since it became a subsidiary.
- 'Goodwill arising on consolidation' represents the value of the ability of the subsidiary to generate additional profits as a result of an established workforce and valuable cost and/or sales synergies.

- Goodwill remains on the group statement of financial position, but is subject to an 'impairment review' annually and written down in value if it is established that its value has diminished.

- Negative goodwill should be immediately credited to the group income statement.

- It is permissible for a company to show the entire value of the goodwill of its subsidiaries, not just the parent's share of that value.

- Inter-group company balances (receivables and payables) must be eliminated from the group statement of financial position.

Group income statement

- Group income statements are derived by adding like items (revenues and expenses).

- The non-controlling (minority) shareholders' share of the after-tax profit is deducted from the group total to reflect the fact that not all of the subsidiary's profit belongs to the parent company's shareholders.

- Inter-group company trading transactions (revenues and expenses) must be eliminated from the group income statement.

Group statement of comprehensive income

- Group statements of comprehensive income are derived by adding like items.

- The statement must distinguish between comprehensive income that is attributable to non-controlling interests and that which is attributable to the shareholders of the parent company.

Group statement of cash flows

- Group statements of cash flows are derived by adding like items (cash flows).

- Inter-group company cash transfers must be eliminated from the group statement of cash flows.

Associate companies

- An 'associate company' is one in which a company has less than a controlling interest, but yet is able to exert significant influence over it, often indicated by representation on the board of directors.

- The investing company will be required to produce consolidated financial statements that reflect not only its own performance and position, but those of its associate company/companies as well.

- In the consolidated income statement, the investing company's share of the operating profit of the associate company is added to the operating profit of the investing company. Any interest payable and tax relating to the associate company will also be shown.

- In the consolidated statement of financial position, the investment made in the associate company will be shown and the investing company's share of any post-acquisition reserves will be added to the investment.

- Dividends received by the investing company from the associate company are not included in the consolidated income statement.

Key terms

parent company p. 296	non-controlling interests p. 311
subsidiary company p. 296	minority interests p. 311
group (of companies) p. 296	goodwill arising on consolidation
group financial statements p. 296	p. 314
takeover p. 296	negative goodwill arising on
holding company p. 296	consolidation p. 314
target company p. 299	group income statement p. 334
group statement of financial position	group statement of cash flows
p. 305	p. 337
consolidated financial statements	associate company p. 338
p. 306	

Further reading

If you would like to explore the topics covered in this chapter in more depth, we recommend the following books:

Alexander, D., Britton, A. and Jorissen, A., *International Financial Reporting and Analysis*, 5th edn, Cengage Learning, 2009, Chapters 25 and 26.

Elliott, B. and Elliott, J., *Financial Accounting and Reporting*, 13th edn, Financial Times Prentice Hall, 2009, Chapters 21 to 24.

Review questions

Solutions to these questions can be found at the back of the book on page 488.

9.1 When does a group relationship arise and what are its consequences for accounting?

9.2 What does a group statement of financial position show?

9.3 Quite often, when an existing company wishes to start a new venture, perhaps to produce a new product or render a new service, it will form a subsidiary company as a vehicle for the new venture. Why would it choose not to have the new venture conducted by the original company?

9.4 What is an associate company and what are the consequences for accounting of one company being the associate company of a group of companies?

Exercises

Exercises 9.1 to 9.4 are more advanced than 9.5 to 9.8. Those with coloured numbers have solutions at the back of the book, starting on page 514.

If you wish to try more exercises, visit the students' side of the Companion Website.

9.1 Giant plc bought a majority shareholding in Jack Ltd, on 31 March. On that date the statements of financial position of the two companies were as follows:

Statements of financial position as at 31 March

	Giant plc £m	Jack Ltd £m
ASSETS		
Non-current assets		
Property, plant and equipment		
Land	27	12
Plant	55	8
Vehicles	18	7
	100	27
Investment		
10 million shares of Jack Ltd	30	–
	130	27
Current assets		
Inventories	33	13
Trade receivables	42	17
Cash	22	5
	97	35
Total assets	227	62

	Giant plc £m	Jack Ltd £m
EQUITY AND LIABILITIES		
Equity		
Called-up share capital:		
ordinary shares of £1 each, fully paid	50	10
Share premium account	40	5
Revaluation reserve	–	8
Retained earnings	46	7
	136	30
Non-current liabilities		
Borrowings – loan notes	50	13
Current liabilities		
Trade payables	41	19
Total equity and liabilities	227	62

Required:

Assume that the statement of financial position values of Jack Ltd's assets represent 'fair' values. Prepare the group statement of financial position immediately following the takeover.

9.2 The statements of financial position of Jumbo plc and of Nipper plc, on the date that Jumbo plc bought the shares in Nipper plc, were as follows:

Statements of financial position as at 31 March

	Jumbo plc £m	Nipper plc £m
ASSETS		
Non-current assets		
Property, plant and equipment		
Land	84	18
Plant	34	33
Vehicles	45	12
	163	63
Investment		
12 million shares of Nipper plc	24	–
	187	63
Current assets		
Inventories	55	32
Trade receivables	26	44
Cash	14	10
	95	86
Total assets	282	149
EQUITY AND LIABILITIES		
Equity		
Called-up share capital:		
ordinary shares of £1 each, fully paid	100	20
Share premium account	–	12
Retained earnings	41	8
	141	40
Non-current assets		
Borrowings – loan notes	100	70
Current liabilities		
Trade payables	41	39
Total equity and liabilities	282	149

Required:

Assume that the statement of financial position values of Nipper plc's assets represent fair values. Prepare the group statement of financial position immediately following the share acquisition.

9.3 An abridged set of consolidated financial statements for Toggles plc is given below.

Toggles plc
Consolidated income statement for the year ended 30 June

	£m
Revenue	172.0
Operating profit	21.2
Taxation	(6.4)
Profit after taxation	14.8
Non-controlling interests	(2.4)
Profit for the year	12.4

Consolidated statement of financial position as at 30 June

	£m
ASSETS	
Non-current assets	
Property, plant and equipment	85.6
Intangible asset	
Goodwill arising on consolidation	7.2
	92.8
Current assets	
Inventories	21.8
Trade receivables	16.4
Cash	1.7
	39.9
Total assets	132.7
EQUITY AND LIABILITIES	
Equity	
Share capital	100.0
Retained earnings	16.1
	116.1
Non-controlling interests	1.3
	117.4
Current liabilities	
Trade payables	15.3
Total equity and liabilities	132.7

Required:
(a) Answer, briefly, the following questions:
   1 What is meant by 'non-controlling interests' in both the income statement and the statement of financial position?
   2 What is meant by 'goodwill arising on consolidation'?
   3 Why will the 'retained earnings' figure on the consolidated statement of financial position usually be different from the 'retained earnings' as shown in the parent company's statement of financial position?
(b) Explain the purposes and advantages in preparing consolidated financial statements for the parent company's shareholders.

9.4 Arnold plc owns 75 per cent of the ordinary shares of Baker plc. The outline income statements of the two companies for the year ended on 31 December are as follows:

Income statements for the year ended 31 December

	Arnold plc £m	Baker plc £m
Revenue	83	47
Cost of sales	(36)	(19)
Gross profit	47	28
Administration expenses	(14)	(7)
Distribution expenses	(21)	(10)
Profit before taxation	12	11
Taxation	(4)	(3)
Profit for the year	8	8

Required:

Prepare the consolidated (group) income statement for Arnold plc and its subsidiary for the year ended 31 December.

9.5 The summary statements of financial position for Apple Limited and Pear Limited are set out below.

Statements of financial position as at 30 September

	Apple Limited £000	Pear Limited £000
ASSETS		
Non-current assets		
Property, plant and equipment	950	320
Investment		
Shares in Pear Limited	240	–
	1,190	320
Current assets		
Inventories	320	160
Trade receivables	180	95
Cash at bank	41	15
	541	270
Total assets	1,731	590
EQUITY AND LIABILITIES		
Equity:		
£1 fully paid ordinary shares	700	200
Reserves	307	88
	1,007	288
Non-current liabilities		
Loan notes	500	160
Current assets		
Trade payables	170	87
Taxation	54	55
	224	142
Total equity and liabilities	1,731	590

Apple Ltd purchased 150,000 shares in Pear Ltd at a price of £1.60 per share on 30 September (the above statement of financial position date). The statement of financial position of Pear Ltd reflects all of the assets of the company, net of liabilities, stated at their fair values.

Required:
Prepare a consolidated statement of financial position for Apple Ltd as at 30 September.

9.6 Abridged financial statements for Harvest Limited and Wheat Limited as at 30 June this year are set out below. On 1 July last year Harvest Limited acquired 800,000 ordinary shares in Wheat Limited for a payment of £3,500,000. Wheat Ltd's share capital and share premium were each the same throughout. Similarly, the assets in the statement of financial position of Wheat Limited were shown at fair market values, throughout.

Statements of financial position as at 30 June this year

	Harvest Limited £000	Wheat Limited £000
ASSETS		
Non-current assets		
Property, plant and equipment	10,850	4,375
Investment		
Shares of Wheat Limited	3,500	–
	14,350	4,375
Current assets	3,775	1,470
Total assets	18,125	5,845
EQUITY AND LIABILITIES		
Equity		
Share capital (£1 shares)	2,000	1,000
Share premium account	3,000	500
Revenue reserves at 1 July last year	2,800	375
Profit for the current year	399	75
Total equity	8,199	1,950
Non-current liabilities		
Bank loans	7,000	2,500
Current liabilities	2,926	1,395
Total equity and liabilities	18,125	5,845

Required:
Prepare the consolidated statement of financial position for Harvest Ltd as at 30 June this year, using the data given above.

9.7 A year ago Pod Limited bought 225,000 £1 fully paid ordinary shares of Pea Limited for a consideration of £500,000. Pea Limited's share capital and share premium were each the same as at today's date. Simplified statements of financial position for both companies as at today's date, after having traded as a group for a year, are set out below. The statement of financial position of Pea Ltd reflects all of the assets of the company, net of liabilities stated at their fair values.

Statements of financial position as at today

	Pod Limited £	Pea Limited £
ASSETS		
Non-current assets		
Property, plant and equipment	1,104,570	982,769
Investments		
Shares in Pea Limited	500,000	–
	1,604,570	982,769
Current assets		
Inventories	672,471	294,713
Trade receivables	216,811	164,517
Amounts due from subsidiary company	76,000	–
Cash	2,412	1,361
	967,694	460,591
Total assets	2,572,264	1,443,360
EQUITY AND LIABILITIES		
Equity		
Share capital: £1 ordinary shares	750,000	300,000
Share premium	250,000	50,000
Reserves as at a year ago	449,612	86,220
Profit for year	69,504	17,532
Total equity	1,519,116	453,752
Non-current liabilities		
Bank loan	800,000	750,000
Current liabilities		
Trade payables	184,719	137,927
Amounts owing to holding company	–	76,000
Borrowings – overdraft	68,429	25,681
	253,148	239,608
Total equity and liabilities	2,572,264	1,443,360

Required:

Prepare a consolidated statement of financial position for Pod Ltd and its subsidiary company as at today's date.

9.8 The statements of financial position for Maxi Limited and Mini Limited are set out below.

Statements of financial position as at 31 March this year

	Maxi Limited £000	Mini Limited £000
ASSETS		
Non-current assets		
Property, plant and equipment	23,000	17,800
Investment		
1,500,000 shares in Mini Limited	5,000	–
	28,000	17,800
Current assets		
Inventories	5,000	2,400
Trade receivables	4,280	1,682
Amounts owed by Maxi Limited	–	390
Cash at bank	76	1,570
	9,356	6,042
Total assets	37,356	23,842
EQUITY AND LIABILITIES		
Equity		
10,000,000 £1 ordinary shares fully paid	10,000	
2,000,000 50p ordinary shares fully paid		1,000
Share premium account	3,000	2,000
Retained earnings at beginning of year	3,100	2,080
Profit for the year	713	400
	16,813	5,480
Non-current liabilities		
Bank loans	13,000	14,000
Current liabilities		
Trade payables	3,656	2,400
Other payables	1,047	1,962
Amounts owed to Mini Limited	390	–
Short-term borrowings – overdraft	2,450	–
	7,543	4,362
Total equity and liabilities	37,356	23,842

On 1 April last year, Maxi Limited bought 1,500,000 shares of Mini Limited for a total consideration of £5 million. At that date Mini Limited's share capital and share premium were each the same as shown above. The statement of financial position of Mini Ltd reflects all of the assets of the company, net of liabilities stated at their fair values.

Required:

Prepare a consolidated statement of financial position for Maxi Limited at 31 March this year.

10

Increasing the scope of financial reporting

Introduction

Over the years, there has been a trend towards greater disclosure of information regarding the performance and position of businesses. Various reasons can be suggested for this trend. They include the increasing complexity of business, the increasing sophistication of users and an increasing recognition that other groups, apart from shareholders, have a stake in the success of a business.

In this chapter we consider additional financial reports that may be provided by businesses. Some of these simply expand on the information contained within the annual financial report while others offer a different perspective on how business success is defined and measured.

Learning outcomes

When you have completed this chapter, you should be able to:

● explain the purpose of segmental reports and describe their main features;

● discuss the benefits of narrative reporting and describe the main features of the business review;

● discuss the role of interim financial statements and outline the key measurement and reporting requirements of IAS 34;

● explain the purpose of the value added statement and prepare a simple value added statement from available information;

● describe the impact of inflation on the measurement of financial position and performance and outline the two main approaches to dealing with inflation in financial statements.

The development of financial reporting

Let us begin by placing the additional financial reports in historical context. Financial reporting has been around for many hundreds of years. It seems to have emerged as a result of one or more persons having custody and management of assets belonging to one or more others. Examples might include a farm manager looking after land owned by another and a merchant ship's captain taking goods, owned by another, overseas and selling them. The owners would normally require that the steward (that is, the person looking after the assets) report on how the assets were deployed and how successfully. These reports were often expressed in financial terms and gave rise to what is known as 'stewardship accounting'.

Limited liability companies first came into being during the middle of the nineteenth century. Their advent gave added impetus to assets being owned by one group of people (the shareholders) and managed by another group (the directors). The creation of these new legal entities was not accompanied by stringent requirements either to publish financial statements or to have them audited. Nevertheless, many companies did so. This was largely in response to pressure from investors who were reluctant to part with their money without relevant feedback, in the form of periodic financial reports, from the directors.

These financial reports reduced uncertainty in the minds of investors, who then became more willing to provide funds and to scale down their expectations of financial returns. There is quite strong, and recent, evidence that greater disclosure of financial information tends to lower a company's cost of capital and, furthermore, that directors understand this relationship. (See reference 1 at the end of the chapter.)

Relying on market forces to determine the form and content of financial reports is, however, a risky business. Directors control access to financial information and it is not always in their interests to ensure that the truth is revealed in a timely and accurate way. Furthermore, investors are often dispersed and find it difficult to act collectively. They are, therefore, in a weak position to exert pressure on the directors. Given these problems, it is not surprising that the 'market model' resulted in abuses and led, inevitably, to calls for regulation.

The past century and a half has been characterised by a movement away from market-led financial reporting towards a highly elaborate regulatory framework. The UK government started the ball rolling with the Companies Act 1862, which recommended the preparation of a rudimentary income statement and statement of financial position each year (as well as an audit of the latter). This was followed by a succession of Companies Acts, with each requiring greater financial disclosure. Since the 1970s accounting standard-setting bodies, and in particular the IASB, have become major forces in financial reporting regulation and have added considerably to the mountain of rules. The IASB, for example, has nearly forty standards currently in existence.

The relentless increase in reporting requirements has created some disquiet. Doubts have been raised as to whether the increasing complexity of financial statements has led to an improvement in their usefulness. There is a concern that accounting regulators and businesses have lost a sense of focus and forgotten the purpose for which financial statements are prepared. Thus, a major challenge for the future is to produce better, rather than simply more, regulation. The quality of financial statements is dependent on regulators ensuring that rules are clearly targeted and are proportionate to the problems that they address. It is also dependent on businesses providing as clear, open and understandable financial statements as possible within the rules that exist.

It is worth mentioning as a footnote to this section that financial reports of many businesses, including many well-known ones like British Airways plc, provide much more information than is required by the regulations. This is done, presumably, with the aim of making the businesses' activities more transparent and so reducing uncertainty.

From stewardship to decision making

We have seen that, in the early days of financial reporting, stewardship was the key issue. The main aim was to recount what had happened so as to make stewards (managers) accountable and perhaps, therefore, more careful in deploying the assets of the owner. As financial reporting developed, however, its decision-making potential was increasingly exploited. In modern times, the decision-oriented aspect has become increasingly important and regulation has become more targeted on making financial statements useful as decision-making tools.

Decision making involves making predictions about the future and it is argued that, to help users, financial reporting should have both a *predictive role* and a *confirmatory role*. That is to say, it should enable a user to make reliable predictions about future earnings and cash flows. It should also enable a user to confirm whether past predictions were reliable.

We are now going on to look at three more recent developments in company financial reporting statements. All three of these go beyond the routine financial statements, yet preparing them is obligatory for many larger and/or listed companies. The statements concerned are segmental reports, business reviews and interim financial statements.

Segmental financial reports

Most large businesses are engaged in a number of different operations, with each having its own levels of risk, growth and profitability. Information relating to each type of business operation, however, is normally added together (aggregated) in the financial statements so as to provide an overall picture of financial performance and position. For example, the revenue figure at the top of the income statement represents all of the company's revenues added together. This will be true even where the revenues come from quite different activities. Although this aggregation of information can help to provide a clearer broad picture, it can make it difficult to undertake comparisons over time or between businesses. Some idea of the range and scale of the various types of operation must be gained for a proper assessment of financial health. Thus, to undertake any meaningful analysis of financial performance and position, it is usually necessary to disaggregate the information contained within the financial statements. These dis-
→ aggregated information are disclosed in **segmental financial reports**.

By breaking down the financial information according to each type of business operation, or operating segment, we can evaluate the relative risks and profitability of each segment and make useful comparisons with other businesses or other business operating segments. We can also see the trend of performance for each operating segment over time and so determine more accurately the likely growth prospects for the business as a whole. We should also be able to assess more easily the impact on the overall business of changes in market conditions relating to particular operating segments.

Disclosure of information relating to the performance of each segment may also help to improve the efficiency of the business by keeping managers on their toes. Operating segments that are performing poorly will be revealed and this should put pressure on managers to take corrective action. Finally, where an operating segment has been sold, the shareholders will be better placed to assess the wisdom of the managers' decision to sell it.

Segmental reporting rules

An IASB standard (IFRS 8 *Operating Segments*) requires listed companies to disclose information about their various operating segments. Defining an operating segment, however, can be a tricky business. The IASB has opted for a 'management approach', which means that an operating segment is defined by reference to how management has segmented the business for internal reporting and monitoring purposes. An operating segment is, therefore, defined as a part of the business that

● generates revenues and expenses,
● has its own separate financial statements, and
● has its results regularly reviewed for resource-allocation and assessment purposes.

Not all parts of the business will meet the criteria identified. The headquarters of the business ('head office'), for example, is unlikely to do so.

Activity 10.1

What do you think are the main advantages of adopting the management approach?

Under the management approach, shareholders will receive similar reports to the internal reports produced for management, which means that they can assess business performance from the same viewpoint as management. It should also mean that businesses will avoid heavy reporting costs as the information will already have been produced.

There are, of course, other ways of identifying an operating segment. One approach would be to define a segment according to the industry to which it relates. This, however, may lead to endless definition and classification problems.

To be reported separately, an operating segment must be of significant size. This normally means that it must account for 10 per cent or more of the combined revenue, profits or assets of all operating segments. A segment that does not meet this size threshold may be combined with other similar segments to produce a reportable segment, or separately reported despite its size, at the directors' discretion. If neither of these options is chosen, it should be reported with other segments under a separate category of 'all other segments'.

Segmental disclosure

Financial information to be disclosed includes some profit (/loss) measure (for example, operating profit) for each segment along with the following income statement items:

● revenue, distinguishing between revenue from external customers and revenue from other segments of the business;

- interest revenue and interest expense;
- depreciation and other material non-cash items;
- material items of income and expense;
- any profit (loss) from associate companies or joint ventures;
- segment profit (loss);
- income tax (where it is separately reported for a segment).

The business must also disclose the total assets for each segment and, if they are reported to management, the total liabilities. Any additions to non-current assets during the period must also be reported.

Example 10.1 provides an illustrative segmental financial report for a business.

Example 10.1

Goya plc
Segmental report for the year ended 31 December 2009

	Publishing £m	Film-making £m	All other £m	Totals £m
Revenue from external customers	150	200	25	375
Inter-segment revenue	20	10	–	30
Interest revenue	10	–	–	10
Interest expense	–	15	–	15
Depreciation	40	20	5	65
Reportable segment profit	15	19	4	38
Other material non-cash items:				
Impairment of assets	–	10	–	10
Reportable segment assets	60	80	12	152
Expenditures for reportable segment				
non-current assets	12	18	2	32
Reportable segment liabilities	25	32	4	61

We can see that information relating to each segment as well as a combined total for all operating segments is shown. This information may be simply set out in the form of a table, as shown above, with no headings or totals.

Key items, which include revenues, profits, assets, and liabilities, must be reconciled with the corresponding amounts for the business as a whole. For example, Goya plc's income statement should show revenue of £375 million for the business as a whole. When carrying out a reconciliation, we should bear in mind that:

- inter-segment revenues should be eliminated as no transaction with external parties occurs;
- any profit arising from inter-segment transfers should also be eliminated;
- assets and liabilities that have not been allocated to a particular segment should be taken into account.

The last item normally refers to assets and liabilities relating to business-wide activities. Thus, head office buildings may provide an example of unallocated assets and staff pension liabilities may provide an example of unallocated liabilities.

IFRS 8 requires certain non-financial information concerning segments to be disclosed including the basis for identifying operating segments and the types of products and services that each segment provides. It also requires business-wide information to be disclosed such as geographical areas of operations, and reliance on major customers.

Segmental reporting problems

Various problems arise when preparing segmental reports, not least of which is that of identifying a segment. We have already seen that the relevant IFRS identifies operating segments according to the internal reporting and monitoring procedures of the business. While this may be the most sensible course of action, comparisons between segments in other businesses may be impossible because of the different ways in which they are defined.

→   Another problem may arise where there is a significant amount of sales between operating segments. Where this occurs, the **transfer price** of the goods or services between segments can have a substantial impact on the reported profits of each segment. (The transfer price is the price at which sales are made between different segments of the business.) A potential risk is that revenues and profits will be manipulated for each segment through the use of particular transfer pricing policies.

Activity 10.2

Why might a business wish to do this?

Where a business operates in different countries, it may try to report high profits in a country that has low tax rates and to report low profits (or even losses) in a country with high tax rates.

Real World 10.1 reveals how Her Majesty's Revenue and Customs (HMRC) is taking an increasingly hard line towards the transfer pricing policies that businesses adopt, including DSG, the business that owns Currys, Dixons and PC World.

Real World 10.1

A taxing issue

The taxman is ramping up a major offensive on companies it suspects of avoiding the UK's tax coffers when they shift goods from one place to another as 1,000 transfer pricing disputes remain in the pipeline.

HMRC is looking to haul UK companies over the coals if it believes the price has been set artificially low in moves to reduce taxable profits, according to leading tax advisers. The DSG case earlier this year, which saw the Dixons' parent company shell out a £52.7 million settlement, was seen as a key victory for the taxman.

Transfer pricing sees multinationals put a price on the value of assets or goods which are sent from one subsidiary to another, most often across international borders, and covers everything from sales or purchases of goods and services to intellectual property, debt or deemed transactions that are not reflected in any accounts.

Companies are supposed to ensure an arm's-length policy is maintained when assigning values. HMRC, which has a dedicated transfer pricing group with about 70 specialists, is continuing its clampdown to help maximise tax take in the uncertain economic conditions. Shiv Mahalingham, managing director at Alvaraz and Marsal Taxsand, said the money flowing in from transfer pricing issues has doubled to about £470 million between 2006 and 2007 and HMRC's clampdown meant errant companies would continue to find themselves under the cosh.

Source: 'HMRC pursues tax avoiders in transfer pricing clampdown', David Jetuah, *Accountancy Age*, 19 November 2009.

IFRS 8 recognises the impact of transfer pricing policies on segmental revenues and profit by stating that the basis for accounting for transactions between segments must be disclosed.

A third problem is that some expenses and assets may relate to more than one operating segment and their allocation between segments may vary between businesses. Again, this may hinder comparisons of segmental profits and profitability between businesses.

Business review

A business, particularly a large business, may have extremely complex organisational arrangements, financing methods and operating characteristics. The financial statements must, however, reflect this complexity if they are to provide a faithful portrayal of financial health. As a consequence, the statements can often be lengthy, detailed and difficult to understand.

To provide a clearer picture for users, a narrative report can be provided that reviews the business and its results. UK law now requires all except the smallest companies to include a *business review* in their annual financial report. This review, which is prepared by the directors, must provide a balanced and comprehensive analysis of the year's performance and of the position at the year end. The review must also set out information concerning

- the principal risks and uncertainties that are faced;
- key performance indicators;
- the main trends and factors likely to affect the future;
- the company's employees;
- environmental, social and community issues; and
- persons with whom the company has essential contractual or other arrangements, unless disclosure is prejudicial to the person or to the public interest.

Activity 10.3

What do you think are the main qualitative characteristics that information contained within the business review should possess? (*Hint*: Think back to Chapter 1.)

To be useful, the information should exhibit the characteristics for accounting information in general, which we identified in Chapter 1. Thus the information should be relevant, understandable, reliable and comparable. The fact that we are dealing with narrative information does not alter the need for these characteristics to be present.

To contain the quality of reliability, the information provided must be complete. This means that it should include all significant information that will help assess business performance. Information that places the business in an unfavourable light must not be omitted.

The reporting framework

The particular form that a business review should take is left to the discretion of the directors. In searching for a suitable framework, the directors may look to the Reporting

Standard RS 1 issued by the UK Accounting Standards Board (ASB). This statement precedes the legal requirement for a business review but nevertheless covers the same sort of ground. It is not mandatory; it simply aims to provide guidance on best practice.

The framework set out in RS 1 rests on the disclosure of information relating to four key elements of a business.

Figure 10.1 shows these four key elements.

Figure 10.1   The key elements of the business review

Reporting Standard RS1, issued by the UK ASB, recommends basing the business review on four key elements.

The information to be reported for each of these elements is discussed below.

The nature of the business

This part of the review should describe the environment within which the business operates. As might be imagined, this can cover a wide range and may include a commentary on key operational matters such as the products sold, business processes, business structure and competitive position. It can also include a commentary on the legal, economic and social environment.

This part should also describe the objectives of the business and the strategy adopted to achieve those objectives. **Real World 10.2** indicates how one well-known business deals with this topic in its business review.

Real World 10.2

Reviewing the situation

In its 2009 annual report, Tesco plc's business review discusses the business's strategy as follows:

> Tesco has a well-established and consistent strategy for growth, which has allowed us to strengthen our core UK business and drive expansion into new markets. The rationale for the strategy is to broaden the scope of the business to enable it to deliver strong, sustainable long-term growth

Real World 10.2 continued

by following the customer into large expanding markets at home – such as financial services, non-food and telecoms – and new markets abroad, initially in Central Europe and Asia, and more recently in the United States.

The strategy to diversify the business was laid down in 1997 and has been the foundation of Tesco's success in recent years. The new businesses which have been created and developed over the last 12 years as part of this strategy now have scale, they are competitive and profitable – in fact we are now market leader in many of our markets outside the UK.

The objectives of the strategy are:

- to be a successful international retailer;
- to grow the core UK business;
- to be as strong in non-food as in food;
- to develop retailing services – such as Tesco Personal Finance, Telecoms and tesco.com; and
- to put community at the heart of what we do.

Source: Tesco plc Annual Report and Financial Statements 2009, Business Review, www.Tesco.com.

Finally, this part of the business review should include a commentary on the key performance indicators (KPIs) used to assess the success of the business strategy. KPIs will vary between businesses but will normally comprise a combination of financial and non-financial measures. Key financial measures may be based upon sales revenue growth, profit, total shareholder return, dividends and so on. Key non-financial measures may relate to market share, employee satisfaction, product quality, supplier satisfaction and so on.

Business performance

This part of the review considers the development and performance of the business for the year and for the future. It should include comments on anything affecting performance, such as changes in market conditions or the launch of new products or services. It should also identify trends and anything else that may affect future prospects. **Real World 10.3** provides an extract from Tesco's business review, which sets out details of new store openings and store extensions in its core UK business.

 Real World 10.3

Extra growth

We opened a total of 2.0 million square feet of new sales area in 2008/9, of which 362,000 square feet was in store extensions, principally for Extra. We opened another 11 Extra hypermarkets – six from extensions to existing stores and five new stores, bringing the total to 177, with a further 15 planned this year. Extra now represents 40% of our total sales area. We also opened 21 new superstores and 125 new Express stores, bringing the overall total number of Tesco stores to 2,282.

In the current year, we aim to open a similar amount of new space across our formats – equivalent to an additional 6.4% of sales area.

Source: Tesco plc Annual Report and Financial Statements 2009, Business Review, www.Tesco.com.

Resources, risks and relationships

This part should comment on the resources of the business and how they are managed. The resources discussed should not be confined to items shown in the statement of financial position and may include such things as corporate reputation, patents, trademarks, brand names, market position and the quality of employees.

This part should also include comments on the main risks and uncertainties facing the business and how they are managed. **Real World 10.4** shows how Tesco plc comments on one important risk in its business review.

Real World 10.4

A risky business

In its 2009 business review, Tesco plc identified nearly twenty forms of risk that the business must consider. These cover a wide range and include competition, IT systems, reputational, environmental, fraud, terrorism and currency risks. The risk posed by product safety is described as follows:

> The safety and quality of our products is of paramount importance to Tesco as well as being essential for maintaining customer trust and confidence. A breach in confidence could affect the size of our customer base and hence financial results.
>
> We have detailed and established procedures for ensuring product integrity at all times, especially for our own-label products. There are strict product safety processes and regular management reports. We work in partnership with suppliers to ensure mutual understanding of the standards required. We also monitor developments in areas such as health, safety and nutrition in order to respond appropriately to changing customer trends and new legislation. We have clear processes for crisis management, pulling together expert teams should we need to respond quickly on issues.

Source: Tesco plc Annual Report and Financial Statements 2009, Business Review, www.Tesco.com.

Finally, this part of the business review should include a commentary on key relationships with stakeholders, apart from shareholders, that may affect the business. The stakeholders may include customers, suppliers, employees, contractors and lenders as well as other businesses with which the business has strategic alliances. **Real World 10.5** shows how, in its 2009 business review, Tesco plc describes feedback received from customers.

Real World 10.5

Every little helps

This year hundreds of thousands of customers have told us what they want from an 'Every Little Helps' shopping trip. We've held over 200 'Customer Question Time' forums in our stores in addition to many other focus groups. We have also launched 'Shopper Thoughts', a proprietary online panel of 64,000 customers who provide us with rapid and detailed feedback on everything from the range of products we sell to the friendliness of our staff. Our latest trial feedback initiative is called Fizzback, which allows customers to tell us what they think via free text message, phone, email or comment card. Clubcard also helps us to understand what our customers want, whilst allowing us to thank them for shopping with us.

Source: Tesco plc Annual Report and Financial Statements 2009, Business Review, www.tesco.com.

Financial position

This final part of the of the business review should describe events that have influenced the financial position of the business during the year and those that are likely to affect the business in the future. It should also include a discussion of the capital (financial) structure, cash flows and liquidity of the company. **Real World 10.6** shows how, in its 2009 business review, Tesco plc comments on its funding.

Real World 10.6

Finding the funds

The Group finances its operations by a combination of retained earnings, long and medium-term debt, capital market issues, commercial paper, bank borrowings and leases. The objective is to ensure continuity of funding. The policy is to smooth the debt maturity profile, to arrange funding ahead of requirements and to maintain sufficient undrawn committed bank facilities, and a strong credit rating so that maturing debt may be refinanced as it falls due.

Tesco Group has a long-term rating of A3 by Moody's and A– by Standard and Poor's with a stable outlook. New funding of £5.6bn was arranged during the year, including a net £0.7bn from property transactions and £4.9bn from medium-term notes (MTNs). At the year end, net debt was £9.6bn (last year £6.2bn).

Source: Tesco plc Annual Report and Financial Statements 2009, Business Review, www.tesco.com.

This final part of the business review should also comment on the treasury policy of the business, which is concerned with managing cash, obtaining finance and managing relationships with financial institutions. Possible areas for discussion can include major financing transactions and the effects of interest charges, or interest rate changes, on the business. **Real World 10.7** shows how, in its 2009 business review, Tesco plc comments on interest rates.

Real World 10.7

Any interest?

Tesco plc manages its interest rates in various ways and the business review states:

The objective is to limit our exposure to increases in interest rates while retaining the opportunity to benefit from interest rate reductions.

A combination of fixed rate and floating rate debt is used by the business and

The average rate of interest paid on an historic cost basis excluding joint ventures and associates this year was 5.2% (last year 4.5%).

Source: Tesco plc Annual Report and Financial Statements 2009, Business Review, www.tesco.com.

The quality of business reviews

Business reviews are still at an early stage of development and problems concerning their quality are, perhaps, to be expected. A major risk is that these reports will paint too rosy a picture. If they are to be useful, managers must resist this temptation and must be honest about any failings. However, in a world where there is no real incentive for managers to behave in this way and no independent scrutiny, we should not be surprised if this does not occur.

In 2006, the ASB carried out a survey of narrative reporting practice. It found that, generally, businesses provided a good account of the nature of the business and its markets as well as of their business strategy and objectives, but the reporting of principal risks, KPIs and the resources of the business needed improvement. The greatest problem area for businesses, however, was the reporting of forward-looking information. (See reference 2 at the end of the chapter.)

Activity 10.4

Why might the reporting of forward-looking information be a problem for the directors of a business?

The directors may be concerned that the information will be of use to competitors and so damage the competitive position of the business. There is also a risk that the information may turn out to be incorrect and users may then feel that they have been misled.

Interim financial statements

Interim financial statements were first published in the US at the turn of the last century and began to appear in the UK in the 1950s. The main impetus for their publication came from progressive managers who felt that the interval between annual financial statements is too long for users to be without information. These days, interim financial statements are an integral part of the financial reporting cycle of most large businesses. Regulatory authorities, particularly Stock Exchanges, have been the major reason for this. Producing half-yearly or quarterly interim financial statements is usually an important listing requirement.

Activity 10.5

The London Stock Exchange requires listed businesses to produce half-yearly interim financial statements. The US Securities and Exchange Commission (SEC), on the other hand, requires listed businesses to produce quarterly financial statements.

What are the advantages and disadvantages of producing interim financial statements on a quarterly, rather than a half-yearly, basis?

Quarterly statements will track more closely financial progress throughout the year and will provide more timely information to users than half-yearly statements. This may, however, be achieved at the expense of reliability. The shorter the reporting period, the greater the need for estimates as there is not enough time for events to unfold. This leads to a greater risk of inaccuracy and error. The costs of quarterly reporting will also be greater.

The precise role of interim financial statements has proved to be a source of contention. Some believe that they are simply a supplement to the annual financial statements;

their purpose being to provide timely information that can help in predicting annual profits or losses. Others, however, believe that they should not focus simply on helping to predict the future. They should also help to confirm the results of earlier predictions. Like annual financial statements, they should have both a predictive and a confirmatory role and there is no reason why they should not. A year, after all, is an arbitrary reporting period and annual financial statements rarely cover the operational cycle of a business.

Measuring interim profit

The role of interim financial statements has important implications for the measurement of interim profit. Two methods of measuring interim profit have been proposed, with each reflecting one side of the debate. The **integral method** of profit measurement sees the interim period as being simply part of the annual reporting period. It seeks to provide a measure of interim profit that can be used to help predict the annual profit. To do this, annual expenses are predicted and then a proportion of these are allocated to the interim period based on the proportion of annual sales revenue generated in that period. Under this approach, interim and annual profit margins are maintained at a fairly consistent level. The **discrete method** of profit measurement, on the other hand, treats the interim period as quite separate and distinct from the annual period. It is not primarily concerned with predicting annual profit and adopts accounting methods and policies for measuring interim profit that are the same as those used to measure annual profit.

Example 10.2 below should make the differences between the two methods clear.

Example 10.2

Varna plc is a large retailer that produces interim financial statements on a half-yearly basis. The business has produced the following estimates for the forthcoming year.

1 Revenue will be £40 million for the first half-year and £100 million for the whole year.
2 Cost of sales will be 50 per cent of sales revenue.
3 Administration expenses will be fixed at £1.5 million per month for the first six months of the year and £2.5 million per month thereafter.
4 The business will sponsor a sports event at a total cost of £5 million in the first half year. The benefits from the sponsorship deal are expected to benefit the whole year.

The estimated interim profit for the first half year, calculated using the integral and discrete methods will be as follows:

	Estimated interim profit	
	Integral	*Discrete*
	£m	*£m*
Revenue	40.0	40.0
Cost of sales (50%)	(20.0)	(20.0)
Administration – (40/100 × £24m)	(9.6)	
– (6 × £1.5m)		(9.0)
Sponsorship – (40/100 × £5m)	(2.0)	
		(5.0)
Interim profit	8.4	6.0

Notes

1 The discrete method uses the same approach to profit measurement as for the annual period. Expenses are assigned to the particular period in which they are incurred. The sponsorship cost will be written off in the first half year even though the benefits are expected to extend into the second half year. This cost does not meet the definition of an asset at the year end and so is not deferred at the end of an interim period.
2 The integral method 'smooths out' the total annual expenses between the two half-year periods based on the level of activity. Thus, the first half year is charged with 40% (that is, £40m/£100m) of the total expenses for the year.

Let us now calculate annual profit to see how interim profit, when derived using the integral method, may be helpful for prediction purposes.

	Estimated annual profit £m
Revenue	100.0
Cost of sales (50%)	(50.0)
Administration [(6 × £1.5m) + (6 × £2.5m)]	(24.0)
Sponsorship	(5.0)
Profit for the year	21.0

Interim profit, based on the integral method, represents 40 per cent of the annual profit. (That is, £8.4m/£21m = 40%) This, of course, is the same as the percentage of interim sales to annual sales (£40m/£100m = 40%). In other words, (interim sales/annual sales)% = (interim profit/annual profit)%. (See reference 4 at the end of the chapter.) If users can predict sales for the second half of the year, this should provide a good basis for predicting profit. (Having ploughed through this example, you may wonder whether, instead of adopting the integral approach, it would be better simply to provide external users with a profit forecast for the year.)

The International Accounting Standards Board (IASB) has produced a standard for interim financial statements (IAS 34 *Interim Financial Reporting*). It applies to all businesses that are either required, or wish, to prepare these statements in line with international standards. The standard favours the discrete approach to income measurement and states that accounting policies and methods adopted at the interim stage should be in line with those adopted at the annual stage. One problem, however, is that certain items, such as tax, can only be considered in the context of the year as a whole. The standard deals with the tax problem by stating that the tax rate applied to interim profit should be based on the average, effective tax rate for the year as a whole.

Interim financial disclosure

There is nothing to stop a business producing a comprehensive set of financial statements for the interim period, although considerations of cost and timeliness will normally make this impractical. IAS 34 recognises that a full reporting option is available to businesses and therefore sets out the *minimum* components of interim financial statements. The standard requires

- a condensed statement of financial position,
- a condensed statement of comprehensive income (either as a single statement or as a separate income statement plus a statement of comprehensive income),
- a condensed statement of changes in equity,
- a condensed statement of cash flows, and
- selected explanatory notes.

Headings and sub-totals appearing in the condensed financial statements should be in line with those appearing in the most recent annual financial statements. This should help users to track events occurring since the annual statements were published.

Activity 10.6

What do you think is the main risk of preparing condensed interim financial statements? (*Hint*: Think back to Chapter 5 where we considered summary financial statements.)

The main risk is that, if an attempt is made to simplify complex reality, important information may be lost and the message may become distorted.

The standard assumes that users will have access to the most recent annual report and so explanatory notes focus on issues relating specifically to the interim reporting period. These include

- confirmation that the interim financial statements use the same accounting policies and methods as those used for the annual financial statements,
- suitable explanations concerning the seasonality and cyclicality of business operations,
- the nature and amount of any unusual items affecting assets, liabilities, income and cash flows,
- details of the issue/redemption of loans or share capital and dividends paid,
- information relating to business segments,
- details of significant events, including changes in the composition of the business, changes in contingent assets or liabilities, and material events affecting the business after the end of the interim period.

These disclosure requirements should enable users to glean a fair amount of information concerning the financial progress of the business.

We shall now consider two approaches to financial reporting that also go beyond the routine financial statements. These approaches are not mandatory, though they have been adopted by some businesses. They are the value added statement and accounting for inflation.

The value added statement

→ The **value added statement (VAS)** came to prominence in the mid 1970s following publication of an influential discussion document entitled *The Corporate Report* (see reference 3 at the end of the chapter). This report argued for the inclusion of the VAS within the annual report. It regarded the VAS as an important financial statement and went so far as to suggest that the VAS might one day become more important than the income statement. Following publication of *The Corporate Report*, two government reports lent further support for the inclusion of the VAS within the annual reports of large businesses.

The VAS is similar to the income statement insofar that they are both concerned with measuring wealth created by a business over time. The key difference between the two, however, is the way in which wealth is defined and measured. The VAS measures *value added* whereas the income statement measures *profit earned*.

What is value added?

Value added is an alternative measure of the wealth generated by a business over time. A business can be seen as buying in goods and/or services to which it then 'adds value'. The amount of value added is derived by calculating the total output of the business and then deducting the cost of total inputs. This is shown diagrammatically in Figure 10.2 below.

Figure 10.2 Calculating value added by a business

Like profit, value added is a residual figure. It represents the amount remaining after the cost of total inputs has been deducted from the value of total outputs received by the business.

The total output of the business will normally be the sales revenue for the period. The total inputs will be the bought-in materials and services such as the purchase of inventories, rent, rates, electricity, telephone, postage and so on. The difference between total output and total inputs, which is the value added, represents the wealth generated from the collective effort of those with a stake in the business – that is, employees, suppliers of capital and government.

Value added is a broader measure of wealth than profit. It recognises that various groups contribute to, and have a stake in, the wealth generated by a business and it seeks to measure how much wealth is attributable to these 'stakeholders'. This is in contrast to the measure of profit, which is concerned only with the wealth attributable to the owners (that is, the shareholders).

Preparing a value added statement

The VAS begins by measuring the value added by a business and then goes on to show how it is distributed among the key 'stakeholders'. Example 10.3 shows the layout for a value added statement.

Example 10.3

Value added statement for the year ended 30 June

	£m
Revenue	130.6
Bought-in materials and services	(88.4)
Value added	42.2
Applied in the following way:	
To employees	
Wages, pensions and fringe benefits	28.1
To suppliers of capital	
Interest payable on loans	2.6
Dividends to shareholders	3.8
	6.4
To pay government	
Tax payable	3.2
To provide for maintenance and expansion of assets	
Depreciation of non-current assets	3.0
Retained earnings	1.5
	4.5
	42.2

We can see that, in the first part of the VAS, valued added is derived by deducting the cost of bought-in materials and services from sales revenue. The second part then shows how much value added is divided between the various stakeholder groups and how much is retained within the business. (Depreciation and retained earnings represent amounts reinvested to maintain and expand the asset base.)

The VAS does not provide any information that is not already contained within the conventional income statement. It is, in fact, a rearrangement of the income statement. It is claimed, however, that through this rearrangement new insights concerning the performance of the business may be gained.

Activity 10.7

Ray Cathode (Lighting Supplies) plc has produced the following income statement for the year to 31 December:

Income statement for the year ended 31 December

	£m
Revenue	198
Cost of sales	(90)
Gross profit	108
Salaries and wages	(35)
Rent and rates	(18)
Insurance	(3)
Light and heat	(10)
Postage and stationery	(1)
Advertising	(4)
Depreciation	(19)
Operating profit	18
Interest payable	(6)
Profit before taxation	12
Taxation	(4)
Profit for the year	8

During the year a dividend of £3 million was announced and paid.

From the above information, see if you can produce a value added statement for the year to 31 December. (Use the format in Example 10.3 above to guide you.)

Your answer should be as follows:

Value added statement for the year ended 31 December

	£m
Revenue	198
Bought-in materials and services (90 + 18 + 3 + 10 + 1 + 4)	(126)
Value added	72
Applied in the following way:	
To employees	
Salaries and wages	35
To suppliers of capital	
Interest payable on loans	6
Dividends to shareholders	3
	9
To pay government	
Tax payable	4
To provide for maintenance and expansion of assets	
Depreciation of non-current assets	19
Retained profits (8 − 3)	5
	24
	72

Activity 10.8

What useful information can you glean from the VAS in Activity 10.7?

The VAS in Activity 10.7 reveals that nearly half of the value added generated by the business during the year was distributed to employees in the form of salaries and wages. This proportion is much higher than that distributed to suppliers of capital. A relatively high proportion of value added being distributed to employees is not unusual. The business retained one-third of the value added to replace and expand the assets. A high proportion of value added retained may suggest a concern for growth to be financed through internally generated sources. The proportion of value added required to pay tax is relatively small.

Benefits of the VAS

The VAS helps to promote the message that a business is a coalition of interests and that business success depends on co-operation between the various stakeholders. It may even foster better relations by encouraging a team spirit among those with a stake in the business. If employees are identified as important stakeholders, they may feel more part of the business team and respond by showing greater co-operation and commitment. The VAS may also help managers to appreciate that employees are team members and not simply an expense, as portrayed in the conventional income statement.

A further benefit claimed for the VAS is that some useful ratios can be derived from this statement. These include

● value added to sales revenue (per cent);
● value added per £1 of wages and salaries (£);
● dividends to value added (per cent);
● tax to value added (per cent);
● depreciation and retentions to value added (per cent);
● value added to capital employed (per cent).

Activity 10.9

Calculate each of the above ratios using the information contained in the solution to Activity 10.7 above. How could these ratios be useful? (For purposes of calculation, assume that the business's capital employed is £80 million.)

Your answer should be as follows:

$$\text{Value added to sales revenue} = \frac{72}{198} \times 100\% = 36.4\%$$

The lower this ratio is, the greater will be the reliance on outside sources of materials and services. For example, a wine retailer that purchases its wine from a wholesaler will have a lower ratio than a wine retailer that owns its own vineyards and bottling facilities. A low ratio may indicate vulnerability to difficulties caused by external suppliers.

$$\text{Value added per £1 of wages} = \frac{72}{35} = £2.06$$

This ratio is a measure of labour productivity. In this case, the employees are generating £2.06 of value added for every £1 of wages expended: the higher the ratio, the higher the level of productivity. Normally, the ratio would be higher than 1.0. A ratio of less than 1.0 would indicate that employees are being paid more than the value of their output.

$$\text{Dividends to value added} = \frac{3}{72} \times 100\% = 4.2\%$$

This ratio shows the portion of value added that will be received in cash, more or less immediately, by shareholders. The trend of this ratio may provide an insight into the distribution policy of the business over time. It is important to remember, however, that shareholders also benefit, in the form of capital growth, from amounts reinvested in the business. Thus, the ratio is only a partial measure of the benefits received by shareholders.

$$\text{Tax to value added} = \frac{4}{72} \times 100\% = 5.6\%$$

This ratio indicates that portion of the value added which is payable to government in the form of taxes. It may be useful in assessing whether or not the business has an unfair burden of taxation.

$$\text{Depreciation and retentions to value added} = \frac{24}{72} \times 100\% = 33.3\%$$

This ratio provides some indication of the way that finance is raised. A high ratio may indicate that finance for new investment tends to be raised from internal sources rather than from external sources, such as borrowing or new share issues.

$$\text{Value added to capital employed} = \frac{72}{80} \times 100\% = 90\%$$

This ratio is a measure of the productivity of capital employed. A high ratio is, therefore, normally preferred to a low ratio.

Problems of the VAS

The proposal to include a VAS as part of the annual report was initially greeted with enthusiasm. At the peak of its popularity, it was included in the annual reports of almost one-third of the hundred largest listed businesses. This peak has long passed, however, and now the VAS has become a rare sighting in the financial reporting landscape.

Although the VAS simply rearranges information contained in the conventional income statement, the effect of this rearrangement is to raise a number of thorny theoretical and practical problems. Many of these problems remain unresolved, leaving doubts over its usefulness. The more important of these problems are:

● *The team concept.* Some dismiss the idea of a business being a team of stakeholders working together as no more than a public relations exercise. It is seen as a misguided attempt to obscure the underlying conflict between suppliers of capital and employees.
● *Team membership.* Even if the team concept is accepted, there is room for debate about the nature and composition of the team. Suppliers, for example, may work closely with a business to ensure the timely flow of goods and services, yet cannot be treated as team members because of the way in which value added is calculated. They may,

however, have a stronger case for being considered team members than, say, government, which may have little contact with a business, apart from when collecting taxes.

● *The classification of items.* The VAS is beset with classification problems. For example, gross wages paid to employees (that is, wages before tax and national insurance payments are deducted) are normally shown under the heading 'To employees'. Yet it is the government that receives the taxation and National Insurance payments. Employees will receive their wages net of taxation and National Insurance, with the employer paying the deductions directly to the government.

● *The importance of profit.* Within a capitalist economy, profit will always be at the heart of financial reporting. Shareholders, who are the owners and principal risk-takers, are concerned with the returns from their investment. If managers do not keep this firmly in mind and provide shareholders with acceptable returns, they are likely to be replaced by managers who will.

● *Loss of focus.* There is a danger that if managers become too concerned with increasing value added this may have an adverse effect on profit. To illustrate this point, consider Activity 10.10 below.

Activity 10.10

Ray Von plc is considering whether to make a particular component or to purchase the item from an outside supplier. The component can be sold by Ray Von for £40. Making the component would involve Ray Von in a labour cost of £12 a unit and a material cost of £18. The cost of buying the item from an outside supplier would be £26. Calculate both the value added and profit arising from one unit of the component under each option.

Your answer should be as follows:

	Buy-in	Make
	£	£
Selling price	40	40
Bought-in materials	(26)	(18)
Value added	14	22
Labour costs	(–)	(12)
Profit	14	10

We can see that making the item will provide a higher value added but a lower profit than buying in. Thus, a decision to maximise value added would be at the expense of profit.

Finally, it is worth making the point that the profit generated by a business is likely to be important to various stakeholders and not simply to shareholders. Lenders will be interested in the profit generated to enable them to assess the riskiness of their loan; governments will be interested for taxation purposes; and employees will be interested for the assessment of likely future pay increases and job security. So far, there has been a failure to demonstrate that value added is as useful for decision-making purposes as profit.

Reporting value added

Although the VAS now rarely appears in the annual reports, some businesses still use this statement when reporting business performance to employees. It may then be portrayed in diagrammatic form for ease of understanding. For example, the application of total value added of Ray Cathode (Lighting Supplies) plc that we met earlier in Activity 10.7 (see page 369) can be represented in the form of a pie chart, as in Figure 10.3.

| Figure 10.3 | Distribution of total value added by Ray Cathode (Lighting Supplies) plc |

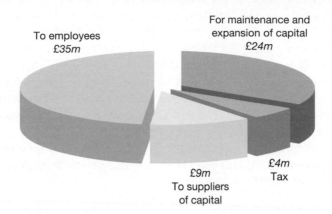

Total value added £72m

For maintenance and expansion of capital £24m

To employees £35m

£9m
To suppliers of capital

£4m
Tax

The pie chart shows clearly how value added by the business has been distributed to the various stakeholders. We can see, for example, that almost half of the total value added is distributed to employees.

Reporting value added only to employees, however, raises an issue of credibility. Employees may well ask why a financial report that is not regarded as being important to other users is being provided to them. They may feel the major motivation is to demonstrate the extent to which value added is taken up in salaries and wages. As mentioned earlier, a sizeable proportion of total value added is usually distributed to employees.

It is interesting to note that the UK government regards value added as an important measure of wealth creation and business competitiveness. Each year, it produces an annual report known as the Value Added Scoreboard, as **Real World 10.8** explains.

Real World 10.8

Keeping score

The Value Added Scoreboard sets out details of value added by the top 800 UK businesses and the top 750 European businesses, based on an analysis of their most recent annual reports. The 2009 Value Added Scoreboard examined annual reports for the accounting year ending before 5 January 2009. For most businesses this means an accounting year ending in 2008 and so pre-dates the recent economic downturn.

The report found that the UK businesses generated total value added of £757bn and the European businesses (which include UK businesses) generated total value added of £2,717bn. It also found that 67 per cent of the total valued added by the UK businesses came from the top ten industrial sectors, compared to 60 per cent for the European businesses. A breakdown of value added by UK businesses according to industrial sector is shown in Figure 10.4.

Source: The 2009 Value Added Scoreboard, Department for Business Innovation and Skills, www.innovation.gov.uk.

Real World 10.8 continued

Figure 10.4	Breakdown of value added of UK businesses by industrial sector

The figure reveals that oil and gas producers generated the largest percentage of value added, followed by banks. The report shows, however, that oil and gas producers accounted for only 31 (4 per cent) of the top 800 UK businesses; banks accounted for only 17 (2 per cent).

Self-assessment question 10.1

Rose Limited operates a small chain of retail shops. An abbreviated income statement for this year is given below.

Income statements for the year ended 31 March

	£000
Revenue	12,080
Cost of sales	(6,282)
Gross profit	5,798
Labour costs	(2,658)
Depreciation	(625)
Other operating costs	(1,003)
Operating profit	1,512
Interest payable	(66)
Profit before tax	1,446
Taxation	(259)
Profit for the year	1,187

Dividends announced and paid were £300,000.

Required:
Prepare a value added statement for the year ended 31 March this year.

The solution to this question can be found at the back of the book on page 480.

Inflation accounting and reporting

We saw in Chapter 2 that there is an assumption in accounting that money, which is the unit of measurement, will remain stable over time. This, however, is an unrealistic assumption as the value of money changes. Usually, it is inflation that is the culprit. This occurs when the general purchasing power of money is reduced because of a rise in prices. Occasionally, however, it is because of deflation, which occurs when the general purchasing power of money is increased because of a fall in prices.

The measurement of financial performance and position is complicated by changes in the value of money and this, in turn, can undermine the usefulness of financial statements. In the following sections, we focus on the distorting effect of inflation as it is this, rather than deflation, that has been the more persistent problem over the years. We shall see that inflation results in an overstatement of profit and an inadequate portrayal of financial position. We shall also consider two broad approaches that attempt to correct for the distorting effects of inflation in the financial statements.

Inflation and profit measurement

During a period of inflation, profit tends to be overstated. This is because time elapses between buying a particular resource and its subsequent use. Inventories are a good example of this problem, as illustrated in Example 10.4 below.

Example 10.4

Kostova Car Sales Ltd acquired a new Mercedes motor car for £25,000 as part of its showroom inventories. The car was held for three months before being sold to a customer for £30,000. The cost of replacing the vehicle from the manufacturer increased during the three-month inventories holding period to £26,250. This was in line with the general rate of inflation for that period. What is the profit made on the sale of the motor car?

The conventional approach to measuring profit is to match the selling price of the vehicle with the original cost of acquisition. Thus, the conventionally derived profit will be:

	£
Sale of motor car	30,000
Cost of acquisition	(25,000)
Profit	5,000

Where the value of money is constant, this approach can produce a valid result. Where, however, prices are rising, there is a problem. The original acquisition cost will understate the resources consumed. During the inventories holding period, the cost of replacing the car increased in line with the rate of inflation. (This is to say that the *average* purchasing power of money, as measured by the general rate of inflation, and the *specific* purchasing power of money, as measured by changes in the cost of the car, decreased by the same amount during the inventories holding period.) Given this loss of purchasing power, the original cost of the car is no longer a meaningful measure of the resources consumed during the period. It would be more realistic to calculate the profit for the period by taking the difference between the selling price and cost of the new car *expressed in current terms*.

→

Example 10.4 continued

This means the inflation-adjusted profit will be:

	£
Sale of motor car	30,000
Current purchase cost of car	(26,250)
Profit	3,750

We can see that, by substituting the original cost with the current purchase cost of the car, the profit for the period is lower. It can be argued that, unless this is done, profits will be overstated.

The problem of time elapsing between the acquisition of a resource and its ultimate use is even more acute in the case of non-current assets. A non-current asset, such as a building, may be held for many years and the income statement for each of these years will be charged with its depreciation. Where this charge is based on the acquisition (historic) cost of the asset, it will become increasingly out of date and so will not reflect the resources consumed during the period. Unless revenues are matched with depreciation charges expressed in current terms, profits will be overstated.

Inflation and financial position

During a period of rising prices, financial statements based on historic cost do not adequately portray financial position. There are three potentially serious problems:

● an erosion of the equity base may not be clearly recognised;
● the assets of the business will tend to be understated; and
● any gains and losses from holding monetary items will not be recognised.

Below we consider each of these problems.

Maintaining the equity base

If the owners are to maintain the purchasing power of their investment and the business is to maintain its scale of operations, the equity base of the business must be kept intact. There is a risk, however, that inflation will erode this base and that the statement of financial position will fail to indicate that this erosion has occurred. To illustrate this point, let us consider Example 10.5.

Example 10.5

Habbad Enterprises sells software packages to small businesses. The statement of financial position of the business at the beginning of a period is:

Statement of financial position at beginning of the period

	£
ASSETS	
Inventories (20 packages @ £100)	2,000
EQUITY	
Opening equity	2,000

During the period, the business managed to sell all of the software packages for cash for £150 each. The conventionally derived profit for the period would be £1,000 (that is, 20 × £(150 − 100)) and the statement of financial position at the end of the period would be:

Statement of financial position at the end of the period

	£
ASSETS	
Cash (20 × £150)	3,000
EQUITY	
Opening equity	2,000
Profit for the period	1,000
	3,000

When prices are constant, it would be possible for Habbad Enterprises to distribute the whole of the reported profit for the period to the owners and still retain the equity base intact. That is, the distribution would not have an adverse effect on the purchasing power of the owners' investment in the business, or the ability of the business to maintain its scale of operations. Following the distribution of profits, £2,000 would still remain, representing the equity at the start of the period.

Let us assume, however, that the general rate of inflation during the period was 10 per cent and the cost of the software packages increased in line with this rate. To ensure that the owners' investment in the business is kept intact and the business is able to continue its current scale of operations, it would not now be possible to distribute all of the profits as conventionally measured.

Activity 10.11

What amount of profit do you think could be distributed to the owners of Habbad Enterprises without any adverse effect on the equity base?

As the general rate of inflation was 10 per cent during the period, and the cost of software packages increased in line with this rate, the equity base must be increased by this amount to preserve the owners' investment and to ensure that the existing scale of operations can be maintained. The equity at the end of the period should, therefore, be

$$£2,000 + (10\% \times £2,000) = £2,200$$

As the equity at the end of the period is £3,000, the amount that can be distributed will be

$$£3,000 - £2,200 = £800$$

Calculating profit by matching revenue with the cost of purchases expressed in current terms will also provide a measure of the amount that can be safely distributed to owners. Hence:

	£
Sales revenue (20 @ £150)	3,000
Cost of packages in current terms (20 @ £110)	(2,200)
Profit	800

Maintaining the equity base and profit measurement are really two sides of the same coin. Profit can be defined as the amount that may be distributed to the owners without eroding the equity base.

Reporting assets

During a period of rising prices, the acquisition (historic) cost of assets acquired becomes outdated. Current values will be higher and so reporting assets using their original costs will tend to understate financial position: the higher the rate of inflation, the greater this understatement.

It is worth remembering that assets held at the end of an accounting period will normally be acquired at different dates. Equipment (a non-current asset), for example, may be held at the end of an accounting period and acquired as follows:

Equipment at cost

	£
Acquired 31 March 2004	38,000
Acquired 30 June 2007	54,000
Acquired 20 September 2009	62,000
	154,000

During a period of inflation, the purchasing power of the pound will be quite different at each acquisition date. The total cost of this group of assets (£154,000) appearing on the statement of financial position will, therefore, be meaningless. In effect, the pounds spent at the various dates represent different currencies, each with different purchasing power.

Activity 10.12

What will be the effect of inflation on the calculation of key profitability ratios such as the operating profit margin and return on capital employed (ROCE)?

As profit is normally overstated during a period of inflation, profitability ratios will tend to be higher. Where profit is related to capital employed (net assets), such as in the ROCE ratio, this problem is compounded. This is because the capital employed (net assets) of the business tends to be understated.

Monetary items

Some items appearing on a statement of financial position have a fixed number of pounds assigned to them. The particular amount may be fixed by contract or by statute and will not change as a result of inflation. These are known as **monetary items**.

Activity 10.13

Can you think of any assets or liabilities appearing on a statement of financial position that would be categorised as monetary items?

Examples of monetary assets would be trade receivables and cash. Examples of monetary liabilities would be loans, bank overdrafts, trade payables and tax owing.

It is important to identify monetary items as holding monetary assets during a period of inflation will result in a loss of purchasing power. Holding monetary liabilities, on the other hand, will lead to a gain. Example 10.6 illustrates this point.

Example 10.6

A business holds a constant £1,000 in cash during a year when inflation is at the rate of 20 per cent. As a result, the purchasing power of the cash held will be lower at the end of the year than at the beginning. Those goods and services which would have cost £1,000 at the beginning of the period would, on average, cost £1,200 by the end of the period. This represents a loss of purchasing power of £200 (in terms of end-of-period £s) over the period.

This loss of purchasing power will have a real effect on the business's ability to preserve the capital invested by the owners and on its ability to maintain its scale of operations.

The reverse situation will apply where a monetary liability is held during a period of inflation. The liability will be reduced, in real terms, and so the owners will make a gain at the expense of the lenders. These monetary gains and losses may be significant but will not be reported in the conventional financial statements. This is because money is the unit of measurement and it cannot measure changes in its own purchasing power.

Reporting the effects of inflation

The distorting effects of inflation on the conventional financial statements can be severe. Even relatively low inflation rates can have a significant cumulative effect over time. To combat the problem, various methods of accounting for inflation have been proposed and there has been much debate as to which should be adopted. At the heart of the debate lies the problem of equity maintenance and, in particular, how equity maintenance should be defined. By resolving this problem, other problems, such as the way in which profit is measured and how assets should be reported, can then be resolved.

Approaches to equity maintenance

Two broad approaches to equity maintenance have competed for acceptance. These are now discussed.

Maintaining the owners' investment

The first approach is concerned with ensuring that the *general purchasing power of the owners' investment in the business* is maintained during a period of inflation. To do this, a general price index, such as the Retail Price Index (RPI), is used to measure changes in the purchasing power of the pound. (A general price index is constructed by taking a basket of goods and services at a particular point in time and expressing their total cost at a base value of 100. The prices of these goods and services are then measured regularly over time and any changes are expressed in relation to the base value.) A set of financial statements is then prepared using the price index measures for different dates.

Financial transactions occurring at different dates will be expressed in terms of their purchasing power at a single, common date – the end of the accounting period. This is done by adjusting for the change in the price index between the date of the transaction and the end of the accounting period. Profit available for distribution will be derived by expressing both the revenue received and the cost of the goods sold for the period in terms of their current (end-of-accounting-period) purchasing power. The cost of assets acquired will also be expressed in terms of their current purchasing power.

→   To illustrate how **current (or constant) purchasing power (CPP) accounting** works, let us look at Example 10.7.

Example 10.7

Konides and Co. commenced trading on 1 August when the RPI stood at 110. The conventional financial statements of the business showed the opening statement of financial position as follows:

Statement of financial position as at 1 August

	£
ASSETS	
Cash	280,000
EQUITY	
Opening equity	280,000

On 1 August, inventories were purchased for cash at a cost of £200,000 and land was acquired at a cost of £80,000. The inventories were sold on 31 August for £250,000 cash when the RPI stood at 121. No other transactions took place during the month.

The CPP profit for the period is calculated by matching revenues and costs of goods sold *after* the amounts have been expressed in terms of their purchasing power at the end of August. Thus, the CPP income statement will be as follows.

CPP income statement for the period to 31 August

	CPP £
Sales revenue (250,000 × 121/121) (Note 1)	250,000
Cost of sales (200,000 × 121/110) (Note 2)	(220,000)
Profit for the period	30,000

Notes:
1 The sales revenue is already expressed in terms of current purchasing power as the sale of inventories took place on the last day of the accounting period.
2 The cost of sales figure is adjusted as the inventories were acquired at an earlier date. [Note that where there are lots of sales and purchases that accrue evenly over the period, an average index for the period is used as the denominator (bottom figure) when making adjustments.]

The CPP statement of financial position at the end of August will be as follows.

CPP statement of financial position as at 31 August

	CPP £
ASSETS	
Non-current assets	
Land (£80,000 × 121/110) (Note 1)	88,000
Current assets	
Cash (Note 2)	250,000
Total assets	338,000
EQUITY	
Equity (£280,000 × 121/110) (Note 3)	308,000
Retained earnings	30,000
Total equity	338,000

Notes:

1 The value for land has been adjusted to reflect changes in the purchasing power of the pound since the date of acquisition.
2 Cash has not been adjusted as it is a monetary item that stays fixed irrespective of changes in the purchasing power of the pound. (There is no loss on holding cash during the period as it was received at the end of the month.)
3 To maintain the equity base, the opening equity will have to be increased by £280,000 × 121/110 = CPP£308,000. This has been achieved and so the owners' investment in the business has been maintained.

Activity 10.14

We have seen that maintaining the owners' investment relies on the use of a *general* price index. Can you think of a problem with this?

The main problem is that a general price index may not reflect the particular cost of goods and services for individual owners.

Maintaining business operations

The second approach to maintaining equity intact is concerned with ensuring that the *business is able to maintain its scale of operations*. To do this, the specific price changes that affect the business must be taken into account when preparing the financial statements. **Current cost accounting (CCA)** is an important method of accounting for specific price changes. It is mainly, but not exclusively, based on the current cost of replacing an item. In other words, the current costs rather than the historic costs of items are reported.

Under CCA, the profit available for distribution is normally calculated by matching revenue with the cost of replacing the goods that were sold. In many cases, price changes that affect a business will not correspond to general price changes occurring within the economy (although, for the sake of convenience, we assumed in earlier examples that the specific price of goods changed in line with the general rate of inflation).

Example 10.8

Referring to Konides and Co. (see Example 10.7 on pages 380–381), let us assume that the cost of replacing the inventories sold rose by 20 per cent and the land rose by 5 per cent during August. Using the specific purchasing power approach to accounting for inflation, the profit for the period would be:

CCA income statement for the period to 31 August

	£
Sales revenue	250,000
Cost of sales (£200,000 + (20% × £200,000))	(240,000)
Profit for the period	10,000

We can see that the cost of sales is increased by 20 per cent to reflect the current replacement cost of the goods sold.

CCA statement of financial position as at 31 August

	£
ASSETS	
Non-current assets	
Land (£80,000 + (5% × £80,000) (Note 1)	84,000
Current assets	
Cash (Note 2)	250,000
Total assets	334,000
EQUITY	
Equity (£280,000 + £4,000 + £40,000) (Note 3)	324,000
Retained earnings	10,000
Total equity	334,000

Notes:

1 Land has been adjusted to reflect changes in replacement cost since the date of acquisition.
2 Cash has not been adjusted as it is already shown at replacement cost.
3 To maintain the equity base, the opening equity must be increased to reflect the increase in the replacement cost of the land (£4,000) and inventories (£40,000). That is (£280,000 + £4,000 + £40,000) = £324,000. This allows the business to maintain its scale of operations. Konides and Co. could pay out £10,000 to its owners and still be left with £240,000 to replace the inventories just sold. Thus it would be able to maintain the same level of operations.

Activity 10.15

We have seen that CCA regards maintaining the operating capacity of the business as important. Can you think of any circumstances where it would not be important?

There would be no point in maintaining operating capacity if demand for the goods or services produced by the business was falling.

Which method is better?

There is a clear philosophical divide between the two approaches regarding the issue of equity maintenance. We have seen that the CPP approach seeks to protect the general purchasing power of the owners' investment, so that the owners would still have the same command over goods and services generally. The CCA approach, on the other hand, seeks to maintain the scale of business operations, so that the business can continue operating at the same level. Choosing between the two approaches will inevitably involve a value judgement as to whether it is the owners' investment or the business entity that is of paramount importance.

It could be argued that the two approaches are not mutually exclusive and that annual financial reports could incorporate both. In other words, the business could produce CPP, CCA and historic cost financial statements. This would provide users with a fuller picture. This, however, ignores, or at least underplays, the reporting costs involved and the problems likely to be created for less sophisticated users of financial statements.

The two approaches (CPP and CCA) reflect, to some extent, the familiar tension in accounting between reliability and relevance. The CPP approach is often commended for its reliability. The historic cost of items is normally used as the basis for making adjustments and the adjustments are made using an objective index. The relevance of some of the CPP information produced, however, is questionable. In Example 10.7 above we saw that land had been adjusted to take account of the general rise in prices. We also saw, however, that the current value (replacement cost) of the land did not rise in line with the general rate of inflation. We may well ask, therefore, what is the point of reporting the CPP figure relating to the land? How can it be used for decision-making purposes?

The CCA approach is often commended for its relevance. The current value of land appearing on the statement of financial position, for example, may help in decisions as to whether to hold or to sell this item. The reliability of the information, however, may be an issue, particularly where assets are unique and where there is no market for them. Sometimes, the spectre is raised of unscrupulous directors manipulating CCA figures to portray a picture of financial health that they would like users to see. This risk, however, may be mitigated by hiring independent, professional valuers to provide the CCA information.

CPP and CCA differ in their choice of measurement unit. The CPP approach abandons money as the unit of measurement. Instead, items are expressed in terms of pounds of current purchasing power. Many users, however, may find this measurement unit difficult to understand and so may struggle to interpret the significance of CPP financial statements. The CCA approach, on the other hand, continues to use money as the unit of measurement. (A consequence of using different measurement units is that the profit calculated under each approach cannot be easily compared.)

The vital importance of money for business transactions, and for accounting measurement, cannot be overstated. It is, after all, money that is received from customers and that is used to pay dividends, suppliers, taxes and so on. This means that, if the CPP approach is adopted, it can only provide information in the form of supplementary reports. The conventional financial statements, on which the CPP adjustments are based, will remain the centrepiece of financial reporting. CCA financial statements, on the other hand, could replace, rather than be supplementary to, the conventional financial statements.

Activity 10.16

Now that we have considered the two broad approaches to dealing with inflation, can you think of any arguments for adopting neither and, instead, sticking with financial statements based on historic costs? Try to think of at least three arguments.

Various arguments exist, including the following:

- Historic cost accounting is a 'tried and tested' approach with which users are familiar.
- It provides objective, verifiable information that can help reassure users of the integrity of the financial statements.
- It is based on actual transactions that have been carried out.
- It avoids some of the key weaknesses of CPP and CCA. (For example, it uses money as the unit of measurement and does not rely on valuations that may prove to be incorrect.)
- There is a lack of unanimity concerning which of the two approaches to dealing with inflation should be adopted.

You may have thought of others.

The inflation accounting debate has lost its intensity in recent years as most of the industrialised world has enjoyed relatively low rates of inflation. Accounting regulators have therefore given the issue low priority and have, instead, grappled with more pressing issues.

The weaknesses of the historic cost approach, however, are widely recognised. Currently, a number of international accounting standards either allow or require current values to be used instead of historic costs. It is possible that further progress in developing a conceptual framework for accounting will see current values taking centre stage in the measurement of profit and the portrayal of financial position.

Summary

The main points of this chapter may be summarised as follows:

Developments in financial reporting

- Initially, financial reports were unregulated and were only prepared in response to investors' demands for information.
- Abuses arising from the provision of unregulated reports led to financial reporting regulation and the need for independent audit.
- Financial reporting regulation from government, and more recently from standard-setters, has increased dramatically over the past 150 years.
- In the future the challenge is to provide better, rather than more, regulation.

Segmental reports

- Segmental reports disaggregate information on the financial statements to help users to achieve a better understanding of financial health.
- An operating segment is defined by the IASB using the 'management approach'.

- IFRS 8 requires certain information relating to each segment to be shown.
- The way in which an operating segment is defined can hinder comparisons of segments between businesses.

Business review

- A business review is a narrative report that requires the directors to provide a balanced and comprehensive analysis of the development and performance of the business. It should also set out the principal risks.
- In the UK, the ASB has issued a Reporting Standard (RS 1) that provides useful guidance when producing a business review.

Interim financial statements

- Interim financial statements may be viewed as supplements to the annual financial statements or as separate financial statements in their own right.
- The integral method of interim profit measurement reflects the predictive role of interim financial statements. It aims to smooth out annual expenses between interim periods in order to enhance the ability of interim statements to help users to predict annual profit.
- The discrete method of interim profit measurement reflects the role of interim financial statements in both confirming past predictions and predicting the future. It uses the same accounting policies and methods as those used for annual financial statements.
- IAS 34 favours the discrete method but requires the tax rate applied to interim profit to reflect the average effective tax rate for the year.
- IAS 34 sets out minimum disclosure requirements for interim reports. These consist of condensed financial statements and explanatory notes.

Value added statements

- Value added = total outputs less total inputs.
- The VAS consists of two parts: a calculation of value added and a description of how value added was applied.
- The VAS has a number of problems, including the team concept, team membership and the classification of items.
- Within a capitalist economy, value added has only limited usefulness as a measure of wealth creation.

Inflation accounting and reporting

- Inflation tends to lead to an overstatement of profit.
- Inflation undermines the portrayal of financial position. Problems include obscuring erosion of the equity base, understatement of asset values, and failure to show gains and losses on holding monetary items.
- Two broad approaches to accounting for inflation have been proposed. Each reflects a different view about how equity is maintained.
- Current purchasing power (CPP) accounting focuses on the general purchasing power of the owners' investment.
- Current cost accounting (CCA) focuses on maintaining a business's scale of operations.

→ **Key terms**

segmental financial reports   p. 354
transfer price   p. 357
integral method   p. 364
discrete method   p. 364
value added statement (VAS)   p. 366

monetary items   p. 378
current (or constant) purchasing
   power (CPP) accounting   p. 380
current cost accounting (CCA)
   p. 381

References

1   Armitage, S. and Marston, C., 'Corporate disclosure, cost of capital and reputation: evidence from finance directors', *British Accounting Review*, December 2008, pp. 314–36.

2   Accounting Standards Board, *A Review of Narrative Reporting by UK Listed Companies in 2006*, January 2007.

3   Accounting Standards Committee, *The Corporate Report*, ASC, 1975.

4   Green, D., 'Towards a theory of interim reports', *Journal of Accounting Research*, Spring 1964, pp. 35–49. (Note: Variations to this integral model can be found in the literature.)

Further reading

If you would like to explore the topics covered in this chapter in more depth, we recommend the following books:

Reporting Statement: Operating and Financial Review, Accounting Standards Board, 2006.

Alexander, D., Britton, A. and Jorissen, A., *International Financial Reporting and Analysis*, 3rd edn, Thomson Learning, 2007, Chapters 4 to 7.

Elliot, B. and Elliot, J., *Financial Accounting and Reporting*, 13th edn, Financial Times Prentice Hall, 2009, Chapters 3 to 5.

IASC Foundation Education, *A Guide through International Financial Reporting Standards*, September 2009, IFRS 8 and IAS 34.

Morley, M., *The Value Added Statement*, Gee Publishing, 1978.

Review questions

Solutions to these questions can be found at the back of the book on pages 488–489.

10.1 'Including a VAS as part of the annual financial reports will undermine their credibility.' What might be the basis for such criticism and do you think that it is valid?

10.2 'CCA is not a method of accounting for inflation. There is really only one method and that is CPP.' What might be the justification for such a statement?

10.3 Can you think of any drawbacks in providing interim financial statements for users?

10.4 What problems does a user of segmental financial statements face when seeking to make comparisons between businesses?

Exercises

Exercises 10.5 to 10.8 are more advanced than 10.1 to 10.4. Those with coloured numbers have solutions at the back of the book, starting on page 517.

If you wish to try more exercises, visit the students' side of the Companion Website.

10.1 It has been suggested that too much information might be as bad as too little information for users of annual reports. Explain.

10.2 'The value added statement simply rearranges information contained within the conventional income statement. As a result it is of little value to users.' Discuss the validity of this statement.

10.3 The following information has been taken from the accounts of Buttons Ltd for the year ended 30 September.

	£
Revenue	950,000
Materials	(220,000)
Wages and salaries	(160,000)
Other expenses	(95,000)
Depreciation	(80,000)
Operating profit	395,000
Interest	(45,000)
Profit before taxation	350,000
Taxation	(110,000)
Profit for the year	240,000

During the year a dividend of £120,000 was announced and paid.

Required:
(a) Prepare a value added statement for Buttons Ltd for the year ended 30 September.
(b) State and comment upon the reasons why a business may present a value added statement to its shareholders in addition to an income statement.

10.4 Refer to your answer to Exercise 10.3 above. Calculate ratios that you believe could be used to interpret the VAS for Buttons Ltd. Explain the purpose of each ratio.

10.5 Segmental information relating to Dali plc for the year to 31 December 2009 is shown below.

	Car parts £m	Aircraft parts £m	Boat parts £m	Total £m
Revenues from external customers	360	210	85	655
Inter-segment revenues	95	40	–	135
Interest revenue	34	–	–	34
Interest expense	–	28	8	36
Depreciation	80	55	15	150
Reportable segment profit	20	24	18	62
Other material non-cash items				
Impairment of assets	–	39	–	39
Reportable segment assets	170	125	44	339
Expenditures for reportable segment:				
Non-current assets	28	23	26	77
Reportable segment liabilities	85	67	22	174

Required:

Analyse the performance of each of the three main business segments for the year and comment on your results.

10.6 Alkrom plc, an oil trader, commenced trading on 1 January and had the following opening statement of financial position.

Statement of financial position as at 1 January

	£m
ASSETS	
Cash	20.0
EQUITY	
Opening equity	20.0

On 1 January Alkrom plc acquired offices at a cost of £4m and 320,000 barrels of oil at £50 per barrel: both acquisitions were paid for immediately. The company held on to the oil as oil prices were expected to rise in the following months. On 31 March all the oil was sold on credit for £60 per barrel.

The RP1 stood at 115 on 1 January and 120 on 31 March.

Required:

Prepare a CPP income statement for the three-month period to 31 March and a CPP statement of financial position as at 31 March. (Ignore taxation and depreciation and work to one decimal place.)

10.7   Segmental information relating to Turner plc for the year to 30 April 2010 is shown below.

	Software £m	Electronics £m	Engineering £m	Totals £m
Revenues from external customers	250	230	52	532
Inter-segment revenues	45	25	–	70
Interest revenue	18	–	–	18
Interest expense	–	25	–	25
Depreciation	60	35	10	105
Reportable segment profit	10	34	12	56
Other material non-cash items				
Impairment of assets	–	5	–	5
Reportable segment assets	140	90	34	264
Expenditures for reportable segment:				
Non-current assets	22	12	10	44
Reportable segment liabilities	55	38	4	97

Required:

Analyse the performance of each of the three main business segments for the year and comment on your results.

10.8   Obtain a copy of the business review for two separate companies within the same industry. Compare the usefulness of each. In answering this question, consider the extent to which each of the two business reviews incorporate the recommendations made by the Accounting Standards Board in RS 1.

11

Governing a company

Introduction

We saw in Chapter 4 that corporate governance, which concerns the way in which companies are directed and controlled, has become an important issue. Strenuous efforts have been made in recent years to improve standards of corporate governance, particularly for large listed companies. In this final chapter, we consider the framework of rules that has been created to try to protect the interests of shareholders. We also consider some of the key issues and problems associated with monitoring and controlling the behaviour of directors.

Learning outcomes

When you have completed this chapter, you should be able to:

- discuss the need for corporate governance rules and the principles upon which such rules should be based;

- explain the role and composition of the board of directors and discuss the issues and problems associated with the roles of chairman and non-executive director;

- describe the audit process and the contribution of the key players to this process;

- explain the main issues and problems associated with the remuneration of directors;

- discuss the importance of shareholder involvement in the corporate governance process and outline the different forms of shareholder involvement that may be found.

Corporate governance

We saw in Chapter 4 that with large companies there tends to be a separation of ownership from day-to-day control of the business. A conflict of interest can, therefore, arise between directors and shareholders. There is a risk that directors will pursue their own interests rather than those of shareholders. If this occurs, it is clearly a problem for the shareholders; however, it may also be a problem for society as a whole. Where investors feel that their funds are likely to be mismanaged, they will be reluctant to invest. A shortage of funds will mean that companies can make fewer investments. Furthermore, the costs of finance will increase as companies compete for what funds are available. Thus, a lack of concern for shareholders can have a profound effect on the performance of individual companies and, with this, the health of the economy. To avoid these problems, most competitive market economies have a framework of rules to help monitor and control the behaviour of directors.

These rules are usually based around three guiding principles:

- *Disclosure*. This lies at the heart of good corporate governance. An OECD report (see reference 1 at the end of the chapter) summed up the benefits of disclosure as follows:

  > Adequate and timely information about corporate performance enables investors to make informed buy-and-sell decisions and thereby helps the market reflect the value of a corporation (company) under present management. If the market determines that present management is not performing, a decrease in stock [share] price will sanction management's failure and open the way to management change.

- *Accountability*. This involves defining the roles and duties of the directors and establishing an adequate monitoring process. In the UK, company law requires that the directors of a company act in the best interests of the shareholders. This means, among other things, that they must not try to use their position and knowledge to make gains at the expense of the shareholders. As we saw in Chapter 5, the law also requires larger companies to have their annual financial statements independently audited. The purpose of an independent audit is to lend credibility to the financial statements prepared by the directors. We shall consider this point in more detail later in the chapter.

- *Fairness*. Directors should not be able to benefit from access to 'inside' information that is not available to shareholders. As a result, both the law and the London Stock Exchange place restrictions on the ability of directors to buy and sell the shares of the company. One example of these restrictions is that the directors cannot buy or sell shares immediately before the announcement of the annual trading results of the company or before the announcement of a significant event, such as a planned merger or the loss of the chief executive.

These principles are set out in Figure 11.1.

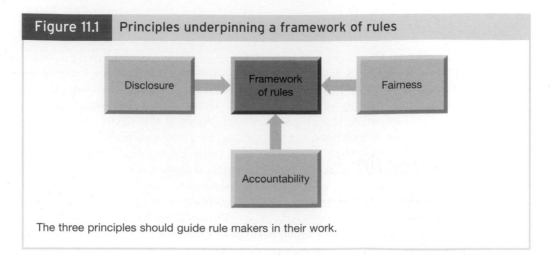

Figure 11.1   Principles underpinning a framework of rules

The three principles should guide rule makers in their work.

Strengthening the framework of rules

The number of rules designed to safeguard shareholders has increased considerably over the years. This has been in response to weaknesses in corporate governance procedures, which have been exposed through well-publicised business failures and frauds, excessive pay increases to directors and evidence that some financial reports were being 'massaged' so as to mislead shareholders. (This last point about 'creative accounting' was discussed in some detail in Chapter 5.)

Many believe, however, that the shareholders must shoulder some of the blame for any weaknesses. Not all shareholders in large companies are private individuals owning just a few shares each. In fact, ownership, by market value, of the shares listed on the London Stock Exchange is dominated by investing institutions such as insurance businesses, banks, pension funds and so on (see Real World 11.14 on pages 432–433). These are often massive operations, owning large quantities of the shares of the companies in which they invest. These institutional investors employ specialist staff to manage their portfolios of shares in various companies. It has been argued that the large institutional shareholders, despite their size and relative expertise, have not been very active in corporate governance matters. Thus, there has been little monitoring of directors. We shall see in a later section, however, that things seem to be changing. There is increasing evidence that institutional investors are becoming more proactive in relation to the companies in which they hold shares.

The board of directors

Before we consider corporate governance issues in more detail, it might be helpful to clarify the role and composition of the board of directors. The board governs the company on behalf of the shareholders and is responsible for promoting their interests. It is led by a chairman and, for a listed public company, the board will normally include both executive and non-executive directors.

The chairman

→ The **chairman** is the senior director. This individual is elected by the other directors and chairs board meetings.

Executive directors

→ **Executive directors** are salaried employees with senior management responsibilities. The finance director of most large companies, for example, is a full-time employee. In addition to being a board member and taking part in board decisions, this individual is responsible for managing the finance function within the company.

Non-executive directors

→ **Non-executive directors** act purely as directors; they are not full-time employees of the company. They often have business experience gained from past or present activities concerned with businesses and/or administration, apart from the company concerned. Many non-executive directors are, at the same time, directors of other companies. The role of non-executive directors has taken on increasing significance in recent years and reflects the increased importance given to corporate governance issues.

→   The **UK Corporate Governance Code** draws a distinction between non-executive directors and *independent* non-executive directors. The term 'independent' in this context implies freedom from other significant links to the company, to its directors and to major shareholders. According to the UK Code, for example, a non-executive director could not be regarded as independent if that person had been an employee of the company concerned in the previous five years.

Both types of non-executive, however, should need to take an independent attitude towards their roles. Independence of mind is vital for any non-executive director. They should be able to bring an objectivity of approach that can be difficult for executive directors whose working life is so bound up in the affairs of the company. Indeed, this is a major reason for having non-executive directors.

To try to ensure an effective presence of independent non-executive directors, the UK Code states that, for large listed companies, at least half the board, excluding the chairman, should consist of independent non-executive directors. The chairman should also be an independent non-executive director, at the time of being appointed. For smaller listed companies, at least two independent non-executive directors should be on the board.

Although executive directors are much more deeply involved in running a company than non-executive directors, both have the same legal obligations towards the shareholders of the company. The role of the non-executive directors will be discussed in more detail later in the chapter.

The UK Corporate Governance Code

During the 1990s there was a real effort by the accountancy profession and the London Stock Exchange to address the problems of poor corporate governance mentioned earlier. A Code of Best Practice on Corporate Governance emerged in 1992. This was concerned with accountability and financial reporting. In 1995, a separate code of practice emerged which dealt with directors' pay and conditions. These two codes were revised, 'fine tuned' and amalgamated to produce the Combined Code, which was issued in 1998. Every few years, the impact and effectiveness of the Code has been reviewed and this has resulted in revisions being made. In 2010, the Combined Code changed its name to the 'UK Corporate Governance Code'.

The UK Corporate Governance Code has the backing of the London Stock Exchange. This means that companies listed on the London Stock Exchange must 'comply or explain'. That is, they must comply with the requirements of the UK Code or must give their shareholders good reason why they do not. Failure to do one or other of these can lead to the company's shares being suspended from listing.

Activity 11.1

Why might this be an important sanction against a non-compliant company?

A major advantage of a Stock Exchange listing is that it enables investors to sell their shares whenever they wish. A company that is suspended from listing would find it hard and, therefore, expensive to raise funds from investors because there would be no ready market for the shares.

An example of a failure to comply with the code is given in Real World 11.3 on page 400.

The UK Code sets out a number of principles relating to such matters as the role of the directors, their relations with shareholders, and their accountability. **Real World 11.1** outlines some of the more important of these.

Real World 11.1

The UK Corporate Governance Code

The key elements of the UK Code are as follows:

- Every listed company should have a board of directors that is collectively responsible for its success.
- There should be a clear division of responsibilities between the chairman and the chief executive officer of the company to try to ensure that a single person does not have unbridled power.
- There should be an appropriate balance of skills, experience, independence and knowledge to enable it to carry out its duties effectively.
- The board should receive timely information that is of sufficient quality to enable it to carry out its duties. All board members should refresh their skills regularly and new board members should receive induction.
- Appointments to the board should be the subject of rigorous, formal and transparent procedures and should be drawn from a broad talent pool.
- All directors should submit themselves for re-election at regular intervals, subject to satisfactory performance.
- All directors should allocate sufficient time to the company's business to carry out their duties effectively.

- Remuneration levels should be sufficient to attract, retain and motivate directors of the appropriate quality and should take account of individual and company performance.
- There should be formal and transparent procedures for developing policy on directors' remuneration.
- The board should present a balanced and understandable assessment of the company's position and prospects.
- The board should try to ensure that a satisfactory dialogue with shareholders occurs.
- Boards should use the annual general meeting to communicate with investors and encourage their participation.
- Institutional shareholders should use their votes and enter into a dialogue with the company based on a mutual understanding of objectives.
- The board should define the company's risk appetite and tolerance and should maintain a sound risk management system.
- Formal and transparent arrangements for applying financial reporting and internal control principles and for maintaining an appropriate relationship with auditors should be in place.
- The board should undertake a formal and rigorous examination of its own performance each year, which will include its committees and individual directors.

Source: www.fsa.org.uk.

Strengthening the framework of rules in this way has been generally agreed to have improved the quality of information available to shareholders, resulted in better checks on the powers of directors, and provided greater transparency in corporate affairs. However, rules can only be a partial answer. A balance must be struck between the need to protect shareholders and the need to encourage the entrepreneurial spirit of directors – which could be stifled under a welter of rules. This implies that rules should not be too tight, and so unscrupulous directors may still find ways around them.

Activity 11.2

Rules are not the only answer. What could shareholders do to try to ensure that the directors act in the shareholders' best interests?

Two ways are commonly used in practice:

- Shareholders may insist on monitoring closely the actions of the directors and the way in which they use the resources of the company.
- They may impose incentive schemes on directors, which link their pay to changes in shareholder wealth. In this way, the interests of the directors and shareholders will become more closely aligned.

Real World 11.2 provides some idea of the make-up of the board of directors of a major UK retail business, J Sainsbury plc. It is fairly typical for a large listed company.

The Sainsbury's board as at June 2009

Chairman

Sir Philip Hampton   Former group finance director of LloydsTSB Group plc (2002 to 2004)

Non-executive chairman of The Royal Bank of Scotland plc

Non-executive director of Belgacom S A

Chief executive officer (executive director)

Justin King   Non-executive director of Staples Inc

Board member of London Organising Committee of the Olympic games and Paralympic Games

Chief financial officer (executive director)

Darren Shapland   Chairman Sainsbury's bank plc

Formerly Group Finance Director of Carpetright plc

Trading director

Mike Coupe   Former managing director of Iceland Food Stores and director of Big Food Group plc

Independent non-executive director

Val Gooding   Member of BBC's Executive Board

Non-Executive Director of the Lawn Tennis Association

Trustee British Museum

Independent non-executive director

Gary Hughes   Chief financial officer of Gala Coral Group

Independent non-executive director

Bob Stack   Trustee and non-executive director of Earthwatch International

Non-executive Director of IMI plc

Visiting Professor Henley Management College

Senior independent non-executive director

Dr John McAdam   Chairman of Rentokil Initial plc and United Utilities plc

Non-executive director Rolls-Royce Group plc and Sarah Lee Corporation

Independent non-executive director

Anna Ford   Former BBC newsreader

Non-executive director N Brown Group plc

Trustee Royal Botanical Gardens

Independent non-executive director

Mary Harris   Member supervisory board of TNT NV and Unibail-Rodamco S A

Note that of the ten directors, three are executives each with their own clear role in the management of the company. All of the other seven (including the chairman) are independent non-executive directors. Most of the directors also hold directorships of other major companies and/or have senior roles in non-business organisations. They also have experience of management/administration at a high level.

Source: 'The Board', J Sainsbury plc, www.j-sainsburyc. co.uk, June 2009.

Tasks of the board

To try to ensure that the company succeeds in its purpose, the board is charged with various tasks. The main tasks are to:

1 *Decide on the strategic direction of the company.* The degree of involvement in strategy-setting tends to vary between boards. In some cases, the full board will establish the strategic aims but will delegate responsibility for developing a strategic plan to an **executive committee**. This is a committee made up of particular members of the board, which usually includes the **chief executive officer**, who leads the management team, and the other executive directors. Once the committee has developed a plan, it will be put before the full board for approval.

2 *Exercise control.* To try to ensure that things go according to plan and resources are properly allocated, the board must exercise control. This is often done through board committees. Each committee is made up of board members who report to the full board on their progress and findings. The key committees are mentioned below.

   The main areas over which the board must exercise control include:

   ● *Carrying out the strategic plan.* Having developed a strategic plan, the executive committee will usually be charged with its successful implementation.
   ● *Checking the integrity of the financial statements.* The UK Corporate Governance Code states that a separate board committee, known as the **audit committee**, should be set up to promote the reliability of the financial reporting systems.
   ● *Evaluating and managing risk.* Although a separate **risk management committee** may be formed, the audit committee may take on this responsibility.
   ● *Nominating and remunerating directors.* The UK Corporate Governance Code states that a **nomination committee** and a **remuneration committee** should each be established to help provide formal and transparent procedures in these areas.
   ● *Assessing board performance.* Appraisals based on contributions made, or outcomes achieved, should be carried out on individual directors and on the board as a whole.

   The control function of the board will be discussed in more detail in later sections.

3 *Maintain external relations.* The board is responsible for promoting the interests of the company and establishing good relationships with shareholders. Relationships with major shareholders are often helped through informal meetings involving key board members. These meetings, which usually involve a free exchange of views between board members and shareholders, may help the shareholders to adopt a long-term perspective to company performance. They may also help in securing support when the board has to make difficult decisions.

Chairing the board

We have seen that the role of chairman is to lead and manage the board of directors. The chairman should try to ensure that the board operates as an effective decision-making body and that board meetings are conducted in a business-like manner. To fulfil the role, the chairman will normally be expected to

● hold frequent board meetings so that key issues and problems can be dealt with at the appropriate time;
● try to ensure that the board agenda properly reflects the key issues and problems confronting the company;

- provide board members with relevant, reliable and timely information to help in their deliberations;
- provide enough time at board meetings for key issues and problems to be discussed thoroughly;
- allow all directors the opportunity to voice their opinions at board meetings;
- guide discussions so that the focus does not deviate from key strategic issues and problems.

The chairman plays a crucial role in defining the culture of the board and, through this, the company as a whole. It is important, therefore, that the chairman tries to foster a good working relationship between board members by providing a supportive environment where directors feel valued and where a climate of trust prevails.

Activity 11.3

In trying to establish good working relations, should the chairman try to ensure that boardroom conflict is avoided?

No. There are occasions when conflict between board members is beneficial. It can help ensure that issues are thoroughly aired and that important proposals are given proper scrutiny.

The chairman will act as an important link between the board and the shareholders. When the board wishes to inform shareholders of its recent proposals and decisions, the chairman will normally take a lead role. Similarly, when shareholders wish to respond to board proposals and decisions, or to raise concerns, they will often relay their views to the board through the chairman. Good communication skills are, therefore, a vital ingredient of a successful chairman.

Finally, the chairman must try to ensure that board performance is subject to proper scrutiny and that improvements are made where necessary. The performance of individual directors, as well as the board as a whole, should be evaluated on a regular basis, at least annually. The criteria for assessing board performance will be considered in a later section. To try to ensure effective board performance, the UK Code requires the chairman to agree and review development needs with individual directors.

Separating the roles of chairman and CEO

We have seen that the role of the chairman is to lead the board of directors and the role of the chief executive officer (CEO) is to lead the management team. The UK Corporate Governance Code states that both roles should not be occupied by the same individual.

Activity 11.4

What risks are associated with a single individual occupying both roles?

Where the two roles are combined, too much power may be concentrated in the hands of a single individual. This power may be used to dominate the board and to marginalise the contribution of others. It may also be used to plunder the company's resources through excessive pay, bonuses and 'perks'. When the company is performing well these abuses of power may be overlooked, but when things turn sour, questions regarding accountability will inevitably surface. Thus, there is a need to maintain appropriate checks and balances.

Having a separate chairman may provide a number of benefits. The chairman may be a useful source of support for the chief executive when the occasion demands. Where, for example, problems that create controversy among board members arise, they are more likely to be resolved when the chairman and chief executive adopt the same stance. A chairman can also act as a sounding board for new ideas and provide advice for the chief executive. In many cases, chairmen have occupied the position of chief executive at an earlier point in their careers and are older than the chief executive of the company. They are often, therefore, well placed to undertake these supportive roles.

Having a separate chairman may also help in smoothing the path of succession. Where a chief executive leaves the company, the continued presence of the chairman can help to 'steady the ship' and provide a sense of continuity during the period of transition. (See reference 2 at the end of the chapter.) The chairman can also help a newly-appointed chief executive to settle in and to become familiar with the issues and challenges to be faced.

Finally, a separate chairman may help the company to cope more effectively with the demands of modern business. The skills and time required to fulfil both roles are likely to be beyond the capacity of a single individual. It is argued that only by separating the roles can proper attention be given to corporate governance matters and to managing the company.

Is separation always the best solution?

There is little doubt that a powerful chairman/chief executive can create problems for a company. What is less certain, however, is whether a 'one size fits all' approach is the best solution for dealing with this issue. There may be circumstances where combining the roles may be appropriate. A company in difficulties, for example, may benefit from a single, strong leader who has a clear vision and who can act in a decisive and fairly unconstrained manner. A company that has just appointed a young and relatively inexperienced chief executive, on the other hand, may benefit from an experienced non-executive chairman who can support the new appointee.

Those in favour of separating the roles often ignore, or at least underplay, the potential problems of adopting this approach.

Activity 11.5

Can you think of potential problems that may arise from separating the two roles?

Responsibilities may become hazy and this, in turn, may result in a lack of clear direction. There is also a risk that the two individuals occupying the roles simply do not get on. They may have conflicting personalities. They may also have conflicting views over the way in which each role should be carried out and the general direction in which the company should be heading. A breakdown in relationships can lead to endless power struggles, which may badly affect the performance of the company.

Despite considerable pressure to comply with the UK Corporate Governance Code, a number of listed UK companies have a single individual occupying both roles. **Real World 11.3** examines the controversy created for one well-known company by combining the roles.

Real World 11.3

2 for 1 deal at M&S

FT

Marks and Spencer shareholders gave Sir Stuart Rose a bloody nose on Wednesday when more than a fifth of those voting refused to support his elevation to executive chairman. In one of the biggest protest votes in recent City history, 22 per cent of the voting shareholder base abstained or opposed his re-election to the board, making clear their displeasure at its decision to merge the chairman and chief executive roles. The vote at the retailer's annual meeting at the Royal Festival Hall in London challenged his authority as the company tries to recover from last week's shock profit warning.

'The vote shows there is discernible level of unease about what has happened and the company needs to take steps to consult with shareholders about ways of mitigating the unease', said Peter Montagnon of the Association of British Insurers, representing large institutions. 'The company said it wants to strengthen the independent presence on the board and it needs to examine what this means in consultations with shareholders', he said. The company also needs to make clear that it has got succession for Sir Stuart in hand at a reasonably early stage.'

The revolt was bigger than those faced by Arun Sarin of Vodafone in 2006 and Richard Lapthorne of Cable and Wireless last year. Concerns at the M&S board structure have been exacerbated by the sharp downturn in sales and plunging share price. Sir David Michels, deputy chairman, said he was 'sensitive' to shareholders' concerns but insisted that the 'route we chose was the right one . . . We are convinced that history will show we made the right decision.'

Before the vote, Sir Stuart tried to disarm his critics by saying 'I have this week been called the Robert Mugabe of retail, a kitten strangler. I have been accused of having the hide of an armadillo and being arrogant, and today I have been accused of being Gordon Brown. This is a flurry of insults.'

In November 2009, Marks and Spencer plc announced the appointment of a new chief executive, with Sir Stuart Rose staying on as part-time chairman until June 2011. It seems that, in the end, the company took heed of shareholders' concerns.

Source: 'M&S shareholders give Rose a dressing down', Tom Braithwaite, Elizabeth Rigby and Kate Burgess, *Financial Times*, 9 July 2009.

Perhaps a clinching argument in favour of separating the two roles would be that it leads to superior shareholder returns. There is, however, no evidence to support this.

Making separation work

Separating the two roles will only be successful if the two individuals concerned strike up a good working relationship. To maximise the chances of success, the board should appoint to the roles individuals whose personalities appear to mesh. The board should also appoint two individuals with complementary skills and knowledge. (See reference 3 at the end of the chapter). This will help to fill any gaps and should help to build mutual respect between the chairman and chief executive.

The board of directors should try to define the two roles and should make everyone aware of the responsibilities and duties associated with each role. Defining these roles, however, is easier said than done. It is impossible for all situations to be covered. Some overlaps are likely to occur and there is likely to be some uncertainty about who is responsible for certain tasks. This brings the inevitable risk of boundary disputes. Where the company operates in a highly dynamic environment, new tasks are continually emerging and so this will be a particular problem. In this situation, constant renegotiations of the two roles may have to occur. For any chance of success, both parties must enter into any renegotiations with mutual respect for each other's abilities and for the authority vested in each role.

To avoid misunderstanding and to build mutual trust, there should be frequent communications between the two parties. Important information should be shared and there should be no 'surprises'.

Activity 11.6

Will the chairman or the chief executive normally have the most information to share?

As the person responsible for leading the management team, the chief executive will normally have the most information to share. So, it is particularly important for this individual to be open and transparent.

Finally, the chairman, who is often a former chief executive, must resist any temptation to intervene in the management of the business. The role of chairman demands that a different approach be taken. It requires a willingness to operate in the background and to keep ego and ambition firmly in check.

Should the chief executive go on to become chairman?

The UK Corporate Governance Code recommends that the chief executive should not go on to become chairman of the same company.

Activity 11.7

Can you think of a potential problem that may arise from allowing the chief executive to relinquish this post and then become the chairman?

The main risk here is that the individual will be unable to give up the reins of management easily and will still become involved in operating decisions.

The chairman's involvement in day-to-day management issues can create disharmony and can have a detrimental effect on company performance. It can lead to confusion and divided loyalties among the management team and can also undermine the decisions of the current chief executive. There is also a risk, however, that the opposite may occur. The chairman may be too sensitive to the risk of intervening and so may withdraw too far. As a result, the new chief executive may be given too free a hand in managing the company. (See reference 4 at the end of the chapter.)

Allowing the chief executive to become chairman can also increase the risk of defensive behaviour. The new chief executive may feel that points can be scored by criticising the decisions made, and results achieved, when the former chief executive (and now chairman) was managing the company. This is likely to be more of a problem where the new chief executive has been recruited from outside the company and is keen to establish authority. The chairman, on the other hand, may seek to justify past decisions and actions. This may lead to criticism of the new chief executive and attempts to undermine any proposals for change.

Real World 11.4 provides the results of a survey of directors on their attitudes towards this issue.

Real World 11.4

The wrong move

FT

A survey of 430 directors serving on more than 900 boards by Directorbank, a UK specialist recruitment agency, found that 58 per cent of respondents opposed the idea of the chief executive going on to take over the role of chairman.

One said there would be too much baggage, another that they would be too concerned to defend their past record. BA's Lord Marshall, chief executive before becoming chairman of the airline, says he would now come down marginally against making such a transition in the same company. He recognises that at times he has consciously not intervened to give the newcomer 'space', when with hindsight he should have done. 'I certainly found myself biting my tongue. I'd been CEO for thirteen years and a lot of staff continued to look to me as the leader.'

Steve Norris, Jarvis chairman, says moving from chief executive to chairman could be dangerous, especially in private companies. 'I can't tell you the number of people I know who decided they would like to take a "back seat" – that's the expression they use – and hired someone to be chief executive, but actually can never give up driving, and when that happens, that's just lethal; lethal for them and lethal for the business.'

Some of the directors doubted whether the chief executive role was good preparation for chairing the board, which required a 'completely different mindset' to be successful. 'There are a lot of very good chief executives who do make outstanding chairmen,' says Sir Rob Margetts of Legal & General. 'But unquestionably, chief executive-type behaviours, which tend to be control-type behaviours, are not the characteristics you need in a chairman. Or put the other way round, a chairman who has those characteristics and hasn't actually modified them is unlikely to get on very well with his chief executive. . . .'

Source: 'An expert hand behind the scenes', John Willman, *Financial Times*, 30 September 2008.

It seems that few companies allow the chief executive to become chairman. Nevertheless, there may be disadvantages in not doing so.

Activity 11.8

Can you think what these disadvantages might be?

The most important is the loss to the company of the chief executive's expertise and experience. This loss can be particularly severe where the company's operations are unique or highly complex. In these circumstances, recruiting a suitable outside chairman may be extremely difficult. A further disadvantage of not allowing the chief executive to become chairman is that a sense of continuity may be lost.

The role of non-executive directors

Not so long ago, the image of the non-executive director was that of an avuncular figure offering kindly guidance and advice to the board concerning the direction of the company. This was not seen as an unduly onerous role and any time spent on the company's affairs could be confined to board meetings and in perusing background documents for the various agenda items. Whatever truth such an image may have contained, it is not a faithful portrayal of the current role of the non-executive director of a UK listed public company. An important consequence of strengthening corporate governance standards, which was referred to earlier, has been to increase the demands placed on the non-executive directors.

Non-executive directors are expected to contribute towards each of the functions of the board mentioned above and the contribution they make will largely depend on their background, experience and personal qualities. As we have seen, often non-executive directors of a listed public company are, or have been, executive directors of another listed public company and so will usually have experience of the commercial world as well as expertise in a particular field, such as finance or marketing. As a result non-executive directors can often play a valuable role in discussions on strategy. They may make useful suggestions or may constructively challenge the assumptions and decisions of the executive directors.

Activity 11.9

How might the fact that non-executive directors are not engaged in the day-to-day running of the company help in board discussions?

They are more detached from company problems and this allows them to provide a more objective view. This may be of particular value during periods of change or crisis, when an objective view can help executive directors to maintain perspective.

Non-executive directors can also play an important role in monitoring and controlling the activities of the company. In working towards the strategic plan, control mechanisms involving plans, budgets, quality indicators and benchmarking may be used. The experience and skills of non-executive directors may enable them to identify weaknesses in the current control systems and to suggest ways of improving them. They may also be able to highlight areas of poor performance.

Non-executives have an important role in the various board committees that are set up to control the activities of the company. It was mentioned earlier that, to promote the integrity of financial information, an audit committee is usually set up. The UK Corporate Governance Code states that this committee should consist entirely of non-executive directors, the majority of whom should be independent non-executive directors. It was also mentioned earlier that listed companies normally have a remuneration committee that is charged with recommending to the board the remuneration of the executive directors and the chairman. The UK Code states that this committee should also consist of independent non-executive directors. This means that non-executives have enormous influence over the remuneration of executive directors, and where there are performance-related elements, will be involved in setting targets and in monitoring the performance of the executive directors. The roles of both the audit committee and the remuneration committee will be considered in more detail later in the chapter.

Finally, we have seen that listed companies normally have a nominations committee. Its role is to lead the nomination process by identifying the skills, knowledge and experience required for the board and by preparing appropriate job specifications. The UK Code states that this committee should have a majority of independent non-executive directors as members.

The board and large shareholders often maintain a dialogue through informal meetings, which non-executives may attend. This can help them to appreciate the concerns of shareholders. At times, non-executives may become the shareholders' communications channel to the board of directors. Shareholders may be particularly reliant on this channel if they have already voiced concerns to the chairman, or to the executive directors, and have not received satisfactory replies.

Finally, non-executive directors may help to raise the profile of the company. They often enjoy a good reputation within their particular field and may have strong links with a wide range of bodies, including government agencies and foreign companies. These links may be extremely valuable in developing new contacts and in promoting the company's interests.

Role conflict

The different roles that non-executives are expected to play provide potential for conflict. In developing strategy, co-operation between the executive and non-executive directors is essential. All directors are expected to work together as part of a team in pursuit of a common purpose. However, the monitoring role that non-executive directors also have means that they must assess the performance of executive directors. Disputes between executive and non-executive directors can easily arise over the company's financial systems, control systems and remuneration systems. Given this potential conflict, non-executive directors must tread carefully and should retain a certain distance from the executive directors to maintain their independence.

Relations with the executive directors

The potential for disputes may make the non-executive and executive directors wary of each other. Executive directors may resent the presence of non-executives on the board because they believe that the non-executives

- are monitoring their behaviour and, effectively, acting as 'corporate policemen';
- do not fully understand the nature of the company's business; and
- do not devote enough time and effort in carrying out their duties.

Non-executives, on the other hand, may sense that executives are acting in an unhelpful or guarded manner towards them. They may feel that executive directors are seeking to undermine their position by

- withholding key information or reports;
- failing to provide important information at the required time; and
- holding informal meetings on important matters to which the non-executives are not invited.

The chairman of the board can play an important part in overcoming these suspicions and problems.

Activity 11.10

What do you think the chairman could do? (Try to think of at least two possible initiatives the chairman could take.)

The chairman can take various initiatives, such as trying to ensure that the board's procedures are transparent and that informal meetings of cliques are discouraged. Where doubts exist over the competence of particular directors, the chairman should see that appropriate training and development opportunities are made available. To allow any suspicions and problems to be aired, the chairman should arrange meetings between executive and non-executive directors. Finally, the chairman should try to ensure that all directors receive timely and relevant information.

Maintaining independence

There is a danger that non-executive directors will not provide an independent voice. They may come under the influence of the executive directors and fail to challenge decisions and so promote proper accountability. The fact that non-executives are often executive directors of other companies may lead them to develop some empathy with the executive directors on the board.

Activity 11.11

How might shareholders intervene in an attempt to ensure that this risk is avoided, or at least reduced?

Shareholders could become involved in the appointment of the non-executive directors, perhaps by identifying and proposing suitable candidates. Once appointed, regular meetings with shareholders may help to strengthen their independence from the executive directors, as well as their commitment to the shareholders' interests.

The increasing burdens placed on non-executive directors mean that a lot of time must be spent in dealing with company affairs. Some, however, have been accused of accepting too many non-executive director appointments, which undermines their ability to devote time to increasingly complex board issues. The UK Code does not recommend any minimum time commitments for directors, but does state that *all* directors should allocate sufficient time to be able to carry out their duties effectively.

To encourage a diligent attitude, non-executives should be properly rewarded for the time spent on company business. There is a risk, however, of paying non-executives too handsomely for their efforts.

Activity 11.12

What problem may arise from paying non-executive directors large salaries?

It may compromise their independence. Where non-executives are paid fairly modest salaries, based on the time spent carrying out their duties, the amounts will usually form only a small proportion of their total income. This may help them retain a higher degree of independence when making decisions.

There is normally a large gulf between the total remuneration received by part-time, non-executive directors and that of full-time, executive directors. The 2009 annual report for Tesco plc showed that non-executive directors (excluding the chairman) were paid between £10,000 and £129,000 each and executive directors between £1.6 million and £5.1 million each. (These figures exclude those employed for part of the year only.)

Listed companies recognise the increasing burden placed on non-executives and in recent years their pay has been rising. **Real World 11.5** gives an indication of the average fees paid to non-executive directors of the UK's largest listed companies.

Real World 11.5

Time to get on board   FT

Falling share prices and a wave of profit warnings and dividend cuts failed to prevent non-executive directors of FTSE 100 companies from receiving hefty pay increases last year. Fees paid to non-executive directors at all FTSE 100 companies rose 6.3 per cent on average in the 12 months to July 2008, climbing to £57,056, according to Incomes Data Services, the pay specialists. However, some companies froze directors' pay altogether. At those FTSE 100 groups that did deliver an increase, salaries paid to non-executive directors jumped by an average of 15 per cent.

Lloyds Banking Group and Barclays, which both reported share price falls of more than 65 per cent last year, paid a particularly high flat fee to non-executive directors of £65,000 in 2008.

Fees offered to outside directors by Kazakhmys, the struggling mining and metals group, whose shares fell 83 per cent last year, and Vodafone, which saw shares slump 25 per cent, were even grander. Kazakhmys gave £120,000 each to its non-executive directors, while Vodafone offered £110,000.

Source: 'Hefty pay rises for non-executives', Ellen Kelleher, *Financial Times*, 15 February 2009.

The audit process

External audit

→ **External audit** forms an important element of corporate governance. To understand what it entails, we must first be clear about the roles and responsibilities of directors and auditors concerning the published financial statements.

As we saw in Chapter 5, company law requires that the directors prepare annual financial statements that provide a true and fair view of the state of affairs of the company. This will involve

- selecting suitable accounting policies and applying them consistently;
- making estimates and judgements that are prudent and practical;
- stating whether appropriate accounting standards have been adopted; and
- applying the going concern convention where it is appropriate to do so.

The annual financial statements must be published and made available to shareholders, lenders and others. In addition to preparing the annual financial statements, the law also obliges the directors to keep proper accounting records and to safeguard the assets of the company.

External auditors are appointed by, and report to, the shareholders. They are normally an independent firm of accountants and their role is to examine the annual financial statements prepared by the directors. They must assess the reliability of these statements by examining the underlying accounting records and by reviewing the key assumptions and estimates used in their preparation. Following this, the auditors will provide shareholders with an independent opinion as to whether the financial statements provide a true and fair view of the state of affairs of the company and comply with legal and other regulatory requirements. This opinion is contained within an audit report, which becomes part of the published annual report.

The external auditors must inform shareholders of any significant problems that have been unearthed during the audit process and so the audit report must include instances where

- proper accounting records have not been kept;
- information and explanations required to undertake the audit have not been received;
- information specified by the law or by regulatory bodies, such as the UK listing authority, has not been disclosed; and
- the directors' report contains information that is inconsistent with the financial statements.

For companies listed on the London Stock Exchange, the auditors must also review the corporate governance statement, which is also prepared by the directors, to see whether it complies with the provisions of the UK Corporate Governance Code. Where the auditors have no concerns over the reliability and integrity of the financial statements, an 'unqualified' opinion is provided, which should lend credibility to the statements.

Internal audit

Many large companies have an **internal audit** function, although there is no legal requirement to have one. The main purpose of internal audit is to provide the directors with reassurance concerning the reliability of the company's control and financial reporting systems. Internal auditors are employees of the company and so do not have the same independence as external auditors. They will normally report to the directors, who will determine the nature and scope of the internal audit.

Although some variation will be found in practice, internal audit will usually involve a review of

- the internal control systems to see whether they are effective in safeguarding the company's assets and in preventing errors and fraud;

- the accounting systems to see whether they provide reliable information, which meets the needs of management and complies with relevant regulations;
- internal operations and processes to see whether they are efficient and provide value for money.

Real World 11.6 reveals how serious failures in the internal control systems of one major carmaker put its business plan at risk.

Real World 11.6

Losing control at GM

Struggling carmaker General Motors has warned that ineffective internal controls over financial reporting might make it difficult for it to execute on its business plan.

GM said weaknesses include poor 'maintenance of records that, in reasonable detail, accurately and fairly reflect the transactions and dispositions of the assets of the corporation', as well as failing to ensure that 'receipts and expenditures of the corporation are being made only in accordance with authorisations of management and directors of the corporation'.

GM said that its management recognised the problems and is taking steps to correct them – but declined to comment further on the matter.

Source: 'Ineffective Internal Controls Hurting GM', AccountancyAge.com, 16 May 2007.

In recent years, the risk management processes of a company have been identified as a further element of good corporate governance. An important consequence of this has been to widen the remit of the internal audit function to include a review of these processes. Thus, internal auditors are now often expected to provide assurances to the directors concerning the adequacy and effectiveness of the company's risk management procedures. They may also be involved in promoting a risk management philosophy within the company through employee risk awareness and risk management programmes.

Real World 11.7 sets out the particular internal controls and risk management systems used to protect shareholder wealth at Marks and Spencer plc, the retailer, during the 2009 financial year.

Real World 11.7

Keeping control at M&S

Internal control

The Board maintains control and direction over appropriate strategic, financial, operational and compliance issues. It has put in place an organisational structure with formally defined lines of responsibility and delegation of authority.

There are also established procedures for financial planning, capital expenditure, information and reporting systems and for monitoring the Group's business and their performance.

Plans and policies
- communication of the Group's strategy, objectives and targets, values and standards;
- annual operating and capital plans and future projections;
- operating policies and procedures;

- clearly defined capital investment control guidelines;
- review of treasury policies by the Board; and
- review of social, environmental and ethical matters by the How We Do Business Committee.

Competent people
- appointment and development of employees of the necessary calibre to fulfil their allocated responsibilities; and
- clear roles and accountabilities with regular performance reviews.

Monitor and control
- review by operating divisions and their plans with the relevant director prior to submission to the Board for approval, including identification and assessment of risks;
- monthly comparison of operating divisions' actual financial performance against budget; and
- regular consideration by the Board of year end forecasts.

Regulatory update
- reporting of accounting and legal developments; and
- regular briefings on latest best practice corporate governance to the Board.

Risk assessment

Every six months the Board reviews the Group Risk Profile – the tool that drives risk assessment and action planning. This is supported by an ongoing process for identifying, evaluating and managing the significant risks faced by the Group.

As an integral part of planning and review, managers from each business area and minor projects:

- identify the risks to their plans;
- evaluate the risks using likelihood and impact; and
- document the actions being taken to manage those risks.

This process has been in place for the year under review and up to the date of approval of the Annual report and financial statements. It has been regularly reviewed by the Board and accords with the Internal Control Guidance for directors on the Combined Code (now UK Corporate Governance Code) produced by the Financial Reporting Council.

Source: Marks and Spencer plc Annual Report 2009, p. 55.

As internal auditors regularly review the reliability of the company's accounting and internal control systems, the external auditors are likely to take this into account when planning the scope and nature of the external audit work to be undertaken. Although the external auditors must retain full responsibility for the external audit, it may be possible to place confidence in certain work carried out by a well-resourced and competent internal audit team.

Audit committees

The UK Corporate Governance Code places audit committees at the heart of the financial reporting process and they are seen as vital to good corporate governance. The responsibilities of the audit committee have increased in recent years following the introduction of international financial reporting standards and tougher overseas corporate governance rules, such as the Sarbanes–Oxley Act in the US. This Act was introduced in the wake of accounting scandals and applies to a number of large UK listed companies that also list their shares in the US.

The role of the audit committee

There is a danger that the role of the directors as preparers of the financial statements and the role of external auditor as 'watchdog' will not be properly carried out. We saw in Chapter 5 that there have been several accounting scandals involving directors preparing financial statements that portray a company's financial health in a way that bears little resemblance to economic reality (creative accounting). External auditors have sometimes failed to spot irregular accounting practices used by directors to obscure the true position. This has cast doubt over the quality of the audit process and, in some cases, over the independence of auditors. It has been argued that where an accountancy firm carries out a large amount of non-audit work for a client company, its ability to audit the financial statements on behalf of the shareholders will be compromised. Non-audit work is awarded by the directors and may include tax advice, IT support, financial and management consultancy.

Activity 11.13

Why might undertaking non-audit work compromise an accountancy firm's ability to audit?

Non-audit work is often very well paid and, as we have seen, awarded by the directors. The auditors may not, therefore, wish to upset the directors. There is a risk that this will influence the way in which they conduct the audit.

The UK Corporate Governance Code recommends that an audit committee should have delegated authority for trying to ensure that financial reporting and internal control principles are properly applied and for maintaining an appropriate relationship with the external auditors. The committee should consist of at least three, or in the case of smaller companies, two, independent, non-executive directors. The main role and responsibilities of the audit committee should be as follows:

- to monitor the integrity of the financial statements;
- to review the company's internal controls;
- to make recommendations concerning the appointment and removal of the external auditor and to approve the terms of engagement;
- to review and monitor the independence, objectivity and effectiveness of the external auditor; and
- to establish and implement policies concerning the supply of non-audit services by the external auditor.

In addition to these duties, the audit committee may also take responsibility for reviewing the risk management systems of the company where the board, or a separate risk committee, does not address this issue.

Fulfilling the role

The audit committee will receive its terms of reference from the board of directors. In practice, these terms are normally in line with the role and responsibilities set out above. The board of directors must also seek to ensure that the committee has the authority and resources to carry out its responsibilities: without these, the committee will have no real 'teeth'.

It is important to establish the right membership of the committee. It should consist of individuals with the integrity, judgement and strength of character to deal with difficult issues that may have to be confronted. They must be prepared to pursue enquiries, even when faced with determined opposition from senior managers or executive directors.

Activity 11.14

Do you think that members of the committee should all be qualified accountants?

There is a case for having qualified accountants on the committee as it will often have to grapple with complex accounting issues. The UK Corporate Governance Code, however, makes the fairly modest recommendation that at least one member should have 'recent and relevant financial experience,' It is worth stating that committee members may be put under enormous pressure to agree to controversial accounting policies. When faced with such pressure, the personal qualities mentioned above will be more important than formal accounting qualifications.

The audit committee should meet regularly and adequate time should be allocated to each meeting. Some meetings should be planned to coincide with important events such as the start of the annual audit, the publication of interim financial statements and the announcement of the preliminary results for the year. In practice, it seems that audit committees of most large UK listed companies meet at least four times a year. Those companies that are also registered with the US Securities and Exchange Commission (SEC) must comply with strict US requirements and are likely to meet more frequently. Figure 11.2 below shows the frequency of meetings of SEC-registered and non-SEC-registered companies that are in the FTSE 100.

Figure 11.2   Frequency of audit committee meetings

The audit committees of SEC-registered companies tend to meet more frequently than those of non-SEC-registered companies.

Source: Based on a survey of annual reports of 84 companies from the FTSE 100 that were published between the beginning of November 2004 and the end of June 2005, Independent Audit Ltd, 'Audit Committee Reporting in 2005', www.boydeninterim.co.uk.

To be effective, the audit committee should have clear lines of communication with key individuals such as the chief executive, the finance director and the heads of the internal and external audit teams. These individuals should provide the audit committee with timely and relevant information and, where appropriate, attend meetings of the audit committee.

When reviewing internal controls, the audit committee should receive details of the effectiveness of the processes put in place by both the internal and external audit teams. The committee must be satisfied that the internal controls have operated satisfactorily during the year and that any recommendations for improvement were implemented. When reviewing the company's risk management systems, the committee will need to check that key risk areas are being monitored and that any control failures or emerging risks are quickly identified and dealt with. The committee must also be satisfied that risk management is not seen as simply a 'box-ticking' exercise and that everyone recognises its importance.

Internal auditors should help the audit committee by reporting on the effectiveness of internal control and risk management procedures. They can become the 'eyes and ears' of the audit committee and may be invaluable in providing necessary assurances. The internal auditors can benefit from a close relationship with the audit committee as it can strengthen their independence and status within the company. The audit committee can help foster greater independence through meetings with the internal auditors where management is excluded. The committee can also strengthen the authority of internal auditors by insisting that management co-operates with them. (See reference 5 at the end of the chapter.)

When reviewing the external audit process, the audit committee should consider the experience and expertise of the audit team. It should also review the audit plans and procedures and seek to ensure that they mesh with the work of the internal audit team. It will need to check that sufficient time is spent on the audit and that key risks are being addressed. To help monitor progress, meetings with the external auditor should be held to compare actual performance against earlier planned performance. The amount of non-audit services undertaken by the external auditors should also be monitored. To maintain a fresh perspective to the audit process, the committee may regularly rotate the head of external audit and/or the audit firm.

When reviewing the financial statements, the audit committee should pay particular attention to the following:

- the accounting policies adopted and whether they conform to the industry norm;
- any changes to accounting policies;
- the estimates and judgements made in key areas such as bad debts, provisions, depreciation and so on;
- any unusual items, such as large write-offs, or unusual relationships, such as a very high bad debts to sales revenue figure; and
- any unusual trends in financial performance or position.

This should help to identify irregular accounting practices or fraudulent behaviour. Any questions arising should be capable of being answered by the chief executive, finance director and external auditors.

The audit committee will normally produce a report for shareholders to be contained within the annual report. In practice, the quality of these reports varies considerably. In some cases, they simply describe the main features of the committee such as its constitution and membership, its role, the frequency of meetings and so on. This kind of information, however, offers little insight as to the way in which the committee has gone about its work. The audit committee report will be presented to the annual general meeting, which the chairman of the audit committee should attend. This will give shareholders the opportunity to question the chairman on any matters for which the committee has responsibility.

Are audit committees worthwhile?

Audit committees are fairly new and it is difficult to say just how effective they are in dealing with the problems discussed. It seems, however, that at least many audit committee members *believe* that these committees are effective. A survey by the Audit Committee Institute asked audit committee members of leading UK and US companies whether they believed that the high-profile financial reporting scandals of the last few years could have been avoided, or reduced, if there had been an effective audit committee in place. The results are shown in Figure 11.3.

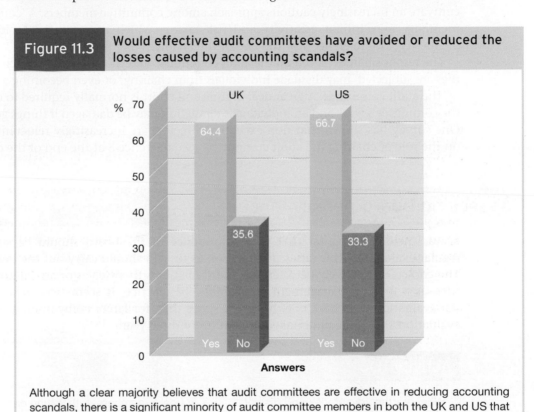

Figure 11.3 Would effective audit committees have avoided or reduced the losses caused by accounting scandals?

Although a clear majority believes that audit committees are effective in reducing accounting scandals, there is a significant minority of audit committee members in both the UK and US that do not believe that this is so.

We can see that roughly two-thirds of audit committee members believe that effective audit committees would have helped. There seems to be little difference between the responses of UK and US committee members. (See reference 6 at the end of the chapter.)

Activity 11.15

How might a sceptic respond to the above results? Why might the results give some cause for concern?

Only the passage of time will reveal whether audit committees can really offer some protection from accounting scandals.

There are potential costs in placing heavy responsibilities on the audit committee and in scrutinising its activities and decisions. There is always a risk that such pressure will cultivate an increasingly cautious approach among committee members. A 'compliance' mentality may inhibit creativity and risk taking, which are essential to long-term prosperity. (See reference 7 at the end of the chapter.)

The responsibilities placed on the audit committee, and the scrutiny to which its activities are subjected, may dissuade individuals from chairing, or even becoming a member of, the audit committee. A great deal of time and effort is normally required to carry out the committee's work and an individual's reputation may be damaged if things go wrong. One survey has shown that non-executive directors are increasingly reluctant to take on the role of chairing the audit committee. (See reference 8 at the end of the chapter.)

Assessing board performance

It was mentioned earlier that the performance of the board should be subject to regular evaluation. This raises the question as to who should carry out the evaluation. The choice is effectively between the board members themselves or an external party, such as a firm of management consultants. In practice, it seems that boards prefer self-evaluation. The UK Code, however, states that, for larger companies, an external evaluation should be undertaken at least every three years.

A second question raised concerns the areas of performance that should be evaluated. As the evaluation of board performance is a fairly new process, there is still no consensus on this matter. However, some possible areas, based on the UK Corporate Governance Code and other sources of good practice are set out in Table 11.1.

Table 11.1 Evaluating board performance

Company objectives	● Are the objectives of the company clearly set out? ● Is the board fully committed to these objectives? ● Are the objectives used as a framework for board decisions? ● Is there a regular board review of progress towards the achievement of the objectives?
Controlling the company	● Is the system of internal control and reporting regularly reviewed by the board? ● Are the risk management and reporting systems regularly reviewed by the board?
Board structure and roles	● Are the roles and responsibilities of the board clearly defined? ● Is the relationship between the board and key board committees appropriate and clear? ● Are the roles of the chairman and non-executive directors appropriate and clear?
Board meetings	● Are board meetings called with sufficient frequency to permit timely decisions? ● Is relevant material, including written agendas and minutes of previous meetings, sent to directors prior to a board meeting? ● Are all directors required to attend board meetings and what is their attendance record? ● Do the discussions at board meetings focus on strategic rather than operational issues? ● Are urgent problems arising between board meetings properly managed and reported?
Board composition	● Is there a separation of the roles of chairman and chief executive? ● Does the board reflect an appropriate balance between executive and non-executive directors? ● Does the board membership reflect an appropriate mix of age, skills and experience? ● Is the membership of important board committees, such as remuneration and audit committees, appropriate? ● Do the tenure agreements of board members provide the opportunity to refresh the board over time?
Board discussions and decisions	● Does the board work together in an effective manner? ● Do board discussions result in appropriate decisions being made? ● Are board decisions implemented and monitored? ● Are board members given the time and opportunity to express their views on key issues? ● Is the contribution of all directors at board meetings satisfactory? ● Are board discussions and decisions dominated by key individuals?
Board relations with shareholders	● Are there appropriate policies in place for communicating with shareholders? ● Are the communication channels established between the board and institutional and private shareholders appropriate? ● Are shareholders satisfied that their views are heard and considered by the board?
Board appointments and development	● Are rigorous procedures in place for the appointment of new directors? ● Are there clearly defined and appropriate procedures in place for appraising the performance of individual directors? ● Are appropriate training and development programmes (including induction programmes) available to board members? ● Has the board developed clear succession plans?

Self-assessment question 11.1

You have been asked to evaluate the performance of the board of directors of a large listed company and intend to use the checklist set out in Table 11.1 as the basis for carrying out this task.

What sources of information would you use to help you undertake your evaluation?

The answer to this question can be found at the back of the book on page 480.

Remunerating directors

Setting directors' remuneration at an appropriate level is not an easy task. Nevertheless, it is often vitally important to the success of the company. In this section we consider some of the key issues and problems that must be considered.

Remuneration policy

The UK Corporate Governance Code states that the level of directors' remuneration should be sufficient to attract, retain and motivate individuals of the right quality. The UK Code also states that remuneration should be linked to long-term performance and to the risk policy of the company. A significant proportion of the total remuneration awarded to executive directors should be based on company and individual performance.

By linking pay to performance, some of the risks and rewards of being a shareholder are passed to the directors. If a particular course of action yields good returns, the directors will benefit; if it fails to make a return the directors will not. This may encourage them to think more like shareholders and to take tough decisions that are likely to benefit shareholders.

The remuneration package of an executive director of a large listed company is usually made up of two elements:

- a fixed element, which is largely in the form of a base salary but will also include benefits such as pension contributions, medical insurance and so on; and
- a variable element, which rewards directors on the basis of both short-term and long-term performance.

The variable element is normally dependent on the executive directors achieving clear targets that reflect the goals of the company. The rewards for achieving these targets are usually taken in the form of cash and/or shares.

The main elements of the remuneration package for an executive director of a listed public company are shown in Figure 11.4.

Figure 11.4   The main elements of remuneration for an executive director of a listed public company

An executive director will normally receive a fixed element and a variable element, with the latter being performance-related.

The UK Code discourages performance-related payments to non-executives.

Activity 11.17

Should non-executive directors, as well as executive directors, have a performance-related element to their remuneration?

In the UK, non-executive directors are rewarded on the basis of the time spent and responsibilities undertaken on behalf of the company. The view is that if performance-related remuneration is offered, there is a risk that their independence will be compromised. Not all countries, however, adopt this view.

In large listed businesses, performance-related awards often account for more than half the total rewards given to executive directors. **Real World 11.8** indicates the importance that Tesco plc places on performance when rewarding directors.

 ## Real World 11.8

Tesco rewards

The executive directors of Tesco plc receive a fixed base salary (plus benefits) and a variable reward based on the achievement of performance targets. These targets reflect the responsibilities of individual directors and the objectives of the business.

The performance-related element of Tesco plc's executive directors represents a large proportion of total remuneration. Depending on individual incentive arrangements and performance, the base salary will represent between 12% and 33% and performance-related rewards will represent between 67% and 88% of total remuneration.

Source: Tesco plc Annual Report and Financial Statements 2009, p. 51.

The targets and rewards that might be included in directors' incentive schemes will be discussed in more detail later in the chapter.

Tenure and service contracts

The UK Corporate Governance Code recommends that all directors submit themselves for re-election, by shareholders, at regular intervals. For larger companies, it is recommended that all directors be subject to annual re-election. For smaller companies, re-elections should take place at least every three years. Non-executive directors that have served more than nine years, however, should be subject to annual re-election. The annual re-election of directors of larger companies is designed to ensure greater accountability. There are, however, concerns that it is potentially disruptive and may encourage short-term thinking among board members.

Remuneration committee

The remuneration committee is the cornerstone of the UK Code's attempt to ensure that directors' rewards are appropriate. The UK Code states that this committee should be responsible for setting remuneration for executive directors and the chairman. The committee should consist entirely of independent, non-executive directors. For larger businesses there should be at least three directors, and for smaller businesses at least two. The UK Code also states that no director should be allowed to determine his or her own level of rewards.

Although this committee is meant to prevent executive directors from being over-rewarded, critics point out that in recent years directors' pay and benefits have increased at a much faster rate than have corporate profits and sales (or the pay and benefits in other occupations). Furthermore, studies have shown that the relationship between directors' pay and performance is not a very clear one. (See reference 9 at the end of the chapter.)

An inherent problem of the remuneration committee is that non-executive directors are responsible for the rewards of executive directors. We have seen that non-executive directors are often executive directors of other companies and so there is a risk that they will be sympathetic to a high-reward culture. There may also, however, be problems with the way in which the committee goes about its business – as we shall now see.

Problems with the process

Various studies have pointed out problems in the way in which remuneration committees operate. One study by Main and others (see reference 10 at the end of the chapter) interviewed 22 independent non-executive directors with experience of remuneration committees and found that the businesses for which they served held, on average, 4.8 committee meetings per year. These meetings were tightly scheduled and often fairly brief (on average 1.5 hours). Despite the importance of their role, it seems that these committees do not devote much time to carrying it out. The study also found that it was quite common for the chief executive officer (CEO) and chairman to be present at remuneration committee meetings.

Activity 11.18

Why might the presence of these individuals be a problem?

Although it may be useful for the committee to receive their input at times, there is a danger that the independence of the committee will be compromised by their continual presence.

It seems that committee members are rarely selected on the basis of their experience in negotiating or developing reward packages or given training in these matters once appointed. (See reference 11 at the end of the chapter.) This can be a particular problem when hiring a new chief executive officer. The pool of talent for chief executives is small and it is a 'seller's market'. Thus, to recruit a suitable candidate, the committee may be tempted to offer more than is necessary. Incumbent chief executive officers may also be over-rewarded. They are often powerful personalities with considerable influence over other board members. There is a risk that committee members will be too deferential and will err on the side of generosity in contract negotiations.

A further problem arises from the process by which remuneration schemes for directors are developed. The committee is often not responsible for the initial development of these packages; the time spent by non-executive directors on committee meetings is simply not long enough. Instead, the human resource department will often gather data from within the business and commission market data from outside remuneration consultants. Proposals will be produced, which may then be sent to the chief executive officer and other senior directors for approval. After this has been done, they may be passed to the remuneration committee for consideration. Jenson and Murphy make the point that 'The fact that the committee only sees plans that have already been "blessed" by top managers creates an environment that invites abuse and bias.' (See reference 12 at the end of the chapter.)

The remuneration committee must be careful when using market data to formulate appropriate reward packages. Too great a focus on market trends and statistics has been held responsible, at least in part, for a ratcheting effect on directors' rewards. Such data can often be used to justify an increase in rewards: usually businesses do not want to be seen paying below-average rewards to directors. This can result in upward pressure on the average level of rewards without a corresponding increase in performance.

Improving the process

A strong chairman is vital for promoting the integrity and independence of the remuneration committee. The chairman should set the agenda and should attempt to ensure that the committee has the opportunity for open discussions without other directors being in attendance. The chairman should also try to ensure that the committee has access to appropriate information and expertise.

The remuneration committee should take direct responsibility for crafting reward packages for directors. To do this, committee members must invest time and effort in carrying out their role and adequate training must be provided. To help to stiffen the resolve of committee members, regular meetings with shareholders should be arranged. It is inappropriate for the human resources department, in conjunction with outside consultants, to prepare reward packages for the remuneration committee simply to rubber stamp. It is also inappropriate for the chief executive officer and chairman to approve these packages before they are passed to the remuneration committee.

Non-executive directors

Setting up a remuneration committee does not deal with the problem of who determines the pay of the non-executive directors.

Activity 11.19

Who do you think should determine the pay of the non-executive directors?

The UK Corporate Governance Code states that the board of directors, or perhaps the shareholders, should take responsibility for doing this. Where the board sets their pay, the executive directors will have an influence over the pay of the non-executive directors (a point which may not be lost on those non-executive directors serving on the remuneration committee!).

Real World 11.9 warns of the fate that may await the chairman of the remuneration committee when shareholders are dissatisfied with the committee's decisions.

Real World 11.9

In the firing line   FT

Royal Dutch Shell has unveiled a big boardroom shake-up and the departure of Sir Peter Job, the head of its remuneration committee, as the company moved to placate top shareholders angered by excessive executive pay.

The restructuring comes after extensive discussions with leading investors during the summer over their mounting unhappiness about Shell's pay policy in recent years. Ructions with investors came to a head in May at the annual shareholder meeting when 59 per cent of them voted against Shell's remuneration report. They were protesting at the board's decision to use discretionary powers to pay bonuses to five senior directors even though the group had failed to meet set targets. Jeroen van der Veer, the outgoing chief executive, received a 58 per cent rise in his total pay for 2008, taking it to €10.3m (£9m).

Since May, Jorma Ollila, Shell's chairman, has met many of the group's top shareholders. One said: 'We made clear we expected to see the chairman of the remuneration committee move on. The company is paying the price for two years of contentious pay schemes.'

Source: 'Shake-up at Shell after pay backlash', Kate Burgess, *Financial Times*, 11 September 2009.

Reporting directors' remuneration

The law requires that UK listed companies prepare an annual directors' remuneration report. This report must be submitted to shareholders for approval, which will normally take place at the annual general meeting. The report should set out the remuneration of each director with details of salaries and other benefits received. The chairman of the remuneration committee will normally attend the shareholders' meeting to deal with any issues that may arise.

Setting performance targets

We saw earlier that a large proportion of the remuneration received by executive directors should be performance-related. There are various performance targets that can be used as a basis for rewarding directors and below we consider some of the more popular of these. Before we do so, however, it is useful to identify the characteristics, or qualities, a good performance target should possess. Perhaps the key characteristics are that it should

- be in line with the goals of the company;
- lead to a convergence of directors' and shareholders' interests;
- reflect the achievement of the directors; and
- be robust and not easily distorted by particular policies, financing arrangements or manipulative practices.

No single performance target will perfectly encapsulate all of these qualities. Nevertheless, a number of potentially useful performance targets exist, as we shall now see.

Total shareholder return

A widely-used performance target is based on **total shareholder return (TSR)**. The total return from a share is made up of two elements: the increase (or decrease) in share value over a period plus any dividends paid during the period. To illustrate how total shareholder return is calculated, let us assume that a company commenced trading by issuing shares of £0.50 each at their nominal value (P_0) and by the end of the first year of trading the shares had increased in value to £0.55 (P_1). Furthermore, the company paid a dividend of £0.06 (D_1) per share during the period. We can calculate the total shareholder return as follows:

$$\text{Total shareholder return} = \frac{D_1 + (P_1 - P_0)}{P_0} \times 100\%$$

$$= \frac{0.06 + (0.55 - 0.50)}{0.50} \times 100\%$$

$$= 22\%$$

The figure calculated has little information value when taken alone. It can only really be used to assess performance when compared with some benchmark.

Activity 11.21

What benchmark would be most suitable?

Perhaps the best benchmark to use would be the returns from similar businesses operating in the same industry over the same period of time.

The reason that this benchmark is usually suitable is because it will compare the returns generated by the company with those generated from other investment opportunities that have the same level of risk. As a general rule, the level of return from an investment should be related to the level of risk that has to be taken.

Many large companies now publish total shareholder returns in their annual reports. **Real World 11.10** provides an example.

Real World 11.10

Tesco's TSR

Tesco plc publishes its total shareholder returns (TSR) for a five-year period, along with movements in the FTSE 100 index for the same period. The company uses this index as a benchmark as it reflects the performance of companies of similar size. However, when using TSR as a basis for rewarding directors, the company also uses other leading food retailers as a benchmark.

The TSR for the company is displayed graphically in Figure 11.5.

Figure 11.5	Tesco plc: total shareholder returns February 2004 to February 2009

Shareholder returns vary over time and so a measure of TSR is likely to be sensitive to the particular time period chosen.

Source: Tesco plc Annual Report and Financial Statements 2009.

British Sky Broadcasting Group (BSkyB) plc also uses TSR as a performance target for its executive directors. **Real World 11.11** explains how awards are made, or 'vested', using this target.

Real World 11.11

Sky high rewards

BSkyB awards 30 per cent of the performance-related element of executive directors' remuneration using a TSR target. TSR is measured over a three-year period and compared to the TSR of the FTSE 100 companies. If the TSR is below the median of the FTSE 100 companies, no awards are vested to the directors. If the TSR achieves the median, one-third of awards available is vested. If the TSR is in the upper quartile, the whole of the awards available is vested. If the TSR lies somewhere between the median and upper quartile of the TSR of FTSE 100 companies, the awards available are vested on a straight-line basis. This is shown graphically in Figure 11.6.

Figure 11.6   TSR vesting schedule for BSkyB

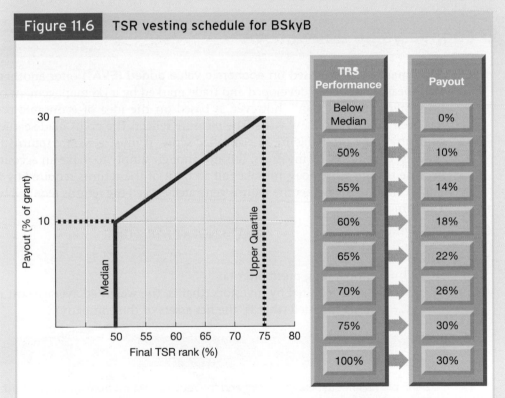

Awards based on TSR account for 30 per cent of the total performance-related awards for executive directors. If TSR achieves the upper quartile range of FTSE 100 companies, all of the award (that is, 30 per cent of the total awards) is vested. If TSR achieves the median, one-third of the award (that is, 10 per cent of the total awards) is vested. If the TSR lies somewhere between the median and the upper quartile, the awards are vested on a straight-line basis.

Note that BSkyB compares TSR performance against companies of a similar scale, presumably because it is impossible to find companies with similar operations.

Source: British Sky Broadcasting Group plc Annual Report 2009, p. 62.

Problems with TSR

TSR measures changes in shareholder wealth and, therefore, has obvious appeal as a basis for rewarding executive directors. It is also a fairly robust measure which can accommodate different operating and financing arrangements. Nevertheless, care must be taken when using it. In particular, the issue of risk must be considered. Higher returns may be achieved by simply taking on higher-risk projects and directors should not necessarily be remunerated for increasing returns in this way.

To assess relative performance, TSR must be compared to that of similar companies. There may, however, be difficulties in finding similar companies as a suitable basis for comparison, as with BSkyB for example. (There is also a risk that unsuitable companies will be deliberately chosen to make the company's performance seem better than it is.) Other problems such as the inability to identify the contributions of individual directors to overall company performance, the inability to identify share price changes that are beyond the directors' control, and the fact that TSR can be manipulated over the short term, all conspire to make this a less than perfect measure.

Economic value added (EVA®)

→ Performance targets based on **economic value added (EVA®)** offer another approach. This measure has been developed and trade marked by a US management consultancy firm, Stern Stewart. EVA®, however, is based on the idea of economic profit, which has been around for many years. The measure reflects the point made earlier that for a company to be profitable in an economic sense, it must generate returns that exceed the returns required by investors. It is not enough simply to make an accounting profit because this measure does not take full account of the returns required by investors.

EVA® indicates whether the returns generated exceed the returns required by investors. The formula is:

$$EVA^® = NOPAT - (R \times C)$$

where
NOPAT = Net operating profit after tax
    R = Returns required by investors (that is, the weighted average cost of capital)
    C = Capital invested (that is, the net assets of the company).

Activity 11.22

Dena plc has net assets of £250m and the required return from investors is 10 per cent. The company made a net operating profit of £50m for the year and the appropriate tax rate is 20 per cent. What is the EVA® for the year?

EVA® will be

$$(£50m - (20\% \times £50m)) - (10\% \times £250m) = £15m$$

Only when EVA® is positive can we say that the company is increasing shareholder wealth. To maximise shareholder wealth, managers must increase EVA® by as much as possible.

Activity 11.23

What can managers do in order to increase EVA®? (*Hint*: use the formula shown above as your starting point.)

The formula suggests that in order to increase EVA®, managers may try to:

- Increase NOPAT. This may be done either by reducing expenses or by increasing sales revenue.
- Use capital invested more efficiently. This means selling off assets that are not generating returns that exceed their cost and investing in assets that do.
- Reduce the required rates of return for investors. This may be achieved by changing the capital structure in favour of long-term borrowing (which is cheaper to service than share capital).

EVA® relies on conventional financial statements to measure the wealth created for shareholders. However, the NOPAT and capital figures shown on these statements are used only as a starting point. They have to be adjusted because of the problems and limitations of conventional measures. According to Stern Stewart, the major problem is that profit and capital are understated because of the conservative bias in accounting measurement. Profit may be understated as a result of arbitrary write-offs such as research and development expenditure written off and as a result of excessive provisions being created (such as allowances for trade receivables). Capital may also be understated because assets are reported at their original cost (less amounts written off), which can produce figures considerably below current market values. In addition, certain assets such as internally generated goodwill and brand names are normally omitted from the financial statements because no external transactions have occurred.

Stern Stewart has identified more than a hundred adjustments that could be made to the conventional financial statements to eliminate the conservative bias. However, it believes that, in practice, only a handful of adjustments to the accounting figures of any particular business tend to be needed. Unless an adjustment is going to have a significant effect on the calculation of EVA® it is really not worth making. The adjustments made should reflect the nature of the particular business. Each business is unique and so must customise the calculation of EVA® to its particular circumstances. (This aspect of EVA® can be seen as either indicating flexibility or as being open to manipulation depending on whether you support this measure!)

Under EVA®, managers can receive bonuses based on actual achievement during a particular period. If management rewards are linked to a single period, however, there is a danger that managers will place undue attention to increasing EVA® during this period rather than over the long term. This might be achieved in the short term, for example, by cutting back on necessary investment. The objective should be to maximise EVA® over the longer term. Where a business has a stable level of sales revenue, operating assets and borrowing, a current-period focus is likely to be less of a problem than where these elements are unstable over time. A stable pattern of operations minimises the risk that improvements in EVA® during the current period are achieved at the expense of future periods. Nevertheless, any reward system for managers must encourage a long-term perspective and so rewards should be based on the ability of managers to improve EVA® over a number of years rather than a single year.

The amount of EVA® generated during a period is rarely reported to shareholders. This means that shareholders will be unable to check whether rewards given to directors are appropriate.

Earnings per share

The earnings per share (EPS) ratio was considered in Chapter 8 and we may recall that it is calculated as follows:

$$\text{Earnings per share} = \frac{\text{Earnings available to ordinary shareholders}}{\text{Number of ordinary shares in issue}}$$

When used as a basis for directors' incentive plans, a particular level of growth in earnings per share is usually required in order to trigger rewards.

EPS poses problems when used as a performance target for rewarding directors. A major difficulty is that an increase in EPS does not necessarily lead to an increase in shareholder wealth. EPS may be increased by embarking on risky ventures and an increased level of risk may be reflected in a decrease in share price. A further difficulty is that EPS can be increased in the short term by simply changing certain decisions and policies.

Activity 11.24

Can you think how EPS could be increased by changes in decisions and policies?

It may be done by restricting expenditure on discretionary items such as training, research and in nurturing brands. Accounting policy changes, such as changing the point at which revenue is recognised, can also increase EPS.

An annual EPS target would be inappropriate where a company is suffering losses, caused perhaps by uncontrollable changes in economic conditions. It may take time to turn around the company's fortunes. The directors may have to make tough decisions and work hard over many years before there is any real prospect of generating a profit.

Real World 11.12 describes how one large listed company uses EPS and EVA® to reward its managers.

Real World 11.12

Targeting a bonus

SSL International plc, the condom and footcare products manufacturer, offers performance-related rewards for its executive directors. These rewards are made up of two elements: an annual cash bonus and a share-based, long-term incentive plan. Performance targets for each of these elements are based on EPS and EVA.

For 2009/10, the annual bonus is based one-third on EVA and two-thirds on EPS. For the long-term incentive plan, it is the other way around.

Directors become eligible for an annual cash bonus (based on a percentage of base salary) when the actual performance matches target performance as follows:

Performance vs target	97.5%	100%	102.5%
% of salary for Chief Executive	12.5%	57.5%	125%
% of salary for Executive Directors	11.5%	52.9%	115%

No bonus is payable on results below the threshold. We can see that the maximum bonus is paid upon the achievement of 102.5 per cent of target performance.

Directors become eligible for shares under the long-term incentive plan when actual performance matches target performance as follows:

	EPS (one-third) Compound annual growth rate (CAGR) over the three financial years ending March 2012		EVA (two-thirds) Aggregate generated over the three financial years ending March 2012	
	Percentage of salary vesting	Performance scale	Percentage of salary vesting	Performance scale
Below threshold	Nil	<13.5%	Nil	<£160m
Threshold	5%	13.5%	10%	£160m
Maximum	33.3%	>/=16.3%	66.7%	>/=£170m

A sliding scale of payment will operate between the points in the target range.

Source: SSL International plc Annual Report and Accounts 2009, pp. 44–5.

Other accounting ratios

In practice, other ratios based on profits, such as return on capital employed and return on shareholders' funds, may be used to reward executive directors. They suffer, however, from the same sort of problems that afflict EPS.

Directors' share options

→ One way in which long-term performance can be rewarded is through the granting of **directors' share options**. This type of reward, however, has provoked considerable controversy. For years a debate has raged over whether granting share options to directors is consistent with good corporate governance. Peter Drucker, an eminent management thinker, has been a vociferous critic of this practice and has referred to it as 'an encouragement to loot the corporation'. We shall now consider the main features of directors' share options and then go on to explore the case for and against using options to reward directors. We shall see that a company implementing a directors' share option scheme must grapple with a variety of issues and problems.

What are directors' share options?

A directors' share option scheme gives directors the right, but not the obligation, to buy equity shares in their company at an agreed price. The conditions of the scheme will usually stipulate that the option to buy must be exercised either on, or after, a specified future date. A final date for exercising the option will also usually be specified. Share options are normally awarded only to executive directors. The UK Corporate Governance Code states that non-executive directors should not be rewarded in this way.

Directors' share options will only be exercised if the market value of the shares exceeds the option price. Where the option is exercised, the company must issue the agreed number of shares to the director, who will make a profit from the transaction. The option differs from most financial options in that a director will not normally be required to pay for the option rights: they are granted at no cost to the directors concerned. Directors' share options, however, cannot be traded and will usually be forfeited if the person leaves the company before the option can be exercised.

In the UK, directors' share options are normally issued at the current market price of the underlying shares. In the past, share options were sometimes issued at a discount to the market price; however, the UK Corporate Governance Code has discouraged this practice. The terms of a share option scheme often allow the directors to exercise their option no earlier than three years, but no later than ten years, after the option has been granted. Inland Revenue rules and best practice guidelines from institutional investors limit the value of options to £100,000 or four times current salary (see reference 13 at the end of the chapter). The exercise of the option may be subject to certain performance targets, such as growth in earnings per share, being met (see reference 14 at the end of the chapter).

What are the benefits of granting options?

Directors' share option schemes have been a popular method of rewarding the directors of large listed companies and various arguments have been put forward to support their use. It is often suggested, for example, that a well-designed scheme will benefit shareholders as it will help to align the interests of directors with those of shareholders.

Activity 11.25

How might this alignment of interests occur?

It is argued that share options give directors an incentive to increase the value of the company's shares and, thereby, to increase the wealth of shareholders.

Some argue that share options may even help to strengthen the psychological bond that a director has with the company. Through exercising an option and acquiring shares, the directors may identify more closely with the company and feel a sense of shared purpose with other shareholders. This argument does depend, however, on the directors retaining, rather than selling, the shares acquired under the option agreement.

It has also been suggested that share options may help to retain board members. The fact that a director's share options are normally forfeited if a director leaves the company can provide a strong incentive to stay. Thus, options can provide a set of 'golden handcuffs' for talented directors who have other employment opportunities.

Unlike other forms of directors' remuneration, share options involve no financial outlay for the company at the time that they are granted. If the share price does not perform well over the option period, the option will be allowed to lapse and the company will incur no cost. If, on the other hand, the shares perform well and the options are exercised, they represent a form of deferred payment to the directors. This deferral of rewards may be particularly attractive to a growing company that is short of cash.

Where directors exercise their options and the company, therefore, issues shares at below their current market value, there is a very real cost to the company. Were the company to issue those same shares to an ordinary investor, it would receive the current market price for them.

What are the problems of options?

Many see share options as a poor means of rewarding directors. Warren Buffett, one of the world's shrewdest and most successful investors, has made clear his opposition to their use. One problem that concerns him is that share option schemes cannot differentiate between the performances achieved by individual directors. He argues:

> Of course stock (share) options often go to talented, value-adding managers and sometimes deliver them rewards that are perfectly appropriate. (Indeed, managers who are really exceptional almost always get far less than they should.) But when the result is equitable, it is accidental. Once granted, the option is blind to individual performance. Because it is irrevocable and unconditional (so long as a manager stays in the company), the sluggard receives rewards from his options precisely as does the star. A managerial Rip Van Winkle, ready to doze for ten years, could not wish for a better 'incentive' system. (See reference 15 at the end of the chapter.)

A further problem concerning the incentive value of share options, to which Buffett refers, is that, where the share price falls significantly below the exercise price, the prospects of receiving benefits from the share options may become remote and any incentive value will be lost.

Both rises and falls in share price may be beyond the control of the directors and may simply reflect changes in economy-wide or industry-wide factors. Any incentive scheme that is subject to the vagaries of the stock market is, therefore, likely to present problems. There is always a risk that directors will either be undercompensated or over-compensated for their achievements.

Buffett's criticism of share options is not confined to their dubious incentive value. He also challenges the view that share options place directors in the same position as that of shareholders. He argues:

> . . . the rhetoric about options frequently describes them as desirable because they put owners and managers in the same financial boat. In reality, the boats are far different. No owner has ever escaped the burden of capital costs, whereas a holder of a fixed-price option bears no capital costs at all. An owner must weigh upside potential against downside risk: an option holder has no downside. In fact, the business project in which you would wish to have an option frequently is a project in which you would reject ownership. (I'll be happy to accept a lottery ticket as a gift – but I'll never buy one.) (See reference 15 at the end of the chapter.)

This latter point, concerning the lack of 'downside' risk associated with the acquisition of options, may have an impact on the directors' risk-taking behaviour.

Activity 11.26

How might this affect the risk-taking behaviour of directors?

As options are granted to directors at no cost to them, the directors have an incentive to take risks when these options are 'underwater' (that is, when they cannot be exercised at a profit). By taking risks, there is a prospect of a rise in share prices and resulting benefits. If, on the other hand, by taking risks there is a fall in share prices, the directors will incur no financial loss.

Where share options are exercised, the directors may find themselves holding a large proportion of their total wealth in the form of company equity. The concentration of wealth in this form may have a number of unintended consequences. For example, it may lead to risk-averse behaviour as directors may be concerned with maintaining their wealth intact. This behaviour may not, however, find favour with the shareholders, who are likely to have a more diversified portfolio of investments and so may be more willing to take risks.

Share option schemes are based on the assumption that shareholders are concerned with share price increases and that directors' behaviour and incentives should reflect this concern. An excessive focus on share price, however, may not be in the best interests of shareholders. Share price represents only one part of the shareholders' total return from the company: the other part is dividend income.

Activity 11.27

How might directors behave as a result of this focus on share price increases rather than dividends?

There is a risk that this may lead the directors to restrict dividend payments so that profits are retained to fuel share price growth. Indeed, as directors are rewarded on the basis of share price growth rather than dividend growth, they have an incentive to act in this way. (This potential problem has led some companies to incorporate dividend protection conditions in the share option schemes offered to directors.)

Using similar reasoning, it can be argued that directors also have an incentive to have the company re-purchase its own shares as this too may lead to increases in share price.

In the UK, directors' share options have declined in popularity, which is partly due to the changes in the corporate governance environment. An influential report on directors' remuneration discouraged the use of share option schemes and a number of large institutional investors have voiced their concern over their cost and effectiveness. Furthermore, international accounting standards now require the 'fair value' of share option schemes to be included in the financial statements. Shareholders can now see more clearly the cost incurred by granting share options as it is shown as a charge against profits.

Share option schemes are open to abuse. The particular forms of abuse that have been identified usually relate to the conditions of the share option scheme and to the pricing of options. A share option scheme will often include a condition that certain performance targets, such as earnings per share, must be met before the directors can exercise their options. There have been allegations, however, that some companies have set performance targets too low for them to have any real incentive effect.

The pricing of options has often been a target for manipulation by unscrupulous individuals and, in the US, several scandals have been unearthed. Some high-profile US companies have been found to have reissued share options to directors at a lower price when the share price of the company fell below the option price. This practice effectively eliminates any risks for directors and may also eliminate any incentive effect that share options may have. (See reference 16 at the end of the chapter.)

Activity 11.28

Can you think of any circumstances under which reissuing share options at a lower price to directors might be justified?

It is sometimes argued that, by 'repricing' options in this way, it may re-incentivise directors, particularly when stock market prices are falling.

Real World 11.13 describes one high-profile case concerning the repricing of options.

Real World 11.13

Buy now at Ebay   **FT**

In a move likely to rekindle the debate over controversial pay practices in Silicon Valley, Ebay yesterday asked its shareholders for permission to reset the terms of its employee stock (share) options. The plan would allow employees whose options are 'underwater', or have exercise prices that are significantly higher than the current share price, to exchange them for restricted stock (share) units.

Repricing stock (share) options is controversial because it benefits employees even as shareholders suffer from a depressed share price. Despite its unpopularity on Wall Street, it became common during the technology bust earlier this decade. Now, with the share prices of technology companies down because of the recession, options repricing may become common once again.

In January, Google unveiled a similar plan, responding to its own devalued share price. Sandeep Aggarwal, an analyst with Collins Stewart, said he believed additional companies would follow suit. 'I think there will be several more technology companies to do this,' he said. The window of opportunity to exchange under the Google plan ran out yesterday and the company said employees exchanged about 93 per cent for new options with a lower exercise price.

Stock [share] options, a common part of Silicon Valley pay packages, are meant to encourage employees to work hard, stay with a company, and share in its profits. But when the market price of the share dips below the exercise price, the options lose their value.

In a filing with the US Securities Exchange Commission, Ebay said the plan would help boost morale in the company: 'Because of the continued challenging economic environment and the uncertain impact of our efforts to change our business, we believe these underwater stock options are no longer effective as incentives to motivate and retain our employees.'

Source: 'Ebay seeks to alter terms of stock options', David Gelles, *Financial Times*, 11 March 2009.

An even more controversial practice is when directors benefit from the backdating of options. One study found that 1,400 directors of 460 US companies benefited from the backdating of share options to the lowest price in a monthly period. (See reference 17 at the end of the chapter.)

Deciding on a target measure

Given the strengths and weaknesses of each of the target measures described, reliance on a single measure can pose problems. Many companies, therefore, employ a range of target measures in the hope of capturing various aspects of performance and of overcoming the weaknesses of a particular measure. We saw earlier, in Real World 11.12 (pages 426–427), how SSL International plc employed two measures to capture the performance of its executive directors.

The rise of shareholder activism

Improving corporate governance has tended to focus on developing a framework of rules. Whilst rules are important, it is also important for shareholders to play their part by actively monitoring and controlling the behaviour of directors. In this section, we identify the main shareholders of listed companies and discuss their role in establishing good corporate governance. We also consider why there has been greater shareholder activism in recent years.

Who are the main shareholders?

Real World 11.14 provides some impression of the ownership of London Stock Exchange listed shares.

Real World 11.14

Becoming institutionalised

At 31 December 2006, 40 per cent of the shares (by market value) of London Stock Exchange listed companies were owned by investors (individuals and institutions) that are based overseas. Of those owned by UK residents (individuals and institutions), the breakdown of ownership is as shown in Figure 11.7.

| Figure 11.7 | Beneficial ownership of UK shares by UK investors, end of 2006 |

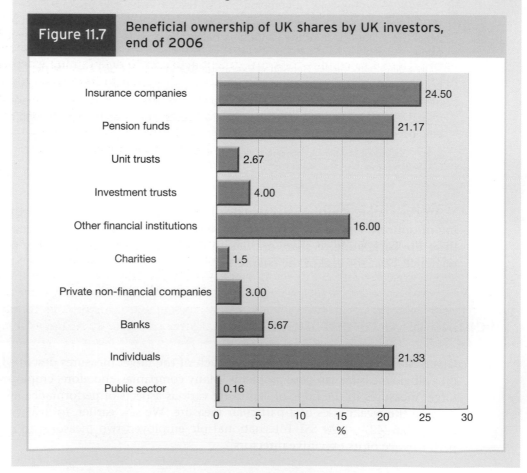

Large financial institutions, such as insurance companies, banks, pension funds, unit trusts and investment trusts, are now the most important investors in shares listed on the London Stock Exchange. These institutions have increased their hold on the ownership of Stock Exchange listed shares over time, whilst the proportion of listed shares held directly by individuals has decreased. The proportion of shares (by market value) owned by various financial institutions is now around 79 per cent of the total market value of those London Stock Exchange listed shares, with only 21 per cent held by individuals.

Looking at the changes in the ownership of listed shares over the past four decades shows two striking features:

1 The value of listed shares owned by overseas residents has gone up progressively from just 7 per cent in 1963 to 40 per cent in 2006; and
2 Of those held by UK residents, the value of listed shares held by individuals has fallen from 58 per cent in 1963 to 21 per cent in 2006.

Source: Office for National Statistics.

The rise of the institutions does not mean that individuals have less investment in listed shares. It is simply that individuals are now tending to invest through the institutions, for example by making pension contributions, rather than by buying shares directly. Ultimately, all of the investment finance must come from individuals.

This concentration of ownership of listed shares means that financial institutions have enormous voting power and, as a result, the potential to exercise huge influence over the way in which Stock Exchange companies are directed and controlled. In the past, however, they have been reluctant to exercise this power and have been criticised for being too passive and for allowing the directors of companies too much independence.

Most financial institutions have chosen to take a non-interventionist approach and have preferred to confine their investment activities to determining whether to buy, hold or sell shares in particular companies. They appear to have taken the view that the costs of actively monitoring directors and trying to influence their decisions are too high in relation to the likely benefits. It is also worth pointing out that these costs are borne by the particular financial institution undertaking the monitoring whereas the benefits are spread across all of the company's shareholders. (This phenomenon is often referred to as the 'free-rider' problem.)

Waking the sleeping giants

In recent years, however, financial institutions have begun to play a more active role in corporate governance. More time is being devoted to monitoring the actions of directors and in engaging with the directors over key decisions. This change of heart has occurred for a variety of reasons. One important reason is that the increasing concentration of share ownership has made it more difficult for financial institutions simply to walk away from an investment in a poorly performing company by selling its shares.

Activity 11.29

Why might it be difficult for financial institutions to simply sell their shares?

A substantial number of shares may be held and so a decision to sell would have a significant impact on the market price, leading to heavy losses.

A further reason why it may be difficult to sell is that a company's shares may be included in a stock market index (such as the FTSE 100 or FTSE 250). Certain types of financial institutions, such as investment trusts or unit trusts, may offer investments that are designed to 'track' the particular index. They may, therefore, become locked into a particular company's shares in order to reflect the index. In both situations outlined, therefore, a financial institution may have little choice but to stick with the shares held and try to improve performance by trying to influence the actions and decisions of the directors.

It is also worth mentioning that financial institutions have experienced much greater competitive pressures in recent years. There have been increasing demands from clients for them to demonstrate their investment skills and, thereby, justify their fees, by either outperforming benchmarks or beating the performance of similar financial institutions. These increased competitive pressures may be due, at least in part, to the fact that economic conditions have not favoured investors in the recent past; they have experienced a period of relatively low stock market returns. Whatever the reason, the increased pressure to enhance the wealth of their clients has led financial institutions, in turn, to become less tolerant towards underperforming boards of directors.

The regulatory environment has also favoured greater activism on the part of financial institutions. The UK Corporate Governance Code, for example, urges institutional shareholders to use their votes and to enter into a dialogue with companies.

Activity 11.30

What might a financial institution wish to discuss with the directors of a company? Try to identify at least two financial and two non-financial aspects of the company.

Financial institutions are likely to take an interest in various aspects of a company. Some of the more important include:

- objectives and strategies adopted;
- trading and profit performance;
- internal controls;
- policies regarding mergers and acquisition;
- major investments and disinvestments;
- adherence to the recommendations of the UK Corporate Governance Code;
- corporate social responsibilities; and
- directors' incentive schemes and remuneration.

This is not an exhaustive list. As shareholders of the company, anything that might have an impact on their wealth should be a matter of concern.

It is worth pointing out that listed companies have become more vulnerable to takeover, particularly by private equity funds. Takeovers very often lead to existing directors losing their positions. This makes the directors particularly sensitive to the views and aspirations of the large shareholders that have the power to resist a takeover by refusing to sell their shares.

Forms of activism

It is important to be clear as to what is meant by the term 'shareholder activism' as it can take various forms. In its simplest form it involves taking a more active role in voting for or against the resolutions put before the annual general meeting or any extraordinary general meeting of the company. This form of activism is seen by the government as being vital to good corporate governance. The government is keen to see a much higher level of participation than currently exists and expects institutional shareholders to exercise their right to vote. In the past, financial institutions have often indicated their dissent by abstaining from a vote rather than outright opposition to a resolution. There is some evidence, however, that they are now more prepared to use their vote to oppose resolutions of the board of directors. Much of the evidence, however, remains anecdotal rather than based on systematic research.

A particularly rich source of contention between shareholders and directors concerns directors' remuneration and there have been several shareholder revolts over this issue. **Real World 11.15** provides an example of a fairly recent falling out.

Real World 11.15

Revolting shareholders

FT

Cable and Wireless suffered one of the biggest shareholder revolts of the year at a FTSE 100 company yesterday with a heavy protest vote by investors over the telecommunications group's controversial pay policy. Nearly 38 per cent of votes on the policy at C&W's annual meeting failed to back it in a further sign of an increasing activist stance by investors on pay. Royal Dutch Shell and Royal Bank of Scotland recently both had their remuneration reports rejected by shareholders.

Some 21.3 per cent of votes on the C&W remuneration report were against and 16.2 per cent abstained. The Association of British Insurers, which represents shareholders that account for almost 20 per cent of investments in the UK stock market, made its strongest possible objection to C&W's pay policy by issuing a 'red top' alert.

The ABI said the C&W vote was a 'clear and significant sign of shareholder concern', adding that the company's non-executive directors 'must now engage constructively with shareholders to address their obvious concerns'. At the annual meeting, one smaller investor claimed C&W's long-term incentive plan amounted to 'unbridled greed'. 'You are demeaning a great and historic company,' said the investor, prompting limited applause from fellow shareholders.

However, C&W signalled it would not amend its pay policy, including a private equity-style long-term incentive plan, which offers potentially large rewards to the company's managers. C&W said it was 'pleased our proposals received strong support' following 'extensive consultation' with shareholders.

Richard Lapthorne, C&W chairman, rejected the suggestions of greed and said the scheme, which is based on total shareholder return, was underpinning the company's revival. He highlighted how C&W had made a 44 per cent return to investors over the first three years of the scheme, which was put in place in 2006.

Source: 'Shareholders revolt over C&W pay', Andrew Parker, Financial Times, 18 July 2009.

Although shareholder revolts are widely reported and catch the newspaper headlines, they do not happen very often. Nevertheless, the benefits for shareholders of flexing their muscles and voting against resolutions put forward by the directors may go beyond their immediate, intended objective: other boards of directors may take note of shareholder dissatisfaction and adjust their behaviour in order to avoid a similar fate.

The cost of voting need not be high as there are specialist agencies which offer research and advice to financial institutions on how their votes should be cast.

Another form of activism involves meetings and discussions between representatives of a particular financial institution and the board of directors of a company. This requires a fairly high degree of involvement with the company and some of the larger financial institutions have dedicated teams for this purpose. This can be, therefore, a costly exercise. **Real World 11.16** is an extract from a report published by one major financial institution that is committed to this form of activism and which gives an insight to the approach taken.

Real World 11.16

Getting active

Jupiter International Group plc, a major provider of unit trusts and investment trusts, believes that, when monitoring investments:

> an important part of this process is the dialogue (usually private) between institutional share-holders and the companies in which they invest. As such, its fund managers and analysts host and attend regular meetings with the management of companies, with a high percentage of companies being seen twice a year where corporate strategy, performance and other management issues are discussed.

Source: Corporate Governance and Voting Policy January 2008, www.jupiteronline.co.uk, p. 14.

Such meetings can be a useful mechanism for exchanging views and for gaining a greater understanding of the needs and motivations of each party. This may help to pre-empt public arguments between the board of directors and financial institutions, which is rarely the best way to resolve issues.

The final form of activism involves intervention in the affairs of the company. This, however, can be very costly, depending on the nature of the problem. Where strategic and operational issues raise concerns, intervention can be very costly indeed. Identifying the weaknesses and problems relating to these issues requires a detailed understanding of the nature of the business. This implies close monitoring by relevant experts who are able to analyse the issues and then propose feasible solutions. The costs associated with such an exercise would normally be prohibitive, although the costs may be mitigated through some kind of collective action by financial institutions.

Not all forms of intervention in the affairs of a company, however, need be costly. Where, for example, there are corporate governance issues to be addressed, such as a failure to adhere to the recommendations of the UK Corporate Governance Code, a financial institution may nominate individuals for appointment as non-executive directors who can be relied upon to see that necessary changes are made. This should involve relatively little cost for the financial institution.

The future of shareholder activism

The rise of shareholder activism raises two important questions that have yet to be answered. Firstly, is it simply a passing phenomenon? It is no coincidence that share-holder activism took root during a period when stock market returns were fairly low.

There is a risk that financial institutions will become less active and less vigilant in monitoring companies when stock market returns improve. Secondly, does shareholder activism really make a difference to corporate performance? The research on this topic so far has been fairly sparse but early research in the US is not encouraging for those who urge financial institutions to take a more active approach. We may have to wait some while, however, for clear answers to these questions.

Summary

The main points of this chapter may be summarised as follows:

Corporate governance

- Corporate governance issues arise because of the separation of ownership from control of the company.
- Corporate governance rules are based around the principles of disclosure, accountability and fairness.
- The UK Corporate Governance Code, which applies to UK Stock Exchange listed companies, adopts a 'comply-or-explain' approach to the rules that it sets out.

The board of directors

- The board governs the company on behalf of the shareholders.
- The board is responsible for setting the strategic direction of the company, controlling the company and nurturing relations with shareholders and other parties.
- The chairman must lead and manage the board of directors.
- The chairman's role involves trying to ensure that the board operates effectively, providing advice and support to directors, communicating with shareholders and trying to ensure that the performance of the board and the directors is subject to regular scrutiny.
- The UK Corporate Governance Code states that the roles of chairman and chief executive should not be occupied by the same person. Furthermore, the chief executive should not go on to become chairman of the same company.
- The board is made up of executive and non-executive directors, all of which have the same legal obligation to the shareholders of the company.

Non-executive directors

- Non-executive directors are part-time and do not engage in the day-to-day running of the company.
- This more detached role allows them to take a more objective view of the issues confronting the company.
- Non-executive directors are meant to contribute to the main tasks of the board identified earlier and will play a key role in board committees concerned with the nomination of directors, the remuneration of executive directors and the integrity of financial statements.
- The role of non-executive directors contains the potential for conflict between the need to work with executive directors as part of a team and the need to monitor and assess the performance of executive directors on behalf of the shareholders.

The audit process

- An external audit is required by all but the smallest companies.

- External auditors are appointed by, and report to, the shareholders and their role is to examine the annual financial statements that have been prepared by the directors.

- Many large companies have an internal audit function, the main purpose of which is to provide the directors with reassurance concerning the reliability of the company's control and financial reporting systems.

- The presence of internal auditors can help the external auditors, who may be able to place reliance on some of the work undertaken by them.

- The UK Corporate Governance Code states that an audit committee should be created with delegated authority for ensuring that financial reporting and internal control principles are properly applied and for maintaining an appropriate relationship with the external auditors.

- The terms of reference of the committee will be determined by the board of directors.

- An audit committee report will be prepared for shareholders and presented at the AGM.

- The value of audit committees in preventing audit scandals is, so far, unproven.

Assessing board performance

- The board should be subject to regular evaluation, which may be carried out by the board itself or by an external party, such as a firm of management consultants.

- Areas of performance to be evaluated may include achievement of company objectives, control exercised over the company's activities, board structure and roles, board meetings, board composition, board discussions and decisions, relations with shareholders and board appointments and development.

Remunerating directors

- The UK Corporate Governance Code states that directors' remuneration should be sufficient to recruit and retain directors of the right calibre and that a significant proportion of total remuneration should be linked to performance.

- The remuneration package of executive directors will usually have a fixed element and a variable element, with the latter being linked to the achievement of clearly defined performance targets.

- The remuneration committee is the cornerstone of the UK Corporate Governance Code's attempt to ensure that directors' rewards are appropriate.

- Various problems in the way in which a remuneration committee functions may have contributed to excessive rewards being paid to directors.

- Performance targets should be consistent with the overall aims of the company, align the interests of directors with those of shareholders, reflect the achievement of the directors and be robust.

- TSR (total shareholder return) is a popular performance target and measures changes in shareholder wealth. To assess relative performance, similar companies must be used as a benchmark.

- EVA® (economic value added) indicates whether the returns generated exceed the returns required by investors. It relies on conventional financial statements to measure the wealth created but adjusts these to reflect the conservative bias in accounting measurement.

- EPS (earnings per share) can be used as a performance target by setting a particular level of growth required.

- Share options may be used to reward directors. However, these have been criticised for their failing to align the interests of directors with those of shareholders.

- Most listed public companies use a variety of measures and incentives to reward executive directors rather than relying on a single measure.

The rise of shareholder activism

- Institutional shareholders, who dominate the London Stock Exchange, have taken a more active role in the affairs of listed companies in recent years.

- Activism takes the form of using their votes, meetings with directors and intervention in a company's affairs.

- It is not clear whether such activism will continue when share prices rise and returns from the stock market increase.

 Key terms

chairman p. 392
executive directors p. 393
non-executive directors p. 393
UK Corporate Governance Code p. 393
executive committee p. 397
chief executive officer p. 397
audit committee p. 397
risk management committee p. 397

nomination committee p. 397
remuneration committee p. 397
external audit p. 406
internal audit p. 407
total shareholder return (TSR) p. 421
Economic value added (EVA®) p. 424
directors' share options p. 427

References

1 OECD, *Corporate Governance: Improving Competitiveness and Access to Capital in Global Markets*, report by Business Sector Advisory Group on Corporate Governance, Organisation for Economic Co-operation and Development (OECD), 1998, p. 14.

2 Kimbell, D. and Neff, T., 'Separating the roles of chairman and chief executive: looking at both sides of the debate', Spencer Stuart Research and Insight, July 2006, p. 2.

3 Stiles, P. and Taylor, B., *Boards at Work*, Oxford University Press, 2001, p. 108.

4 Owen, G. and Kirchmaier, T., *The Changing Role of the Chairman: Impact of Corporate Governance Reform in the UK 1995–2005 on Role, Board Compensation and Appointment*, March 2006.

5 Haigney, N., 'Relationship between Audit Committee and Internal Audit', HM Treasury, www.nationalschools.gov.uk.

6 Independent Audit Ltd, *Audit Committee Reporting in 2005*, www.boydeninterim.co.uk.

7 Sulkowicz, K., 'New organisational and psychological challenges of the audit committee', *Audit Committee Quarterly*, Issue 8, 2003, Audit Committee Institute.

8 Reported in Tucker, S., 'UK chiefs reluctant to take on audit role', FT.com, 30 January 2005.

9 Girma, S., Thompson, S. and Wright, P., 'Corporate governance reforms and executive compensation determination: evidence from the UK', *The Manchester School*, Vol. 75, 2007, pp. 65–81.

10 Main, B., Jackson, C., Pymm, J. and Wright, V., 'Questioning the remuneration committee process', 2007.

11 Lincoln, D., Young, D., Wilson, T. and Whiteley, P., *The Role of the Board Remuneration Committee*, PARC Research Report, March 2006.

12 Jenson, M. and Murphy, K., *Remuneration: Where We've Been, How We Got Here, What Are the Problems and How to Fix Them*, European Corporate Governance Institute Working Papers in Finance, 2004, p. 22.

13 Pope, P. and Young, S., 'Executive share options: an investor's guide', www.manifest.co.uk.

14 Bender, R., 'Just rewards for a new approach to pay', *Financial Times*, 2 June 2005.

15 Buffet, W. *Annual Report to Shareholders*, Berkshire Hathaway, Inc., 1985, p. 12.

16 Monks, R. and Minow, N., *Corporate Governance*, 2nd edn, Blackwell, 2001, p. 226.

17 Quoted in Guerrera, F., 'Study links directors to options scandal', *Financial Times*, 18 December 2006.

Further reading

If you would like to explore the topics covered in this chapter in more depth, we recommend the following books:

Elliott, B. and Elliott, J., *Financial Accounting and Reporting*, 13th edn, Financial Times Prentice Hall, 2009, Chapter 30.

Mallin, C., *Corporate Governance*, 2nd edn, OUP, 2007, Chapters 3, 6, 8 and 9.

Monks, R. and Minow, N., *Corporate Governance*, 4th edn, John Wiley and Sons Ltd, 2007, Chapters 2–4.

Solomon, J., *Corporate Governance and Accountability*, 2nd edn, John Wiley and Sons Ltd, 2007, Chapters 3–6.

Review questions

Solutions to these questions can be found at the back of the book on pages 489–490.

11.1 What are the main tasks of the board of directors?

11.2 What are the benefits of separating the roles of chairman and chief executive?

11.3 A large public company wishes to improve its payroll accounting systems and is seeking outside help to do this. The external auditors of the company are a large firm of accountants that has a consultancy arm. What are the advantages and disadvantages of allowing the external auditors to undertake this task?

11.4 Why have institutional shareholders become more active in corporate governance issues in recent years?

Exercises

Exercises 11.4 and 11.5 are more advanced than 11.1 to 11.3. Those with coloured numbers have solutions at the back of the book, starting on page 520.

If you wish to try more exercises, visit the students' side of the Companion Website.

11.1 Identify the main ways in which a large listed company may communicate with its shareholders.

11.2 Assume that the chairman of the board of directors of a large public listed company has asked you to develop a set of criteria against which the performance of a non-executive director could be appraised. Try to identify at least six criteria, based on the discussion of the role found in the chapter, which you might select.

11.3 Reviewing the risk management systems within a company goes beyond the traditional role of internal audit. What changes may have to be made to the internal audit function to enable it to carry out this enhanced role?

11.4 The board of directors of a listed company is likely to place considerable emphasis on maintaining good communications and strong relationships with its institutional shareholders. What are the main benefits and problems of doing this?

11.5 The newly appointed chairman of Vorak plc has been told that considerable tension and suspicion exists between the executive and non-executive directors on the board. The executive directors question the competence of the non-executive directors and the non-executive directors believe that important information is being withheld from them. Assuming that the concerns of each group are well founded, what advice would you give to the chairman concerning how to ease the tension and promote a better working relationship between the two groups?

Appendix A
Recording financial transactions

Introduction

In Chapters 2 and 3, we saw how the financial transactions of a business may be recorded by making a series of entries on the statement of financial position (balance sheet) and/or the income statement. Each of these entries had its corresponding 'double', meaning that both sides of the transaction were recorded. However, adjusting the financial statements, by hand, for each transaction can be very messy and confusing. With a reasonably large number of transactions it is pretty certain to result in mistakes.

For businesses whose accounting systems are on a computer, this problem is overcome because suitable software can deal with a series of 'plus' and 'minus' entries very reliably. Where the accounting system is not computerised, however, it would be helpful to have some more practical way of keeping accounting records. Such a system not only exists but, before the advent of the computer, was the routine way of keeping accounting records. It is this system that is explained in this appendix. We should be clear that the system we are going to consider follows exactly the same rules as those that we have already met. Its distinguishing feature is its ability to provide those keeping accounting records by hand with a methodical approach that allows each transaction to be clearly identified and errors to be minimised.

Learning outcomes

When you have completed this appendix, you should be able to:

- explain the basic principles of double-entry bookkeeping;

- write up a series of business transactions and balance the accounts;

- extract a trial balance and explain its purpose;

- prepare a set of financial statements from the underlying double-entry accounts.

The basics of double-entry bookkeeping

→ When we record accounting transactions by hand, we use a recording system known as **double-entry bookkeeping**. This system does not use plus and minus entries on the face of a statement of financial position and income statement to record a particular transaction, in the way described in Chapters 2 and 3. Instead, these are recorded in accounts.

→ An **account** is simply a record of one or more transactions relating to a particular item, such as cash, fixtures and fittings, borrowings, sales revenue, rent payable or equity. A business may keep few or many accounts, depending on the size and complexity of its operations. Broadly, businesses tend to keep a separate account for each item that appears in either the income statement or the statement of financial position.

An example of an account, in this case the cash account, is as follows:

Cash

£	£

We can see that an account has three main features:

- a title indicating the item to which it relates;
→ - a left-hand side, known as the **debit** side; and
→ - a right-hand side, known as the **credit** side.

One side of an account will record increases in the particular item and the other will record decreases. This, of course, is slightly different from the approach we used when adjusting the financial statements. When adjusting the statement of financial position, for example, we put a reduction in an asset or claim in the same column as any increases, but with a minus sign against it. However, when accounts are used, a reduction is shown on the opposite side of the account.

The side on which an increase or decrease is shown will depend on the nature of the item to which the account relates. For example, an account for an asset, such as cash, will show increases on the left-hand (debit) side of the account and decreases on the right-hand (credit) side. However, for claims (that is, equity and liabilities) it is the other way around. An increase in the account for equity or for a liability will be shown on the right-hand (credit) side and a decrease will be shown on the left-hand (debit) side.

To understand why this difference exists, we should recall from Chapter 2 that the accounting equation is:

$$\text{Assets} = \text{Equity} + \text{Liabilities}$$

We can see that assets appear on one side of the equation and equity and liabilities appear on the other. Recording transactions in accounts simply expresses this difference in the recording process. Increases in assets are shown on the left-hand side of the account and increases in equity and liabilities are shown on the right-hand side of the account. We should recall the point made in Chapter 2 that each transaction has two aspects. Thus, when we record a particular transaction, two separate accounts will be affected. Recording transactions in this way is known as double-entry bookkeeping.

It is worth going through a simple example to see how transactions affecting statement of financial position items would be recorded under the double-entry bookkeeping system. Suppose a new business started on 1 January with the owner putting £5,000 into a newly opened business bank account, as initial equity. This entry would appear in the cash account as follows:

Cash

	£		£
1 January Equity	5,000		

The corresponding entry would be made in the equity account as follows:

Equity

	£		£
		1 January Cash	5,000

It is usual to show, in each account by way of note, where the other side of the entry will be found. Thus, someone looking at the equity account will know that the £5,000 arose from a receipt of cash. This provides potentially useful information, partly because it establishes a 'trail' that can be followed when checking for errors. Including the date of the transaction provides additional information to the reader of the accounts.

Now suppose that, on 2 January, £600 of the cash is used to buy some inventories. This would affect the cash account as follows:

Cash

	£		£
1 January Equity	5,000	2 January Inventories	600

This cash account, in effect, shows 'positive' cash of £5,000 and 'negative' cash of £600, a net amount of £4,400.

Activity A.1

As you know, we must somehow record the other side of the transaction involving the acquisition of the inventories for £600. See if you can work out what to do in respect of the inventories.

We must open an account for inventories. Since inventories are assets, an increase in it will appear on the left-hand side of the account, as follows:

Inventories

	£		£
2 January Cash	600		

What we have seen so far highlights the key rule of double-entry bookkeeping: each left-hand entry must have a right-hand entry of equal size. Using the jargon, we can say that *every debit must have a credit*.

It might be helpful at this point to make clear that the words 'debit' and 'credit' are no more than accounting jargon for left and right, respectively. Generally, in English, when not referring to accounting, people tend to use 'credit' to imply something good and 'debit' to imply something undesirable. Debit and credit have no such implications in accounting. Each transaction requires both a debit entry and a credit one. This is equally true whether the transaction is a 'good' one, like being paid by a credit customer, or a 'bad' one, like having to treat a credit customer's balance as worthless because that customer has gone bankrupt.

Recording trading transactions

The rules of double entry also extend to 'trading' transactions, that is, making revenue (sales and so on) and incurring expenses. To understand how these transactions are recorded, we should recall that in Chapter 3 the accounting equation was extended as follows:

$$\text{Assets} = \text{Equity} + (\text{Revenues} - \text{Expenses}) + \text{Liabilities}$$

This equation can be rearranged so that

$$\text{Assets} + \text{Expenses} = \text{Equity} + \text{Revenues} + \text{Liabilities}$$

We can see that increases in expenses are shown on the same side as assets and this means that they will be dealt with in the same way for recording purposes. Thus, an increase in an expense, such as wages, will be shown on the left-hand (debit) side of the wages account and a decrease will be shown on the right-hand (credit) side. Increases in revenues are shown on the same side as equity and liabilities and so will be dealt with in the same way as them. Thus, an increase in revenue, such as sales, will be shown on the right-hand (credit) side and a decrease will be shown on the left-hand (debit) side.

To summarise, therefore, we can say that:

- **Debits (left-hand entries) represent increases in assets and expenses and decreases in claims and revenues.**
- **Credits (right-hand entries) represent increases in claims and revenues and decreases in assets and expenses.**

Let us continue with our example by assuming that, on 3 January, the business paid £900 to rent business premises for the three months to 31 March. To record this transaction, we should normally open a 'rent account' and make entries in this account and in the cash account as follows:

Rent

		£			£
3 January	Cash	900			

Cash

		£			£
1 January	Equity	5,000	2 January	Inventories	600
			3 January	Rent	900

The fact that assets and expenses are dealt with in the same way should not be altogether surprising since assets and expenses are closely linked. Assets transform into expenses as they are 'used up'. Rent, which, as here, is usually paid in advance, is an asset when it is first paid. It represents the value to the business of being entitled to occupy the premises for the forthcoming period (until 31 March in this case). As the three months progress, this asset becomes an expense; it is 'used up'. We need to remember that the debit entry in the rent account does not necessarily represent either an asset or an expense; it could be a mixture of the two. Strictly, by the end of the day on which it was paid (3 January), £30 would have represented an expense for the three days; the remaining £870 would have been an asset. As each day passes, an additional £10 (that is, £900/90 (there are 90 days in January, February and March altogether)) will transform from an asset into an expense. As we have already seen, it is not necessary for us to make any adjustment to the rent account as the days pass.

Assume, now, that on 5 January the business sold inventories costing £200 for £300 on credit. As usual, when we are able to identify the cost of the inventories sold at the time of sale, we need to deal with the sale and the cost of sales as two separate issues, each having its own set of debits and credits.

First, let us deal with the sale. We now need to open accounts for both 'sales revenue' and 'trade receivables' – which do not, as yet, exist. The sale gives rise to an increase in revenue and so there is a credit entry in the sales revenue account. The sale also creates an asset of trade receivables and so there is debit entry in trade receivables:

Sales revenue

	£			£
		5 January	Trade receivables	300

Trade receivables

	£		£
5 January Sales revenue	300		

Let us now deal with the inventories sold. Since the inventories sold have become the expense 'cost of sales', we need to reduce the figure on the inventories account by making a credit entry and to make the corresponding debit in a 'cost of sales' account, opened for the purpose:

Inventories

	£			£
2 January Cash	600	5 January	Cost of sales	200

Cost of sales

	£		£
5 January Inventories	200		

We shall now look at the other transactions for our hypothetical business for the remainder of January. These can be taken to be as follows:

8 January   Bought some inventories on credit costing £800
11 January   Bought some office furniture for £600 cash
15 January   Sold inventories costing £600 for £900, on credit

18 January   Received £800 from trade receivables
21 January   Paid trade payables £500
24 January   Paid wages for the month £400
27 January   Bought inventories on credit for £800
31 January   Borrowed £2,000 from the Commercial Finance Company

Naturally, we shall have to open several additional accounts to enable us to record all of these transactions in any meaningful way. By the end of January, the set of accounts would appear as follows:

Cash

		£			£
1 January	Equity	5,000	2 January	Inventories	600
18 January	Trade receivables	800	3 January	Rent	900
31 January	Comm. Fin. Co.	2,000	11 January	Office furniture	600
			21 January	Trade payables	500
			24 January	Wages	400

Equity

		£			£
			1 January	Cash	5,000

Inventories

		£			£
2 January	Cash	600	5 January	Cost of sales	200
8 January	Trade payables	800	15 January	Cost of sales	600
27 January	Trade payables	800			

Rent

		£		£
3 January	Cash	900		

Sales revenue

	£			£
		5 January	Trade receivables	300
		15 January	Trade receivables	900

Trade receivables

		£			£
5 January	Sales revenue	300	18 January	Cash	800
15 January	Sales revenue	900			

Cost of sales

		£		£
5 January	Inventories	200		
15 January	Inventories	600		

Trade payables

		£			£
21 January	Cash	500	8 January	Inventories	800
			27 January	Inventories	800

Office furniture

		£		£
11 January	Cash	600		

Wages

		£		£
24 January	Cash	400		

Borrowings – Commercial Finance Company

	£			£
		31 January	Cash	2,000

All of the transactions from 8 January onwards are quite similar in nature to those up to that date, which we discussed in detail, and so we should be able to follow them using the date references as a guide.

Balancing accounts and the trial balance

Businesses keeping their accounts in the way shown would find it helpful to summarise their individual accounts periodically – perhaps weekly or monthly – for two reasons:

- to be able to see at a glance how much is in each account (for example, to see how much cash the business has left), and
- to help to check the accuracy of the bookkeeping so far.

Let us look at the cash account again:

Cash

		£			£
1 January	Equity	5,000	2 January	Inventories	600
18 January	Trade receivables	800	3 January	Rent	900
31 January	Comm. Fin. Co.	2,000	11 January	Office furniture	600
			21 January	Trade payables	500
			24 January	Wages	400

Does this account tell us how much cash the business has at 31 January? The answer is partly yes and partly no.

We do not have a single figure showing the cash **balance** but we can fairly easily deduce this by adding up the debit (receipts) column and deducting the sum of the credit (payments) column. However, it would be better if a cash balance were provided for us.

To summarise or balance this account, we add up the column with the larger amount (in this case, the debit side) and put this total on *both* sides of the account. We then put in, on the other side, the figure that will make that side add up to the total that appears in the account. We cannot put in this balancing figure only once, as the double-entry rule would be broken. Thus, to preserve the double entry, we also put it in on the other side of the same account below the totals, as follows:

Cash

		£			£
1 January	Equity	5,000	2 January	Inventories	600
18 January	Trade receivables	800	3 January	Rent	900
31 January	Borrowings	2,000	11 January	Office furniture	600
			21 January	Trade payables	500
			24 January	Wages	400
			31 January	Balance carried down	4,800
		7,800			7,800
1 February	Balance brought down	4,800			

Note that the balance carried down (usually abbreviated to 'c/d') at the end of one period becomes the balance brought down ('b/d') at the beginning of the next. Now we can see at a glance what the present cash position is, without having to do any mental arithmetic.

Activity A.2

Try balancing the inventories account and then say what we know about the inventories position at the end of January.

The inventories account will be balanced as follows:

Inventories

		£			£
2 January	Cash	600	5 January	Cost of sales	200
8 January	Trade payables	800	15 January	Cost of sales	600
27 January	Trade payables	800	31 January	Balance c/d	1,400
		2,200			2,200
1 February	Balance b/d	1,400			

We can see at a glance that the business held inventories that had cost £1,400 at the end of January. We can also see quite easily how this situation arose.

We can balance all of the other accounts in a similar fashion. However, there is no point in formally balancing accounts that have only one entry at the moment (for example, the equity account) because we cannot summarise one figure; it is already in as summarised a form as it can be. After balancing, the remaining accounts will be as follows:

Equity

	£			£
		1 January	Cash	5,000

Rent

		£		£
3 January	Cash	900		

Sales revenue

		£			£
31 January	Balance c/d	1,200	5 January	Trade receivables	300
			15 January	Trade receivables	900
		1,200			1,200
			1 February	Balance b/d	1,200

Trade receivables

		£			£
5 January	Sales revenue	300	18 January	Cash	800
15 January	Sales revenue	900	31 January	Balance c/d	400
		1,200			1,200
1 February	Balance b/d	400			

Cost of sales

		£			£
5 January	Inventories	200	31 January	Balance c/d	800
15 January	Inventories	600			
		800			800
1 February	Balance b/d	800			

Trade payables

		£			£
21 January	Cash	500	8 January	Inventories	800
31 January	Balance c/d	1,100	27 January	Inventories	800
		1,600			1,600
			1 February	Balance b/d	1,100

Office furniture

		£		£
11 January	Cash	600		

Wages

		£		£
24 January	Cash	400		

Borrowings – Commercial Finance Company

	£			£
		31 January	Cash	2,000

Activity A.3

If we now separately total all of the debit balances and the all of the credit balances, what should we expect to find?

We should expect to find that these two totals are equal. This must, in theory be true since every debit entry was matched by an equally sized credit entry.

Let us see if our expectation in Activity A.3 works in our example, by listing the debit and credit balances as follows:

	Debits £	Credits £
Cash	4,800	
Inventories	1,400	
Equity		5,000
Rent	900	
Sales revenue		1,200
Trade receivables	400	
Cost of sales	800	
Trade payables		1,100
Office furniture	600	
Wages	400	
Borrowings		2,000
	9,300	9,300

→   This statement is known as a **trial balance**. The fact that it agrees gives us *some* indication that we have not made bookkeeping errors.

This situation, does not, however, give us total confidence that no error could have occurred. Consider, for example, the transaction that took place on 3 January (paid rent for the month of £900). In each of the following cases, all of which would be a wrong treatment of the transaction, the trial balance would still have agreed:

- The transaction was completely omitted from the accounts, that is, no entries were made at all.
- The amount was misread as £9,000 but then (correctly) debited to the rent account and credited to cash.
- The correct amount was (incorrectly) debited to cash and credited to rent.

Nevertheless, a trial balance that agrees does give some confidence that accounts have been correctly written up.

Activity A.4

Why do you think the words 'debtor' and 'creditor' are used to describe those who owe money or are owed money by a business?

The answer simply is that debtors have a debit balance (that is, a balance brought down on the debit side) in the books of the business, whereas creditors have a credit balance.

Preparing the financial statements (final accounts)

If the trial balance agrees and we are confident that there are no errors in recording, the next stage is to prepare the income statement and statement of financial position. Preparing the income statement is simply a matter of going through the individual accounts, identifying those amounts that represent revenue and expenses of the period, and transferring them to the income statement, which is itself also part of the double-entry system.

We shall now do this for the example we have been using. The situation is complicated slightly for three reasons:

- As we know, the £900 rent paid during January relates to the three months January, February and March.
- The business's owner estimates that the electricity used during January is about £110. There is no bill yet from the electricity supply business because it normally bills customers only at the end of each three-month period.
- The business's owner believes that the office furniture should be depreciated by 20 per cent each year (straight-line).

These three factors need to be taken into account. As we shall see, however, the end-of-period adjustments of these types are very easily handled in double-entry accounts. Let us deal with these three areas first.

The rent account will appear as follows, after we have completed the transfer to the income statement:

Rent

		£				£
3 January	Cash	900	31 January	Income statement		300
				Balance c/d		600
		900				900
1 February	Balance b/d	600				

At 31 January, because two months' rent is still an asset, this is carried down as a debit balance. The remainder (representing January's rent) is credited to the rent account and debited to a newly opened income statement. As we shall see shortly, the £600 debit balance remaining will appear in the 31 January statement of financial position.

Now let us deal with the electricity. The electricity account will be as follows after the transfer to the income statement:

Electricity

	£			£
		31 January	Income statement	110

Because there has been no cash payment or other transaction recorded so far for electricity, we do not already have an account for it. It is necessary to open one. We need to debit the income statement with the £110 of electricity used during January and credit the electricity account with the same amount. At 31 January, this credit balance reflects the amount owed by this business to the electricity supplier. Once again, we shall see shortly that this balance will appear on the statement of financial position.

Next we shall consider what is necessary regarding the office furniture. The depreciation for the month will be $20\% \times £600 \times \frac{1}{12}$, that is £10. Normal accounting practice is to charge (debit) this to the income statement, with the corresponding credit going to a 'provision for depreciation of office furniture' account. The latter entry will appear as follows:

Provision for depreciation of office furniture

	£		£
		31 January Income statement	10

This £10 balance will be reflected in the statement of financial position at 31 January by being deducted from the office furniture itself, as we shall see.

The balances on the following accounts represent straightforward revenue and expenses for the month of January:

- Sales revenue
- Cost of sales
- Wages.

The balances on these accounts will simply be transferred to the income statement.

To transfer balances to the income statement, we simply debit or credit the account concerned, such that any balance amount is eliminated, and make the corresponding credit or debit in the income statement. Take sales revenue, for example. This has a credit balance (because the balance represents a revenue). We must debit the sales revenue account with £1,200 and credit the income statement with the same amount. So a credit balance on the sales revenue account becomes a credit entry in the income statement. For the three accounts, then, we have the following:

Sales revenue

		£			£
31 January	Balance c/d	1,200	5 January	Trade receivables	300
			15 January	Trade receivables	900
		1,200			1,200
31 January	Income statement	1,200	1 February	Balance b/d	1,200

Cost of sales

		£			£
5 January	Inventories	200	31 January	Balance c/d	800
15 January	Inventories	600			
		800			800
1 February	Balance b/d	800	31 January	Income statement	800

Wages

		£			£
24 January	Cash	400	31 January	Income statement	400

The income statement will now look as follows:

Income statement

		£			£
31 January	Cost of sales	800	31 January	Sales revenue	1,200
31 January	Rent	300			
31 January	Wages	400			
31 January	Electricity	110			
31 January	Depreciation	10			

We must now transfer the balance on the income statement (a debit balance of £420).

Activity A.5

What does the balance on the income statement represent, and to where should it be transferred?

The balance is either the profit or the loss for the period. In this case it is a loss as the total expenses exceed the total revenue. This loss must be borne by the owner, and it must therefore be transferred to the equity account.

The two accounts would now appear as follows:

Income statement

		£			£
31 January	Cost of sales	800	31 January	Sales revenue	1,200
31 January	Rent	300			
31 January	Wages	400			
31 January	Electricity	110			
31 January	Depreciation	10	31 January	Equity (loss)	420
		1,620			1,620

Equity

		£			£
31 January	Income statement (loss)	420	1 January	Cash	5,000
31 January	Balance c/d	4,580			
		5,000			5,000
			1 February	Balance b/d	4,580

The last thing done was to balance the equity account.

Now all of the balances remaining on accounts represent either assets or claims as at 31 January. These balances can now be used to produce a statement of financial position, as follows:

Statement of financial position as at 31 January

	£
ASSETS	
Non-current assets	
Property, plant and equipment	
Office furniture: cost	600
depreciation	(10)
	590
Current assets	
Inventories	1,400
Prepaid expense	600
Trade receivables	400
Cash	4,800
	7,200
Total assets	7,790
EQUITY AND LIABILITIES	
Equity (owners' claim)	4,580
Non-current liability	
Borrowings	2,000
Current liabilities	
Accrued expense	110
Trade payables	1,100
	1,210
Total equity and liabilities	7,790

The income statement could be written in a more stylish manner, for reporting to users, as follows:

Income statement for the month ended 31 January

	£
Sales revenue	1,200
Cost of sales	(800)
Gross profit	400
Rent	(300)
Wages	(400)
Electricity	(110)
Depreciation	(10)
Loss for the month	(420)

The ledger and its division

→ The book in which the accounts are traditionally kept is known as the **ledger**, and 'accounts' are sometimes referred to as 'ledger accounts', even where they are computerised.

In a handwritten accounting system, the ledger is often divided into various sections. This tends to be for three main reasons:

● Having all of the accounts in one book means that it is only possible for one person at a time to use the accounts, either to make entries or to extract useful information.

- Dividing the ledger along logical grounds can allow specialisation, so that various individual members of the accounts staff can look after their own part of the system. This can lead to more efficient record-keeping.
- It can also lead to greater security, that is, less risk of error and fraud by limiting an individual's access to only part of the entire set of accounts.

There are no clear, universal rules on the division of the ledger, but the following division is fairly common:

- *The cash book*. This tends to contain all of the accounts relating to cash either loose (petty cash) or in the bank.
- *The sales (or trade receivables) ledger*. This contains the accounts of all of the business's individual trade receivables.
- *The purchases (or trade payables) ledger*. This consists of the accounts of all of the business's individual trade payables.
- *The nominal ledger*. The accounts in this tend to be those of expenses and revenue, for example, sales revenue, wages, rent and so on.
- *The general ledger*. This contains the remainder of the business's accounts, mainly those to do with non-current assets and long-term finance.

Summary

The main points in this appendix may be summarised as follows:

Double-entry bookkeeping is a system for keeping accounting records by hand, such that a relatively large volume of transactions can be handled effectively and accurately.

- There is a separate account for each asset, claim, expense and revenue that needs to be separately identified.
- Each account looks like a letter T.
- The left-hand (debit) side of the account records increases in assets and expenses and decreases in revenues and claims.
- The right-hand (credit) side records increases in revenues and claims and decreases in assets and expenses.
- There is an equal credit entry in one account for a debit entry in another, in respect of each transaction.
- Double-entry bookkeeping can be used to record day-to-day transactions.
- It can also follow through to generate the income statement.
- The statement of financial position is a list of the net figure (the 'balance') on each of the accounts after appropriate transfers have been made to the income statement.
- The accounts are traditionally kept in a 'ledger', a term that persists even with computerised accounting.
- The ledger is traditionally broken down into several sections, each containing particular types of account.

Key terms

double-entry bookkeeping p. 443   **balance** p. 448
account p. 443   **trial balance** p. 451
debit p. 443   **ledger** p. 455
credit p. 443

Further reading

If you would like to explore the topics covered in this appendix in more depth, we recommend the following books:

Bebbington, J., Gray, R. and Laughlin, R., *Financial Accounting*, 3rd edn, Thomson Learning, 2001, Chapters 2 to 7.

Benedict, A. and Elliott, B., *Practical Accounting*, Financial Times Prentice Hall, 2008, Chapters 2 to 5.

Thomas, A., *An Introduction to Financial Accounting*, 5th edn, McGraw-Hill, 2005, Chapters 3 to 8.

Exercises

The answers to all three of these exercises are at the back of the book, starting on page 521. If you wish to try more exercises, visit the students' side of the Companion Website.

A.1   In respect of each of the following transactions, state in which two accounts an entry must be made and whether the entry is a debit or a credit. (For example, if the transaction were buying inventories for cash, the answer would be debit the inventories account and credit the cash account.)

(a) Bought inventories on credit.
(b) Owner made cash drawings.
(c) Paid interest on business borrowings.
(d) Bought inventories for cash.
(e) Received cash from a credit customer.
(f) Paid wages to employees.
(g) The owner received some cash from a credit customer, which was taken as drawings rather than being paid into the business's bank account.
(h) Paid a credit supplier.
(i) Paid electricity bill.
(j) Made cash sales.

A.2   (a) Record the following transactions in a set of double-entry accounts:

1 February	Lee (the owner) put £6,000 into a newly-opened business bank account to start a new business
3 February	Bought inventories for £2,600 for cash
5 February	Bought some equipment (non-current asset) for cash for £800
6 February	Bought inventories costing £3,000 on credit
9 February	Paid rent for the month of £250
10 February	Paid £240 for electricity for the month
11 February	Paid general expenses of £200
15 February	Sold inventories for £4,000 in cash; the inventories had cost £2,400
19 February	Sold inventories for £3,800 on credit; the inventories had cost £2,300
21 February	Lee withdrew £1,000 in cash for personal use
25 February	Paid £2,000 to trade payables
28 February	Received £2,500 from trade receivables

(b) Balance the relevant accounts and prepare a trial balance (making sure that it agrees).
(c) Prepare an income statement for the month and a statement of financial position at the month end. Assume that there are no prepaid or accrued expenses at the end of the month and ignore any possible depreciation.

A.3 The following is the statement of financial position of David's business at 1 January of last year.

ASSETS		£
Non-current assets		
Property, plant and equipment		
Buildings		25,000
Fittings: cost	10,000	
depreciation	(2,000)	8,000
		33,000
Current assets		
Inventories of stationery		140
Trading inventories		1,350
Prepaid rent		500
Trade receivables		1,840
Cash		2,180
		6,010
Total assets		39,010
EQUITY AND LIABILITIES		£
Equity		25,050
Non-current liabilities		
Borrowings		12,000
Current liabilities		
Trade payables		1,690
Accrued electricity		270
		1,960
Total equity and liabilities		39,010

The following is a summary of the transactions that took place during the year:

1 Inventories were bought on credit for £17,220.
2 Inventories were bought for £3,760 cash.
3 Credit sales revenue amounted to £33,100 (cost £15,220).
4 Cash sales revenue amounted to £10,360 (cost £4,900).
5 Wages of £3,770 were paid.
6 Rent of £3,000 was paid. The annual rental amounts to £3,000.
7 Electricity of £1,070 was paid.
8 General expenses of £580 were paid.
9 Additional fittings were purchased on 1 January for £2,000. The cash for this was raised from additional borrowings of this amount. The interest rate is 10 per cent a year, the same as for the existing borrowings.
10 £1,000 of the borrowing was repaid on 30 June.
11 Cash received from trade receivables amounted to £32,810.
12 Cash paid to trade payables amounted to £18,150.
13 The owner withdrew £10,400 cash and £560 inventories for private use.

At the end of the year it was found that:

- The electricity bill for the last quarter of the year for £290 had not been paid.
- Trade receivables amounting to £260 were unlikely to be received.
- The value of stationery remaining was estimated at £150. Stationery is included in general expenses.
- The borrowings carried interest of 10 per cent a year and was unpaid at the year end.

Depreciation is to be taken at 20 per cent on the cost of the fittings owned at the year end. Buildings are not depreciated.

Required:

(a) Open ledger accounts and bring down all of the balances in the opening statement of financial position.

(b) Make entries to record the transactions 1 to 13 (above), opening any additional accounts as necessary.

(c) Open an income statement (part of the double entry, remember). Make the necessary entries for the bulleted list above and the appropriate transfers to the income statement.

(d) List the remaining balances in the same form as the opening statement of financial position (above).

Appendix B

Glossary of key terms

Account   A section of a double-entry bookkeeping system that deals with one particular asset, claim, expense or revenue. *p. 443*

Accounting   The process of identifying, measuring and communicating information to permit informed judgements and decisions by users of the information. *p. 2*

Accounting information system   The system used within a business to identify, record, analyse and report accounting information. *p. 10*

Accounting period   The time span for which a business prepares its financial statements. *p. 72*

Accruals accounting   The system of accounting that follows the accruals convention. This is the system followed in drawing up the statement of financial position and income statement. *p. 86*

Accruals convention   The convention of accounting that asserts that profit is the excess of revenue over expenses, not the excess of cash receipts over cash payments. *p. 86*

Accrued expenses   Expenses that are outstanding at the end of an accounting period. *p. 82*

Acid test ratio   A liquidity ratio that relates the liquid assets (usually defined as current liabilities less inventories) to the current liabilities. *p. 240*

Allotted share capital   *See* Issued share capital.

Allowance for trade receivables   An amount set aside out of profit to provide for anticipated losses arising from debts (trade receivables) that may prove irrecoverable. *p. 102*

Amortisation   A measure of that portion of the cost (or fair value) of a non-current asset that has been consumed during an accounting period. The word 'amortisation' tends to be used where the particular non-current asset is an intangible one, whereas 'depreciation' is normally used with tangible assets. *p. 93*

Assets   Resources held by a business, that have certain characteristics. *p. 36*

Associate company   A company over which considerable influence, but not full control, may be exercised by another company. *p. 338*

Audit committee   A committee of the board of directors, comprising non-executive directors, that is charged with ensuring that financial reporting and internal control principles are properly applied and with maintaining an appropriate relationship with the external auditors. *p. 397*

Auditors Professionals whose main duty is to make a report as to whether, in their opinion, the financial statements of a company do what they are supposed to do, namely show a true and fair view and comply with statutory, and financial reporting standard, requirements. *p. 171*

AVCO *See* Weighted average cost.

Average inventories turnover period ratio An efficiency ratio that measures the average period for which inventories are held by a business. *p. 232*

Average settlement period for trade payables ratio The average time taken for a business to pay its trade payables. *p. 234*

Average settlement period for trade receivables ratio The average time taken for trade receivables to pay the amounts owing. *p. 233*

Bad debt An amount owed to the business that is considered to be irrecoverable. *p. 101*

Balance The net of the debit and credit totals in an account in a double-entry book-keeping system. *p. 448*

Bonus shares Reserves that are converted into shares and issued 'free' to existing shareholders. *p. 128*

Business entity convention The convention that holds that, for accounting purposes, the business and its owner(s) are treated as quite separate and distinct. *p. 51*

Business review Part of the directors' report that helps shareholders to assess how well the directors have performed. It provides an analysis of financial performance, position and cash flows. It also sets out the principal risks and uncertainties facing the business. *p. 172*

Called-up share capital That part of a company's share capital for which the shareholders have been asked to pay the agreed amount. It is part of the claim of the owners against the business. *p. 131*

Capital reserves Reserves that arise from an unrealised 'capital' profits or gains rather than from normal realised trading activities. *p. 126*

Carrying amount The difference between the cost (or fair value) of a non-current asset and the accumulated depreciation relating to the asset. The carrying value is also referred to as the written-down value (WDV) and the net book value (NBV). *p. 89*

Cash generated from operations per ordinary share ratio An investment ratio that relates the cash generated from operations and available to ordinary shareholders to the number of ordinary shares. *p. 264*

Cash generated from operations to maturing obligations ratio A liquidity ratio that compares the cash generated from operations to the current liabilities of the business. *p. 241*

Chairman The director who is appointed to lead the board of directors. *p. 392*

Chief executive officer The director who is appointed to lead the management team. *p. 397*

Claims Obligations on the part of a business to provide cash or some other benefit to outside parties. *p. 36*

Common-sized financial statements   Financial statements (such as the income statement, statement of financial position and statement of cash flows) that are expressed in terms of some base figure. *p. 273*

Comparability   The requirement that items which are basically the same should be treated in the same manner for measurement and reporting purposes. Lack of comparability will limit the usefulness of accounting information. *p. 7*

Consistency convention   The accounting convention that holds that, when a particular method of accounting is selected to deal with a transaction, this method should be applied consistently over time. *p. 101*

Consolidated financial statements   *See* Group financial statements.

Consolidating   Changing the nominal value of shares to a higher figure (from, say, £0.50 to £1.00) and then reducing the number of shares in issue so that each shareholder has the same total nominal value of shares as before. *p. 125*

Conventions of accounting   A set of generally accepted rules that accountants tend to follow when preparing financial statements. They tend to have evolved over time in order to deal with practical problems rather than to reflect some theoretical ideal. *p. 14*

Corporate governance   Matters concerned with directing and controlling a company. *p. 123*

Corporation tax   Taxation that a limited company is liable to pay on its profits. *p. 122*

Cost of sales   The cost of the goods sold during a period. Cost of sales can be derived by adding the opening inventories held to the inventories purchases for the period and then deducting the closing inventories held. *p. 74*

Creative accounting   Adopting accounting policies to achieve a particular view of performance and position that preparers would like users to see rather than what is a true and fair view. *p. 173*

Credit   An entry made in the right-hand side of an account in double-entry bookkeeping. *p. 443*

Current assets   Assets that are held for the short term. They include cash itself and other assets that are held for sale or consumption in the normal course of a business's operating cycle. *p. 45*

Current cost accounting (CCA)   An approach to preparing financial statements that is concerned with ensuring that the business is able to maintain its scale of operations during a period of inflation. *p. 381*

Current liabilities   Claims against the business which are expected to be settled within the normal course of the business's operating cycle or within twelve months of the statement of financial position date, or which are held primarily for trading purposes, or for which the business does not have the right to defer settlement beyond twelve months of the statement of financial position date. *p. 47*

Current (or constant) purchasing power (CPP) accounting   An approach to preparing financial statements this is concerned with ensuring that the general purchasing power of the owners' investment in the business is maintained during a period of inflation. *p. 380*

Current ratio   A liquidity ratio that relates the current assets of the business to the current liabilities. *p. 239*

Debit   An entry made in the left-hand side of an account in double-entry bookkeeping. *p. 443*

Depreciation   A measure of that portion of the cost (or fair value) of a non-current asset that has been consumed during an accounting period. *p. 86*

Direct method   An approach to deducing the cash flows from operating activities, in a statement of cash flows, by analysing the business's cash records. *p. 195*

Directors   Individuals who are appointed (normally by being elected by the shareholders) to act as the most senior level of management of a company. *p. 123*

Directors' report   A report containing information of a financial and non-financial nature that the directors must produce as part of the annual financial report to shareholders. *p. 172*

Directors' share options   The right given to directors to buy equity shares in their company at an agreed price. This right will only be exercised if the value of the shares exceeds the agreed price at the time that the right may be exercised. *p. 427*

Discrete method   An approach to interim profit measurement that treats the interim period as quite separate and distinct from the annual period. *p. 364*

Discriminate function   A boundary line, produced by multiple discriminate analysis, which can be used to identify those businesses that are likely to suffer financial distress and those that are not. *p. 279*

Dividend   The transfer of assets (usually cash) made by a company to its shareholders. *p. 124*

Dividend cover ratio   An investment ratio that relates the earnings available for dividends to the dividend announced, to indicate how many times the former covers the latter. *p. 262*

Dividend payout ratio   An investment ratio that relates the dividends announced for the period to the earnings available for dividends that were generated in that period. *p. 262*

Dividend per share   An investment ratio that relates the dividends announced for a period to the number of shares in issue. *p. 263*

Dividend yield ratio   An investment ratio that relates the cash return from a share to its current market value. *p. 263*

Double-entry bookkeeping   A system for recording financial transactions where each transaction is recorded twice, once as a debit and once as a credit. *p. 443*

Dual aspect convention   The accounting convention that holds that each transaction has two aspects and that each aspect must be recorded in the financial statements. *p. 53*

Earnings per share   An investment ratio that relates the earnings generated by the business during a period, and available to shareholders, to the number of shares in issue. *p. 263*

Economic value added (EVA®)   A measure of business performance that concentrates on wealth generation. It is based on economic profit rather than accounting profit and takes full account of the costs of financing. *p. 424*

Equity   The owners' claim; in the case of a limited company, the sum of shares and reserves. *p. 39*

Executive committee   A committee of the board of directors, comprising the executive directors and normally chaired by the chief executive officer. The committee may be given the task of developing and implementing the strategic plan of the company. *p. 397*

Executive directors   Directors who normally work for the company on a full-time basis and have executive responsibilities for certain key business functions, such as finance, marketing and so on. *p. 393*

Expense   A measure of the outflow of assets (or increase in liabilities) incurred as a result of generating revenue. *p. 71*

External audit   An independent examination of the accounting records to see whether the financial statements provide a true and fair view of the state of affairs of the company and comply with legal and other regulatory requirements. The person conducting this examination will express an opinion, which is contained within an audit report and which becomes part of the published annual report. *p. 406*

Fair values   The values ascribed to assets as an alternative to historic cost. They are usually the current market value (that is, the exchange values in an arm's-length transaction). *p. 58*

Final accounts   The income statement, statement of cash flows and statement of financial position taken together. *p. 35*

Financial accounting   The measuring and reporting of accounting information for external users (those users other than the managers of the business). *p. 12*

Financial gearing   The existence of fixed payment-bearing sources of finance (for example, borrowings) in the capital structure of a business. *p. 244*

First in, first out (FIFO)   A method of inventories costing which assumes that the earliest acquired inventories are used (in production or sales) first. *p. 96*

Framework of principles   The main principles that underpin accounting, which can help in identifying best practice and in developing accounting rules. *p. 166*

Fully paid shares   Shares on which the shareholders have paid the full issue price. *p. 131*

Gearing ratio   A ratio that relates the contribution of finance that requires a fixed return (such as borrowings) to the total long-term finance of the business. *p. 246*

Going concern convention   The accounting convention that holds that it is assumed that the business will continue operations for the foreseeable future, unless there is reason to believe otherwise. In other words, it is assumed that there is no intention, or need, to liquidate the business. *p. 53*

Goodwill arising on consolidation   An amount paid in excess of the underlying net asset value of the subsidiary's shares. *p. 314*

Gross profit   The amount remaining (if positive) after the cost of sales has been deducted from trading revenue. *p. 73*

Gross profit margin ratio   A profitability ratio relating the gross profit to the sales revenue for a period. *p. 229*

Group (of companies)   A situation that arises where one company is able to exercise control over another or others. *p. 296*

Group financial statements   Sets of financial accounting statements that combine the performance, position and cash flows of a group of companies under common control. Also known as consolidated financial statements. *p. 296*

Group income statement   An income statement for a group of companies, prepared from the perspective of the parent company's shareholders. *p. 334*

Group statement of cash flows   A statement of cash flows for a group of companies, prepared from the perspective of the parent company's shareholders. *p. 337*

Group statement of financial position   A statement of financial position for a group of companies, prepared from the perspective of the parent company's shareholders. *p. 305*

Historic cost convention   The accounting convention that holds that assets should be recorded at their historic (acquisition) cost. *p. 51*

Holding company   *See* Parent company.

Horizontal analysis   An approach to common-sized financial statements where all the figures in equivalent statements over time are expressed in relation to an equivalent figure for the base period (year, month and so on). So, for example, the sales revenue figure for each year will be expressed in terms of the sales revenue figure for the base year. *p. 275*

Income statement   A financial statement (also known as profit and loss account) that measures and reports the profit (or loss) the business has generated during a period. It is derived by deducting from total revenue for a period, the total expenses associated with that revenue. *p. 32*

Indirect method   An approach to deducing the cash flows from operating activities, in a statement of cash flows, by analysing the business's other financial statements. *p. 195*

Intangible assets   Assets that do not have a physical substance (for example, patents, goodwill and trade receivables). *p. 38*

Integral method   An approach to interim profit measurement that regards the interim period as being simply part of the annual reporting period, whereby annual expenses are predicted and then a proportion of these are allocated to the interim based on the proportion of annual sales revenue generated in the interim period. *p. 364*

Interest cover ratio   A gearing ratio that divides the operating profit (that is, profit before interest and taxation) by the interest payable for a period. *p. 247*

Internal audit   Investigations carried out by employees of the company to provide the directors with reassurance concerning the reliability of the company's control and financial reporting systems. *p. 407*

International Accounting Standards   *See* International Financial Reporting Standards.

International Financial Reporting Standards   Transnational accounting rules that have been adopted, or developed, by the International Accounting Standards Board and which should be followed in preparing the published financial statements of listed limited companies. *p. 153*

Issued share capital   That part of the share capital that has been issued to shareholders. Also known as allotted share capital. *p. 130*

Last in, first out (LIFO)   A method of inventories costing which assumes that the most recently acquired inventories are used (in production or sales) first. *p. 96*

Ledger   The book in which accounts are traditionally kept. *p. 455*

Liabilities   Claims of individuals and organisations, apart from the owner, that have arisen from past transactions or events such as supplying goods or lending money to the business. *p. 39*

Limited company   An artificial legal person that has an identity separate from that of those who own and manage it. *p. 18*

Limited liability   The restriction of the legal obligation of shareholders to meet all of the company's debts. *p. 118*

Loan notes   Long-term borrowings usually made by limited companies. *p. 131*

Management accounting   The measuring and reporting of accounting information specifically for the managers of a business. *p. 12*

Matching convention   The accounting convention that holds that, in measuring income, expenses should be matched to revenue which they helped generate in the same accounting period as that revenue was realised. *p. 81*

Materiality   The requirement that material information should be disclosed to users in financial statements. *p. 7*

Materiality convention   The accounting convention that states that, where the amounts involved are immaterial, only what is expedient should be considered. *p. 85*

Minority interests   *See* Non-controlling interests.

Monetary items   Items that appear on a statement of financial position that have a fixed number of pounds assigned to them. *p. 378*

Multiple discriminate analysis   A statistical technique that can be used to predict financial distress; it involves using an index based on a combination of financial ratios. *p. 279*

Negative goodwill arising on consolidation   The amount by which the underlying net asset value of the subsidiary's shares exceeds the amount paid for the shares. *p. 314*

Net book value   *See* Carrying amount.

Nominal value   The face value of a share in a company. Also called par value. *p. 124*

Nomination committee   A committee of the board of directors, comprising a majority of independent, non-executive directors, that is charged with leading the process for nominating new directors. *p. 397*

Non-controlling interests   That part of the net assets of a subsidiary company that is financed by shareholders other than the parent company. Also known as minority interests'. *p. 311*

Non-current assets   Assets held that do not meet the criteria of current assets. They are held for the long-term operations of the business rather than continuously circulating within the business. Non-current assets can be seen as the tools of the business. Also known as fixed assets. *p. 46*

Non-current liabilities   Those amounts due to other parties that are not current liabilities. *p. 47*

Non-executive directors   Directors who normally work for the company on a part-time basis and who do not have executive responsibilities but nevertheless have the same legal obligations towards the shareholders as executive directors. *p. 393*

Operating cash cycle (OCC)   The period between the outlay of cash to buy supplies and the ultimate receipt of cash from the sale of goods. *p. 242*

Operating profit   The profit achieved during a period after all operating expenses have been deducted from revenues from operations. Financing expenses are deducted after the calculation of operating profit. *p. 74*

Operating profit margin ratio   A profitability ratio relating the operating profit to the sales revenue for the period. *p. 228*

Ordinary shares   Shares of a company owned by those who are due the benefits of the company's activities after all other stakeholders have been satisfied. *p. 124*

Overtrading   The situation arising when a business is operating at a level of activity that cannot be supported by the amount of finance that has been committed. *p. 270*

Paid-up share capital   That part of the share capital of a company that has been called and paid. *p. 131*

Par value   *See* Nominal value.

Parent company   A company that has a controlling interest in another company. *p. 296*

Partnership   A form of business unit where there are at least two individuals, but usually no more than twenty, carrying on a business with the intention of making a profit. *p. 17*

Preference shares   Shares of a company owned by those who are entitled to the first part of any dividend that the company may pay. *p. 126*

Prepaid expenses   Expenses that have been paid in advance at the end of the accounting period. *p. 84*

Price/earnings ratio   An investment ratio that relates the market value of a share to the earnings per share. *p. 265*

Private limited company   A limited company for which the directors can restrict the ownership of its shares. *p. 119*

Profit   The increase in wealth attributable to the owners of a business that arises through business operations. *p. 70*

Profit before taxation   The result when all of the appropriately matched expenses of running a business have been deducted from the revenue for the year, but before the taxation charge is deducted. *p. 138*

Profit for the year   The result when all of the appropriately matched expenses of running a business have been deducted from the revenue for the year and then, in the case of a limited company, the taxation charge deducted. *p. 74*

Property, plant and equipment   Those non-current assets that have a physical substance (for example, plant and machinery, motor vehicles). *p. 58*

Prudence convention   The accounting convention that holds that financial statements should err on the side of caution. *p. 52*

Public limited company   A limited company for which the directors cannot restrict the ownership of its shares. *p. 119*

Reducing-balance method   A method of calculating depreciation that applies a fixed percentage rate of depreciation to the carrying amount of an asset in each period. *p. 89*

Relevance   The ability of accounting information to influence decisions; regarded as a key characteristic of useful accounting information. *p. 6*

Reliability   The requirement that accounting information should be free from significant errors or bias and should represent what it purports to represent. Reliability is regarded as a key characteristic of useful accounting information. *p. 6*

Remuneration committee   A committee of the board of directors, comprising independent, non-executive directors, that is charged with the task of setting the pay and benefits for the executive directors and the chairman. *p. 397*

Reserves   Part of the owners' claim (equity) of a limited company that has arisen from profits and gains, to the extent that these have not been distributed to the shareholders or reduced by losses. *p. 123*

Residual value   The amount for which a non-current asset is sold when the business has no further use for it. *p. 88*

Return on capital employed ratio (ROCE)   A profitability ratio expressing the relationship between the operating profit (that is, profit before interest and taxation) and the long-term funds (equity and borrowings) invested in the business. *p. 226*

Return on ordinary shareholders' funds ratio (ROSF)   A profitability ratio that compares the amount of profit for the period available to the ordinary shareholders with their stake in the business. *p. 225*

Revenue   A measure of the inflow of assets (for example, cash or amounts owed to a business by credit customers), or a reduction in liabilities, arising as a result of trading operations. *p. 70*

Revenue reserve   Part of the owners' claim (equity) of a company that arises from realised profits and gains, including after-tax trading profits and gains from disposals of non-current assets. *p. 124*

Risk management committee   A committee of the board of directors that is charged with reviewing the adequacy and effectiveness of the company's risk management procedures. *p. 397*

Sales revenue per employee ratio   An efficiency ratio that relates the sales revenue generated during a period to the average number of employees of the business. *p. 236*

Sales revenue to capital employed ratio   An efficiency ratio that relates the sales revenue generated during a period to the capital employed. *p. 235*

Segmental financial reports   Financial reports that break down the operating results of a business according to its business or geographical segments. *p. 354*

Share   Portion of the ownership, or equity, of a company. *p. 5*

Share premium account A capital reserve reflecting any amount, above the nominal value of shares, that is paid for those shares when they are issued by a company. *p. 128*

Sole proprietorship An individual in business on his or her own account. *p. 17*

Splitting Changing the nominal value of shares to a lower figure (from, say, £1.00 to £0.50) and then issuing sufficient shares so that each shareholder has the same total nominal value of shares as before. *p. 125*

Statement of cash flows A statement that shows a business's sources and uses of cash for a period. *p. 32*

Statement of changes in equity A financial statement, required by IAS 1, which shows the effect of gains/losses and capital injections/withdrawals on the equity base of a company. *p. 160*

Statement of comprehensive income A financial statement that extends the conventional income statement to include other gains and losses that affect shareholders' equity. *p. 158*

Statement of financial position A statement that shows the assets of a business and the claims on those assets. Also known as balance sheet. *p. 32*

Straight-line method A method of accounting for depreciation that allocates the amount to be depreciated evenly over the useful life of the asset. *p. 88*

Subsidiary company A company over which another (parent) company is able to exercise control, usually, but not necessarily, because more than 50% of its shares are owned by the parent company. *p. 296*

Summary financial statements A summarised version of the complete annual financial statements, which shareholders may choose to receive as an alternative to the complete statements. *p. 173*

Takeover The acquisition of control of one company by another, usually as a result of acquiring a majority of the ordinary shares of the former. *p. 296*

Tangible assets Those assets that have a physical substance (for example, plant and machinery, motor vehicles). *p. 38*

Target company A company that has been identified by another company as a suitable target for a takeover. *p. 299*

Total shareholder return (TSR) A measure of the total return from a share, which is made up of two elements: the increase (or decrease) in share value over a period plus (or minus) any dividends paid during the period. *p. 421*

Transfer price The price at which goods or services are sold, or transferred, between divisions of the same business. *p. 357*

Trial balance A totalled list of the balances on each of the accounts in a double-entry bookkeeping system. *p. 451*

UK Corporate Governance Code A code of practice for companies listed on the London Stock Exchange that deals with corporate governance matters. *p. 393*

Understandability The requirement that accounting information should be understood by those for whom the information is primarily compiled. Lack of understandability will limit the usefulness of accounting information. *p. 7*

Univariate analysis   A statistical technique that can be used to help predict financial distress, which involves the use of a single ratio as a predictor. *p. 279*

Value added statement (VAS)   A financial statement that takes the revenue for a period and deducts the cost of external inputs to determine the value added by the business. *p. 366*

Vertical analysis   An approach to common-sized financial statements where all of the figures in the particular statement are expressed in relation to one of the figures in that same statement, for example, sales revenue or total long-term funds. *p. 275*

Weighted average cost (AVCO)   A method of inventories costing, which assumes that inventories entering the business lose their separate identity and any issues of inventories reflect the weighted average cost of the inventories held. *p. 96*

Working capital   Current assets less current liabilities. *p. 197*

Written-down value (WDV)   *See* Carrying amount.

Appendix C

Solutions to self-assessment questions

Chapter 2

2.1 The statement of financial position you prepare should be set out as follows:

Simonson Engineering
Statement of financial position as at 30 September 2010

	£
ASSETS	
Non-current assets	
Property, plant and equipment	
Property	72,000
Plant and equipment	25,000
Motor vehicles	15,000
Fixtures and fittings	9,000
	121,000
Current assets	
Inventories	45,000
Trade receivables	48,000
Cash in hand	1,500
	94,500
Total assets	215,500
EQUITY AND LIABILITIES	
Equity	
Closing balance*	120,500
Non-current liabilities	
Long-term borrowings	51,000
Current liabilities	
Trade payables	18,000
Short-term borrowings	26,000
	44,000
Total equity and liabilities	215,500

*The equity is calculated as follows:

Opening balance	117,500
Profit	18,000
	135,500
Drawings	(15,000)
Closing balance	120,500

Chapter 3

3.1

TT and Co.
Income statement for the year ended 31 December 2009

	£
Sales revenue (152,000 + 35,000)	187,000
Cost of goods sold (74,000 + 16,000)	(90,000)
Gross profit	97,000
Rent	(20,000)
Rates (500 + 900)	(1,400)
Wages (33,500 + 630)	(34,130)
Electricity (1,650 + 620)	(2,270)
Bad debts	(400)
Van depreciation ((12,000 − 2,000)/4)	(2,500)
Van expenses	(9,400)
Profit for the year	26,900

Statement of financial position as at 31 December 2009

	£
ASSETS	
Delivery van (12,000 − 2,500)	9,500
Inventories (143,000 + 12,000 − 74,000 − 16,000)	65,000
Trade receivables (152,000 − 132,000 − 400)	19,600
Cash at bank (50,000 − 25,000 − 500 − 1,200	
− 12,000 − 33,500 − 1,650 − 12,000 + 35,000	
+ 132,000 − 121,000 − 9,400)	750
Prepaid expenses (5,000 + 300)	5,300
Total assets	100,150
EQUITY AND LIABILITIES	
Equity (50,000 + 26,900)	76,900
Trade payables (143,000 − 121,000)	22,000
Accrued expenses (630 + 620)	1,250
Total equity and liabilities	100,150

The statement of financial position could now be rewritten in a more stylish form as follows:

Statement of financial position as at 31 December 2009

	£
ASSETS	
Non-current assets	
Property, plant and equipment	
Delivery van at cost	12,000
Accumulated depreciation	(2,500)
	9,500
Current assets	
Inventories	65,000
Trade receivables	19,600
Prepaid expenses	5,300
Cash	750
	90,650
Total assets	100,150
EQUITY AND LIABILITIES	
Equity	
Closing balance	76,900
Current liabilities	
Trade payables	22,000
Accrued expenses	1,250
	23,250
Total equity and liabilities	100,150

Chapter 4

4.1 Dev Ltd

(a) The summarised statement of financial position of Dev Ltd, immediately following the rights and bonus issue, is as follows:

Statement of financial position

	£000
Net assets (235 + 40 (cash from the rights issue))	275
Equity	
Share capital: 100,000 shares @ £1 ((100 + 20) + 60)	180
Share premium account (30 + 20 − 50)	–
Revaluation reserve (37 − 10)	27
Retained earnings	68
	275

Note that the bonus issue of £60,000 is taken from capital reserves (reserves unavailable for dividends) as follows:

	£000
Share premium account	50
Revaluation reserve	10
	60

More could have been taken from the revaluation reserve and less from the share premium account without making any difference to dividend payment possibilities.

(b) There may be pressure from a potential lender for the business to limit its ability to pay dividends. This would place lenders in a more secure position because the maximum buffer or safety margin between the value of the assets and the amount owed by the business is maintained. It is not unusual for potential lenders to insist on some measure to lock up shareholders' funds in this way as a condition of granting the loan.

(c) The summarised statement of financial position of Dev Ltd, immediately following the rights and bonus issue, assuming a minimum dividend potential objective, is as follows:

Statement of financial position as at 31 December 2009

	£000
Net assets [235 + 40 (cash from the rights issue)]	275
Equity	
Share capital: 100,000 shares @ £1 ((100 + 20) + 60)	180
Share premium account (30 + 20)	50
Revaluation reserve	37
Retained earnings (68 − 60)	8
	275

(d) Before the bonus issue, the maximum dividend was £68,000. Now it is £8,000. Thus the bonus issue has had the effect of locking up an additional £60,000 of the business's assets in terms of the business's ability to pay dividends.

(e) Before the issues, Lee had 100 shares worth £2.35 (£235,000/100,000) each or £235 in total. Lee would be offered 20 shares in the rights issue at £2 each or £40 in total. After the rights issue, Lee would have 120 shares worth £2.2917 (£275,000/120,000) each or £275 in total.

   The bonus issue would give Lee 60 additional shares. After the bonus issue, Lee would have 180 shares worth £1.5278 (£275,000/180,000) each or £275 in total.

   None of this affects Lee's wealth. Before the issues, Lee had £235 worth of shares and £40 more in cash. After the issues, Lee has the same total wealth but all £275 is in the value of the shares.

(f) The things that we know about the company are as follows:

   - It is a private (as opposed to a public) limited company, for it has 'Ltd' (limited) as part of its name, rather than plc (public limited company).
   - It has made an issue of shares at a premium, almost certainly after it had traded successfully for a period. (There is a share premium account. It would be very unlikely that the original shares, issued when the company was first formed, would have been issued at a premium.)
   - Certain of the assets in the statement of financial position have been upwardly revalued by at least £37,000. (There is a revaluation reserve of £37,000. This may just be what is left after a previous bonus issue had taken part of the balance.)
   - The company has traded at an aggregate profit (though there could have been losses in some years), net of tax and any dividends paid. (There is a positive balance on retained earnings.)

Chapter 5

5.1 (a) Dividends announced between the end of the reporting period and the date at which the financial reports are authorised for publication should *not* be treated as a liability in the statement of financial position at the end of that period. IAS 1 specifically precludes the treatment of such dividends as liabilities.

(b) IAS 1 provides support for three key accounting conventions – accruals, going concern and consistency. It does not specifically support the historic cost convention.

(c) IAS 1 does not permit bank overdrafts to be offset against positive bank balances when preparing the statement of financial position. For the sake of relevance they should be shown separately.

(d) IAS 8 states that accounting policies should be changed if it is required by a new financial reporting standard or if it leads to more relevant and reliable information being reported.

(e) IAS 10 states that *significant* non-adjusting events occurring between the end of the reporting period and the date at which the financial statements are authorised should be disclosed by way of note. The standard requires the nature of the event and its likely financial effect to be disclosed.

(f) The law only requires that Stock Exchange listed companies publish an annual directors' remuneration report.

Chapter 6

6.1   Touchstone plc

Statement of cash flows for the year ended 31 December 2010

	£m
Cash flows from operating activities	
Profit before taxation (after interest) (see Note 1 below)	60
Adjustments for:	
Depreciation	16
Interest expense (Note 2)	4
	80
Increase in trade receivables (26 − 16)	(10)
Decrease in trade payables (38 − 37)	(1)
Decrease in inventories (25 − 24)	1
Cash generated from operations	70
Interest paid	(4)
Taxation paid (Note 3)	(12)
Dividend paid	(18)
Net cash from operating activities	36
Cash flows from investing activities	
Payments to acquire tangible non-current assets (Note 4)	(41)
Net cash used in investing activities	(41)
Cash flows from financing activities	
Issue of loan notes (40 − 20)	20
Net cash used in financing activities	20
Net increase in cash and cash equivalents	15
Cash and cash equivalents at 1 January 2010	
Cash	4
Cash and cash equivalents at 31 December 2010	
Cash	4
Treasury bills	15
	19

To see how this relates to the cash of the business at the beginning and end of the year it can be useful to provide a reconciliation as follows:

Analysis of cash and cash equivalents during the year ended 31 December 2010

	£m
Cash and cash equivalents at 1 January 2010	4
Net cash inflow	15
Cash and cash equivalents at 31 December 2010	19

Notes:

1 This is simply taken from the income statement for the year.
2 Interest payable expense must be taken out, by adding it back to the profit before taxation figure. We subsequently deduct the cash paid for interest payable during the year. In this case the two figures are identical.
3 Companies pay 50% of their tax during their accounting year and the other 50% in the following year. Thus the 2010 payment would have been half the tax on the 2009 profit (that is, the figure that would have appeared in the current liabilities at the end of 2009), plus half of the 2010 tax charge (that is, $4 + (\frac{1}{2} \times 16) = 12$).
4 Since there were no disposals, the depreciation charges must be the difference between the start and end of the year's non-current asset values, adjusted by the cost of any additions:

	£m
Carrying amount at 1 January 2010	147
Additions (balancing figure)	41
	188
Depreciation (6 + 10)	(16)
Carrying amount at 31 December 2010	172

Chapter 7

7.1   Ali plc and Bhaskar plc

In order to answer this question, you may have used the following ratios:

	Ali plc	Bhaskar plc
Return on ordinary shareholders' funds ratio	$(99.9/687.6) \times 100 = 14.5\%$	$(104.6/874.6) \times 100 = 12.0\%$
Operating profit margin ratio	$(151.3/1,478.1) \times 100 = 10.2\%$	$(166.9/1,790.4) \times 100 = 9.3\%$
Average inventories turnover period ratio	$(592/1,018.3) \times 12 = 7.0$ months	$(403/1,214.9) \times 12 = 4.0$ months
Average settlement period for trade receivables ratio	$(176.4/1,478.1) \times 12 = 1.4$ months	$(321.9/1,790.4) \times 12 = 2.2$ months
Current ratio	$\dfrac{853}{422.4} = 2.0$	$\dfrac{816.5}{293.1} = 2.8$
Acid test ratio	$\dfrac{(853 - 592)}{422.4} = 0.6$	$\dfrac{(816.5 - 403)}{293.1} = 1.4$
Gearing ratio	$\dfrac{190}{(687.6 + 190)} \times 100 = 21.6\%$	$\dfrac{250}{(874.6 + 250)} \times 100 = 22.2\%$
Interest cover ratio	$\dfrac{151.3}{19.4} = 7.8$ times	$\dfrac{166.9}{27.5} = 6.1$ times

(Note: It is not possible to use any average ratios because only the end-of-year figures are provided for each business.)

Ali plc seems more effective than Bhaskar plc at generating returns for shareholders indicated by the higher ROSF ratio. This may be partly caused by Ali plc's higher operating profit margin.

Both businesses have a very high inventories turnover period; this probably needs to be investigated, particularly by Ali plc. Ali plc has a lower average settlement period for trade receivables than Bhaskar plc.

Ali plc has a much lower current ratio and acid test ratio than Bhaskar plc. The acid test ratio of Ali plc is substantially below 1.0: this may suggest a liquidity problem.

The gearing ratios of the two businesses are quite similar. Neither business seems to have excessive borrowing. The interest cover ratios are also similar. The ratios indicate that both businesses have good profit coverage for their interest charges.

To be able to draw really helpful comparisons between the two businesses, it would probably be necessary to calculate other ratios from the 2010 financial statements. It would also be helpful to have access to the ratios for both businesses over recent years and, possibly, the ratios of other businesses operating in the same industry.

Chapter 8

8.1 Ali plc and Bhaskar plc

	Ali plc	Bhaskar plc
Dividend payout ratio	(135/99.9) × 100 = 135%	(95/104.6) × 100 = 91%
Dividend yield ratio	[(135/320)/(1 − 0.1)]/6.5 × 100 = 7.2%	[(95/250)/(1 − 0.1)]/8.20 × 100 = 5.1%
Earnings per share	99.9/320 = £0.31	104.6/250 = £0.42
P/E ratio	6.5/0.31 = 21.0	8.2/0.42 = 19.5

Both of these businesses seem to have a rather imprudent dividend policy, with Ali paying out more than its profit for the year and Bhaskar most of it. If the current year's level of profit is abnormally low and the businesses have the funds available this may not be quite as reckless as it seems at first sight. The average payout ratio for all retailers listed on the London Stock Exchange is 48 per cent – much lower than either Ali or Bhaskar.

Given the high level of dividends paid by the two businesses, it is not surprising that the dividend yields are also high. The average dividend yield ratio for food and drug retailers listed on the London Stock Exchange is 2.91 per cent – again very much lower than either Ali or Bhaskar.

The EPS values are impossible to interpret without a historical series of past EPS values for each business. The EPS value is not directly comparable between businesses. This is partly because the nominal value of the shares (which varies from one business to another) and how each business is financed have profound effects on the EPS value.

The P/E ratios for both businesses are somewhat above the average for food and drug retailers listed on the London Stock Exchange, which is 16.98. This ratio is seen as a measure of the level of confidence that investors have in the business's future. On the face of it, Ali is more highly regarded than Bhaskar, but both are better regarded than retailers generally.

Chapter 9

9.1 Great plc

Group statement of financial position as at 31 December last year

	£m
ASSETS	
Non-current assets	
Property, plant and equipment (at cost less depreciation)	
Land (80 + 14 + 5)	99
Plant (33 + 20)	53
Vehicles (20 + 11)	31
	183
Intangible asset	
Goodwill arising on consolidation (Note 1)	5
	188
Current assets	
Inventories (20 + 9)	29
Trade receivables (21 + 6)	27
Cash (17 + 5)	22
	78
Total assets	266
EQUITY AND LIABILITIES	
Equity	
Called-up share capital: ordinary shares of £1 each, fully paid	100
Retained earnings (Note 2)	81
	181
Non-controlling interests (Note 3)	13
	194
Non-current liabilities	
Loan notes	50
Current liabilities	
Trade payables	22
Total equity and liabilities	266

Notes

1 Goodwill arising on consolidation: 53 − (80% × (20 + 35 + 5)) = 5.

2

	£m
Great plc's retained earnings balance	77
Great plc's share of Small plc's post-acquisition profits (40 − 35) × 80%	4
	81

3 Non-controlling interests: (60 + 5) × 20% = 13

Group income statement for last year

	£m
Revenue (91 + 27)	118
Cost of sales (46 + 13)	(59)
Gross profit (45 + 14)	59
Administration expenses (8 + 3)	(11)
Distribution expenses (6 + 2)	(8)
Operating profit (31 + 9)	40
Interest payable (3 + 0)	(3)
Profit before taxation (28 + 9)	37
Taxation (12 + 4)	(16)
Profit for the year (16 + 5)	21
Attributable to non-controlling interests (20% × 5)	(1)
Profit for the year attributable to Great plc shareholders	20

Chapter 10

10.1   Rose Ltd

Value added statement for the year ended 31 March

	£000
Revenue	12,080
Bought-in materials and services (6,282 + 1,003)	(7,285)
Value added	4,795
Applied as follows:	
To employees	2,658
To pay government	259
To suppliers of capital:	
Interest	66
Dividends	300
	366
For maintenance and expansion of assets:	
Depreciation	625
Retained profit (1,187 − 300)	887
	1,512
	4,795

Chapter 11

11.1   The sources of information that may be used could include the following:

- Documents setting out
  - the strategic plan of the company;
  - board structure and roles;
  - board appointments procedures;
  - operations of the board;
  - minutes of board meetings;
  - meeting agendas and background information;
  - criteria for directors' appraisal.
- Interviews with board members.
- Interviews with and/or questionnaires sent to senior management and shareholders.
- Attendance and observation at board meetings.
- Attendance and observation at meetings with shareholders, including the AGM.
- Company website and published material, including the annual reports.
- CVs of board members.
- Performance reports (such as monthly budget reports and sales reports) received by the board.
- Information relating to training and development programmes carried out.

This is not an exhaustive list. You may have thought of other sources of information.

Appendix D
Solutions to review questions

Chapter 1

1.1 The purpose of providing accounting information is to enable users to make more informed decisions and judgements about the organisation concerned. Unless it fulfils this objective, there is no point in providing it.

1.2 The main users of financial information for a university and the way in which they are likely to use this information may be summed up as follows:

Students	Whether to enrol on a course of study. This would probably involve an assessment of the university's ability to continue to operate and to fulfil students' needs.
Other universities and colleges	How best to compete against the university. This might involve using the university's performance in various aspects as a 'benchmark' when evaluating their own performance.
Employees	Whether to take up or to continue in employment with the university. Employees might assess this by considering the ability of the university to continue to provide employment and to reward employees adequately for their labour.
Government/funding authority	How efficient and effective the university is in undertaking its various activities. Possible funding needs that the university may have.
Local community representatives	Whether to allow/encourage the university to expand its premises. To assess this, the university's ability to continue to provide employment for the community, to use community resources and to help fund environmental improvements might be considered.
Suppliers	Whether to continue to supply the university at all; also whether to supply on credit. This would involve an assessment of the university's ability to pay for any goods and services supplied.
Lenders	Whether to lend money to the university and/or whether to require repayment of any existing loans. To assess this, the university's ability to meet its obligations to pay interest and to repay the principal would be considered.
Board of governors and managers (faculty deans and so on)	Whether the performance of the university requires improvement. Performance to date would be compared with earlier plans or some other 'benchmark' to decide whether action needs to be taken. Whether there should be a change in the university's future direction. In making such decisions, management will need to look at the university's ability to perform and at the opportunities available to it.

We can see that the users of accounting information and their needs are similar to those of a private-sector business.

1.3　In order to be justified in producing a particular piece of accounting information, strictly the person authorising its production should be satisfied that the economic cost of providing it is less than the economic benefit which will be derived from having that information available. This is to say that there should be a net economic benefit of producing it. Otherwise it should not be produced.

There are obvious problems in determining what is the value of the benefit. There are also likely to be difficulties in determining the amount of the cost. Thus, the judgement is not easy to make.

Economics is not the only issue, particularly in the context of financial accounting. Social and other factors may well be involved. It can be argued that society has a right to certain information about a large business, even though the information may not have an economic value to society.

1.4　Since we can never be sure what is going to happen in the future, the best that we can do is to make judgements on the basis of past experience. Thus information concerning flows of cash and of wealth in the recent past is likely to be a useful source on which to base judgements about possible future outcomes.

Chapter 2

2.1　The confusion arises because the owner seems unaware of the business entity convention in accounting. This convention requires a separation of the business from the owner(s) of the business for accounting purposes. The business is regarded as a separate entity and the statement of financial position is prepared from the perspective of the business rather than that of the owner. As a result, funds invested in the business by the owner will be regarded as a claim that the owner has on the business. In the standard layout of the statement of financial position, this claim will be shown alongside other claims on the business from outsiders.

2.2　A statement of financial position does not show what a business is worth, for two major reasons:

- Only those items that can be measured reliably in monetary terms are shown on the statement of financial position. Thus, things of value such as the reputation for product quality, skills of employees and so on will not normally appear in the statement of financial position.
- The historic cost convention results in assets normally being recorded at their outlay cost rather than their current value. In the case of certain assets, the difference between historic cost and current value may be significant.

2.3　The accounting equation is simply the relationship between a business's assets, liabilities and equity. For the standard layout, it is:

Assets (current and non-current) = Equity + Liabilities (current and non-current)

For the alternative layout mentioned in the chapter, the equation is:

Assets (current and non-current) – Liabilities (current and non-current) = Equity

2.4　Some object to the idea of humans being treated as assets for inclusion on the statement of financial position. It can be seen as demeaning for humans to be listed alongside inventories, plant and machinery and other assets. However, others argue that humans are often the most valuable resource of a business and that placing a value on this resource will help bring to the attention of managers the importance of nurturing and developing this 'asset'. There is a saying in management that 'the things that count are the things that get counted'. As the value of the 'human assets' is not stated in the financial statements, there is a danger that managers will treat these 'assets' less favourably than other assets that are on the statement of financial position.

Humans are likely to meet the first criterion of an asset listed in the chapter, that is, that a probable future benefit exists. There would be little point in employing people if this were not the case. The second criterion concerning exclusive right of control is more problematic. Clearly a business cannot control humans in the same way as most other assets. However, a business can have the exclusive right to the employment services that a person provides. This distinction between control over the services provided and control over the person makes it possible to argue that the second criterion can be met.

Humans normally sign a contract of employment with the business, and so the third criterion is normally met. The difficulty, however, is with the fourth criterion, that is, whether the value of humans (or their services) can be measured with any degree of reliability. To date, none of the measurement methods proposed enjoy widespread acceptance.

Chapter 3

3.1 At the time of preparing the income statement, it is not always possible to determine accurately the expenses that need to be matched to the sales revenue figure for the period. It will only be at some later point in time that the true position becomes clear. However, it is still necessary to try to include all relevant expenses in the income statement and so estimates of the future will have to be made. The income statement would lose much of its usefulness were the business to wait for all of the unkowns to become clear.

Examples of estimates that may have to be made include:

- expenses accrued at the end of the period such as the amount of telephone expenses incurred since the last quarter's bill
- the amount of depreciation based on estimates of the life of the non-current asset and future residual value
- the amount of bad and doubtful debts incurred.

3.2 Depreciation attempts to allocate the cost or fair value, less any residual value, of the asset over its useful life. Depreciation does not attempt to measure the fall in value of the asset during a particular accounting period. Thus, the carrying amount of the asset appearing on the statement of financial position normally represents the unexpired cost of the asset rather than its current market value.

3.3 The convention of consistency is designed to provide a degree of uniformity concerning the application of accounting policies. We have seen, that in certain areas, there may be more than one method of accounting for an item, for example inventories. The convention of consistency states that, having decided on a particular accounting policy, a business should continue to apply the policy in successive periods. While this policy helps to ensure that users can make valid comparisons concerning business performance *over time*, it does not ensure that valid comparisons can be made *between businesses*. This is because different businesses may consistently apply different accounting policies.

3.4 An expense is that element of the cost incurred that is used up during the accounting period. An asset is that element of cost which is carried forward on the statement of financial position and which will normally be used up in future periods. Thus, both assets and expenses arise from costs being incurred. The major difference between the two is the period over which the benefits (resulting from the costs incurred) accrue.

Chapter 4

4.1 It does not differ. In both cases they are required to meet their debts to the full extent that there are assets available. This means that they both have a liability that is limited to the extent of their assets. This is a particularly important fact for the shareholders of a limited company because they know that those owed money by the company cannot demand that the shareholders contribute additional funds to help meet debts. Thus the liability of the shareholders is limited to the amount that they have paid for their shares, or have agreed to pay in the case of partially unpaid shares. This contrasts with the position of the owner or part owner of an unincorporated (non-company) business. Here all of the individual's assets could be required to meet the unsatisfied liabilities of the business.

Thus, while there is a difference between the position of a shareholder (in a limited company) and that of a sole proprietor or partner, there is no difference between the position of the company itself and a sole proprietor or partner.

4.2 A private limited company may place restrictions on the transfer of its shares, that is, the directors can veto an attempt by a shareholder to sell his or her shares to another person to whom the directors object. Thus, in effect, the majority can avoid having as a shareholder someone that they would prefer not to have. A public company cannot do this.

A public limited company must have authorised share capital of at least £50,000. There is no minimum for a private limited company.

4.3 A reserve is that part of the equity (owners' claim) of a company that is not share capital. Reserves represent gains or surpluses that enhance the claim of the shareholders above the nominal value of their shares. For example, the share premium account is a reserve that represents the excess over the nominal value of shares that is paid for them on a share issue. The retained earnings balance is a reserve that arises from ploughed-back profits earned by the company.

Revenue reserves arise from realised profits and gains. Capital reserves arise from unrealised profits and gains (for example, the upward revaluation of a non-current asset) or from issuing shares at a premium (share premium).

4.4 A preference share represents part of the ownership of a company. Preference shares entitle their owners to the first part of any dividend paid by the company, up to a maximum amount. The maximum is usually expressed as a percentage of the nominal or par value of the preference shares.

(a) They differ from ordinary shares to the extent that they only entitle their holders to dividends to a predetermined maximum value. Dividends to ordinary shareholders have no predetermined maximum. Were the company to be liquidated, the preference shareholders would normally receive a maximum of the nominal value of their shares, whereas the ordinary shareholders receive the residue after all other claimants, including the preference shareholders.

(b) They differ from loan notes in that these represent borrowings for the company, where normally holders have a contract with the company that specifies the rate of interest, interest payment dates and redemption date. They are often secured on the company's assets. Preference shareholders have no such contract.

Chapter 5

5.1 The general rule is that the relevant figures for the earlier period(s) in which the error occurred should be restated for comparison purposes. The nature of the error and its effect on relevant items and on earnings per share for the current and the prior period should also be disclosed.

5.2 Accounting policies are the principles, rules and conventions used to prepare the financial statements. Wherever possible, they should be determined by reference to an appropriate accounting standard. In the absence of an appropriate standard, managers must make suitable judgements to ensure that users receive relevant and reliable information.

5.3 Accounting rules help to ensure that unscrupulous directors do not exploit their position and portray an unrealistic view of financial health. It is also important for the purpose of comparability, both over time and between businesses.

5.4 The main methods of creative accounting are misstating revenues, massaging expenses, misstating assets, concealing 'bad news' and inadequate disclosure.

Chapter 6

6.1 Cash is normally required in the settlement of claims. Thus, employees and contractors want to be paid for their work in cash. A supplier of non-current assets or inventories will normally expect to be paid in cash, perhaps after a short period of credit. When businesses fail, it is their inability to find the cash to pay claimants that actually drives them under. These factors lead to cash being the pre-eminent business asset and, therefore, the one that analysts and others watch carefully in trying to assess the ability of the business to survive and/or to take advantage of commercial opportunities.

6.2 With the direct method, the business's cash records are analysed for the period concerned. The analysis reveals the amounts of cash, in total, that have been paid and received in respect of each category of the statement of cash flows. This is not difficult in principle, or in practice if it is done by computer, as a matter of routine.

The indirect method takes the approach that, while the profit (loss) for the year is not equal to the net inflow (outflow) of cash from operations, they are fairly closely linked to the extent that appropriate adjustment of the figure for profit (loss) for the year will produce the correct figure for cash flow. The adjustment is concerned with depreciation charge for, and movements in relevant working capital items over, the period.

6.3 (a) *Cash flows from operating activities.* This would normally be positive, even for a business with small profits or even losses. The fact that depreciation is not a cash flow tends to lead to positive cash flows in this area in most cases.

(b) *Cash flows from investing activities.* Normally this would be negative in cash flow terms since assets become worn out and need to be replaced in the normal course of business. This means that, typically, old items of property, plant and equipment are generating less cash on their disposal than is having to be paid out to replace them.

(c) *Cash flows from financing activities.* There is a tendency for businesses either to expand or to fail. In either case, this is likely to mean that, over the years, more finance will be raised than will be redeemed or retired.

6.4 There are several reasons for this, including the following:

- Changes in inventories, trade receivables and trade payables. For example, an increase in trade receivables during an accounting period would mean that the cash received from credit sales would be less than the credit sales revenue for the same period.
- Cash may have been spent on new non-current assets or received from disposals of old ones; this would not directly affect profit.

Chapter 8

8.1 The statement of financial position is drawn up at a single point in time – the end of the financial period. As a result, the figures shown on the statement of financial position represent the position at that single point in time and may not be representative of the position during the period. Wherever possible, average figures (perhaps based on monthly figures) should be used. However, an external user may only have access to the opening and closing statements of financial position for the year and so a simple average based on these figures may be all that it is possible to calculate. Where a business is seasonal in nature or is subject to cyclical changes, this simple averaging may not be sufficient.

8.2 Factors that could affect a company's decision on the level of dividend to pay include the following:

- The level of profit for the period concerned. Businesses tend to be reluctant to pay dividends at a higher level than that of after-tax profits. They may be prepared to exceed this limit occasionally, when they have an abnormally poor year, but over a period of years, dividends typically fall well below profit levels.
- The amount of cash available. Businesses tend not to borrow to pay dividends though this would be perfectly legal. Only if they have sufficient liquidity will they normally pay dividends.
- Other demands on funds. Linked to the liquidity point, businesses may be constrained from paying dividends by the extent of other calls on their funds, particularly for investment. In theory businesses will pay out any cash remaining only after all profitable investments have been undertaken.
- Past practice. Businesses tend to adopt a fairly consistent dividend policy, from which they are often reluctant to vary. This is because it is believed that changes in dividend policy can send misleading 'signals' to investors. For example, cutting the level of dividends might signal that the business is in difficulties.

8.3 The P/E ratio may vary between businesses within the same industry for the following reasons:

- Accounting policies. Differences in the methods used to compute profit (for example inventories valuation and depreciation) can lead to different profit figures and, therefore, different P/E ratios.
- Different prospects. One business may be regarded as having a much brighter future due to factors such as the quality of management, the quality of products, location and so on. This will affect the market price investors are prepared to pay for the share and hence it will also affect the P/E ratio.
- Different asset structure. The business's underlying asset base may be much higher and this may affect the market price of the shares.

8.4 Three ratios that could be affected by overtrading are:

- Acid test ratio. This is likely to fall if overtrading is occurring because the trade payables settlement period is likely to increase and overdraft finance is likely to exist. At the same time, inventories and trade receivables levels could well fall.
- Cash generated from operations to maturing obligations ratio. This is likely to fall. Cash generated is likely to rise more slowly than maturing obligations if the business is overtrading.
- Interest cover ratio. This is likely to fall despite rising profits because interest, perhaps on short-term borrowing (for instance, overdrafts), is likely to rise more steeply.

Chapter 9

9.1   A group is said to exist when one company is in a position to exercise control over another company. This almost always means that the parent owns more than 50% of the voting shares of the subsidiary.

Where a group relationship exists, all companies in the group must prepare annual financial statements in the normal way, but, in addition, the parent company must prepare and publish a set of group financial statements.

9.2   The group statement of financial position shows the assets and external claims of all members of the group (including the parent company) as if they were those of the parent company. Where there are minority shareholders in any of the subsidiary companies, the fact that the parent company shareholders do not supply all of the equity finance of the group is recognised. This recognition takes the form of an item 'non-controlling interests' in the financing area of the group statement of financial position.

9.3   There are probably two reasons for this:

1   *Limited liability*. Each company has its own limited liability. Thus, one company's financial collapse will not affect the others directly. The group is a number of independent units as far as liability is concerned.
2   *Individual identity*. Operating a large business as a group of separate semi-autonomous departments is generally seen as good management. One means of emphasising the autonomy is to establish each department or division as a separate company. This arrangement may also be seen as a good marketing ploy since customers may prefer to deal with (what they see as) a smaller unit.

9.4   One company will be treated as an associate of another where another company or group has a long-term interest and can exercise significant influence over the operating and financial policies of that company. Influence is usually demonstrated through representation on the board of directors of the associated company and is supported by a substantial interest in the voting shares in that company. Usually ownership of 20% or more of the voting shares will represent a substantial interest in the voting shares.

The accounting consequences are that the group must include its share of the post-acquisition reserves of the associate, as well as the cost of the shares, in its own statement of financial position. It must also show its share of the operating profit, interest charges and tax charges relating to the associate in the income statement.

Chapter 10

10.1   This criticism may arise because of the problems mentioned in the chapter. It can be argued that the VAS promotes a view that the business is a coalition of interests. It can be seen as trying to foster a team spirit among key interest groups and trying to get employees 'on side' by treating them as team members. Critics argue that this is mere propaganda, which tries to obscure the underlying conflict between capital and labour. They argue that, as the main purpose of the statement is persuasive rather than informative, the integrity of the financial statements could be damaged in the eyes of users.

Problems relating to team membership and the classification of key items also undermine the usefulness of the statement and this may have a more general adverse effect on the credibility of the financial reports. Supporters of the VAS would dispute these claims. They would argue that value added offers an alternative measure of wealth creation that may provide new insights into business performance. Furthermore, most financial statements have to overcome theoretical or classification problems and the VAS is no exception.

10.2 Inflation may be defined as a general rise in prices or a fall in the general purchasing power of money. The level of inflation is measured by using a general price index, such as the Retail Price Index (RPI). The CPP approach is concerned with maintaining the general purchasing power of the owners' investment in the business and uses the RPI as the basis of making adjustments. It can, therefore, be described as a method of accounting for inflation.

The CCA approach is concerned with specific price changes rather than general price changes. It is concerned with ensuring that a business can maintain its scale of operations. Specific price increases, however, can occur even when there is no inflation. In a dynamic economy there will always be price movements. Thus, even during a period of zero inflation (and deflation) there will be price increases in certain goods and service, which will be offset by price decreases in others. Supporters of CCA, however, would argue that the key issue is not which method is the 'true' method of accounting for inflation, but rather which method is more helpful for decision-making purposes.

10.3 There are a number of possible drawbacks, which include the following:

- The reporting costs may be considerable.
- Reports covering a short period are more likely to be inaccurate because of estimation errors.
- Condensing complex information may result in a distorted portrayal of performance and position.
- It may encourage users to take a short-term perspective when evaluating performance.

10.4 There are various problems associated with the measurement of business segments. These include:

- the definition of a segment;
- the treatment of inter-segmental transactions, such as sales;
- the treatment of expenses and assets that are shared between segments.

There is no single correct method of dealing with these problems and variations will arise in practice. This, in turn, will hinder comparisons between businesses.

Chapter 11

11.1 The main tasks of the board are to:

- set the strategic direction of the company;
- exercise control; and
- maintain external relations.

11.2 The main benefits are that:

- it ensures that a single individual does not have too much power;
- the chairman can offer support and act as a mentor to the CEO;
- it can smooth the path of succession; and
- it can ensure that the responsibilities of both roles will be carried out more effectively than would be the case if a single individual occupied both roles.

11.3 The external auditors will have an intimate knowledge of the accounting and payroll systems that are currently in operation and should be well placed to suggest improvements that will suit the company's needs. There may therefore be a saving of time and cost if they are given the task. However, there is always a risk that the external auditors will receive too high a proportion of the total fees received from the company in the form of consultancy work. This runs the risk of compromising the auditors' independence.

11.4   Institutional investors have become more active for the following reasons:

- *Difficulties of disinvesting in a large public company*. Institutional shareholders tend to have significant shareholdings in companies and attempting to sell a large quantity of shares may provoke a fall in price. Furthermore, an institutional shareholder may be locked into a company's shares if it offers funds to investors which attempt to track the market.
- *Pressure to perform*. Poor stock market returns in recent years have increased pressures on institutional shareholders to provide good returns. One way in which this may be done is through intervention in a company's affairs.
- *Changed regulatory environment*. There is pressure on large institutional shareholders through the UK Corporate Governance Code and government exhortations to engage with companies over corporate governance issues.

Appendix E

Solutions to selected exercises

Chapter 2

2.1 Paul

Statement of cash flows for Thursday

	£
Opening balance (from Wednesday)	59
Cash from sale of wrapping paper	47
Cash paid to purchase wrapping paper	(53)
Closing balance	53

Income statement for Thursday

	£
Sales revenue	47
Cost of goods sold	(33)
Profit	14

Statement of financial position as at Thursday evening

	£
Cash	53
Inventories of goods for resale (23 + 53 − 33)	43
Total assets	96
Equity	96

2.2 Equity

	£
Cash introduced by Paul on Monday	40
Profit for Monday	15
Profit for Tuesday	18
Profit for Wednesday	9
Profit for Thursday	14
Total business wealth (total assets)	96

Thus the equity, all of which belongs to Paul as sole owner, arises from the cash he put in to start the business plus the profit earned each day.

2.3 Helen

Income statement for day 1

	£
Sales revenue (70 × £0.80)	56
Cost of sales (70 × £0.50)	(35)
Profit	21

Statement of cash flows for day 1

	£
Opening balance	40
Cash from sales	56
Cash for purchases (80 × £0.50)	(40)
Closing balance	56

Statement of financial position as at end of day 1

	£
Cash balance	56
Inventories of unsold goods (10 × £0.50)	5
Total assets	61
Equity	61

Income statement for day 2

	£
Sales revenue (65 × £0.80)	52.0
Cost of sales (65 × £0.50)	(32.5)
Profit	19.5

Statement of cash flows for day 2

	£
Opening balance	56.0
Cash from sales	52.0
Cash for purchases (60 × £0.50)	(30.0)
Closing balance	78.0

Statement of financial position as at end of day 2

	£
Cash balance	78.0
Inventories of unsold goods (5 × £0.50)	2.5
Total assets	80.5
Equity	80.5

Income statement for day 3

	£
Sales revenue (20 × £0.80) + (45 × £0.40)	34.0
Cost of sales (65 × £0.50)	(32.5)
Profit	1.5

Statement of cash flows for day 3

	£
Opening balance	78.0
Cash from sales	34.0
Cash for purchases (60 × £0.50)	(30.0)
Closing balance	82.0

Statement of financial position as at end of day 3

	£
Cash balance	82.0
Inventories of unsold goods	–
Total assets	82.0
Equity	82.0

2.5   Crafty Engineering Ltd

(a)   **Statement of financial position as at 30 June last year**

	£000
ASSETS	
Non-current assets	
Property, plant and equipment	
Property	320
Equipment and tools	207
Motor vehicles	38
	565
Current assets	
Inventories	153
Trade receivables	185
	338
Total assets	903
EQUITY AND LIABILITIES	
Equity (which is the missing figure)	441
Non-current liabilities	
Long-term borrowings (loan from Industrial Finance Co.)	260
Current liabilities	
Trade payables	86
Short-term borrowings	116
	202
Total equity and liabilities	903

(b) The statement of financial position reveals a high level of investment in non-current assets. In percentage terms, we can say that more than 60% of the total investment in assets (565/903) has been in non-current assets. The nature of the business may require a heavy investment in non-current assets. The investment in current assets exceeds the current liabilities by a large amount (approximately 1.7 times). As a result, there is no obvious sign of a liquidity problem. However, the statement of financial position reveals that the business has no cash balance and is therefore dependent on the continuing support of short-term borrowing in order to meet obligations when they fall due. When considering the long-term financing of the business, we can see that about 37% (that is, 260/(260 + 441)) of the total long-term finance for the business has been supplied by borrowings and about 63% (that is, 441/(260 + 441)) by the owners. This level of long-term borrowing seems quite high but not excessive. However, we would need to know more about the ability of the business to service the borrowing (that is, make interest payments and repayments of the amount borrowed) before a full assessment could be made.

2.8 (a) The income statement shows the increase in wealth, as a result of trading (revenue), generated during the period, the decrease in wealth caused by the generation of that revenue (expenses) and the resulting net increase (profit) or decrease (loss) in wealth for the period. Though most businesses hold some of their wealth in cash, wealth is held in many other forms: non-current assets, receivables and so on.

(b) Assets, to be included in a statement of financial position, must be judged as likely to produce future economic benefits. The economic benefit may come from selling the asset in the short term, in which case the statement is broadly true for those assets that it is the intention of the business to liquidate (turn into cash) in the short term. Many assets have an economic benefit that is not related to liquidation value but to use – for example, in production. For these types of asset, the statement is certainly not true.

There are other conditions that must be met in order for an item to be included in the statement of financial position. These are:

1 The business must have a right to control the asset.
2 The benefit must arise from some past transaction or event.
3 The asset must be measurable in monetary terms.

(c) The accounting equation is:

$$\text{Assets} = \text{Equity} + \text{Liabilities}$$

(d) Non-current assets are assets that do not meet the criteria for current assets. They are normally held for the long-term operations of the business. Some non-current assets may be immovable (for example, property) but others are not (for example, motor vans).

(e) Goodwill may or may not have an infinite life – it will depend on the nature of the goodwill. There are no hard and fast rules that can be applied. Where this asset has a finite life, it should be amortised. Where it is considered to have an infinite life, it should not be amortised but should be tested annually for impairment.

Chapter 3

3.1 (a) Equity does increase as a result of the owners introducing more cash into the business, but it will also increase as a result of introducing other assets (for example, a motor car) and by the business generating revenue by trading. Similarly, equity decreases not only as a result of withdrawals of cash by owners but also by withdrawals of other assets (for example, inventories for the owners' personal use) and through trading expenses being incurred. For the typical business, in a typical accounting period, equity will alter much more as a result of trading activities than for any other reason.

(b) An accrued expense is not one that relates to next year. It is one that needs to be matched with the revenue of the accounting period under review, but that has yet to be met in terms of cash payment. As such, it will appear on the statement of financial position as a current liability.

(c) The purpose of depreciation is not to provide for asset replacement. Rather, it is an attempt to allocate the cost, or fair value, of the asset (less any residual value) over its useful life. Depreciation is an attempt to provide a measure of the amount of the non-current asset that has been consumed during the period. This amount will then be charged as an expense for the period in deriving the profit figure. Depreciation is a book entry (the outlay of cash occurs when the asset is purchased) and does not normally entail setting aside a separate amount of cash for asset replacement. Even if this were done, there would be no guarantee that sufficient funds would be available at the end of the asset's life for its replacement. Factors such as inflation and technological change may mean that the replacement cost is higher than the original cost of the asset. It is not necessarily the case that a particular asset will be replaced, in any case.

(d) In the short term, it is possible for the current value of a non-current asset to exceed its original cost. However, nearly all non-current assets will wear out over time as a result of being used to generate wealth for the business (land being one of the rare exceptions). This will be the case for freehold buildings. As a result, some measure of depreciation should be calculated to take account of the fact that the asset is being consumed. Some businesses revalue their freehold buildings where the current value is significantly different from the original cost. Where this occurs, the depreciation charged should be based on the revalued amount (fair value). This will normally result in higher depreciation charges than if the asset remained at its historic cost.

3.3 The existence of profit and downward movement in cash may be for various reasons, which include the following:

- the purchase of assets for cash during the period (for example, motor cars and inventories), which were not all consumed during the period and are therefore not having as great an effect on expenses as they are on cash;
- the payment of an outstanding liability (for example, borrowings), which will have an effect on cash but not on expenses in the income statement;
- the withdrawal of cash by the owners from the equity invested, which will not have an effect on the expenses in the income statement;
- the generation of revenue on credit where the cash has yet to be received. This will increase the sales revenue for the period but will not have a beneficial effect on the cash balance until a later time.

3.5 (a) Rent payable – expense for period   £9,000
     (b) Rates and insurance – expense for period   £6,000
     (c) General expenses – paid in period   £7,000
     (d) Interest payable on borrowings – prepaid   £500
     (e) Salaries – paid in period   £6,000
     (f) Rent receivable – received during period   £3,000

3.7   WW Associates

Income statement for the year ended 31 December 2009

	£
Sales revenue (211,000 + 42,000)	253,000
Cost of goods sold (127,000 + 25,000)	(152,000)
Gross profit	101,000
Rent (20,000)	(20,000)
Rates (400 + 1,500)	(1,900)
Wages (−1,700 + 23,800 + 860)	(22,960)
Electricity (2,700)	(2,700)
Machinery depreciation (9,360)	(9,360)
Loss on disposal of the old machinery (13,000 − 3,900 − 9,000)	(100)
Van expenses (17,500)	(17,500)
Profit for the year	26,480

WW Associates
Statement of financial position as at 31 December 2009

	£
ASSETS	
Machinery (25,300 + 6,000 + 9,000 − 13,000 + 3,900 − 9,360)	21,840*
Inventories (12,200 + 143,000 + 12,000 − 127,000 − 25,000)	15,200
Trade receivables (21,300 + 211,000 − 198,000)	34,300
Cash at bank (overdraft) (8,300 − 23,000 − 25,000 − 2,000 − 6,000 − 23,800 − 2,700 − 12,000 + 42,000 + 198,000 − 156,000 − 17,500)	(19,700)
Prepaid expenses (400 − 400 + 5,000 + 500)	5,500
Total assets	57,140
EQUITY AND LIABILITIES	
Equity (owner's capital) (48,900 − 23,000 + 26,480)	52,380
Trade payables (16,900 + 143,000 − 156,000)	3,900
Accrued expenses (1,700 − 1,700 + 860)	860
Total equity and liabilities	57,140

	£
* Cost less accumulated depreciation at 31 December 2008	25,300
Carrying amount of machine disposed of (£13,000 − £3,900)	(9,100)
Cost of new machine	15,000
Depreciation for 2009 (£31,200 × 30%)	(9,360)
Carrying amount (written-down value) of machine at 31 December 2009	21,840

The loss on disposal of the old machinery is the carrying amount (cost less depreciation) less the disposal proceeds. Since the machinery had only been owned for one year, with a depreciation rate of 30%, the depreciation on it so far is £3,900 (that is, £13,000 × 30%). The effective disposal proceeds were £9,000 because, as a result of trading it in, the business saved £9,000 on the new asset.

The depreciation expense for 2009 is based on the cost less accumulated depreciation of the assets owned at the end of 2009. Accumulated depreciation must be taken into account because the business uses the reducing-balance method.

The statement of financial position could now be rewritten in a more stylish form as follows:

WW Associates
Statement of financial position as at 31 December 2009

	£
ASSETS	
Non-current assets	
Property, plant and equipment	
Machinery at cost less depreciation	21,840
Current assets	
Inventories	15,200
Trade receivables	34,300
Prepaid expenses	5,500
	55,000
Total assets	76,840
EQUITY AND LIABILITIES	
Equity	
Closing balance	52,380
Current liabilities	
Trade payables	3,900
Accrued expenses	860
Borrowings – Bank overdraft	19,700
	24,460
Total equity and liabilities	76,840

3.8 Nikov and Co

An examination of the income statements for the two years reveals a number of interesting points, which include:

- An increase in sales revenue and gross profit of 9.9% in 2009.
- The gross profit expressed as a percentage of sales revenue remaining at 70%.
- An increase in salaries of 7.2%.
- An increase in selling and distribution costs of 31.2%.
- An increase in bad debts of 392.5%.
- A decline in profit for the year of 39.3%.
- A decline in the profit for the year as a percentage of sales revenue from 13.3% to 7.4%.

Thus, the business has enjoyed an increase in sales revenue and gross profits, but this has failed to translate to an increase in profit for the year because of the significant rise in overheads. The increase in selling costs during 2009 suggests that the increase in sales revenue was achieved by greater marketing effort, and the huge increase in bad debts suggests that the increase in sales revenue may be attributable to selling to less creditworthy customers or to a weak debt-collection policy. There appears to have been a change of policy in 2009 towards sales, and this has not been successful overall as the profit for the year has shown a dramatic decline.

Chapter 4

4.1 Limited companies can no more set a limit on the amount of debts they will meet than can human beings. They must meet their debts up to the limit of their assets, just as we as individuals must. In the context of limited companies, 'reserves' mean part of the owners' claim against the assets of the company. These assets may or may not include cash. The legal ability of the company to pay dividends is not related to the amount of cash that it has.

Preference shares do not carry a guaranteed dividend. They simply guarantee that the preference shareholders have a right to the first slice of any dividend that is paid.

Shares of those companies that have gained a Stock Exchange listing can, in effect, be bought by one investor from another through the Stock Exchange. (Listed companies represent a very small proportion of all companies.)

One shareholder selling shares to another has no direct effect on the company. These are not new shares being offered by the company, but existing shares that are being sold 'second-hand'.

4.2 (a) The first part of the quote is incorrect. Bonus shares should not, of themselves, increase the value of the shareholders' wealth. This is because reserves, belonging to the shareholders, are used to create bonus shares. Thus, each shareholder's stake in the company has not increased.

(b) This statement is incorrect. Shares can be issued at any price, provided that it is not below the nominal value of the shares. Once the company has been trading profitably for a period, the shares will not be worth the same as they were (the nominal value) when the company was first formed. In such circumstances, issuing shares at above their nominal value would not only be legal, but essential to preserve the wealth of the existing shareholders relative to any new ones.

(c) This statement is incorrect. From a legal perspective, the company is limited to a maximum dividend of the current extent of its revenue reserves. This amounts to any after-tax profits or gains realised that have not been eroded through, for example, payments of previous dividends. Legally, cash is not an issue; it would be perfectly legal for a company to borrow the funds to pay a dividend – although whether such an action would be commercially prudent is another question.

(d) This statement is partly incorrect. Companies do indeed have to pay tax on their profits. Depending on their circumstances, shareholders might also have to pay tax on their dividends.

4.4 **Iqbal Ltd**

Year	Maximum dividend £	
2006	0	No profit exists out of which to pay a dividend.
2007	0	There remains a cumulative loss of £7,000. Since the revaluation represents a gain that has not been realised, it cannot be used to justify a dividend.
2008	13,000	The cumulative net realised gains are derived as (–£15,000 + £8,000 + £15,000 + £5,000).
2009	14,000	The realised profits and gains for the year (net figure).
2010	22,000	The realised profits and gains for the year.

4.6 Pear Limited

Income statement for the year ended 30 September 2010

	£000
Revenue (1,456 + 18)	1,474
Cost of sales	(768)
Gross profit	706
Salaries	(220)
Depreciation (249 + 12)	(261)
Other operating costs (131 + (2% × 200) + 2)	(137)
Operating profit	88
Interest payable (15 + 15)	(30)
Profit before taxation	58
Taxation (58 × 30%)	(17)
Profit for the year	41

Statement of financial position as at 30 September 2010

	£000
ASSETS	
Non-current assets	
Property, plant and equipment	
Cost (1,570 + 30)	1,600
Depreciation (690 + 12)	(702)
	898
Current assets	
Inventories	207
Trade receivables (182 + 18 – 4)	196
Cash at bank	21
	424
Total assets	1,322
EQUITY AND LIABILITIES	
Equity	
Share capital	300
Share premium account	300
Retained earnings (104 + 41 – 25)	120
	720
Non-current liabilities	
Borrowings – 10% loan notes (repayable 2014)	300
Current liabilities	
Trade payables	88
Other payables (20 + 30 + 15 + 2)	67
Taxation	17
Dividend approved	25
Borrowings (bank overdraft)	105
	302
Total equity and liabilities	1,322

4.7 Chips Limited

Income statement for the year ended 30 June 2010

	£000
Revenue (1,850 − 16)	1,834
Cost of sales (1,040 + 23)	(1,063)
Gross profit	771
Depreciation ((220 − 2 − 5 + 8) + (94 × 20%))	(240)
Other operating costs	(375)
Operating profit	156
Interest payable (35 + 35)	(70)
Profit before taxation	86
Taxation (86 × 30%)	(26)
Profit for the year	60

Statement of financial position as at 30 June 2010

ASSETS	Cost £000	Depreciation £000	£000
Non-current assets			
Property, plant and equipment			
Buildings	800	(112)	688
Plant and equipment	650	(367)	283
Motor vehicles (102 − 8); (53 − 5 + 19)	94	(67)	27
	1,544	(546)	998
Current assets			
Inventories			950
Trade receivables (420 − 16)			404
Cash at bank (16 + 2)			18
			1,372
Total assets			2,370
EQUITY AND LIABILITIES			
Equity			
Ordinary shares of £1, fully paid			800
Reserves at beginning of the year			248
Retained profit for year			60
			1,108
Non-current liabilities			
Borrowings (secured 10% loan notes)			700
Current liabilities			
Trade payables (361 + 23)			384
Other payables (117 + 35)			152
Taxation			26
			562
Total equity and liabilities			2,370

Chapter 5

5.1 Principles

Accounting is an evolving subject. It is not static and so the principles that are laid down at any particular point in time may become obsolete as a result of changes in our understanding of the nature of accounting information and its impact on users and changes in the economic environment within which accounting is employed. We must accept, therefore, that accounting principles will continue to evolve and that existing principles must be regularly reviewed.

5.2 Accountants' judgement

The quotation probably overstates the case. It is true that choice has been removed in some areas but there is still plenty of scope for accountants to make choices and to exercise judgement. Many decisions involving the valuation of assets and liabilities and the treatment of unusual items can involve difficult judgements. We have also seen that some accounting standards require judgements to be made (for example, those dealing with inventories and valuation).

5.5 I. Ching (Booksellers) plc

Statement of comprehensive income for the year ended 31 December 2009

	£m
Revenue	943
Cost of sales	(460)
Gross profit	483
Distribution expenses	(110)
Administrative expenses	(212)
Other expenses	(25)
Operating profit	136
Finance charges	(40)
Profit before tax	96
Taxation	(24)
Profit for the year	72
Other comprehensive income	
Revaluation of property, plant and equipment	20
Foreign currency translation differences for foreign operations	(15)
Tax on other comprehensive income	(1)
Other comprehensive income for the year, net of tax	4
Total comprehensive income for the year	76

5.6 Manet plc

Statement of changes in equity for the year ended 31 December 2009

	Share capital £m	Share premium £m	Revaluation reserve £m	Translation reserve £m	Retained earnings £m	Total £m
Balance as at 1 January 2009	250	50	120	15	380	815
Changes in equity for the 2009						
Dividends (Note 1)					(80)	(80)
Total comprehensive income for the year (Note 2)			30	(5)	160	185
Balance at 31 December 2009	250	50	150	10	460	920

Notes:

1 Dividends have been shown in the statement rather than in the notes. Either approach, however, is acceptable.

2 The effect of each component of comprehensive income on each component of shareholder equity must be shown. The revaluation gain and loss on exchange translation are each transferred to a specific reserve and the profit for the year is transferred to retained earnings.

5.7   Accounting regulation

Here are some points that might be made concerning accounting regulation and accounting measurement:

For

- It seems reasonable that companies, particularly given their limited liability, should be required to account to their members and to the general public and that rules should prescribe how this should be done – including how particular items should be measured. It also seems sensible an effort should be made through these rules to establish some uniformity of practice. Investors could be misled if the same item appeared in the financial statements of two separate companies but had been measured in different ways.
- Companies would find it difficult to attract finance, credit and possibly employees without publishing credible information about themselves. An important measure of performance is profit, and investors often need to make judgements concerning relative performance within an industry sector. Without clear benchmarks by which to judge performance, investors may not invest in a company.

Against

- It could be argued that it is up to the companies to decide whether or not they can survive and prosper without publishing information about themselves. If they can, so much the better, as, by not doing so, they will save large amounts of money. If it is necessary for a company to provide financial information in order to be able to attract investment finance and other necessary factors, then the company can make the necessary judgement as to how much information is necessary and what forms of measurement are required.
- Not all company managements view matters in the same way. Allowing companies to select their own approaches to financial reporting enables them to reflect their particular personalities. Thus, a conservative management will adopt conservative accounting policies, such as writing off research and development expenditure quickly, whereas more adventurous management may adopt less conservative accounting policies, such as writing off research and development expenditure over several years. The impact of these different views will have an effect on profit and will give the reader an insight to the approach adopted by the management team.

Chapter 6

6.1   (a) An increase in the level of inventories would, ultimately, have an adverse effect on cash.

(b) A rights issue of ordinary shares will give rise to a positive cash flow, which will be included in the 'financing' section of the statement of cash flows.

(c) A bonus issue of ordinary shares has no cash flow effect.

(d) Writing off some of the value of the inventories has no cash flow effect.

(e) A disposal for cash of a large number of shares by a major shareholder has no cash flow effect as far as the business is concerned.

(f) Depreciation does not involve cash at all. Using the indirect method of deducing cash flows from operating activities involves the depreciation expense in the calculation, but this is simply because we are trying to find out from the profit before taxation (after depreciation) figure what the profit before taxation *and* depreciation must have been.

6.3

Torrent plc
Statement of cash flows for the year ended 31 December 2010

	£m
Cash flows from operating activities	
Profit before taxation (after interest) (see Note 1 below)	170
Adjustments for:	
Depreciation (Note 2)	78
Interest expense (Note 3)	26
	274
Decrease in inventories (41 – 35)	6
Increase in trade receivables (145 – 139)	(6)
Decrease in trade payables (54 – 41)	(13)
Cash generated from operations	261
Interest paid (Note 3)	(26)
Taxation paid (Note 4)	(41)
Dividend paid	(60)
Net cash from operating activities	134
Cash flows from investing activities	
Payments to acquire plant and machinery	(67)
Net cash used in investing activities	(67)
Cash flows from financing activities	
Redemption of loan notes (250 – 150) (Note 5)	(100)
Net cash used in financing activities	(100)
Net decrease in cash and cash equivalents	(33)
Cash and cash equivalents at 1 January 2010	
Bank overdraft	(56)
Cash and cash equivalents at 31 December 2010	
Bank overdraft	(89)

To see how this relates to the cash of the business at the beginning and end of the year it can be useful to provide a reconciliation as follows:

Analysis of cash and cash equivalents during the year ended 31 December 2010

	£m
Cash and cash equivalents at 1 January 2010	(56)
Net cash outflow	(33)
Cash and cash equivalents at 31 December 2010	(89)

Notes:
1 This is simply taken from the income statement for the year.
2 Since there were no disposals, the depreciation charges must be the difference between the start and end of the year's plant and machinery values, adjusted by the cost of any additions.

	£m
Carrying amount at 1 January 2010	325
Additions	67
Depreciation (balancing figure)	(78)
Carrying amount at 31 December 2010	314

3 Interest payable expense must be taken out, by adding it back to the profit before taxation figure. We subsequently deduct the cash paid for interest payable during the year. In this case the two figures are identical.
4 Companies pay 50% of their tax during their accounting year and 50% in the following year. Thus the 2010 payment would have been half the tax on the 2009 profit (that is, the figure that would have appeared in the current liabilities at the end of 2009), plus half of the 2010 tax charge (that is, $23 + (\frac{1}{2} \times 36) = 41$).
5 It is assumed that the cash payment to redeem the loan notes was simply the difference between the figures on the two statements of financial position.

6 It seems that there was a bonus issue of ordinary shares during the year. These increased by £100m. At the same time, the share premium account balance reduced by £40m (to zero) and the revaluation reserve balance fell by £60m. This had no impact on cash.

6.6

Blackstone plc
Statement of cash flows for the year ended 31 March 2010

	£m
Cash flows from operating activities	
Profit before taxation (after interest)	
(see Note 1 below)	1,853
Adjustments for:	
Depreciation (Note 2)	1,289
Interest expense (Note 3)	456
	3,598
Increase in inventories (2,410 – 1,209)	(1,201)
Increase in trade receivables (1,173 – 641)	(532)
Increase in trade payables (1,507 – 931)	576
Cash generated from operations	2,441
Interest paid (Note 3)	(456)
Taxation paid (Note 4)	(300)
Dividend paid	(400)
Net cash from operating activities	1,285
Cash flows from investing activities	
Proceeds of disposals	54
Payment to acquire intangible non-current asset	(700)
Payments to acquire property, plant and equipment	(4,578)
Net cash used in investing activities	(5,224)
Cash flows from financing activities	
Bank borrowings	2,000
Net cash from financing activities	2,000
Net decrease in cash and cash equivalents	(1,939)
Cash and cash equivalents at 1 April 2009	
Cash at bank	123
Cash and cash equivalents at 31 March 2010	
Bank overdraft	(1,816)

To see how this relates to the cash of the business at the beginning and end of the year it can be useful to provide a reconciliation as follows:

Analysis of cash and cash equivalents during the year ended 31 March 2010

	£m
Cash and cash equivalents at 1 April 2009	123
Net cash outflow	(1,939)
Cash and cash equivalents at 31 March 2010	(1,816)

Notes:

1 This is simply taken from the income statement for the year.
2 The full depreciation charge was that stated in Note 2 to the question (£1,251m), plus the deficit on disposal of the non-current assets. According to Note 2, these non-current assets had originally cost £581m and had been depreciated by £489m, that is a net carrying amount of £92m. They were sold for £54m, leading to a deficit on disposal of £38m. Thus the full depreciation expense for the year was £1,289m (that is, £1,251m + £38m).
3 Interest payable expense must be taken out, by adding it back to the profit before taxation figure. We subsequently deduct the cash paid for interest payable during the year. In this case the two figures are identical.

4 Companies pay tax at 50% during their accounting year and the other 50% in the following year. Thus the 2010 payment would have been half the tax on the 2009 profit (that is, the figure that would have appeared in the current liabilities at 31 March 2009), plus half of the 2010 tax charge (that is, $105 + (\frac{1}{2} \times 390) = 300$).

6.7

York plc
Statement of cash flows for the year ended 30 September 2010

	£m
Cash flows from operating activities	
Profit before taxation (after interest) (see Note 1 below)	10.0
Adjustments for:	
Depreciation (Note 2)	9.8
Interest expense (Note 3)	3.0
	22.8
Increase in inventories and trade receivables (122.1 – 119.8)	(2.3)
Increase in trade payables (82.5 – 80.0)	2.5
Cash generated from operations	23.0
Interest paid (Note 3)	(3.0)
Taxation paid (Note 4)	(2.3)
Dividend paid	(3.5)
Net cash from operating activities	14.2
Cash flows from investing activities	
Proceeds of disposals (Note 2)	5.2
Payments to acquire non-current assets	(20.0)
Net cash used in investing activities	(14.8)
Cash flows from financing activities	
Increase in long-term borrowings	3.0
Share issue (Note 5)	5.0
Net cash from financing activities	8.0
Net increase in cash and cash equivalents	7.4
Cash and cash equivalents at 1 October 2009	
Cash at bank	9.2
Cash and cash equivalents at 30 September 2010	
Cash at bank	16.6

To see how this relates to the cash of the business at the beginning and end of the year it can be useful to provide a reconciliation as follows:

Analysis of cash and cash equivalents during the year ended 30 September 2010

	£m
Cash and cash equivalents at 1 October 2009	9.2
Net cash inflow	7.4
Cash and cash equivalents at 30 September 2010	16.6

Notes:

1 This is simply taken from the income statement for the year.

2 The full depreciation charge was the £13.0m, less the surplus on disposal (£3.2m), both stated in Note 1 to the question. (According to the table in Note 4 to the question, the non-current assets disposed of had a net carrying amount of £2.0m. To produce a surplus of £3.2m, they must have been sold for £5.2m.)

3 Interest payable expense must be taken out, by adding it back to the profit before taxation figure. We subsequently deduct the cash paid for interest payable during the year. In this case the two figures are identical.

4 Companies pay 50% of their tax during their accounting year and the other 50% in the following year. Thus the 2010 payment would have been half the tax on the 2009 profit (that is, the figure that would have appeared in the current liabilities at 30 September 2009), plus half of the 2010 tax charge (that is, $1.0 + (\frac{1}{2} \times 2.6) = 2.3$).

5 The share issue must have been for cash since it could not have been a bonus issue – the share premium account is untouched and 'Reserves' had altered over the year only by the amount of the 2010 retained earnings (profit for the year, less the dividend). The shares seem to have been issued at par (that is, at their nominal value). This is a little surprising since the business has assets that seem to be above that value. On the other hand, were this a rights issue, the low issue price would not have disadvantaged the existing shareholders since they were also the beneficiaries of the advantage of the low issue price.

6.8

Axis plc
Statement of cash flows for the year ended 31 December 2010

	£m
Cash flows from operating activities	
Profit before taxation (after interest) (see Note 1 below)	34
Adjustments for:	
Depreciation (Note 2)	19
Interest payable expense (Note 3)	2
Interest receivable (Note 4)	(2)
	53
Decrease in inventories (25 – 24)	1
Increase in trade receivables (26 – 16)	(10)
Increase in trade payables (36 – 31)	5
Cash generated from operations	49
Interest paid (Note 3)	(2)
Taxation paid (Note 5)	(15)
Dividend paid	(14)
Net cash from operating activities	18
Cash flows from investing activities	
Interest receivable	2
Proceeds of disposals (Note 2)	4
Payments to acquire non-current assets (Note 6)	(25)
Net cash used in investing activities	(19)
Cash flows from financing activities	
Issue of loan notes	20
Net cash from financing activities	20
Net increase in cash and cash equivalents	19
Cash and cash equivalents at 1 January 2010	
Cash at bank	nil
Short-term investments	nil
	nil
Cash and cash equivalents at 31 December 2010	
Cash at bank	7
Short-term investments	12
	19

To see how this relates to the cash of the business at the beginning and end of the year it can be useful to provide a reconciliation as follows:

Analysis of cash and cash equivalents during the year ended 31 December 2010

	£m
Cash and cash equivalents at 1 January 2010	nil
Net cash inflow	19
Cash and cash equivalents at 31 December 2010	19

Notes:
1 This is simply taken from the income statement for the year.
2 The full depreciation charge for the year is the sum of two figures labelled 'depreciation' and the deficit on disposal of non-current assets (that is, £2m + £16m + £1m = £19m). These were detailed in the income statement.

According to the note in the question, the non-current assets disposed of had a net carrying amount of £5.0m (that is, £15m – £10m). To produce a deficit of £1m, they must have been sold for £4m.

3 Interest payable expense must be taken out, by adding it back to the profit before taxation figure. We subsequently deduct the cash paid for interest payable during the year. In this case the two figures are identical.

4 Interest receivable must be taken away to work towards the profit before crediting it, because it is not part of operations but of investing activities. The cash inflow from this source appears under the 'Cash flows from investing activities' heading.

5 Companies pay 50% of their tax during their accounting year and the other 50% in the following year. Thus the 2010 payment would have been half the tax on the 2009 profit (that is, the figure that would have appeared in the current liabilities at 31 December 2009), plus half the 2010 tax charge (that is, $7 + (\frac{1}{2} \times 16) = 15$).

6 The cost of the newly acquired non-current assets (plant and machinery) can be deduced as follows:

	£m
Cost of plant and machinery at 1 January 2010	70
Plant disposed of	(15)
Plant acquired	25
Cost of plant and machinery at 1 January 2010	80

Chapter 7

7.1 I. Jiang (Western) Ltd

The effect of each of the changes on ROCE is not always easy to predict.

1 On the face of it, an increase in the gross profit margin would tend to lead to an increase in ROCE. An increase in the gross profit margin may, however, lead to a decrease in ROCE in particular circumstances. If the increase in the margin resulted from an increase in sales prices, which in turn led to a decrease in sales revenue, a fall in ROCE can occur. A fall in sales revenue can reduce the operating profit (the numerator (top part of the fraction) in ROCE) if the overheads of the business did not decrease correspondingly.

2 A reduction in sales revenue can reduce ROCE for the reasons mentioned above.

3 An increase in overhead expenses will reduce the operating profit and this in turn will result in a reduction in ROCE.

4 An increase in inventories held would increase the amount of capital employed by the business (the denominator (bottom part of the fraction) in ROCE) where long-term funds are employed to finance the inventories. This will, in turn, reduce ROCE.

5 Repayment of the borrowings at the year end will reduce the capital employed and this will increase the ROCE, assuming that the year-end capital employed figure has been used in the calculation. Since the operating profit was earned during a period in which the borrowings existed, there is a strong argument for basing the capital employed figure on what was the position during the year, rather than at the end of it.

6 An increase in the time taken for credit customers to pay will result in an increase in capital employed if long-term funds are employed to finance the trade receivables. This increase in long-term funds will, in turn, reduce ROCE.

7.2 Amsterdam Ltd and Berlin Ltd

The ratios for Amsterdam Ltd and Berlin Ltd reveal that the trade receivables turnover ratio for Amsterdam Ltd is three times that for Berlin Ltd. Berlin Ltd is therefore much quicker in collecting amounts outstanding from customers. On the other hand, there is not much difference between the two businesses in the time taken to pay trade payables.

It is interesting to compare the difference in the trade receivables and payables collection periods for each business. As Amsterdam Ltd allows an average of 63 days' credit to its customers, yet pays suppliers within 50 days, it will require greater investment in working capital than Berlin Ltd, which allows an average of only 21 days to its customers but takes 45 days to pay its suppliers.

Amsterdam Ltd has a much higher gross profit margin than Berlin Ltd. However, the operating profit margin for the two businesses is identical. This suggests that Amsterdam Ltd has much higher overheads (as a percentage of sales revenue) than Berlin Ltd. The inventories turnover period for Amsterdam Ltd is more than twice that of Berlin Ltd. This may be due to the fact that Amsterdam Ltd maintains a wider range of inventories in an attempt to meet customer requirements. The evidence therefore suggests that Amsterdam Ltd is the one that prides itself on personal service. The higher average settlement period for trade receivables is consistent with a more relaxed attitude to credit collection (thereby maintaining customer goodwill) and the high overheads are consistent with incurring the additional costs of satisfying customers' requirements. Amsterdam Ltd's high inventories levels are consistent with maintaining a wide range of inventories, with the aim of satisfying a range of customer needs.

Berlin Ltd has the characteristics of a more price-competitive business. Its gross profit margin is much lower than that of Amsterdam Ltd, that is, it has a much lower gross profit for each £1 of sales revenue. However, overheads have been kept low, the effect being that the operating profit margin is the same as Amsterdam Ltd's. The low inventories turnover period and average collection period for trade receivables are consistent with a business that wishes to minimise investment in current assets, thereby reducing costs.

7.6 Bradbury Ltd

(a)

	2009	2010
1 Operating profit margin	$\dfrac{914}{9,482} \times 100\% = 9.6\%$	$\dfrac{1,042}{11,365} \times 100\% = 9.2\%$
2 ROCE	$\dfrac{914}{11,033} \times 100 = 8.3\%$	$\dfrac{1,042}{13,943} \times 100\% = 7.5\%$
3 Current ratio	$\dfrac{4,926}{1,508} = 3.3{:}1$	$\dfrac{7,700}{5,174} = 1.5{:}1$
4 Gearing ratio	$\dfrac{1,220}{11,033} \times 100\% = 11.1\%$	$\dfrac{3,675}{13,943} \times 100\% = 26.4\%$
5 Days trade receivables	$\left[\dfrac{2,540}{9,482}\right] \times 365 = 98$ days	$\left[\dfrac{4,280}{11,365}\right] \times 365 = 137$ days
6 Sales revenue to capital employed	$\dfrac{9,482}{(9,813 + 1,220)} = 0.9$ times	$\dfrac{11,365}{(10,268 + 3,675)} = 0.8$ times

(b) The operating profit margin was slightly lower in 2010 than in 2009. Although there was an increase in sales revenue in 2009, this could not prevent a slight fall in ROCE in that year. The lower operating margin and increases in sales revenue may well be due to the new contract. The capital employed by the company increased in 2010 by a larger percentage than the increase in revenue. Hence, the sales revenue to capital employed ratio decreased over the period. The increase in capital employed during 2010 is largely due to an increase in borrowing. However, the gearing ratio is probably still low in comparison with other businesses. Comparison of the premises and borrowings figures indicates possible unused borrowing (debt) capacity.

The major cause for concern has been the dramatic decline in liquidity during 2010. The current ratio has more than halved during the period. There has also been a similar decrease in the acid test ratio, from 1.7:1 in 2009 to 0.8:1 in 2010. The statement of financial position shows that the business now has a large overdraft and the trade payables outstanding have nearly doubled in 2010.

The trade receivables outstanding and inventories have increased much more than appears to be warranted by the increase in sales revenue. This may be due to the terms of the contract that has been negotiated and may be difficult to influence. If this is the case, the business should consider whether it needs more longer-term finance. If the conclusion is that it does, acquiring more may be a sensible policy.

7.7   Harridges Ltd

(a)

	2009	2010
ROCE	$\dfrac{310}{1,600} = 19.4\%$	$\dfrac{350}{1,700} = 20.6\%$
ROSF	$\dfrac{155}{1,100} = 14.1\%$	$\dfrac{175}{1,200} = 14.6\%$
Gross profit margin	$\dfrac{1,040}{2,600} = 40\%$	$\dfrac{1,150}{3,500} = 32.9\%$
Operating profit margin	$\dfrac{310}{2,600} = 11.9\%$	$\dfrac{350}{3,500} - 10\%$
Current ratio	$\dfrac{735}{400} = 1.8{:}1$	$\dfrac{660}{485} = 1.4{:}1$
Acid test ratio	$\dfrac{485}{400} = 1.2{:}1$	$\dfrac{260}{485} = 0.5{:}1$
Trade receivables settlement period	$\dfrac{105}{2,600} \times 365 = 15$ days	$\dfrac{145}{3,500} \times 365 = 15$ days
Trade payables settlement period	$\dfrac{300}{1,560^*} \times 365 = 70$ days	$\dfrac{375}{2,350^*} \times 365 = 58$ days
Inventories turnover period	$\dfrac{250}{1,560} \times 365 = 58$ days	$\dfrac{400}{2,350} \times 365 = 62$ days
Gearing ratio	$\dfrac{500}{1,600} \times 100\% = 31.3\%$	$\dfrac{500}{1,700} \times 100\% = 29.4\%$

* Used because the credit purchases figure is not available.

(b) There has been a considerable decline in the gross profit margin during 2010. This fact, combined with the increase in sales revenue by more than one-third, suggests that a price-cutting policy has been adopted in an attempt to stimulate sales. The resulting increase in sales revenue, however, has led to only a small improvement in ROCE and ROSF.

The operating profit margin ratio has fallen by about 16 per cent, slightly less than the nearly 18 per cent fall in the gross profit margin ratio. This must mean that overheads have not risen in proportion to sales revenue. This may suggest that overheads have been better controlled during 2010. On the other hand many overheads do not increase in proportion to sales revenue. Staff costs (wages and salaries) are an example of a cost that does not necessarily rise in proportion to sales revenue.

The current ratio has fallen, and the acid test ratio has fallen by more than half. Even though liquidity ratios are lower in retailing than in manufacturing, the liquidity of the business should now be a cause for concern. However, this may be a passing problem. The business is investing heavily in non-current assets and is relying on internal funds to finance this growth. When this investment ends, the liquidity position may improve quickly.

The trade receivables period has remained unchanged over the two years, and there has been no significant change in the inventories turnover period in 2010. The gearing ratio seems quite low and provides no cause for concern given the profitability of the business.

Overall, the business appears to be financially sound. Although there has been rapid growth during 2010, there is no real cause for alarm provided that the liquidity of the business can be improved in the near future. In the absence of information concerning share price, it is not possible to say whether an investment should be made.

7.8   Freezeqwik Ltd

The OCC may be calculated as follows:

Number of days

Average inventories holding period:

$$\frac{\text{(Opening inventories + Closing inventories)/2}}{\text{Cost of sales}} \times 365 = \frac{(142 + 166)/2}{544} \times 365 \qquad 103$$

Average settlement period for trade receivables:

$$\frac{\text{Trade receivables}}{\text{Credit sales}} \times 365 = \frac{264}{820} \times 365 \qquad \underline{118}$$

$$221$$

Average settlement period for trade payables:

$$\frac{\text{Trade payables}}{\text{Credit purchases}} \times 365 = \frac{159}{568} \times 365 \qquad \underline{(102)}$$

OCC $\underline{119}$

The business can reduce the length of the OCC in a number of ways. The average inventories holding period seems quite long. At present, average inventories held represent more than three months' sales requirements. Lowering the level of inventories held will reduce this. Similarly, the average settlement period for trade receivables seems long, at nearly four months' sales. Imposing tighter credit control, offering discounts, charging interest on overdue accounts and so on, may reduce this. However, any policy decisions concerning inventories and trade receivables must take account of current trading conditions.

Extending the period of credit taken to pay suppliers could also reduce the OCC. However, because of the risk of losing supplier goodwill, this option must be given careful consideration.

Chapter 8

8.1   Next plc

The Next plc dividend yield is very close to that for the general retailers section average. This might imply that Next pays out about the same proportion of its earnings as the section average. In fact this is not the case with Next paying out a substantially smaller proportion of its profit (cover of 2.8 times, compared with the 2.07 average). This implies that Next has a relatively low share price, compared to other retailers.

Compared to current (most recently reported) earnings, the current market price (P/E ratio) of Next is rather lower than the average for listed retailers. This again implies that the investing public has less confidence in the future prospects of Next than in listed retailers generally. However, both dividend yield and P/E ratios can be difficult to interpret.

8.2   **Telford Industrial Services plc**

Common-sized statement of financial position at 31 December

	2007 £m	2008 £m	2009 £m	2010 £m
Non-current assets	100	83	106	102
Current assets				
Inventories	44	36	38	41
Trade receivables	71	69	56	46
Cash	–	5	–	–
	115	110	94	87
Total assets	215	193	200	189
Equity	100	100	100	100
Non-current liabilities	63	49	49	48
Current liabilities				
Trade payables	42	44	41	28
Short-term borrowings	10	–	10	13
	52	44	51	41
Total equity and liabilities	215	193	200	189

[The individual figures are calculated by dividing each of the original figures by the equity value for the year concerned and multiplying the result by 100. For example, the inventories figure for 2007 is $(21/48) \times 100 = 44$. Since the revised values have been expressed in whole numbers (no decimal places), it was necessary to adjust to make the statement of financial position agree, despite rounding errors.]

Summary of common-sized income statements for years ended 31 December

	2007 £m	2008 £m	2009 £m	2010 £m
Sales revenue	100	100	100	100
Operating profit	19	24	6	10
Interest payable	(3)	(2)	(4)	(3)
Profit before taxation	16	22	2	7
Taxation	(8)	(9)	–	(3)
Profit for the period	8	13	2	4

[The individual figures are calculated by dividing each of the original figures by the sales revenue value for the year concerned and multiplying the result by 100. For example, the operating profit figure for 2007 is $(28/152) \times 100 = 19$.]

8.3   **Ali plc and Bhaskar plc**

(a) The Altman Z-score model is as follows:

$$Z = 0.717a + 0.847b + 3.107c + 0.420d + 0.998e$$

where a = Working capital/Total assets
   b = Accumulated retained profits/Total assets
   c = Operating profit/Total assets
   d = Book (statement of financial position) value of ordinary and preference shares/Total liabilities at book (statement of financial position) value
   e = Sales revenue/Total assets

For Ali plc, the Z-score is:

$$0.717[(853.0 - 422.4)/1,300.0] + 0.847(367.6/1,300.0) + 3.107(151.3/1,300.0)$$
$$+ 0.420[320.0/(190.0 + 422.4)] + 0.998(1,478.1/1,300.0) = 2.193$$

For Bhaskar plc, the Z-score is:

$$0.717[(816.5 - 293.1)/1,417.7] + 0.847(624.6/1,417.7) + 3.107(166.9/1,417.7)$$
$$+ 0.420[250.0/(250.0 + 293.1)] + 0.998(1,790.4/1,417.7) = 2.457$$

(b) The Z-scores for these two businesses are quite close, with Bhaskar looking slightly safer. They are both in the category of businesses in the 'zone of ignorance' and, therefore, difficult to classify (a Z-score between 1.23 and 4.14). This is quite unusual in that the Altman model is able confidently to classify 91 per cent of businesses. Clearly, these two businesses fall into the remaining 9 per cent.

It is questionable whether the Altman model is strictly applicable to UK businesses, since it was derived from data relating to US businesses that had failed. On the other hand, it probably provides a useful insight.

8.5 Green Ltd

(a)

		2008		2009		2010	
(1)	Return on capital employed ratio	(0.2)/(8.4 + 6.5) × 100	(1.3)%	(2.0)/(4.0 + 8.2) × 100	(16.4)%	1.9/(4.4 + 7.4) × 100	16.1%
(2)	Acid test ratio	2.8/4.1	0.68:1	2.6/5.8	0.45:1	4.1/6.1	0.67:1
(3)	Trade receivables settlement period ratio*	2.8/11.5 × 12	2.9 months	2.6/8.0 × 12	3.9 months	4.1/9.5 × 12	5.2 months
(4)	Interest cover ratio		no cover		no cover	1.9/1.5	1.3 times
(5)	Gearing ratio	6.5/(6.5 + 8.4) × 100	43.6%	8.2/(8.2 + 4.0) × 100	67.2%	7.4/(7.4 + 4.4) × 100	62.7%

* The year-end trade receivables figures were used because it would not have been possible, with the information provided in the question, to use the average for the years.

In terms of profitability, Green Ltd seems to have improved in 2010, relative to the previous two years, particularly 2009. This has probably been the main reason for the improvement in liquidity since 2009. The increase in the time taken to collect the cash from credit customers is a concern. This has almost doubled since 2008. Over five months seems a very long time.

Gearing, which increased in 2009, has dropped a little in 2010. Given the level of profit, gearing still looks high, with the interest obligations not being very well covered by operating profit.

(b) Possibly the most useful help that your business could offer Green Ltd is some advice on reducing its level of working capital (current assets less current liabilities). As mentioned in (a), the trade receivable level in 2010 seems very high. This seems also to be true of inventories. At the same time, trade payables seem quite low (only 50% of the level of inventories in 2010). It seems perfectly plausible that a combination of taking longer to pay suppliers, getting in cash from customers more quickly and reducing the level of inventories could generate sufficient funds to eliminate the bank overdraft.

Your business may be reluctant to involve itself in providing finance. It is not, presumably, in the business of doing so. It may prefer to suggest that Green Ltd looks for some bank or equity finance from a more traditional source. Given the already high level of gearing, even assuming that the overdraft can be eliminated, as suggested above, equity looks a better bet than loan financing. Given that it is your business's only source of some of its needs, you may feel that supplying finance, and gaining the influence that this may bring, is the best way to protect your business's interests.

If your business is able and willing to advance equity finance (buy new shares issued by Green Ltd), the following points need to be addressed:

- *Future profitability*. How profitable can Green Ltd be in the future, with the new machinery?
- *Influence*. If your business is to buy shares, it will need to be sure of considerable influence over Green Ltd's management. A seat on Green Ltd's board of directors seems a minimum requirement.
- *Exit route*. How will your business be able to liquidate its investment, as and when it wishes to do so? Green Ltd is not a plc and cannot, therefore be Stock Exchange listed. This means that there is no ready and obvious market for the shares.

8.8 Genesis Ltd

(a) Current ratio $= \dfrac{232}{550} = 0.42:1$

Acid test ratio $= \dfrac{104}{550} = 0.19:1$

Inventories turnover period $= \dfrac{128}{1,248} \times 365 = 37$ days

(To be consistent with the last two ratios, the inventories turnover period ratio has been calculated using the year-end inventories figure.)

Average settlement period for trade receivables $= \dfrac{104}{1,640} \times 365 = 23$ days

Average settlement period for trade payables $= \dfrac{184}{1,260} \times 365 = 53$ days

It is difficult to make a judgement about such matters with no equivalent ratios for past periods, other businesses or the business's own plans, but there is some evidence that this business is, in fact, overtrading. Both of the liquidity ratios look weak. The acid test ratio should probably be around 1:1. Customers are paying more than twice as quickly as suppliers are being paid. This suggests that pressure may be being applied to the former to pay quickly, perhaps with adverse results. It may also imply that payments are being delayed to suppliers because of a lack of available finance.

(b) Overtrading must be dealt with either by increasing the level of funding to match the level of activity, or by reducing the level of activity to match the funds available. The latter option may result in a reduction in operating profit in the short term but may be necessary to ensure long-term survival.

Chapter 9

9.1

Group statement of financial position of Giant and its subsidiary as at 31 March

	£m
ASSETS	
Non-current assets (at cost less depreciation)	
Property, plant and equipment	
Land (27 + 12)	39
Plant (55 + 8)	63
Vehicles (18 + 7)	25
	127
Current assets	
Inventories (33 + 13)	46
Trade receivables (42 + 17)	59
Cash (22 + 5)	27
	132
Total assets	259
EQUITY AND LIABILITIES	
Equity	
Called-up share capital:	
ordinary shares of £1 each, fully paid	50
Share premium account	40
Retained earnings	46
	136
Non-current liabilities	
Loan notes (50 + 13)	63
Current liabilities	
Trade payables (41 + 19)	60
Total equity and liabilities	259

Note that the group statement of financial position is prepared by adding all like items together. The investment in 10 million shares of Jack Ltd (£30m), in the statement of financial position of Giant plc, is then compared with the equity (in total) in Jack Ltd's statement of financial position. Since Giant paid exactly the fair values of Jack's assets *and* bought all of Jack's shares, these two figures are equal and can be cancelled.

9.2   The statement of financial position of Jumbo plc and its subsidiary will be as follows:

Statement of financial position as at 31 March

	£m
ASSETS	
Non-current assets (at cost less depreciation)	
Property, plant and equipment	
Land (84 + 18)	102
Plant (34 + 33)	67
Vehicles (45 + 12)	57
	226
Current assets	
Inventories (55 + 32)	87
Trade receivables (26 + 44)	70
Cash (14 + 10)	24
	181
Total assets	407
EQUITY AND LIABILITIES	
Equity	
Called-up share capital:	
ordinary shares of £1 each, fully paid	100
Retained earnings	41
	141
Non-controlling interests	16
	157
Non-current liabilities	
Loan notes (100 + 70)	170
Current liabilities	
Trade payables (41 + 39)	80
Total equity and liabilities	407

Note that the normal approach is taken with various assets and external claims (that is, adding like items together). The 'non-controlling interests' figure represents the minorities' share (8 million of 20 million ordinary shares) in the equity of Nipper plc (40 per cent of £40 million).

9.3 Toggles plc

(a) 1 'Non-controlling interests' represents the portion, either of net assets (statement of financial position) or profit for the year (income statement), which is attributable to minority shareholders. Minority shareholders exist where the parent company does not own all of the shares in its subsidiary. Since, by definition, the parent company is the major shareholder in each of its subsidiaries, any other shareholders in any other subsidiary must be a minority, in terms of number of shares owned.

2 'Goodwill arising on consolidation' is the difference, at the time that the parent acquires the subsidiary, between what is paid for the subsidiary company shares and what they are 'worth'. 'Worth' normally is based on the fair values of the underlying assets (net of liabilities) of the subsidiary. These are not necessarily, nor usually, the statement of financial position values. Goodwill, therefore, represents the excess of what was paid over the fair values of the (net) assets of the subsidiary. As such goodwill arising on consolidation is an intangible asset that represents the amount that the parent was prepared to pay for the value of the fact that the subsidiary has a workforce in place and any possible synergies that will arise from the parent and the subsidiary having a close relationship.

3 The retained earnings of the parent company will be its own cumulative profits net of tax and dividends paid.

When the results of the subsidiaries are consolidated with those of the parent, the parent's share of the post-acquisition retained earnings of its subsidiaries is added to its own retained earnings figure. In this way the parent is, in effect, credited with its share of the subsidiaries' after-tax profit that has arisen since the takeover.

(b) The objective of preparing consolidated financial statements is to reflect the underlying economic reality that the assets of the subsidiary companies are as much under the control of the shareholders of the parent, acting through their board of directors, as are the assets owned directly by the parent. This will be true despite the fact that the subsidiary is strictly a separate company from the parent. It is also despite the fact that the parent may not own all of the shares of the subsidiaries.

Consolidated financial statements provide an example where accounting tends to put 'content' before 'form'. That is to say that it tries to reflect economic reality rather than the strict legal position. This is done in an attempt to provide more useful information.

9.4 Arnold plc

Group income statement for the year ended 31 December

	£m
Revenue (83 + 47)	130
Cost of sales (36 + 19)	(55)
Gross profit (47 + 28)	75
Administration expenses (14 + 7)	(21)
Distribution expenses (21 + 10)	(31)
Profit before taxation (12 + 11)	23
Taxation (4 + 3)	(7)
Profit for the year (8 + 8)	16
Attributable to minorities (25% × 8)	(2)
Profit for the year attributable to Arnold plc shareholders	14

9.5 The statement of financial position of Apple Ltd and its subsidiary will be as follows:

Statement of financial position as at 30 September

	£000
ASSETS	
Non-current assets (at cost less depreciation)	
Property, plant and equipment (950 + 320)	1,270
Goodwill arising on consolidation (see Note 2)	24
	1,294
Current assets	
Inventories (320 + 160)	480
Trade receivables (180 + 95)	275
Cash at bank (41 + 15)	56
	811
Total assets	2,105
EQUITY AND LIABILITIES	
Equity	
£1 fully paid ordinary shares	700
Reserves	307
	1,007
Non-controlling interests (see Note 3)	72
	1,079
Non-current liabilities	
Loan notes (500 + 160)	660
Current liabilities	
Trade payables (170 + 87)	257
Taxation (54 + 55)	109
	366
Total equity and liabilities	2,105

Notes

1 The normal approach is taken with various assets and external claims.
2 The goodwill arising on consolidation is the difference between what Apple Ltd paid for the shares in Pear Ltd (150,000 × £1.60 = £240,000), less the fair value of the net assets acquired (150,000/200,000 × £288,000 = £216,000). That is £24,000.
3 The non-controlling interests figure is simply the minority shareholders' stake in the net assets of Pear Ltd. This is 50,000/200,000 × £288,000 = £72,000.

Chapter 10

10.1 **Information**

Some believe that the annual reports of companies are becoming too long and contain too much information. A few examples of the length of the 2008 reports of large companies are as follows:

Marks and Spencer plc	104 pages
Tesco plc	112 pages
National Grid plc	196 pages
3i Group plc	128 pages

There is a danger that users will suffer from information overload if they are confronted with an excessive amount of information and that they will be unable to cope with it. This may, in turn, lead them to

- fail to distinguish between important and less important information;
- fail to approach the analysis of information in a logical and systematic manner;
- feel a sense of confusion and avoid the task of analysing the information.

Lengthy annual reports are likely to be a problem for the less sophisticated user. This problem has been recognised and many companies publish summarised financial statements for private investors, which include only the key points. However, for sophisticated users the problem may be that the annual reports are still not long enough. They often wish to glean as much information as possible from the company in order to make investment decisions.

10.5   Dali plc

A striking feature of the segmental reports is that the car parts segment generates the highest revenue – more than the other two segments combined. Nevertheless, it is the aircraft parts segment that generates the highest profit. We can use some simple ratios at this point to help evaluate performance.

Table of key results

	Car	Aircraft	Boat
Total revenue	£360m	£210m	£85m
Segment profit	£20m	£24m	£18m
Net assets (assets less liabilities)	£85m	£58m	£22m
Segment profit as a percentage of sales revenue	5.6%	11.4%	21.2%
Segment profit as a percentage of net assets employed	23.5%	41.4%	81.8%
Expenditure on non-current assets	£28m	£23m	£26m
Depreciation as a percentage of segment assets	47.1%	44.0%	34.1%

We can start by considering the profit generated in relation to the sales revenue for each operating segment. We can see from the table that the boat parts segment generates the most profit in relation to sales revenue. Around 21 per cent, or £0.21 in every £1, of profit is derived from the sales revenue generated. The total revenue for this segment, however, is much lower than for the other two segments. Although the car parts segment generates the most revenue, less than 6%, or £0.06 in every £1, of profit is derived from the sales revenue generated. It is worth noting that the aircraft parts segment suffered a large impairment charge during the year, which had a significant effect on profits. The reasons for this impairment charge should be investigated.

We can also compare the profit generated with the net assets employed (that is, total assets less total liabilities) for each segment. We can see from the table above that the boat parts segment produces the best return on net assets employed by far: around 82 per cent, that is, £0.82 for every £1 invested. Once again, the car parts segment produces the worst results with a return of less than 24 per cent.

The relatively poor results from the car parts segment may simply reflect the nature of the market in which it operates. Compared with car parts segments of other businesses, it may be doing very well. Nevertheless, the business may still wish to consider whether future investment would not be better directed to those areas where greater profits can be found.

The investment in non-current assets during the period in relation to the total assets held is much higher for the boat parts segment. This may reflect the faith of the directors in the potential of this segment.

The depreciation charge as a percentage of segment assets seems to be high for all of the operating segments – and highest for the car parts division. This should be investigated as it may suggest poor buying decisions.

10.6

Alkrom plc
CPP income statement for the three-month period to 31 March

	CPP£m
Sales revenue (120/120 × £19.2m)	19.2
Cost of sales (120/115 × £16.0m)	16.7
Profit for the period	2.5

CPP statement of financial position as at 31 March

	CPP£m
ASSETS	
Non-current assets	
Property, plant and equipment	
Offices (£4m × 120/115)	4.2
Current assets	
Receivables	19.2
Total assets	23.4
EQUITY	
Equity (20.0 × 120/115)	20.9
Retained earnings	2.5
Total equity	23.4

10.7 **Turner plc**

Table of key results

	Software	Electronics	Engineering
Total revenue	£250m	£230m	£52m
Segment profit	£10m	£34m	£12m
Net assets (assets – liabilities)	£85m	£52m	£30m
Segment profit as a percentage of sales revenue	4.0%	14.8%	23.1%
Segment profit as a percentage of net assets employed	11.8%	65.4%	40.0%
Expenditure on non-current assets	£22m	£12m	£10m
Depreciation as a percentage of segment assets	42.9%	38.9%	29.4%

We can see from the table that the software segment generates the highest revenue, but also generates the lowest profit. We can use some simple ratios at this point to help evaluate segmental performance. We can start by considering the profit generated in relation to the sales revenue for each operating segment. We can see from the table that the engineering segment generates the most profit in relation to sales revenue. Around 23 per cent, or £0.23 in every £1, of profit is derived from the sales revenue generated. However, for the software segment, only 4%, or £0.04 in every £1, of profit is derived from the sales revenue generated.

We can also compare the profit generated with the net assets employed (that is, total assets – total liabilities) for each segment. We can see from the table that the electronics segment produces the best return on net assets employed: around £0.65 for every £1 invested. Once again, the software segment produces the worst results.

The reasons for the relatively poor results from the software segment need further investigation. There may be valid reasons; for example, it may be experiencing severe competitive pressures. The results for this segment, however, are not disastrous: it is making a profit. Nevertheless, the business may wish to re-evaluate its long-term presence in this market.

It is interesting to note that the software segment benefited most from the investment in non-current assets during the period – as much as the other two segments combined. The reason for such a large investment in such a relatively poorly performing segment needs to be justified. It is possible that the business will reap rewards for the investment in the future; however, we do not have enough information to understand the reasons for the investment decision.

Depreciation charges in the software segment are significantly higher than for the other operating segments. This may be because the segment has more non-current assets, although we do not have a figure for the non-current assets held. The depreciation charge as a percentage of segment assets is also higher and the reasons for this should be investigated.

10.8   Business review

No solution provided as answers will vary according to the business reviews examined.

Chapter 11

11.1   Communication with shareholders

A large listed company may communicate with shareholders through:

- the published annual report;
- announcements made through the Stock Exchange concerning major events such as new contracts, new directors, proposed takeovers or mergers and so on;
- the annual general meeting (AGM);
- a dedicated company website;
- informal meetings with major shareholders;
- presentations to investment analysts.

11.2   Non-executive directors

The following criteria may be used to evaluate the performance of a non-executive director:

- willingness to spend time in understanding the business and in acquiring additional skills to improve effectiveness;
- contribution made to board discussions on key issues such as strategy development;
- effectiveness in challenging proposals made by identifying key weaknesses and assumptions;
- independence of mind and ability to resist undue pressure from other directors;
- perseverance in following up unresolved issues and in defending positions taken;
- ability to work as part of a team, when required, and to establish effective relations with key individuals, including other board members.

This is not an exhaustive list; you may have thought of other criteria.

11.4   Institutional shareholders

The benefits that may accrue from the maintenance of close ties with institutional shareholders are as follows:

- It provides the board of directors with the opportunity to explain the future direction of the company, which may lead to a better understanding of board proposals and decisions that have been made. This may, in turn, make institutional shareholders more willing to offer support during difficult times.

- It may encourage institutional shareholders to take a long-term view. If the board can provide a clear vision and strategy for the company, the shareholders may become less concerned with any short-term setbacks and become more concerned with achieving long-term goals.
- It can provide an external discipline on the board. The directors will be subjected to considerable scrutiny when meeting institutional shareholders. They will have to justify their decisions and be prepared to answer tough questions. This can, however, improve the quality of decisions made.
- It can provide valuable feedback on board proposals. Institutional investors may be sounded out on particular ideas that are under review. Their views can then be taken into account when making a final decision.
- It can help in future funding. Where institutional shareholders have good relations with the board and have confidence in the future direction of the company, they are more likely to be sympathetic to requests for additional funding.

There are various problems that can arise from close links with institutional shareholders. For example, there is a risk that certain commercially sensitive information provided to them will not be treated in confidence. There is also a risk in upsetting small shareholders, who may feel that large institutional shareholders are given undue influence over decisions. Finally, there is a problem in determining what are the acceptable limits to the discussions and information that is offered.

Appendix A

A.1
Account to be debited	Account to be credited
(a) Inventories	Trade payables
(b) Equity (or a separate drawings account)	Cash
(c) Interest on borrowings	Cash
(d) Inventories	Cash
(e) Cash	Trade receivables
(f) Wages	Cash
(g) Equity (or a separate drawings account)	Trade receivables
(h) Trade payables	Cash
(i) Electricity (or heat and light)	Cash
(j) Cash	Sales revenue

Note that the precise name given to an account is not crucial so long as it is clear to those who are using the information what each account deals with.

A.2 (a) and (b)

Cash

		£			£
1 Feb	Equity	6,000	3 Feb	Inventories	2,600
15 Feb	Sales revenue	4,000	5 Feb	Equipment	800
28 Feb	Trade receivables	2,500	9 Feb	Rent	250
			10 Feb	Electricity	240
			11 Feb	General expenses	200
			21 Feb	Equity	1,000
			25 Feb	Trade payables	2,000
			28 Feb	Balance c/d	5,410
		12,500			12,500
1 Mar	Balance b/d	5,410			

Equity

		£			£
21 Feb	Cash	1,000	1 Feb	Cash	6,000
28 Feb	Balance c/d	5,000			
		6,000			6,000
			28 Feb	Balance b/d	5,000
28 Feb	Balance c/d	7,410	28 Feb	Income statement	2,410
		7,410			7,410
			1 Mar	Balance b/d	7,410

Inventories

		£			£
3 Feb	Cash	2,600	15 Feb	Cost of sales	2,400
6 Feb	Trade payables	3,000	19 Feb	Cost of sales	2,300
			28 Feb	Balance c/d	900
		5,600			5,600
1 Mar	Balance b/d	900			

Equipment

		£		£
5 Feb	Cash	800		

Trade payables

		£			£
25 Feb	Cash	2,000	6 Feb	Inventories	3,000
28 Feb	Balance c/d	1,000			
		3,000			3,000
			1 Mar	Balance b/d	1,000

Rent

		£			£
9 Feb	Cash	250	28 Feb	Income statement	250

Electricity

		£			£
10 Feb	Cash	240	28 Feb	Income statement	240

General expenses

		£			£
11 Feb	Cash	200	28 Feb	Income statement	200

Sales revenue

		£			£
28 Feb	Balance c/d	7,800	15 Feb	Cash	4,000
			19 Feb	Trade receivables	3,800
		7,800			7,800
28 Feb	Income statement	7,800	28 Feb	Balance b/d	7,800

Cost of sales

		£			£
15 Feb	Inventories	2,400	28 Feb	Balance c/d	4,700
19 Feb	Inventories	2,300			
		4,700			4,700
28 Feb	Balance b/d	4,700	28 Feb	Income statement	4,700

Trade receivables

		£			£
19 Feb	Sales revenue	3,800	28 Feb	Cash	2,500
			28 Feb	Balance c/d	1,300
		3,800			3,800
1 Mar	Balance b/d	1,300			

Trial balance as at 28 February

	Debits	Credits
	£	£
Cash	5,410	
Capital		5,000
Inventories	900	
Equipment	800	
Trade payables		1,000
Rent	250	
Electricity	240	
General expenses	200	
Sales revenue		7,800
Cost of sales	4,700	
Trade receivables	1,300	
	13,800	13,800

(c) **Income statement**

		£			£
28 Feb	Cost of sales	4,700	28 February	Sales revenue	7,800
28 Feb	Rent	250			
28 Feb	Electricity	240			
28 Feb	General expenses	200			
28 Feb	Equity (profit)	2,410			
		7,800			7,800

Statement of financial position as at 28 February

	£
ASSETS	
Non-current assets	
Equipment	800
Current assets	
Inventories	900
Trade receivables	1,300
Cash	5,410
	7,610
Total assets	8,410
EQUITY AND LIABILITIES	
Equity (owners' claim)	7,410
Current liabilities	
Trade payables	1,000
Total equity and liabilities	8,410

Income statement for the month ended 28 February

	£
Sales revenue	7,800
Cost of sales	(4,700)
Gross profit	3,100
Rent	(250)
Electricity	(240)
General expenses	(200)
Profit for the month	2,410

A.3 (a) and (b)

Buildings

		£			£
1 Jan	Balance brought down	25,000			

Fittings – cost

		£			£
1 Jan	Balance brought down	10,000	31 Dec	Balance carried down	12,000
	Cash	2,000			
		12,000			12,000
1 Jan	Balance brought down	12,000			

Fittings – depreciation

		£			£
31 Dec	Balance carried down	4,400	1 Jan	Balance brought down	2,000
			31 Dec	Income statement	
				(£12,000 × 20%)	2,400
					4,400
		4,400			
			1 Jan	Balance brought down	4,400

General expenses

		£			£
1 Jan	Balance brought down	140	31 Dec	Income statement	570
	Cash	580		Balance carried down	150
		720			720
1 Jan	Balance brought down	150			

Inventories

		£			£
1 Jan	Balance brought down	1,350	31 Dec	Cost of sales	15,220
31 Dec	Trade payables	17,220		Cost of sales	4,900
	Cash	3,760		Equity	560
				Balance carried down	1,650
		22,330			22,330
1 Jan	Balance brought down	1,650			

Cost of sales

		£			£
31 Dec	Inventories	15,220	31 Dec	Income statement	20,120
	Inventories	4,900			
		20,120			20,120

Rent

		£			£
1 Jan	Balance brought down	500	31 Dec	Income statement	3,000
31 Dec	Cash	3,000		Balance carried down	500
		3,500			3,500
1 Jan	Balance brought down	500			

Trade receivables

		£			£
1 Jan	Balance brought down	1,840	31 Dec	Cash	32,810
31 Dec	Sales revenue	33,100		Income statement (bad debt)	260
				Balance carried down	1,870
		34,940			34,940
1 Jan	Balance brought down	1,870			

Cash

		£			£
1 Jan	Balance brought down	2,180	31 Dec	Inventories	3,760
31 Dec	Sales revenue	10,360		Wages	3,770
	Borrowings	2,000		Rent	3,000
	Trade receivables	32,810		Electricity	1,070
				General expenses	580
				Fittings	2,000
				Borrowings	1,000
				Trade payables	18,150
				Equity	10,400
				Balance carried down	3,620
		47,350			47,350
1 Jan	Balance brought down	3,620			

Equity

		£			£
31 Dec	Inventories	560	1 Jan	Balance brought down	25,050
	Cash	10,400		Income statement (profit)	10,900
	Balance carried down	24,990			
		35,950			35,950
			1 Jan	Balance brought down	24,990

Borrowings

		£			£
30 June	Cash	1,000	1 Jan	Balance brought down	12,000
31 Dec	Balance carried down	13,000		Cash	2,000
		14,000			14,000
			1 Jan	Balance brought down	13,000

Trade payables

		£			£
31 Dec	Cash	18,150	1 Jan	Balance brought down	1,690
	Balance carried down	760	31 Dec	Inventories	17,220
		18,910			18,910
			1 Jan	Balance brought down	760

Electricity

		£			£
31 Dec	Cash	1,070	1 Jan	Balance brought down	270
31 Dec	Balance carried down	290	31 Dec	Income statement	1,090
		1,360			1,360
			1 Jan	Balance brought down	290

Sales revenue

		£			£
31 Dec	Income statement	43,460	31 Dec	Trade receivables	33,100
				Cash	10,360
		43,460			43,460

Wages

		£			£
31 Dec	Cash	3,770	31 Dec	Income statement	3,770

Interest on borrowings

		£			£
			31 Dec	Income statement (((6/12 × 14,000) + (6/12 × 13,000)) × 10%)	1,350

(c) **Income statement for the year to 31 December**

		£			£
31 Dec	Cost of sales	20,120	31 Dec	Sales revenue	43,460
	Depreciation	2,400			
	General expenses	570			
	Rent	3,000			
	Bad debts (Trade receivables)	260			
	Electricity	1,090			
	Wages	3,770			
	Interest on borrowings	1,350			
	Profit (Equity)	10,900			
		43,460			43,460

(d) **Statement of financial position as at 31 December last year**

	£
ASSETS	
Non-current assets	
Property, plant and equipment	
Buildings	25,000
Fittings: cost	12,000
depreciation	(4,400) 7,600
	32,600
Current assets	
Inventories of stationery	150
Inventories	1,650
Prepaid rent	500
Trade receivables	1,870
Cash	3,620
	7,790
Total assets	40,390
EQUITY AND LIABILITIES	£
Equity (owners' claim)	24,990
Non-current liabilities	
Borrowings	13,000
Current liabilities	
Trade payables	760
Accrued electricity	290
Accrued interest on borrowings	1,350
	2,400
Total equity and liabilities	40,390

Index